KONFRONTASI
The Indonesia-Malaysia Dispute
1963-1966

KONFRONTASI
The Indonesia-Malaysia Dispute
1963-1966

J.A.C. MACKIE
Research Director
Centre of Southeast Asian Studies
Monash University

Published for the Australian Institute of International Affairs

KUALA LUMPUR
OXFORD UNIVERSITY PRESS
LONDON NEW YORK MELBOURNE
1974

Oxford University Press, Ely House, London W. 1

GLASGOW NEW YORK TORONTO MELBOURNE WELLINGTON
CAPE TOWN IBADAN NAIROBI DAR ES SALAAM LUSAKA ADDIS ABABA
DELHI BOMBAY CALCUTTA MADRAS KARACHI LAHORE DACCA
KUALA LUMPUR SINGAPORE JAKARTA HONG KONG TOKYO

Bangunan Loke Yew, Kuala Lumpur
● *Australian Institute of International Affairs 1974*

*Having as its object the scientific study of International
questions, the Australian Institute of International Affairs,
as such, does not express opinions or advocate policies.
The views expressed in this book are therefore
the author's own.*

Printed in Malaysia by
CHARLES GRENIER SDN BHD KUALA LUMPUR,
and bound by
ART PRINTING WORKS, KUALA LUMPUR

*To my mother
and the memory of my father*

Preface

THIS book has grown out of a project sponsored by the Australian Institute of International Affairs, with the aid of a grant from the Ford Foundation, which was originally conceived as a study of the international relations of the Indonesia-Malaysia-Philippines-Australia area in the mid-1960s. When I started work on it in 1964, Indonesia's confrontation of Malaysia had already begun to overshadow other aspects of the problem and it soon became apparent that the problems of how to interpret Indonesia's actions in the dispute were of central importance to any such undertaking. However, I have tried to preserve a balance between the Indonesian and the Malaysian side of the story, tracing the interaction of domestic and international developments in both countries. The full history of the complex domestic politics of Indonesia in those turbulent years still has to be unravelled in far more detail than I have attempted here.

I have put more emphasis on the early development of the conflict rather than the later stages, mainly because the issues were more controversial—and the choices made more fateful—at that period than later, when the logic of events was more rigid. I was able to visit Indonesia, Malaysia (including Sarawak and Sabah) and the Philippines at the end of 1964 to make first-hand enquiries into the course of the conflict, but have relied more on the writings of others for the later stages. While this has resulted in some imbalance of narrative detail, I do not think the central analytical purpose of the study has been weakened thereby.

It has unfortunately been necessary, for reasons of length, to exclude or minimize discussion of several aspects of the problem which deserved much closer attention, such as the role of the Philippines in the dispute and the nuances of British, Australian, American and Russian policy. Their importance is undeniable, but I have felt it more fruitful to stress the domestic background on both sides rather than treat the conflict merely as part of a larger international chess-game with a circumscribed set of rules and relationships. A striking feature of confrontation was that the traditional rules and relationships simply were not applicable.

In referring to the various parts of Borneo, I have used the familiar anglicized form when referring to what was once called 'British Borneo' — i.e. Sarawak, North Borneo and Brunei, although the tiny Sultanate of Brunei was strictly a protectorate, not a colony — North Borneo in reference to the former colony of that name, now called Sabah, and the latter name when referring to it as a state of Malaysia. The Indonesian name, Kalimantan, has generally been retained when referring to the Indonesian segment of the island, the provinces thereof being characterized as West Kalimantan, East Kalimantan etc.

The spelling of Indonesian and Malaysian words and names in a book such as this presents an almost insuperable problem of standardization, which has been complicated by the change to a common, standardized spelling just as this book went to press. Because of the unfamiliarity of the latter, it seemed preferable to retain the pre-1971 spelling of Indonesian or Malay words or names in most cases. (A few exceptions such as Java, Surabaya, Majapahit and Srivijaya have been accepted as beyond standardization by now.) Proper names have been left as their owners use them: thus, we have a *Party Rakyat* in Malaya and a *Party Ra'ayat* in Brunei, not to mention *Harian Rakjat* in Indonesia. Here, as elsewhere, it seems preferable to respect the diversity of the region rather than to try to impose an arbitrary unity upon it. Personal titles have been standardized, to the best of my knowledge, according to the form appropriate at the time to which reference is made.

I wish to acknowledge gratefully the assistance I have been given in various ways by a large number of people during the writing of this book. Some cannot be mentioned because of their official positions. I benefitted greatly from discussions with Alex Alatas, Sir Garfield Barwick, Ganis Harsono, the late Tun Ismail bin Abdul Rahman, Syed Jaffar Albaar, Jek Yuen Thong, Ambassador Howard P. Jones, Lim Cheong Eu, A. M. Mackenzie, Martono Kadri, Alex Marentek, Senator Manglapus, Vice-President Pelaez, Tun Abdul Razak, S. Rajaratnam, Ambassador Narcisco Reyes, Sir Robert Scott, Soedjatmoko, Suwito Kusumowidagdo and Senator L. Sumulong.

For research assistance and secretarial help I wish to thank Michael Leigh, Suzanne Nichterlein, Jane Pyke, Pam Sayers, Gwen Wheeler and Diane Zijlstra. For other kinds of help I wish to thank Susan Osborne, Creighton Burns, Lance Castles, Herbert Feith, Bruce Grant, John Hoffman, George Kahin, Daniel Lev, John Legge, Michael Leifer, Lee Kok Liang, Colonel and Mrs. J. Mackay, Douglas Miles, Rex Mortimer, Ruth McVey, Douglas Paauw, Frank Palmos, Peter Polomka, Bill and Margaret Roff, J. P. Sarumpaet, Alan Smith, K. D. Thomas, R. K. Vasil, Wang Gungwu, Col. Rais Abin, Frederick Bunnell and my wife, Onnie. Responsibility for the statements herein rests, of course, solely with the author.

Centre of Southeast Asian Studies,   J. A. C. MACKIE
Monash University,
January 1973

Contents

Maps

Tables

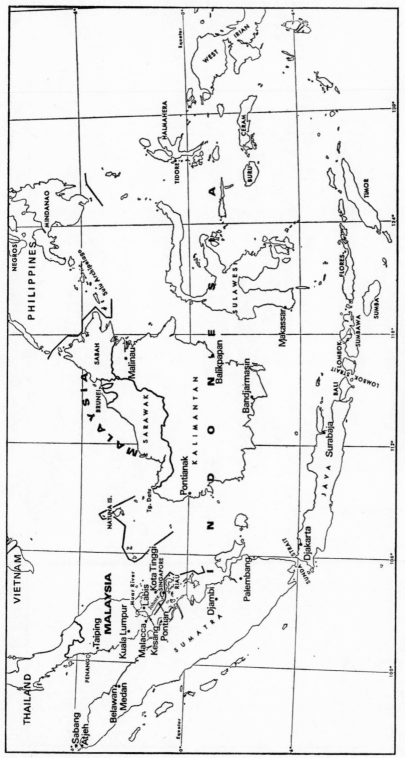

1. SOUTH-EAST ASIA

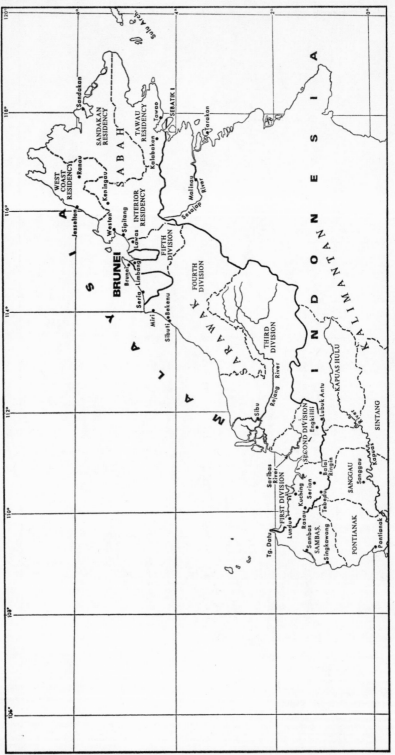

2. EAST MALAYSIA AND KALIMANTAN

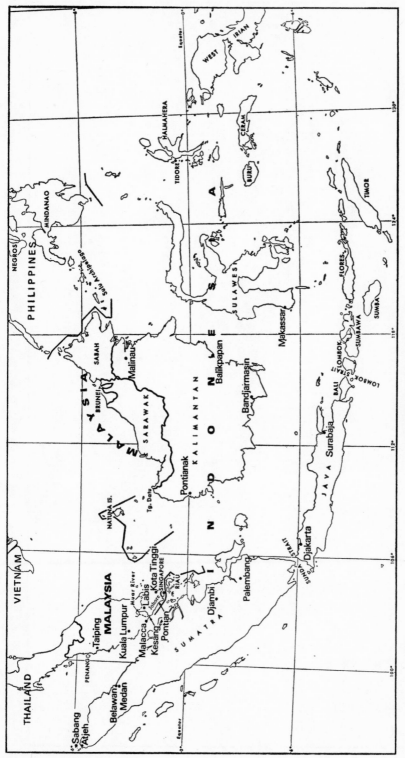

1. SOUTH-EAST ASIA

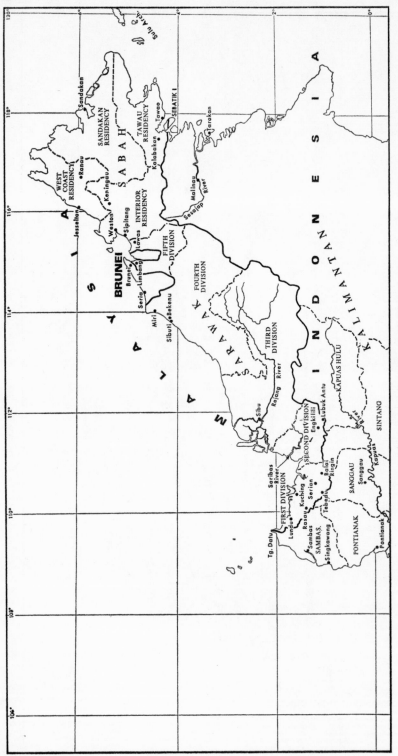

2. EAST MALAYSIA AND KALIMANTAN

I
Introduction

INDONESIA's confrontation of Malaysia during the years 1963 to 1966 was
an enigmatic affair, less than a war but something more than a mere
diplomatic dispute. It began, as it ended, cryptically, hesitantly and
shrouded in ambiguities. In military terms, it was a miniscule conflict,
yet the political stakes at issue seemed important enough to influence the
destiny of the entire South-East Asian region. The whole campaign bore
the stamp of President Soekarno's personality and political philosophy
so strongly that it is tempting to regard it, in retrospect, as essentially an
affair of his contriving. In fact, the term 'confrontation' itself may almost
be regarded as one of Soekarno's distinctive contributions to the lexicon
of modern diplomacy.[1] The origins and character of the conflict were
inextricably bound up with the development of the doctrine of the New
Emerging Forces, which Soekarno was at that time elevating to the status
of a major pillar of Indonesia's foreign policy and domestic ideology:
its end came within a matter of weeks after Lieutenant-General Suharto's
assumption of effective power from him in March 1966 — to be accepted
with surprisingly little protest by the politicians and public who had been
enthusiastically applauding the slogans of confrontation only a short
time before.

At the time, however, it seemed that confrontation was something more
than merely a campaign engineered by Soekarno to serve his own political purposes. Its dynamics were obviously far more complex than that,
for Soekarno was by no means an all-powerful autocrat, as he was sometimes depicted; other influential groups in the Indonesian political system
also played prominent parts in launching and maintaining the campaign
against Malaysia, most notably the Indonesian Communist Party (PKI),
but also many of the foremost anti-Communists, including the Army
leaders and most of the other political parties — although nearly all of
them had reservations about the lengths to which the struggle should be
pursued. In 1963–4 the most widely-accepted accounts of the conflict
depicted it as the expression of far more deep-seated forces than the mere
whims of an impulsive autocrat. Some saw it as a projection of under-

lying tensions and instability, others as the manifestation of an inherent expansionism or Pan-Malay chauvinism of the *Indonesia Raja* variety.[2] The most persuasive explanations were those which stressed the influence of the ideological imperatives behind the actions of the major participants in the Indonesian drama, both in its external and domestic aspects. Since the ending of confrontation in 1965–6, it has been easier to assess the relative importance of these factors than it was while the conflict was still in progress, although this creates some dangers of over-simplifying the complexities and uncertainties of the moment. In the account which follows, the strengths and weaknesses of the various explanatory hypotheses which have been put forward will be assessed against the evidence we can derive from the historical record, but the explanation given will be couched in terms of the interaction of many factors in a steadily unfolding drama rather than of any overriding set of determinants.

To interpret what significance we should attach to confrontation is, however, a more difficult exercise than merely accounting for why and how it came about. Can it be regarded simply as an aberration into which Soekarno led his country in his final frenetic years of power, a deviation from Indonesia's traditional foreign policy of non-alignment? Or should it be seen as a manifestation of deep-rooted expansionist tendencies which are likely to recur? How far should we regard it as a portent for the future, as an example of the regional instability and conflicts which are likely to arise in South-East Asia in the aftermath of the withdrawal of the former colonial powers and the transformation of the Western-based international order they created in the region into something new and characteristically Asian?

Certainly the previous half-century of relative international tranquillity in this part of the world (prior to the Japanese occupation in 1941–5) can be regarded as an aspect of what Harry J. Benda has called the 'colonial deviation' in South-East Asian history, while the disputes between Malaya, Indonesia and the Philippines in 1962–3 were quite directly connected with the processes of decolonization and the search for a new pattern of international relations in the region.[3] Those processes have by no means completely worked themselves out and it will not be clear whether a new regional balance of power has been established until the withdrawal of British and American forces has been completed. Even then, the assessment we make of the confrontation episode will not be a final one, for writers in different times and circumstances will inevitably see it from different angles, stressing whichever of the various causal factors seem most significant to them at the time.

In 1963–4, explanations in terms of Indonesia's self-aggrandizement or her propensity towards foreign adventures for reasons of domestic political instability had a strong *prima facie* appeal. By 1965, more stress was being put on the role of the Communist Party and the Chinese government's manipulation of Soekarno in their desire to draw him into conflict with the Western powers over the Malaysia issue. Later, it was more readily apparent that the causes of confrontation were complex and heterogeneous; one set of factors gave rise to the dispute, but a rather different set kept the conflict simmering.[4] Before we can explain confrontation, however, it is necessary to determine what it is we are trying to explain, what confrontation entailed and how it should be described. Some of the early interpretations in terms of Pan-Malay chauvinism or an inherent expansionism fell down on this score, partly because they 'explained' more than the facts required, or else they failed to account for the enigmatic, hot-and-cold character of Soekarno's opposition to Malaysia.[5] It will help to define our problem, therefore, if we begin with a brief characterization of the main stages of the conflict.

The Indonesia government began to express opposition to the Malaysia scheme shortly after the Brunei revolt of December 1962, more than eighteen months after the proposal by the Malaysia Prime Minister, Tunku Abdul Rahman, to extend the Malayan Federation to embrace Singapore, Sabah and Sarawak. From then until Malaysia came into being on 16 September 1963, Indonesians criticized the scheme vehemently as a British 'neo-colonialist project' and as a threat to their country's security. But the proclamation of a 'confrontation' policy in January did not mean immediate or open conflict. During this first stage, Soekarno's objective was apparently a very limited one, to forestall the creation of Malaysia if possible, either by encouraging further uprisings from within, like the Brunei revolt, by means of a propaganda offensive and covert military aid to the 'freedom fighters' of northern Borneo, or by a diplomatic strategy aimed at delaying Malaysia's creation. The diplomatic strand of Soekarno's policy seemed to be assuming greater importance than the more radically confrontative aspects in the middle of the year, when the series of Manila Conferences held out hopes of an amicable compromise which would reconcile some of Indonesia's objections to the Malaysia scheme with Tunku Abdul Rahman's insistence on pressing ahead with it as planned. But these hopes were dashed in September after a series of pin-pricking incidents which led Indonesia to charge Malaysia with a 'breach of the Manila Agreements' and to refuse to recognize the new Federation when it was formed. Attacks on the Malayan and British embassies in Djakarta, followed by the cutting of all commercial ties between Indonesia and Malaysia, sharply intensified the quarrel between the two countries.

While the events of September 1963 marked a major watershed in the development of Indonesia's struggle to 'crush Malaysia', the next phase was still characterized by the singular ambiguity of President Soekarno's aims and methods. He did not dramatically increase the degree of military activity on the land frontier in Borneo, nor did he abandon the diplomatic strand of confrontation. Attempts were made to rediscover the basis for a 'return to the Manila Agreements' in conferences at Bangkok (February-March 1964) and Tokyo (June 1964), but without success. Yet this second period of the conflict was of crucial importance, for it was marked by a major shift in the domestic balance of power within Indonesia to the disadvantage of the right-wing elements whose hopes had been pinned largely on the success of a US-backed economic stabilization programme in 1963;

but that programme had been undermined almost irrevocably by the commitment to confrontation in September 1963, however ambivalent Soekarno and his senior ministers may have been about that commitment. By March 1964, it was becoming clear that there was no hope of obtaining further US aid, which was an essential condition of any effective attack on Indonesia's almost endemic inflation. Soon afterwards, as America's capacity to restrain Indonesia diminished in effectiveness, the campaign against Malaysia was stepped up to a new level. Soekarno's proclamation of the 'People's Twofold Command' *(Dwikora)* and summons to a nation-wide mobilization of 'volunteers' to fight Malaysia in May, followed by the failure of the Tokyo Conference in June, may be taken as symbolic of the hardening of Indonesia's opposition to Malaysia, though these symbols made little difference to the course of events.

The third phase of confrontation, between July and December 1964, was marked by an intensification of the military conflict. Two attempted landings by small Indonesian forces on the Malayan peninsula itself, which coincided with race riots in Malaysia, posed a much more serious threat than the earlier ineffective border raids in the Borneo jungles. In September, a sharp crisis was precipitated, with Malaysia appealing to the UN Security Council against 'blatant Indonesian aggression' and British forces threatening a counter-strike against Indonesian naval and air bases. Indonesia's vulnerability to any such attack made it necessary for her to avoid any further escalation of the military conflict, although she continued to send occasional raiding parties across the Malacca Straits from time to time. A military stalemate persisted from then onwards, with no major new developments. But confrontation remained a serious threat to Malaysia because of mounting racial tensions between the Malays and the Chinese, which could easily have burst into a conflagration. Indonesia was also attempting to put diplomatic pressure on Malaysia to negotiate a return to the Manila Agreements (on terms favourable to Indonesia, of course) by manoeuvring to have her excluded from the Afro-Asian family of nations at the 2nd Afro-Asian Conference in 1965.

A rather different phase of confrontation may be discerned from January 1965, when Soekarno abruptly withdrew Indonesia from the UN and moved towards a much closer association than hitherto with China, straining Indonesia's relations with USA almost to breaking point in the process. During the next nine months, more energy was devoted to verbal confrontation of the *Nekolim* ('neo-colonialists and imperialists') in terms of a vast world-wide dialectical process of struggle between the New Emerging Forces and the Old Established Forces than to any specific action to crush Malaysia. Paradoxically, it was just at this stage that the separation of Singapore from Malaysia in August 1965 seemed likely to give Indonesia much opportunity to exploit the rifts in the Federation. But by then, however, political tensions were mounting to a crisis point in Indonesia as well as Malaysia, partly because of the accelerating price inflation and associated social tensions, partly because the steady increase of PKI influence over the previous year had greatly alarmed the anti-communists. Soekarno now seemed to be inclining the weight of his great influence more and more to the left, with the 'Djakarta-Peking axis' symbolizing the trend and adding greatly to the apprehensions of the anti-Communists. The explosion of violence that burst out after the coup attempt of 1 October 1965, which resulted in the destruction of the PKI and the eventual collapse of Soekarno's system of Guided Democracy, marked the culmination of this mounting tension — and changed the course of Indonesian history.

The coup also brought about the gradual ending of the Malaysia conflict. Thereafter, the Indonesian Army was too preoccupied with domestic problems to pose any serious military threat to Malaysia. Even before the destruction of the PKI and Lt.-Gen. Suharto's takeover of power from Soekarno, in March 1966, the new military leaders of Indonesia had started to make covert moves to restore peace with Malaysia, although confrontation was not formally ended until August 1966.

The proximate causes of these developments will become clearer, even if not always fully explicable, as the story unfolds. But it is well to remember that, as with icebergs, we see only a small part of the whole. We still know very little about the importance of the underlying dispositions and motivations of individuals, such as the intensity of *Indonesia Raja* chauvinism or anti-colonialist sentiments, or even of the effectiveness of the ubiquitous ideological indoctrination which so pervaded the political climate of the late Soekarno era. We cannot gauge how far Indonesia's leaders believed the sometimes specious arguments they advanced against the Malaysians and British whom they angrily blamed for the conflict, or how far their views of the outside world had been coloured by the ideological filter of the doctrine of New Emerging Forces through which they saw it.

For the Malaysians, one of the problems created by this strongly ideological cast of thought was that of identifying just what the aims of Indonesia's leaders really were in their conflict with Malaysia. It was never at all clear from Soekarno's cryptic utterances what his ultimate objectives were in the various negotiations that took place, while the stated aims of the PKI and Army leaders were frequently quite different from his and sometimes incompatible with each others'. This obscurity of purpose was made even more confusing by the fact that Indonesia's conduct of the struggle against Malaysia often seemed surprisingly half-hearted and ineffective, a matter of threats and bluster rather than real military pressure. There were political and military reasons why that was so, which were not fully apparent at the time; yet it would be utterly misleading to infer that the whole conflict was just a storm in a teacup or a *sandiwara*, a piece of play-acting. The outcome might easily have been very different if, for example, racial conflict had broken out in Malaysia, or if the Indonesian coup attempt of 30 September 1965 had not occurred for another twelve months and a more serious trial of military strength had developed in Sarawak. In reconstructing what happened, it is necessary to take account of the uncertainties of the time and to remember that while we now know the outcome of the struggle — and see it in the light of that knowledge —

the participants in the drama did not. 'History is lived forwards, but is written in retrospect', commented C. V. Wedgwood.[6] 'We know the end before we consider the beginning and we can never wholly recapture what it was to know the beginning only'. In interpreting the motives and strategies of the principal actors in this drama, it is vitally important to remember this, for our perspective on the struggle has been drastically altered by the downfall of Soekarno and the destruction of the PKI in 1965–6.

In the account of confrontation that follows, the main political developments within both Malaysia and Indonesia will be sketched in as a background to the conflict between them. The emphasis will fall mainly on the interrelationship between Indonesia's domestic politics and her foreign policies during this period; but while it is hoped that this will clarify some of the problems of explaining or interpreting Soekarno's policies in these crucial years, a more comprehensive and detailed study of Indonesia's domestic politics at that time is still badly needed. Without question, the instability of her politico-economic system after 1961 was an important factor predisposing Indonesia towards an assertive, adventurous foreign policy. But this does not mean that the development of confrontation was in any way predetermined, at least in its early stages. The conflict with Malaysia developed tentatively and unpredictably throughout 1963 as a series of *ad hoc* responses to a most delicately poised domestic balance of power and an unusually fluid international situation. Chance, accident and fortuitous coincidences of timing — what H.A.L. Fisher called 'the contingent and the unforeseen' — also played an important part, particularly at the time of the open break between Indonesia and Malaysia in September 1963, when Soekarno's government was carried by events over which it had imperfect control to a more extreme position than it initially intended to assume. One could also argue that it was simply an ill-starred coincidence of timing that the British withdrawal from South-East Asia happened to be entering its final phase in 1962–3 just when Soekarno's regime was at the peak of its power and self-confidence after the West Irian campaign, flushed by victory and the recent acquisition of great quantities of arms from the Soviet bloc. At just that time, too, the Brunei revolt provided a providential opportunity and inducement for Soekarno to assert the applicability of his recently developed doctrine of the New Emerging Forces, no doubt with the hope of hastening the departure of the British by either frustrating or wrecking the Malaysia experiment. The doctrine, too, seemed more plausible in the international environment of the years 1963–5 than it did either before or after. If Malaysia had been brought into existence without any untoward incidents before the end of the West Irian campaign (when Indonesia could not afford to express any opposition to it), events might have turned out very differently in both countries.

Some attention must be given to the Malaysian side of the story before we proceed further with the reasons for Indonesia's hostility to the new federation. The central purpose behind the creation of Malaysia was to make possible the merger of Singapore and the Malayan Federation, without creating a Chinese majority which would have endangered the existing political primacy of the Malays in an enlarged state. A closer association between the two was becoming essential, said the Tunku, since a developing split between the non-Communist and pro-Communist wings of Singapore's ruling party, the People's Action Party (PAP), was raising the spectre of a Communist accession to power there. Singapore was due to obtain full independence from the British in 1963 and that would have meant the end of the Internal Security Council through which the British and Malayan governments had previously been able to keep the Communist activities there under tight control during and after the 'Emergency' of 1948–60. Hence the Tunku's proposal to incorporate Singapore within an expanded federation of Malaysia which would include also the two Borneo colonies and the Brunei protectorate, for it was commonly assumed in early discussions of the political arithmetic of this exercise in nation-building that the indigenous people of Borneo would act as a counter-balance to the Chinese of Singapore and thus help to preserve the dominant position of the Malays within the new federation.

This assumption has turned out, in fact, to be an extremely dubious one, like several other of the initial assumptions made about Malaysia. It is certainly true that the politics of Malaysia have essentially been communal politics: its main political conflicts since 1963 have centred round the communal problems of language, education and special rights for 'natives', epitomized in the broader question of whether the new state should be an essentially 'Malay Malaysia' or a 'Malaysian Malaysia' — a somewhat pejorative phrasing of the issues whose significance we will examine more fully in due course. But the non-Malay indigenes of Borneo have not for the most part sided with the Malays in the post-1963 disputes: if anything rather the reverse. In fact, the political alignments there have by no means been straightforward cleavages between two racial groups. They have been much more tangled than that, even though the basis of political organization and party support has remained very largely communal. The cause of tensions within Malaysia since 1963 has not been the crude arithmetic of ethnic populations, but differences of opinion within the various states of the new federation about the appropriate pattern of party organization and social integration in a democratic, multi-racial Malaysia. It is easy to be wise after the event about the Malaysia experiment by pointing to its subsequent troubles, such as the exclusion of Singapore, the several race riots and the suspension of parliamentary democracy in 1969–70. In the circumstances that prevailed in 1961–2, however, no other realistic formula for achieving the decolonization of Singapore and the Borneo territories was foreseeable, so the Tunku's plan seemed the most effective way of achieving what then appeared to be the thoroughly logical step of merging Singapore and Malaya. (Some might argue that a preferable solution would have been for left-wing Chinese elements to have taken over in Singapore and the Borneo territories, looking towards Peking for economic and political support rather than Kuala Lumpur; but such a solution would have aroused widespread communal antagonism among the non-Chinese and was out of the question in 1961.)

Historians will probably argue for years whether the former British colonies could have become independent on different terms which might have produced fewer tensions. But it is not easy to visualize better arrangements which would have been politically practicable at the time. A British proposal in 1958 for a united and ultimately independent British North Borneo had failed to generate much response. By 1961, however, a degree of urgency was created by the very logic of the political situation; many people accepted the argument that unless the Borneo territories united with Malaysia then and there, they might not get another opportunity to do so because of the rising tide of 'Chinese chauvinism', as it was then called. (Indonesia was only a peripheral worry.) In Singapore, Lee Kuan Yew's PAP had long been committed to the goal of 'independence through merger with Malaysia', but after the emergence of the *Barisan Sosialis* in June-July 1961 as the most formidable force opposed to the Tunku's concept of Malaysia in any of the territories concerned, it became politically essential to Lee (and important to the Tunku also) to achieve merger by 1963. The two chief difficulties in the way were to win acceptance for the proposal in Singapore and to devise a means of bringing the Borneo territories rapidly towards self-government within an enlarged federation. In Malaya itself the Tunku faced no significant obstacles, for the Alliance government had a substantial majority over the opposition parties, so long as the main Malay party, UMNO, was prepared to back the scheme. (Even UMNO had misgivings, however, and the Tunku had to play his cards more carefully than has been generally recognized.) It did not take much persuasion to overcome some initial British reservations about the Tunku's plan; in fact, Malaysia suited the British government very well, both as an opportunity for withdrawing from its Borneo commitments with a minimum of difficulty and because Britain might have been saddled with the choice between accepting a left-wing government in Singapore, with incalculable results, or suspending the constitution and re-imposing colonial rule, if the Malaysia plan had been forestalled after Lee Kuan Yew had committed his political life to it in 1961. In the background, too, was the possibility that the Malayan Communist Party might re-kindle the embers of the 1948–60 Emergency in order to frustrate its opponents. Communal tensions always provided highly combustible fuel for such a holocaust. So Malaysia was certainly the easiest way out for all concerned. Perhaps in their anxiety to achieve it, its advocates gave too little thought to what would follow.

The course of developments within the component parts of Malaysia in in the years 1961–5 will later be sketched out more fully for two reasons. In the first place, the belief that Malaysia was merely a ramshackle neo-colonialist creation of the British and that it would fall apart under the strain of confrontation played an important part in Indonesian thinking, so we need to realize why Soekarno's analysis of Malaysia's internal dynamics proved to be so wildly wrong. Secondly, because the Indonesians regarded Malaysia as a neo-colonialist puppet regime imposed upon the people against their will, their strategy was largely based on an assumption that there would be substantial domestic opposition to Tunku Abdul Rahman's government. But their assessments of the Malaysian situation were sometimes weirdly distorted by the ideological lens through which they saw it. The two governments had such very different socio-political perspectives that they were frequently talking at cross-purposes. And because their political and moral frames of reference were so different, misunderstanding and mistrust were easily compounded. Each felt a high degree of moral indignation against the other which frustrated efforts to reach a negotiated settlement of the conflict. Consequently, their views about the rights and wrongs of the dispute that developed in 1963–4 also have to be taken into account as factors which influenced the actions of both governments to a considerable extent, no less than the political and military considerations which swayed them.

There was no particular reasons to expect Indonesian hostility to the Malaysia notion when it was first mooted. In fact, the scheme was well under way before any criticism of it was expressed in Djakarta. Indonesia's preoccupation with her own struggle for West Irian was initially a major reason for not advancing any objection to Malaysia. Her opposition to Malaysia, first aroused by the Brunei revolt of December 1962, developed gradually and to some extent capriciously into Soekarno's commitment to 'crush Malaysia' after the open breach in September 1963. Paradoxically, this decision was made just after the series of Manila Conferences which brought forth the vision of Malay brotherhood, or Maphilindo, embracing the three nations of Malay stock, Malaya, the Philippines and Indonesia. The story of the Manila Agreements and the collapse of the Maphilindo ideal, which briefly seemed to offer the basis for a solution to the quarrel between Indonesia and Malaya, constitutes one of the most important and controversial chapters in the whole affairs. Arguments in 1963–4 about the question of who was responsible for the breach of the Manila Agreements and the wrecking of the Maphilindo venture were not mere diplomatic hair-splitting. They aroused strong passions on either side and were crucial to the negotiating positions of each, hence not easily susceptible to compromise without entailing fundamental concessions on matters of principle by one side or other.

While the aim of this book will be primarily to explain why and how the conflict between Indonesia and Malaysia developed, it will be impossible to avoid some assessment of the rights and wrongs of the case. In particular, the negotiations leading up to the Manila Agreements are of peculiar importance in this story because of the light they throw on the intentions of the signatories to those Agreements.[7] Subsequent differences of interpretation about what was meant by several ambiguous clauses of the Manila Agreements added greatly to the difficulties of reaching a negotiated settlement of the dispute in 1964. The period between the Manila Summit meeting of July-August 1963 and the open break between Indonesia and Malaysia six weeks later may be regarded as an equivalent to the *peripeteia* of classical Greek tragedies, 'the sudden reversal of circumstances on which the plot of a tragedy hinges'. Just at a stage when conflict between Indonesia and Malaysia seemed likely to be averted by the vision splendid of Maphilindo and Pan-Malay brotherhood, which might have transformed the political relationship between the three nations involved, the affair took a very different turn. Misunderstandings, mutual suspicions and recriminations, as well as deliberate attempts to sabotage the Maphilindo policy by various elements on both sides, brought about the dramatic *bouleversement* which brought Indonesia and Malaysia into an open conflict. And the events of September 1963 had far-reaching consequences in Indonesian politics, consequences which proved to be irreversible until the coup of October 1965.

In the debates which ensued about who was responsible for the breach of the Manila Agreements and dissipation of the 'Maphilindo spirit' at that time, each side argued vehemently that the other was in the wrong, for each interpreted the agreement within a very different ideological frame of reference from the other. The intensity of this conviction on both sides, Malaysian and British as well as Indonesian and Filipino, was a major obstacle to compromise during the search for a negotiated settlement in late 1963 and early 1964. Differing accounts about the precise nature and intent of the Manila Agreements made it difficult at the time even for a relatively impartial outsider to discover the truth about what happened at Manila and immediately afterwards. In Chapter VII an attempt is made to reconstruct the course of events in those two crucial months and to assess the validity of the differing interpretations. This seems to establish beyond reasonable doubt that the Malaysian interpretation of what was intended by the controversial paragraph 4 of the Manila Joint Statement (regarding the United Nations Mission of Enquiry into opinion in the Borneo territories about Malaysia) comes much closer to the truth than the Indonesian-Filipino versions, which were in some cases quite deliberately distorted. But it is almost impossible to discuss these tangled events with complete impartiality or in a manner that will be considered satisfactory on both sides. All we can try to do is to achieve a sufficient degree of empathy with the various participants to be able to see the situation as it appeared to them, before we resort to critical judgements of their motives. The judgements have to be made at some point, of course, and they undoubtedly colour our views about the affair. My own sympathies for the Malaysian case throughout this dispute will be apparent in the account that follows, but I have tried to do justice to the Indonesian side of the story and to comprehend the motives for Indonesian actions.

But to understand is not always to excuse, although it may temper condemnation. Many of Indonesia's actions in the Malaysia dispute cannot be condoned unless one uncritically accepts Soekarno's interpretation of world politics on the basis of the doctrine of the New Emerging Forces and agrees with the conclusions he drew from it. Unfortunately, brilliant though his political and ideological talents may have been, Soekarno's methods were often opportunistic, cynical, inconsistent with each other — and, in the final test, disastrous for Indonesia, for the course on which he steered Indonesia after September 1963 led inexorably towards the upheavals of October 1965. Although Soekarno's leadership could, until then, be extolled for his contributions towards Indonesia's national unity and the avoidance of religious conflict, or even admired for sheer political virtuosity, his style of leadership in the later years brought out many of the most disturbing features of Indonesian political life at that time. His ideological doctrines provided Indonesia with an ingenious mélange of half-truths which seemed to provide them with a coherent picture of their place in the world, but failed to help them resolve their most basic socio-economic problems and made Indonesia into a dangerously unstable force in South-East Asia, perilously isolated from most of the international community except Communist China and her closest allies. There can be little doubt that Indonesia needed an ideology, but the ideology Soekarno gave her served his own immediate political purposes, external as well as internal, better than it met Indonesia's need for guidance towards a way out of her difficulties.

[1]The word konfrontasi had been in general currency in Indonesia for many years, generally to refer to the contrast between traditional and modern modes of thought and cultural expression. The eternal conflict between two parties in the wayang drama was depicted very literally as a 'confronting' of one by the other, the characters being grouped opposite each other on stage in highly formalized array and engaging either in verbal debate or physical battle in which their supernatural power was the decisive weapon. In 1960, during the struggle to regain West Irian, Soekarno had threatened to 'confront' the Dutch with whatever means they employed — military force if they chose military force (for the Dutch had just sent out the aircraft carrier Karel Doorman to reinforce their defences), or political or economic measures, as necessary. The term was bafflingly ambiguous to foreigners, but an Indonesian would have found it quite familiar.

[2]See the answers given to the question 'What really were the mainsprings of Indonesia's opposition to Malaysia?' in Arnold C. Brackman, Southeast Asia's Second Front, The Power Struggle in the Malay Archipelago (Frederick A. Praeger, 1966), pp. 150–4 and passim. The 'expansionist' theory is most bluntly stated by Bernard K. Gordon in 'The Potential for Indonesian Expansionism', Pacific Affairs, vol. XXXVI, no. 4, Winter 1963–4, pp. 378–93 and in The Dimensions of Conflict in Southeast Asia (Prentice Hall Inc., 1966), ch. 3. Both writers are inclined to overstrain their central hypotheses and ignore the domestic political dynamics (or else, in Brackman's case, treat the latter so obsessively in terms of a Communist drive for power that other important factors are seriously neglected). Former US Ambassador Howard P. Jones puts the stress primarily on Soekarno and his 'emotionalism' in Indonesia: the Possible Dream (Harcourt, Brace, Jovanovich, New York, 1971), pp. 271–2. For a more subtle interpretation by the former Assistant Secretary of State for Far Eastern Affairs in the State Department, couched in terms of 'the new nationalism' of the Afro-Asian world, the need for national identity and the focusing of power at the centre in loosely articulated nations, see Roger Hilsman, To Move a Nation, The Politics of Foreign Policy in the Administration of John F. Kennedy (Doubleday & Co., New York, 1967), ch. 25–7.

[3]The notion that South-East Asia's history may now be returning to its natural course after the 'colonial deviation' is an extension of Harry J. Benda's ideas on this subject: see his 'Decolonisation in Indonesia: the Problem of Continuity and Change', American Historical Review, vol. LX, no. 4, July 1965, pp. 1058–73.

[4]One of the best early accounts of how the conflict came about, giving the Indonesian side of the story more sympathetically than most, was that by George McT. Kahin, 'Malaysia and Indonesia', Pacific Affairs, vol. XXXVII, no. 3, Fall 1964, pp. 253–70. A useful analysis of the influence of Indonesian domestic politics on the early development of confrontation was given by Donald Hindley, 'Indonesia's Confrontation of Malaysia: the Search for Motives', Asian Survey, vol. IV, no. 6, June 1964, pp. 904–13.

For a lively but somewhat tendentious account, see Robert Curtis, 'Malaysia and Indonesia', *New Left Review*, no. 28, November-December 1964, pp. 5–32.

[5]This is an obvious weakness of Bernard Gordon's writings on the dispute and, to a lesser extent, of the Robert Curtis article. Even Hindley's article can give rise to a similar misconception that the support for confrontation was more widespread and more intense in Indonesia, particularly in the Army, than it was in the later stages.

[6]C. V. Wedgwood, *William the Silent* (Jonathan Cape, London, 1967), pp. 35, 212–14.

[7]See Appendix I for the text of the Manila Agreements. According to Kahin (who was at the Manila Summit conference and in close contact with the Indonesian delegation) the Joint Statement was intended to provide a 'face-saving formula' for a UN Mission of Enquiry in Borneo to enable Soekarno to acquiesce in the formation of Malaysia and abandon confrontation without loss of face. This seems to have been only part of the story. The Philippines Ambassador to Djakarta, Narciso Reyes, insisted during the course of an interview he kindly gave me in December 1964 that Paragraph 4 of the Joint Statement was intended to imply a very different kind of UN enquiry, but I find it hard to reconcile this claim with the available evidence of the Manila Conference for reasons set out below (pp. 157–65).

II

Indonesians and Malays:
the Legacy of the Past

RACIALLY, the inhabitants of Malaysia, Indonesia and the Philippines have close affinities — they are 'blood brothers' in the language of platform orators — although within all three countries ethnic and linguistic differences still create serious communal problems amongst the indigenous peoples, as well as between them and the immigrant Chinese, Indians and Europeans. Historically, they have been exposed to broadly similar influences from outside the region, cultural, political and economic. Yet the past has left a legacy of diversity rather than unity. And the idea of the solidarity of the Malay peoples, towards which the concept of 'Maphilindo' raised such high hopes in mid-1963, has had a slender basis in the actual history of the past 1,500 years, despite the claims of the *Indonesia Raja*' myth-makers. The peninsula and the archipelago have frequently had divergent politico-economic interests, as also have their various component parts. Neither regional unity nor national integration have been inevitable or historically necessary, highly desirable though they may be today. Unifying and disintegrating forces have waxed and waned in strength during recent years, as through the centuries preceding, in accordance with changes in the political and economic circumstances of the region.

The political unity of the three nations resulted from the consolidation of the Dutch, British and Spanish colonies during the nineteenth century, when colonial rivalries led to the delineation of the international boundaries which still exist. While there is a certain logic in these boundaries (the Malacca Straits, the main north-south watershed in Borneo, the Sulu Sea) which makes them as sensible as any others, they do not coincide neatly with ethnic divisions. Malays have long lived on both sides of the Malacca Straits which, until 1870, had rarely been a clear-cut dividing line between the principalities of Sumatra and the peninsula; the sea was an easy means of communication as well as a barrier. The Dayak peoples of Borneo's interior straddled the present-day frontier and some groups have long been moving to and fro across it. The Sultans of the Sulu archipelago formerly asserted sovereignty over north-east Borneo, and on this basis the Philippines laid claim on Sabah in 1962 — a reminder that nationalists do not regard colonial agreements about frontiers as sacrosanct.[1]

For centuries before the international boundaries were settled in the last decades of the nineteenth century, seafaring Malays, Buginese, Sumatrans and Javanese roamed and settled at will throughout the archipelago. They had little regard for frontiers in the modern sense, although some might have had to swear personal allegiance to a ruler who was strong enough to insist on it. Land was plentiful and population scanty, so additions to the labour force were welcomed rather than excluded until well into the twentieth century. Political boundaries have not been a very substantial barrier to the movement of the various peoples throughout the region even during the last one hundred years — and have probably never been, except where they have coincided with other barriers, geographical, linguistic, religious or racial.[2] Much of the appeal of Pan-Malay sentiment and the short-lived Maphilindo concept of 1963–4 was based on the feeling that the unifying pull of ethnic affinity could and should offset the division of the region into national states with divergent interests. These notions also underlay the latent antagonism towards the Chinese and China among the Malays and the Indonesians. We therefore need to begin by looking briefly at the ethnic background in order to set the problems of unity and diversity in the region in perspective, then at the course of historical relationships between the various peoples of Indonesia and Malaysia and their attitudes towards each other.

HISTORICAL RELATIONS

Relations between the various states of the peninsula and the archipelago have rarely been stable or clearcut throughout the 1,500 years or so for which we have some reliable knowledge, except in the last half-century or so of the colonial era. Perhaps if we were to trace the waxing and the waning of the old kingdoms, sultanates and harbour principalities and analyse their links with their vassals, tributaries and rivals we might find that these kaleidoscopic relationships should be regarded as the traditional or natural pattern of South-East Asian history towards which the Indonesia-Malaysia conflict marked a return after the abnormal circumstances of the 'colonial deviation'. But this would take us too far from our story here. Three aspects of the story deserve some attention, however.

The first is that the very mixed feelings which Indonesians and Malays have shown towards each other in the last decade — pride in their common Malay cultural heritage, yet at the same time mutual suspicions: admiration tinged with apprehension on the Malay side, disdain spiced with both envy and contempt on the Indonesian — are a complex amalgam derived from both recent experience and folk-memories of the past which we find embodied in their myths and legends. To characterize these tangled sentiments baldly would, of course, be as perilous as it would be to summarize French and British attitudes to each other in a few words: but to disregard the ambivalence they signify would be just as misleading.

Second, the notion of unity of the Malay-Indonesian peoples, which some mythologists have sought to invoke as a political symbol, is no better supported by the historical record than the idea of European unity under the Holy Roman Empire. It is more accurate to describe their past within a pattern of intrinsically unstable relationships, oscillating periodically from conflict to complementarity between two major politico-economic systems, one based on Javanese manpower and agricultural production, the other based on the maritime network of trading ports around the Malacca Straits, on the Sumatran side as well as on the peninsula.[3]

Third, the very striking differences of outlook and values which characterized the modern Indonesian and Malaysian elites in the early 1960s and which contributed significantly to their mutual misunderstandings and suspicions at the time of confrontation result in large part from their very different historical experiences, particularly in late colonial times. There are also, of course, many important differences amongst the several elite groups in each of the two nations. Some of the internal instability in each country, which is itself a contributing factor behind the instability of the international order, derives from the fissures and tensions within these elites.[4]

*   *   *   *

Pride in the greatness of the ancient Malay-Indonesian kingdoms is taught in the schoolrooms of both nations without much concern about the boundaries created by the colonial powers — pride in Srivijaya and Majapahit, in the Sultanates of Malacca, Brunei, Atjeh and Mataram, to mention only the most eminent. But there are differences of emphasis from place to place, of course, as in any part of the world: Malays are more likely to look back to Malacca Sultanate or even Srivijaya as the golden age, Javanese to Majapahit or Mataram, the great centres of the high courtly civilization they have inherited. The Malay chronicles attest the magnificence of the fourteenth century Javanese kingdom of Majapahit, which seems to have experienced an 'empire-building' phase for a brief period under the great minister Gadjah Mada, though its power was probably based not on military and political prowess so much as on superior religious and cultural achievements.[5] Majapahit seems not to have exercised effective control over the Straits of Malacca, where piracy was becoming a problem in the late fourteenth century: nor did it prevent the rise of the Malacca Sultanate in the early fifteenth century. However, the Malacca view of the relationship between them, as depicted in their legends, indicates ambiguities and ambivalences which are remarkably similar to present-day attitudes.

The Malacca Sultans seem to have acknowledged a younger-brother relationship, but not subordination. In the Malay chronicle, *Sejarah Melayu*, the pomp and splendour of the Majapahit court are recounted with admiration. It was not beneath the dignity of the Sultan to send envoys there or even to pay a visit personally in the hope of marrying the Maharaja's beautiful daughters, although we do not hear of such visits being reciprocated. Yet in the Malay accounts, the hero, Hang Tuah, always contrives to outwit and outfight his Javanese adversaries (just as the deer outwits the tiger in the *kanchil* stories), despite the advantages the latter enjoy on their home ground: he even foils the devious plots laid by the crafty Gadjah Mada, whose reputation in the Malay stories is perhaps characteristic of a more general Malay attitude toward the Javanese — there are elements of admiration and awe, but little warmth or trust.

After Majapahit's decline, the founding of the Portuguese, Spanish and Dutch colonial empires in the sixteenth and seventeenth centuries (later, also the British) forestalled any further development of an archipelago-wide empire within the Malay world. This is not the place to look into the tangled history of power relationships within the region since that time, but it is worth noticing briefly two significant consequences of colonial rule which have a direct relevance to the Malaysia-Indonesia conflict of 1963–5.

The consolidation of the Dutch and British colonial empires during the last century or so before their collapse in World War II accentuated several of the striking differences which are today discernible between the societies and cultures of Indonesia and Malaya. At the same time, they fused these two regions into distinct political entities with an unprecedented degree of political cohesiveness. The mechanics of this process of political integration have a bearing upon the arguments which later developed about whether Indonesia and Malaysia constituted 'natural' or cohesive nation-states. Singapore's peculiar position as a thorn in the side of both countries also needs to be seen in the same context of the unfolding politico-economic trends of the past hundred years.

Djakarta (then Batavia) became the economic and political focal point of the Dutch colony, binding together the many discrete parts of the outer islands within a network of commercial interdependence based on trade routes, shipping lines, telegraph links and credit services, a partially unified legal and administration system, and, in the last resort, military control. Singapore likewise became the economic focal point of the British colony, although Kuala Lumpur was a rival political centre. The incorporation of Sumatra within the Dutch economic system based on Java, after the 1870 Treaty of London delineated the boundary between the two colonial spheres of influence, is a matter of particular interest, for most of Sumatra had previously had closer commercial links with Singapore than Batavia. In 1888, the Dutch government set up its own inter-island shipping line, KPM, in order to break the British dominance in shipping services throughout the archipelago. By establishing a network of small feeder services to the ports from which the main Dutch lines plied to Europe, notably Batavia, and providing also credit facilities and other ancillary services needed by the small traders of the islands, the Dutch succeeded in gradually redirecting the trade of much of the archipelago away from Singapore and British ships towards Batavia and Dutch ships. This process involved a bitter and expensive struggle between Dutch and

British commercial interests, but by the 1930s the Dutch had won and Singapore's role as the entrepot of the entire archipelago was seriously threatened in the long term.[6]

Fortunately for her, however, and disastrously for Indonesia, Singapore received a new lease of life after the Second World War, when a great deal of Indonesian export trade was channelled out through Singapore, including the lucrative 'smuggling' or 'barter trade' which resulted from the breakdown of Indonesia's administrative and commercial services. Indonesia's difficulties were compounded by both the nationalization of KPM in 1958 and the economic disintegration accompanying the inflation of the following decade, which have therefore dangerously weakened one of the most important integrating forces in Indonesia. Hence smuggling became a very real threat to the country's strength and unity — and insofar as the mere existence of Singapore constituted a veritable haven for smugglers in the midst of Indonesia's territory, it aggravated that threat. The Indonesians would have liked to be able to divert their trade away from Singapore and the Chinese merchants there, many of them related to the Chinese in Indonesia, for whom they felt no great love in any case; but all their efforts to achieve this objective prior to confrontation had failed. Yet the belief persisted that somehow or other the Singapore problem could be solved and the grip of her 'capitalistic Chinese blood-suckers' on Indonesia's trade broken once and for all if only Indonesia could summon up enough will-power and drive. This belief was a very potent factor impelling many Indonesians to support confrontation in 1963.

The colonial era brought rapid economic development to the two colonies, but at very uneven rates within different parts of them. The pattern of development was determined mainly by the interests of the colonizers, not by needs of the local societies. One result of this has been that the social systems which were moulded by the powerful new influences of the late colonial era have not been well adjusted to the maintenance of the economic and political institutions inherited with independence: hence the ruling elites which took over the reins of government from their former masters have held their power uneasily as they have striven to legitimize and buttress their authority in new ways more appropriate to the post-colonial circumstances. This underlying instability has obviously been a far more serious problem in Indonesia than in Malaya — hence the restless, 'revolutionary' aspect of her political and social life over the past two decades, the shaky authority of her ruling elite, and the superheated ideological controversies there, which were deflected by Soekarno towards external enemies in order to restore national unity. The ruling elite in Malaya, by contrast, has so far been conservative in its socio-economic programme and relatively secure from any serious challenge from below, although that tranquillity could at any time be shattered if anything should happen to upset the precarious racial balance there.[7] Malaya's economic and political problems were generally manageable (until 1969, at least) and her relative prosperity took the edge off social discontents. On the other hand, Indonesia's problems have proved peculiarly intractable for a variety of reasons, not least among them being the peculiar imbalance of population and resources between Java and the rest of Indonesia, which is a legacy of the distorted pattern of economic and social development in the late colonial era. These difficulties were later aggravated greatly by the administrative incompetence and financial irresponsibility of the Soekarno regime; but it must be admitted that there are no easy solutions to the most deepseated of her economic and political problems, which tend to interact upon each other in a series of vicious circles. It was largely because no other solutions appeared to be available that Soekarno's millenarian fantasies made the appeal they did.

PAN-INDONESIAN INCLINATIONS, 1945–1957

Indonesia's struggle for national independence made a powerful appeal to restless young Malays in the last decade before the Second World War and in the years of her revolutionary conflict against the Dutch between 1945–9. An organized nationalist movement had barely emerged in Malaya before 1941, although the doctrines of nationalism and Islamic modernism emanating from the Dutch colony were beginning to send ripples across the calm surface of Malayan life.[8] But the proclamation of Indonesian independence in August 1945 coincided with traumatic political changes within Malaya in the wake of the Japanese collapse to bring about a quickening of political consciousness among both the Malays and Chinese of the peninsula. Indonesia's example of determined struggle and sacrifices for independence during the following years has frequently been acknowledged by Malays (but more ambivalently by Malayan Chinese) as an inspiration to them in their own efforts to achieve their freedom from colonial rule.[9] Soekarno and Hatta were regarded as national heroes in Malaya as well as in Indonesia, and it has often been reported that their photos were hung in many Malay and Bornean households in the years before independence.

How far all this was pride of race at a time of national awakening, or solidarity in the shared struggles to end colonial rule (not a very important factor in Borneo, apparently), or a yearning for the unity of the Malay-Indonesian people it would be perilous to guess. The idea of *Indonesia Raja* (or, in Malay terminology, *Melayu Raya*) did arouse some interest in 1945 when it was not at all clear whether the authority of the colonial powers would be re-established or how the political boundaries of South-East Asia would be redrawn after the collapse of the Japanese Greater East Asia Co-prosperity Sphere. Yet it is easy to exaggerate its subsequent importance to both countries.

It is appropriate to give some attention to the strength and significance of this Pan-Indonesian sentiment, since some commentators inferred that Indonesians harboured irredentist and expansionist ambitions, mainly on the basis of one particular episode in 1945, which the Malaysian government used later as propaganda for the view that Soekarno and other Indonesian politicians believed that Malaya and northern Borneo should form part of Indonesia. During confrontation, excessive emphasis was put on this episode, the debate on the territory of the future nation in the Investigating Committee for Preparation of Indonesian Independence. On the other hand, there seems to be no doubt that the sense of brotherhood between the Indonesian and Malayan nationalists was stronger during the years of anti-colonial struggle in and after 1945 than at any other period.

We should remember that during the first decade after the end of the war, anti-British and anti-colonial sentiment waxed strong among all the Malays, aristocrats as well as low born radicals. Even the Sultans had cause to distrust the British after the attempt in 1945 to impose the Malayan Union upon them (which would have relegated the Malays virtually to a position of political inferiority in what they considered their own land), although the revised Federation arrangements of 1948 favoured the 'feudal' elements among the Malays at the expense of the other communities.[10] British colonial rule seemed likely to last at least until a stable political basis for representative government could be devised — something which still seemed a long way off during the crisis years of the Emergency when communal antagonisms were running high. It is hardly surprising that some young Malays were impatient to throw off the colonial yoke and seize power for themselves, throwing in their lot with the Indonesians in their struggle for independence, which seemed much closer to success in the early post-war years when Malayan independence was not yet within sight. Pro-Indonesian sentiment was strongest amongst those who had least to lose and most to gain from a revolutionary upheaval, whereas the Sultans and their dependants must have been alarmed by the radicalism engendered by the Indonesian struggle for independence. Many had family ties with the aristocracies of East Sumatra and Atjeh which were destroyed in the bloody *jacqueries* of 1945–6.[11] In Java, the revolutionaries deposed the Sunan of Surakarta and rejected the feudal claims of the old *prijaji* aristocracy in the name of revolutionary egalitarianism. The progressive Marxist element that was such a prominent feature of the Indonesian revolution could hardly make the same appeal to peninsular Malays, to whom it raised the spectre of Chinese domination. Ideological radicalism has generally been a Chinese rallying point in Malaya since 1945, whereas the Malays have been more responsive to appeals to ethnic solidarity.

Nevertheless, it was among a small group of radical, ideologically-inclined, anti-colonialist Malays that pro-Indonesian sentiment was strongest. The leaders of this group, Ibrahim Ya'acob, Ishak bin Haji Mohammed and Ahmad Boestamam, play a particularly interesting part in our story, which goes back well before 1945 and extends right through to 1965 when two of them ended up in detention for alleged involvement in pro-Indonesian subversion. They were strongly attracted by Pan-Malay or Pan-Indonesian doctrines, yet they ultimately became associated with parties (Partindo in Indonesia and the Socialist Front in Malaya) on an ostensibly multi-racial appeal and a Marxist ideology, which brought them into political alliance with Chinese radicals and Communists in both countries.

Ibrahim Ya'acob and Ishak bin Haji Mohammed had been prominent in the establishment of the *Kesatuan Melayu Muda* (Union of Malay Youths — KMM) in 1937, a radical nationalist and anti-British organization, described by a historian of Malay nationalism as a counterpart of such movements as *Jong Java, Jong Sumatra* etc. in Indonesia.[12] They were in touch with exiled Indonesian nationalists who, like themselves, were mostly journalists or school teachers of relatively low social origin, whose prospects of employment or political advancement under the colonial regimes were extremely limited. Both men were arrested by the British when the war broke out, along with many other members of KMM. They collaborated with the Japanese but at the same time maintained links with the Communist-led Malayan People's Anti-Japanese Army. Ibrahim Ya'acob became commander of the PETA, the Japanese-created Malay militia: thus he had strong reasons for wanting to forestall a restoration of British rule at the end of the war. He therefore endeavoured to link Malaya's future with Indonesia's and in July 1945 played a prominent part in the establishment of a new organization called the Union of Peninsular Malays or KRIS (*Kesatuan Ra'ayat Indonesia Semenanjong*). It was a short-lived body, whose main claim to fame is that on 12 August 1945, when Soekarno and Hatta were returning to Djakarta after talks with the Japanese regional commander about immediate Indonesian independence, they discussed the inclusion of Malaya in an Indonesian declaration of independence with the KRIS leaders. At a brief meeting in Taiping with Soekarno and Hatta, Ibrahim Ya'acob declared that KRIS was preparing to send a delegation to Djakarta for the independence ceremony and to take part in the formation of the Republic of Indonesia. In Ya'acob's account of the meeting, Soekarno shook hands with him and said 'Let us form one single Motherland for all the sons of Indonesia', to which he replied that 'we, the Malays in Malaya are with loyalty in full support of the idea of a single Motherland, with Malaya as part of Free Indonesia'.[13] Nothing came of all this, however, because the Japanese surrender followed too suddenly and the Indonesians went ahead with their Proclamation of Independence without bothering about Malaya. (Soekarno does not even refer to the incident in his 'autobiography'.) But it is interesting to note that the delegation which was to have gone to Djakarta would have included four Sultans as well as the radicals from KRIS. Conceivably a broadly-based Pan-Indonesian movement might have developed at that critical juncture if the Japanese collapse had not occurred so quickly. There was certainly support for it on the Indonesian side, as we shall see. But KRIS collapsed along with the plans for obtaining independence from the Japanese. Ibrahim Ya'acob fled to Indonesia to continue the struggle from there. Soon afterwards a new party appeared, the Malayan Nationalist Party (MNP), which had

many of the same characteristics and personnel as the old KMM —
radical anti-colonialism, strongly pro-Indonesian sentiment, ideological
links with the Communists and a desire to unite the left-wing groups of
all races. We shall return shortly to its relations with Indonesia during
the turbulent years 1945-9 after turning briefly to the Indonesian side
of the story.

After the Japanese had offered Indonesia the prospect of early independence in mid-1945 and work on the political and constitutional structure
of the new state came under discussion, the question of whether Malaya
and the British Borneo colonies should be included in the national territory of Indonesia was debated in the Investigating Committee for Preparation of Indonesia's Independence (*Badan Penjelidik Kemerdekaan
Indonesia,* or BPKI) on 11 July 1945.[14] By a vote of 39 out of 66, the
Committee accepted the arguments for their inclusion put forward by
Mr. Mohammed Yamin and Ir. Soekarno. The debate has a certain
historical interest as an expression of the views which influenced Indonesians on this matter, although it had no practical significance, since
the decision rested at that time in the hands of the Japanese authorities:
the final preparations for independence went ahead under the auspices
of a different committee in such great haste that no formal consideration
was given to the question of Indonesia's boundaries. It was tacitly assumed
that they were the boundaries of the former Netherlands Indies — the
view of the minority in the BPKI — but the 1945 Constitution did not
even define this point.

The debate was interesting mainly for the fact that Soekarno sided with
Yamin in his essentially historical and geo-political approach to the
problem against the more cautious arguments of Hatta, who advocated
that the matter be determined by international law, i.e. that Indonesia
be confined to the territory of the Netherlands Indies. Yamin's basic
principle was simple — '... that the areas which should be included in
Indonesian territory are those which have given birth to Indonesian
people: the motherland of a people will be transformed into the territory
of a State'. The areas he listed as inhabited by Indonesians were the
islands of the Netherlands Indies (including West New Guinea), Timor,
North Borneo and Malaya. In addition to this ethnic criterion, he also
advanced an argument based on the earlier unity of the archipelago under
Majapahit, as revealed in the *Nagarakrtagama,* and the will to unity felt
by the Indonesian people since pre-historic times. By restoring the four
northern states of Malaya (which Japan had transferred to Thailand,
from which they are 'as different as night is from day, whereas they are
no different from Indonesia') to their motherland, Indonesia would be
righting a wrong. Yamin felt no doubts that 'the whole population of
Malaya wants to join with us' — although his concern with this point
seemed to be secondary to his emphasis on the geopolitical necessity of
reuniting the archipelago and the peninsula. Soekarno, in his brief endorsement of Yamin's arguments, put a little more weight on the wishes
of the Malayans, referring not only to scores of letters and telegrams he

had received from Malays asking that Malaya be included in Indonesia, but also to a visit several days earlier (9 July) by three young men from Singapore, including 'Lt.-Col. Abdullah Ibrahim' (presumably Ibrahim Ya'acob) conveying the same request on behalf of the youth of Malaya. Apart from that, he went on, 'I am convinced that the people of Malaya feel themselves as Indonesians, belonging to Indonesia and as one of us'.

Soekarno's case rested squarely on anti-imperialism, not Pan-Indonesianism: he admitted that he had once dreamt of a 'Pan-Indonesia' embracing the Philippines as well as Malaya, 'but the Philippines is now independent, so we must respect the sovereignty of the Philippine nation, so we need no longer talk of a Pan-Indonesia'. He also briefly mentioned the need to control both sides of the Straits of Malacca if Indonesia were to become strong and secure. There was no need to be confined to the former territory of the Dutch, he said, because 'we are not having talks with the Dutch or the British, but we are having talks with the Imperial Japanese Government, and the hands of the Japanese government will decide what shall form the future State of Indonesia'. Hatta also regarded the question as one for the Japanese to determine, but took his stand on the former territory of the Dutch, preferring to see Malaya an independent state within Greater East Asia — though he went on to add that 'if the people of Malaya themselves desire to join with us, I shall have no objection to that'. Another moderate leader, Hadji Agus Salim, also urged that the decision be made 'not on the basis of the desire expressed by only two or three emissaries who happen to come, but on the basis of the desire expressed by the general population in those territories'. This view did not prevail, however, against the more appealing doctrines of Yamin and Soekarno, which played upon the notions of Muslim and Malay unity, as well as historical greatness.

The existence of these sentiments should not be ignored, but the extent of their political significance is quite another matter. When it came to the point, they had little influence on political behaviour. The proclamation of independence did not mention the inclusion of Malaya, while the Taiping plan to include a Malayan delegation in the ceremony was abandoned. In the tumultuous circumstances of August 1945 it could hardly have been otherwise. But there is no indication that the idea of merging the Indonesian and Malayan struggles for independence was ever again considered seriously by the Indonesian leaders. They had problems enough in fighting the Dutch and no desire to add the British as their adversaries. Hatta's view that the national territory should embrace the former Netherlands Indies simply came to be accepted tacitly. During the later dispute with the Dutch over West Irian, the Indonesian government argued its case solely on this basis and repeatedly denied any wider claims (although several embarrassing statements were made by individuals, which the government had to repudiate subsequently).[15] The claim to West Irian was generally not argued on the basis that Indonesia was the successor state to Majapahit or even, as could have been argued, of the Sultanate of Tidore. Perhaps this was merely a tactical precaution, however, an elaborate diplomatic facade behind which the ideal of *Indonesia Raja* still aroused powerful irredentist feelings. But if that were the case, it is extraordinary that no Indonesian political party or individual political leader, with the solitary exception of Mohammed Yamin, attempted to capitalize on such sentiments. Nor was any serious effort made in later years to intervene in Malayan politics or draw Malaya into a union with Indonesia, although contact seems to have been maintained with a few individuals in Malaya and Borneo who harboured Pan-Indonesian visions (such as Azahari, Ibrahim Ya'acob and Zaidi) or who had participated in the Indonesian struggle for independence, with the aim, no doubt, of utilizing them or encouraging them if the circumstances were propitious.

Yamin was unique among the major Indonesian politicians in his eagerness to seize every opportunity to extol the historic greatness of the Indonesian people. He wrote copiously on their past glories and his books were widely circulated to schools, although they can be classed as poetic fantasies rather than serious histories. He was something of a rogue elephant in Indonesian politics, deriving his influence more from his association with Soekarno than from any party or personal following, for his romantic view of history and sweepingly geo-political, historicist view of Indonesia's place in the world was very similar to the President's; in fact, he played a role somewhat similar to that of a traditional *pudjangga* or court historian-chronicler who contributed to the creation of the state-myth.

But no other politician of note attempted to take up Yamin's themes and after he died in 1962 no one emerged to assume his mantle as the great *pudjangga* at Soekarno's court. Even Soekarno, who frequently larded his speeches with references to the historic glories of Indonesia in an attempt to conjure up the spirit of national greatness, never made the same use of the *Indonesia Raja* theme as Yamin. His nationalism sprang more from other sources, anti-colonialism and an ideology of revolution. It was eclectic and diffuse, however, and Soekarno could doubtless have incorporated irredentist elements into it if he had needed to. But the significant point is that he did not need to stimulate sentiments of this kind, as Hitler and Mussolini did, and that the diffuse feeling that North Borneo 'naturally belonged' to Indonesia in much the same way as Malaya and Indonesia 'naturally' shared one motherland was never exploited politically, simply because it was not necessary or expedient at any point between 1945 and 1965.

Since there were many Sumatrans, Boyanese and even Javanese in Malaya and Singapore, the Indonesian government endeavoured to contact them, organize them and utilize their aid during the Indonesian struggle for independence against the Dutch (1945–9). Various Indonesian representatives were established in Singapore and Malaya to act as trading and arms-buying agencies and establish contact with outside sources of support. If the Malaysian government's White Paper can be believed, some of these activities veered in the direction of intelligence work on the one hand and, on the other, of spreading the appeal of *Indonesia Raja* and urging Indonesian residents in Malaya to look upon Indonesia still as their homeland.[16] The evidence presented in the White Paper is hardly sufficient to warrant the conclusion that there was any overriding government policy to subvert Malaya and draw it into Indonesia's embrace, however. During the period when the Indonesians were fighting colonialism and Malaya was still under colonial rule, the activities of Indonesia's representatives there were bound to be unorthodox and must often have had a sinister and conspiratorial quality. Their most fruitful contacts were almost inevitably with left-wing groups in bad odour with the colonial authorities. That some of these men were encouraged and even financed by the Indonesian consulates is neither surprising nor particularly shocking, for most countries seem to engage in similar pursuits and they do not necessarily imply expansionist aims. The peculiar geographical and demographic circumstances of Malaya created unusual opportunities for Indonesian influence and propaganda, of course, and it would be naive to assume that these were not exploited to some extent by zealous officials fishing in troubled waters. There is probably a great deal yet to be revealed about this subterranean aspect of Indonesian-Malayan relations in the turbulent post-war years, but it seems that in the calmer decade after 1950 the Indonesian government itself did not pursue any very specific policies towards Malaya, except insofar as it may have continued to assist opponents of colonial rule and kept in touch with dissident pro-Indonesian Malays.

In 1947 the Sjahrir government appointed Dr. Oetojo, former Secretary-General of the Foreign Ministry, to be the first official diplomatic representative in Singapore (not recognized as such by the British government, of course) to coordinate the activities of the various Indonesian Associations in Malaya. According to the later Malaysian White Paper on the subject,[17] he was also engaged in intelligence activities in order

...to penetrate Malay and Indonesian organizations with the object of spreading the doctrine of Greater Indonesia within which Malaya would find its 'freedom'.... The direction of intelligence activities was to change with the needs of the Indonesian Republican leaders. At first when Indonesia was struggling for survival, action was defensive. Intelligence was sought on the activities (political, diplomatic, economic and military) of dissident Indonesian groups, and on black market and smuggling activities which drained the economic energy from the new Republic. Once the Republic became strong, intelligence was sought about political activities within the Malaysia-to-be territories, either of groups of Indonesians, which were not amenable to Indonesian pressure or blandishments or, on the other hand, groups in which Indonesian officials could play the role of back-seat driver to Indonesia's interest.

No less important was the aim to turn public opinion in Malaya in an Indonesian direction. Attention was concentrated on the fringe of Malay extremist youths on racial grounds: on youth groups whose enthusiasm and frustrations could be worked on, who could be mobilized for training, and who would take the risks of subversive action; on Communist groups because of their anti-colonial policy, and on groups of Indonesian-born, or Malayan-born groups of Indonesian origin, who, like the Boyanese, kept close links with their island of origin, who could be brought to respond to the appeal of *Indonesia Raya*, and who could influence local-born Malays by the appeal of identity of culture, race and religion. The argument was at times anti-colonial and anti-European, at others anti-Chinese, always with the suggestion that Indonesia had shown the way to power and wealth for the Malays.

The political situation was very confused on both sides of the Malacca Straits in the years 1945–8. In Indonesia the Republican governments of the time were having difficulty enough, apart from their struggles with the Dutch, in establishing their authority over rival aspirants for power, particularly over the followers of Tan Malaka, with whom some of the Malay radical nationalists were in contact.[18] Singapore was at that time a veritable hotbed of political intrigue by politicians from both sides of the Straits.

In Malaya, a storm of protest which stirred Malay nationalism into vigorous life for the first time was aroused by the British attempt in 1945–6 to impose the Malayan Union constitution in place of the former ramshackle set of separate administrative arrangements for the Straits Settlements, the Federated Malay States and the Unfederated Malay States. (Neither Sarawak, Brunei nor British North Borneo was formally a colony until 1946, it should be remembered.) These old arrangements had persisted down to the Second World War in spite of occasional efforts by empire-building pro-consuls to weld the region into a single colony under centralized control. Although British rule had for over half a century been binding the various parts of the peninsula together relentlessly in a web of legal, administrative and economic institutions, the fiction of indirect rule through the Sultans who were merely 'advised' by British Residents was still preserved in the Malay states, largely because of the political inconvenience of antagonizing the leaders of Malay society. After the War, however, the old policy was abruptly reversed by the Labour government in its attempt to create a Malay Union, under which the residual sovereignty of the conservative Sultans would simply have been abolished and the structure of government unified under direct Colonial Office rule.

The Malayan Union scheme provided for a common citizenship in the peninsula (but not in Singapore, whose political development subsequently diverged from Malaya's in various respects) and a common citizenship. It aroused vehement Malay opposition, partly because of the abrasive manner of its introduction, but also because 'the whole conception of the Malay Rulers as the embodiment of sovereignty and the Malays as a privileged indigenous community was to be replaced by a system of equal rights for all under a colonial regime heading for democratic self-government'. To justify the abrogation of Malay rights it was argued that the Malays were now a minority community in Malaya.[19] In the storm of controversy aroused by the proposal, the United Malay Nationalist Organization (UMNO) emerged as the major exponent of a new Malay nationalism. At the same time several other political organizations arose in opposition to UMNO, notably the Malayan Nationalist Party as the voice of radicalism among the Malays and the Malayan Democratic Union among the non-Malays, recruited largely from the Western-educated middle classes of Singapore and the major towns. These groups opposed the Malayan Union scheme as a continuation of colonial rule, but they did not carry much weight against the colonial authorities (as UMNO now began to do) and did not long survive the chilly political winds of 1948. In that year the British dropped the Union scheme in favour of a Federation Agreement negotiated with the Sultans, who were left a greater degree of sovereignty in their states in return for their willingness to accept a strong federal government in Kuala Lumpur and a compromise formula for extending Malayan citizenship to those non-Malays who had made their homes there. The left wing denounced the Federation Agreement as a reactionary step and soon afterwards the Malayan Communist Party (MCP) embarked upon the armed revolt which came to be known as 'The Emergency'.

During the fighting which continued throughout the next twelve years, the Communists failed, however, to divert the British from their course of gradual political advance towards independence on a basis which virtually took the primacy of the Malays for granted. The Emergency retarded the pace of that advance and worked to the serious disadvantage of the Malayan Chinese, since they came under suspicion of sympathy with the Malayan Communist Party which was largely Chinese in its membership and leadership and drew its support from the rest of the Chinese community, partly out of sympathy, partly out of sheer blackmail.

In the storm over the Malayan Union in 1945–6, a prominent part was played by the radicals of the Malay Nationalist Party (MNP), Ahmad Boestamam and Ishak bin Haji Mohammed, who were the most strongly inclined to merge their struggle against colonial rule with Indonesia's on political, ideological and racial grounds. They found themselves making common cause with the Malayan Communist Party and the Malayan Democratic Union in the struggle over the Malayan Union scheme in 1946–7. Strange bedfellows though Communists and advocates of Pan-Malay solidarity were to seem later, they would not have been so far apart in their aims at that time when anti-colonialism was the dominant theme of both ideologies. Even the relatively moderate Indonesian governments of 1946–7 would have felt themselves to have more in common with these groups than with the Sultans and UMNO conservatives. The MNP allegedly went so far in its anti-colonial stand that it identified itself entirely with the Indonesian struggle for independence and 'accepted the necessity for a period of outright rule by Indonesia'.[20] Boestamam and Ibrahim Ya'acob (the latter safely ensconced in Indonesia after 1945) had close contacts with Tan Malaka, the Indonesian Trotskyist or national-communist leader, in 1945–6 (until he was gaoled in June 1946), while other MNP members who were Communists were in contact with the PKI leader of that time, Alimin. The PKI was in a state of disarray in the first months of Indonesian independence, still taking the Moscow line of opposition to 'bourgeois nationalists' such as Soekarno and Hatta, but Tan Malaka's stature as an old time Comintern agent for South-East Asia made him one of the most prominent Indonesian leaders after Soekarno; so he would have been a natural ally for radical young Malay revolutionaries. Probably neither he nor they felt much concern about national boundaries established by the colonial powers. Their primary concern was to mobilize revolutionary forces in both colonies to overthrow colonial rule: national boundaries would be determined thereafter according to the real will of the people.

After 1948, the situation was considerably changed by the Communist insurgency in Malaya and the abortive Communist revolt in Indonesia at Madiun in September 1948. The parties which came to power in Indonesia after the confusion of 1948–9 (the second Dutch 'military action' following close behind the Communist revolt) were strongly anti-Communist in outlook during the first years of the 1950s. And on the Malayan side, the MNP disappeared in 1950 (Boestamam and Ishak having been arrested since 1948); the old left-wing coalition of 1946–7 disintegrated and by 1952 political leadership in the Malayan struggle for independence was taken over by UMNO under the new leadership of Tunku Abdul Rahman.[21] Both the radical nationalists and the more conservative Malay politicians who looked towards Dato Onn bin Ja'afar or the Sultans for leadership were shouldered aside as the UMNO-MCA Alliance established a firm basis of electoral support in 1952–5. Although both the Tunku and the Alliance have later been characterized as politically conservative it is worth recalling that the Tunku himself was regarded by the British at that time as too brash and impatient in his anti-colonialism and political strategy. The British looked on communal parties like UMNO with disfavour, preferring Dato Onn and his multi-racial IMP as the potential vehicle of Malayan nationalism — until his political prospects were dashed in the elections of July 1955, at which the Alliance swept the poll and the Tunku became Chief Minister. The Tunku was still shackled by the limitations of a colonial constitution, but it was certain by then that Malaya (though not Singapore) would achieve independence in 1957.[22]

Shortly after the 1955 elections in Malaya and Indonesia, the Tunku was invited to pay an official visit to Indonesia by the Burhannuddin Harahap government, a Masjumi-led, strongly anti-Communist 'caretaker' government which welcomed the opportunity to make this gesture of solidarity with a fellow-Malay leader who was opposing colonial rule. Otherwise there were few notable landmarks in Indonesian-Malayan relations during the early 1950s, about which little has been written. Malaya was not officially represented at the Bandung Afro-Asian Conference in April 1955, just before the Malayan elections, although an UMNO member who happened to be in Indonesia at the time attended in a private capacity.[23] Dr. Burhanuddin al-Helmy, Ibrahim Ya'acob and others were there, lobbying strenuously for official recognition as the true voice of Malayan nationalism, but the Ali Sastroamidjojo government appears to have been reluctant to commit itself on this matter, although Burhanuddin's expenses were allegedly paid by the Indonesian consulate in Singapore.[24] While in Indonesia, he discussed his political plans with Ibrahim Ya'acob, who had now been in Indonesia for ten years and had close links with certain radical nationalist elements there. On his return to Malaya Burhanuddin participated in the founding of the Party Ra'ayat, but withdrew in 1956 to become leader of the Pan-Malayan Islamic Party (PMIP) after Boestamam, newly released from detention, was elected chairman of the former.

The PMIP was often categorized as a 'right-wing' party, because of its Islamic ideological base and its strength among the more conservative Malay communities of the east coast where UMNO was relatively weak, but Burhanuddin's career shows that such labels are not very meaningful in a society where politics is essentially communal rather than ideological. Later the PMIP became virtually a party of the poorer Malays alienated by UMNO's establishment character. Even when Soekarno's flirtation with the Communists was provoking cries of alarm from UMNO politicians at the time of confrontation, the PMIP clung to the ideal of Malay solidarity as the basis for *musjawarah* (consultation) with Indonesia. Seen in a broader perspective, there was a thread of consistency in the attitudes of these non-establishment Malays throughout these two decades.

UNEASY NEIGHBOURS, 1957–1962

When Malaya became independent in August 1957, its new government's relations with the Indonesian government were outwardly cordial, although somewhat clouded by doubts on both sides about the political complexion of the other. Very quickly, however, these doubts began to harden into mistrust and positive suspicion. Within a few months, the Tunku's government had to make decisions on a number of issues which, although not in themselves sufficient to create open enmity, were bound to confirm each government's stereotype of the other as potentially unfriendly. These issues were Malaya's attitude to the PRRI-Permesta rebellion which broke out in February 1958, the smuggling problem, the West Irian dispute between Indonesia and Holland and the two governments' very different policies on matters of regional security and Communism.[25]

The political conflict between certain outer island dissidents and the Djakarta government, which grew into overt rebellion in February 1958, had been developing for more than six months at the time when Malaya received her independence. The Tunku was immediately faced with the disagreeable necessity of making a long-term assessment about the future stability and political complexion of Soekarno's new Guided Democracy. It was not an easy guess to make, for Soekarno's position seemed to be very shaky in the middle of 1957. Few impartial observers would have found it credible at the time that, if a showdown developed between the central government and the regionalists, the latter would utterly fail or that Soekarno would succeed as quickly and completely as he did in re-establishing the authority of the central government and concentrating political power in his own hands as a result. The balance of advantages seemed to favour the regionalists in too many respects.

There were many signs that the Malayan government (like that of Britain, Australia and the USA) simply backed the wrong horse at this stage.[26] Soekarno was regarded in Kuala Lumpur as dangerously sympathetic to the PKI and politically beholden to it. Because the long struggle against the Communists in Malaya was not yet over, Communism loomed large in the thinking of the Tunku and his colleagues, to an extent which Soekarno later described as 'Communist-phobia'. The activities of the Indonesian rebels in Malaya and Singapore in 1958 and the Malayan government's attitude towards them greatly irritated the Indonesian government. In March, the Malayan government formally proclaimed a policy of non-involvement in the PRRI affair, which it said was an internal matter for the Indonesian government.[27] But it gave a considerable measure of sympathy and assistance to the rebels, many of whom passed in and out of Singapore and Malaya freely during 1957–8. The Malayan government argued that so long as these men held valid Indonesian travel documents 'the Federal government was bound to honour them' — though it was simultaneously excluding Indonesian Communists carrying similar documents. When the Indonesian government cancelled the passports of persons known to be actively engaged in the rebellion, the Malayan government finally refused further entry to them: but it did not take any action to expel those who were already in the country and it granted asylum to a number of rebels and rebel sympathizers who had defected from Indonesian embassies abroad, merely demanding assurances from them that they would not engage in activities against the Indonesian government while residing in Malaya. While the lack of an extradition treaty absolved the Malayan government from any legal obligation to hand over the rebels, there was no doubt where its sympathies lay and it is hardly surprising that Indonesians regarded the Malayans as hypocritical in their protestations of non-involvement. They could have made life much more difficult for the rebels and given far more assistance to the Indonesian government if they had chosen to do so and as the latter felt they should have done.

On the other hand, some of the Indonesian demands for an extradition treaty were unrealistic and abrasive. After the signing of a Treaty of Friendship in 1959, in which provision had been made for the signing of an extradition agreement, Subandrio wrote to the Malayan Minister for External Affairs in January 1960 proposing such a treaty; but he evidently envisaged that political refugees should be covered, not just criminal offenders, as is normal under international law, for his proposal was linked to the case of thirty rebels who had fled to Penang shortly before. Malaya proposed a regular treaty covering only criminal offenders, but the Indonesian government did not respond to this. Malaya's refusal of the broader request was regarded by the Indonesian press, however, as further evidence that she was simply giving aid and encouragement to the rebels.[28]

Both sides went on behaving in ways which increased the other's suspicions about its motives. The appointment of Brig.-Gen. Djatikusumo as Indonesian Consul-General in Singapore late in 1958 gave rise to alarm on several counts. He was undiplomatically blunt and forthright in his utterances against the rebels and their sympathizers in Malaya and Singapore: he also made vigorous efforts to contact Indonesian groups there and allegedly laid the basis of an Indonesian intelligence organization which continued to function actively under his successor, Colonel Soegih Arto, until 1963. According to the Malaysian White Paper on Indonesian subversive activities during these years, they carried out military espionage (but on a rather trivial scale, unless there was far more to it than the White Paper revealed), made contact with pro-Indonesian groups among the Malayan government's political opponents and utilized the West Irian issue as an opportunity to recruit Malayan volunteers for the struggle against colonialism who were later indoctrinated in Indonesia for use against Malaysia.[29] It could hardly be claimed that these activities amounted to any very sinister design before 1962, although they seem to have been intensified in 1962-3, to the discomfort of the Malaysian government.

Another source of friction which was aggravated by the rebellion was the smuggling problem. The dissident provinces of Indonesia engaged in 'barter trade' with Singapore and Malaya very extensively in 1957-8, to the great profit of Singapore's shipowners and merchants. Smuggling continued to cause a serious loss of foreign exchange even after the central government restored its control over the dissident provinces, for it was never able to suppress it forcibly by naval patrols or to check it at the source through its own officials, many of whom were underpaid and easily corrupted by illegal traders, many of them Chinese with business contacts in Singapore. According to a very common Djakarta opinion, the Singapore and Malayan authorities ought to have been cooperating with the Indonesian government to apprehend the law-breakers; even though there was no obligation in international law for them to do so, it was frequently argued in Indonesia that economic pressure could be brought to bear on Singapore to make her do so. Singapore merchants were anxious to increase their entrepot trade by shipping more manufactured goods into Indonesia and the appropriate licences were controlled by Djakarta. Officials in Singapore reacted contemptuously to such crude pressures; it was no concern of theirs to cut the throats of their own hard-working traders by acting as Indonesia's customs officials, they would say, and even if they did, the illegal export of Indonesia's rubber would merely be deflected to Malaya and elsewhere. They tended to despise the Indonesians for their inability to manage their own affairs better and for their corruptibility, while Indonesians waxed morally indignant that Singapore merchants were growing fat at their expense on the basis of illegal trading and mere 'middleman' activities.

The tragedy of the smuggling problem was that each country had a degree of right on its side. It was practically impossible to check smuggling from the Indonesian side so long as the economy was in such disorder and

Singapore-Malaya provided such an easy haven for smugglers. Only superhuman government officials in Indonesia could have been expected to resist the temptations to corruption created by the large profits of illegal trade. Even the high patriotic fervour and intensified suppression of 'barter trade' after the trade break with Malaysia in September 1963 caused only a brief cessation of smuggling. By mid-1964, 'barter trade' was back to its old levels, until it was stopped, ironically, by a ban from the Malaysian side, imposed simply to keep out subversives.

The West Irian issue, on which the two nations might have been drawn together in common opposition to colonialism, also aroused resentments on both sides. In September 1957, Malaya abstained in a vote at the UN on an Indonesian motion to inscribe the West Irian issue on the agenda for that session: the government said it was too preoccupied by domestic problems arising from its newly-won independence and would vote only on issues directly affecting Malaya, remaining neutral on all others. The Indonesian government took a very poor view of this, since it desperately needed every vote it could muster. When the next vote was taken in November, Malaya supported the Indonesian cause and her government continued to do so in public statements throughout the next five years until the West Irian question was settled. Moreover, the Tunku made several personal attempts to bring about a peaceful settlement, partly because the dispute was constantly creating embarrassments for the Malayan government by facing it with invidious decisions on various minor matters, about which it could not afford to antagonize Indonesia.[30] The dispute was also working to the domestic advantage of the PKI at the expense of the moderates in Indonesian politics, like Hatta and Djuanda, with whom the Malayan leaders felt the strongest sympathy.[31] There was little prospect of normalizing relations with Indonesia until this potentially explosive problem was settled. But Malaya's efforts to mediate aroused more ire in Djakarta than gratitude.

The Tunku's most important attempt to act as a mediator between the Indonesians and the Dutch occurred towards the end of 1960, evidently with the encouragement of Nasution and Djuanda, as well as the Indonesian press. But in the middle of his 'sacred mission' to bring the two sides closer together, he was bitterly attacked by Subandrio for exceeding his mandate as a negotiator; this torpedoed the entire operation. The vehemence of Subandrio's outburst seemed quite disproportionate to the alleged transgression, however, and it is hard to avoid the conclusion that the Tunku was an unwitting victim of Indonesian factional in-fighting between 'hawks' and 'doves' on the Irian issue. In any case, the episode rankled on both sides for a long time.[32] Malaya continued to support the Indonesians in their struggle with the Dutch, denying the latter transit facilities and backing Indonesia in UN votes on the issue, for her leaders were still anxious to see the dispute settled as soon as possible. No objection was raised to Indonesia's recruitment of volunteers for West Irian in Singapore and Malaya, who were taken to Indonesia for military training and indoctrination, although these volunteers, who would have been motivated by either strongly pro-Indonesian or anti-colonialist sentiments, were likely to be highly receptive to Indonesian indoctrination about the neo-colonialist nature of Malaysia and the Alliance government.

Soekarno and the Tunku also held radically different views of Communism and colonialism as factors affecting the security of South-East Asia. Soekarno regarded colonialism and neo-colonialism as a more persistent and imminent threat to Indonesia's independence than Communism. To the Tunku, Communism had been the great threat to Malaya between 1948 and 1957, while in the subsequent years his most serious problems were posed by Peking-oriented Chinese and the opponents of his Malaysia scheme whom he regarded as Communist agents or dupes. He was very much a Muslim insofar as his thinking embodied a sharp dichotomy between wicked Communists and virtuous anti-Communists, in contrast to Soekarno's very Javanese syncretism in such matters. Colonialism seemed a far less sinister threat to the Tunku, for he had experienced it in its most benign form and had never had to generate the intensity of passion to fight against it that Soekarno had. Both experience and ideology inclined the two men to opposing views on the two most sensitive issues involving the security of the region.

Among the nations of the Afro-Asian world, Malaya belonged for reasons of both policy and ideology to the right wing, while Indonesia was moving steadily towards the extreme left. Indonesia had the prestige of having been host to the Bandung conference and one of the oldest non-aligned nations. Malaya sought to prove herself a good Afro-Asian by her zeal on issues like opposition to apartheid in South Africa and contributing to the UN Congo force. The Tunku sided firmly with India against China in the border war of October 1962. Malayan foreign policies frequently diverged from Indonesia's even on questions like the Congo while on matters of more direct importance to them involving security and Cold War problems they were generally opposed.

Malaya did not join SEATO when she became independent in 1957 and her leaders always took care not to be directly associated with it, although probably not so much out of conviction as to avoid affronting other Afro-Asians. But she depended almost entirely for the military underpinnings of her security on the Anglo-Malayan defence agreement of October 1957 and the related arrangements with Australia and New Zealand.[33] Her ministers ritually scoffed at SEATO from time to time and they took care not to be too closely identified with American policies on Cold War issues, but despite their claims to have an independent foreign policy, and to be no more 'aligned' by their defence treaty than Cuba, she was not invited to the Belgrade or Cairo Conferences of Non-Aligned Nations in 1961 or 1964.

Indonesia raised no objection to the Anglo-Malayan defence agreement in 1957. The Malayan Ambassador took pains to forestall any criticism there by stressing that it would not involve Malaya in any commitments contrary to her national interests or inimical to Indonesia, nor draw her into SEATO. But in Indonesian eyes Malaya was not really independent so long as she was militarily dependent on another power. However, it was generally expected that British forces would sooner or later be withdrawing from the region, so the Indonesians were not deeply concerned by the Anglo-Malayan defence agreement at a time when the West Irian issue was still dominating their horizons. SEATO and the American presence in South-East Asia generally attracted far more attention in the years up to 1962. One reason for Indonesia's eleventh-hour opposition to the British presence in 1963-4 was the realization that extension of the 1957 agreement to cover Malaysia might entail an indefinite prolongation of the British military arrangements there.

Another symbol of the differences between the two governments was the contrast between the Tunku's enthusiasm for regional cooperation, as embodied in the Association of South-East Asian States (ASA) and Soekarno's disdain for it. The Tunku favoured it as a pragmatic association for specific economic purposes, but he also saw that no regional grouping made much sense unless Indonesia was included and he hoped that she would eventually join. Soekarno refused to participate because he regarded it as virtually an extension of SEATO and a veiled threat to non-alignment, since Malaya, Thailand and the Philippines all had close ties with the Western powers.[34] The latter consideration did not inhibit Soekarno from participating in Maphilindo in 1963, however, when he could see some political advantage in doing so. Malay brotherhood was to him an instrument of political manipulation rather than of deep conviction.

[1]The diplomatic rivalries and negotiations which led up to the definition of these frontiers are outlined, in the case of the Malacca Straits, in Nicholas Tarling, 'British Policy in the Malay Peninsula and Archipelago, 1824–71', *Journal of the Malayan Branch, Royal Asiatic Society*, vol. XXX, part 3, 1957; in the case of the Borneo frontier in Graham Irwin, 'Nineteenth Century Borneo. A Study in Diplomatic Rivalry', *Verhandelingen van het Koninklijk Instituut voor Taal-, Land- en Volkenkunde*, deel XV, 1955: and in regard to the North Borneo-Sulu region Leigh R. Wright, 'Historical Notes on the North Borneo Dispute', *Journal of Asian Studies*, vol. XXV, no.3, May 1966, pp. 471–84.

[2]For a traditional account of the various 'waves of migration' into the archipelago, see Fay Cooper-Cole, *The Peoples of Malaysia* (van Nostrand, 1945); a stimulating new approach to the matter is suggested by Felix Keesing, 'Some Notes on Early Migrations in the Southwest Pacific Area', *Southwestern Journal of Anthropology*, vol. XI, no. 2, Summer 1950, pp. 101–19: an excellent summary of his argument, clarifying the concept of 'race' is given by Clark Cunningham, *The Postwar Migration of the Toba-Bataks to East Sumatra* (Yale Southeast Asia Studies, Cultural Report Series, 1958), Appendix 1.

[3]This pattern of relationships has been spelled out more elaborately by C.D. Cowan in 'Continuity and Change in the International History of South-East Asia', *Journal of Southeast Asian History*, vol. IX, no. 1, March 1968, pp. 1–11. For a fuller history of the various states of South-East Asia, see D. G. E. Hall, *A History of Southeast Asia*, (Macmillan, 2nd ed., 1964).

[4]'There tends to be a correlation between international instability and the domestic insecurity of elites' concludes Richard Rosecranz from a study of the roots of international conflict in Europe over the last two centuries; *Action and Reaction in World Politics: International Systems in Perspective* (Boston, Houghton Mifflin, 1963).

[5]The extent of Majapahit's political power has been challenged by the Dutch historian, C. C. Berg, who attributes the 'empire-building' phase of Javanese power in the thirteenth and fourteenth centuries more to magico-spiritual strength based on Tantric rituals rather than military might: his theory is summarized in Hall, op. cit. pp. 77–89.

[6]The role of KPM in the economic unification of the Netherlands Indies is in G. C. Allen and Audrey Donnithorne, *Western Enterprise in Malaya and Indonesia. A Study in Economic Development* (Allen and Unwin, 1957), ch. 12. For Sumatra's earlier links with Singapore, see Tarling, op. cit.

[7]An excellent picture of the development of the Malayan elite under colonial rule is given in W. R. Roff, *The Origins of Malay Nationalism* (Yale University Press, 1967). On the Indonesian elite, see Robert van Niel, *The Emergence of the Modern Indonesian Elite* (The Hague, van Hoeve, 1960) and Hildred Geertz, 'Indonesian Cultures and Communities' in Ruth McVey (ed.), *Indonesia* (New Haven, Human Relations Area Files Press, 1963), ch. 2.

[8]Roff, op. cit. passim; Radin Soenarno, 'Malay Nationalism, 1900–45', *Journal of Southeast Asian History*, vol.I, no. 1, March 1960, pp. 1–28.

[9]Tunku Abdul Rahman acknowledged the point frankly to President Soekarno even at the height of confrontation, during the course of the Tokyo Conference.

[10]The Malayan Union constitution of 1946 represented an attempt by the British Labour Party government to impose some order on the untidy three-tier arrangement of Straits Settlements, Federated Malay States and Unfederated Malay States (but not Singapore; see below p. 37) by compelling the Sultans to transfer their sovereignty almost entirely to the British Crown. Although it did not provide for immediate political democracy, it did offer citizenship to both non-Malays and Malays on an equal basis.

[11]This point is brought out well in Robert Curtis, 'Malaysia and Indonesia', pp. 12–16.

[12]Soenarno, op. cit. pp. 22 ff; Roff, op. cit. pp. 222 ff.

[13]Ibid. p. 25.

[14]For fuller details of the Investigating Committee, see Benedict Anderson, *Some Aspects of Indonesian Politics under the Japanese Occupation: 1944–1945* (Cornell Modern Indonesian Project, Interim Report Series, 1961), pp. 18–32. The speech by Yamin on 31 May and the full debate on the subject on 11 July have been reprinted by the Malaysian Department of Information as *Background to Indonesia's Policy Towards Malaysia* (Kuala Lumpur, 1964), from which the extracts herein have been taken.

[15]In the first and fullest statement of Indonesia's claim to West New Guinea, the *Report of the Committee New Guinea (Irian) of the Netherlands-Indonesian Union* (The Hague, 1950), the historical argument was advanced by the Indonesian delegation (which included Mr. Yamin), but in the later United Nations General Assembly debates of 1954–7 Indonesian officials carefully refrained from using it.

[16]*Indonesian Intentions Towards Malaysia* (Kuala Lumpur, Penchetak Kerajaan, 1964), para. 6–14.

[17]Ibid. para. 7–8.

[18]For the story of Indonesian domestic politics in 1945–7 and Tan Malaka's threat to the Soekarno-Sjahrir alliance of those years, see G. McT. Kahin, *Nationalism and Revolution in Indonesia* (Cornell University Press, 1952), ch.6.; a much fuller account of the 1945–6 period, tracing the complexities of Indonesian politics in far more detail, is Benedict R. O'G. Anderson, *Java in a Time of Revolution: Occupation and Resistance, 1944–1946* (Ithaca, Cornell University Press, 1972).

[19]J. M. Gullick, *Malaya* (London, Benn, 2nd ed., 1964), p. 89. The complex background to the Malayan and Singapore politics of 1945–8 is outlined in T. H. Silcock and Ungku Abdul Aziz, 'Nationalism in Malaya', in W. L. Holland (ed.), *Asian Nationalism and the West* (Macmillan, New York, 1953), pp. 298 ff. See also J. de V. Allen, *The Malayan Union* (Yale Southeast Asian Studies, 1967).

[20]*Indonesian Intentions Towards Malaysia*, p. 9; the MNP adopted the Indonesian flag and national anthem and proclaimed its objective as 'Dominion Status within the Greater Indonesian Empire'.

[21]The emergence of UMNO and formation of the Alliance is well described in Margaret F. Clark, 'The Malayan Alliance and its Accommodation of Communal Pressures, 1952–62' (University of Malaya, MA thesis, 1964), to which I am considerably indebted for material in this section.

[22]On Singapore's constitutional relationship with Malaya after 1945, see pp. 37–9 below.

[23]A rather bizarre account of the Malayan groups at the Bandung Conference may be found in the compilation by the *Perikatan Pemuda Melayu di Luar Tanah Air* (Overseas Malay Youths Association) entitled *Anak Melayu Di Indonesia* (Djakarta, Gunung Agung, 1957), pp. 117 ff.

[24]*Indonesian Intentions Towards Malaysia*, p.10. Burhanuddin had been prominent at an All-Malay Youth Conference in Kuala Lumpur in April 1955. His biography is briefly set out in a preface to his *Azas Falsafah Kebangsaan Melayu* (Djakarta, Fa. Tekad, 1963) which is a Roman-script version of a pamphlet published in Malaya in Jawi script in 1950.

[25]The dissident movements in West Sumatra and North Sulawesi which culminated in the proclamation of the Revolutionary Republic of Indonesia (*Pemerintah Revolusioner Republik Indonesia* — PRRI) in Feb. 1958, supported by the distinct but parallel *Permesta* (*Perdjuangan Semesta* — Universal Struggle) movement in Sulawesi, are outlined in H. Feith, *Decline of Constitutional Democracy in Indonesia*, pp. 520–55, 578–91.

[26]Fuller surveys of American and Australian policy towards Indonesia at the time of the PRRI-Permesta revolt may be found in Daniel S. Lev, 'America, Indonesia and the Rebellion of 1958', *United Asia*, vol. XVII, no. 4, July-August 1965, pp. 305–9; and J. A. C. Mackie, 'Australian-Indonesian Relations', in G. Greenwood and N. D. Harper, *Australia in World Affairs 1956–1960* (Melbourne, F. W. Cheshire, 1963), pp. 296–304.

[27]Indonesia did not issue a declaration of insurgency, so the Malayan government claimed that it was under no obligation to take any action against the rebels: *Malayan-Indonesian Relations* (Kuala Lumpur, Jabatan Penerangan, 1964), para. 19.

[28]Ibid. para. 21–5.

[29]*Indonesian Intentions Towards Malaysia*, para. 15 ff.

[30]In June 1960 the Tunku had discussed the question of West New Guinea during a visit to Holland, but provoked some sharp comments in Indonesia for his pains: Subandrio commented that: 'The Tunku has a rather inflated opinion of his position in world politics'. After his major attempt at mediation in November 1960, discussed below, he again raised the issue at the 1961 Commonwealth Prime Ministers' Conference, but without significant result. There was no Indonesian reaction on that occasion.

[31]See Robert Curtis, op. cit. p. 15. Hatta visited Malaya in 1962 as a private citizen: his impressions of the Malaysia experiment, very critical of its implications for the Malays, are set out in 'One Indonesian View of the Malaysia Issue', *Asian Survey*, vol. V, no. 3, March 1965, pp. 139–43. Djuanda was liked by the Malayan leaders for his quiet and pragmatic approach to politics: the title *Tun* was bestowed upon him during his goodwill visit in 1959.

[32]*Malayan-Indonesian Relations*, paras. 38–9: see also paras. 34–45 for the Tunku's offer to mediate and Djuanda's acceptance of the offer and the Tunku's report to Soekarno on his mission.

[33]The status of British and Australian forces in Malaya, which might at any time be required elsewhere for SEATO purposes, was ambiguous, but the issue was unimportant in practice, except on one occasion. In 1962, when RAAF planes from Butterworth had to be sent to Thailand on a SEATO operation, they were flown to Singapore first, so that technically it could be said that the units stationed in Malaya had not been used for SEATO purposes. The Malayan government made no objection at that time to the use of Singapore bases and the units based there for SEATO purposes: Gullick, op. cit. pp. 147–8. See also R. W. Winks, 'Malaysia and the Commonwealth', in Wang Gungwu (ed.), *Malaysia. A Survey* (Singapore, Donald Moore Books, 1964), pp. 380–1.

[34]Further details on ASA (and the Tunku's earlier SEAFET proposal, South-East Asian Friendship and Economic Treaty) may be found in Lalita Prasad Singh, *The Politics of Economic Co-operation in Asia* (University of Missouri Press, 1966), pp. 215–21. Subandrio initially expressed interest in the SEAFET proposal and Yamin was enthusiastic about it, according to one informant, but Soekarno could not afford to antagonize the USSR by associating with SEATO governments at a time when he was hoping for substantial financial and military aid from her.

III

The Creation of Malaysia

BECAUSE of the great stress Indonesians put on the charge that Malaysia was a neo-colonialist creation, imposed on the people concerned without reference to their wishes by the wily British and their puppets, it is necessary to give some attention to the processes through which it came into being. While such allegations came uncomfortably close to the truth in some respects, they were far from it in others. One of the most striking features of Malaysia's birth was the utter ineffectiveness of the opponents of the scheme, both before and after Indonesia's intervention. Another was the paradox that the incorporation of Malaya, Singapore and the Borneo territories, which had been in the minds of British officials at least since 1892, but which the colonial authorities had never been able to achieve in the heyday of their power, could so readily be brought about by the government of independent Malaya.[1] The explanation of this paradox is to be found in the politics of ethnic diversity in the states concerned rather than in the machinations of the colonialists.

Whether or not the 'Malaysia experiment' was the best solution to the problems of terminating colonial rule in Singapore and British Borneo — or even a viable solution in the long run — is a question which cannot be adequately considered here. The rifts which have subsequently developed between Kuala Lumpur and Singapore and within the Borneo states have seemed to bear out some of the prophecies of gloom, though one might reply that prophecies of gloom are all too easy in such racially heterogeneous states as these and that the separation of Singapore in 1965 could have been avoided by greater forebearance on both sides. It was by no means unavoidable. And it is difficult to envisage any other formula that would have represented a more satisfactory compromise between the diverse interests of the peoples concerned and that would have had a chance of being accepted in the circumstances of 1961. In this and the following chapter, we will look briefly at the political dynamics of Malaysia's creation, without delving too deeply into the story, which has been told fully elsewhere.[2]

The British had administered Singapore separately from the Malay

TABLE 1

ETHNIC COMPOSITION OF THE MALAYSIAN POPULATION: DECEMBER 1961

(in thousands)

	Malaya	Singapore	Sarawak	Sabah	Total	%
Indigenous people	3,620	238	529	320	4,707	46.2
Chinese	2,670	1,279	243	110	4,302	42.2
Indians and Pakistanis	813	142	–	–	955	9.4
Others	129	41	8	45	223	2.2
Total	7,232	1,700	780	475	10,187	100.0
Percentage of distribution	70.9	16.7	7.7	4.7	100	

Source: Table from *Malaysia, Buku Tahunan Resmi, 1963* (Kuala Lumpur, Government Printer, 1964): 'Supplement, An Introduction to Malaysia', pp. 11–12.

states in colonial times and did not include it in either the abortive Malayan Union scheme in 1945 or the 1948 Federation, since they already had difficulties enough with the peninsular states because of Malay apprehensions about the rapid increase in the numbers and wealth of the Chinese (and to a lesser extent, Indian) population.[3] (See Table 1.) Malaya was pushed ahead towards independence more rapidly than Singapore after 1945, partly because of British sensitivity to the Malays' case, partly because it suited Britain to maintain direct colonial rule in the latter so long as the Singapore bases were important to her.[4] When Tunku Abdul Rahman emerged as head of an independent Malaya in 1957, he made it clear on several occasions that he was not at that time prepared to contemplate a merger of Singapore and the Federation. Chinese 'chauvinism' and radicalism in Singapore seemed to be too closely linked to the activities of the predominantly Chinese Malayan Communist Party (MCP) for Malay tastes. And there was no sign of any change in the Malayan government's attitude on the matter during the following years, until the Tunku's historic speech to the Foreign Correspondent's Association in Singapore on 27 May 1961.

'INDEPENDENCE THROUGH MERGER'

In Singapore, the People's Action Party (PAP) had consistently advocated merger with Malaya as the only feasible basis for Singapore's independence since its foundation in 1954. But the question did not become a prominent issue in Singapore politics, for the PAP was able to gain ground steadily over all its opponents on the basis of its broadly Socialist and anti-colonialist platform on domestic problems. With its sweeping victory in 1959, the PAP assumed office under a constitution providing for virtually full internal self-government, except over internal security, defence and foreign affairs, with the expectation that complete independence for Singapore would be granted when a review of the constitutional arrangements was made in 1963.[5] The new government therefore put great emphasis on the need for Singapore to demonstrate its 'Malayan' character and culture, so as to convince the Kuala Lumpur government that 'independence through merger with Malaya' could be now contemplated, since Singapore Chinese accepted Malaya as their homeland and were neither Chinese chauvinists nor Communists. But although the merger question was coming more and more prominently into the forefront throughout 1960, there was no sign whatever that the Tunku or his government was willing to consider it. It was a big step forward when the Tunku and Lee Kuan Yew exchanged visits in early 1961 for discussions of the problem over some diplomatic golf, after which the Tunku spoke more favourably than ever before about the PAP leaders ('as good Malayans as we are'), though he still insisted that merger would have to wait until some distant date 'when the people of Singapore are completely loyal to Malaya'.[6] Even in mid-May, Lee Kuan Yew spoke as if an early merger was out of the question, though he was hoping for some kind of common market arrangement with Malaya. What changed the Tunku's mind over the next few weeks was the development of a split in the PAP between the moderate English-educated leaders and the predominantly Chinese-educated radicals of the rank and file, which raised the spectre of Lee's downfall and a 'Chinese Cuba' on Malaya's very doorstep. So he held out the vague prospect of merger in his speech of 27 May and within two months found himself fully embarked on a campaign to achieve it. Ironically, the prospect of merger probably did more than anything else to precipitate the split within the PAP which made the achievement of merger essential for the political survival of Lee Kuan Yew.

The split within the PAP had various causes, stemming back ultimately to the diverse socio-cultural bases of the party's following. Ever since Lee Kuan Yew and his colleagues had founded the PAP in 1954 as an anti-colonialist, Socialist party on the far left of the political spectrum, it had drawn its support mainly from the Chinese-educated working class of Singapore and from a handful of English-educated intellectuals attracted by its reputation for efficiency and honesty. According to Lee, the former group included under-cover Communists and open-front pro-Communists who were both using the PAP at that time in the common struggle against colonial rule and trying to gain control of it from the non-Communists. In 1957 the left-wing group led by Lim Chin Siong came within an ace of capturing control, but were imprisoned by Lim Yew Hock's government just in time to allow Lee to reconstitute the party structure in a way which consolidated his control of the Central Executive Committee.[7] After the

PAP's overwhelming victory in the 1959 elections Lee arranged the release of the most prominent detainees from the party's left wing, who were given official jobs and some honour, but little power within the party, in the hope that they would be politically neutralized. Their frustrations soon made them restless, however, and within two years of its sweeping victory the PAP was again under severe strain from the tensions between its two wings. Some disillusionment was being felt among the rank and file, too, for the party leaders who had talked like fire-eating radicals when in opposition were now striving to show themselves moderate, pragmatic and realistic as ministers. They were all well aware that Singapore's economic prospects were too uncertain to permit the luxury of frightening away capitalist investors by too much talk of Socialism. Their attempt to create a 'Malayan' culture (in effect, a multi-racial culture) clashed with some of the aspirations of the China-oriented Chinese, to whom both Malay and English were foreign tongues. The great danger to the PAP leaders in 1960–1 was that 'Chinese chauvinism' allied to political radicalism might be mobilized by some new party to the left of the PAP — presumably with Communist backing — and thus outflank the PAP on a platform of militant anti-colonialism, just as the PAP had outflanked the Workers' Party before it.

That was why an otherwise unimportant defeat for the PAP at the Hong Lim by-election of April 1961 was regarded by Lee as such a critical danger signal. The seat was won by Ong Eng Guan, an erratic but ambitious ex-PAP Minister who had been expelled in the middle of 1960 after trying to outflank the leadership in a bid for party support with a set of strongly anti-colonial resolutions. Ong fought the by-election in his former electorate of Hong Lim in April 1961 and soundly defeated the official PAP candidate, blatantly and successfully appealing to radical anti-colonialism and Chinese self-consciousness, campaigning for complete independence and accusing the government of compromise with colonialism. It was a serious set-back to Lee Kuan Yew, who later said that he even considered resigning because of it.[8] (He soon turned the set-back to his own advantage, however, by playing on the Tunku's fear of the dangers to Malaya if Singapore fell under the domination of Communists or Chinese radicals.) Ong had not been supported by Lim Chin Siong and the left-wing trade union leaders who later split from the PAP, for they had their differences with him on other grounds. But they must have realized the implications of the PAP's loss of popular support. Six weeks later, Lim Chin Siong and his five colleagues ('the trade union six' as they came to be called) issued their first open challenge to the PAP leadership. In the meantime, the Tunku's proposal of merger through Malaysia had injected a new and controversial element into the Singapore political scene.

The showdown between Lee Kuan Yew and the left wing of the PAP came to a head during another by-election for the Anson constituency in June and July. This seat should have been easy for the PAP to hold in normal circumstances, but it was being contested by the flamboyant former Chief Minister, David Marshall, whose tiny Workers' Party was able to claim to be more radically anti-colonialist than the PAP by advocating independence in 1963. Lim Chin Siong and his colleagues seized this opportunity to launch a challenge to Lee Kuan Yew on the question of abolishing the Internal Security Council, threatening that they would only support the PAP in the Anson by-election if the government agreed to press for abolition of the Council in the 1963 negotiations on the Singapore constitution. This demand was tactically shrewd, for it was known to be unacceptable to the Malayan government, which held the controlling vote in the Internal Security Council. So if Lee accepted their demand, he would destroy his chances of achieving merger, whereas if he refused he would risk a split within his party. Lee decided to take the risks involved in a break with the PAP left wing and pin his hopes on the possibility of merger. Opening the Anson campaign on 9 June, the PAP leaders stated categorically that in the 1963 negotiations they would seek 'complete independence through merger with the Federation or merger with a larger federation'.[9]

During the Anson campaign, the 'trade union six' seemed to be as much concerned about these domestic questions as with the merger issue, on which they carefully avoided an open clash with the PAP leadership, even though they were now adding a strongly anti-colonialist slant to official party policy. But Lee Kuan Yew had already concluded that Lim Chin Siong had 'received his instructions from his organisation, the communist underground'[10] and it was Lee who now brought the issue to a head. Shortly before the election, the PAP leaders threatened a complete break with the dissidents, accusing them of confusing the voters and not giving the party their full support, for Lim Chin Siong had criticized the way the Tunku had launched the Malaysia proposal. Two days later 8 PAP assemblymen announced their support for the 'trade union six' and Lee demanded the resignation of Lim Chin Siong, Sandra Woodhull and Fong Swee Suan as political secretaries. Next day, Marshall narrowly won the Anson seat. When the Assembly met a week later, Lee had a bare majority of one on a motion of confidence in his government.[11]

Lim Chin Siong and his colleagues then proceeded to form themselves into the *Barisan Sosialis* (Socialist Front) as the major opposition party. Lee's position was now very precarious and his difficulties in steering Singapore towards merger seemed formidable. Although he could count on the support of the more conservative opposition parties on votes affecting merger, which the latter favoured, they would not have been averse from toppling his government and forcing a general election if they felt the opportunity was ripe for it. Moreover, Lee could not altogether rely on the Tunku's help in his new predicament, since UMNO and the Singapore People's Alliance had a prior claim on his affections. If Lee was to survive, he had to push the merger proposal through to a successful conclusion before 1963 without losing any further PAP supporters in the Assembly and without being out-manoeuvred by his opponents on the right or the left.[12] It was a gamble at long odds.

TABLE 2
PARTY STRENGTHS IN SINGAPORE

	May 1959 election	July 1961 PAP split	September 1963 election
Peoples' Action Party ⎫	–	26	37
Barisan Sosialis ⎬	43	13	13
United Peoples' Party ⎭	–	3	1
Workers' Party	–	1	–
SPA (Singapore Peoples' Alliance)	4	4	–
UMNO	3	3	–
Independent	1	1	–
	51	51	51

Note: In the 1955 Singapore election, the Labour Front (headed originally by David Marshall, later by Lim Yew Hock), which later became the nucleus of the SPA, had won only 10 seats out of 24; other small, right-wing parties and independents, 8, the Alliance 3 and PAP 3 (out of the 4 seats it contested).

THE MALAYSIA HARD SELL

The Tunku's brief reference in his speech of 27 May to the possibility, sooner or later, of 'an understanding with Britain and the peoples of Singapore, North Borneo, Brunei and Sarawak' had a catalytic effect on the politics of all the territories mentioned. The campaign to translate the idea into a reality gathered momentum so quickly that within three months the Tunku's vague hint was being discussed in quite specific detail as an objective to be achieved by 1963. In the Borneo territories, political parties were for the first time stirred into vigorous life, as we shall see in the next chapter. In Singapore, the question of merger soon became the dominant political issue, bringing the rift within the PAP into the open and very nearly causing the downfall of Lee Kuan Yew's government. Yet more than anything else it was the PAP split which transformed the Tunku's nebulous idea into an urgent political issue.

Once the movement to establish Malaysia got under way, it proceeded so rapidly that the Tunku did not even have an opportunity to consult his own party stalwarts who were uneasy about its far-reaching implications for Malay hegemony in the Federation. For the first few weeks, however, the Tunku's suggestion was discussed as if it were little more than a vague possibility in the distant future; speculation about the terms on which it might be practicable nearly all implied a very different form of associa-tion from the one which finally came into being. Moreover, the first reactions of nearly all the political parties except those in Singapore differed a good deal from the policies they later adopted when the issue

became one of immediate practical politics. In most of the original comments on the Tunku's proposal, a loose confederation of the five territories
was assumed, not the kind of close association actually achieved. Prior
unification of the Borneo states was regarded by some as an essential first
step, with self-government preceding entry into Malaysia.[13]   The whole
process was generally expected to take five to six years or more: the possibility that it might be complete before the 1963 talks on Singapore's constitution was not scouted seriously in public until well into July, after the
split in the PAP.

The Tunku himself said little to indicate what his ideas on the subject
were until he paid a visit to Brunei at the beginning of July. There he
spoke enthusiastically about the possibility of Brunei entering the Federation as a twelfth state — but was both non-committal and tactless regarding the other Borneo states, thus giving rise to fears of Malay or Brunei
domination over them.[14] Just after his visit, the first major statement of
opposition to the scheme was uttered by three Borneo politicians, A. M.
Azahari of the Brunei *Party Ra'ayat*, Ong Kee Hui of the Sarawak United
Peoples' Party and Donald Stephens, North Borneo's most vocal indigenous political leader. Although the first two of these represented the
most long-established political parties in the island (five and two years
respectively!) nobody could have predicted at the time whether or not they
reflected popular opinion on the matter in Borneo — if indeed one could
talk about such a thing. Shortly afterwards the Malay leaders in Sarawak
pronounced firmly in favour of the scheme and the great debate began to
get under way there. The Tunku did his best to remedy the impression that
Malaya was intending to 'colonize' Borneo, but his remarks implying that
all non-Chinese were Malays rankled with Dayaks and Kadazans for some
time after.

Towards the end of July 1961, ten days after the Anson by-election, the
Tunku invited Lee for talks on the conditions of merger between Singapore
and Malaysia. This was the first distinct sign that merger had become an
urgent political issue, not just a long-range ideal. A few days later informal
discussions on the idea were held with representatives from Sarawak and
North Borneo who were in Singapore for a meeting of the Commonwealth
Parliamentary Association and plans made to hold a Malaysia Solidarity
Consultative Committee meeting in Jesselton during August.[15] The
Tunku warmly welcomed these moves and the Malaysia bandwagon soon
began to roll. Donald Stephens was quickly converted to active support
for Malaysia. And a stream of visitors from Sarawak and Sabah were
brought to the Federation on junketing tours during the following months
to see the good things which Malaysia was to bring them.

The Tunku and Lee Kuan Yew reached agreement in principle on the
broad terms of merger on 23 August. Several months later the two
governments published the Heads of Agreement embodying these terms.[16]
Singapore would become

...a state within the Federation, but on special conditions and with a larger
measure of local autonomy than the other States forming the Federation.

Defence, External Affairs and Security will be the responsibility of the Federation Government; Education and Labour that of the Singapore Government ... while the Federation will be responsible for the conduct of external relations, the special position of Singapore in relation to entrepot trade will be safeguarded.

Further details were still to be worked out on many points, but no great difficulty had been encountered in reaching agreement up to this point. Nor did the Tunku or Lee meet any serious difficulties in winning acceptance in their respective Parliaments for merger on these conditions.

The British government's response to the Tunku's plan was initially cautious; it avoided either enthusiasm or firm commitment to it. Contrary to Indonesian charges that British neo-colonialists were the *dalang* (puppet-master) manipulating the whole affair from behind the scenes, the evidence seems to indicate that the British government (and the Australian) were distinctly sceptical about Malaysia until the prospects of success became much brighter.[17] Malayan and British interests in the scheme were, of course, very nearly complementary, but they were not entirely identical. Lord Selkirk, the Commissioner General for South-East Asia, merely commended it as a 'sound long-term plan' in his first statement about it on June 14. The British Prime Minister remarked only that the idea was 'striking and merited the widest discussion'. When the Governors of Sarawak and North Borneo and the High Commissioner for Brunei met Lord Selkirk in Singapore on 26 June, they were noticeably lukewarm in their attitudes to Malaysia. Sir William Goode, of North Borneo, found it 'interesting' and 'constructive' as a future possibility, but added that for the immediate future 'we are thinking very much more in terms of getting close to our immediate friends, Sarawak and Brunei'. His colleague from Sarawak spoke a little more warmly of it, but also implied that more immediate problems were occupying the Sarawak government's attention.[18]

The Tunku later told the Malayan Parliament that he had forced the British authorities to agree to two principles as a basis for future discussion of the Malaysia issue. First, that sovereignty over the Borneo territories should be transferred directly to the Federation (i.e. there would be no prior grant of independence, which might have entailed the possibility of Chinese-dominated governments there) and, second, in the future Anglo-Malaysian defence arrangements, the use of Singapore for SEATO purposes would be prohibited, just as the use of the Malayan forces and bases were under the 1957 Anglo-Malaya defence agreement.[19] There certainly was some difference of emphasis and interests between them on these issues, particularly the latter. Neither the Tunku nor Lee Kuan Yew could afford to leave himself open to the charge of being associated with SEATO. Hence in the joint statement issued by the Malayan and British governments after talks between the Tunku and Mr. Macmillan in November, no mention was made of SEATO (leaving open to divergent interpretations the question of whether troops in Malaysia under the Defence Agreement could be used for SEATO purposes); the existing defence agreement with Malaya was to be extended to the other territories, with the stipulation that the United Kingdom would be granted the right to retain bases at Singapore 'for the purpose of assisting in the Defence of Malaysia and for Commonwealth Defence and for the preservation of peace in Southeast Asia' — a phrase which the Indonesians later objected to violently.[20] In these talks the British government acknowledged that the creation of a Federation of Malaysia was 'a desirable aim' and agreed to set up a joint Commission of Malayan and British members 'to ascertain the views of the peoples of North Borneo and Sarawak on this question: and ... to make recommendations' before any final decision was made. But neither the British nor the Australian government expressed support for the scheme in other than carefully qualified terms.

With those aspects of the problem clarified, Britain's support for Malaysia became more whole-hearted. The colonial authorities in Borneo saw the writing on the wall and abandoned their initial hesitations. In general, the threat of Communism, or Chinese dominance, in the whole area was simply taken for granted, not only in official propaganda, but even in the Cobbold Report, which seems to have been in other respects a judicious and fair-minded assessment of the Borneo situation. By August 1962, shortly after the Cobbold Commission's generally favourable report on the Borneo reaction, the British and Malayan governments decided in principle that Malaysia should be brought into being on 31 August 1963, subject to the necessary legislation being passed in the parliaments concerned.[21] In short, Britain's adherence to the Malaysia scheme became more binding as it came closer to fruition. Paradoxically, Indonesia's threat to Malaysia in 1963 probably had more influence in cementing the British commitment than mere intellectual conviction would ever had had.

The governments concerned may have been quickly convinced that Malaysia was 'a desirable aim', but the people had to be convinced also. There were all kinds of doubts and fears to be assuaged, many of them substantial and understandable, about the consequences for the citizens of all five territories. The propaganda campaigns in favour of Malaysia varied in intensity from one place to another; Singapore's was by far the most formidable, for there the opposition was most vigorous, whereas in Brunei the Sultan seems to have made little attempt to counter the *Party Ra'ayat's* campaign against Malaysia. It can hardly be denied that the people of Singapore and the Borneo colonies were 'bulldozed' to some extent into accepting the Malaysia scheme by the weight of government propaganda — although there was no lack of opposition propaganda also. But there were other reasons why it was accepted as well.

The opposition parties found the odds heavily weighted against them in terms of political opportunities to obstruct the scheme, almost impossibly so in the case of the Singapore referendum on merger. In Malaya itself, with 25 seats in parliament against 74, they had virtually no hope of out-voting the Tunku's government on any issue. Yet the impotence of the opposition parties was not due just to the heavy-handedness of the governments in power (in Singapore, the Barisan came within an ace of unseating the PAP government in July 1961 and in the Sarawak elections of 1963 SUPP nearly achieved power), but also to the inability of the various opponents of the Malaysia scheme to devise more effective means of mounting a popular, vote-catching campaign against it. If they had been able to offer convincing alternatives to the Tunku's plan, or if they had even been able to attract sufficient supporters away from the parties in power to create a threat that the achievement of Malaysia might prove a Pyrrhic victory for the Tunku or Lee, the affair might have developed very differently. As it happened, the opposition parties in Malaya were pitifully divided and confused in their strategy on the issue, and were outmanoeuvred into tactical mistakes which weakened their case seriously, as also the *Barisan Sosialis* in Singapore. (This was not true in Sarawak, however, where SUPP was in a strong position on the Sarawak political chessboard until Indonesian confrontation compromised its position seriously in 1963.) It would be hard to make a convincing case against the proposition that by 1963 the supporters of the Malaysia scheme outnumbered its opponents in each of the constituent states, except Brunei. The various elections of 1962–4 in the Borneo colonies, Singapore and the Federation all resulted in substantial defeats for opponents of Malaysia.[22] Confrontation was partly responsible for these defeats, but there are signs that political support for the Malaysia scheme had begun to prevail over the opposition to it in all the territories concerned well before confrontation — in fact, even before the Singapore referendum of September 1962, which was the first major setback for the anti-Malaysia forces.

The rapid swing of political opinion in Sarawak and North Borneo from initial rejection of the Malaysia scheme to a cautious acceptance of it by 1962 can be related to two factors. One was the political dynamics of the two colonies which we will need to examine more closely in the next chapter. The other was the clever campaign of persuasion and coaxing carried out by the Malayan and Singapore governments during the six months between the first Malaysian Solidarity Consultative Committee meeting in August and the fourth in February 1962, at which the general principles on which the new federation would be based were adopted. Those meetings were supplemented by an effective public relations campaign conducted by the two governments — tours for Borneo political leaders to see Malaya's rural development program in action and Singapore's 'Malaysia scholarships'.[23] Equally striking was the ineffectiveness of opposition to Malaysia within Singapore and Malaya to which we must now turn.

THE SINGAPORE REFERENDUM

The Singapore political scene during the year that preceded the referendum on merger on 1 September 1962 was marked by acute tension and uncertainty, as the PAP had a bare majority of only one seat in the Assembly. The *Barisan Sosialis* was incessantly attacking Lee Kuan Yew's 'phony merger' and bidding uninhibitedly for the support of the militant Chinese-educated section of the population on the basis of appeals which were not easy for the PAP to counter on the same emotional plane. Lee Kuan Yew's tactics in surviving the parliamentary pitfalls of that year and steering the merger proposal successfully through the referendum were a triumph of nerve, political skill and sheer ruthlessness.[24]

It has frequently been charged that the 1962 referendum was rigged or meaningless or, at the very least, heavily loaded against the opponents of the Tunku's scheme, since the voters were not given an opportunity simply to vote 'No' to merger.[25] The PAP justified the form of the referendum—a choice between three alternative conditions of merger with the Federation — on the ground that all parties in Singapore supported the principle of merger and only differed on the question of the terms on which it should be brought about. *Barisan* spokesmen had foolishly argued in the early stages of the discussions on Malaysia that Singapore should enter the Federation on the same terms as Penang and Malacca had done earlier: they overlooked the fact that on those terms Malaysian citizenship laws would have disenfranchised a very large number of Singapore citizens, so the *Barisan* was left in the awkward position of having to argue that the Federation should amend its citizenship laws in order to incorporate Singapore. Lee Kuan Yew may have had logic on his side in arguing that the referendum should offer voters a choice of alternatives, not a direct invitation to accept or reject merger, but he played his cards in a way which was calculated to give his opponents almost no opportunity to mobilize an effective expression of popular opinion against Malaysia. Even the decision to hold a referendum appears to have been based upon the PAP leaders' realization that it would be suicidal to seek a popular mandate on this great issue by holding a general election.[26]

In the debates on this question in the Singapore Assembly throughout 1962, Lee could generally count on the support of the right-wing parties (SPA and UMNO) to ensure a safe majority for his government against attacks from the *Barisan* and its allies, Ong Eng Guan's UPP and David Marshall, the sole representative of the Workers' Party. But Lee had to tread a delicate path during the crucial stages, as the PAP lacked a secure majority in the Assembly for several months. He was therefore not in a position to bulldoze the referendum bill through against all opposition, but had to be able to ensure the rather grudging support of Lim Yew Hock's SPA.[27]

The *Barisan* mounted a big publicity campaign against the referendum in April and May 1962, with attempts to demonstrate massive opposition to the government's proposals through protest moves in trades unions and schools, including an attempted boycott of schools on 21 May and a minor showdown with the government when it refused a union request to stage a demonstration on National Day. These measures failed, insofar as their purpose was to convince the government that the *Barisan* could muster overwhelming mass support in a showdown or tie up Singapore by mass action. The government's refusal to be either browbeaten by them or provoked into an unduly repressive response seems to have marked something of a watershed in the campaign, for if mass action was not successful, the *Barisan* was deprived of its potentially most powerful weapon. It was already blocked in its first move to discredit, if not defeat, the government over the referendum, for when the *Barisan* threatened to urge its followers to cast blank votes in protest at the terms of the referendum, the PAP incorporated in the bill (even before the Assembly had considered the form of the alternatives to be offered to the electors) a provision which ensured that blank or defaced ballots would be deemed to imply willingness to 'accept the decision of the Legislative Assembly on the matter referred for the Referendum' — and there was no prospect of the *Barisan* obtaining a majority there. Nevertheless, a substantial protest vote of blank ballots would certainly have shaken Lee Kuan Yew's moral authority and left his government dangerously vulnerable to later defeat. It was this that the *Barisan* did, in fact, campaign for in the referendum, but without much success.

The form of ballot paper which finally emerged from the hard-fought Assembly debates in July offered the voters of Singapore a choice between three alternative formulas for merger, the first based on the government's Heads of Agreement with Malaya announced in November 1961, the second based on the alleged *Barisan* proposal for merger on a basis of equality with the other eleven states of the Federation (i.e. the Penang-Malacca conditions) and the third — included on the insistence of Lim Yew Hock in the final stages of the Assembly debate — entry on terms 'no less favourable than the terms for the Borneo territories' (although these had not yet been finally determined). Lee Kuan Yew was later able to play a further 'trump card' which greatly strengthened the PAP campaign for the first alternative when he managed to induce the Tunku to concede common citizenship of Malaysia to Singapore citizens, instead of merely Malaysian 'nationality' as the November 1961 agreement had provided.[28] Revealing this melodramatically on 14 August on his return from a trip to London, he also announced that the referendum would be held on 1 September, thus leaving the *Barisan* very little time to devise any alternative strategy to defeat or discredit the government.

The results of the referendum were a triumph for Lee which apparently exceeded even his expectations. Of those who voted (90 per cent of Singapore's 624,000 registered electors), 397,000 or 71 per cent voted for alternative A and only 3 per cent for the other two alternatives, while only 144,000 votes (25 per cent) were blank or spoiled. It was not even necessary for Lee to rely on the Assembly's right to determine the disposal of the blank votes. Just how this result should be interpreted is, of course, a contentious issue.[29] Some *Barisan* supporters may have voted for alternative A reluctantly and only because only they had been alarmed by the consequences of using their ballots differently, lest they find themselves disenfranchised. Nevertheless, it is difficult to resist the conclusion that the PAP must have succeeded in convincing a large percentage of the voters, however grudgingly, that there was no real alternative to its own proposals for Malaysia and that these proposals were broadly acceptable. If the *Barisan* had a-massed a really substantial protest vote of blank ballots, the significance of the result would have been highly questionable. It campaigned with that aim, but it failed. The referendum was not a shining example of the democratic process, but it did signify something about the political support for the two sides. Willard Hanna has summarized the matter neatly in his comment on Lee's strategem of 'head I win, tails you lose' in quoting Lee's own comment to the Legislative Assembly: 'I say without the slightest sense of moral embarrassment. We were meeting card-sharpers and we were not going in like spring chickens.'[30]

The referendum result restored the PAP government's drooping prestige and represented a very severe set-back for the *Barisan*, although the PAP still held only the barest majority in the Assembly and could not yet contemplate the future with complete confidence. But the way was now cleared towards the final detailed negotiations on entry into Malaysia, for the only possibility for the *Barisan* to forestall it thereafter would have been the extremely risky course of stirring up riots within Singapore in the hope of inducing the Tunku to change his mind or forcing the British to assume control under emergency powers. The Brunei revolt and Indonesia's proclamation of confrontation (described below in chapter VI) heightened the risks of such eventualities, but also provided Lee with justification for action to forestall them. On 2 February 1963, a large number of *Barisan* leaders, including Lim Chin Siong, Woodhull, the Puthucheary brothers and others were arrested or detained under the Internal Security Regulations, a blow to the *Barisan* which appears to have greatly weakened its capacity to mount any successful opposition to the government either in the Assembly or outside during 1963. How far the *Barisan* was implicated in the plans for the Brunei revolt we can only judge from the allegations of the security services.[31] Lim Chin Siong was in touch with Azahari a few days before the revolt and presumably knew that something was afoot, but the *Barisan's* public support for the rebellion was lukewarm — a public meeting in support of the rebels on 23 December and some predictable statements that this 'popular rising against colonialism' deserved the support of all anti-colonialists.[32] The *Barisan* leaders were also alleged to have discussed plans to mount violent actions against Malaysia in the various territories concerned, a charge for which there may well have been some substance, although little evidence for it was made public. But Indonesian confrontation created an atmosphere of emergency in which opposition to Malaysia was easily made to look suspect and the *Barisan* was unable to regain the political initiative against Lee Kuan Yew.

THE OPPOSITION IN MALAYA

Commenting on the reaction of the opposition parties to the Tunku's plan, Willard Hanna has observed that 'the opposition was generally bumbling and inconclusive at first, for, like the support, it was taken by surprise by the proposal'. Of the Malayan parties, the PMIP (Pan-Malayan Islamic Party) crystallized its attitude most quickly, opposing the proposal as a threat to the Malays and demanding instead that the scope of Malaysia should be widened to bring in (ultimately) the Philippines and Indonesia as well. In the debate in the Malayan parliament on 17 October on a motion to accept the Malaysia plan in principle, the PMIP leader, Dr. Burhanuddin (whose Pan-Malay inclinations have already been mentioned), moved an amendment to this effect which was ruled out of order. But the PMIP was the only party to oppose the scheme unequivocally. The Socialist Front accepted it in principle while criticizing the manner of its introduction and certain of the terms of association. The Vice-President of the Labour Party of Malaya, Ramanathan, had supported the Tunku's call for unity of Malaya and Singapore as early as 28 May, although demanding merger of these two prior to the incorporation of the Borneo territories. In the October debate, Lim Kean Siew, secretary of the Labour Party, expressed support in principle for Malaysia while expressing reservations on the conditions. Ahmad Boestaman, chairman of the Socialist Front and of its predominantly Malay wing, the *Party Rakyat*, stated that the Malaysia proposed by the Tunku was not *Melayu Raya* (which he did not define further) and said he would support it only if it was a first step to *Malaysia Raya*, not if it was to be an instrument of British interests.

The Socialist Front was at this stage uncertain of the stand it should take — and there must have been some difficulty created for it by the Pan-Malay inclinations of the *Party Rakyat*, which would hardly have appealed to the essentially Chinese supporters of the Labour Party. After a Socialist Front delegation visited Borneo in November, a report drafted by Lim Kean Siew stated the party's position on Malaysia in surprisingly moderate terms, by no means as militantly antagonistic to the Tunku's scheme as the party was to become in 1962. It advised the party to accept Malaysia, but to direct its attention to the details of its structure.[33] The report first approached the problem in a broad geographical context:

As we look down, we see that Sarawak, Brunei and North Borneo form but a very small portion of the whole land mass of Borneo, whilst Singapore is a little dot right at the tip of Asia, wrapped round by Malaya, Sumatra, Java, Borneo and the Philippines, which sit like a crescent around a star. Above Singapore and Malaya are the South East Asian States of Cambodia, Laos, and Indo-China, which are non-Muslim States.... Taking the picture as a whole we can only answer the question 'Where do we belong?' by saying that we belong to the islands of Malaysia rather than to the Cambodian and Indo-China States. Therefore we must accept the idea of Malaysia as a logical one and that the Malaysian concept of the Prime Minister of Malaya, which includes only the territories of the Federation of Malaya, Singapore, Sarawak, Brunei and British North Borneo, is but a step towards this greater Malaysia. How the concept of Greater Malaysia is going to shape and what form it will take is another question, but there is no doubt that there must be a form of integration which should include all these territories I have mentioned, because, geographically, linguistically, culturally, and economically we belong to one another.

Lim then touched lightly on two notes which later could be developed into more strident demands for regional association and resistance to neo-colonialism.

Therefore, I say, that the Malaysian concept of the Federation and the North Bornean States is a proper concept, but it is only part of a greater concept and must lead towards this greater concept without which there can be no reality. Secondly, since the Malaysia as conceived today, consists of only a few territories in a vast complex, and since it will cause uneasiness to its neighbouring countries if it aligns itself to any power bloc, it must, in order to survive in peace and democracy, stand very strongly for non-alignment in order not to cause friction within Malaysia so that one day we could all get together again as a Malaysian bloc of nations having its own independent way of life, without suppression and domination from external countries.

The essential argument against the Tunku's scheme, which the Socialist Front and its allies were later to stress with all their might, was that self-determination for the Borneo territories must precede federation. The association should be based on the consent of the people, not on the *fiat* of the colonial rulers. There should be no discrimination in matters of citizenship, migration or civil rights between one state and another, since this would mean that the smaller states could be dominated by the larger ones, which would be domination and imperialism: all must come in as equals. (This argument was well calculated to provide grounds for opposing the special conditions for Singapore's entry, which Lee Kuan Yew had just negotiated with the Tunku.) Full integration was necessary, with a common educational programme, said Lim, without any elements of racialism or discrimination. As a statement of principles, all this was admirable. As a piece of political dialectics, it was skilful in providing a basis for opposing both the Tunku and Lee Kuan Yew. But it was quite unrealistic as an alternative political programme, for there was no chance that UMNO would ever have agreed to merger on those terms.

In January 1962, the Malaysian Socialist Conference in Kuala Lumpur brought together the various parties opposed to the Tunku's scheme, *Party Rakyat* and Labour Party of Malaya, *Party Ra'ayat* of Brunei, Sarawak United Peoples Party, the *Barisan Sosialis*, Workers Party, United Peoples Party and *Party Rakyat* of Singapore — and the one Socialist Party supporting the Tunku's scheme, the PAP. Lee Kuan Yew later said that the PAP's only purpose in attending was to show the conference up in its true colours as a Communist front. The PAP put up a working paper which defended the Malaysia proposal and when the conference (predictably) rejected it, the PAP delegates walked out and the PAP was solemnly expelled as not truly Socialist. If there had ever been any prospect that the Socialist Front in Malaya might seek to strengthen its political prospects at the 1964 elections by drawing the PAP into some sort of working alliance with it (a strategy which some of its members had certainly contemplated during the previous year or so), it was now lost. The Socialist Front was henceforth aligned in the struggle against Malaysia with the *Barisan*, SUPP and Azahari's *Party Ra'ayat*.

The tone of the Joint Communique issued by the Conference was quite restrained (reflecting the moderating hand of David Marshall no doubt) and merely expressed 'concern' and 'regret' at the haste being shown to rush the Malaysia scheme through without proper care to ensure the consent of the people.[34] It was strikingly different from the resolution put forward by Boestamam's *Party Rakyat*, which while favouring the closer association of the Malaysian peoples 'as one step towards the realization of *Melayu Raya*' went on to 'strongly condemn' the Tunku's proposal as 'hostile to the concept of Melayu Raya, directed against progressive forces in this region and aimed as a military threat to Indonesia'. The *Party Rakyat* went on to demand negotiation with 'the true representatives of the people and not with the British government' and couched its entire statement in strongly pro-Indonesian and anti-colonialist terms. By contrast, the statement of Brunei's *Party Ra'ayat* was a quaintly naive call for the conference to 'decide and fight for Kalimantan Utara to be re-unified, and that [sic] Sri Paduka Baginda Maulana Al-Sultan Brunei be placed on the throne of Kalimantan Utara within the structure of constitutional monarchy'. The Tunku's concept of Malaysia 'could be considered a great insult to the people of Kalimantan Utara', it protested, for it alleged that the people there were accepting Communism! Marxism in Malaysia has had some strange bedfellows.

It can hardly have been a sheer coincidence that the hardening of the Socialist Front's attitude to Malaysia at this time followed so closely on the Partindo conference in Indonesia which Boestamam attended and which was soon followed by the PKI's declaration of its opposition to the scheme. On the other hand, we need not assume that Boestamam was taking orders from the PKI, or that he was specifically expecting Indonesian help in his opposition to Malaysia. The anti-colonialist attack was a logical one, for by this time the general pattern of response to the Malaysia proposal was becoming clearer and it must have been obvious to all opponents of the Malaysia scheme that they might have great difficulty in overthrowing Lee Kuan Yew and frustrating the Tunku's scheme, something that had earlier seemed quite possible. If Malaysia was to be forestalled, it would not happen in the parliaments of Singapore or Kuala Lumpur, but in the streets, or the jungle. Brunei and Sarawak offered better prospects — and it was not surprising that by May 1962 there were reports of a North Borneo National Army training in Indonesian territory near Malinau.

Throughout the rest of 1962, few other opportunities arose for the Malayan opponents of Malaysia to block the scheme effectively. Attention was largely focused on what was happening in Singapore and Borneo. The PMIP continued to attack the threat to the special position of the Malays implicit in the Malaysia proposal (or so Dr Burhanuddin argued), but fissures were becoming visible within the PMIP and the Tunku had little to fear from that quarter.[35] The Socialist Front supported the arguments of the *Barisan Sosialis* about the allegedly undemocratic means by which Malaysia was being created, but there was not much sign that this argument, or the charge that Malaysia was a mere continuation of British dominance in new guise, was winning any new popular support for the Socialist Front. (It was, however, playing into the hands of the radical wing of the Labour Party which was weakening the grip of its moderate leadership by early 1963 and, by committing the party to more militant support for the *Barisan Sosialis*, increasing the risks of a crackdown against it under the Internal Security Regulations on charges of Communist affiliations, a risk which the more moderate leaders were most anxious to avoid.) The Tunku was actively engaged in the campaign for Malaysia in Borneo and Singapore, presenting the issues sometimes crudely and heavy-handedly as if it were solely a struggle with Communism. On several occasions he even threatened that he would close the causeway between Singapore and Johore if the Malaysia proposal was rejected in Singapore. From time to time he brandished the threat to use the government's extensive powers under the Internal Security Regulations against Communists and 'extremists' in Malaya, although little use was in fact made of them until after the Brunei revolt.[36]

After the Brunei revolt, nine Socialist Front leaders in Malaya were promptly detained and on 13 February Boestamam himself, although a member of parliament, was arrested on charges of forming a secret underground movement for subversive purposes and maintaining contact with the Indonesian Communist Party.[37] The vulnerability of the opposition parties was greatly increased, for pro-Indonesian sentiment was now as suspect as pro-Communist sentiments had been. Indonesian confrontation undoubtedly strengthened the Malayan government's hand against its domestic critics (as the Singapore arrests in February had shown) by creating the atmosphere of national emergency in which the use of its sweeping powers under the Internal Security Regulations was more easily justified.

The PMIP tried to turn its sense of kinship with the Indonesians to advantage by attacking the Tunku's government for pursuing a policy which had brought Malaya into conflict with Indonesia. In March 1963 it moved a motion in parliament that the government and people should 'pursue all avenues of maintaining peaceful relations with its neighbours' and calling for referral of the dispute to the United Nations in the event of a crisis. But the embarrassing predicament of the opponents of Malaysia was merely highlighted by this motion, for both the PPP and UDP attacked the PMIP for opposing Malaysia. An attempt was made by Aziz Ishak to bring all the opposition parties together on a common programme of no confidence in the Lansdowne report, a call for a referendum on Borneo and condemnation of arbitrary arrests.[38] A common statement was issued, attributing the blame for the Brunei revolt and friction with Indonesia to the Malayan government's methods of pursuing the goal of Malaysia and insisting on the right of self-determination for Singapore and the Borneo states. This statement was sent to U Thant with the claim that the parties concerned represented 49 per cent of the votes cast in the 1959 general elections. But the bald fact remained that they carried few votes in the parliament and had little hope of conjuring up a wave of popular support in the face of Indonesia's expressed hostility to Malaysia.

Instead of being able to convert the Tunku's international embarrassments in 1963 into a political asset to themselves, the opposition parties found that they had lost support as a result of their identification with the anti-Malaysia cause (as the 1964 election was to show to their great cost) and were themselves divided in their attitudes to the Indonesian threat. The PMIP was attracted by the Maphilindo proposal in June, whereas the Labour Party, PPP and UDP were deeply uneasy about it. However, the prospect of a *rapprochement* with Indonesia on the basis of the Manila Accords was a momentary relief to them all; both the PMIP and the other parties supported the plan for a UN ascertainment of Borneo opinion as being in accordance with their policy on the matter. But by this stage the opposition parties in Malaya could only react passively to events, not do anything to shape them.

[1]Amalgamation of the various British territories had been suggested by Lord Brassey in the House of Lords in 1892. The Minister for Colonies in the Attlee government, Mr. Creech Jones, mentioned that the idea had been under discussion during his term of office: *Hansard*, vol. 681, p. 973 (19 July 1963). See also statements in 1954–5 by Lord Boothby and Mr. Lennox Boyd in *Straits Times*, 7 September 1954, and *New York Times*, 20 August 1955.

[2]See Sir Richard Allen, *Malaysia: Prospect and Retrospect* (Oxford University Press, London, 1968); Willard A. Hanna, *The Formation of Malaysia* (American Universities Field Staff Inc., New York, 1964); T. E. Smith, *The Background to Malaysia* (Royal Institute of International Affairs, London, 1963); R. S. Milne, *Government and Politics in Malaysia* (Houghton Mifflin, Boston, 1967); Milton Osborne, *Singapore and Malaysia* (Cornell University, Southeast Asia Program, Data Paper no. 53, 1964).

[3]The Chinese have made up nearly 75 per cent of Singapore's population throughout the last sixty years; see Roff, op. cit. p. 33; Norton Ginsburg and Chester F. Roberts, Jr., *Malaya* (University of Washington Press, 1958), p. 57. The immigration of Chinese, Indians and Indonesians into Malaya is analysed in T. E. Smith, *Population Growth in Malaya* (Royal Institute of International Affairs, London, 1952).

[4]See J. de V. Allen, *The Malayan Union* (Yale University, Southeast Asia Studies, Monograph Series, no. 10, 1967), pp. 94–5.

[5]The Internal Security Council consisted of 3 Singapore government representatives, 3 British and 1 Malayan government representative, which left the latter in a position to cast the decisive vote in the event of any deadlock.

[6]Milton Osborne, op. cit. pp. 4, 8–15; Michael Leifer, 'Politics in Singapore', *Journal of Commonwealth Political Studies*, vol. II, no. 2, May 1964, pp. 103–4. Lee Kuan Yew has said that he told 'the Plen' (the mysterious underground plenipotentiary of the Malayan Communist Party) on 11 May that there was no immediate likelihood of merger, but that he was hoping for common market arrangements: *The Battle for Merger* (Singapore, Government Printing Office, 1961), p. 47. Extensive extracts from Lee's speeches are given in Alex Josey's biography, *Lee Kuan Yew* (Donald Moore, Singapore, 1968) but the selection is misleadingly erratic and quite uninformative on many crucial issues.

[7]Leifer, op. cit. pp. 105–6.

[8]Lee Kuan Yew, *The Battle for Merger* (Singapore Government Printing Office, 1961), p. 51.

[9]See Leifer, p. 108. The 'trades union six' did not demand independence, either immediately or in 1963, as Ong had done in April and as Marshall was to do in the Anson campaign, since that would have been a violation of PAP policy and exposed them to the risk of expulsion. Nor did they demand that the British abandon control of foreign affairs and defence. When pressed, Lim Chin Siong simply called for 'genuinely full internal self-government' and he avoided the trap of opposing merger,

though he asserted that the terms on which merger was attained would be all-important. See *Straits Times*, 24 June 1961; Osborne, op. cit. p. 17.

[10]*The Battle for Merger*, p. 47.

[11]For fuller accounts of these events, see Leifer, op. cit. and Josey, op. cit. pp. 173–86.

[12]One PAP member crossed over to the *Barisan Sosialis* in July, 1962, leaving Lee without a majority, but by this point he could rely on the support of the right-wing parties in crucial votes on the Malaysian issue.

[13]*Straits Times*, 29 May, 5, 24, 27 June, 6 July.

[14]For the Tunku's speeches during his visit to Brunei (4 July) and on 11 July in Kuala Lumpur, see *Straits Times*, 5, 6 and 12 July. Although not as tactless as they have sometimes been characterized, they definitely stressed the role of Malays and the Malay language, while the emphasis on Brunei aroused suspicions of Brunei dominance in Borneo.

[15]The MSCC meetings have been outlined more fully in an unpublished study by Professor Zainal Abidin bin Wahid, part of which was read at the 1971 Orientalists Congress in Canberra.

[16]*Memorandum setting out Heads of Agreement between the Federation of Malaya and Singapore*, 15 November 1961, reprinted in *Malaysia* (Select Documents on International Affairs, no. 1 of 1963, Department of External Affairs, Canberra), pp. 29–37. The Tunku had suggested in the Malayan Parliament earlier that a relationship similar to that of Northern Ireland and Great Britain was envisaged for Singapore and Malaya.

[17]See ibid. p. 38, for Mr. Menzies' first official statement, which was carefully qualified ('this imaginative and far-sighted concept ... if it proved practicable, it could contribute significantly to stability and progress in the area ...'). Sir Garfield Barwick, Australian Foreign Minister from 1962–4, stressed these qualifications in Australia's initial response during an interview in December 1964. For Mr. Macmillan's statement of 20 June, see *Straits Times*, 21 June.

[18]*Straits Times*, 26 June.

[19]*Official Report, Dewan Ra'ayat*, 16 October 1961, pp. 1611–13.

[20]The Joint Statement by the Governments of the United Kingdom and the Federation of Malaya is reprinted in *Malaysia, Select Documents*, pp. 38–9.

[21]Discussions between the Tunku and the British Government in July 1962 after the submission of the Cobbold Report ran into difficulties because of a British preference for an indeterminate transitional stage during which North Borneo and Sarawak would be prepared for self-government and merger. The British finally gave way, however: *Straits Times*, 23–8 July 1962.

[22]See below, pp. 70–1, 74–5, 250–3.

[23]Milton Osborne, op. cit. p. 65; Willard A. Hanna, *The Formation of Malaysia* (American Universities Field Staff, 1964), pp. 15–18, 26.

[24]Leifer, op. cit. pp. 110–13: *State of Singapore Annual Report, 1962* (Government Printing Office, Singapore, 1964), ch. 1.

[25]For fuller accounts of the referendum campaigns, see ibid. and Osborne, op. cit. pp. 23–8: Hanna, op. cit. ch. 13. For another view from the opposition's side, see Karim, 'The Left Wing in Singapore', *Eastern World*, January 1964.

[26]Lee argued in the Legislative Assembly that the government was under no constitutional obligation to hold a referendum, but had decided to do so in order to rebut charges that Singapore was being 'sold out': *Singapore Annual Report*, 1962, pp. 3–4.

[27]Ibid. pp. 2–9.

[28]Many Singapore citizens would not have been eligible for citizenship of the wider Federation under former Malayan law; it had been agreed earlier that they would have Malaysian 'nationality' after merger, but not Malaysian 'citizenship' (which would have entailed voting rights in other territories). But after the Cobbold Report had recommended common Malaysian citizenship for the Borneo territories, the discrimination against Singapore could not be upheld.

[29]Hanna, op. cit. pp. 115–16, 120–2.

[30]Ibid. p. 113.

[31]See Osborne, op. cit. pp. 30–4 for a judicious summary of this episode.

[32]*Singapore Annual Report*, 1962, p. 27.

[33]Lim Kean Siew, *Report to the Socialist Front* (cyclostyled document, Penang, 16 November 1961, in the possession of the author).

[34]See Appendix II below. Extracts from the other resolutions submitted to the Conference are from documents made available to the author by a member of the Socialist Front.

[35]Indications of a pro-Malaysia faction in the PMIP are mentioned in *Straits Times*, 2 July 1962.

[36]*Straits Times*, 26, 28, 31 March 1962.

[37]*Straits Times*, 14 February 1963.

[38]*Straits Times*, 17 March 1963.

IV
The Borneo Territories

INCORPORATION of the former British colonies in North Borneo within the Malaysian federation was the most controversial aspect of the Tunku's scheme, although its purpose was essentially secondary to his main concern, merger with Singapore. The wisdom and justice of rushing the Borneo states headlong into the Federation has been queried then and since on various grounds. One was that it was not 'natural' or sensible to unite the Borneo territories with Malaya and Singapore when they were separated by such a vast expanse of water and such great disparities in their levels of political and educational advancement. Another was that the people of Borneo were being bulldozed against their will into a perilous experiment whose outcome might not be to their advantage. Developments there since 1965 have tended to bear out many of the doubts that were expressed earlier, so some consideration ought to be given to Indonesian charges that Malaysia was an artificial neo-colonialist stratagem imposed on the people of Borneo by the wily British and their puppets. This will require an examination of the political dynamics of the two Borneo states and of the processes by which they were brought into Malaysia. But before we look in detail at the politics of each state (and of Brunei, which finally decided not to join) several general observations need to be made.

THE DYNAMICS OF CLOSER ASSOCIATION

The argument that it is unnatural on geographical or geo-political grounds to unite the former British colonies in Borneo with the Malay peninsula rather than with the rest of Borneo has not been very persuasive in a century when some rather peculiar 'states' have been constructed out of the relics of former colonial empires. If the matter is judged mainly on the basis of historical, commercial and administrative ties, there is quite a strong case for uniting them with Malaya, although the political difficulties created may yet prove to be greater than were initially foreseen. In a region where the sea has long been an easier highway for communications than the land, mere geographical separateness is not an insuperable obstacle to political integration — as witness Indonesia and the Philippines themselves. The partition of Borneo between the British and Dutch or between Malaysia and Indonesia is readily explained by reference to the geography and history of the island. Borneo has never been united politically: historically, the former British territories of Borneo have rarely had more than the slightest contacts with the Indonesian part. The watershed which was used to demarcate the British segment of Borneo from the Dutch in 1891 happened to coincide broadly with ethnological boundaries, except amongst the scattered tribal peoples in the deep interior who have long been on the move from the headwaters of one river system to another.[1] The coastal peoples who have largely dominated the political history of Borneo in the past have generally kept to their own distinct communities on either side of today's international frontiers. The Brunei Sultanate, which was for centuries the most powerful political entity in the island, never exercised much influence to the south of Tanjong Datu (the westernmost tip of modern Sarawak), while the Sultanate of Sambas on the Indonesian side of the modern border seems to have been at odds with the Brunei *pengirans* of Sarawak throughout its heyday during the century before Brooke rule. In the northeast, the Sultanate of Sulu claimed authority over parts of both British and Dutch Borneo, but the region was very thinly populated, in any case, and there are no indications of substantial political structures above the most rudimentary communities.

Indonesians had occasionally urged that British Borneo should be liberated from colonial rule, but few ever suggested publicly that it should be annexed to Indonesia. They could argue persuasively that the border dividing the island into two segments was merely a historical legacy from colonial times and took little account of the wishes of the people concerned, but the Indonesian government carefully avoided irredentist arguments. Even at the height of confrontation it merely demanded self-determination in northern Borneo and an opportunity for the people of the area deliberately to choose their own destiny, either within an independent state or states, or through union with one of their larger neighbours. Although President Soekarno was inclined towards arguments of the kind that 'even a child can see that West Irian is an integral part of Indonesia's national territory', he never applied that logic to Borneo, at least in public.

To assert that Malaysia was an artificial creation just because the Borneo states are separated from the peninsula by 400 miles of sea (claimed as territorial water by Indonesia as far north as the Natuna Islands) is, in itself, to assume rather arbitrarily that propinquity is essential. But more important than such formalist questions are the political ones. Did the people of Borneo (and Malaya) want unification and did they know what alternatives there were to it? Was unification administratively and politically feasible?

In 1962–3 it seemed reasonable to answer 'Yes' to both these questions (though some colonial officials had reservations which, in retrospect, merit more respect than they received at the time). On one plane, the common heritage from British colonial rule of broadly similar legal, administrative, commercial and educational institutions in the modern 'nation-building' segments of society seemed likely to provide a ready-made infrastructure for a larger political unit, even though high transport costs and widely differing economic conditions created some problems. On another plane, the presumption that the Malay and Borneo peoples were closely related seemed to imply a disposition towards unity, if only to forestall Chinese dominance. This assumption was commonly made in discussions of the communal arithmetic of the Malaysia scheme in 1961. Subsequent events have shown that matters were by no means as simple as that — non-Malay indigenes such as the Dayaks and Kadazans have proved acutely sensitive to any suggestion of Malay hegemony. But the crucial fact is that the Malaysia proposal, by arousing vigorous political life in Borneo for the first time, stimulated the growth of political parties and political activity there. It also intensified ethnic self-consciousness and compounded the difficulties of attaining a nation-wide consensus on the character of the multi-racial political system, difficulties which have subsequently led to second thoughts in some circles about the benefits of the union.

Except among the Malay ruling classes, political life at the town level in northern Borneo had barely begun to stir until the mid-1950s. Elections were still unknown and the only vestige of a representative principle in the Legislative Councils of Sarawak and North Borneo was the inclusion amongst the nominated members (not yet a majority in either Council) of the most prominent leaders of the various communities.[2] The ordinary people were apparently willing to trust their traditional leaders to conduct whatever dealings were necessary with the colonial authorities. (The leaders generally took care to preserve a broad degree of consensus within their communities on such matters, of course.) Since educational facilities were rudimentary, there was little social change and virtually no challenge to the authority of traditional leaders.

Among the Malays and Chinese a wider political consciousness was beginning to develop in the 1950s as echoes from Indonesia and China were heard in the colony. But most of the other communities were not anxious to see British rule end before they had caught up with their more advanced neighbours. Even when the British tried to speed up the advance towards representative government and, in 1958, to urge the three Borneo territories into some sort of closer association, almost no political response was evoked from the indigenous peoples, who mostly feared that any moves in these directions would benefit only the Chinese. Because of the essentially communal overtones of virtually all political and social issues, it could hardly have been otherwise. Perhaps the British should have started earlier and more energetically to stimulate social and political changes within their two colonies, but they can hardly be accused of re-tarding the advance to self-government. The response to their attempt in

1958 to bring about a closer association of the Borneo territories in anticipation of further political advance illustrates the difficulties confronting
them.

The impetus behind the call for closer association in February 1958 came
solely from the colonial authorities.[3] The Governors of Sarawak and
North Borneo spoke by radio to their two colonies suggesting that the
possibilities of closer association (but not amalgamation) should be considered and discussed by the people as a first step towards action on the
matter by the governments concerned, including Brunei also. The proposals
each put forward, although spelling out quite fully the possible forms of
association, were intended simply as the basis for such discussion, not as a
specific plan to be adopted. Since there were no formal assemblies in
which discussions could be held, district officers and officials had been
instructed to give assistance and information in village and town deliberations throughout the colonies, but 'it is for you to consider...to accept, to
refuse or to amend'. The Sultan of Brunei had been consulted in advance
and it was envisaged that Brunei would form part of whatever new structure should be formed. At an inter-territorial conference of officials in
March, the Commissioner General for South-East Asia, Sir Robert Scott,
hinted that political association might grow out of administrative cooperation, but this point was not pressed at all hard.

The response to the proposal was disappointing to the colonial government. The only enthusiastic support for it came from the Chinese of Sarawak and, to a lesser extent, of North Borneo. Most other communities
were apprehensive or opposed to any such change. Worst of all, the
Sultan of Brunei stood aloof for many months and then turned his back
on the scheme. Although the North Borneo Legislative Council passed a
motion establishing a committee to discuss the matter further with
representatives of Sarawak and Brunei, nothing came of it and the scheme
was virtually shelved during 1959.

The particular reasons for the lack of enthusiasm for closer association
in each of the three territories are to be found amidst their own political
complexities, but one general observation is appropriate here. Admirably
benevolent and even democratic in intent as the Governors' proposal was,
it could hardly have any dynamic effect in societies which lacked the
essential framework of modern representative institutions. It did not jolt
the communities into political activity as the 1961 proposal did, for it was
too vague to threaten any imminent change in the *status quo* and it held
out no incentive to political action by the non-Chinese communities. In
fact, quite the contrary: the latter were unlikely to act energetically in
support of a move that would hasten the removal of their British protective
umbrella if there were any danger that the Chinese would benefit mostly.

The Tunku's call in 1961 for the Borneo territories to be merged within
Malaysia aroused a much more positive response than the 1958 proposal,
essentially for three reasons. First, it appealed strongly to the Malays of
Sarawak and North Borneo (but not of Brunei, paradoxically) for the very
reason that it alarmed the Chinese — it diminished the likelihood of

Chinese dominance in Borneo by buttressing the political power of the Malays and other indigenous peoples with the backing of Kuala Lumpur. Thus the Malays were stirred into political activity and became strong supporters of the scheme. Second, it highlighted the fact that British rule could not be expected to last much longer; hence that the more backward communities could no longer rely on the colonial authority to hold the ring and discourage communal politics until they had caught up with the others. Third, as a result of both these considerations, even the non-Malay indigenes now recognized the necessity to organize politically and negotiate for the best terms they could get in the new political system.

After initial hesitations, the broad lines of the Borneo reaction to the Tunku's proposal soon became clear. The Malay-Muslim groups of Sarawak and Sabah nearly all supported it enthusiastically. The principal leaders of the other indigenous communities supported it with qualifications. Most of the Chinese in both colonies opposed it initially, though the more realistic of them soon began to accept it as inevitable, particularly in North Borneo, and began to accommodate themselves so as to make the best of the situation as the Chinese of the Nan-yang have so often had to do. Some of the smaller, more backward indigenous groups preferred that British rule should continue, fearing that they would be at the mercy of their more advanced and populous neighbours if the protection of the

TABLE 3
NORTH BORNEO AND SARAWAK:
TOTAL POPULATION BY COMMUNITY AND SUB-GROUP, 1960

NORTH BORNEO			SARAWAK		
All communities		454,421	All communities		744,529
Dusun		145,229	Malay		129,300
Murut		22,138	Melanau		44,661
Bajau		55,779	Sea Dayak		237,741
Ilanun		3,931	Land Dayak		57,619
Other indigenous		79,421	Other indigenous		37,931
Brunei	23,450		Bisayah	2,803	
Kedayan	7,871		Kedayan	7,207	
Orang Sungei	15,112		Kayan	7,899	
Bisayah	10,053		Kenyah	8,093	
Sulu	11,080		Kelabit	2,040	
Tidong	4,417		Murut	5,214	
Sino-Native	7,438		Punan	4,669	
			Other indigenous	6	
Chinese		104,542	Chinese		229,154
Hakka	57,338		Cantonese	17,432	
Cantonese	15,251		Foochow	70,125	
Hokkien	11,924		Hakka	70,221	

Source: *Cobbold Report*, p. 83.

colonial authority were withdrawn. (In Brunei, however, this clearcut pattern did not apply: Azahari and his Party Ra'ayat opposed the idea of merger within a Malaysia that would be 'British dominated', while the Sultan wavered uneasily on the fence.)[4] The Cobbold Commission's often-quoted assessment of opinion in Borneo in early 1962 gives a picture of the situation in Sabah and Sarawak that is probably a fair one, since it broadly conforms with the conclusions to be drawn from the growth of political parties there, the elections of 1963 and the subsequent UN Mission of Enquiry:

...about one-third of the population in each territory strongly favours an early realization of Malaysia without too much concern about terms and conditions. Another third, many of them favourable to the Malaysia project, ask, with varying degrees of emphasis, for conditions and safeguards varying in nature and extent.... The remaining third is divided between those who insist on independence before Malaysia is considered and those who would strongly prefer to see British rule continue for some years to come. If the conditions and reservations which they have put forward could be substantially met, the second category referred to above would generally support the proposals. Moreover once a firm decision was taken quite a number of the third category would be likely to abandon their opposition and decide to make the best of a doubtful job. There will remain a hard core, vocal and politically active, which will oppose Malaysia on any terms unless it is preceded by independence and self-government; this hard core might amount to near 20 per cent of the population of Sarawak and somewhat less in North Borneo.[5]

If anything this assessment may have over-estimated the amount of 'hard core' opposition in Sabah, which had virtually evaporated within the year. Brunei was not included in the Cobbold Commission's terms of reference, however, and the opposition which underlay the Brunei revolt of December 1962 forms part of a rather different story to which we must return in due course.

SARAWAK

Sarawak is the poorest of the states of Malaysia and the most diverse in both ethnic composition and settlement patterns.[6] Even before Malaysia was created it seemed likely to be the weakest link in the chain of new states, for its best organized party was opposed to the scheme and Chinese radicalism posed almost as dangerous a threat in Kuching and Sibu as in Singapore. After confrontation was launched, Sarawak was by far the most vulnerable state; the capital, Kuching, is only about forty miles from the Indonesian border at a point where it is easily accessible from Pontianak. Yet Sarawak was less volatile politically than Sabah in the first three years after colonial rule ended, in spite of greater social and economic tensions. Even Indonesian border raids and attempts at subversion did not succeed in sparking off ethnic conflict or provoking violent hostility towards the government in Kuala Lumpur. On the contrary, Sarawak's peaceful absorption into Malaysia was made considerably easier by the external threat. And, by an odd quirk of fate, the ending of confrontation in 1966 happened to coincide almost exactly with the first major crisis within the Sarawak Alliance and between the State and Federal governments. In order to sort out these paradoxes, we need to look briefly at the ethnic and historical background of Sarawak's political life.

Under the rule of the three White Rajahs, Charles Brooke and his two successors (1841–1946), Sarawak was little more than a benevolent autocracy; even its transfer to the Colonial Office in 1946 did not bring very rapid political changes until 1959.[7] Brooke rule had brought peace and population growth, the suppression of piracy and feuding, establishment of trading facilities (almost entirely in Chinese and British hands) and the development of new crops like pepper and rubber. Yet the regime was highly paternalistic and by the mid-twentieth century it was an historical anachronism. Admirable though the Brookes' Nine Cardinal Principles of government were in their way, they did not promote the welding together of a single political community from the diverse and largely isolated communities scattered along the coast and up the rivers of Sarawak nor hasten them towards modernization or self-government. To have sought any such goals would, of course, have seemed fantastically premature thirty years ago. Even in the decade after Brooke rule ended in 1946, significant stirrings of political life were discernible only among the previously dominant Malays and, to a lesser extent, among the Chinese, who now hoped that they would be permitted equal opportunities for civic advancement under the impartial governance of the Colonial Office and became the most enthusiastic advocates of rapid progress towards self-government. The Dayaks and other indigenous groups, on the other hand, clung to the benevolent protection afforded by British rule until such time as they could catch up with the more advanced races educationally and economically.

The largest ethnic group in Sarawak at the time of the 1960 census were the Iban ('Sea Dayaks'), with over 237,000 souls, or 31 per cent of the population, mainly from the 2nd and 3rd divisions.[8] The Chinese then numbered 229,000 but their rate of increase has been very high and they may now outnumber the Iban. Educationally and economically they are by far the most advanced people, but their political status has been a subordinate one both under the Brooke Raj and since. The 'Malays' of Sarawak numbered only 129,000. Next of the indigenous groups came the Land Dayaks (58,000) and Melanau (45,000): other much smaller groups were the Kenyahs, Kayans, Kedayans, Kelabits and Bisayas, many of whom are related to larger communities beyond the Sarawak border in Indonesian Kalimantan, Brunei or Sabah. Most of these peoples tend to be concentrated in particular regions — the last-mentioned smaller communities in the 4th and 5th Divisions in the north of Sarawak; the Land Dayaks almost entirely in the interior of the 1st Division, south-west of Kuching; Melanau in the coastal stretches of the 3rd; the Iban rather widely dispersed through the 2nd and 3rd Divisions, into which they have been migrating throughout the last century, and even into the 1st Division, where they now outnumber the Land Dayaks. Most of the Malays are to be found in the 1st Division, around Kuching, others in coastal areas further north, with an important concentration on the lower Rejang. The Chinese, too, are clustered mainly around Kuching, in the other main towns, and particularly up the Rejang, around Sibu.

The Malays of Sarawak were the dominant ethnic group throughout the centuries of Brunei rule and the Brooke Raj, being regarded by the latter as a privileged and trusted aristocracy, 'apparent rulers and coastally the "owners" of the country'.[9] They had enjoyed an unchallenged position of superiority there, until the growth of representative institutions and the emergence of Chinese and Dayak claimants to a greater share of power occurred after World War II. The transfer of Sarawak to Colonial Office rule in 1946 had produced a deep split within the Malay community, the anti-cession faction fearing that the ending of Brooke rule would bring wider opportunities to the Chinese at their expense. Personal antagonisms between the pro- and anti-cession factions ran high for many years, the tensions culminating in the murder of the British governor by a young Malay in December 1949. Hostility to the leader of the pro-cession group, the Datu Bandar, who was elevated by the British to the highest posts and honours ever held by a native official, continued to plague the Malay community of Sarawak right down to the period of party formation after 1960. He was largely responsible for the creation of *Party Negara Sarawak* (PANAS) in 1960 as a riposte by the indigenous communities to the formation of the *Sarawak United People's Party* (SUPP), which was essentially Chinese in membership. But a rival Malay party appeared soon afterwards, the *Barisan Ra'ayat Jati Sarawak* (BARJASA), based primarily on the anti-cessionist groups of the 3rd and 4th Divisions,whereas PANAS derived its following mainly from the 1st Division, principally Kuching. Although both parties warmly supported the Malaysia scheme in 1961, the rivalry between them persisted until late in the 1960s and produced constant difficulties for the Malaysian government in its efforts to find a stable Alliance-type coalition of parties in Sarawak.[10]

The division in the Malay community was not purely a matter of personal antagonisms, however. Among the anti-cessionists, there seems to have been a stronger element of Malay cultural nationalism during the 1950s, nurtured by anti-colonial and anti-British sentiments, along with more openly expressed resentment of the Chinese, which found expression in the *Barisan Pemuda Sarawak* (Sarawak Youth Front). Young Malays who felt politically frustrated under British rule looked yearningly towards Brunei, Kuala Lumpur and Djakarta for inspiration and hope, or back towards the past greatness of the Brunei and Malacca Sultanates and the Majapahit empire. Vague and diffuse though these sentiments were, they made a strong appeal to young Malay school-teachers and it is not insignificant that among these ardent nationalists were several with a great admiration for Indonesia and her successful struggle for independence. One of the ablest of these was Ahmad Zaidi, the senior government education official in Sibu, who had a great influence among the Malays of the lower Rejang: he later defected to the Indonesians in 1963, one of the relatively few Sarawak Malays to do so. And when, in the course of confrontation, the Indonesians later attempted to send infiltrators into that region to exploit these old *Barisan Pemuda* sentiments, at least one raiding party was given some protection and succor there.[11]

The Iban were not politically organized or prominent outside their own areas before 1961. Only about 4 per cent were categorized as 'literate' in the 1960 census and only forty-seven had completed secondary education. After initial hesitations, they generally expressed support for the Malaysia proposal, but subject to safeguards on certain matters such as language and education policies. They objected to any proposal that smacked of a mere replacement of their former British rulers by Malays, who were educationally more advanced than they were. (Few Iban are Muslims and most of those who had received secondary education at Christian schools had an interest in keeping English rather than Malay as the vehicle of communication and education.) They are a vigorous and enterprising people, with a relatively flexible social structure, who for generations have been pressing down the great rivers towards the coast from their original homeland along the upper Kapuas, on the Indonesian side of the modern frontier.[12] Many have adapted themselves to new modes of settled cultivation of rice and rubber and even to urban employment. Since 1961, they have also achieved a crucially important political role in Sarawak as the largest ethnic group, although they too have been divided into two parties based on the Saribas and Rejang rivers respectively, as will be described below. The Land Dayaks of the 1st Division, by contrast, have been associated with no one political party and have not come down to the coast from their longhouses in the interior to anything like the same extent. One of the harsh ironies of confrontation was that the accidents of geography and history left such an unaggressive and politically acquiescent people as the Land Dayaks so vulnerable to the main thrust of Indonesian border raids and terrorism. Presumably Indonesia's military leaders had not read Geddes' delightful account of them in *Nine Dayak Nights*.

The Chinese of Sarawak have played a central part in the politics of the past decade, for it was their prominence in the establishment of the *Sarawak United People's Party* (SUPP) in 1959 which precipitated the politicization of Sarawak's ethnic communities and the opposition to the Malaysia concept among young Chinese radicals of the 'Clandestine Communist Organization' (CCO — later officially referred to as Sarawak Communist Organization, or SCO) which gave the Indonesians reason to hope in 1963 that the scheme could be wrecked by provoking insurrection from within.[13] During the century of Brooke rule, the hard-working Chinese miners, farmers and traders who settled there were generally China-oriented in their desire to make some money and then return to China, hence little concerned to play a political role or to remedy the discriminations against non-indigenes. After World War II, however, return to China was no longer attractive and they became more concerned to achieve equality of civic rights through participation in the representative institutions which the colonial government was cautiously introducing.

Their increasing numbers, economic and educational advancement compared with the other communities and pride in the emergence of Communist China as a great power must have heightened their political aspirations. At the same time, problems were arising from shortage of cultivable land and restricted employment opportunities for a swelling population of youthful Chinese who had received some education but could not find jobs they considered suitable, all of which added urgency to their quest for political influence and power.[14] Hence, too, the appeal of the SCO to these discontented and frustrated Chinese-educated youths. It is not surprising that the Chinese were the most enthusiastic supporters of moves towards independence like the 1958 Governors' call for closer association, nor that SUPP was set up soon after it to contest local council elections. Inevitably, too, many Chinese saw the Tunku's call for Malaysia as a move to frustrate their aspirations. On the other hand, it would be as misleading to exaggerate the extent and intensity of opposition to Malaysia among the Sarawak Chinese (which the Indonesians tended to do) as it would to characterize the political sentiments of the entire community in terms of the revolutionary and chauvinistic sentiments of the SCO. The Chinese of Sarawak consist of several distinct communities and it is unwise to generalize too broadly about them.

The Malaysia proposal was a death-blow to the hopes any Chinese may have entertained of hegemony in Sarawak, but it is questionable whether this would ever have been achieved in any case. For the creation of SUPP as a predominantly Chinese party in 1959 and the events which gave rise to it were bound willy-nilly to stimulate the emergence of other political parties and draw the leaders of the more retarded communities into the arena of state politics. Malaysia merely hastened the formation of communal parties which had already started by early 1961. Political life had begun to stir soon after the constitution was amended in 1956 to provide for a majority of elected unofficial members in the *Council Negri* (Legislative Council), to be elected indirectly from District Councils, and for elections to the latter. Local government councils had only in a few cases been elected before that time, but in 1959 general elections to these District Councils were held throughout Sarawak. Moreover, the 1958 proposal for closer association with North Borneo and Brunei presaged a more rapid advance towards self-government in the whole area. These changes started a process of political ferment which would certainly have created a demand for self-government sooner or later.

Sarawak reactions to the 1958 call for closer association revealed the reluctance of the indigenous peoples to take any leaps in the dark. Chinese organizations and politicians in the Kuching Municipal Council supported the proposal warmly as a major step towards the political emancipation they desired. But Malay and Dayak spokesmen were either opposed or non-commital. When the *Council Negri* debated the Governor's proposal in May 1958 it came to no decision, for the unofficial members were generally suspicious. The best reason Temenggong Jugah could give for his cautious approval of it was that the government would not have made the suggestion if it had not been to the good of Sarawak! Some months later the government felt there was sufficient backing for the proposal to warrant the appointment of a committee of enquiry to discuss the matter with a North Borneo committee (which had been set up more promptly and enthusiastically), but the committees never met.[15]

Despite this hesitancy to plunge into the political unknown, all communities in Sarawak were beginning to organize politically by 1959–60, for the evident desire of the colonial authorities to hasten constitutional advance and the local council elections of 1959 were signs that the British would not continue to hold the ring in Borneo much longer. The *Sarawak United People's Party* (SUPP) was set up especially to fight the 1959 local elections, under predominantly Chinese leadership and largely dependent on Chinese money and votes, although it professed and still professes to be a multi-racial party. Soon after, *Party Negara Sarawak* (PANAS) was established under a Malay leader, the Datu Bandar.[16] PANAS was intended by its founders to be a non-communal party, embracing all racial groups: in addition to the Malays who made up its hard core, the party also attracted the most prominent Dayak leaders, notably Temenggong Jugah, and even a small group of prominent Chinese who had been appointed to the *Council Negri*. PANAS had the blessing of the colonial authorities (to put it mildly) as a potential counter-weight to SUPP and was initially regarded in some circles as just a British front party. But it soon became virtually the major Malay party. Early in 1961, some of the more sophisticated younger Dayaks of the Saribas River, in the 2nd Division, began to set up a distinctively Dayak party of their own, the *Sarawak National Party* (SNAP) under the leadership of Stephen Kalong Ningkan. They initially tried to win the support of Temenggong Jugah and other traditional leaders of the Dayak communities of the Rejang in the 3rd Division, but decided to go ahead without them when the Temenggong declined to leave PANAS. Just at that point, the Tunku put forward his proposal regarding Malaysia.

The Tunku's call for Malaysia in May 1961 had a catalytic effect on these developments. It accentuated the tendency towards party proliferation and communalization, for it was soon clear that the British were anxious to seize the opportunity to withdraw from Borneo. After initial hesitations, community and party attitudes to the Malaysia proposal crystallized fairly quickly. The first Sarawak politician to speak out in favour of Malaysia was, naturally enough the Malay leader of PANAS, the Datu Bandar — although even he initially favoured a Borneo federation as a first step. SUPP and most of the Chinese leaders opposed the Malaysia idea from the outset, calling instead for independence before merger. The attitude of the Dayaks and other smaller groups was more complex. They were initially as uneasy about the possibility of Malay dominance as of Chinese; hence they asked for a number of specific safeguards and, in some cases, expressed concern about the ending of British rule.[17] Many of these fears were assuaged by the Malaysia Solidarity Consultative Committee deliberations, particularly as Lee Kuan Yew went out of his way to win over the Borneo delegations. And as the smoke cleared, the political dialectics of opposition to SUPP, which was aligning itself with the left-wing parties of Singapore and Malaya in strong opposition to the Tunku's scheme, impelled the non-Chinese parties to support it simply on prudential calculations of political interest. Better to share power with Kuala Lumpur than to lose it to the Chinese. By the time the Cobbold Commission reached Sarawak early in 1962, the Iban leaders had swung around to qualified support for Malaysia, although in the 1963 elections SUPP won some followers among Iban and Land Dayaks who presumably opposed the scheme. Malaysia was a 'vital necessity', the SNAP leaders told the Cobbold Commission because 'Sarawak cannot stand alone ... Malaysia will bring greater prosperity and will provide protection against the threat of Communism'.[18]

The reasons for SUPP's opposition to the Malaysia concept were varied and will only be briefly summarized here. As a contemporary account put it: 'Certainly, many fears are widely held amongst Chinese. Opposition is partly Chinese communal and partly Communist inspired. They do feel that Malaysia means a privileged status for the native and an inferior status for the Chinese.'[19] They feared disadvantageous conditions of citizenship (later remedied by safeguards to a large extent), a threat to their schools and culture, and discrimination against them in employment opportunities and access to land. Some of SUPP's leaders, such as Ong Kee Hui, indicated a willingness to consider a federation with Malaya, provided that independence were conceded first.[20] There was little likelihood that such a state of affairs would eventuate, however, for prior independence would have offered too great an opportunity for Communist subversion or for the Chinese to achieve political dominance.

The *Council Negri* in September 1962 endorsed in principle the earlier decision of the British and Malayan governments to proceed towards the creation of Malaysia by August 1963 on the basis of constitutional arrangements which were to be worked out in an Inter-governmental Committee under Lord Lansdowne. Negotiations in this committee went forward during the latter part of the year without giving rise to any serious difficulties. When the Lansdowne Committee reported in February 1963, it was apparent that most of the constitutional safeguards which had earlier seemed to the Cobbold Commission necessary to win over the waverers in Sarawak had been incorporated; in fact, Sarawak's representation in the Federal parliament and the financial provisions to subsidize her from Federal revenues were quite generous. But it was the political rather than the purely constitutional problems standing in the way of Malaysia's realization which posed the biggest uncertainties towards the end of 1962. Sarawak's new-born political parties were so young and inexperienced that it was by no means certain that the Alliance, which they were beginning to establish, would succeed in the elections due in mid-1963, even though the system of indirect elections was expected to work to the disadvantage of SUPP. If SUPP emerged strong enough to form a government the whole future of Malaysia would be in doubt.

Three new parties had emerged in 1962 to take part in the coming struggle for control of independent Sarawak. The *Barisan Ra'ayat Jati Sarawak* (BARJASA) strongly supported Malaysia, appealing directly to the Malay-Muslim communities in rivalry with PANAS without making any pretence at being multi-communal, as the latter did. In mid-1962 Temenggong Jugah withdrew from PANAS in order to build up his own party (*Party Pesaka Anak Sarawak*, generally known as PESAKA) among the 3rd Division Dayaks, in anticipation of the coming election. A little later the two Dayak parties announced the formation of a United Front (the forerunner of the Sarawak Alliance Party) to consolidate Dayak unity 'regardless of Divisions, Districts or Rivers'. During 1962 the few Chinese who had earlier joined PANAS withdrew to form a Sarawak Chinese Association (SCA), with much the same outlook as the MCA in Malaya. Thus PANAS was left as a Malay party essentially, although it still retained some support among Land Dayaks and a few individuals of other communities.[21]

By the end of 1962, each of Sarawak's main communities had two parties bidding for popular support within an essentially communal framework — SNAP and PESAKA for the Dayaks, PANAS (though it still claimed to be multi-racial) and BARJASA for the Malays, SCA and SUPP for the Chinese. The only party opposed to Malaysia by this time was SUPP — also an ostensibly non-communal party, although its strength was basically Chinese. The threat posed by SUPP to the other parties contributed in large part to their coming together to form the Sarawak Alliance late in 1962 as state-wide elections loomed closer. The unity of the Alliance was perilously fragile, however, and its prospects of defeating SUPP by no means certain. In March 1963, only three months before the elections, the Datu Bandar impulsively led PANAS out of the Alliance after a dispute about the allocation of positions in the post-independence government. The Sarawak Alliance was a marriage of convenience, as was the Alliance in Malaya; but it was to prove an even more heterogeneous compound of very diverse parties, united by little more, initially, than their fears of SUPP. It managed to win the elections in mid-1963, as we will see in due course, but it was a matter of touch and go.[22]

Because SUPP was by far the best organized of the Sarawak parties, the challenge it posed to the Malaysia scheme until the elections seemed formidable. It has always claimed to be a multi-racial party and it had some success in the early years in winning non-Chinese members, despite its predominantly Chinese leadership and electoral backing. Later, however, its non-Chinese following was eroded away by the formation of other communal parties and by the complicity of young Chinese radicals from SUPP in Indonesian confrontation, which inevitably brought the whole party under suspicion. Whether the party was controlled by these young SCO activists who dominated at the branch level or by its respectable, middle-class leaders in Kuching, Ong Kee Hui and Stephen Yong, has been a matter of endless dispute. According to the colonial authorities,

SUPP was merely an open front organization through which the SCO was waging a broader struggle against the British imperialists and 'anti-independence, right-wing proportied classes'. Ong Kee Hui, on the other hand, described it as 'an outlet through which the energies of the frustrated young Chinese could be channelled and re-oriented', his strategy being, like Lee Kuan Yew's in former days, to work alongside the Communists and contain them rather than abandon the field to them.[23] But the left-wing Chinese-speaking activists in SUPP were much closer in their political sympathies to the *Barisan Sosialis* than they were to Lee Kuan Yew.

However important the question of SCO influence within SUPP may have been from the security angle at the time of confrontation, it is of secondary relevance in an assessment of the party's appeal in 1962–3. SUPP was the only party opposing the Malaysia scheme unequivocally and it was bound to make a strong appeal to the Chinese while it had some prospect of success. Whether it was trying to prevent Sarawak's incorporation in Malaysia as part of a broader Communist strategy to wreck the project or because inclusion would prevent any possibility of the Chinese gaining power in Sarawak through SUPP is a question of no great consequence. Both lines of reasoning would have pushed SUPP along the course it took: it would 'never abandon its anti-colonialism and anti-Malaysia stand'. It may certainly be doubted whether the 'moderate' leaders could have retained their positions at the head of the party if they had not been willing to speak the language of radicalism: on the other hand, they were essential to the radicals if the party was to appear respectable and may have been able to act as a brake upon their militancy.

The Brunei revolt and subsequent declarations of Indonesian support for the rebels added greatly to fears that the left-wing militants in SUPP might resort to violence in order to frustrate the creation of Malaysia. Although the revolt momentarily overflowed Brunei's boundaries into Sarawak, where Limbang and Sibuti were both seized by the rebels, it was essentially an uprising of the Brunei Malays and Kedayans of a very small area in the north of the colony. The leaders of the pro-Malaysia parties immediately condemned the revolt, as also did Ong Kee Hui on behalf of SUPP, but only after several weeks of debate in the party about the attitude it should adopt. Some members of SUPP were said to be involved in the revolt and many others were doubtless sympathetic towards the Brunei rebels and may have been inspired to follow their example, but it would seem that the affair came as a surprise to the SCO leaders; though they advocated an armed revolt in theory, they were unprepared at that time, through lack of arms, equipment, provision dumps and basic guerrilla warfare training, to give practical expression to their theoretical concepts. The situation posed dilemmas for both radicals and conservatives in SUPP. Open support for the rebels was now likely to incur a much more severe reaction from the security services, which had been alerted and strengthened by the increase of British military forces in Borneo, but the temptation to spark off a similar revolt among the discontented young Chinese of Sarawak must have been very strong. To the moderates in SUPP this posed the danger of losing political backing among the non-Chinese and the wealthier sections of the Chinese community. Some members of SUPP resigned soon after the Brunei revolt, while some SCO elements were arrested. There are reports that the moderates in SUPP were alarmed by Indonesia's support for the anti-Malaysia cause and even more by her announcement of 'confrontation' in January: the secretary of SUPP was quick to deny an *Antara* report in Djakarta that 50,000 SUPP members were ready to take up arms against Malaysia.[24]

Nevertheless, in the first half of 1963, the Communist leaders ordered considerable numbers (as many as 1,000 according to some reports) of their cadres to withdraw to Indonesia for practical training and equipment and to avoid arrest. Others, within Sarawak, were ordered to redouble recruitment, commence basic military training and reconnoitre suitable hidden areas for camps and dumps. Indonesian incursions into Sarawak from April onwards were intended to support these groups by enabling them to set up 'liberated areas', but because of harassment by the security forces they proved to be a failure. Those SCO activists who were members of SUPP were a constant source of embarrassment to the moderate leadership, for the party could be accused of condoning their actions because the party's left wing refused to condemn them. The situation was further aggravated by the policy of the Communists in ordering border-crossers to sport SUPP badges. Ong Kee Hui evaded the dilemma by announcing that SUPP members who left Sarawak automatically forfeited their membership, but his difficulties persisted well into 1964, when at one point the government came perilously close to proscribing SUPP altogether.

In the critical period between the Brunei revolt and the three-stage indirect elections of May-July 1963, SUPP still posed a formidable electoral threat which made it impossible to take Sarawak's inclusion in Malaysia for granted. As it happened, the pro-Malaysia parties emerged victorious from the elections and the Sarawak Alliance was able to form a government without any major political troubles.[25] But the contest turned out to be a very close one in which the disunity and political immaturity of SUPP's opponents was nearly fatal. The withdrawal of PANAS earlier in 1963 had not only deprived the Alliance of its most experienced politician, the Datu Bandar, but also gave rise to bitter attacks between the PANAS and Alliance leaders which did no good to the electoral prospects of either. More seriously, on 1 July, soon after the first (District Council) stage of the elections, the Datu Bandar further complicated the situation by entering into an agreement with SUPP in order to strengthen the bargaining power of the two parties in the later indirect elections to the *Council Negri;* this rather unnatural alliance was formed on the basis of a surprising and rather disingenuous new demand that 'the Malaysia issue be determined by a referendum conducted by the United Nations ... before the implementation of Malaysia'. If this anachronistic PANAS-SUPP coalition had polled slightly better in one 3rd Division district it would have commanded a majority in the *Council Negri* and been in a position to form a government — with quite unpredictable results for the Malaysia scheme. However, after a tense two months of electioneering at the District and Divisional Council level Alliance control of the *Council Negri* was assured by 15 July.[26] Thereafter only the final processes of ratifying the Malaysia agreement in the *Council Negri* and forming a government remained to be completed before Malaysia Day.

SABAH

In Sabah, formerly British North Borneo, the pattern of response to the Malaysia scheme was broadly similar to Sarawak's, but with several noteworthy differences. Communism was never a significant threat in Sabah. It is a far more prosperous state than Sarawak, without the pockets of unemployment which contributed to Chinese radicalism there: in fact, Sabah is chronically short of labour for the plantations and timber industry of its east coast.[27] Nor was it seriously threatened by Indonesian confrontation, despite occasional apprehensions about subversion among the 20,000 Indonesian migratory workers employed near Tawau. Sabah did not offer as much scope for the exploitation of communal divisions as Sarawak, though they have played just as important a part in its political life and its response to the Malaysia proposal.

Sabah has many ethnic groups, but they can broadly be classified into three — the Malay-Muslim peoples, the Kadazan (formerly Dusun) group, comprising most of the other indigenous peoples, and the Chinese — to which the three political parties of the Sabah Alliance correspond. The Malays, in the strict sense, are relatively few in number (about 25,000 in 1960), mostly of Brunei origin. However if all the Muslim peoples are added, notably the Bajaus and Ilanuns, the total number is about five times as great. Politically, they have all tended to support one party, the United Sabah National Organization (USNO), led by Datu Mustapha, which is virtually the Sabah counterpart of UMNO, having managed to avoid the internal cleavages suffered by the Sarawak Malays. The Kadazans and ethnically related Muruts are a more numerous group, numbering 145,229 or 32 per cent of the total population in 1960. They are concentrated along the west coast plain around Jesselton and the rice-growing valleys of Tambunan and Ranau, across the ranges, in this respect differing somewhat from the more dispersed Muslim peoples. Relatively few of them have embraced Islam: Christian missions and schools have been influential among them and in some areas there has been a high rate of intermarriage with immigrant Hakka Chinese farmers, many of them also Christian. The literacy rate among Kadazans was a little over 10 per cent in 1960, but less than forty had completed secondary education and many were apprehensive about the danger of being outpaced economically and politically by the Chinese if British rule ended. However, their most prominent leader, Donald Stephens, played a crucial part in bringing Sabah into Malaysia in 1961–3, after founding the first Kadazan political organization and later persuading it to accept Malaysia.[28]

The Chinese of Sabah numbered 104,542 in 1960. They were only a slightly smaller fraction of the total population than their counterparts in Sarawak (23 per cent as against 31 per cent), but their political role has been very different. No party of comparable strength to SUPP has emerged among them, nor have Communism or 'Chinese Chauvinism' made much appeal to them. The only Chinese party is a rather conservative one: it has been in the Sabah Alliance since 1962 and even provided the Chief Minister for several years. While they have shared some of the same problems as the Sarawak Chinese — social problems of a high birthrate and an abnormally youthful population; legal difficulties over citizenship and minor civic discriminations — their relations with the other communities seem to have been strikingly more cordial, both before and since incorporation in Malaysia.[29]

Until 1961, the North Borneo colony was politically dormant, as if oblivious of developments in the world beyond its borders. There had been surprisingly little 'come and go' even with Sarawak, the Cobbold Commissioners observed. Little love was lost between the White Rajahs and the British North Borneo Chartered Company, which governed the territory from 1881 until 1941. And even when both areas came under Colonial Office rule after World War II, change came very slowly. Representative institutions were established only in the most rudimentary form in the district centres and hardly at all in Jesselton, the capital.[30] The colonial authorities were apprehensive that political parties and elections would aggravate ethnic differences in a country which took great pride in its record of good race relations. Hence there was an understandable reluctance to take the plunge towards self-government on the part of any ethnic group.

The proposal for closer association put forward by the two governors in February 1958 caused slight ripples of interest in Sabah, but because of the political *immobilisme* prevailing up to that time, it had even less effect than in Sarawak and Brunei. Only the Chinese showed much enthusiasm for the idea as a step towards self-government. The Muslim leaders were non-commital about it, since political advance seemed likely to benefit the Chinese most: and the Kadazans preferred to maintain the *status quo* until they had caught up with the Chinese. (Some also feared that the scheme might lead to Malay domination under the Brunei Sultanate.) The colonial officials and the Legislative Council in Sabah seem to have endorsed the proposal a little more warmly than their colleagues in Sarawak, but as no community or political party was organized to take an initiative on the matter, little was done about it.[31] Donald Stephens tried to revive interest in the question again at the end of 1960. He had travelled abroad extensively in the meantime and had been warned by the British Colonial Secretary that British rule must soon come to an end, but he seems to have been well in advance of his own people in his thinking on the matter. The winds of change may have been stirring gently in Sabah, but they blew from outside rather than from within.

The Tunku's 1961 call for Malaysia had a very different effect. Initial reactions in Sabah were again lukewarm, but soon changed towards strong support for the scheme. Donald Stephens at first opposed the proposal, preferring that self-government be granted before any decision was made: on July 9, he joined Ong Kee Hui and Azahari of Brunei in the first public statement of opposition to the Tunku's scheme.[32] The Chinese did not like the idea and even the leaders of the Malay-Muslim communities were slower to endorse it than their Sarawak counterparts. But after assurances were given in the Malaysia Solidarity Consultative Committee that adequate safeguards of the special interests of the Borneo states could be written into the terms of federation with Malaya, the earlier fears began to diminish. By August, Stephens had been won over to enthusiastic support for the scheme; there seemed to be no better alternative in sight for North Borneo or for his own Kadazan community than to negotiate the best terms of entry he could obtain and to stake a claim to leadership in the new state by joining the Malaysia bandwaggon at an early stage.[33]

Political parties began to spring up on an almost completely communal basis in the latter part of the 1961, as soon as Malaysia began to loom as a practical possibility. The *United National Kadazan Organization* (UNKO), under Stephens' leadership, was founded in August, the *United Sabah National Organization* (USNO), under Datu Mustapha, soon after. (The latter 'welcomes' Malaysia, according to the delicate terminology of the 1961 *Annual Report*, while the former 'favours' it.) Opposed to Malaysia were the smaller *Pasok Momogun* party, drawing its support from the Kadazan and Murut population of the interior, around Keningau, and the two essentially Chinese parties, which advocated self-government before Malaysia was established — the United Party based on Sandakan and the Democratic Party in Jesselton. (These two came together during 1962 to form the *Sabah National Party*, SANAP.)[34] The party system was much simpler than Sarawak's, since there were virtually no rival parties within each ethnic group, no opposition party comparable with SUPP. The leadership in establishing all these parties came, naturally enough, mainly from the unofficial members of the Legislative Council. Frequent shifts in allegiance and alignment were reported during the early months before the general pattern of attitudes to Malaysia crystallized at the end of 1961.

By the time the Cobbold Commission visited North Borneo in February 1962, public opinion there was beginning to swing in favour of the Malaysia proposal fairly generally, for the series of Malaysia Solidarity Consultative Committee conferences had just reached agreement on the broad lines of an acceptable constitutional structure for Malaysia and the North Borneo government had issued an official paper explaining and advocating the proposal for the people of the colony in anticipation of the Cobbold Commission hearings. The Commission's opinion that the opposition to the Malaysia concept was not very intense in North Borneo (as compared with Sarawak) was soon confirmed by the fact that the three smaller parties which had initially expressed opposition to the scheme decided to 'reassess their attitudes'. Seeing the writing on the wall, they dropped their demand for prior self-government and began to concentrate, instead, on achieving adequate safeguards in the forthcoming constitutional talks. All the

North Borneo parties came together in a common front to present their state's 'Twenty Points' to the later Lansdowne Committee in August 1962.[35]

Discussions leading up to the formation of a Sabah Alliance began at about the same time between the leaders of UNKO and USNO. Sufficient progress had been made by September 1962 for these two parties to agree on a national council of twelve members from each, with a joint chairman presiding alternately. The other parties were then invited to join. In October, the two predominantly Chinese parties, Democratic Party and United Party, merged and applied to join the Alliance. The *Pasok Momogun*, too, dropped its earlier opposition to Malaysia and joined the Alliance bandwagon, for it was by then becoming obvious that the disposition of power in the new state would be determined within the Alliance.

No serious problems were experienced in the initial distribution of offices. Datu Mustapha was elected as the first Chairman of the National Council of the Alliance, with Stephens chairman of its Executive Committee. Later, it was similarly agreed that Datu Mustapha should become the Head of State *(Yang di-Pertua Negara)* and Stephens the first Chief Minister; but soon after that political and personal antagonisms gravely strained this tandem relationship between them.

The first big task confronting the Alliance was to contest the local council elections planned for November, from which indirect elections for the Legislative Council were to take place in 1963. Since there were no other parties contesting the election and there was a high probability that Alliance candidates would sweep the polls (as they did, winning all but 6 of the 137 seats), the allocation of candidacies amongst the several Alliance parties might have been expected to cause serious friction. Apparently it did not do so at that stage, even though intra-alliance contests occurred in some wards, while there were also some cases where candidates of parties belonging to the Alliance opposed official Alliance candidates.

TABLE 4

SARAWAK: DIVISIONAL COUNCIL ELECTIONS, 1963

	Local Councils	Legislative Council
USNO	53	8
UNKO	39	5
BUNAP (later SANAP)	27	4
Pasok Momogun	12	1
Independent	6	–

The Brunei revolt broke out a few days before the elections, but apart from necessitating their postponement for several months in the border district of Sipitang, it had almost no effect elsewhere in Sabah. Nor did

Indonesia's declaration of confrontation in early 1963 arouse any serious concern about Sabah's incorporation in Malaysia, as it did in Sarawak. The local council elections were completed in all except three districts by May, preparations then began to go ahead for the establishment of four Residency Electoral Colleges and the indirect election of eighteen members to the Legislative Council in June-July. The final result was a complete sweep for the Alliance at all levels, with the distribution of seats between parties as shown on page 74.

Can the election results be taken as a reliable indication of support for the Malaysia scheme? The UN Mission of Enquiry later concluded so, noting that there was little evidence of articulate and organized opposition except among some groups in the interior and individual members of the *Pasok Momogun*. The voting figures are not conclusive evidence in themselves in this case, since many wards were uncontested and out of a registered adult population of about 160,000 only 74,633 votes were actually cast, nearly all for candidates favouring Malaysia.[36] More significant is the fact that the voting reflected the communal divisions of a plural society, in which the vast majority of voters appear to have voted for their kinsmen and community leaders, taking on trust their advocacy of the Malaysia scheme. (The scheme had, indeed, been widely discussed during the extensive campaign of education or propaganda — according to one's viewpoint — over the previous year, however, and the election was a more meaningful affair than the mockeries which occurred in the Dutch 'puppet' states of East Indonesia and Madura in 1948-9, with which Indonesians instinctively compared them.) It is quite another matter to ask whether the Sabah leaders were right in their conviction that incorporation in Malaysia was in the best interests of the former colony.

Was there any real alternative to Malaysia for an independent Sabah? The UNKO leaders seem to have been convinced in 1962 that there was not, for they told the Cobbold Commission:

> For the Kadazans there can be no other guarantee for their future than for North Borneo to obtain independence by joining Malaysia.... Self government first would mean that the heirs, when the British leave, would be the Chinese owing to their education and economic superiority. This in turn could lead to domination by Communism.... The best security for the future of all the former and present British territories in Southeast Asia lies in their getting together to form Malaysia, a strong viable unit which can play a real part in Commonwealth defence.[37]

The leaders of USNO hardly bothered with such elaborate arguments, for they simply saw the matter in terms of unity with their fellow-Malays. The Chinese simply accepted Malaysia as an unavoidable necessity, after they saw that the other parties favoured it. But would it have been unavoidable if Stephens and the UNKO leaders had not swung round in favour of Malaysia in 1961? And would they have done so if they had foreseen the troubles that were to arise after Malaysia had been formed? By 1965, it was not uncommon to hear wistful speculations that perhaps a Borneo federation on 1958 lines would have been a more satisfactory political solution after all. Incorporation with Indonesia or the Philippines were apparently never considered as realistic alternatives.

It should be remembered that Donald Stephens had favoured a Borneo federation in 1958, and only dropped his insistence on self-government before entering Malaysia after he had been convinced in August 1961 that the Tunku's scheme was the only practical course for Sabah. It was largely the threat of Chinese dominance that led him to change his mind. In mid-1961, the prospect of a victory for Communism or Chinese radicalism in Singapore and Sarawak seemed all too near and the establishment of Malaysia the only counter to it. It was not the threat of Indonesian or Malay dominance that loomed large on the horizon at that time but Chinese. In an independent Borneo federation, the Chinese would have been by far the largest racial group, as well as the richest, best educated, most sophisticated politically and most radical. Even if the Kadazan, Dayak and Malay-Muslim communities all made common cause against them (and that would have been an uneasy coalition), demographic arithmetic alone was no guarantee of political dominance. One can hardly blame Stephens for deciding in favour of Malaysia — which, incidentally, offered him more immediate prospects of local leadership. A further consideration for him must also have been the realization that the 1958 proposal for closer association in Borneo had bogged down in political apathy, whereas the Tunku's call for Malaysia had set in train a set of dynamic political responses in all the territories concerned. It seemed to entail an answer, also, to the Brunei problem — both the Sultan's lack of enthusiasm for the 1958 scheme and the widespread distrust of Brunei dominance in the other Borneo territories. Only if he had possessed supernatural clairvoyance could Stephens have foreseen that by 1964 the Chinese threat would have been contained, that Brunei was to opt out of the game just as Indonesia entered it and that within Sabah itself Kadazan-Malay rivalry would almost outweigh Kadazan fears of the Chinese.

---

[1]K. G. Tregonning, *Under Chartered Company Rule: North Borneo 1881–1946*, (University of Malaya Press, Singapore, 1958), p. 105. See also Tom Harrisson, 'The Malays of South-West Sarawak before Malaysia', *Sarawak Museum Journal*, vol. XI, nos. 23–4, December 1964.

[2]See below, pp. 65, 72.

[3]The 1958 proposal for closer association is described in J. R. Angel, 'The Proposed Federation of Sarawak, North Borneo and Brunei' (MA thesis, University of Sydney, 1965).

[4]See below, pp. 115–17.

[5]*Cobbold Report*, paragraph 144. The main criticism of the Cobbold Report at the time was that it disregarded a collection of signatures and thumb prints (over 112,000) attached to anti-Malaysia statements: but the total SUPP vote in the 1963 election was less than half of that number, so scepticism was not unjustified. The anti-Malaysia vote was estimated at 22.2 per cent of the electorate, with 16.8 per cent neutral or unattributable, according to the later *UN Malaysia Mission Report*, paragraph 117.

[6]Tom Harrisson (ed.), *The Peoples of Sarawak* (Sarawak Museum, Kuching, 1959); Malcolm MacDonald, *Borneo People* (Jonathan Cape, London, 1956); T. H. Silcock, *The Commonwealth Economy in Southeast Asia* (Duke University, North Carolina, 1959), pp. 18–36.

[7]Steven Runciman, *The White Rajahs: A History of Sarawak from 1841 to 1946* (Cambridge University Press, 1960). A lively account of the Iban is given by Robert Pringle, *Rajahs and Rebels. The Ibans of Sarawak under Brooke Rule* (Macmillan, London, 1970).

[8]These figures are taken from the *Cobbold Report*, p. 83.

[9]Harrisson, 'The Malays of South-West Sarawak', p. 432.

[10]The background to the 'Cession Controversy' of 1946–9 is given in MacDonald, op. cit. ch. 19, and Runciman, op. cit. pp. 259–67.

[11]For these details about Zaidi and for much other background information on Sarawak politics, I have drawn upon an unpublished paper by Michael Leigh, 'Sarawak in Malaysia' (mimeographed, 1965).

[12]See A. J. N. Richards, 'The Ibans', in Harrisson (ed.), *The Peoples of Sarawak*, pp. 10–25. The Iban have been described as 'a confident people, masters ... of their environment, boastful but bold, and restless innovators for gain, prestige or sheer enjoyment of change': W. R. Geddes, *Nine Dayak Nights* (Oxford Paperbacks, no. 36, 1961), p. 3.

[13]See Ju K'an T'ien, *The Chinese of Sarawak* (London School of Economics and Political Science Press, 1953); Michael B. Leigh, *The Chinese Community of Sarawak: a Study of Communal Relations* (Malaysia Publishing House Ltd., Singapore Studies in History, no. 6, 1964); Y. L. Lee 'The Chinese in Sarawak (and Brunei)', *Sarawak Museum Journal*, vol. XI, no. 23–4, December 1964.

[14]The number of Chinese rose from about 45,000 in 1909 to 123,000 by 1939 and 229,154 in 1960. The birth rate (3.5 per cent p.a.) has been substantially higher than that of other ethnic groups and in 1960 over 44 per cent of the Chinese population was aged less than 15, so that the demand for schooling, employment and land was beginning to pose serious economic and social problems.

[15]Angel, op. cit. pp. 345–60.

[16]See Tilman 'The Sarawak Political Scene', *Pacific Affairs*, vol. XXXVII, no. 4, Winter 1964–5. In early 1962, PANAS claimed a membership of 10,000 Land Dayaks, 20,000 Iban and 20,000 Malays, according to the *Cobbold Report*, paragraph 86.

[17]For a summary of initial reactions, see *Cobbold Report*, paragraphs 25–77.

[18]Ibid. para. 79.

[19]Leigh, *The Chinese Community of Sarawak*, p. 61.

[20]Ibid. *Cobbold Report*, para. 79.

[21]Tilman, op. cit.; Leigh, 'Sarawak in Malaysia', pp. 9–23. See also Michael Leigh, 'The Development of Political Organisation and Leadership in Sarawak, East Malaysia' (Cornell University, Ph.D. dissertation, 1971), ch. 1.

[22]See Tilman, 'Elections in Sarawak', *Asian Survey*, vol. III, no. 10, October 1963, pp. 507–18.

[23]Leigh, op. cit. pp. 11–14. The official view that SUPP was simply an open-front party controlled by the Sarawak Communist Organization is exemplified in the White Paper entitled *The Danger Within* (Sarawak Information Service, Kuching, 1963).

[24]*Sarawak Tribune*, 31 Dec. 1962; Ong Kee Hui 'deplored' and 'condemned' the Brunei revolt, according to Hanna, op. cit. p. 146.

[25]For the three-tiered election results, see Tilman, 'Elections in Sarawak', *Asian Survey*, vol. III, no. 10 October 1963, pp. 507–18.

[26]The system of indirect elections, which had been designed partly to ensure that SUPP would not just sweep the polls with its superior organization, resulted in distinctly distorted relationship between the number of seats won by each party at the District Council level and the final composition of the Council Negri. The results were as follows:

	District Councils	Divisional Councils	Council Negri
Alliance	138	40	19
PANAS-SUPP	175	34	8
Independents	116	34	9

[27]Figures on *per capita* income are given in the Rueff Mission *Report on the Economic Aspects of Malaysia*, International Bank for Reconstruction and Development (Government Printer, Kuala Lumpur, July 1963), pp. 2–7 and 102–5. A good brief survey of the economic prospects may be found in T. H. Silcock, *The Commonwealth Economy in Southeast Asia* (Duke University Press, 1959), pp. 34–8. The standard accounts of Sabah's history and administration are by K. G. Tregonning, *Under Chartered Company*

Rule and his *North Borneo* (London, HMSO, Corona Library Series, 1960). The former has been reissued in expanded form as *A History of Sabah* but references will be given hereunder to the former work.

[28]The people formerly called 'Dusun' have increasingly preferred to be called Kadazan in recent years since the former word (meaning, literally, 'garden' or 'inland') had derogatory overtones. The new term was popularized by Donald Stephens, the leader of the United National Kadazan Organization and one of the founders of the Society of Kadazans: Tregonning, *North Borneo*, pp. 82–7. These people should not be confused with the Kedayan of Brunei and the surrounding regions.

[29]See *Cobbold Report*, paragraph 103.

[30]The four Local Authorities established in 1952 and 1958 were formed by consultation with the leaders of the communities: elections on a basis of universal suffrage were introduced only in the Local Government Elections Ordinance of July 1962: see *Report of the UN Malaysia Mission*, 1963, paragraphs 148–50.

[31]Angel, op. cit. p. 342 ff. Even the Chinese, who generally supported the idea in Sarawak, were not unanimous about it in North Borneo: a group in Kudat feared that it would imply Malay dominance.

[32]Azahari, Stephens and Ong stated that 'so far as the wishes of the three territories are ascertainable, any plan in accordance with the pronouncements made by Tunku Abdul Rahman in Brunei and Sarawak would be totally unacceptable to the people in the three territories': they called instead for elections and a constitutional link between the three territories. See *Straits Times*, 10 July 1961. See Hanna, op. cit. p. 33 for Stephens' role in the episode.

[33]See statements by Stephens in *Straits Times*, 11 and 17 August and 10 October 1963.

[34]*North Borneo Annual Report 1961*, and ibid. 1962: *Cobbold Report*, paragraphs 124–40.

[35]The 'Twenty Points' are set out in *North Borneo Annual Report, 1962*, pp. 24–8.

[36]*UN Malaysia Mission Report*, paragraphs 203, 239–40.

[37]*Cobbold Report*, paragraph 126.

V
Indonesia under Guided Democracy

THE years in which the idea of Malaysia was being brought to fruition coincided with several important developments within Indonesia. She was then embarking on the last stages of her struggle to regain West Irian (Western New Guinea) from the Dutch by a combination of military confrontation and diplomatic manoeuvring. The success of these unorthodox methods in August 1962 gave a fillip to Soekarno's doctrines of the New Emerging Forces and 'revolutionary diplomacy'. But the West Irian campaign also brought serious economic dislocation, resulting from a huge budget deficit which doubled the volume of money and prices in little over twelve months, nullifying the hard-won economic progress of 1960–1.[1] And with these events came a heightening of domestic political tensions between the right and left wing forces in Indonesian domestic politics. Soekarno's system of Guided Democracy proved to be increasingly unstable from 1962 onwards, both economically and politically — and the increasing assertiveness of his foreign policies seemed to be related to this in a number of ways.

Although the West Irian campaign deflected Indonesian attention and energies away from what was happening in Malaysia until late in 1962, it had an important bearing upon the later conflict between the two countries for two reasons. First, it brought in its wake various changes which contributed to the continuation of sabre-rattling policies. Above all, the Indonesian Armed Forces received a great deal of equipment and tasted the delights of very high expenditures for military purposes, while Soekarno and the PKI discovered how to use 'agitational politics' to their advantage by exploiting an issue of this kind. Second, the pattern of the West Irian campaign was in several respects a model for the later campaign against Malaysia. Yet until the end of 1962 there seemed to be little reason for fear that Indonesia harboured any expansionist designs upon other neighbouring territories. West Irian was a special case, it was frequently argued, a nationalist symbol which no good Indonesians were willing to disavow, since it represented a diminution of their country's nationhood and an affront by their former Dutch masters to the central principles of their nationalism and anti-colonialism. In her almost obsessive concern with recovering West Irian from the Dutch, Indonesia had given very little attention to the other colonial territories on her borders, apart from occasional ritual denunciations of colonialism.[2] They did not pose the same issues or arouse the same intensity of emotion as the Dutch retention of West Irian did. And as the creation of Malaysia was specifically intended to bring about the end of British colonial rule, there seemed to be little reason to fear Indonesian hostility to the scheme.

In any case, before 1962 Indonesia was simply not in a position to pose any serious threat to her neighbours. The large Army (of 300,000 or more), Air Force and Navy, which were a legacy of her struggle for independence and which no Indonesian government had ever been able to reduce in size, were very poorly equipped until they began to receive military supplies from Russia under the $1,000 million arms loan negotiated at the end of 1960. She was preoccupied by her own problems of internal security until the *PRRI-Permesta* rebels of Sumatra and Sulawesi 'returned to the fold of the motherland' in mid-1961; *Darul Islam* insurgents in South Sulawesi and West Java, who had defied the government for over a decade, were not pacified until 1962.[3] And there were serious political differences between President Soekarno and the Army leaders which gravely weakened the government's cohesiveness and capacity to take strong action on any matter. Even over the West Irian issue, on which there was a high degree of consensus, disagreements about tactics were obvious, while on economic and administrative matters there were much deeper unresolved conflicts of interests among the heterogeneous groups supporting Soekarno.

THE POLITICAL SYSTEM

Although the system of 'Guided Democracy' established by President Soekarno in July 1959 had various constant features which persisted until its end in 1966, it is not easy to define categorically how the system worked or what precisely its major elements were.[4] It is unsafe even to talk about 'the government' after 1962, as if Soekarno, his ministers and the administration constituted a coherent, unified group exercising a collective responsibility for policy-making. The notion of a 'court' in which every minister was striving to gain influence at the palace was more apposite in the later years. Significant modifications in the power balance and the all-important ideological framework within which the political struggle for power was waged were occurring constantly throughout that period. Political Indonesia embraces other worlds besides the palace political circles of Djakarta, although it is on the latter that our focus mainly falls. We will be largely concerned with the central triangular relationship between the President, the Army leaders and the PKI (to a lesser extent, also, with the other parties), rather than with Djakarta's relations with the regional capitals, or the intra-bureaucratic contests for funds and influence, or the constant struggle for supporters and power at the grass-roots level in regional councils or bodies like the National Front or the numerous quasi-representative or mass mobilization organizations which quickly flourished and faded in the hot-house political climate of Guided Democracy. But these spheres of political activity intermeshed with each other in various ways, so the wider background should also be remembered if we are to avoid the delusion that Djakarta politics made up the entire story.

The four constant features of Guided Democracy in the 1959–66 period which will here be broadly outlined are the so-called 'triangle' of Soekarno-Army-PKI as the central focus of the struggle for power; the concept of *Nasakom* (the trinity of nationalist, religious and Communist streams of political life in Indonesia) as Soekarno's main organizing principle of political representation and manipulation; the prominence of indoctrination and the official ideology: and the propensity towards highly inflationary budgets and serious economic decline.

The notion of a triangular relationship or balance between President, Army and PKI in these years is not an entirely satisfactory one, but it serves to summarize the central features of the power structure — the fact that the two latter institutions alone constituted nation-wide organizations with fairly concrete political aims and that the President, who had no party or organization under his personal control, maintained his predominant position in the political system by playing them off against each other and laying down the terms upon which the political unity of the regime was to be preserved.[5] The relationship was much more subtle and complex than that, of course: it was not just the PKI on which Soekarno relied as a political counterweight to the Army, but the other parties also represented in the groupings of ten recognized political parties. Neither Soekarno nor the Army leaders could entirely override the claims of political parties to a voice in the government of Indonesia, although they had little use for civilian politicians and were far from tender towards democratic rights. Political parties were badly discredited because of their poor record during the earlier period of parliamentary democracy, so they were unable to resist Soekarno's flagrant extension of his formal constitutional powers at their expense. But they could not be abolished or ignored, either, least of all the PKI. Hence their curiously uncertain position throughout this period, sometimes of very minor importance in the Soekarno-Army contest for power (in 1960–1 and during the West Irian campaign) but at other times (1963–4) able to assert themselves far more strongly.

Political parties had played a dominant part on the Indonesian stage during the years 1945–9, the era of the physical revolution against the Dutch, when they were important instruments for mobilizing mass support in the anti-colonialist struggle, and again during the period of parliamentary democracy, 1950–9.[6] In the latter period, Indonesia's constitution was based on the Dutch parliamentary model, so that President Soekarno's position as titular Head of State gave him little direct political influence. His advocacy of 'Guided Democracy' from 1957 on can be attributed in large part to his desire to wield more direct power and, after the regional revolts of 1957–8 which revealed the inability of political parties to resolve some of the country's most pressing problems, Soekarno and the Army leaders successfully pushed through the 'return to the 1945 Constitution' in July 1959 in order to weaken the position of the political parties. Designed for the unpredictable circumstances of the struggle against the Dutch and based broadly on the American model of a presidential system, the 1945 Constitution left a very limited role to representative bodies and vested very extensive powers in the hands of the President. In 1959–60 Soekarno soon made it clear to the political parties that they were allowed to exist only on sufferance: when they dared to exercise their constitutional right to reject a most unsatisfactory budget in 1960, Parliament was promptly 're-tooled' to Soekarno's convenience. Parties opposing him were banned while the others were 'simplified' and reduced in number to ten under the requirements of a new law concerning political parties. In addition to the Parliament, whose functions were purely legislative and fiscal, the Constitution provided also for a People's Consultative Assembly (*Madjelis Permusjawaratan Rakjat Sementara*—MPRS), made up of the members of Parliament and 'representatives of regions and groups'; it was designated as the embodiment of the peoples' sovereignty, with power to elect the President and Vice-President and to lay down the 'general direction of State policy'. Since the members of this body were never elected, however, but merely appointed by the President, it served primarily as a sounding-board for his policies rather than as a countervailing power. (Only in 1966–7, when it was used against the President by the Army leaders, did it acquire an influential role in Indonesian politics.) The realities of power under Guided Democracy were not determined or delimited by the constitution, but by the struggle among his immediate advisers and ministers to exercise influence on the President's policy-making.[7]

The ministers in Soekarno's cabinet were responsible solely to him for their appointment and dismissal. He had to take political pressures into account, of course, in constituting his cabinet, particularly from the Army side. Thus, cabinet reshuffles became the most important manifestations of changes in the power balance and occurred frequently in the years 1962–5. But the 'cabinet' itself was not the centre of decision-making processes like the British cabinet: in fact, it became even less meaningful than the American as its size grew and grew, its meetings became less and less frequent and other bodies were set up by the President to share with him the main responsibilities of decision-making.[8] After 1962 the cabinet had over 45 ministers and by 1966 it had nearly 100 members of ministerial status, although many did not administer departments. Here, as almost everywhere else, power was being split up and diffused, except in a few key ministries which commanded substantial patronage opportunities or financial resources.

The Army leaders were in a position to exercise greater influence than any other political organization during the period when Indonesia was under martial law, because of the wide powers vested in regional military commanders (who have generally been more important than provincial governors in recent years) and because the Army represented the *ultima ratio* of armed force. But General Nasution was reluctant to brandish the threat of force too blatantly, for he and the other General Staff officers were well aware that too open an involvement in politics could imperil the unity of the Army. So long as they obtained representation in the high councils of government and a fair share of the perquisites of office and could limit Soekarno's policies in certain directions, they were content with what Nasution once called the 'middle course' between complete abstention from politics and a complete take-over.[9] Although the Army leaders never showed much enthusiasm for Soekarno's *Nasakom* principle, which implied equality of rights for the PKI, they came to accept it (rather grudgingly) by 1961, partly for lack of any alternative political formula, but in some cases because the efficiency and honesty of the PKI representatives with whom they came into contact in the various deliberative organs of the government impressed them by contrast with the other party representatives.[10] By 1964 some observers were becoming doubtful whether the Army was really such a determined opponent of Communism as it had been considered earlier (perhaps too naively); it seemed to be offering little resistance to policies and doctrines put forward by Soekarno which seemed to be carrying Indonesia towards Communism by a gradual metamorphosis. Others took the view, however, that the Army occupied a position of such power and privilege within the Indonesian political system that it would draw the line against PKI encroachments as soon as it began to feel seriously threatened.[11] But in fact, 'the Army' did not act in the political arena as a tightly-knit force before 1965–6, except perhaps in 1959–60. It was organized in about 20 regional commands broadly corresponding with provinces and every regional commander was keenly aware of local political pressures. The Army was by no means immune from the political and ideological tensions afflicting the country as a whole, even though it had special interests of its own to safeguard.

Moreover, President Soekarno, who was also titular Supreme Commander of the Armed Forces, had considerable influence among some senior officers and the same charismatic appeal to ordinary soldiers and the junior officers as he had among the general public. He was able to play off Lt.-Gen. Yani against General Nasution in 1962 so as to replace the latter as Army Chief of Staff and then achieve a considerable reduction in the influence of Nasution's group of strongly anti-Communist officers. Although Nasution remained Minister of Defence and Security and Chief of Staff of the Armed Forces, his power was steadily reduced. Yani proved to be more compliant to the President, and his relations with Nasution were badly strained at times. Hence the Army leaders were very hesitant to take any firm stand against the President to resist the leftward drift of government policies in 1963–5. Although they were able to insist that no Communists should head ministries (a relatively unimportant precaution after 1962) they were unable to counter policies which worked greatly to the advantage of the PKI or to offset the direct influence which the PKI leaders, Aidit and Njoto, came to exert upon the President by 1964–5.

The Army leaders were caught in a cleft stick, in any case, since their need for big government expenditure on defence could not easily be squared with their interest in sound administration, economic stability and the avoidance of social unrest. The government's attempts to bring the budget into balance in 1961 and 1963 in order to curb inflationary pressures would have entailed severe retrenchment in the size of the Armed Forces, something that no Indonesian government was strong enough to achieve between 1949 and 1966. In order to deflect demands for retrenchment, the Army devised the concept of its 'Civic Mission', the utilization of Army units in support of regional development projects in the provinces. This would not have solved the Army's budgetary problems or immediately boosted production, but it provided a means of creating (or claiming) closer identification of the Army and the civilian population. But the wider problem of the Army's relationship with the civil government was also a thorny one. It has never been successfully resolved and, by its very nature, never can be entirely. Hence the convenience of issues like the West Irian dispute and the confrontation of Malaysia, which legitimized its claims to a special role in national life and to large budget expenditure. Despite a certain ambivalence in the attitude of the Army leaders to both campaigns — in each of which, paradoxically, they suffered a severe loss of political influence — they did provide an escape from some of the immediate political and financial dilemmas facing the leadership.

The role of the PKI in the central power triangle was not as clear-cut as the President's or the Armed Forces'. It controlled no ministries and had few of its members or sympathizers in top civil service positions or the Armed Forces, but it could wield considerable influence in provincial and regency councils, backed by its extensive network of branches and militant cadres. What made it a more considerable political force than the other parties, however, was not so much its formal power as the fact that it had a coherent ideology, political and social objectives to strive for beyond mere office-holding and an appeal to the down-trodden which was likely to win it vastly more support if another election were ever held.[12] It was not tainted with the same record of corruption and incompetence as other parties, whom it was able to embarrass along with the government by urging reforms in the name of democracy as well as Socialism. It could generally use Soekarno's own terminology against its 'reactionary' opponents when it wanted to silence them and identify itself with Soekarno for safety from its enemies. Although estimates of PKI membership (about 2–2½ million in December 1963) were probably somewhat exaggerated for political effect, the party had established an efficient organizational structure throughout Java at least, reaching into many areas where the other parties did not. Its peasant organization claimed 8½ million members, but by the PKI's own admission it was not winning support among the peasants as effectively as it hoped and it was far from having the 'toiling masses' at its beck and call. It claimed steady increases in its membership and its cadres were becoming increasingly militant as it went from strength to strength in the years 1963–5. It behaved as if it represented the wave of the future and because it was able to convince many non-Communist Indonesians of that also, it grew into a formidable political force, despite its exclusion from the main decision-making bodies.[13] The power of the PKI was frequently exaggerated before the 1965 coup and there is now a tendency to belittle it retrospectively because the coup failed. But its advances in 1964–5 were dramatic, as we shall see, although they were confined to the capital rather than the provinces and still left the party in a position of heavy dependence on Soekarno.

The success of the PKI in growing from a shattered and demoralized party after the failure of the 1948 Madiun revolt to the confident and militant force it became in 1965 was due very largely to Aidit's skilful political tactics. The doctrine of the National United Front — i.e. seeking to maintain a close identification with other 'progressive' national forces such as Soekarno and the parties supporting him, exploiting nationalist symbols rather than class consciousness — paid handsome dividends between 1951–60 as the PKI accomplished, first, the isolation of its most bitter enemies, the Masjumi and PSI (Socialist Party), then their exclusion from political life.[14] By 1961 some observers were doubtful whether this policy would enable the PKI to get much closer to the key centres of political power in the face of Army opposition to a *Nasakom* cabinet; the PKI had become 'domesticated' by Soekarno and was caught in a blind alley, it was argued, since it had lost its revolutionary zeal, yet it could not abandon the National United Front policy for fear of repression.[15] But the West Irian campaign (and, later, the Malaysia campaign) provided Aidit with a way out of the difficulties confronting him in 1961, for it was in the realms of foreign policy and national ideology that the PKI was now able to make dramatic new gains, exploiting new opportunities to mobilize the people in mass organizations for the national cause, using militantly anti-imperialist slogans advantageous to the PKI to draw Indonesia away from the USA and closer to China. True, the PKI barely managed to get a foot inside the portals of formal governmental power and never obtained the *Nasakom* cabinet it periodically demanded, but it was able to keep the wheel of Indonesia's revolution turning constantly to the left, it succeeded in wearing away Indonesia's ties to the USA almost to breaking point and it managed to turn all the attacks of its enemies back to their own disadvantage in the years 1964–5. The main factor in its success was not just numbers and mass organization, but skilful political strategy in exploiting the temperament of Soekarno, the disunity of the party's opponents and the changes in the international situation. According to Ruth McVey, the most authoritative commentator on the PKI,

...its policy has been to attempt to integrate the Communist movement with the present regime and with society as a whole, on such a grand scale that it becomes identical with the nation's organizational and ideological backbone. It seeks to become indispensable, for indispensability means invulnerability, and invulnerability means power.[16]

So long as Soekarno lived and the PKI could count on his protection and sympathy, this policy served its purposes excellently. The prospect of Soekarno's demise in 1964–5 opened up new problems, however, and the PKI's disastrous involvement in the coup of October 1965 may well have been precipitated by fears of an Army crackdown when he died, although there are many unanswered questions about the reasons for and extent of PKI complicity in the coup.

From the point of view of the Malaysia story, however, the PKI's influence within the Indonesian political system in 1963 has to be assessed in the light of its generally cautious and limited tactical aims. While it was constantly endeavouring to push the government into an anti-western foreign policy stance by exploiting the Malaysia issue, it was very much aware of the perils to which it would be exposed if its opponents took advantage of any situation of national emergency that might develop to curb or ban the PKI's activities. It also had to be careful not to alarm the military by involving the doctrine of class conflict or openly attacking Army or ex-Army men. Hence the necessity to use the smoke-screen of Soekarno's ideology and slogans, like *Nasakom* and *Nekolim*, to which no exception could be taken.

The *Nasakom* idea was initially put forward in 1960 as a formula for allocating party representatives in the MPRS, Parliament, National Front, regional assemblies and other consultative bodies established by the government. The ten approved parties, said to represent the three main streams in Indonesian life, nationalist, religious (*agama*) and Communist, generally obtained some representation, with the big three, PNI, NU and PKI, obtaining an approximately equal share. Precise numbers were no longer of vital importance in these assemblies, since consensus (*musjawarah*) was the basic principle underlying Guided Democracy, not rule by majority vote. The smaller parties were at least assured of a right to be heard, so there were some advantages for them in the new system. The PKI would have preferred elections and the restoration of democratic rights, but it supported the *Nasakom* idea against the anti-Communists who were unhappy about it, since this aligned them with Soekarno and provided them with opportunities to gain footholds in many new spheres of political activity.

Soekarno found the *Nasakom* principle convenient for his purposes in two ways. It embodied the ideas of consensus and national unity, which he was erecting as the main pillars of his personal authority, both the goal of his endeavours and a means of silencing dissentients. And it enshrined the legitimacy of the constituent parties, including the PKI, against demands for the suppression of Communism or of outright military rule.[17] Opposition to the *Nasakom* idea was rarely heard in public, for any sentiments that could be characterized as 'Communist-phobia' were regarded as anti-revolutionary, so their exponents were likely to come under heavy attack from the left. On the whole, too, *Nasakom* seems to have been fairly widely accepted as a workable principle in the period of Soekarno's personal paramountcy when there was great difficulty in finding any other which would obtain wide acceptance. All the recognized political groups were under heavy ideological pressure to strengthen national unity by the method of *musjawarah*, which meant that they could not hope to achieve sole dominance, but were left with a form of veto power and with opportunities to influence the formulation of official policies through back-stage pressure, bargaining and manipulation. That was the essential weakness of the *musjawarah* principle: it tended to paralyse decision-making on controversial issues. Guided Democracy and *Nasakom* consensus did not result in strong government any more than liberal democracy and majority rule had done. In fact, the result was a series of weak compromises. Either the government had to resort to an elaborate process of political manoeuvring and deception before it could act decisively (as we will see it doing in the matter of the unpopular economic stabilization scheme of May 1963) or it had to engineer a *fait accompli* which could not be reversed.[18] The assertiveness of Soekarno's regime in the 'expressive' aspects of government, ideological indoctrination and foreign policy particularly, and its strongly authoritarian handling of the problems of power-maintenance could not hide or remedy its underlying weakness in tackling the 'instrumental' side of government, involving social, economic and political reforms, more efficient administration or the curbing of inflation.

Soekarno's emphasis on ideology, indoctrination, slogans and symbolism was one of the most striking features of political activity under Guided Democracy. The 'symbol-wielders' and 'solidarity-makers' came to exercise far more influence than the 'administrators', to use Feith's useful dichotomy. The President had set forth the new goals, tasks and slogans of the regime in his Independence Day speech of 17 August 1959 entitled 'The Rediscovery of Our Revolution' which was to become known as the Political Manifesto (generally referred to as *Manipol-Usdek*).[19] Its main doctrines were the renunciation of capitalism, 'liberalism' and related foreign cultural influences, the abandonment of 'text-book thinking', return to Indonesia's national identity, restoration of the spirit of the 1945 Revolution and the national solidarity which it created and the establishment of a 'just and prosperous society' based upon Indonesian Socialism. The social values underlying these slogans were widely endorsed by Indonesians, although a good deal of cynicism was aroused by some of their particular manifestations. But a massive campaign of indoctrination, coupled with 're-tooling' of government employees suspected of mere lip service to the new doctrines, ensured that at least in their public utterances most Indonesians had to express agreement with the national ideology. The necessity for ideological conformity was one of the strongest pillars maintaining the Soekarno regime after 1960, silencing overt criticism of the government (although individual ministers could still be obliquely attacked) and leaving the initiative for the interpreting of his vague doctrines always in the President's hands.

While the ideology was undeniably imposed from above, it also made a considerable appeal in its own right, for Indonesians were looking for a *pegangan* — something to hang on to — a prescribed set of doctrines and objectives at a time when they lacked any clear sense of national purpose. *Manipol-Usdek* was vague enough to mean all things to all men (or nearly all), but its general radical-nationalist character was unmistakeable. And at least it brought temporary relief from the danger of ideological conflict between Islam and Communism, which had seemed perilously imminent on several occasions in the previous decade. A common response to *Manipol-Usdek*, observed Feith, was 'it may not be a very good ideology, but an ideology is certainly what we need'.[20] The efficacy of all this indoctrination is not easily gauged. By 1962 it seemed to have achieved a very considerable influence over the thinking of the vast majority of Indonesians, if only because they had little or no opportunity to obtain any other view of national and international affairs. On the other hand, some critics of the regime believed that its transparent inadequacies and gross hyperbole made it counter-productive. People could not find in it the guidance they were seeking and so had to think out their own solutions to the problems besetting them. Many paid lip-service to the ideology, but became utterly cynical about it behind their outward show of conformity. The vehemence with which the students who had been too young to remember the earlier 'liberal' doctrines repudiated Soekarno's ideology in 1966 is indeed a striking testimony to its evanescence.[21]

The prominence of ideology in the Soekarno regime is directly relevant to the Malaysia story because confrontation came to be the most complete manifestation of the doctrine of the New Emerging Forces and continuing revolution against the neo-colonialist enemy. These gradually superseded *Manipol-Usdek* and *Nasakom* as the main themes of Soekarno's oratory. Slogans soon grow stale and have to be replaced. Soekarno's fertility of imagination in devising new ones which could be presented as logical extensions of their predecessors was one of his most extraordinary but blighting gifts. For it brought its own retribution in due time. Ideology became important just for its own sake, acquiring an almost autonomous life of its own, quite divorced from the real world. By 1965 Soekarno was behaving as if the most important political consideration was to follow out the logic of his doctrines at all costs, rather than to change his political course and modify his ideology — and the costs by then were disastrously high, particularly in the economic sphere.

The economic and administrative performance of the Indonesian government under Guided Democracy suffered disastrously because of the obsession with ideology and the scramble for office and influence around the President. Despite its highly authoritarian character, Soekarno's government was not strong when it came to getting things done. In its efforts to regulate the economy and promote productive investment, the regime proved to be hopelessly ineffective. Inflation and economic stagnation were constant features of the period after 1959, except briefly in 1960-1. Prices and the volume of money roughly doubled every twelve months between September 1961 and October 1965, solely because of budget deficits. As the situation deteriorated, the government's ability to balance the budget also diminished, which in turn eroded its determination to tackle the problem. The counterpart to its neglect of basic economic problems was its obsession with the immediate problems of remaining in power, with simply riding the wave of revolution, since there was little else that could be done. After the collapse of an attempted stabilization programme in 1963, no serious effort was made to bring the inflation under control or restore the economy to rights.[22]

Why was Soekarno's regime so disastrously hamstrung in this respect? The fundamental answer was perhaps best given by Feith in his explanation of why ideological and 'symbolic' concerns so often prevailed over rational solutions to economic problems: 'The basic issue is always the same: is power to be with those who want to gear society to the maximization of production, or is it to be with those, both symbol wielders and military men, who can best sustain the mood of "the Revolution goes on"?'[23]

Two other factors should be mentioned at this point. The first is that the heterogeneous collection of political forces represented in Soekarno's government did not conduce to strength and consensus so much as to intra-governmental political manoeuvring for influence and a debilitating politicization of the bureaucracy which had to carry out most of the government's policies. Thus the degree of commitment felt towards official policies was often low. The PKI frequently criticized government policies obliquely or openly, but it was by no means alone in this respect. There was very little sense of 'collective responsibility' for government policies, no more than was needed to maintain the outward appearance of conformity. Hence the inflation was simply allowed to deteriorate. No political party had a strong interest in stability *per se*, but all had an interest in obtaining the biggest possible allocation of budget allocations for their parts of the bureaucracy or patronage resources for disbursement among their followers. Only a few individual ministers like Djuanda were strongly committed to economic development and budgetary stability, but they carried little weight on their own. Two attempts to hold the budget in balance, in 1961 and 1963, both failed because retrenchment hurt important groups represented in the government. Significantly, both attempts were wrecked by the resort to 'external adventures' — the West Irian campaign of 1962 and the confrontation of Malaysia in 1963.[24]

The second factor to be noted is that budget deficits served as a kind of political safety-valve for the government throughout this period, in much the same way as 'external adventures' functioned as a unifying force and diversion from domestic conflicts. It was easier just to borrow more from the central bank (i.e. to print more money) than to resolve the awkward political problems of priorities that would arise if a determined effort were made to keep government expenditures within the limits set by tax revenues. Inflation enabled the government to side-step the task of over-hauling the tax machinery, which was steadily crumbling. It postponed the need for a conscious choice between divergent political objectives.

The demands of the Armed Forces for big military expenditures could be met without any overt reductions in other sectors, although the declining value of the rupiah achieved reductions in real terms which the government would not have dared to impose as a matter of policy. On the few occasions when it introduced measures with a marked deprivational effect, they were sudden and irreversible measures whose impact was indiscriminate or uncertain; they did not obviously favour one group at the expense of another and no political steadfastness was needed to implement them.[25]

For all its talk about Socialism à la Indonesia and the need for 'blueprints' or a planned economy, Soekarno's regime achieved the reverse of economic planning. It was, in fact, living from hand to mouth in terms of foreign exchange, the resource which was most crucial to it. Its Eight Year Overall Development Plan of 1960 was a sheer fantasy from the outset. Only if the inflation had been checked could economic development have been stimulated. This was well known, but it could not be achieved. Meanwhile Indonesians were becoming accustomed to the problems of living with inflation and by 1964 Soekarno was openly boasting that they could go on doing so indefinitely — or, at least until Malaysia had been crushed. The disastrous consequences became apparent in the course of 1965.

SOEKARNO

The personality of President Soekarno himself coloured Indonesia's foreign policy and influenced her destiny to a remarkable degree in the years 1960–5. It was he who drew the country away from the policy of non-alignment which had been the normally accepted posture of most Indonesian politicians until then, and steered it instead towards the strongly anti-Western commitment implicit in the doctrine of the New Emerging Forces and, ultimately, towards alignment with Peking. His speeches were studded with references to the romanticism, rhythm and dialectic of revolution, which obviously stirred his soul far more deeply than the prosaic tasks of political manipulation of administration ever did. And in the development of a foreign policy based on confrontation of the old established order he was able to give expression to this sense of on-going revolution, whereas in domestic politics he was bogged down and frustrated by the complexity of Indonesia's problems to which there was no simple panacea.

Soekarno has been aptly described as a man 'obsessed with revolutionary elan ... (with) the thrill of a political surfride'.[26] He was bent upon winning recognition of Indonesia's role as a major power in South-East Asia, but he was not seeking regional dominance just for its own sake.

He was preoccupied with changing the established international order, with movement and with the dynamism which he believed Indonesia could generate, commented Bruce Grant. Takdir Alisjahbana has used the term 'monumentalism' as one of the keys to this aspect of his personality:

He is fond of everything spectacular and imposing; even to his children he gave the name of Guntur and Guruh, which both mean thunder. His speeches are full of rhetorical metaphors, taken from terrifying events in nature, such as storm and thunder, the boiling ocean, or from the great war stories of the *wayang* heroes .... Revolution, in which everything is adrift and confused, is a state that gives his dynamism the chance to shake everything and to experiment with society according to his exuberant fantasy.... The Indonesian Revolution he evokes is seen as the greatest revolution of all time: greater than the American Revolution, greater than the French Revolution, and greater than the Communist Revolution in Russia, for in the Indonesian Revolution, according to Soekarno, are included the national revolution, the political revolution, the social revolution, the cultural revolution and the revolution of man, a 'summing up of many revolutions in one revolution.'[27]

Yet if Soekarno sometimes seemed excessive or irrational, there was method in his madness. His vision of world history and Indonesia's place in it was based on a shrewd perception of the changing world situation and of how to exploit it. Moreover, his doctrines served an important cognitive function. 'The Indonesian leaders are intellectuals. They feel they have to act according to an idea. They must rationalise all their actions.' This comment on Soekarno's ideological preoccupations came from a senior Australian politician to whom realism and pragmatism ranked far higher among the political virtues. On the other hand impulse and instinct also seem to have influenced Soekarno's reactions on particular occasions. His policies were sometimes quite unpredictable. He was a shrewd politician, however, despite his erratic whims — which he could restrain if he felt it necessary. His flamboyant and adventurous side expressed itself in his high-flown speeches and grandiose doctrines rather than in daring decision-making: in fact, he was often cautious or even hesitant about committing himself firmly to any particular course of action if there were uncertainties ahead, especially in matters of domestic politics. The ambiguities and hyperbole which characterized some of his high-flown utterances often served to obscure their precise meaning, as if Soekarno himself had not yet decided just what significance he was going to attach to them. In domestic politics he was a master at exploiting the uncertainties and suspense which he created by keeping everyone guessing or apprehensive about his next move, while he watched to see what theirs would be. Rarely did he act decisively in either domestic or international politics — neither at the outbreak of the Indonesian revolution in August 1945, for example, nor in the coup of October 1965, although Indonesia's fate hinged upon his actions on both occasions. Nor did he in precipitating the conflict with Malaysia. (He did, however, when he withdrew from the United Nations in January 1965.) It would be wrong, of course, to exaggerate the impression of indecisiveness. The truth is somewhere in between. Soekarno was an unusually complex and many-sided personality, a man of remarkable abilities and strong feelings, who was the central figure in an unusually complicated political and social drama to which there were no simple solutions.[28]

This is not the appropriate place to attempt a rounded picture of Soekarno in all his colourful and contradictory aspects. Good sketches of him have already been published elsewhere, but the assessment of his real stature and his place in Indonesia's pantheon of national heroes will have to be left to those who have known him more intimately, in conjunction with those who have thoroughly explored the course of recent Indonesian history. His eminence in that pantheon is assured by his role as the foremost national leader between 1927 and 1949, whatever one might think of his subsequent political influence and his inglorious end in 1965–70. Yet he remains an enigma in many respects, despite the very public life he led. His actions often differed greatly from his words, his grandiose political doctrines from the devious compromises through which he executed them. Few politicians can afford the luxury of complete consistency, of course, but Soekarno's inconsistencies seemed unusually flagrant — the contrast between his Socialist, egalitarian doctrines and the extravagantly corrupting court life which he allowed to develop around him; between his fascination with 'blueprints', plans and targets for the nation and his sublime unconcern with the basic mechanics of social and economic change; between his bombastic slogans ('Build the World Anew', 'Crush Malaysia', 'Storm the Last Ramparts of Imperialism') and his care, except on two or three notable occasions, to avoid precipitate action in carrying them out.

Nearly all who have known Soekarno will agree on his great charm, humour and energy, his exceptional oratorical ability, his shrewdness in most political matters, his breadth of interests and ideas (more impressive in his youth than in his declining years, unfortunately) and his creative, artistic temperament, to mention only the most obvious points. Most would agree with Lev's characterization of him as 'romantic, almost utopian, in his ideas ... capable of tremendous abstract anger against historical wrongs as he sees them.... By temperament he is radical and adventurous, virtues which he often proclaims and which he insists Indonesia as a nation must substitute for the permissive psychology he believes was left over from the colonial era'.[29] His sensitivity to the political mood of his people was uncanny in one so isolated from them for so much of his life through exile and the restraints of high office. Soekarno's ability to articulate the resentments, frustrations, insecurities, aspirations and dreams of ordinary Indonesians from many walks of life was the envy of his rivals; he understood and transmuted those sentiments, expressing them in slogans and images which aroused enthusiasm and a sense of personal identification with the national struggle, the revolution that would liberate the nation, the individual and, ultimately, all mankind.

He had not the patience to concern himself with the tedious, prosaic problems of economists and administrators who could offer neither dramatic results nor emotional satisfaction. So he made no bones of the matter and left these problems to others while he concentrated on the political, ideological and psychological reconstruction of his nation.

'Soekarno appears to be the archetype of the pure politician,' observed Lev, 'far more interested in power and leadership than in particular policy goals and broad objectives.' This is true enough, insofar as he showed little real interest in the mechanics of the social changes he talked about and may even have been 'not truly convinced that much in Java ought to be different'.[30] But it would be unfair to leave the impression that he was only interested in maintaining power for its own sake, or for the glorification of himself or the nation. That would be altogether too shallow a judgement of the radical and Socialist sentiments he espoused, of his sympathies for the little man and his desire for continued identification with 'the people' in some vaguely conceived fashion. Soekarno's political sympathies have always been towards the left, not necessarily towards the Communist Party (whose doctrinal rigidities were in many ways distasteful to him) so much as towards the 'national Communists' of the Murba type, such as the young Chairul Saleh and Adam Malik, buccaneering young adventurers and romantics like himself for the most part. Although he spent the last eight years of his power in a balancing role between right and left, he always seems to have been more at ease in association with the latter, whereas he had little liking for conservatism in any of its manifestations.

Progress, revolution, personal identification with the masses, the unity of the whole people, these were the ideas which inspired Soekarno. Government was a matter of leading the people towards a promised land, not merely of reconciling the pressures of various interest groups or indirectly regulating economic and social life to maintain stable conditions in which private initiative could thrive on the basis of the acquisitive instincts. The goal of the journey was perhaps of less importance to him than the journey itself, but there could be no such journey without the vision of a 'just and prosperous society' at the end of it. The vision he offered turned out to be no more than a mirage in the end, for Soekarno never spelled out how the just and prosperous society could be achieved in Indonesia's circumstances, while in his preoccupation with lifting up his countrymen's eyes to the distant hills he took too little account of the economic quicksands they were stumbling into. But to turn around and change course just for the sake of economic stability would have been repugnant to him, a repudiation of the philosophy which had guided his whole life. Some observers concluded that in the last two years of his autocratic power he was actively promoting the PKI to a position from which it could inherit his political mantle when he died. Certainly his close identification with it at that time and his refusal to ban the PKI after the attempted coup of October 1965 reveal how strong his sympathies with it were. But it is highly debatable that he was consciously working to bring the PKI to power, although he may indeed have been trying to make it such an integral part of the political scene that there could be no question of a right-wing reaction to destroy it after he was gone. (In 1964 he was thought by many observers to be favouring the leaders of the non-Communist left who were regarded as anathema by the PKI.) He probably could have done much more to advance PKI interests if that had been his aim, although the risk of precipitating a counter-move by the anti-Communists if he had done so must have been a major consideration restraining him. By 1965, when the 'Djakarta-Peking axis' was being created, Soekarno's political interests came to coincide with the PKI's more than ever before, while the anti-Communists found themselves increasingly on the defensive. But there were still many indications that Soekarno's primary concern was to preserve the precarious national unity his regime was based upon, even if it meant being carried further to the left by the apparently irresistible tide of the PKI's advance.

INDONESIAN FOREIGN POLICY, 1959–1965

Soekarno's yearning to transform the entire international political system in accordance with the demands of the newly independent nations was vividly expressed in the title of his address to the United Nations General Assembly, in September 1960, 'To Build the World Anew'. He did not make it very clear just what he meant by this apart from urging an end to colonialism and the Cold War, but he was quick to discern the changes that were occurring in the wider pattern of international relationships and to adjust Indonesia's policies to take advantage of them. Since these changes were reaching fruition just at the time when the Malaysian dispute began to develop, they form an important element in the background to our story.

During the previous decade, the three main planks of Indonesian foreign policy had been the maintenance of a non-aligned (strictly 'independent and active') foreign policy, opposition to colonialism and prosecution of the West Irian campaign. Differences between one government or party and another on foreign policy issues were little more than differences of emphasis and tactics rather than of basic objectives (except in the case of the PKI, which approved of non-alignment only as an interim tactic). But foreign policy questions did not dominate the political scene during the 1950s as obsessively as the West Irian and Malaysian issues were to do after 1961. There were two main reasons for this. First, although the West Irian claim was the major foreign policy concern of almost every Indonesian government, very little could be done to promote it effectively in the circumstances prevailing until 1961 beyond raising the question in the United Nations and threatening the Dutch (vainly, as it turned out) with economic reprisals. Second, the non-aligned countries could exercise relatively little political leverage vis-à-vis the two major blocs during the Cold War period, except in the matter of playing off one against the other for the sake of financial aid. After 1960, however, this bipolar pattern began to break down and the opportunities for Indonesia to play a more independent role on the world stage began to multiply. By 1964–5, neither the USA nor Russia was able to exert much influence over her if she chose to defy them.[31]

After 1960, Soekarno's foreign policy became increasingly militant and assertive, not only in his handling of the West Irian and Malaysia campaigns, but also in his alignment with the most radical members of the Afro-Asian world and ultimately with Communist China. The change came gradually, almost imperceptibly, under the influence of various factors. One of the most important was the thawing of the Cold War and the split within the Soviet bloc, to which the development of Soek-arno's doctrine of the New Emerging Forces and his swing from a three-camp theory of international relations towards a two-camp theory was in part a response, a recognition of the fact that the ideological rigidities of the Cold War era were breaking down. Just as de Gaulle was quick to perceive the consequences of this change and take advantage of it to increase France's political leverage vis-à-vis the USA so too Soekarno saw the opportunities for the nations of the Third World to exploit the rivalries of the great powers with impunity. He put forward the doctrine of the New Emerging Forces rather tentatively during the years 1961–2, but by 1963 it was becoming a key guideline to Indonesia's foreign policy.

The West Irian campaign of 1961–2 also removed some of the major constraints upon Indonesia's freedom of action in world and regional politics. It was itself made possible by the acquisition of substantial quantities of arms from Russia under loans offered by Premier Khrushchev during his visit early in 1960. For the first time, Indonesia had a sufficient military capability to constitute a serious threat to her immediate neigh-bours and to be able to contemplate the application of pressure against imperialist bases in the area. Moreover, it was no longer necessary for her after 1962 to avoid giving offence to nations whose votes in the UN on the West Irian issue might be vital to her. (Her relations with India deteriorated with almost indecent haste, although Soekarno's coolness towards Nehru had originated some years earlier.) As J. D. Legge commented shortly afterwards, 'for twelve years Indonesia's demand for the satisfaction of her claim to West Irian has dominated her foreign policy to an extent where it may have obscured effectively her real international position'.[32] What her 'real international position' was to be or the role she should be expected to play in the South-East Asia region, now that the colonial powers were finally leaving, became a puzzle for all concerned in 1963. One of the other consequences of the West Irian campaign was a penchant for 'living dangerously', which was now carried over by Soekarno into the central theory of his foreign policy.

In addition to the changing world situation, another factor contributing to the increasing militancy and stridency of Indonesian statements about foreign policy after 1960 was a very substantial modification of the official doctrines which served as a guide and ideological underpinning to her policies. In the first instance, this entailed a shift from a three-camp view of the world, in which Indonesia and other Afro-Asian nations were regarded as non-aligned in the struggle between the two great ideological blocs, to the two-camp doctrine of inexorable conflict between the New Emerging Forces and the Old Established Forces, which Soekarno began to propagate towards the end of 1962. Later, the implications of this change were developed further when even non-alignment in the over-riding struggle against imperialism was castigated.

The development of Soekarno's ideas on these matters can be illustrated by brief reference to three of his major speeches on foreign policy. In his speech to the UN General Assembly in September 1960, there was no hint of a departure from the old three-camp doctrine: on the contrary, he chided Bertrand Russell for depicting modern history as a conflict between two ideologies and ignoring the contribution of the non-aligned nations. The latter had nothing to do with the two Cold War blocs, from whom the principle threat to peace derived. By the time of the Belgrade Conference of Non-Aligned Nations in September 1961, however, Soek-arno was using many of the phrases and emphases which were later to become part of his stock-in-trade; here we find, the phrase 'new emergent forces for freedom and justice and the old forces of domination' and the notion of tension in the world deriving from inexorable conflict between these two opposing forces (not just from ideological differences, as some were wrongly trying to assert, such as Nehru). The bogey of 'neo-colonial-ism' now began to figure more prominently in Soekarno's speeches along with the assertion that the root cause of the world's conflicts was, in every case, imperialism and the forcible division of nations (the latter point an indirect reference to West Irian). It was not fortuitous that the non-aligned were generally on the same side as the New Emerging Forces which were thrusting into prominence, argued Soekarno, for they had been engaged in the struggle for independence against the imperialists. By April 1963, the whole doctrine had crystallized further into the two categories of

those who want to lead a life in which all nations enjoy independence and people are free from exploitation and oppression, i.e. the group known as 'the new emerging forces': [and] those nations or persons who want to preserve the evil state of the past, to continue the practice of colonial domination and oppression ... the 'old established forces'.[33]

Exactly who fell into each of these two categories was never clarified precisely, except insofar as 'imperialists' and their allies were obviously in the latter camp and anti-imperialists, hence the Communist countries generally, to the former: but Japan and India posed problems and de Gaulle sometimes behaved in a manner befitting an anti-imperialist, so sharp lines were never drawn. Non-alignment was a doctrine that could not easily be accommodated within the new system and it tended to drop out of official usage in 1963. Soekarno's key concepts now became 'continuance of the Revolution' and confrontation of counter-revolutionary elements. By the time of the 1964 Cairo Conference of the Non-Aligned, he was arguing that

...non-alignment must be anti-imperialist. If it is not anti-imperialist, then non-alignment is in reality already aligned, because it favours imperialism . . . it is impossible for one to be 'non-bloc' as between imperialism and anti-imperialism or between the coloniser and those fighting the coloniser.

Later he was to claim of that conference (in blithe disregard for the historical record) that 'revolutionary non-alignment won, equivocal non-alignment lost'.[34]

The ultimate step towards repudiation of the virtues of non-alignment in the old sense was marked by Soekarno's drive in 1965 to organize a Conference of New Emerging Forces, with strong Chinese backing, to work for

...the binding together of all international revolutionary forces...'international Nasakom', that is, a combining of all nationalist states with religious states and communist states on a world scale to batter the Necolim bruised and bloody, to shatter and destroy it and to build the world anew ....[35]

By this time, however, the Afro-Asian bloc was itself disintegrating under the strains of the Cairo Conference in October 1964 and the abortive Second Afro-Asian Conference at Algiers in June 1965.

One might well ask how far these doctrinal sophistries positively influenced the direction in which Indonesia's foreign policy developed during this period and how far they merely reflected changes which were occurring for more basic reasons. There can be no simple answers to these questions. At times it almost seemed as if the main purpose of her foreign policy was to prove the correctness of the ideology. By 1964–5, Soekarno's preoccupation with holding the Second Afro-Asian Conference and the Conference of the New Emerging Forces seemed to bear little relation to any positive political benefits that could be expected of them. But by then there was virtually no other course of action open to him (except humiliating retreat), so the momentum of a dynamic foreign policy had to be maintained. Yet the doctrine of the New Emerging Forces was the servant rather than the master of Soekarno's policies.

One of the striking features of Indonesia's foreign policy in the years 1960–2 was the apparent increase in Russian influence, resulting from Khrushchev's visit and the $1,000 million Soviet arms loans of 1960. This trend coincided with a brief period of serious tension between Indonesia and China in 1959–60 and also with her marked shift away from the American position on most issues at the UN, as if in reaction against the asymmetrical non-alignment of the 1950s when Indonesia's ties with the West were much closer than they were with the Communist countries, mainly for reasons of domestic politics. Now, Soekarno was not averse from allowing the PKI to gain the domestic benefits accruing from closer relations with Russia; in fact, by responding more favourably than previous Indonesian governments to Russian overtures, he was able to enhance his freedom of manoeuvre against the anti-Communists both at home and abroad. He soon made it clear, however, that he was no more prepared to become a puppet of Moscow than of Washington. By early 1963, disputes over Indonesia's difficulties in repaying her loans from Russia for military equipment were becoming a constant source of friction between the two countries, just at the time when the PKI was swinging towards a pro-Peking position in the Sino-Soviet dispute. Soekarno's increasing disposition to do the same left the Russians in an embarrassing and essentially defensive posture, for there was little they could do except attempt to retain what influence they had with the Armed Forces leaders who needed Russian equipment and spare parts.[36]

China did not exercise any significant influence on Indonesian foreign policy before 1963. The main concern of the Peking government was to repair the damage caused by the 1959–60 rift over Indonesia's ban on alien (mostly Chinese) retail stores in rural areas. But this was virtually settled by 1961 and relations slowly began to improve.[37] The dramatic development of the Djakarta-Peking axis in 1964–5 will be outlined in due course, but here it is sufficient to observe that that development was a consequence of Soekarno's new and more aggressive foreign policies, resulting mainly from Indonesia's diplomatic isolation, rather than a cause.

Indonesia's relations with the USA were changing in complex and subtle ways during these years. The election of President Kennedy was greeted by many Indonesians, including Soekarno, as a hopeful sign of better understanding and a more cordial relationship than had existed in the bleak Eisenhower-Dulles era. For his part, Kennedy made several positive moves in this direction by cultivating Soekarno personally, by tilting the weight of American support towards the Indonesian side in the West Irian dispute and by offering substantial economic assistance for the implementation of the 1960 Development Plan. But Kennedy faced difficulties in winning Congressional support for this policy, just as Soekarno faced difficulties with the PKI whenever he seemed to be moving too close to the West. These complexities of domestic and international politics had a significant impact on the course of events in 1963, when Sukarno's confrontation policy was taking shape. But with the intensification of confrontation in September 1963 and the collapse of the Washington-backed stabilization scheme, US-Indonesian relations began to deteriorate steadily, as we shall see in due course. The PKI exploited the Malaysia issue with considerable skill to weaken Indonesia's links with the USA and it came close to breaking them in early 1965. Soekarno was reluctant to go so far as this, but at some point in 1964 he seems to have decided that there was no possibility of repairing the damage that had been wrought in his relations with the USA and it was soon after this that he began to move into a closer association with China.[38]

THE WEST IRIAN CAMPAIGN

In the last stages of the West Irian campaign of 1962, Soekarno achieved success by the unconventional methods of diplomacy and low-level use of force which he later tried to repeat in the campaign against Malaysia. The two episodes had many similar features, but they were also significantly different in certain respects. In the case of West Irian the objective was finite — the incorporation of West Irian within Indonesia. The claim had long been supported by all groups in Indonesia, although there were important differences of opinion about how best to pursue it, and it was a matter of far more importance and prestige to the government to succeed in recovering West Irian into the national territory than it ever was to 'crush Malaysia'. The latter campaign was a more synthetic affair, a matter of ideological suasion rather than deep conviction. Nevertheless, in both cases, an external issue was exploited by Soekarno to achieve certain domestic goals. A combination of diplomacy, threats, bluff and infiltrations of irregular and regular forces was utilized to stretch the resources of the enemy to the limit. And the experience of 'living dangerously', daring to act unconventionally or in ways which had earlier been considered impracticable, proved to be catching. Soekarno's ideas of 'revolutionary diplomacy' developed further in the months after the West Irian success and were soon to be applied against Malaysia.

In December 1961 the campaign to recover West Irian was dramatically intensified after a decade of unsuccessful pressure to induce the Dutch to discuss the Indonesian claim.[39] Tension had been mounting since mid-1960 when Indonesian threats of armed infiltration prompted the Dutch to reinforce their naval and air forces in West New Guinea by sending out the aircraft carrier, 'Karel Doorman'; this in turn led the Indonesians to threaten to 'confront' the Dutch in the military sphere if necessary. During 1961 she began to acquire large quantities of additional arms from the Soviet Union, particularly aircraft, which greatly increased the credibility of her threats to use force. Yet there were many signs that Nasution and the Navy leaders (but not the Air Force commander) were extremely cautious about submitting the issue to the test of arms. The risks involved were considerable, not only for the leaders personally if military action failed, but also for Indonesia's relations with the western world, which would be gravely damaged, so that she would be forced into closer dependence on the USSR. An element of urgency had been injected into the situation, however, by the Dutch 'crash programme' of creating an elite in West New Guinea to whom independence could be granted as soon as possible. By late 1961 Soekarno was beginning to threaten open military action to regain the territory if the Dutch would not negotiate. Statements by Nasution and others were far less bellicose, however, and the peculiar course of the final campaign suggests that Soekarno was trying to create a situation which would make military action inescapable for them. His *Trikora* speech (*Trikomando Rakjat* or 'Peoples' Threefold Command') of 19 December, billed in advance as his 'final command' after a series of threats of military action, exemplified the ambivalence of his tactics. The President's 'commands' were, in fact, something of an anti-climax although they are frequently regarded as the signal for the final, militant phase of the struggle for West Irian — merely vague injunctions to 'defeat the formation of a Dutch-colonial Papuan puppet state', to raise the Indonesian flag in West Irian and to prepare for general mobilization. Despite a lot of belligerent talk, no substantial military action followed immediately, although on 15 January a torpedo-boat of the Indonesian navy was sunk during a clash with Dutch vessels close to the coast of New Guinea, with the loss of fifty lives, including that of the Deputy Chief of Staff of the Navy.[40] Even this did not precipitate more violent action, however, for by then the emphasis was swinging back in favour of negotiations following a significant modification of the Dutch conditions for holding talks, which had previously been utterly uncompromising. Since the failure of the Luns Plan, which might have enabled the Dutch to transfer their expensive and thankless colonial burden to the UN, the prospects facing them were bleak: no alternative was now visible except negotiation or the risk of military conflict in New Guinea and within Holland public opinion was at last beginning to swing round in favour of a negotiated settlement. The terms of such a settlement were going to be the subject of hard bargaining, however, for Indonesia was insisting on a transfer of sovereignty over West New Guinea, whereas the Dutch based their stand on the right of self-determination for the Papuans.

Soekarno's diplomatic strategy in this situation was skilful, for by threatening to use force he succeeded in inducing the American government to put pressure on the Dutch towards a negotiated settlement for the sake of keeping the peace, whereas American neutrality on the issue had previously worked to the advantage of the Dutch by preserving the *status quo*.[41] After an exploratory mission by Robert Kennedy in February, talks began near Washington under the chairmanship of Ellsworth Bunker in March, but broke down after two days. The initial Bunker proposals envisaged a transfer of administrative authority over West New Guinea to the temporary executive authority of the UN, which would administer the territory for between one and two years, gradually phasing the Dutch officials out and Indonesian ones in. Full administrative control was to be transferred to Indonesia after two years. Indonesia was to give the people of West New Guinea an opportunity to exercise freedom of choice by a date to be specified. Indonesia accepted the Bunker proposals in principle, but the Netherlands kept pressing for qualifications which would establish the right of self-determination for the Papuans more strongly. With the breakdown of the talks in March, Indonesians began to resort to small-scale landings of paratroops and sea-borne infiltrators, continuing throughout April and May until the resumption of talks in July. Their purpose was presumably to show the Dutch that the Indonesians were not bluffing and to subject them to increasingly burdensome military pressure in order to weaken Dutch stubbornness in the negotiations. Such tactics were provocative and came perilously close to being counter-productive by stiffening Dutch intransigence and alienating American sympathy; but they finally served their purpose, since the American government was bent upon obtaining a settlement. A substan-

tial paratroop landing during the last days of the final round of negotiations in August (intended, perhaps, to ensure a substantial force of
Indonesians *in situ* at the time of the UN take-over) seemed to be a
gratuitously blatant affront to the Dutch, who were being compelled to
negotiate under the threat of force; but Indonesia was driving as hard a
bargain as she could by that stage. 'Living dangerously' had paid Soekarno
handsomely.

It had also paid him substantial rewards at home. A dour struggle for
power within Indonesia was going on throughout this time, but its interaction with the external struggle is not easy to trace. It is clear, however,
that Soekarno's personal power was enormously enhanced in contrast to
his rival, Nasution. The initial reluctance of the military leaders to be
bulldozed into ill-prepared military adventures appears to have been
overcome by March, when a brigade of para-commandos was put at the
disposal of the West Irian theatre commander (Brigadier-General Suharto).
By August, the Army leaders were prepared to launch a major assault
if the negotiations failed. They had abandoned their earlier policy of
restraint that had allowed them to be outflanked in nationalist fervour by
Soekarno and the left wing. Nasution's influence was reduced sharply by
the elevation of Yani as Army Chief of Staff in June; and Yani soon began
to become identified politically with the President. The old Indonesian
ambivalence between 'diplomacy and struggle' as the twin poles between
which policy oscillated was probably again an underlying factor in the
sometimes inexplicable excesses and divagations of the West Irian campaign, just as it had been in 1945–9 and was to be again during the
confrontation of Malaysia.

The West Irian campaign also had a curious aftermath. Two months
after the conclusion of the New York Agreement a campaign began to
develop in West New Guinea to bring about the shortening of the interim
period of UNTEA (United Nations Temporary Executive Authority)
control so that Indonesia would take over the administration fully on 1
January 1963, instead of 1 May, as the agreement stipulated. Since
there seemed to be no strong reason for hastening the transfer of West
Irian into Indonesian hands, the impression was inevitably created that
Soekarno was simply thirsting for further diplomatic victories to boost
his prestige at home or else to distract attention from domestic to external
issues. There were probably varied motives behind it all. One was to
give the impression of an irresistible wave of enthusiasm among the
inhabitants of West New Guinea for immediate incorporation with their
Indonesian brothers after their release from the dark night of Dutch
slander and lies about Indonesia. By encouraging the development of
something that could be presented to the world as a spontaneous
campaign by the people of West New Guinea for a shortening of the
UNTEA period, with which was coupled a demand for nullification of
the requirement in the New York Agreement of an act of self-determination in 1969, the Indonesians may have been hoping to sweep away
the latter in the momentum of enthusiasm generated in the aftermath

of the Dutch withdrawal. Something very similar had happened in 1950 when the federal state, imposed against the inclinations of the Republicans during the 1949 negotiations with the Dutch, collapsed quickly in the face of a snowballing campaign of mass rallies and resolutions of local representative bodies for a unitary state.[42]

The first suggestion that a plebiscite in 1969 was not necessary came in a statement on 20 October by Wajoi, the leader of the first delegation of pro-Indonesian politicians from the Papuan National Congress to be brought to Indonesia with the object of convincing them that the Dutch had been throwing dust in their eyes about conditions in Indonesia.[43] The early statements to and by this delegation indicate that the Indonesian authorities were proceeding rather cautiously to impress their visitors with the sense of all being blood brothers together. Just before they left, Wajoi made his statement (presumably prompted by the Indonesian authorities) that the people of West Irian already considered themselves to be Indonesians so that a further act of choice was unnecessary. Immediately after the delegation's return, cables began to 'flood in' to Djakarta from various organizations in West New Guinea calling for immediate union with Indonesia, without waiting for a plebiscite. The National Front there, after hearing a report from one of the delegation's members, endorsed this view, adding that it was a sheer lie to say Indonesia was short of food and clothing and that the idea of a plebiscite was merely a Dutch stratagem to divide the people of West New Guinea from the Indonesians. (References to 'Dutch time-bombs' were common in the Indonesian press at the time.) Soon afterwards another delegation came to Indonesia, drawn from the Dutch-established New Guinea Council and led by E. J. Bonay, who had previously stood in an intermediate position between the Dutch and the Indonesians and strongly advocated self-determination for the Papuans. He was more circumspect in his utterances, but also gave some words of support for the campaign to hasten the transfer to Indonesian administration; later, he travelled to New York with a delegation to press for this at the United Nations. However, the UNTEA Administrator stated firmly on 7 November that the transfer would not be speeded up and it was never really on the cards that it would be. The continuance of the campaign in the press and public statements through until January is all the more puzzling for just this reason, for while symbolic victories may have their uses, to court defeat even on a symbolic issue seems quixotic. U Thant finally made it quite clear after a meeting with the Indonesian Representative in West Irian late in January that an earlier transfer was out of the question and the campaign subsided soon after.[44] All that Indonesia managed to gain from the affair was a small symbolic victory by contriving to have the Indonesian flag flying in West New Guinea before the new year dawned. On the debit side, the episode cost her much of the goodwill and trust abroad that she had been able to retain throughout the West Irian campaign, because of the light regard she seemed to be showing for the international agreement she had just signed. Coming hard on top of the discreditable affair of the Asian Games, over which she had also shown a disturbing inclination to flout accepted canons of international behaviour, it helped to create the worst possible background for her stand on the Malaysia question when it developed soon afterwards.

The fourth Asian Games were held in Djakarta in August 1962, just after the triumphant victory in West Irian. But the goodwill of the occasion was marred when Indonesia refused admission to the delegations of Israel and Taiwan, whose governments she did not recognize, although these two countries were both members of the Asian Games Federation and entitled under its rules to participate. When the Indian President of the Executive Committee of the Asian Games Federation, Mr. Sondhi, criticized Indonesia for allowing political considerations to be introduced into a sporting contest and sponsored a move to withhold the title 'Asian Games' from the Djakarta meeting, a violent demonstration was launched, allegedly spontaneously, against the Indian embassy. Sondhi himself had to leave Indonesia hastily to avoid further unpleasantness. (Relations with India cooled rapidly after this time; during the India-China border war in October, Indonesia assumed a neutrality which India regarded as positively pro-Chinese.) The episode typified the new style of 'revolutionary diplomacy' that was beginning to develop in Djakarta—the utilization of 'uncontrollable' outbursts of mob violence or intimidation, the defiance of established rules and protocols, and the assertion of new principles for old ones by way of justification after the event. Thus, the old-fashioned doctrine that politics should not intrude into matters of sport was now challenged openly by Soekarno's proclamation that 'sports cannot be separated from politics. Therefore let us now work for a sports association on the basis of politics ... on the basis of the new emerging forces...'. As a result of the incident, Indonesia found herself suspended by the International Olympic Committee until she apologized to Israel and Taiwan. So Soekarno then set about to organize the Games of the New Emerging Forces in Djakarta in November 1963 in order to show his independence of the International Olympic Committee.[45] The holding of the Games, like the other 'symbolic' issues of foreign policy to which so much importance seemed to be attached in 1962-3, was made to serve a variety of Soekarno's purposes in Indonesia's domestic politics, while the quarrel with the 'old established forces' of international athletics could be presented as further evidence of the need for solidarity among the New Emerging Forces.

INDONESIAN REACTIONS TO
THE MALAYSIA PROPOSAL, 1961–1962

The Malaysia scheme evoked little opposition and not much interest in Indonesia until towards the end of 1962. The Indonesian government could hardly afford to jeopardize its claim to West Irian by making statements which could be interpreted as a sign of covetousness or expansionism on her northern frontier, but it was not just prudence which accounts for its lack of interest. The critical events of 1961 in Malaya, Singapore and Borneo were given surprisingly little attention in the Indonesian press, even in the Communist papers. Hence Indonesian attitudes to Malaysia were formed on the basis of information which was not only scanty but often quite erroneously interpreted. Even after the Brunei revolt, many well-informed Indonesians with whom the author discussed the matter were quite unaware of the Tunku's purpose in bringing in the Borneo territories to balance the Singapore Chinese.

The Tunku's speech on 27 May happened to be mentioned in *Suluh Indonesia*, but merely as an opportunity to attack his thinly disguised sneers at 'neutrals who support Communists': the report made no reference to the Malaysia proposal. Only in early July can a few references to the matter be found, after statements of opposition from the *Party Ra'ayat* of Brunei and others.[46] Even the split within the PAP on the issue attracted almost no attention. An interpretive article on the Malaysia Federation in *Harian Rakjat* on 18 July described it in very mild terms as 'a new form of colonialism, or what is now usually called neo-colonialism .... Our first impression is that this is in accordance with British colonial interests ... colonialism cannot defend itself in the old forms. Certain concessions have to be made to the colonized peoples to save their fundamental colonial interests ....' But even the PKI did not see Malaysia as something that it should definitely oppose until December 1961, after a series of Malayan and Brunei delegates had come to Djakarta for a congress of Partindo, the far-left party with which both Azahari, Ibrahim Ya'acob and Boestamam had close connections.[47] (The Socialist Front in Malaya had not fully determined its policy on Malaysia until November, so the PKI's hesitation is hardly surprising.) *Bintang Timur*, the Partindo paper, put forward a neo-colonialist interpetation of Malaysia on 9 December, along with the charge that the Tunku's aim was to oppose Indonesia. A resolution of the PKI Central Committee on 30–31 December denounced Malaysia as a form of neo-colonialism which would 'strengthen the hands of the imperialists in South-East Asia in implementing their SEATO activities which are also aimed against Indonesia' (the Anglo-Malayan Defence Agreement of the previous month and its alleged SEATO implications were the dominant concern of the whole resolution) and declared that 'the Indonesian people will certainly support the righteous, patriotic and just resistance of the people of Malaya, Singapore, Sarawak, Brunei and North Borneo against the efforts for the establishment of this Federation of Malaysia'.[48] Even so, very little publicity was given to this new development, for the campaign to launch 'military confrontation' in West Irian was at its peak at the end of 1961 and other issues were far more pressing than Malaysia.

Indonesians have subsequently alleged that their government was not adequately consulted on the plans to create Malaysia, but there seems to be no basis for the complaint. Lord Selkirk visited Djakarta in August 1961 for talks with Dr. Subandrio and others. The visit received almost no publicity in Indonesia, and according to *Suluh Indonesia*, Subandrio expressed 'no opposition and no active support'. At the United Nations several months later, Subandrio made the much quoted statement that:

We are not only disclaiming the territories outside the former Netherlands East Indies, though they are of the same island, but — more than that — when Malaya told us of its intentions to merge with the three British Crown Colonies of Sarawak, Brunei and British North Borneo as one Federation, we told them that we had no objections and that we wished them success with this merger so that everyone might live in peace and freedom.

For the sake of clarification, I may tell this Assembly that three-quarters of the island of Borneo is Indonesian territory, while the remainder constitutes the aforementioned three British Crown Colonies. Naturally, ethnologically and geographically speaking, this British part is closer to Indonesia than, let us say, to Malaya. But we still told Malaya that we had no objection to such a merger, based upon the will for freedom of the peoples concerned.[49]

Three years later, Indonesians put great stress upon the last ten words in that statement as evidence that their approval for Malaysia had not been unconditional. Similarly, a letter of Subandrio's to the *New York Times* on the West Irian issue, setting out Indonesia's lack of expansionist intent, had concluded: 'we wish the Malayan government well if it can succeed with this plan'. The qualifications in these statements may have been inserted with far-sighted Machiavellian skill, but little significance can be attributed to them as evidence of Indonesian attitudes to Malaysia at that time. Indonesian officials were being extremely careful to avoid antagonizing those whose diplomatic support it needed over West Irian just then. Lt.-Gen. Djatikusumo praised the Malaysia scheme quite unequivocally when in Kuala Lumpur for a Colombo Plan meeting as 'a new and good idea ... we welcome anything that can bring peace and stability in this area....' (His tune was very different eighteen months later, however, when he became Ambassador in Kuala Lumpur.) And there was no Indonesian official protest or comment on the Anglo-Malayan agreement of 23 November on defence arrangements, even though the section on future use of the Singapore base for SEATO purposes was deliberately left ambiguous. What is more, arrangements were under consideration about this time for President Soekarno to visit London early in 1962 as a state guest at Buckingham Palace. The visit was later cancelled because of a domestic food crisis, but it is hard to believe that if Soekarno and his ministers were already anticipating difficulties over Malaysia he would have been so willing to consort with neo-colonialists so intimately. Later in 1962, the British Supreme Commander, Far East, was an official guest of Nasution's just after the West Irian campaign.

Matters began to change in 1962, however, as the PKI criticisms of Malaysia attracted wider notice. Ali Sastroamidjojo, chairman of the PNI, made a characteristically cryptic comment in April that Malaysia might increase the danger of war in the region because its purpose was to 'give military bases to big powers'. Ali's position in the government at that time was too peripheral for his utterances to have much significance as official policy, but he was a political bellwether with a keen sense of the profitable issues to exploit. Soon after the West Irian campaign was over, he was one of the first to raise the Malaysia question, declaring that Indonesia could not remain indifferent to what happened on her borders and must decide whether Malaysia would be advantageous to Indonesia or not. His words aroused a flurry of protest from the Malayan press, which led on to a sharp exchange of recriminations.[50] More disturbing was the fact that Subandrio said much the same thing in an airport interview in Singapore a day or so later in an ill-considered reply to an ill-conceived question.[51] The press in both countries again drew the worst conclusions about the other, but fortunately the incident was shortlived. No further exchanges at the official level occurred over the next two months before the Brunei revolt, although the PKI was by this time openly attacking the Malaysia idea, while the evidence from various Malaysian sources leaves little doubt that at least some elements within the Indonesian military and intelligence forces were engaging in subversive activities.[52]

If these sources are reliable, it would seem that by the latter half of 1962 the Malayan government had grounds for concern about Indonesia's intentions on two counts. From northern Borneo were coming reports that dissident Malays of the TNKU, mainly from Brunei, were being trained and equipped in Indonesian Borneo and that Indonesian infiltrators were already numerous on the Malaysian side of the border.[53] And within Malaya and Singapore, Indonesian recruitment of volunteers for the liberation of West Irian had some curious aspects, to say the least.[54] The numbers selected were small (50 in Singapore and 73 in the Federation chosen from several thousand volunteers) and, perhaps inevitably, the volunteers included many from suspect left-wing Malay and Chinese organizations. Most left for Indonesia for military training at a very late stage, only a month before the West Irian struggle reached its conclusion. They did not return until November and December. Meanwhile, in addition to military training they were given political indoctrination with strongly anti-colonialist overtones. That is no less than one would have expected in Indonesia at that time. The Malaysian White Paper also describes attempts to recruit the volunteers into an *Angkatan Pemuda Revolusioner Melayu* (Malayan Revolutionary Youth Force) for subsequent use within Malaya and Singapore in Indonesia's interests. It would be more surprising if this had not been attempted, for such volunteers would be the natural material for intelligence services to try to recruit and use. (Most countries engage in such intelligence activities to a greater or less degree, but the circumstances gave the Indonesian officials richer opportunities in Malaya-Singapore than usual and they seem to have been rather unsubtle in trying to take advantage of them.) It is questionable, however, whether there was any specific purpose behind the rather peculiar activities of Indonesian consular officials among the Indonesian communities in Singapore and Malaya and among Indonesian-oriented citizens of those places before 1963. Most of the activities recorded for the period up to the Brunei revolt could be interpreted in several ways. Even if they may be regarded as evidence of potentially revolutionary activities against Malaya, they were hardly sufficient to establish that there was already a plan to subvert Malaysia and they do not justify Brackman's conclusion that, with the ending of the West Irian campaign, 'arrows pointing to Malaysia as the next destination were nailed to the Indonesian signpost'.

[1]On the economic background to the events of 1960–3, see J. A. C. Mackie, *Problems of Inflation in Indonesia*, pp. 30–7.

[2]On West Irian, see below, pp. 98-103. One or two ambiguously anti-colonialist comments about the British in northern Borneo were made by prominent Indonesians, but they were unofficial and exceptional.

[3]Most of the Russian loan was spen on the Navy and the Air Force. H. Feith, 'Indonesia's Military Hardware', *Nation* (Sydney), 3 November 1962. On the PRRI-Permesta rebellion, see Herbert Feith and Daniel Lev, 'The End of the Indonesian Rebellion', *Pacific Affairs*, vol. XXXVI, no. I, Spring 1963, pp. 32–46.

[4]The best general accounts of the system up to 1962 are Herbert Feith, 'The Dynamics of Guided Democracy', in Ruth McVey (ed.), *Indonesia*, ch. 8, and Kahin's section on 'Indonesia' in G. McT. Kahin (ed.), *Major Governments in Asia* (Cornell University Press, 2nd edition, 1963), ch. 22–3.

[5]Herbert Feith, 'President Soekarno, the Army and the Communists: the Triangle Changes Shape', *Asian Survey*, vol. IV, no. 8, August 1964, pp. 904–13. The Army was not identical with the rest of the Armed Forces in its political outlook: the Air Force was generally much closer to Soekarno, as also the Police, to a lesser extent. For a comprehensive survey of PKI policies during the Soekarno era, see Rex Mortimer, 'The Ideology of the Indonesian Communist Party, under Guided Democracy' (Monash University, Ph.D. thesis, 1970).

[6]The standard works on party politics of the pre-1959 period are G.McT. Kahin, *Nationalism and Revolution in Indonesia* (Cornell University Press, 1962); Herbert Feith, *The Decline of Constitutional Democracy in Indonesia* (Cornell University Press, Ithaca, 1963) and Daniel S. Lev, *The Transition to Guided Democracy: Indonesian Politics, 1957–59* (Cornell Modern Indonesia Project, 1966).

[7]The role of parties after 1960 is outlined in Feith, 'Dynamics of Guided Democracy', pp. 325–48. The constitutional framework is summarized in J. A. C. Mackie, 'Indonesian Constitutions, 1945-60', in R. N. Spann (ed.) *Constitutionalism in Asia* (Asia Publishing House, Bombay, 1963), ch. 9.

[8]After April 1962, a small inner group of ministers known as KOTI (*Komando Operasi Tertinggi* — Supreme Operations Command) functioned as the principal formal decision-making body. At the same time a much larger State Leadership Body was established (*Musjawarah Pimpinan Negara*) and in 1964 a Cabinet Presidium. Details of the formal changes may be found in *Republic of Indonesia Cabinets 1945–1965*, compiled by Susan Finch and Daniel S. Lev (Cornell Modern Indonesia Project, 1965).

[9]By eschewing a direct political role for the Army, while ensuring that individual officers were appointed to policy-making and executive positions at all levels, says Lev, the Army elite was integrated into the political structure of the nation and easily satisfied. This was essentially why the 'middle course' avoided the temptations of a military coup: Daniel S. Lev, 'The Political Role of the Army in Indonesia', *Pacific Affairs*, XXXVI, no. 4, Winter 1963-4, pp. 359–60. For a more general picture of the Army, see Guy Pauker, 'The Role of the Military in Indonesia' in J. J. Johnston (ed.), *The Role of the Military in Underdeveloped Countries* (Princeton University Press, Princeton, 1962).

[10]For an explanation of *Nasakom*, see below pp. 86-7.

[11]Pauker, who had seen the Army as the great anti-Communist hope for Indonesia in 1958, later became very pessimistic about its prospects of averting a PKI take-over 'by acclamation' when the latter seemed to be establishing an irresistible claim to power as Indonesian's 'last hope': see Pauker, *Communist Prospects in Indonesia* (Rand Corporation Memorandum, RM-4135-PR, November 1964), pp. 4–7. On the other hand, as Lev put it, the Army had such a huge stake in the outcome of the power struggle, that it was inconceivable that it would passively tolerate a PKI take-over if it could possibly prevent it.

[12]Ibid. pp. 1 and 17–21 for estimates of PKI numerical strength up to 1964. The most balanced assessment of the PKI position up to 1962 is Ruth McVey, 'Indonesian Communism and the Transition to Guided Democracy', in A. Doak Barnett (ed.), *Communist Strategies in Asia* (Praeger, New York, 1963), ch. 5: for her assessment of the 1964 situation see her chapter on 'Indonesia' in 'The State of the Parties', *Survey*, no. 54, January 1965, pp. 113–22.

[13]Exclusion of the PKI from the cabinet became less and less significant as the cabinet became bigger and more diffuse: PKI vice-chairmen of the Provisional People's Consultative Assembly and the Gotong-Rojong Parliament became members of the State Leadership Body after 1962 and bore the rank of Minister. One of them, Njoto, was attached to the Presidium in 1964–5. Probably more serious was their exclusion from the regional *Tjatur Tunggal*, the quadrumvirate of Military Commander, Provincial Governor, Police Chief and Chief Attorney which inherited a position similar to the Regional War Administrator's Council under State of Emergency regulations until 1963.

[14]The story is told by Donald Hindley, *The Communist Party of Indonesia: a Decade of the Aidit Leadership 1951–1961* (California University Press, Berkeley, 1964).

[15]Donald Hindley, 'President Soekarno and the Communists: the Politics of Domestication', *American Political Science Review*, vol. LVI, no. 4, December 1962, pp. 915–26.

[16]Ruth McVey, 'Indonesia', in *Survey*, no. 54, January 1965, p. 114.

[17]Soekarno's 'Political Manifesto' (Manipol) which had been officially declared the ideology of Guided Democracy, came to be merged with the *Nasakom* idea in 1963–4 in the slogan *Manipol-Usdek jang berporoskan Nasakom* ('Manipol-Usked with Nasakom as its axis'), the acronym Usdek referring to the five main elements of Manipol. Soekarno claimed that the origins of this idea stemmed back to one of his earliest pamphlets in 1927: see his *Nationalism, Islam and Communism* (ed. Ruth McVey, Cornell Modern Indonesia Project, Translation Series, 1969).

[18]For examples of such decisions, see Mackie, *Problems of Inflation*, pp. 19 ff.

[19]For the concept of 'administrators' and 'solidarity-makers' as two rival skill-groups seeking to reconstruct the polity in accordance with their own ideas, see Feith, *Decline of Constitutional Democracy in Indonesia*, pp. 113–22 and *passim*. He has elaborated the significance of *Manipol-Usdek* and related slogans in 'Indonesia's Political Symbols and their Wielders', *World Politics*, vol. XVI, no. 1, October 1963, pp. 79–97.

[20]Feith, *Dynamics of Guided Democracy*, p. 368.

[21]For another view of the matter from a more functionalist angle, see Donald E. Weatherbee, *Ideology in Indonesia: Soekarno's Indonesian Revolution* (Yale Southeast Asia Studies, New Haven, 1966).

[22]The 1963 stabilization scheme is discussed below, pp. 136-9. For some explanations of the reasons for inflation and the relevant statistics, see Mackie, *Problems of Inflation*, ch. 2 and pp. 98–101.

[23]Feith, 'Indonesia's Political Symbols and their Wielders', op. cit. p. 94.

[24]The economic background to these episodes is discussed further in Mackie, *Problems of Inflation*, pp. 31–40.

[25]Ibid. pp. 19–21.

[26]Robert Curtis, 'Indonesia and Malaysia', loc. cit. p. 25.

[27]S. Takdir Alisjahbana, *Indonesia: Social and Cultural Revolution* (Kuala Lumpur, Oxford University Press, 1966), p. 141.; Bruce Grant, *Indonesia* (Melbourne University Press, Melbourne, 1964), ch. 3.

[28]A lively picture of the man may be found in *Soekarno: an Autobiography as told to Cindy Adams* (Bobbs Merrill Inc. 1965), unreliable though it is on many historical details. The most scholarly biographies are J. D. Legge, *Soekarno* (The Penguin Press, Harmondsworth, 1972) and Berhard Dahm, *Sukarno and the Struggle for Indonesian Independence* (Cornell University Press, Ithaca, 1969).

[29]Lev, *Transition to Guided Democracy*, pp. 46 ff.

[30]Ibid. p. 47.

[31]Brief summaries of Indonesian foreign policy during the 1950s are given by G. McT. Kahin in Kahin (ed.) *Major Governments of Asia* (Cornell University Press, second edition, 1963), pp. 680-7 and by Herbert Feith in Kahin (ed.), *Governments and Politics of Southeast Asia* (Cornell University Press, 2nd edition, 1964), pp. 265–70. The politics of foreign aid are well described in Alexander Shakow, 'Foreign Economic Assistance in Indonesia, 1950–61' (University of London, Ph. D. thesis, 1962). The best general survey of post-1960 foreign policy is Frederick P. Bunnell, 'Guided Democracy Foreign Policy: 1960–65', *Indonesia* (Cornell Modern Indonesia Project),

II, October 1966, pp. 37–76. For a useful collection of extracts from Soekarno's speeches, see George Modelski (ed.), *The New Emerging Forces* (Australian National University, Department of International Relations, Documents and Data Papers, no. 2, 1963).

[32]J. D. Legge, 'Indonesia after West Irian', *Australian Outlook*, vol. XVII, no. 1, April 1963, p. 5.

[33]Modelski, op. cit. p. 69.

[34]Soekarno's speech to the Second Conference of Non-Aligned Nations, Cairo, 6 October 1964, published in *The Era of Confrontation* (Department of Information, Djakarta, n.d.).

[35]Soekarno's Independence Day Speech, 1965, *Reach to the Stars: A Year of Self-Reliance* (Department of Information, 1965), p. 38.

[36]See Nadia Derkach, 'The Soviet Policy towards Indonesia in the West Irian and Malaysia Disputes', *Asian Survey*, vol. V, no. 11, November 1965, pp. 566–71.

[37]Two comprehensive accounts of Sino-Indonesian relations during this period have been given by David Mozingo; see *Sino-Indonesian Relations: an Overview* (Santa Monica, Rand Memorandum RM-4641-PR, 1965) and 'China's Policy towards Indonesia' in Tang Tsou (ed.), *China in Crisis* (Chicago University Press, Chicago, 1968).

[38]American-Indonesian relations over this period are dealt with in Howard P. Jones, *Indonesia. The Possible Dream* (Harcourt Brace, 1971) and, for the 1961–63 period, by Frederick Bunnell, 'The Kennedy Initiatives in Indonesia, 1962–63' (Cornell University, Ph.D. thesis, 1969), and Roger Hilsman, *To Move a Nation: The Politics of Foreign Policy in the Administration of John F. Kennedy* (Doubleday & Co., New York, 1967).

[39]The exclusion of West New Guinea from the territory which became the Republic of Indonesian at the time of the Round Table Conference at The Hague in October 1949 and the breakdown of subsequent efforts to reach agreement about its future status are outlined in Robert C. Bone, *The Dynamics of the West New Guinea (Irian Barat) Problem* (Cornell Modern Indonesia Project, 1958). For a brief discussion of the issues involved in 1961–2, see J. A. C. Mackie, 'The West New Guinea Argument', *Australian Outlook*, vol. XVI, no. 1, April 1962, pp. 26–46.

[40]The background to these incidents is more fully elaborated in Herbert Feith and J. A. C. Mackie, 'The Pressures on Soekarno', *Nation* (Sydney), 27 January 1962.

[41]The Indonesian-American relationship at this time is well described in Frederick P. Bunnell, op. cit. pp. 50–4.

[42]Feith, *Decline of Constitutional Democracy*, pp. 54–71.

[43]*Suluh Indonesia*, 20, 25 October 1962.

[44]*Suluh Indonesia*, 25 January 1963. A brief survey of the agitation to abbreviate the period of UNTEA administration is given in Legge, op. cit.

[45]Indonesia's 'confrontation' of the established international athletic organizations during the two years between the Asian Games and the Tokyo Olympic Games (June, 1964) was a not unimportant sidelight of Soekarno's new style of diplomacy: it was given enormous publicity in the Indonesian press and the Games of the New Emerging Forces were hailed as an enormous triumph; see Ewa T. Pauker, 'Ganefo I: Sport and Politics in Djakarta', *Asian Survey*, vol. V, no. 4, April 1965, pp. 171–85.

[46]*Suluh Indonesia*, 29 May: Harian Rakjat, 6, 12, 18 July (the latter being the first informative background article) and 31 August ('*Apa Itu Malaysia Raja?*'). *Bintang Timur* carried its first reference to the matter (a protest by the Brunei Party Ra'ayat) on 12 July.

[47]See *Bintang Timur*, 9 and 29 December: this was the Partindo paper and often took up more adventurous policy positions than the more cautious PKI paper, *Harian Rakjat*, although in general their policies were very similar.

[48]The text is published in full in *Malayan-Indonesian Relations*, pp. 52–53. It should be noted, however, that in the long report of the Third Plenum of the CC-PKI, the reference to Malaysia was a very small part.

[49]Ibid. para 48–9; *New York Times*, 13 November 1961.

[50]Associated Press Report, 9 April 1962: *Straits Times*, 25 September 1962.

[51]*Straits Times*, 26, 27 September. Subandrio had been asked what Indonesia would do if Malaysia permitted the Americans to set up a base there and rather impetuously

replied that she would arrange for a Soviet base in Indonesian territory. He subsequently tried to amend matters, stating that 'there is not one controversial issue between Malaya and Indonesia', although he complained about the campaign of insinuations and innuendos against Indonesia.

[52] *Indonesian Intentions Towards Malaysia*, para. 15 ff.

[53] See below, pp. 120-1.

[54] *Indonesian Intentions Towards Malaysia*, para. 29 ff.; Brackman, op. cit. p. 130.

VI
The Beginnings of Confrontation

THE Brunei revolt of 8 December 1962 was a trivial, almost Gilbertian, little uprising, yet it provided the sparks which were in due course to be fanned into the flames of conflict between Indonesia and Malaysia. Although it was suppressed within a few days and did not in itself embroil the governments of the two countries to a serious extent, it revealed how dangerous for the proponents of Malaysia any further uprisings might be, particularly if they were likely to result in the internationalization of the Malaysia issue through the involvement of other countries or through appeals to the United Nations, which might mean delays and opportunities for the obstruction of Malaysia's formation.[1] As it happened, the Brunei revolt was not followed by any other anti-Malaysia uprisings, as was widely feared in early 1963. If anything, its net effect was to embarass and alarm some of the fence-sitters in Sarawak and Sabah towards the pro-Malaysian camp and to make it easier for the authorities to clamp down hard on the opponents of Malaysia under cover of the threat to national security, because of Indonesia's bellicose attitude. But since it also gave Indonesia a heaven-sent opportunity to claim that the revolt proved that Malaysia was a neo-colonialist strategem being imposed by British bayonets against the will of the people concerned (and also encouraged the Philippines government in its prosecution of the Sabah claim), its long-term consequences were far-reaching, for it brought these two nations together in an unlikely partnership in opposition to the Malaysia scheme.

Initially, Indonesia's opposition amounted to little more than a war of words. During the first half of 1963, however, it took on both diplomatic and military aspects as well, the first through the series of conferences at Manila between March and August directed towards finding a peaceful resolution of the contretemps, the second through various probing raids across the Sarawak border from April onwards and attempts to establish contact with subversive elements within Malaysia. But no one either in Djakarta or abroad could anticipate at this stage just how far Soekarno was prepared to go in his efforts to frustrate the formation of Malaysia, which seemed to be his objective — though even that was not entirely clear. His statements and actions were, as always, ambiguous, for he was faced with pressing economic and political problems within Indonesia, so that he had to make concessions to the left in foreign policy even while he was turning towards the right in economic policy. He could not afford to go too far in antagonizing the British at a time when he was negotiating for very substantial loans from a consortium of Western donor countries of which she and the USA were the most prominent members, but nor could he afford to repudiate his opposition to Malaysia entirely. At the Manila Conferences of June-July he seemed to be inclining towards a peaceful settlement of the dispute within the framework of Maphilindo (to the dismay of the PKI), but even there he was careful to keep as many options open as he could until the last. It was the ambiguity and obscurity of his objectives that led to so many differing interpretations of Indonesia's policy towards Malaysia in the early stages of the conflict.

THE BRUNEI REVOLT

On racial, historical and geographical grounds it had seemed perfectly natural to include the tiny Brunei protectorate, with its predominantly Malay population, in the proposed federation of Malaysia. Yet Brunei was to prove in several respects the most awkward of the Borneo territories for Kuala Lumpur to deal with, despite its strongly Muslim and Malay character. The Sultan's courtiers had good reason to feel apprehensive about the prospect of democratization that incorporation in Malaysia was likely to bring, while the Party Ra'ayat, led by Sheikh A. M. Azahari, had other reasons for opposing the scheme.

Some countries seem to be burdened by the grandeurs or good fortune of their past, and unable to adjust to the demands of the present and future. Brunei basks in her former glories as one of the great Malay sultanates, and enjoys the lavish revenues derived from her oil fields during recent decades, which have transformed the sultanate from a condition of seedy decay and declining population in the 1930s to one of outward wealth today. But for all its good fortune, Brunei in 1962 revealed many of the classic symptoms of colonial unrest. Its leaders had shown little sign of capacity to adjust to the modern world, by contrast with neighbouring Sabah, although on a *per capita* basis Sabah's export earnings and public revenues were only about one-seventh of Brunei's.[2] Despite her expensive new mosque with its gold-leaf-covered dome, the impressive Shell Oil Company installations and a four-to-one ratio of government revenues over expenditure, Brunei's was a badly lop-sided economy. Her agriculture was backward and stagnant. Commerce was mostly in the hands of the Chinese. Not far from the mosque, the Malay ra'ayat still lived in their huts on piles over the famous *Kampung Ayer,* which had not changed greatly since Magellan's chronicler, Pigafetta, described it in 1521.

Although the oil industry provided the revenues that had made possible improved health services, one of the highest birth rates in the world (50 per 1,000) and, after 1954, expanding primary and secondary schooling for some, it could not possibly provide sufficient employment for the fast-growing population of young people. Only a tiny handful of the 47,000 Malays in 1960 had completed secondary education and none had graduated from a university.[3] A modest development plan started in the mid-1950s increased public expenditure on social services and buildings, but was hardly sufficient to offset the growing dualism between the traditional and the modern urbanized sectors of the economy and society.

Technically, Brunei was not a colony but merely a protectorate of Britain's under a treaty of 1888 which remained in force until 1959, the Sultans having agreed to accept a British resident whose 'advice' was accepted in all matters except religion and Malay custom, as in the Malay states. During this period the British had effective control of both internal administration and external relations while the foreign-owned oil company had come to dominate economic life. It was a grievous decline for a proud empire which had been a great trading centre in the hey-day of Malacca and the twilight of Majapahit's glory, with a population of 100,000 people at the time of Magellan's visit. Long before Rajah Brooke began to carve out large slices of Brunei territory in the mid-nineteenth century, Brunei's control over the principalities of the west coast of Borneo had begun to crumble. The city's population had declined to a mere 12,000.[4] But for the discovery of oil in the 1920s, Brunei might well have crumbled into complete decay.

Only the most gingerly and hesitant steps towards representative government were taken in the decade before 1962, but even the prospect of more democratic institutions had a significant fermenting effect.[5] The *Party Ra'ayat* was formed by Sheikh Azahari in 1956 and soon began to make its presence felt, threatening to boycott a 'traditional form of election' to District Councils, which had to be postponed and later abandoned, pending talks on more permanent constitutional arrangements. In the official *Annual Report* on Brunei, the party was described superciliously as having a very limited following amongst the 'educated classes', being drawn largely from 'the labouring classes ... mainly dismissed ex-government servants who see in the Party a means of expressing their discontent and dissatisfaction'. Azahari himself had spent the war years in Indonesia studying at the Bogor veterinary school. He stayed on in Indonesia for several years during the revolution and appears to have been considerably influenced by the radical and anti-colonialist political philosophies he imbibed there. Although he engaged without much success in a variety of business enterprises during the 1950s (allegedly with financial support from the Sultan at one stage), he showed considerable political talent in building up the *Party Ra'ayat* by exploiting discontent with the Sultan's regime and, particularly, the British overlordship which sustained it. His party steadily increased in influence as the prospect of representative institutions drew closer, although the Sultan delayed promulgation of an enactment on local councils pending the outcome of drawn-out talks about a permanent constitution. The February 1958 proposals for a federation of the North Borneo territories sent ripples across the pond, however, providing Azahari with a useful issue to recruit support and quickening the Sultan's interest in Malaya, symbolized by the lavish residence he had built for himself in Kuala Lumpur.

The reactions of Azahari's party and the Sultan respectively to the 1958 governor's proposal for a wider Borneo federation were revealing. Azahari, who had earlier advocated a single North Borneo state, was quick to express support for the idea, although withholding his opinion on details, presumably out of distrust for a British-sponsored political structure. The *Borneo Bulletin* commented that although most of the people it had interviewed on the matter favoured a closer association with the neighbouring colonies, the majority of the Executive Council was not in favour of it.[6] In March, the ninth Inter-Territorial Conference of officials was held in Brunei at the Sultan's invitation, during which the Commissioner General for South-East Asia, Sir Robert Scott, said in a broadcast that these conferences, although concerned with administrative cooperation, pointed the way towards closer political association. The Sultan, however, not only gave no sign that he was willing to cooperate with the other governments; he quite blatantly poured cold water on the idea (while not openly opposing it) in his *Idul Fitri* message of 26 April, in which he stressed that Brunei was not a colony and was under no treaty obligation even to participate in the inter-territorial administrative conferences, from which much of the impetus towards closer association had derived. By May, Donald Stephens was urging in Jesselton that the other two territories should press on without Brunei if necessary, which they later proceeded to do. The Sultan made his attitude crystal clear in October in an interview with the *Straits Times*, in which he referred to Brunei's strong religious, racial and family ties with Malaya, with which he wanted closer association.[7] (A loan of $M100 million to the Federation government was announced in the following month.) He said that opinion in Brunei was opposed to federation with the Borneo territories because it would entail spreading Brunei's wealth amongst her poorer neighbours and delay the achievement of independence. Soon after this, with a new-found burst of energy and decisiveness, the Sultan announced his intention to visit London to complete the protracted constitutional discussions on a new Treaty to replace the 1905-6 protectorate agreements.

Under the new constitution of September 1959, supreme executive authority inside Brunei was vested in the Sultan. A British High Commissioner was appointed, in place of the former Resident, with responsibility for Defence and External Affairs, and a seat on the Executive Council. A Legislative Council of officials and nominated members was created and indirect elections for the unofficial members through elected District Councils were to be held within two years. One of the nominees, in April 1962, was to be Azahari himself.

Azahari had continued to press for unification of 'the people' and their political organizations within a united front embracing all the Borneo territories. Only through such unity would political advancement be achieved, he argued. 'The British want to federate the three territories for their own benefit, but we want a merger of the three territories for our own benefit.' In June 1960 he succeeded in forming a 'joint consultative preparatory committee for pan-Bornean congress' with representatives of SUPP and his own *Party Ra'ayat*.[8] By this time he was becoming a political leader whose importance was recognized outside the tiny Sultanate. Lee Kuan Yew met him when he visited Borneo in September 1960. And after the Tunku launched the Malaysia concept in May 1961, Azahari was associated with Donald Stephens and Ong Kee Hui in the first expression of Bornean opposition to it, although the Sultan of Brunei seemed inclined to look sympathetically upon the idea. Thus Azahari's commitment to a Bornean union and his opposition to the Sultan's affiliation with Kuala Lumpur were of long standing and represented a substantial political investment in a policy which must have seemed to him to be steadily winning popular support in Sarawak as well as Brunei. It is hardly surprising that he looked upon the Tunku's wooing of the Sultan as a threat by conservative and British-backed interests to the political prospects of his own *Party Ra'ayat*.

The Sultan was confronted with a delicate problem when the Malaysia proposal became a live political issue in mid-1961, for Azahari immediately expressed opposition on behalf of his party. No matter how confident the Sultan may have been that the loyalty of the Malay *ra'ayat* to their ruler would ultimately prevail when put to the test, the prospect of imminent elections and more rapid democratization must have given him pause. He edged towards Malaysia cautiously, avoiding overt commitment for some months and announcing to the Legislative Council in December 1961 that he found the proposal 'attractive' but that he intended to consult the people before making a decision.[9] Brunei observers were sent to the various Solidarity Conferences over the next two months. A committee of enquiry which included Azahari was set up to determine the wishes of the people, but its findings were not published — and were rumoured to be unfavourable to Malaysia.[10] Azahari moved a resolution against Malaysia in the Legislative Council without success, but nothing was settled before the August 1962 elections which marked an overwhelming victory for Azahari and his party.

The *Party Ra'ayat* carried all before it in the elections, although it had long been opposed to the system of indirect elections in which court influence might have disproportionate advantages. Its conservative rival, the Brunei National Organization, proved to be a disastrous failure, despite the postponement of the elections from 1961 until August 1962 to give it a chance to establish itself. In the meantime, the Malaysia issue had become the focus of political controversy, with the Sultan and his followers rather hesitantly in favour of joining and the *Party Ra'ayat* unequivocally opposed. At the August elections, fifty-four of the fifty-five District Council seats were won by the *Party Ra'ayat*, which consequently gained all sixteen elected seats (out of a total of thirty-three) in the Legislative Council. Its rival was shown to be too incompetent to win any substantial number of votes or even to field an effective team of candidates.[11] Yet the Sultan still exercised supreme power, still ruled through his old, conservative and discredited ministers and still had the decisive voice on whether or not Brunei should join Malaysia.

Was the victory of the *Party Ra'ayat* a measure of popular opposition to the Malaysia proposal in Brunei? One could hardly claim that it was not, although it is paradoxical that a predominantly Malay and Muslim community should have been more nearly aligned with the left-wing Chinese of Sarawak on this issue than with their fellow-Malays of Sarawak and Sabah. Was it due to suspicions that Malaysia meant continuance of the conservative regime of the Sultan and the 'neo-colonialist' status of British administrators and a British oil company? Or to delusions that Malaysia would entail a wider spread of Brunei's oil wealth, which could otherwise be shared among the people when real independence was achieved? Or to dreams of re-establishing Brunei's ancient empire throughout North Borneo as the preferred pattern of independence? Or to fears of being 'taken over' by the better-educated mainland Malays? All these attitudes — particularly the first — probably played a part, however misguided they might have seemed to outsiders.[12]

By the time of the Brunei elections, recruitment and training of a North Borneo National Army (*Tentera Nasional Kalimantan Utara* or TNKU) in and around Brunei had been going on for several months. Not much is known about its composition or plans, or when the decision to launch a revolt in Decembr actually crystallized. All we do know is that by late 1962 the *Party Ra'ayat* had strong reasons for feeling frustrated in its bid for power and in its hopes of preventing incorporation in Malaysia. It had swept the polls in August, yet its sixteen members in the Legislative Council were still outnumbered by the seventeen nominated members. The time was drawing near for a decision to be made on Malaysia and the Sultan still seemed to be in favour of joining. Above all, he seemed determined to make the decision himself — and there was little that Azahari and his followers could do about it. They put forward two anti-Malaysia resolutions for discussion in the Legislative Council on 5 December (with some prospect of winning the support of several nominated members to carry the day), but the meeting was simply postponed by the Sultan. This might in itself seem to constitute an adequate explanation of the rebellion on 8 December, but there are a number of cross-currents which are not accounted for by such a simple theory. Plans for a revolt of some kind or other must have been under consideration for a long time: Azahari had already been out of Brunei for some weeks, while the training of TNKU members had begun many months earlier. In any case, the revolt was apparently not directed against the Sultan and his autocratic power, for Azahari believed that the Sultan would support him; it was directed against Malaysia and against British dominance, in favour of a unified North Borneo.

There are some puzzling aspects of both Azahari's attitude to Malaysia and the Sultan's in the period between the elections and the revolt. Hanna reports that after being received cordially in audience by the Sultan late in the year, Azahari expressed support for the address made by the Sultan in the Legislative Council 'accepting Malaysia in principle' — a remarkable volte-face, if it can be taken at face value, but perhaps intended as an oblique reminder of the Sultan's promise to consult the will of the people on the matter.[13]

It is easy for an outsider to say that if Azahari and his followers had been patient and if Brunei had advanced further towards representative government after joining Malaysia (as she would have been strongly pressed to do), the *Party Ra'ayat* would soon have achieved political power in the state, to which it was obviously entitled. But did Azahari and his colleagues see it in those terms? It is more likely that what they were seeking was control of all north Borneo, perhaps a revival of Brunei's ancient glories, without interference from Kuala Lumpur or London. They may have been hoping for some degree of Indonesian support in this. After all, there was little attraction for Azahari in being *Mentri Besar* of a state even smaller than Perlis, under a federal government with much greater powers than the British Resident in Brunei exercised. Even though the prospect of a Brunei-dominated Borneo federation had little or no appeal in Sabah and Sarawak, he and his followers may well have been blind to this. If Azahari saw the problem primarily in the light of an anti-colonialist struggle, such objections may have seemed unimportant. Probably he had not looked very far beyond getting rid of the British and preventing Malaysia, which must have seemed to him very like a substitution of rule from Kuala Lumpur (with the British still only at one remove as the 'neo-colonialist' masters) instead of from London. Whether or not the Sultan was really in league with Azahari over the revolt, as the latter claimed and the former subsequently denied, is still a matter for conjecture.[14] It is conceivable that the Sultan may have agreed in vague terms to cooperate with Azahari rather than the British if the latter succeeded in subverting the neighbouring colonies away from Malaysia and into a Borneo federation. Each may have misunderstood the other, or even been double-crossing the other at some stage. But the evidence on this is inconclusive.

The uprising began in the early hours of Saturday morning, 8 December, with surprise attacks by elements of the North Borneo National Army (TNKU) in Brunei town and Seria, the centre of the Shell Oil Company's installations, and all small towns along the coast, as well as several in nearby areas of Sarawak and North Borneo, Sibuti, Limbang, Lawas and Weston. But the rebels failed to seize the Sultan or his palace (indeed, they seem not to have tried very hard) and were beaten back from the police station and administrative centre. The Sultan, instead of throwing in his lot with the rebels, as announced by Azahari who was in Manila at the time, proclaimed a state of emergency and a 24-hour curfew; he also called upon the British for assistance to restore law and order. The *Party Ra'ayat* was banned, some hundreds of its members arrested and a warrant for Azahari's arrest issued. Units of a Police Mobile Force were flown in from Jesselton within a few hours, while more substantial reinforcements from Singapore arrived later in the day. Since the rebel forces have been estimated at only 2,000 men, not at all well armed, while the British had more than three powerful mobile battalions in Brunei within three days, the military issue was never really in serious doubt. But the rebels held many British hostages, especially in Seria where 400 European prisoners were held, and they had used 'human shield' tactics in some of their initial attacks, so that a primary military consideration was to save the lives of these people.[15]

Azahari was in Manila with Achmad Zaini, his 'Minister for Economic Affairs', when the revolt broke out, having flown in from Singapore the previous day. Declaring that he spoke as Prime Minister of the Unitary State of North Borneo (NKKU — *Negara Kesatuan Kalimantan Utara*), which had been unified under the Sultan, he announced that seven divisions of the North Borneo National Army, consisting of 20,000 men, had attacked twenty towns and were 'almost certainly surrounding Jesselton'. But from his statements it seems that the revolt took him by surprise and that he had no direct contact with his followers. He initially denied reports that the Sultan had denounced the rebels as mere British propaganda; the Sultan had himself raised the NKKU flag on 8 December, claimed Azahari, and thrown off British domination, which was bent on denying the right of self-determination to the people of Borneo by forcing them into Malaysia.[16] Later, when it became clear that the revolt had failed, Azahari called on the UN Secretary General to intervene, cabled various Afro-Asian heads of state for support and spoke of flying to the UN (or, later, to the Afro-Asian Peoples' Solidarity Organization headquarters in Cairo) to publicize his case. In the end he did not do so: in fact, he was able to give no help to the rebels. His lieutenant, Zaini, defected to the British authorities in Hong Kong and at the end of January Azahari slipped quietly from Manila to Djakarta to continue his struggle under Indonesian auspices.

Actually, the rebel plans seem to have miscarried from the outset. The half-hearted attack on the small town of Weston, at the end of the west-coast railway line in North Borneo, exemplifies the aimlessness of the insurgents.[17] About sixty members of the TNKU from two Brunei Malay villages in the south-western corner of North Borneo, armed with seven shotguns, four cigarette-tin bombs and *parangs*, attacked Weston police station, seized half a dozen more guns and advanced a few miles up the railway line towards Jesselton until they became unnerved by their first casualty (there is some evidence that this may have shattered a belief in their own invulnerability) and by the failure of additional Brunei rebels to reinforce them: they withdrew to their *kampong* and surrendered next day. A few other rebels from the same area had gathered in anticipation, but did not move because of similar lack of support from Brunei. Elsewhere in North Borneo there were no disturbances whatever and it was possible to hold the colony's first District Council elections in the following week everywhere except in the border dist ict of Sipitang. Azahari's claims from Manila that thirty towns in Borneo had been captured, including Jesselton, and that the Sultan was on the side of the rebels, turned out to be grotesquely wide of the mark.

Seria was recaptured and its European hostages released without further loss of life on 11–12 December, Limbang and Lawas (both in the Sarawak Fifth Division) and Kuala Belait by 12 December, after sharp fighting at Limbang. Further south in Sarawak, the small towns of Bekenu and Sibuti were held for a few more days by Kedayans who had seized them, but otherwise the revolt did not spread beyond the Baram valley in the Fourth Division. All major towns in Brunei and Sarawak had been freed of rebels by 16 December, over 3,000 rebels had been captured and the British authorities announced that 'the rebellion as such is over'. Military operations were now concentrated on cutting off any rebels who were trying to flee into the jungle or towards the Indonesian border. This task fell mainly to Sarawak irregulars, from the headwaters of the northern Sarawak rivers, under the redoubtable Tom Harrisson, since the bulk of the British regulars had been occupied in the main centres of Brunei and Limbang. (Brunei is separated from both North Borneo and Indonesian Borneo by strips of Sarawak territory.) Harrisson doubts if any of the rebels got through the cordon of armed Kenyah, Kayan and Kelabit tribesmen who dominated the few passable routes through the rugged terrain of the interior, particularly as the Brunei Malays and Kedayans who were involved in the rebellion are coastal peoples unaccustomed to the jungle.[18]

Why the Kedayans of Sarawak, as well as Brunei, supported the rebels so strongly is also something of a puzzle, but the fact that they did deserves attention. Harrisson points out that they were a neglected ethnic group in Sarawak (where there are about 10,000 of them, with perhaps a slightly larger number in Brunei), 'politically backward ... or what I would call happy fellows', who are 'easily got at and confused'.[19] They are industrious rice-growers, said to be the best in Borneo, a fact which may have something to do with a legend that they are descended from Javanese colonists who accompanied the Javanese bride of a Sultan of Brunei back in the golden era of Majapahit and Brunei. In Brunei, the Kedayans formed 17 per cent of the population in 1947, the biggest ethnic group after the Brunei Malays; but their numbers have grown very slowly since then. In Sarawak, and doubtless also in Brunei, they have not been brought into responsible positions in the government or adequately recognized as a significant ethnic minority. Whether they were seriously discontented with their lot or harbouring visions of re-unification with Java one can only guess. But neither of these assumptions is necessary to explain their susceptibility to the diffuse promises of the Party Ra'ayat and TNKU. All the latter had to do was to persuade them that they would be better off by overthrowing the established authority and taking their fate into their own hands as part of a dimly comprehended wider movement. It is quite likely, as Harrisson asserts, that they were 'completely confused and misled', but in such a situation the causes of a revolt may have very little relationship to the outcome.

The revolt achieved local tactical surprise, but it did not come complete-ly out of the blue, since the British and Malayan authorities had been accumulating information about the North Borneo National Army for some time. The *Borneo Bulletin*, published in Brunei, had carried a front-page story on it as early as May 1962.[20] Reports about parties of twenty to thirty men making their way by jungle tracks from Borneo through the Sarawak Fifth Division to the Indonesian border had been trickling in since March. Training grounds and dummy rifles in jungle clearings had been found, but enquiries into these matters among the local population proved entirely unfruitful. According to Tunku Abdul Rahman, arms and training had been given to TNKU members at Mali-nau in Indonesian Kalimantan, about sixty miles up the Sesajap River from Tarakan and less than one hundred miles as the crow flies from the Indonesian-Sarawak border.[21] There had been frequent warnings of trouble from this quarter, but they had proved unfounded, so the British Secretary of State for Colonies told the House of Commons later in answer to a charge that the British were caught by surprise: 'We were not without information of this particular trouble'. But, explained his deputy later, "Wolf' was being cried so often that it was somewhat discounted'.[22] There had been a number of discoveries of armed camps in all three Borneo territories during November; reports were received that young Brunei Malays were buying up sheath knives, torches and jungle green cloth and rumours were circulating about simultaneous demonstrations in the three territories. On 25 November, ten TNKU members were arrested at Lawas. It is generally believed that these arrests had the effect of precipitating the revolt prematurely on 8 December some weeks earlier than the original plans provided for.[23] The Tunku consulted Lord Selkirk on the matter on 2 December and the latter immediately flew to Brunei and North Borneo to investigate the situation himself. What action he took, if any, has not been revealed; no troops were sent to Borneo, although a British minister later claimed that they were in a state of readiness for immediate action. Possibly the authorities in Malaya expected it to come a few weeks later, after the rains had commenced and transportation become difficult, but the revolt was hastened by the Lawas arrests. It certainly seems to have caught Azahari and the Indonesians by surprise, as well as the British.

The extent of Indonesian complicity in the Brunei revolt, which was rather hysterically exaggerated in much Malayan comment on it, cannot yet be gauged with any precision. (It suited Kuala Lumpur to blame Indonesians for the revolt, either the government or the communists, since the real causes had discomforting implications for the advocates of Malaysia.) There is little reason to doubt Tunku Abdul Rahman's charges that for months previously members of the TNKU had been receiving training and supplies at Malinau, although the Tunku implies that this was being done under Communist auspices rather than by official government agencies. It is quite conceivable that the East Kali-mantan military commander, Colonel Suharjo, was taking action in this matter largely on his own initiative, possibly with some encouragement from PKI or Partindo elements, for he himself had left-wing inclinations and was strongly anti-imperialist.[24] Indonesian Army men are said to have been involved in the training, although it was outwardly disguised as a Partindo-run operation. How far Suharjo had official backing from the Army leaders or any other senior Indonesian authorities remains unclear, however. It is inconceivable that they did not have some inkling of what was afoot, for Azahari visited Djakarta at least twice during 1962. He had maintained connections there ever since his sojourn there during the revolution; some reports say that he was receiving money from Indonesia, but this may have been merely a retainer for a man who might one day turn out to be useful. In any case, this evidence of involvement is hardly sufficient to establish the charge that the revolt was due primarily to Indonesian incitement. Certainly the Indonesians later gave a great deal of moral support, as well as asylum to Azahari and other NKKU leaders and some measure of practical help (of very limited effectiveness) to anti-Malaysian elements in the Borneo territories in the months that followed. Yet the revolt itself caught Indonesia's leaders unprepared. Their reaction was slow and hesitant, as we shall see in due course, and their assistance to Azahari very limited. The constantly feuding leaders of the NKKU were never granted diplomatic recognition, nor even given much personal prominence in Indonesia's extensive propaganda campaign against Malaysia throughout 1963–4.[25]

The Indonesians have subsequently characterized the revolt as 'a natural and spontaneous manifestation by the subject peoples of the three British dependencies to break away from the colonial chains which had held them in bondage for decades'. The independence of the North Borneo Unitary State was proclaimed by 'the acknowledged leaders of the people of Sarawak, Brunei and North Borneo', under Azahari, 'who was, by virtue of his statesmanship, chosen to become the Prime Minister'.[26] But was it, in any significant sense, a broad popular uprising? Certainly such a claim cannot be made in respect of Sabah or Sarawak, despite the widespread opposition to Malaysia among Sarawak Chinese. In Brunei, some of the classic features of a popular revolt against an alien and colonial government were certainly present: Azahari's party could claim extensive popular support and quite a large fraction of the adult male population may have been involved. They had ample grounds for discontent with the Sultan's autocratic regime, as we have seen, as well as for resentment of the British protectorate and the British-owned oil company. But the more closely we examine the revolt and its background, the more questions arise about just what its aims were and at whom it was directed. Not against the Sultan, apparently, for Azahari initially thought he was supporting him in an anti-Malaysia and anti-British rebellion. Loyalty to the Sultan remained a deeply ingrained instinct of the Brunei ra'ayat, despite the rebellion. Against Malaysia certainly — but what was the rationale of this since the Sultan was in favour of Malaysia? Was the Sultan really implicated in the venture, as

Azahari implied — and if so, why? Why, for that matter, did Azahari abandon his advantageous political position just when he was so close to the threshhold of power in the Legislative Council? Did he really intend to set up a client state under Indonesian protection? Until Azahari's own story is more fully revealed we can only offer tentative answers to these questions.

INDONESIA'S RESPONSE: CONFRONTATION AS A WAR OF WORDS

The first Indonesian comments on Azahari's revolt do not give support to the theory that it was anticipated in Djakarta. President Soekarno made no public reference on it until the evening of 10 December — and then only a vague sentence at a diplomatic reception: 'the events in North Borneo could not be separated from the New Emerging Forces which are quickly altering the face of the earth'. The PKI did not immediately seize upon the revolt as an opportunity to generate all-out support for Azahari: its paper, *Harian Rakjat*, on the 10th simply quoted the capitalist news-agencies' reports on the revolt without making much of the issue. It accepted at face value Azahari's statements from Manila that the Sultan had raised the flag of the United States of Borneo and was opposing the entry of British troops to Brunei; but neither then nor on the days following did *Harian Rakjat* attempt to slant the news so as to exaggerate the extent or success of the revolt or to argue that it merited active Indonesian support. Its editorial view was that the revolt proved clearly that imperialism-colonialism was tottering and that the Malaysia idea was unpopular because it was neo-colonialist: hence it was natural for these New Emerging Forces to look to others for support. Stronger statements of support for the 'people's revolution' in Brunei were made by the Partindo leaders, although even their mouthpiece, *Bintang Timur*, which usually took a more adventurous line than *Harian Rakjat*, did not go beyond a vague statement of approval in its editorial columns.[27]

Further expressions of support for the rebels came quickly from the student's federation, PPMI, from the West Kalimantan students' association in Djakarta and from the Minister for Information, Roeslan Abdulgani, who called on the press to support 'colonial peoples fighting for their independence'. Many other organizations, mostly from the left wing, began to clamber on to the bandwagon in the days following. General Nasution commented non-committally that Indonesia had no territorial claim to North Borneo but was opposed to colonialism. In similar vein, the Foreign Affairs commission of Parliament announced that as an independence movement the Brunei revolt must receive the support of the Indonesian people.[28] On the whole, however, these early semi-official statements were little more than non-committal ranging shots prior to a verbal engagement that might or might not develop.

The war of words began to intensify soon after the Tunku's 'accusations' against Indonesia, as the Indonesian press described them, in his statement to the Malayan Parliament on 11 December. Actually the Tunku's references to Indonesian aid to the rebels were extremely brief and oblique. Although he accused the rebels of wanting to incorporate the Borneo territories into Indonesia, he did not implicate the Indonesian government as such, but only the PKI and 'other foreign parties', even in his revelation of the arms and training given to the TNKU at Malinau. It would seem that he was trying to avoid antagonizing Soekarno more than necessary.[29] But the cat was out of the bag and the Malayan press was far less inhibited than he — for Indonesian communism and the Soekarno government were often bracketed together as indistinguishable evils in Malaya. Later the Tunku certainly did make some ill-chosen statements which exacerbated feelings in Djakarta official circles, but by then the hue and cry had been going for some time. The question of who uttered the first insult in the quarrel is not in itself a very significant one, but in our attempt to identify the motivations of the main actors in the drama, we should not underestimate the importance of these mutual provocations and antagonisms in the early stages of the dispute.

The development of the anti-Malaysia campaign in the press during the following weeks deserves some attention for the light it throws on the style of Guided Democracy politics and because it blew up so quickly from a condition of almost total unconcern with the Malaysia idea. Stress was put on the anti-colonialist and revolutionary aspects of the Brunei revolt, the proof it gave to Soekarno's theory of the struggle against neo-colonialism by the New Emerging Forces (whose final victory was not doubted even after the revolt collapsed, because the shaky foundations of Malaysia had been revealed) and the evidence it provided that Tunku Abdul Rahman was a mere lackey of the British. The fact that he sent Malayan police to crush the Brunei 'freedom fighters' alongside the British troops, his reliance on British forces in the crisis and his hostility to Indonesia simply corroborated the worst suspicions about him there. Almost every step the Malaysians took was presented in an unfavourable light. Since most Indonesians had no other source of news and no better framework of interpretation than the doctrine of neo-colonialism, they had little reason to doubt what they read or heard.

The press now began to print a great deal on Malaysia, an extraordinary melange of straightforward news agency reports and weird distortions. Even newspapers which were out of sympathy with the government's general policy and ideology fell into line with the most thoroughly indoctrinated, almost as if it were the natural response.[30] One could easily cite innumerable examples of the half-truths, misleading twists of interpretation and often devious arguments used against Malaysia and its advocates, but to do so might give a misleading impression that a great effort of indoctrination had been necessary, or that the issue was a burning one in Indonesian breasts. Probably neither of these propositions was true. Indoctrination on this issue was barely needed because the groundwork had been well prepared; the neo-colonialist interpretation of the imperialists' behaviour was by now a natural one for most politically aware Indonesians. To say that they felt strongly about Malaysia at that stage, however, is quite another matter. It is questionable whether many did so until much later in 1963, when the nation's prestige was at stake in the campaign to 'crush Malaysia'. This was not the case immediately after the Brunei revolt. It suited some Indonesians to build up a campaign against Malaysia in the hope of getting good seats on the band-wagon, while there were certain advantages for the President and those who shared his views that such a campaign should develop, although in a tentative, non-committal way. His own arguments and sentiments naturally inclined him towards Azahari's cause, but he gave the Brunei rebels little more than moral support in the early months. His strategy as it unfolded appears to have been one of exploiting any opportunities that might arise within Borneo or Singapore to forestall the creation of Malaysia rather than of commitment to prevent it. It was a combination of a war of nerves, a probing action to discover weaknesses that could be exploited, a series of ambiguous threats to the Tunku and signals of moral support and encouragement to dissident elements within Malaysia. There were certainly groups in Indonesia which were anxious to seize any opportunities to push the government into a commitment which it would be unable to disavow but reluctant to embrace unequivocally; yet they were never influential enough to exert a decisive influence on Soekarno's policy towards Malaysia until September 1963.

Soekarno and Subandrio made several further statements during December which contributed further to the intensification of feelings within and between the two countries, although they still left considerable ambiguity about their ultimate intentions regarding Malaysia.[31] In fact their remarks might well have been disregarded as merely declaratory assertions of the New Emerging Forces doctrine had they not been coupled with personal attacks on the Tunku which began to appear deliberately provocative. Subandrio said in Singapore on 15 December that the Tunku's 'hostile statements' about Indonesia were endangering relations between the two countries; he accused him of a persistently unfriendly attitude and of putting all the blame for the revolt on Indonesia, despite the fact that the British forces commander had said there was no evidence of Indonesian participation. On his return to Djakarta, Subandrio added that Indonesia 'would accept the Tunku's challenge' if he continued his slanderous remarks. President Soekarno told a mass rally that Indonesians who did not support the Borneo rebels would be 'traitors to their own souls' — a remark which prompted a diplomatic Note from the British Foreign Office asking an assurance that Indonesia was not supporting the rebels.[32] Charges and counter-charges now became far less inhibited. The Indonesian Department of Information discerned a 'threat' to Indonesia in the 'cruel acts by British troops and Malayan police in efforts to defeat freedom fighters in north Kalimantan'. The first of the mass rallies on the issue was organized in Djakarta on 23 December by a newly-formed National Committee for Solidarity with North Kalimantan under the aegis of Chairul Saleh, with the burning of imperialist effigies. Simultaneously the Tunku was telling an UMNO youth rally that 'Indonesia had committed a lot of treachery against us to crush Malaysia', asserting that very strong influence was exerted on the Indonesian government by the PKI, which was suspicious of the Malaysia idea because it would not then be able to expand its influence in Malaya and Singapore. Soekarno in turn attacked this 'false accusation' of Communist influence as 'Communist-phobia', claiming that Indonesia's attitude to Malaysia was 'a matter of principle' based on the 1955 Bandung Conference principles! Both propositions, needless to say, contained a grain of truth and a rather larger grain of fantasy.[33]

There was a brief lull in the recriminations during early January, when developments in West Irian were occupying the headlines in Indonesia — the final lowering of the Dutch flag there on 31 December, demands in West Irian for a shortening of the UNTEA administration period and negotiations with U Thant about an earlier transfer of West Irian to Indonesian control. Unfortunately the Tunku aroused another outburst of anger in Djakarta when he rashly embellished an attack on a pro-Indonesian organization in Singapore, with the statement; 'The Indonesians look upon us as enemies. But this hatred of Malaya did not originate from the Indonesian people. It originated from the Russians, of whom there are about a thousand in Indonesia.' Only a week after this Dr. Subandrio declared that Indonesia's patience was not inexhaustible and he proclaimed in a speech on 20 January, that 'We cannot but adopt a policy of confrontation against Malaya because at present they represent themselves as accomplices of the neo-colonialists and neo-imperialists pursuing a hostile policy towards Indonesia'.[34]

What 'confrontation' was to mean was not at all clear at that stage. Even Subandrio could not immediately throw any light on the consequences that might follow, when questioned shortly after his speech — except that it did not mean that Indonesia was contemplating war over the issue.[35] But the parallel with Indonesia's earlier confrontation of the Netherlands during the West Irian crisis was obvious, not only in the threat of armed force which had characterized the last stages of that struggle, but also in its conveniently imprecise connotations. After all, confrontation of the Netherlands had been proclaimed as early as June 1960, at the time of the *Karel Doorman* incident, before diplomatic relations with Holland were severed and long before any serious clashes developed. Confrontation, it was frequently asserted, had many aspects — diplomatic and economic, as well as military. The ambiguity was to be exploited to the full!

The purpose of proclaiming confrontation seems to have been as much a matter of internal politics as external. It gave a clear signal to the press and political leaders at home to mount the sort of 'revolutionary' campaign against the confronted which had become a familiar feature of the Indonesian political scene. It enabled Soekarno to test political reactions on the issue at stake both at home and abroad. It was also calculated to arouse uncertainty and alarm in the adversary and among other powers as to Indonesia's real intentions, without irrevocably committing her in any formal way. There was something uniquely Soekarnoesque about this technique; it was a style he had developed with considerable success in dealing with superannuated imperialists and their stooges, a combination of threats, brinkmanship and play-acting, which could be modulated at will to a pitch of fierce hostility at one extreme or, at the other, of patient acquiescence while waiting for favourable opportunities to resume the long-term struggle, whatever its objectives may be. It served Soekarno's purposes in mobilizing the revolutionary energies of the Indonesian people while leaving him a maximum of latitude in determining just what goals these energies should be directed towards. Confrontation was in due course to be dignified with a formal definition, when President Macapagal of the Philippines had to be reassured that it did not have the aggressive connotations attributed to it by the Malaysians:

It is not a policy of aggression, much less a policy of territorial expansion. Its main purpose is to oppose the neo-colonialist policy of an outside power which... is bent on wrecking Maphilindo. This divide and rule policy, backed by preponderant military force, can only be checked by a firm defensive policy of confrontation, lest the national independence and security of the countries of this region succumb to foreign domination.[36]

There are ambiguities and question-begging assumptions in plenty here, but however vague or misleading Soekarno's language of 'revolutionary diplomacy' may have seemed to foreign critics, it articulated ideas which were both familiar and persuasive within the Indonesian (or at least the Javanese) *Weltanschaung.*

Other Indonesian actions within a few days of the Subandrio announcement had the effect, whether intended or not, of underlining its most sinister implications. General Yani, while on a visit to Pontianak, near the exposed southern border of Sarawak, drew headlines with a statement that the Army was only awaiting orders to assist the rebels in North Kalimantan. Antara added that two divisions of volunteers were ready to do likewise.[37] (No such order was issued, of course, although border raids by alleged 'volunteers' were quietly begun several months later.) These early sabre-rattlings could perhaps be disregarded as formalistic utterances of no serious significance, for Subandrio repeated on several occasions that there was not going to be war over Brunei. But what importance was to be attached to confrontation? How far were the Indonesian authorities planning to go on this issue? Were they hoping to provoke Malaya into severing diplomatic relations? That was almost the only interpretation that could be given for several further developments which brought relations between the two countries to a nadir in early February. Ganis Harsono, the Indonesian Foreign Ministry spokesman, issued to the press an extraordinarily abusive written attack on the Tunku just after the arrests of *Barisan Sosialis* leaders in Singapore. In addition to predictable attacks on Malaya as a police state, he described the Tunku as 'around the bend', and gave a long, almost comical list of his insults and hostile actions towards Indonesia, which proved, said Harsono, that the Tunku had become an object of ridicule in South-East Asia.[38]

Using more temperate language, Soekarno added his own endorsement to confrontation on 13 February in a strangely lack-lustre speech to the National Front; he charged the imperialists with attempting to encircle Indonesia and frustrate her revolution in order to protect their stake in the rubber, tin and oil of Malaysia, but beyond expressing sympathy for the struggle of the people of North Kalimantan, he gave no hint as to the form confrontation would take.[39] Subandrio, only a day after he had talked to Lee Kuan Yew about the matter in Singapore, spoke cryptically to an audience of foreign correspondents of the likelihood of armed conflict if Malayan hostility to Indonesia spread to Borneo, so that Indonesia found herself sharing a common land frontier with a hostile neighbour — a remark which may simply have meant that he was casting round for yet another argument to defend a policy which had not been carefully worked out.

At the diplomatic level, confrontation found its most immediate expression at that stage in two rather grotesque episodes, the Afro-Asian People's Solidarity Conference at Moshi in Tanganyika, and an Afro-Asian Journalists' Conference in Djakarta shortly after. Both provided an opportunity to begin the isolation of the 'neo-colonialist' Malaysians-to-be from the A-A bloc. Malayan representatives were bluntly excluded from the Djakarta conference by the simple device of not sending an invitation, so it was not a very famous victory. Moshi had its moments of drama, or perhaps farce, as the Indonesian delegation laboured, first and successfully, to debar representatives from Singapore-Malaya and then unsuccessfully to have a resolution passed condemning Malaysia as neo-colonialist. The latter was too much for the host government, which was reluctant to offend both Britain and Malaya just for the sake of Afro-Asian solidarity. The compromise adopted was an expression of support for 'the just struggle of the people of North Kalimantan against colonialism'. The Malayan delegation mocked at the fact that Brunei was represented by an Indonesian.[40] (Azahari did not turn up, though when he left Manila at the end of January he was reported to be proceeding there. Actually he went to Indonesia instead.) But the whole affair had a Ruritanian quality and was notable mainly for its demonstration of the disproportionate amount of energy put into scoring ritualistic points at such gatherings.

It is easy to exaggerate the intensity of the fears and hostility aroused by this early war of words, which seemed at the time to be little more than shadow-boxing — a threat to *future* relations between the two neighbours, perhaps, but hardly a source of imminent conflict then and there. Much of the feeling aroused was a sense of outrage at the apparent hypocrisy of the other's charges — Malayans and Britons being irked that Indonesians from the mire of their economic and political chaos should presume to criticize an orderly, well-run state; Indonesians irritated that their motives and ideology seemed to be so wilfully misunderstood and distorted. Malayans were also angered by a series of incidents in the narrow Malacca Straits where Indonesian gunboats had pursued Malayan fishermen into Malayan territorial waters.[41] This sort of friction posed a worrying problem for the Kuala Lumpur authorities, for there were divergent interpretations of what constituted 'territorial waters' and the Malayan navy could not possibly protect over 2,000 fishing vessels in the Malacca Straits, even though its patrols were intensified and its defence expenditure increased. The incidents also seemed to be part of a deliberate policy of provoking a quarrel with Malaya.

For the Malayan government the most disturbing effect of confrontation in early 1963 was that it suddenly found itself faced for the first time with difficult problems of coming to terms with a bleak and unfriendly neighbourhood. It had been accustomed to the opposition of the Communists, of course, but now Indonesia was setting out to isolate her from the Afro-Asian family of nations. Moreover, President Macapagal had announced the Philippines' opposition to Malaysia on 29 January (partly on the ground that it was unacceptable to Indonesia), thus compounding the Tunku's annoyance with his earlier claim to part of Sabah in the name of the heirs to the Sultan of Sulu.[42] The only reassuring diplomatic development for Malaysia was President Kennedy's first open statement of support (still a carefully qualified one, designed to avoid offence to Indonesia) on 15 February.[43] Internally, however, the prospects of bringing Malaysia into being were looking brighter in February; the Lansdowne Committee negotiations were almost complete, talks with Brunei and Singapore were going well, the Brunei rebels had nearly all been rounded up, and even the arrests of *Barisan* leaders and Ahmad Boestaman had caused remarkably few repercussions. Only Sarawak was still a serious question mark.

The creation of Malaysia seemed assured, provided that Indonesia did not go too far to forestall it. But how to dissuade her? Calls for international action, either through the UN (as the PMIP wanted) or a summit meeting of the heads of state (proposed by Vice-President Pelaez of the Philippines on his way back from London) had a seductive appeal to some Malays, particularly on the opposition side. U Thant was, in fact, keeping a quiet eye on the Malaysia-Indonesia dispute through one of his deputies, Narasimhan, who stopped briefly in Malaya and Singapore for talks on the matter when he visited Indonesia in mid-February to discuss the West Irian arrangements. But there were perils in allowing the fate of Malaysia to be internationalized in any way, for it opened up limitless prospects of delays and complications, as well as the admission that Indonesia and the Philippines might have some *locus standi* in the matter. Yet the Tunku had to take some slight risks of this sort if Indonesia's attacks were to be diminished. By responding favourably to Pelaez's suggestion of a Summit meeting he opened the way for the important diplomatic initiatives at the Manila ECAFE conference in March, from which developed the various Manila conferences between April and August.

Pelaez put forward his suggestion for a conference of South-East Asian countries in an effort to promote closer regional cooperation; he had earlier shown considerable enthusiasm for ASA (Association of South-East Asian States) although at that moment the prospects of obtaining further progress on ASA seemed very gloomy.[44] An ASA conference at ministerial level had been postponed several times since mid-1962 because of the Tunku's reluctance to proceed while the Philippines' claim to Sabah was hanging over his head; Macapagal's speech of 29 January particularly angered him. Yet Pelaez was keen to keep ASA alive and, if possible, to conjure up some content for the earlier Macapagal concept of a Greater South-East Asian Confederation; hence his proposal to bring the Indonesian President to the conference table with the ASA leaders. Soekarno's initial reaction was non-commital, but the Tunku welcomed the proposal if only because it could 'help Malaya to learn the reasons for Indonesian hostility'. He could not afford to allow the formation of Malaysia to be delayed by any such conference, of course, but something might be achieved if Indonesia could be mollified or if the Philippines could be induced to abate its opposition. At the end of February the Malayan Ambassador to the Philippines let it be known that he was hoping to arrange an ASA meeting in late March and that he was sure the Tunku would attend it. Shortly afterwards, it was also announced that Tun Razak, the Deputy Prime Minister, would lead Malaya's delegation to the ECAFE conference which Subandrio was also to attend, earlier in March, presumably with the object of exploring the possibilities of further negotiations. Formally, the Tunku was not yet committed to anything more than the limited ASA talks with the Philippines, but wider prospects were being opened. Verbal attacks on Indonesia were muted in Malaya in the hope of creating a better atmosphere for talks. And Australia now began to play an active part as a broker in the dispute.[45] Mr. T. K. Critchley, High Commissioner to Malaya, paid an unofficial visit to Djakarta to talk to the President and other Indonesian leaders with whom he had established cordial relations when he was Australia's representative on the Good Offices Committee fifteen years earlier: he then flew home to Canberra where Australia's relations with both Malaya and Indonesia were undergoing an extensive review. Sir Garfield Barwick, Minister for External Affairs, decided to attend the Manila ECAFE conference, partly to try to bring about a peaceful resolution of the dispute that had arisen, partly in order to underline Australia's interest in participating in such regional deliberations. His intervention was not altogether welcome to the British, who took a jaundiced view of the tripartite talks which developed out of the Manila discussions, but Barwick believed that if the Indonesians were genuinely afraid that Malaysia constituted a threat to her security, as they claimed to be, it was worth taking pains to dispel their apprehensions.

The talks held in Manila during the ECAFE conference opened a new and more cordial phase in Indonesian-Malayan relations, as the three governments concerned made plans for the series of Manila conferences which later resulted in the vision splendid of Maphilindo. Outwardly, the March meeting achieved little more than a formula for exploratory talks between officials, as a first step in this direction. But even this degree of progress was quite an accomplishment. Neither the Malayan nor Indonesian government was yet prepared to modify publicly its earlier intransigent attitude to the other. Tun Razak announced before he left Malaya that he did not intend to see Subandrio unless the latter took the initiative in approaching him, and it appears that he did not do so, at least in public. Both of them showed considerable cordiality to their Filipino hosts, though sparing little for each other. Macapagal's official proposal for *pourparlers* between the three nations on 11 March was a tentative, gingerly statement, not at all in character with his grandiloquent proposal of a Confederation of South-East Asian States the previous year, although Macapagal was later to be credited with the bold initiative behind the Manila talks and Maphilindo.[46] His suggestion was not even greeted with immediate and warm approval by the Malayan or Indonesian authorities. The former withheld comment until Subandrio agreed to the talks. Subandrio took two days to do so — and then only with the qualification that before his government would accept Malaysia two conditions must be fulfilled: relations between Malaya and Indonesia must be 'clarified' and Malaya must prove that the proposed Malaysia Federation would not be used to subvert Indonesia.[47]

Why was it so difficult to bring Indonesia and Malaysia together at the conference table, despite the apparent willingness of each to negotiate? One major reason was the purely tactical problem of defining what was to be on the agenda. The Tunku was willing to hold talks if they offered a means to 'learn the reasons for Indonesian hostility' and he was anxious to calm Indonesian apprehensions about threats to their security resulting from the Malaysia scheme; but there were tight limits to the concessions he was prepared to yield, since he could not afford to delay Malaysia's creation or admit that it depended upon Indonesia's approval. But for Indonesia's leaders there was no advantage in high-level negotiations if the Malaysia scheme was to be excluded from the agenda or if one of the preconditions was abandonment of confrontation. Part of the difficulty for the Malayan government and the would-be mediators, moreover, was to discover just what Soekarno's real aims were in espousing confrontation. If he did not really want to heal the breach that had developed, negotiations would not solve anything and were simply an unnecessary risk from the Kuala Lumpur point of view. But two other interpretations were constantly advanced by Indonesian officials to induce the Malayans to offer concessions of some sort. Confrontation could not easily be repudiated without some face-saving gesture by the Tunku, they argued, for Soekarno was now too firmly committed to it by virtue of the New Emerging Forces doctrine and by popular support in Indonesia for North Kalimantan's 'freedom fighters'. On another level, many Indonesians attributed their opposition to Malaysia to the security aspect. They expressed concern that, instead of bringing an early end to British military bases, the creation of Malaysia was to involve an extension of the existing Anglo-Malayan defence agreement. Macapagal's confederation proposal provided a convenient framework for further discussions of this problem. Hence it suited all concerned to treat the security aspect as the central problem at Manila, as if it were the essential stumbling-block which could soon be cleared away by negotiations and assurances about mutual non-aggression.[48]

The path to the Summit, as it turned out, was by no means the quick and easy series of steps envisaged in the Macapagal proposal. There were delays and pinpricks on both sides. Only a few days after he had accepted Subandrio's two conditions for further talks, the Tunku made a surprise statement that a Summit meeting would not be necessary; a ministerial conference would suffice, since the purpose of any talks would simply be to explain the reasons for Malaysia, not to bargain on the timing or terms on which it would be formed. Although Razak 'clarified' this next day to mean simply that a favourable climate had to be created for a Summit, the Indonesians accused Malaya of being 'not serious' in their approach. However, on 29 March the Malayan government announced that it was ready for talks in Manila at the officials' level on 5 April.[49] Hostile statements against Indonesia were avoided during this period, although the Malayan press was still tending to take the view that a Summit conference was not necessary. But doubts and delays still remained on the Indonesian side.

Macapagal had proposed an officials' conference to prepare the agenda for a Foreign Minister's meeting which would precede the Summit conference. But it was doubtful for some time how the Malaysia question would be included, if at all. Speculation in Manila about some form of 'self-determination process ... and interim UN administration for the Borneo territories' (along the lines of the West Irian formula) indicated to the Malayans what sort of pressure might be put upon them.[50] In the communique issued after an ASA conference on 4 April, referring to the forthcoming talks between the 'three countries of Malay origin', nothing was said about the Malaysia issue although the Tunku commented later that nothing would necessarily be ruled out. The officials' conference had to be postponed when the Indonesian delegate refused to leave Djakarta in protest at a speech by the Tunku which was deemed unfriendly. When it did meet on 15 April, it took over a week to draw up a provisional agenda which, without making any reference to Malaysia, simply listed the broadest generalities such as defence against Communism, the Philippines' proposed Confederation, economic cooperation, an Asian common market and cultural questions.[51] No precise date for the Foreign Ministers' conference was set, but it was expected to be held in mid-May. Even this modicum of agreement was not easily reached and there are indications that Indonesia was still distinctly luke-warm about the series of talks going ahead at all. On 12 April occurred the first major border incursion in Sarawak, at Tebedu, which could easily have led to a breakdown of negotiations if Kuala Lumpur had reacted adversely to it; General Yani made no real attempt to deny Indonesian involvement in the raid, but the Tunku avoided any exacerbating comment on it. On 20 April, in a speech during President Liu Shao-chi's visit to Bali, Soekarno again spoke strongly of Indonesia's determination to prevent Malaysia. And it was at Indonesia's request that the Foreign Ministers' meeting was further postponed from mid-May until early June. For some weeks it was far from certain whether it would ever be held. Then, quite unexpectedly, came a thaw in relations between the two countries on 25 May, when Soekarno invited the Tunku at very short notice to join him in Tokyo for unofficial talks, which led to an agreement to press on with the Foreign Ministers' conference in early June, with the prospect of a Summit meeting to follow if all went well. The reasons for this volte-face are to be found in the domestic politics of both parties, to which we must now give some attention.

INDONESIAN DOMESTIC POLITICS, 1962–1963

Because the Brunei revolt brought the Malaysia problem into prominence in Indonesia so soon after the conclusion of the struggle for West Irian, just when the government in Djakarta was bracing itself to tackle the difficult and unpopular tasks of economic stabilization that had been neglected throughout 1962, its effects in giving Soekarno the excuse and opportunity to turn away from the uncongenial path of economic rehabilitation towards another 'foreign adventure' have been strongly emphasized in many accounts of confrontation and its origins.[52] At a very general level of abstraction one might, indeed, describe the political drama that was being played out in Djakarta throughout 1963 in terms of the necessity to make a choice between these two courses, for the victory of the advocates of more militant confrontation in September 1963 entailed the collapse of the stabilization scheme and a disastrous set-back to the ministers who supported it, such as First Minister Djuanda. But it would be an oversimplification to explain the Indonesian political scene in the first half of 1963 as if this choice had been the main or decisive issue between the left and right wings in the Djakarta power struggle. The interplay of domestic and foreign policy considerations in the politics of that period was extremely complex. Soekarno was obviously hoping to have it both ways, for he initially decided in favour of the stabilization scheme and the heavy dependence on Western bloc financial assistance it entailed even while he was proclaiming his opposition to Malaysia, in order to gain all the political advantages he could from it. Likewise, the PKI welcomed confrontation as an opportunity to undermine the stabilization scheme and prevent a pro-Western foreign policy orientation — yet the PKI was also ambivalent in its attitude to the Malaysia question (especially after September 1963) in case it should result open hostilities which would enable the Army to re-establish martial law. The Army leaders were ambivalent on the matter also, since they were generally in favour of the stabilization scheme, even though it was bound to hurt the Army, but alarmed in case they found themselves outflanked, as they had been over the West Irian issue, on an issue where the PKI could exploit nationalist sentiment to their disadvant-age. Throughout early 1963 the big question was how far Soekarno would lean in either direction, either towards tough measures for economic reform or a radical stand in opposition to Malaysia.

The Brunei revolt introduced this new and unpredictable issue into Indonesian politics at a time when the power struggle in Djakarta was more than usually tense. With the ending of the West Irian campaign in August 1962, a cluster of political and economic problems had been thrust into prominence on which fundamental decisions about national objectives were needed. The most pressing of these were the abolition of the martial law powers of the Armed Forces and measures to curb the inflation and economic deterioration. There were also other questions about the future role of political parties, about holding long overdue elections and about a cabinet reshuffle, whose solutions were bound to bear upon the key issue underlying nearly all the manouvres in the Indonesian political arena — what was to be the power basis of the regime in this new phase of Indo-nesia's history?

Shortly before the West Irian campaign reached its victorious conclusion, Army units had crushed and captured the Darul Islam insurgents in West Java so that peace and security were now restored throughout the whole of Indonesia for the first time since 1945, the Sumatra-Sulawesi rebellion of 1957–8 having petered out about twelve months earlier. There was no longer any convincing justification for the maintenance of martial law (or 'State of Emergency' as it was strictly called).[53] The political parties, which had suffered severe restrictions on their freedom of action at the hands of the military authorities during the preceding year or so, now began to see the opportunity for a revival of civilian institutions. The approaching end of martial law also added a fresh impetus to pressures for the drafting of a new election law in anticipation of long-overdue elections, a second plenary meeting of the People's Consultative Assembly (MPRS) and a cabinet reshuffle in which the parties hoped for a reduction of mili-tary influence. Interspersed with these demands for a new formal frame-work of political institutions were calls for the creation of a *gotong rojong* or *Nasakom* cabinet, which would include Communists as well as the representatives of the other major political *aliran*.[54] These issues were tangled up, moreover, with the political implications of the economic stabilization program that the government was then considering. It was the conflicting pulls of the stabilization scheme and of the Malaysia issue that gave such significance to the outcome of the political tug-of-war that was going on around Soekarno throughout the first nine months of 1963.

The abolition of martial law turned out to be the one of the least controversial of these issues, despite its far-reaching implications for the Army leadership, particularly in the provinces, which had become ac-customed to the exercise of wide powers over civil affairs during the previous five years. The leaders of the Armed Services soon accepted the inevitability of some formal change of status (not without serious misgivings, it seems) and set about buttressing their *de facto* power in other ways, through the utilization of a 'Council to Assist the Revolutionary Leadership' (*Madjelis Pembantu Pimpinan Revolusi,* or MPPR) in Djakarta and in the regions of the *Tjatur Tunggal* (the quadrumvirate of governor, regional military commander, chief of police and chief prosecutor, later 'democratized' into a *Pantja Tunggal* of five men by the addition of a representative of the National Front), who constituted a body with rather indistinct status and functions but virtually identical membership with the old Regional War Administrator's Council, exercising different but very broad powers.[55] It would be wrong to imply, however, that no significant reduction in the powers of the military authorities occurred when martial law was abolished in May 1963. Civil disturbances later in the year were to show that both local officials and Army officers took a markedly literal view of just who was now responsible for the preservation of law and order. Moreover, for other reasons also, the day-to-day power of the Army leaders in Djakarta politics declined perceptibly during the next two years, while that of the political parties increased. This change was not immediately apparent in mid-1963, but the abolition of martial law certainly contributed to the reduction of the Army's influence in civil affairs.[56]

The attempt by the political parties to obtain a new election law and to increase their own influence within the government was less successful. A committee of ministers (including Nasution) and party leaders was set up in November 1962 to draw up an elections bill, but it ran into serious disagreements on various thorny questions about the election or nomination of functional group representatives in Parliament or Consultative Assembly and the President's right to veto candidates. (A meeting of the MPRS, earlier planned for 3 December, had to be postponed until May to allow these problems to be settled first.) In the end, the committee merely referred the various problems back to the President for decision — after which little more was ever heard about the matter, since the parties themselves were divided on it, while more pressing issues were demanding the President's attention.

The main issue around which the struggle for power seemed to hinge at the beginning of 1963 was that of a cabinet reshuffle and the creation of a *Nasakom* cabinet representing all major political currents, including the Communists, which was being demanded insistently by the PKI. The demand for a 're-tooling' of the cabinet had a widespread appeal at a time when prices seemed to be rising uncontrollably, corruption, mismanagement and inefficiency were rampant in nearly all state enterprises and most of Soekarno's ministers seemed utterly incapable of doing anything to remedy the situation. The cry for a *Nasakom* cabinet, which the PKI had long been demanding, was also taken up by some PNI leaders who hoped that a reshuffle would both restore them to positions of greater influence and reduce the dominance of the Armed Services leaders. The latter were stubbornly opposing entry of the PKI into the cabinet — Aidit spoke in December of 'dark forces manipulated by the Imperialists who were resisting the PKI's rightful demands' — although some Army leaders were now less confident on this score than previously.[57] The PKI's campaign for a *Nasakom* cabinet was intensified to an unprecedented pitch in early 1963, largely on the basis of the President's own slogans, so that almost no one dared raise a voice in public against it. If Soekarno had acceded to this demand it would have been an important victory for the left, signifying a major shift in the political centre of balance, even though the PKI's acquisition of two or three ministerial portfolios (in a cabinet of over 50 ministers) would not in itself have entailed any very great accretion of power.[58]

For President Soekarno, however, the problems involved in the creation of a *Nasakom* cabinet went far beyond a mere shift in the domestic balance of power between the PKI and its adversaries. It was tied up also with the international implications of the economic stabilization scheme his government was contemplating, which was likely to be out of the question unless substantial foreign aid could be obtained from the International Monetary Fund and a US-backed consortium of Western countries. The PKI was strongly opposed to this course which it saw as a move to draw Indonesia back towards the Western camp; this was probably the major reason why it was so anxious to gain entry to the cabinet at that time. If it had succeeded, Indonesia's chances of gaining substantial foreign aid from the USA would have been much reduced, in view of the critical attitudes towards Soekarno prevailing in the US Congress and Senate. The Kennedy administration was taking a more sympathetic line towards Indonesia than its predecessor, but was having increasing difficulty in getting its foreign aid appropriations bill through the Congress. In 1961, a survey mission led by Professor D. D. Humphrey had recommended a substantial US-backed aid program to buttress Indonesia's Eight-Year Development Plan.[59] The mission's report was issued just at the end of the West Irian campaign, carrying a clear implication that if the Indonesian government was now prepared to turn its attention towards the economic and administrative problems confronting it, the US was prepared to assist it substantially. Discussions with the IMF during the last quarter of 1962 began to clarify the broad outlines of the stabilization programme needed to bring Indonesia's spiralling inflation under control; they also spelled out the financial conditions for the large scale loans that would have to be sought, of which the most important were a balanced budget, increased taxes and a more realistic foreign exchange rate. The programme was bound to be severely deflationary in the first instance and hurtful to the poor. But it was hoped to sugar the pill by making available additional foreign exchange for imports to check rising prices in the first instance, through loans from the IMF, then to provide for substantial development expenditures by loans from the Development Assistance Committee of the OECD to the tune of $250 million which were under consideration in the middle of 1963. Indonesia could hardly have hoped to check the inflation she was suffering from much less painfully. But the political price was likely to be one which neither Soekarno nor the PKI would find easy to accept.

Above all, the continued exclusion of the PKI from the cabinet was almost bound to be a necessary condition of any scheme dependent on substantial aid from USA at that time. Although the Kennedy administration, including key officials of the State Department, was willing to believe that the Soekarno regime was now determined to tackle its economic problems and to recommend lending him the funds needed for this purpose, it was not easy to convince conservative Congressmen of this. Representative Passman, chairman of a Subcommittee of the House Appropriations Committee, was especially critical of Soekarno's foreign policies and dalliance with the Communists, as he saw it. Moreover, the influential Clay report on the US foreign aid programme, which was published in March 1963, singled out Indonesia as a country to which 'we do not see how external assistance can be granted...unless it puts its internal house in order, provides fair treatment to foreign creditors and enterprises, and refrains from international adventures...' — though it held out the prospect of aid if this path were taken.[60] An even more critical view was being taken by Congressman Bloomfield throughout the 1963 hearings of the Appropriations Committee: he finally succeeded on 25 July in having an amendment added to the foreign assistance authorization bill for 1964 requiring the suspension of military and economic assistance to Indonesia unless the President issued statement determining that such aid was in the US national interest. To a proud and sensitive nationalist like Soekarno, these criticisms and indirect constraints must have been extremely galling, yet he could only afford to disregard them if he could also thumb his nose at the entire stabilization scheme. It may well have been for this very reason that in the first half of 1963 he sought compensation for his uncomfortable dependence on the IMF and OECD governments by demonstrating his independence of them — and even contempt for the *Nekolim* world they represented — by sailing as close to the wind as he could in the confrontation of Malaysia. This enabled him not only to maintain his credentials as a radical anti-colonialist, but also to keep the PKI on-side at a time when he was rejecting its other demands — and to keep everyone guessing about his final intentions. It is not without significance that Soekarno embarked formally on the confrontation policy in February 1963 just at the time when negotiations with the IMF over the terms of the stabilization policy were at a critical stage. In March, Soekarno took the first step towards the promulgation of that policy in his 'Economic Declaration' (*Dekon*) and at much the same time began to develop the diplomatic aspect of confrontation through the negotiations at Manila. But he still avoided any firm move towards the left or right in either sphere. Not until the '26 May regulations' implementing the stabilization scheme and his meeting with Tunku Abdul Rahman in Tokyo did he commit himself to a clearcut 'turn to the right'.[61]

A brief account of the stabilization scheme is necessary at this point, since it became politically entangled with the confrontation issue throughout the decisive months of 1963.[62] Its economic rationale was very simple. Rising prices (which had been spiralling at a rate of roughly 100 per cent per annum since early 1962) were to be curbed by a combination of increased imports, a balanced budget and more effective incentives to production. In order to remedy the distortions of the over-regulated cost structure, which were obstructing trade and production in many fields, the scheme put great stress on the market price mechanism in place of the self-defeating attempts to manage the economy by administrative *fiat*, which had merely aggravated the inflationary tendencies of 1961–2 generated by excessive government spending on the West Irian campaign and over-ambitious projects in the Eight Year Overall Development Plan. Because price-fixing regulations had kept the charges of most public utilities and many state trading enterprises pegged at unrealistically low levels, long after costs and the general price level had soared beyond them, the state budget was in effect being required to subsidize huge losses on the railways, air and shipping services, electricity supply and postal services, and even the government's rice purchase programme. Few state enterprises were running profitably or efficiently, so it was urgently necessary to encourage private business in the productive and export sectors, since Indonesia's need for foreign exchange was now desperate. Effective incentives to increase production were more urgently needed than slogans about 'social control' over the nation's productive apparatus. Thus the stabilization scheme entailed in almost every respect a reversal of the dogmas of Soekarno's 'Guided Economy'.

The President's political strategy for introducing the scheme was, consequently, a very cautious one. Discussions were begun in several of the consultative councils of the government during February and March (roughly coinciding with the crucial negotiations with the IMF and US officials), with the aim of reaching agreement on a set of general principles to be incorporated in a Presidential 'Economic Declaration' of analogous status to his earlier Political Manifesto. In all this Soekarno was careful to ensure that he was in a position to claim assent from all the *Nasakom* groups represented in his government so that a national consensus could be proclaimed and overt criticism muted. The Economic Declaration (*Dekon*) was therefore announced with appropriate fanfare on 29 March as a distillation of the opinions put forward by all political organizations during the preceding weeks.[63] As a statement of economic principles which would serve as guidelines for future policy, it was so eclectic as to mean all things to all men — except insofar as it contained a number of new phrases and emphases which had not been heard in official utterances during the Guided Democracy period, such as recognition of the need to rely on incentives and the price mechanism, or the virtues of private business as well as State enterprise. Enough of the old phrases were used to make it difficult for the Communists to withhold their approval for the *Dekon*, although there were many features of it which they disliked intensely. On the other side of the political spectrum it was immediately welcomed for its relatively more 'liberal' tone. However, the President waited nearly two months to obtain endorsement of the *Dekon* by the political parties before taking any irreversible steps towards implementation of the stabilization scheme. They duly expressed their support, with varying degrees of enthusiasm, although without really having any clear idea what economic strategy the President would choose to derive from the vague generalities they were supporting.

Soekarno had good reason to tread warily on such a contentious matter, for national unity was under severe strain in the early months of 1963. Political tensions had been aggravated by rising prices and apprehensions about the approaching end of martial law. Anti-Communists feared a sharp increase in Communist influence against which the other political parties would be relatively powerless. In the opinions of some right-wing elements, the drift to the left had to be checked by precipitating a show-down which would crystallize the anti-Communists into a solid bloc. This was probably one factor (among many others) behind a chain of anti-Chinese riots which broke out in many parts of Java between March and May, for which various wild and fantastic explanations came into circulation, all tending to aggravate the tension between Communists and anti-Communists.[64] Hints of a cabinet reshuffle in which the PKI would gain further representation were still being thrown out by the President himself, though nothing came of them. His violent denunciations of Malaysia during Liu Shao-chi's visit in the latter part of April, roughly coinciding with the first big raid in Sarawak at Tebedu and a deterioration of the more peaceful mood maintained since the previous month's Manila talks, also seemed to portend a move towards the left.[65] The political future at that time was still far from certain. The choice between consolidation and continuing revolution was not yet settled.

A second, long-delayed session of the People's Consultative Assembly (MPRS) had been scheduled for May, against the triumphant backdrop of West Irian's final transfer to Indonesian control and the abandonment of martial law. It was an appropriate occasion for assertions of national unity and confidence in President Soekarno's leadership. Political strife was momentarily muted, as no very contentious issues were brought before the Assembly. Soekarno was proclaimed President for life in recognition of his services to the nation. The other major business of the session was to endorse the *Dekon* as Indonesia's official Economic Manifesto, to be carried into effect at the discretion of the President as Mandatory of the Assembly. This cleared the way politically for Soekarno to promulgate the '26 May decrees' which constituted the central core of the stabilization programme.[66]

The decrees were hailed in the West as a sign that Soekarno had set his course towards realism and moderation, rather than 'living dangerously'. This impression was confirmed when he flew to Tokyo a few days later by two dramatically new developments. He authorized the settlement on mutually favourable terms of a drawn-out wrangle between his government and the three big foreign oil companies operating in Indonesia. And he invited Tunku Abdul Rahman to meet him for talks which proceeded in an encouragingly friendly atmosphere. There seemed to be reasons for hoping at last that Indonesian politics might be entering a more tranquil phase.

The stabilization scheme did have a dramatic effect in checking the over-all increase of price of the previous eighteen months, but it proved intensely unpopular, for many public utility charges rose sharply. Imports increased, after a slight delay, as also did exports. Inevitably, however, it created a serious liquidity crisis. Speculators had to unload their stocks on to the market, which contributed to the levelling out of the price index between June and August, but did not endear the new policies to the traders concerned. The tight-money policies to which the government was committed were most hurtful to businessmen, who might otherwise have been expected to favour a policy of economic liberalization. Businessmen joined the PKI and many others in the chorus of condemnation of the 26 May regulations. When the 1963 and 1964 Budgets were submitted simultaneously to the Parliament in August, they were passed grudgingly: the PKI dared to abstain on the Budget vote at the end of August, although that was as far as it was prepared to carry its opposition.[67]

TOWARDS MALAYSIA: THE FINAL STAGE

Throughout the first half of 1963 the spectre of a repetition of the Brunei revolt hung ominously over the states of the would-be Malaysia, conjuring up fears of more serious Indonesian efforts to frustrate the scheme. Few substantial obstacles to the creation of Malaysia remained after the Lansdowne Committee completed its deliberations on the constitutional and financial terms for the Borneo territories at the end of 1962. But another uprising could easily have upset the time-table for bringing Malaysia into being on 31 August.

Sarawak was the most uncertain factor in the Malaysia equation at that time, for there was still a possibility that SUPP might win the elections scheduled for May-June, as well as a danger that the young Chinese leftists of the SCO and SUPP might resort to an uprising.[68] Elsewhere the opponents of Malaysia were in disarray. The arrest of over a hundred *Barisan Sosialis* leaders in Singapore and Ahmad Boestamam in Malaya showed that the authorities there were determined to use emergency powers ruthlessly to forestall any mass demonstrations against Malaysia, taking advantage of the atmosphere of crisis that had arisen. Consequently there was little the opposition parties within Malaya and Singapore could do to gain any political benefit from the Brunei revolt, whereas they could now easily be accused of pro-Indonesian sympathies. Their few mild gestures of protest against the arrests were quite ineffectual in such circumstances.

Another big question mark that arose in the first half of 1963 was the tension developing between the governments of Malaya and Singapore over the final economic and commercial terms of merger. The negotiations over these issues were to involve some bitter and dramatic arguments during which the very future of Malaysia seemed to hang in the balance, although this was due to hard bargaining over complex economic questions rather than to deep-seated political obstacles in the way of agreement. They have some relevance to this story, for it was sometimes suggested that President Soekarno and his advisers may have been hoping that the

Malaysia scheme would collapse from its own internal strains.[69] If so, this might help to account for Soekarno's suddenly mild attitude towards Malaysia at the end of May and during the Foreign Ministers' conference in June, followed by his equally unexpected outburst against the Tunku when the London Agreement for the establishment of Malaysia was finally signed on 9 July.

The details of these negotiations have been recounted elsewhere and only two aspects of the affair need to be mentioned here.[70] One is the negotiating tactics of the two parties, which may have given the Indonesians an exaggerated impression of the likelihood that the talks would break down. The other is the legacy of distrust generated between the two governments in the course of the negotiations, which was to embitter relations between Kuala Lumpur and Singapore throughout the following years.

The economic conditions of merger were of crucial importance to Singapore, since it was access to wider markets that she needed most desperately if the PAP government was to succeed in its ambitious plans to provide employment in industries for the island's rapidly increasing population. Yet it also wanted to safeguard the entrepot trade as far as possible, on which Singapore's past prosperity had been based. On the other hand, Malaya had already established higher tariffs on some products than Singapore and had industries of her own to protect. Arrangements for a common market were by no means impossible to devise, but the circumstances were such that it was not easy to find satisfactory compromises. One of the difficulties was that mutual concessions presupposed a substantial measure of agreement about long-range economic objectives — and this was conspicuously lacking. Also lacking was the necessary degree of reciprocal trust, for deep personal antipathies developed during the negotiations. Moreover, at the heart of the matter was an extremely tricky technical problem of working out a satisfactory formula for sharing the work of collecting taxes in Singapore and then allocating the proceeds to the two governments on an acceptable ratio. At stake in these negotiations was not only the question of how these revenues should be allocated between the two governments, but also some very delicate questions about the division of responsibility for determining and executing tax policies.[71] These issues were later to prove one of the sources of friction during the controversies of 1964–5 which preceded the separation of Singapore.

Negotiations on these complex details did not begin until January 1963, after the major political uncertainties about the creation of Malaysia had been cleared away. The talks continued intermittently until July, but they ran into a deadlock in March–April and for some weeks no progress was made. Both sides were waiting on the report of the Rueff Mission on behalf of the International Bank regarding the contentious question of the common market arrangements. When it was finally released, its recommendations on this subject favoured Singapore's case at the expense of Kuala Lumpur's and its reception by the latter was a good deal less than open-hearted. The Singapore government was endeavouring to make the two issues of the common market and the financial arrangements interdependent in the negotiations, since it was primarily concerned to obtain guarantees of a satisfactory common market arrangement in return for concessions on the financial questions, on which it could afford to be more flexible. The Malayan negotiators wanted to treat the two issues separately and settle the financial issues first, since they held the stronger cards on the matter of the common market and could insist that their proposals should be accepted. They stated their terms in the manner of an ultimatum to Singapore on several occasions.[72] All this may well have given Indonesian diplomats the impression that the negotiations were on the brink of collapse, especially as they coincided with reports of bitter personal animosities between the leaders of the two governments.

The final phase of the Malaya-Singapore talks opened on 29 May, after a six-week deadlock. It was announced that 'agreement in principle' on the common market issue had been reached, but this in itself did not mean very much since the details still had to be hammered out: in fact, the announcement appears to have been offered as a concession by the Tunku because Lee was facing difficulties in a forthcoming Legislative Assembly debate, but Lee implied in public that it committed Malaya to more than was intended by the Tunku, and this again angered the Malays intensely. There was muttering about Lee being an impossible man to deal with and hints to the PAP that Goh Keng Swee would be more acceptable to Kuala Lumpur. On 19 June, Malaya's 'final terms' for an agreement were announced and a reply was demanded within two days; if the reply was acceptable, the Tunku would fly to London shortly after for the formal signature of the agreement to establish Malaysia. Evidently Singapore's reply was still not acceptable, for Tun Razak was sent to London instead, in the hope that negotiations with Singapore (and the British authorities) might make more progress there in a calmer atmosphere. The Tunku was to follow only when it was certain that agreement would be reached. Whether or not all this melodrama was really necessary, it served its purpose, for sufficient progress was made in London for Razak to cable the Tunku on 5 July to fly there for the final signature of the Agreement, after Singapore had made concessions on the financial issues.

The question of Brunei's inclusion in Malaysia also came to a head at the London talks. Ironically, the Sultan decided at the last moment against joining, though his decision now caused little dismay, for Brunei's inclusion in Malaysia was no longer regarded as crucial. In fact it would have been something of an embarrassment, unless the Sultan were prepared to democratize the political arrangements within his state.

The issues on which the Sultan decided against joining were the formula for dividing up Brunei's oil revenues between Kuala Lumpur and Brunei and the question of the Sultan's precedence in the Conference of Rulers.[73] If the latter issue were to be determined on the basis of his date of accession to the throne (which was the rule applying at the time and which the Sultan felt should be applied to him), he would have been the fourth in rank. But the Conference of Rulers, to whom the Tunku referred the matter for decision, proposed that his precedence should be determined by the date on which he joined the Conference, which would have left him near the bottom of the list. Whether it was this issue which turned the Sultan away from Malaysia or the issue of oil revenues is a matter on which opinions differ. He was rigidly uncompromising in his insistence on maintaining control over Brunei's oil revenues in perpetuity — unrealistically so, insofar as no other state enjoyed such a right — in return for an annual payment of a mere $40 million to the Federal treasury in recompense. The Malayan authorities offered to leave control in Brunei's hands for ten years after the formation of Malaysia and one would have thought a compromise could have been devised here if the Sultan had really wanted it. Evidently he did not, for one reason or another.

After the signature of the London Agreement and the victory of the pro-Malaysia parties in Sarawak's elections, no major obstacles to the creation of Malaysia on 31 August remained. Indonesia's hostility, suddenly renewed by an outburst from Soekarno on 12 June, in complete contrast to his more peaceful mood during the previous six weeks, was now the only serious problem remaining. But there was to be one final internal contretemps before Malaysia came into being. In trying to allay Soekarno's hostility through the concessions he made at the Manila Conference at the end of July, by agreeing to a brief postponement of Malaysia-day in response to Soekarno's pressure for a UN Mission of Enquiry in Borneo, the Tunku stirred up one final hornets' nest at home. Suspicions were aroused against the proposal to delay Malaysia's formation and against the racial implications of the Maphilindo concept put forward at Manila. The latter was distrusted by the Chinese in general, but particularly by Lee Kuan Yew and the Singapore Chinese who were most alert to the implications of Malay-Indonesian ethnic solidarity. Lee's comments on Maphilindo, in turn, angered some leading Malays. The Secretary General of UMNO, Syed Ja'afar Albar, wrote to the Tunku at the end of August urging second thoughts about the whole Malaysia scheme before it was too late, because of all the problems it had brought in its wake.[74] The Tunku needed calm nerves to weather the storm that blew up around him in the last half of August. Lee was challenging the Tunku's right to commit the governments of Singapore, Sabah and Sarawak to any postponement of their independence just for the sake of mollifying Soekarno; he also made common cause with the other two Chief Ministers-designate in pressing the Tunku to proclaim Malaysia by 31 August as originally intended. The British also were uneasy about the delay, distrusting Soekarno's intentions in the matter and apprehensive about Lee's. Duncan Sandys, Minister for Commonwealth Relations, flew to Kuala Lumpur on 23 August for talks with Lee, Stephens and Ningkan as well as the Malayan leaders, advancing his visit by a week. With the end of August drawing near, they all pressed the Tunku to promulgate an alternative date for Malaysia Day, 16 September, just after U Thant was expected to issue his mission's report.[75] This created a new and more serious rift with Indonesia to which we must return in due course. On 31 August, internal self-government was proclaimed in Sabah and Sarawak, with the new constitutions coming into force, although it was not until 16 September that these territories were formally incorporated in Malaysia, and their own political leaders took over full control of the government from the British. Lee Kuan Yew added further drama by announcing on 31 August that Singapore would take over the powers of defence and foreign affairs, which it did not yet control, in trust until the formation of Malaysia, thus asserting, in effect, her self-government and independence of both Britain and Malaysia.[76] The gesture had little importance, except in strengthening Lee's position in the snap election he then called to catch the *Barisan Sosialis* at a disadvantage just after Malaysia Day. But it irritated the Malayan leaders intensely and was regarded as yet another sign that Lee was too ambitious to be trusted.

[1]A useful account of the Brunei revolt was given by T. E. Smith, 'The Brunei Revolt: Background and Consequences', *The World Today*, vol. XIX, April 1963, pp 135–8; Willard Hanna, *The Formation of Malaysia*, chapters 14–16, gives one of the most informative contemporary accounts of Brunei politics before the revolt.

[2]The figures for 1960 are illuminating:

	Population	Total exports	Govt. revenue
Brunei	83,877	$255 mill.	$127 mill.
North Borneo	454,421	$223 mill.	$ 59 mill.

Figures from *State of Brunei, Report for the year 1960* and *North Borneo Annual Report 1962*.

[3]*State of Brunei, Annual Report 1955, p. 3*. The total population in 1960 slightly exceeded 80,000, of whom 22,000 were Chinese.

[4]The population estimates in this paragraph are based on Lee Yong Leng, 'The City of Many Waters', *Hemisphere* (Sydney), vol. VIII, no. 6, June 1964. For the history of Brunei, see H. R. Hughes Hallett, 'A Sketch of the History of Brunei', *Journal of the Royal Asiatic Society, Malay Branch*, vol. XVIII, no. 2, and Runciman, *The White Rajahs. A History of Sarawak from 1841 to 1946*.

[5]Nominated District Advisory Councils were set up in 1954, with the right to send observers to the State Council and the privilege of addressing it on any matter about which the Sultan might wish them to speak. The *Annual Report, 1954*, accorded this revolutionary advance just slightly more significance than the fact that 'the ancient Malay ceremony of ear piercing *(istiadat bertindek)* of the two princesses' was attended by the British Commissioner General and the two neighbouring governors.

[6]*Borneo Bulletin*, 15 February 1958, cited in J. R. Angel, op. cit. p. 346, upon which much of the information in this paragraph is based.

[7]*Straits Times*, 20 Oct. 1958.

[8]*Borneo Bulletin*, 20 Feb. 1960, and *Straits Times*, 18 June 1960, cited in Angel, op. cit. p. 363–4.

[9]*Straits Times*, 6 Dec. 1961.

[10]Hanna, op. cit. p. 136.

[11]Ibid. pp. 36 and 134.

[12]Some contemporary appraisals of the causes underlying the Brunei revolt are given in Hanna, op. cit. pp. 148–51.

[13]Ibid. p. 126.

[14]Rumours about the Sultan's complicity are discussed briefly (and rejected) by Hamilton Fish Armstrong in 'The Troubled Birth of Malaysia', *Foreign Affairs*, vol. XLI, no. 4, July 1963, pp. 671–93.

[15]Brief official accounts of the revolt as reported to the British House of Commons may be found in *Hansard*, vol. 669, pp. 31–6, 1452–6 and vol. 676, pp. 64–5. A useful summary is given in *Keesings Contemporary Archives*, 1963, pp. 19, 261–3.

[16]According to *Harian Rakjat*, 14 Dec., Azahari still maintained that the Sultan was with the TNKU and challenged the British to prove that he has opposed to the NKKU.

[17]*North Borneo Annual Report 1962*, p. 8.

[18]Tom Harrisson, 'Checking the Revolt', *Malaya*, Feb. 1963, pp. 27–31.

[19]Ibid. p. 31.

[20]See *Straits Times*, 12 Dec. 1962 for information on TNKU activities in North Borneo put before the North Borneo Legislative Council by the Chief Secretary.

[21]See the Tunku's speech to the Malayan Parliament on 11 Dec., *Official Report, Dewan Ra'ayat*, vol. IV, pp. 2,666–83.

[22]See statements to the British Parliament by Duncan Sandys on 10 Dec. and Nigel Fisher on 20 Dec. in *Hansard*, vol. 664, p. 33 and vol. 670, p. 1455: the British intelligence services appear to have been better informed than one would infer from Duncan Sandy's perfunctory statements.

[23]According to Michael Leigh, who visited Kuching in December 1962, the revolt had been planned for Christmas eve, by which time Azahari was to be at the UN.

[24]Col. Suharjo made life very difficult for the British officials of Shell Oil Company on several occasions. After the 1965 coup he was suspected of PKI affiliations and went underground.   He was later arrested.

[25]Although Azahari was constantly described as Prime Minister of the NKKU in Indonesian official statements, he appeared in public with Indonesian leaders on very few occasions. For details of his rift with his Deputy Minister of Defence, Zukifli, in Jan. 1964, see Brackman, *Southeast Asia's Second Front*, pp. 143–6; each denounced the other, but Azahari retained the blessing of the Indonesian government.

[26]'The Problem of Malaysia', *The Indonesian Herald*, Djakarta, n.d. (1964?).

[27]The *Harian Rakjat* editorial on Monday, 10 December commented that it was still too early to know about the Brunei revolt, but that two things were clear: Malaysia was not liked because it was neo-colonialist and imperialism-colonialism was shaky. It was natural for these 'New Emerging Forces' to look to others for help. Aidit's first statement that 'the revolt in North Kalimantan is just and must be supported' was carried in *Harian Rakjat* on 13 December. The *Bintang Timur* editorial of 11 Dec. was more positive in its assertion of Indonesia's support: on 14 Dec. it reported that Partindo was forming an organization to help the revolt: 'Support is continually flaring up and comes from the Murba Party, the Indonesian Peasants' Front (BTI), Tani Marhaen, GMNI, IPPI, Front Pemuda Pusat, Pemuda Rakjat, Pemuda Indonesia, Gerwani and many others'.

[28]*Suluh Indonesia*, 14 and 15 Dec. 1962. The Governor of West Kalimantan was quoted as saying he knew the revolt was going to break out; but this was not taken very seriously. For a fuller analysis of early reactions by the parties, the Army and the government to the revolt, see Frederick P. Bunnell, 'The Kennedy Initiatives in Indonesia, 1962–63'   (Cornell University, Ph.D. dissertation, 1969), ch. 3.

[29]See *Official Report, Dewan Ra'ayat*, pp. 2680–1.

[30]One sometimes wondered whether the anti-Soekarno papers were resorting to the *reductio ad absurdum* to mock the official line. A Surabaya paper used the dramatic headline *Rakjat Inggeris Menentang Malaysia* ('The British People Oppose Malaysia') to highlight a solitary and predictable protest by Fenner Brockway at the arrest of Barisan Sosialis leaders in Singapore in early February 1963.

[31]For relatively mild statements by Soekarno on 15 Dec. ('Indonesia is sympathetic to the struggle of the people of North Borneo'), 20 Dec. and at a mass rally on 23 Dec. and by Subandrio on 15 Dec., *see Harian Rakjat*, 17, 20 and 26 December 1962.

[32]Britain twice sought such assurances from Indonesia, apparently without success: on 4 January Indonesia rejected and returned a Note from her for its 'abusive words': *The Times*, 5 Jan. 1963. Similar assurances were sought from the Philippines and given, for Foreign Minister (and Vice President) Pelaez was due in London in January for talks on the Philippines' claim to North Borneo. Azahari's presence in Manila was becoming an embarrassment to the Philippines government by this time.

[33]*Harian Rakjat*, 28 Dec. 1962. This was Soekarno's strongest statement on the matter up to that date; Subandrio was still tending to put the blame mainly on the Tunku's 'offensive statements'.

[34]A good analysis of the significance of Subandrio's statement of confrontation is given by Bunnell, op. cit. pp. 287–9.

[35]*Suluh Indonesia*, 21 Jan. 'Indonesians are forced in spite of themselves to confront Malaysia, because it is an accomplice of neo-colonialism and neo-capitalism. We are bound to oppose neo-colonialism and capitalism, but we do it regretfully towards Malaya. Confrontation does not include war, because it can be carried on without war.'

[36]For the Soekarno-Macapagal joint statement, Jan. 1964, see *The Malaysia Issue: Background and documents* (Djakarta, Department of Foreign Affairs, 1964).

[37]*Suluh Indonesia*, 1 Feb. 1963.

[38]For different versions of this statement, see *Straits Times*, 7 Feb. 1962 and *Suluh Indonesia*, 7 Feb. 1963.

[39]Soekarno's speech to the National Front was an anti-climax, as a major announcement had been expected — perhaps a *Nasakom* cabinet. Instead, the speech contained nothing of substance regarding domestic politics, which may have been his reason for underlining confrontation: see *Suluh Indonesia*, 14 Feb. 1963.

[40]*Straits Times*, 11 and 13 Feb. 1963.

[41]On 31 Jan. an Indonesian gunboat pursued a smuggling vessel to within a few hundred yards of the Malayan shoreline. The Director of the Anti-Smuggling Section of the Indonesian Customs admitted that violations of Malayan territorial waters had occurred, but said this was justified because Malayan authorities protected smugglers. See *Straits Times*, 26 Jan. and *Berita Minggu*, 10 Feb. 1963.

[42]In June 1962, the Macapagal administration had first advanced the Philippines' claim to part of Sabah by virtue of the claims of the heirs of the former Sultan of Sulu, but the Tunku regarded it as a matter to be discussed with the British at that stage. After the Brunei revolt, during which Azahari evidently had backing from influential Filipinos, followed by Macapagal's charge in his January 1963 State-of-the-Nation message that the incorporation of Borneo in Malaysia posed a danger to the Philippines security by opening the way for Communism to spread to her doorstep, relations between Kuala Lumpur and Manila became distinctly strained. Macapagal's anti-Malaysia policy was largely motivated by domestic considerations: it developed in a singularly opportunistic fashion during 1963 and waned after the middle of 1964 when he found it desirable to reverse his pro-Indonesian course. Brief studies of the general background to Macapagal's foreign policy and the Sulu claim may be found in B. K. Gordon, *The Dimensions of Conflict in Southeast Asia* (Spectrum Books, 1966), Ch. 1, 'Philippines Foreign Policy and the North Borneo Claim' and J. A. C. Mackie 'Party Politics and Foreign Policy in the Philippines', *Australia's Neighbours*, April 1965, 4th Series, no. 25.

[43]President Kennedy's first public statement about Malaysia was limited to the observation that it was 'the best hope of security in that very vital part of the world'. While American sympathy towards Malaysia gradually increased during the next eighteen months, official spokesmen were very reluctant to antagonize Indonesia by expressing open support for Malaysia, until the Johnson – Tunku Abdul Rahman joint communique of July 1964. On American policy at this time see Bunnell, 'Guided Democracy Foreign Policy: 1960–65', and Roger Hilsman, *To Move a Nation* (Doubleday and Co., 1967) ch. 26.

[44]See Bernard K. Gordon, *The Dimensions of Conflict in Southeast Asia*, ch. I and VI, on Macapagal's scheme for a Greater Southeast Asian confederation and on ASA.

[45]Some details of the flurry of activity in Canberra at this time are given in Peter Boyce 'Canberra's Malaysia Policy', *Australian Outlook*, vol. XVIII, no.ii, August 1967, pp. 149–61.

[46]For the text of Macapagal's call for 'the promotion of fraternal and neighbourly relations', see *Malaysia*, Department of External Affairs, Canberra, 1963, p. 132.

[47]*Straits Times*, 11, 13, 14 March 1962 for Subandrio's cautiously qualified acceptance of the Macapagal plan and the Tunku's warm welcome to this Indonesian response.

[48]This aspect of the early talks in Manila was stressed by Sir Garfield Barwick in an interview in December 1964.

[49]*Straits Times*, 20, 21, 29, 30 March 1963.

[50]Robert Trumbull in *New York Times*, 15 March 1963.

[51]Ibid. 5, 16 April 1962.

[52]For one of the most explicit formulations of this interpretation, see Hindley, 'Indonesia's Confrontation with Malaysia: the Search for Motives'; the case against it is briefly put in Howard P. Jones, *Indonesia, The Possible Dream*, pp. 271–2.

[53]Indonesia had been under martial law since March 1957 when the regional dissidence began which was later to issue in the PRRI-Permesta rebellion of Feb. 1958. The various martial law regulations are outlined in Daniel S. Lev, *The Transition to Guided Democracy: Indonesian Politics 1957-59* (Cornell Modern Indonesia Project Monograph Series, 1966), pp. 15-16.

[54]These institutions and terms are explained on pp. 82-7.

[55]The decision to end martial law on 30 April 1963 when West New Guinea would pass fully under Indonesian control, was announced after an MPPR meeting on 25 October. But a month after, General Yani still found it necessary to deny 'that the Army was against abolition'; see *Suluh Indonesia*, 30 Nov. 1962.

[56]Other reasons for the decline in Army influence in 1963-4 were the gradual estrangement of Lt.-Gen. Yani from Gen. Nasution (the former having become more closely associated with Soekarno since his appointment in June 1962); the consequent confusion of political goals and tactics among the senior Army officers; and the fact that the political parties became more assertive and influential elements on the political stage at that period, especially the PKI, of course, but also Murba and elements of the PNI.

[57]Nasution told an interviewer at the end of January 1963 that a *Nasakom* cabinet was 'only a matter of time'. The PKI campaign for a *gotong-rojong* cabinet is briefly sketched in J. M. van der Kroef, *The Communist Party of Indonesia* (University of British Colombia Publishing Centre, Vancouver, 1965), pp. 276-8.

[58]Aidit himself warned the party that attainment of a *Nasakom* cabinet should not be regarded as a panacaea and his speeches in early 1963 were far from suggesting that victory was near at hand in the struggle against the 'reactionary and diehard forces', who were seeking to introduce American, Japanese or West German neo-colonialism. For a characteristic PKI analysis of the political situation and the appropriate strategy for the PKI, see D. N. Aidit, '*Dare, Dare, Dare and Dare Again*', *Political Report presented on 10 Feb. 1963 to the First Plenary Session of the Control Committee of the Communist Party of Indonesia* (Foreign Languages Press, Peking, 1963), p. 73.

[59]A full account of the political background to the stabilization scheme is given in Bunnell, op. cit. ch. 4. The US Economic Survey Team to Indonesia, led by Prof. D. D. Humphrey, had been appointed in mid-1961 soon after Soekarno's meeting with President Kennedy, who had offered to assist Indonesia with the financing of her Eight-Year Development Plan. Its report, recommending U.S. assistance of $200-235 million and multilateral finance of $125-155 million, was issued in mid-1962: it has been published under the title *Indonesia: Perspective and Proposals for United States Economic Aid: a Report to the President of the United States* (Yale University Southeast Asia Studies, 1963).

[60]Bunnell, op. cit. pp. 317-21.

[61]See below pp. 138-9, 177-8.

[62]For a fuller account, see Mackie, *Problems of the Indonesian Inflation*, pp. 37-40.

[63]K. D. Thomas, 'Recent Developments in Indonesia', *Australia's Neighbours*, 4th series, no. 11-12, Jan-Feb 1964.

[64]A valuable set of reports into the social and political background to the worst of the May riots (in Sukabumi, West Java) is contained in a publication of the Lembaga Ekonomi dan Kemasjarakatan Nasional, edited by Selosoemardjan, *Pilot Projek Survey 'Pusaka Djiwa' Tentang Faktor-Faktor jang mengandung Gerakan Kerukunan dalam Masjarakat dikota Sukabumi'*.

[65]For Soekarno's statements about Malaysia during Liu Shao-chi's visit, see Modelski, op. cit. pp. 69-70. Ambassador Jones suggests that the Tebedu raid was intended merely as a warning of what might be in store if Kuala Lumpur did not adopt a less inflexible position.

[66]The stabilization programme rested essentially on five pillars:

i. the rigid price controls of the Guided Economy era were dismantled and sharp increases announced (of 400-600 per cent) in charges for transport, postal, electricity and other public utility services which had been imposing a heavy burden on the budget as costs soared in 1961-2.

ii. the foreign exchange regulations were overhauled in what amounted to a devaluation to something nearer the free market value of the Rupiah, partly to increase the return to exporters, but partly also to increase the government's receipts from taxes on foreign trade.

iii. a 'crash programme' of imports of urgently needed spare parts and raw materials was announced to be financed by an immediate release of $40 million of foreign exchange provided by the IMF as the first stage of its loan programme to Indonesia.

iv. salaries and allowances to civil servants were roughly doubled to give them some slight recompense for the price increases they were suffering.

v. the budgets for 1963 and 1964 (announced in July) were to be brought into eventual balance by a tight curb on expenditure increases and a rise in tax revenue from increased imports.

[67]See Thomas, op. cit. The price index for 19 foodstuffs in Djakarta tells the story of the impact of this stabilization scheme on the inflation of prices as vividly as words can do.

Jan.	2319	July	3041
Feb.	2543	Aug.	3133
Mar.	2682	Sept.	3569
Apr.	2700	Oct.	3786
May	3010	Nov.	4617
June	3096		

[68]See above pp. 70–1.

[69]See *Indonesian Herald*, editorial, 27 May 1963.

[70]Milton E. Osborne, *Singapore and Malaysia*, ch. 5.

[71]Ibid. pp. 52–61: Hanna, op. cit. pp. 224–6. See also the *Report on the Economic Aspects of Malaysia by a Mission of the International Bank for Reconstruction and Development* (Kuala Lumpur, Government Printer, 1963).

[72]See the reference to Malaya's 'final terms' on 19 June, *The Times*, 24 June: also *Sydney Morning Herald*, 5 July for a statement by the Tunku that Singapore might be excluded from Malaysia if her ministers remained obdurate in the London negotiations.

[73]See Hanna, op. cit. pp. 225–6. The Tunku attributed the breakdown solely to issue of the Sultan's precedence in the Conference of Rulers, but a Brunei spokesman denied this: *The Times*, 16 July 1963.

[74]Interview with Syed Ja'afar Albar, January 1965.

[75]*The Times*, 23, 24, 26 August.

[76]Osborne, op. cit. pp. 46–7.

VII
The Manila Spirit

AT the end of May, unexpectedly and at very short notice, Soekarno invited the Tunku to join him in Tokyo for private talks. The cordial atmosphere of their meeting raised hopes that further conflict might be avoided. Although Soekarno did not go so far as to renounce his confrontation policy as such, the air was cleared to some extent, the two leaders agreeing in the communique issued at the end of the talks that their respective governments would 'take every possible measure to refrain from making acrimonious attacks and disparaging references to each other'. They also agreed to settle 'any outstanding differences directly and exclusively affecting them ... in a spirit of neighbourliness and goodwill' in accordance with the 1959 Treaty of Friendship. (Nothing further was heard of this treaty in the following months, however.) More significantly, they cleared the way for the Foreign Ministers' meeting on 7 June as the precursor of a Summit conference. As an Indonesian account later put it,

...in spite of the earlier 'war of words' it proved possible for the two leaders to find common ground and the Tunku expressed his willingness to discuss both the problems of the region in general and the Malaysia project in particular with President Soekarno and President Macapagal. With the lessening of tension, the ground was now cleared for a tripartite Ministerial conference....[1]

The Tokyo meeting occurred at the same time as Soekarno finally agreed to conclude the drawn-out negotiations over an oil agreement with the three big international oil companies operating in Indonesia, and shortly after the 26 May decrees which marked a dramatic liberalization of economic controls in Indonesia. Optimists felt justified in drawing the conclusion that he had finally decided to embark on the pro-Western policies implicit in the IMF-sponsored stabilization programme; the scaling down of confrontation appeared to be a logical corollary of that decision, although this could not be done too suddenly and some face-saving gesture might still be required of Malaya in order to 'get Soekarno off the hook', on which he had been caught by his espousal of confrontation. Pessimists were sceptical that his intentions were as simple as that, but it was not easy at the time to fathom just what they might be.

The Tunku told the press that he had insisted to Soekarno that there could be no question of changing the date of Malaysia's formation from 31 August, nor of negotiating conditions for its establishment. Soekarno subsequently claimed that the Tunku *did* agree in Tokyo to an investigation of the wishes of the people of north Borneo before the creation of Malaysia and that he accepted Soekarno's explanation of the reasons for confrontation.[2] Whatever the exact truth of the matter may be, it seems likely that some kind of discussion might have taken place between them along these lines (perhaps in vague or hypothetical terms), since the two Manila conferences which followed the Tokyo meeting proceeded towards a compromise formula involving Malaya's acceptance of an ascertainment of Borneo opinion in return for Indonesia's undertaking to 'welcome' Malaysia. What we will probably never know with any certainty, of course, is the extent to which Soekarno bluffed the Tunku into believing that he merely wanted this as a symbolic gesture of acquiescence by Malaya in the principle of self-determination in order to deal with his domestic problem of drawing back from confrontation.

THE FOREIGN MINISTERS' CONFERENCE AND MANILA ACCORD

The Foreign Ministers' 'Conference of 7–11 June marked the highest peak of cordiality and optimism reached during the entire series of Manila talks, giving promise of a fruitful outcome to the Summit meeting foreshadowed in the following month. Razak and Subandrio had known each other since their London days in the late 1940s and each appears to have been pleased with the results of their talks. Pelaez also had reason for satisfaction, since the Filipino idea of a loose confederation of the three nations (Maphilindo) was warmly endorsed by the other ministers and for the first time began to seem more than a mere pipedream. Yet there were still major difficulties in the way of finding common ground for any such association, as the opening addresses revealed, since they epitomized the very different foreign policy concerns of the three countries. The Malayan statement was a stereotyped homily on the Communist threat to the area. The Philippines stressed the common interests of the three nations in the security of the region as a whole and the advantages of closer association between them, all in the vaguest terms. Indonesia's contribution, however, had a quite different character, being focused mainly on the unconventional nature of the Indonesian revolution, which was related to 'mental development' based on discovery of one's national identity — obviously a veiled allusion to the continued cultural and political dependence of her neighbours on other nations. A press report on the first day commented that it was doubtful if the tensions could be resolved sufficiently for the confederation idea to be acceptable.[3] However, it suited the three governments to try to make the Maphilindo idea work at this stage, if only to provide a new framework within which they could pursue their diverse Malaysia policies without reaching complete deadlock.

Both Subandrio and Pelaez attempted to induce Razak to delay the creation of Malaysia so that opinion in the Borneo territories could be tested. Razak rejected this as impossible for reasons of domestic politics. When he turned the question on Subandrio to ask whether he wanted the postponement of Malaysia Day or the confirmation of popular opinion in Borneo, Subandrio replied that it was the latter, which enabled Razak to quote Narasimhan's conclusions on the matter.[4] Subandrio then went on to say that it was not a formal UN enquiry that he wanted, but merely some sort of gesture to the principle of self-determination, which he could refer to within Indonesia, so that he could willingly accept the creation of Malaysia, not feel obliged to oppose it. He said that he expected the decision to go in favour of Malaysia: in fact, he wanted it to, for he did not regard an independent North Borneo state as a satisfactory alternative at all. Just how the ascertainment of Borneo opinion was to be carried out was not specified in the Manila Accord, however, but was left to the Summit meeting to wrangle over in July. Consequently, Razak was able to return home feeling satisfied that he had committed his government to nothing more than some brief process of formal verification of Borneo opinion. Subandrio, for his part, had succeeded in making the Malayan government specifically affirm its commitment to the principle of self-determination in the North Borneo context and persuading it to accept the desirability of some form of ascertainment.[5]

The Manila Accord embodied four major points: agreement that 'the three countries share a primary responsibility for the maintenance of the stability and security of the area from subversion in any form or manifestation' (clause 3), support for initial steps towards the 'Macapagal plan', which was later designated as '*musjawarah Maphilindo*', an admission by Malaya that the Philippines' claim to Borneo would not be prejudiced by its incorporation in Malaysia and, most crucially, an affirmation of adherence to the self-determination principle in relation to the formation of Malaysia, which was spelled out in clauses 10 and 11 as follows:

10.   The Ministers reaffirmed their countries' adherence to the principle of self-determination for the peoples of non-self-governing Territories. In this context, Indonesia and the Philippines stated that they would welcome the formation of Malaysia provided the support of the people of the Borneo Territories is ascertained by an independent and impartial authority, the Secretary-General of the United Nations or his representative.

11.   The Federation of Malaya expressed appreciation for this attitude of Indonesia and the Philippines and undertook to consult the British Government and the Governments of the Borneo Territories with a view to inviting the Secretary-General of the United Nations or his representative to take the necessary steps in order to ascertain the wishes of the people of those Territories.[6]

The Accord also referred briefly to the Philippines' claim to North Borneo in clause 12, the Ministers 'noting' the claim and agreeing that it would not be prejudiced by the inclusion of North Borneo in Malaysia, while committing themselves to a solution by peaceful means. Nothing was said specifically, however, about the matter of military alliances and foreign bases; only the vague reference to sharing 'primary responsibility for the maintenance of the stability and security of the area' alluded to that in any way. The key issue was obviously the incorporation of the Borneo states in Malaysia.

This agreement may not have formally committed Malaya to very much, certainly not as much as Indonesians later asserted it did. But it could easily be interpreted as meaning a good deal more than it said, and this was to be the source of great difficulties later. Later Indonesian accounts of the Manila conferences make great play of the fact that on each occasion it was possible for the three countries to find common ground and a basis for closer cooperation, but that 'British interference worked to undo what had been done .... Hence the repeated spectacle of agreements reached in good faith being broken almost before the ink was dry.' At the Foreign Minister's conference, agreement was 'no sooner reached than it became impossible to implement it' since the Tunku went off and signed the London Agreement of 9 July 'prepared by the Colonial Office ... according to the neo-colonial formula'; hence it was difficult to see how a Summit could take up the threads of the Foreign Ministers' meeting and still proceed in an anti-colonial direction. One early Indonesian account contrasts the 'brotherly atmosphere that pervaded the discussions', which created high expectations of a new chapter in relation between the two countries, with the Tunku's unilateral action in 'brazenly' signing the London Treaty, instead of working out a solution in close harmony with his neighbours.[7]

How much truth is there in these charges? Indonesians have claimed that at least two provisions of the Manila Accord were flouted by the London Agreement of 9 July — article 3 by the continuance and extension of the Anglo-Malayan Defence agreement and articles 10–11 by the stipulation that Malaysia would definitely be brought into being on 31 August. According to the *Indonesian Herald* version, this 'unilateral' act by the Tunku flouted the 'common understanding and complete agreement on how to solve the problems of common concern' regarding Malaysia.[8] Neither of these charges can be sustained by reference to the actual text of the Accord, although, as with the agreements reached at the later Summit conference, it is necessary to consider what each party seems to have believed the text meant as well as the words of the text themselves. Was there a greater degree of 'common understanding and complete agreement' than we can discern in the carefully vague phrases of the text? The question is not unimportant, for articles 10–11 of the Manila Accord turn out to be the key statements in the entire set of Manila agreements regarding the question of an ascertainment of opinion in the Borneo territories: the more detailed provisions in the later Manila

Joint Statement regarding the implementation of the Accord still refer to them as the starting point.[9] A literal reading of them reveals clearly that the Accord imposed a more specific commitment on Indonesia and the Philippines than upon Malaya. The former were definitely to 'welcome' the formation of Malaysia if the support of the Borneo people was ascertained independently and impartially. On the other hand, Malaya was to 'consult' the British and colonial authorities with a view to inviting U Thant to conduct the ascertainment. By implication, Malaya was thereby committed to an ascertainment process prior to the formation of Malaya — but only by implication, not by specific word. She was committed also by her reaffirmation of the principle of self-determination, but the Malayan view was that this principle had already been honoured in the Borneo territories by the political processes of the two preceding years. The Malayan government could plausibly assert, in fact, that it was not specifically committed in any way to refrain from proceeding with the necessary constitutional processes towards the establishment of Malaysia until an ascertainment had found Borneo opinion to be in favour of Malaysia — although it would have been more tactful politically not to argue along these lines. A Malayan might even have argued (and Ghazali on 30 August did assert) that Malaya had not undertaken that she would not establish Malaysia until and unless the ascertainment was completed and found favourable to her; the undertaking to bring in the UN Secretary General to conduct an ascertainment had been agreed upon only to ensure that Indonesia and the Philippines would 'welcome' Malaysia — it was not a legal condition of its establishment. Obviously no Malayan government could have conceded *that* in any event, no matter how confident it felt about the outcome. On the other hand it would be rather disingenuous to argue the Malaysian case on purely legalistic grounds based solely on the text of the Manila Accord. Although Malaya's commitment to accept an ascertainment mission was not clearly spelled out, it was more than just a *quid pro quo* for the promise of a 'welcome' to Malaysia by Indonesia and the Philippines. (There was, for instance, the juxtaposed reference to 'self-determination'.) The text was deliberately vague, as agreements often have to be, if they are to prove acceptable for home consumption; after all, the Foreign Ministers were merely feeling their way towards amicable agreement on certain general principles which their Heads of State still had to negotiate in detail.

What implications did the signatories intend to be read into the text of the agreement? It cannot be denied that Malaya accepted some commitment to an ascertainment process before the formation of Malaysia in return for the promise of a peaceful welcome: the question at issue hinges around the terms of her commitment. This can be inferred fairly confidently from what we know about the course of the negotiations at the Foreign Ministers' conference. On the Malayan side Razak was adamant at the June conference that Malaysia Day could not be postponed to allow for a full-scale plebiscite in the Borneo territories, although he was prepared to contemplate some limited process of confirmation of the wishes of the people there. Subandrio did not press him very hard on this issue: there was no reference in the Accord to the relevance for this purpose of General Assembly Resolution 1541, which was later to become a major bone of contention at the Summit meeting. Subandrio was apparently content to gain general acceptance of the principle, leaving the details to be negotiated by Soekarno in July. He seems to have been primarily concerned in June to win Razak's confidence through a display of cordiality and apparent frankness, appealing to him for help from Kuala Lumpur in enabling the Indonesian government to drop confrontation. The very friendly ('brotherly') atmosphere of the conference,[10] engendered partly by the new enthusiasm for Maphilindo, was very different from the strain evident at the later Summit conference. It would all have helped to convince Razak that the advantages of co-operating with the Indonesian government would outweigh any slight risks there might be in trying to humour Soekarno. His continued hostility to the new federation would not just be a potential threat which could become dangerous if another revolt broke out in Brunei or Sarawak; it could be also a positive inducement to potential insurgents to take desperate action in the hope of precipitating her intervention before it was too late.

In his closing speech, Subandrio described the conference as 'not just good, but very, very good' and he spoke enthusiastically of 'more or less complete agreement on all questions which affect the interests and attention' of the three countries.[11] Soekarno is said to have been very pleased, also, when Subandrio reported to him in Rome on the outcome. We can only speculate whether they were pleased because the Manila Accord provided the basis for a face-saving gesture if they had to abandon the confrontation policy, or whether they saw possibilities that Soekarno could use the Accord as a lever to push the Tunku further in the direction of a meaningful ascertainment when they met at the Summit conference in July. (Probably it suited them to keep both options open.) On the other hand, the PKI was distinctly unhappy about the communique, charging Subandrio with lack of candour in revealing just what he had agreed to in Manila.[12] How could Indonesia's undying opposition to Malaysia be reconciled, it asked, with Subandrio's assertion that 'more or less complete agreement had been reached on *all* matters which affect our interests'? Had the formation of Malaysia been forestalled, or not? Were the people of Sabah to be allowed to determine their own future, or join the Philippines if they so preferred? Aidit queried the reference to 'mutual understanding' (*pengertian bersama*) in clause 1, for the PKI was still very suspicious of the Philippines for its '*ja Bandung, ja SEATO*' attitude and for its subservience to US Imperialism, which the PKI was trying to brand as 'enemy no 1' for Indonesia.[13]

The PKI Central Committee issued a policy statement about Malaysia on 20 June which ran entirely contrary to the implications of the Manila Accord. It even opposed the suggestion that an expression of self-determination might be sought in the Borneo territories, arguing that the people of North Kalimantan had made their choice on 8 December 1962 (Azahari's rebellion): if a plebiscite was to be *imposed* there, certain conditions must be guaranteed — and the conditions it laid down were obviously unacceptable to the British and Malayan governments.[14]

Strangely, however, the PKI did not react very strongly at this stage against the Maphilindo proposal, at least in public, although it must have been seriously alarmed by the anti-Chinese implications of this new policy development and it certainly regarded Maphilindo as an American inspired move to draw Indonesia into her orbit. Little was said about it in *Harian Rakjat* until mid-July, when Aidit seized the opportunity provided by Soekarno's outburst against the London Agreement to argue strongly that a Summit conference was now out of the question.[15] There was no basis for a Maphilindo confederation, he said: mere similarity of race was not a sufficient reason for it, especially when there were such differences of domestic and foreign policy.

The cordial mood prevailing in June lasted only until the signing of the London Agreement on 9 July, by which it was finally settled that Malaysia would come into being on 31 August. Soekarno's reaction to this was so vehement that earlier hopes of averting Indonesia's hostility to the new federation suddenly receded again. In a speech next day he attacked the Tunku as a man who did not keep his promises. The holding of a Summit conference was now in doubt, he added, alleging that it had been clearly agreed at the Foreign Ministers' conference that the wishes of the people of North Kalimantan should be investigated before Malaysia was established. His attack on the London Agreement implied that the Manila Accord had ruled out any further steps by the Malayans towards the establishment of Malaysia prior to the Summit meeting, an interpretation which could not conceivably have been conceded by Razak and was hardly compatible with theories that the purpose of the Manila talks was simply to find a face-saving formula. By his apparent denial that he meant any such thing, Soekarno left everyone guessing just what his purposes really were.

The Indonesian press and public responded quickly to this signal of a new line towards Malaysia. The PKI now argued strongly that there was no longer any basis for a Summit meeting. It began to stress the slogan '*Ganjang Malaysia*', which was later to be taken up by Soekarno after the final break in September. But the very urgency of PKI assertions that it would be dangerous for Indonesia to become involved again in the Manila talks betrays a fear that this had still not been ruled out, that Soekarno had simply not yet made up his mind.[16] The reaction in other quarters made this abundantly clear. A meeting of the main executive organs of government (the MPPR, KOTI and MPN) on 15 July expressed support for the President's ambiguous statements of 10 and 11 July in characteristically ambiguous fashion, leaving entirely to the President's discretion the decision whether or not he should attend the Summit. The various political and mass organizations did likewise, taking their cue from the President and not daring, except in the case of the PKI, to try to anticipate or determine his decision.[17] For nearly a fortnight, almost until the eve of the proposed Summit meeting, no one could be sure whether Soekarno was prepared to attend or not. Even the Filipino hosts seemed apprehensive and uncertain.[18] Soekarno had not actually said he would *not* attend the Summit, merely that it was in doubt. It was up to the Tunku to show by his actions whether the conference would be held, he added, a few days after his initial outburst. When it came to the point, of course, he did finally announce that he would attend, even though the Tunku had given no further sign of any willingness to change his stand.

How are we to explain these erratic changes of course in July? It is sometimes suggested, although barely credible, that Soekarno was taken by surprise when the Malaya-Singapore-UK negotiations were brought to a successful conclusion in the London Agreement and that his angry reaction was due to pique at the realization of defeat. Soekarno and Subandrio may have been seriously hoping that the tense Malaya-Singapore negotiations of June-July would break down entirely; hence it is possible that they were grievously disappointed when the last major obstacle in the way of Malaysia's creation was surmounted. (The Sarawak elections had finally ruled out the possibility of a SUPP victory there.)[19] Indonesian press reports on the intense bargaining that preceded the London Agreement frequently exaggerated the likelihood of a breakdown, which makes one wonder how much similar wishful thinking prevailed in official circles, or how accurately Soekarno had been informed about the whole matter.[20] More plausible is the hypothesis that it suited Soekarno tactically to switch to a harder line, partly to keep everyone guessing what his real intentions were (domestic critics as well as his Malayan adversaries), partly to unsettle and unnerve the Tunku before the Summit meeting, partly to signal to the world that confrontation was not being abandoned for the sake of a mere 'gesture' on the matter of the Borneo ascertainment. In other words, if he were to attend the Summit, it must not be presupposed that he was there merely to devise a face-saving formula. Soekarno may have felt that the atmosphere of cordiality established at the Tokyo and Manila meetings was being taken too much for granted, as if Indonesia's acquiescence in Malaysia's formation would not involve any substantive concessions from the Malayan side.

Moreover, Soekarno was faced at home by widespread hostility to the government's new course because of the sharp price rises and severe liquidity crisis brought about by the stabilization programme and an intensely suspicious PKI which was eager to take advantage of his embarrassments. The PKI was charging Subandrio with evasiveness about what had been agreed at Manila, hinting that American pressure was being applied to make Indonesia drop her opposition to Malaysia behind the veil of double-talk at Manila, and that the US was pressing her into 'reactionary' economic policies as the price to be paid for the foreign aid needed for the stabilization programme. Thus it would be unwise for Soekarno to appear completely committed to a right-wing course. In mid-July he found it expedient to throw out yet another hint that a cabinet reshuffle (i.e. a *Nasakom* cabinet) might be in the offing. Whether it was to protect his flanks from political sniping, or a mere blind to keep the PKI guessing, the 10 July statement strengthened his hand domestically precisely because it upset predictions that confrontation was about to be quietly abandoned.

The war of nerves against Malaysia in these weeks was a curious interlude. It was intensified by a Navy announcement on 16 July that an *Armada Siaga* ('Alert Fleet') had been formed 'especially to oppose Malaysia', followed on 26 July by joint naval-air manoeuvres in the South China Sea and Malacca Straits which were described as organized 'on a war footing'.[21] Nasution also made some very fiery speeches (which, however, got far less prominence in the Djakarta press than overseas) in the course of a visit to Pontianak, Singkawang and Sanggau, in the West Kalimantan border region, only 40 km. from Sarawak.

We must oppose Malaysia because it represents a direct threat to Indonesia. For the areas to be included in Malaysia have been, and still are, bases for foreign subversive activities in the economic, political and cultural fields, which openly and constantly threaten to eat away the Indonesian Revolution .... We must defeat Malaysia with the Trikora spirit .... Be prepared for general mobilization: continue to help the people of North Borneo, if necessary train them and give them the equipment they need. The final victory will be decided in North Borneo itself and by the patriots of North Borneo who will never surrender.[22]

Despite the vagueness and ambiguity of this speech, which made it impossible to infer just how much or how little it portended, the underlying note of hostility to Malaysia was entirely out of character with the Maphilindo spirit. Were the Indonesians hoping to provoke the Tunku into a refusal to attend the Summit meeting, so that they could justify the maintenance of confrontation by blaming him for the breakdown? It is quite possible — although, oddly enough, no military excursions across the Borneo frontier occurred during the latter part of July.[23] Perhaps all the sound and fury was purely 'symbolic', an elaborate facade to make confrontation seem more real than it was. But it was not quite as simple as that. A contretemps with the British over the expulsion of two Indonesian diplomats from Jesselton on 19 July for subversive activities helped to aggravate matters[24] by providing an opportunity for vehement anti-British speeches and a small demonstration outside the British embassy. Finally, a '*ganjang Malaysia*' rally was announced for 27 July, at which Soekarno was to reveal whether or not he was going to attend the Summit conference and indicate what actions were appropriate for the next stage of confrontation. His speech on that occasion was truculent and defiant towards the Tunku and the British, the theme being that confrontation would be continued in the conference halls of the Maphilindo Summit meeting as in all other fields. But the essential fact of the matter turned out to be that he had decided to attend after all.[25]

The purely tactical consideration of alarming and unnerving the Tunku in advance of the Summit meeting may also have played a part. Hard bargaining on the precise nature of the Borneo ascertainment still lay ahead, so Soekarno's chilly and cavalier attitude to the conference, so much in contrast to the cordiality of the earlier meetings, may well have been calculated to serve notice to the Tunku that he was not going to be let off with a mere outward charade in Borneo — or, at least, not without paying his pound of flesh in return. No doubt Soekarno's mercurial temperament also had a good deal to do with these sudden changes of attitude, but there was a great deal of method in his moodiness.

THE MANILA SUMMIT

Because of the warlike sounds coming from Indonesia, the Summit conference opened under gloomy auspices. President Soekarno had shown little sign of any change in attitude since his denunciation of the Tunku earlier in the month, except insofar as he had agreed to attend the Summit. He still appeared to be in stormy mood and Indonesia's spokesman struck a cold note when he said on arrival in Manila: 'We are not doing any confronting now. President Soekarno is quietly waiting to see what will happen tomorrow. If tomorrow's session shows the Malays are continuing to violate the spirit of the earlier Manila and Tokyo accords, we will pack our bags and go.'[26] In effect, this put the Tunku on notice that if he wanted the Summit meeting to lead anywhere, he would have to make the first concessions.

At the formal opening of the conference on Tuesday, 30 July, only President Macapagal spoke, Soekarno and the Tunku having waived the right to do so at this stage. It was an ominous sign of the tension between them, even though some encouragement could be found in the fact that both men were reluctant to take any risks of aggravating it by uttering provocative words in public. But next morning the atmosphere had changed dramatically by the time the three Heads of Government got down to business in their first closed session. Before the meeting the Tunku paid a brief courtesy call on President Soekarno at his residence (ostensibly to 'clarify his misunderstandings of the London Agreement') and a more conciliatory note was immediately injected into the entire proceedings.[27] A 'cordial and brotherly atmosphere' was reported in the communique issued after the meeting, in which the three leaders approved the Manila Accord agreed upon at the Foreign Ministers' meeting in June, which included the reference to Maphilindo: they also reaffirmed their determination to establish the closest cooperation between their three countries. Paragraph 10 of the Manila Accord (see Appendix I) had envisaged that the opinion of the people of the Borneo territories regarding Malaysia would be 'ascertained by an independent and impartial authority, the Secretary General of the UN or his representative', so the communique went on to reveal that 'the Secretary General of the United Nations has been informed of this decision in order to advise him of the role he would be expected to play in implementing the relevant clauses of the agreement'. U Thant's representative at the conference, Mr. Alfred Mackenzie, the

Canadian head of the UN technical aid mission in Manila, had been called in towards the end of the meeting and 'I was told to inform U Thant to carry out the request outlined in article 10 of the Foreign Ministers' agreement. I did accordingly.' It would be interesting to know in just what terms his cable was drafted. One report mentioned that it sought a reply from U Thant on whether and how he would conduct an ascertainment in accordance with that agreement and, in particular, how long it would take.[28] Another added that the cable made reference to self-determination 'in the letter and spirit of UN General Assembly Resolution 1541' — a highly contentious point since that resolution strongly implied the desirability of some form of plebiscite or referendum.[29] Much of the drama of the next few days was to hinge around that issue and around the three cables sent by U Thant in reply to the requests and information he received from Manila through Mr. Mackenzie.

It is necessary to trace the course of the Manila negotiations in some detail for the light they throw on the intentions of the three signatories to the vague compromise finally embodied in paragraph 4 of the Joint Statement. But before we plunge into the details, it may be helpful to summarize the chronology of developments after the relatively optimistic session of the three Heads of Government on the Wednesday morning. At that stage it was expected that only three days of negotiation would be necessary and a formal concluding ceremony would be held on the Saturday. The Heads of Government were to convene again on Thursday morning, following a Foreign Ministers' meeting on Wednesday afternoon to draft the cable to U Thant. However it was decided at that meeting to postpone the Thursday session of the Heads until the afternoon, presumably to allow time for U Thant's reply; later, it was again postponed until the Friday. Signs of strain began to appear again on the Thursday. The British Charge d'Affaires, who called on the Tunku and Mackenzie in the morning, did not help matters when he let it be known that 31 August was 'unalterable' as the date for Malaysia Day.[30]

This prompted an attack on the British by Ganis Harsono for interfering in the affairs of the Maphilindo countries. Indonesian and Filipino suspicions that the British were trying to wreck the conference and undermine the 'spirit of Maphilindo' played a big part in colouring their interpretations of events at that time. On Thursday, the Foreign Ministers spent a long day in conference, towards the end of which U Thant's first cable was received. A hint of disagreement over the terms of the ascertainment became discernible after the meeting, when an exuberant announcement by Lopez, the Philippines Foreign Minister, that 'we have completed discussions on the clauses on Malaysia and North Borneo' in the Manila Accord (clauses 10–13, dealing with self-determination and the Philippines claim on Sabah) was denied by his Malayan counterpart, Ghazali.[31] Discussions on the foreign military bases had also begun to create friction, with Subandrio repeating Indonesia's objections to the Anglo-Malaysian defence provisions of the London Agreement on Malaysia — although this issue seems at no point to have become as critical a problem as the

Borneo assessment was. Friday was a day of crisis, during which Malaya's stand hardened, although the three Heads of Government met for a second time to sign the eloquent generalities of the Manila Declaration establishing Maphilindo. An extension of the conference until Sunday was announced. U Thant's second cable, in reply to a request for clarification of his first message, did little to resolve the deadlock that was looming. On Friday evening Mackenzie phoned Narasimhan in New York to inform him that the conference would collapse unless some alternative suggestion was forthcoming from U Thant. Next day, U Thant's third cable arrived, suggesting a different type of assessment of Borneo opinion on Malaysia of the kind that was finally undertaken, requiring a much shorter time than his earlier proposals implied and clearly not entailing a plebiscite. This did not immediately solve the problem, for further hard bargaining continued right through until Sunday night, but it transformed the picture as far as Malaya was concerned, since it provided the basis for a compromise which the Tunku could accept without committing himself to a referendum. The final compromise reached between the Tunku and Dr. Subandrio on the Sunday evening, after a long meeting of the Foreign Ministers, amounted to an agreement by Malaya to permit some slight delay in the formation of Malaysia in return for Indonesia's abandonment of her previous demand for a full plebiscite.

Until the participants in the Manila Conference reveal the full story with corroborating documents, it will not be possible to establish with finality just what they intended by their adoption of the ambiguous wording of paragraph 4 of the Joint Statement, around which so much controversy has since raged. But we can infer a good deal about the course of the negotiations, and hence the nature of the compromise reached, from a careful reconstruction with the few fragments of information which have become available publicly.[32] We must begin by considering the overall bargaining position of the two main protagonists.

It is possible that Soekarno's sharp change of attitude on the second day was merely part of a subtle war of nerves against the Malayans; after keeping them apprehensive and uncertain until the eleventh hour with threats to boycott the conference, his abrupt change of the mood may have been intended to stampede the Tunku into offering concessions. It was probably also due to Soekarno's realization of the strong negotiating position he was in if the Tunku showed himself willing to make some concessions for the sake of allaying Indonesia's hostility towards Malaysia, as he did. For the Tunku had little choice but to try and humour Soekarno, even though he could not afford to give much away on the two key issues, the form of ascertainment to be undertaken and the postponement of Malaysia Day. His only alternative would have been to repudiate, in effect, paragraph 10 of the Manila Accord and face Indonesia's inevitable hostility. It was worth his while to pay some small price if Soekarno could be induced to settle for a face-saving formula which he could present to the Indonesian people as a vindication of Indonesia's demand for self-determination in the Borneo territories. (A constant difficulty for the Malayans at this stage was to decide whether Soekarno did just want a face-saving formula with which he could abandon confrontation — which the Indonesians assured many observers, including George Kahin, was their object[33] — or whether he was looking also towards more concrete objectives, the elimination of British bases and 'imperialist' influence, perhaps even the frustration of the Malaysia scheme, as the British officials suspected.) All that Soekarno needed to do in these circumstances was to commit the Tunku as firmly as possible to the doctrine of self-determination for the Borneo colonies. For this purpose he had a valuable instrument at hand in United Nations General Assembly Resolution 1541, since neither Malaya nor even the British could outrightly repudiate it. The Tunku could answer (and presumably did) that the requirements of the Resolution had already been met through elections in Sarawak and Sabah, but the onus was still on him to suggest how the ascertainment mentioned in the Manila Accord was to be carried out by U Thant.

Malaya obviously wanted nothing more than a cursory and minimal form of ascertainment and was resisting the attempt to specify it by reference to Resolution 1541, which would have committed U Thant to a more comprehensive form of plebiscite. It is significant in this regard that the formula finally adopted did not call straightforwardly for an ascertainment of the wishes of the people of North Borneo 'in accordance with' the Resolution, but merely 'within the context of (Resolution 1541) ... by a fresh approach, which in the opinion of the Secretary General is necessary to ensure complete compliance with the principle of self-determination within the requirements embodied in Principle 9, taking into consideration ... etc.' Such flaccid and woolly language, which contrasts sharply with the relatively crisp sentences of the other clauses of the Joint Statement and Manila Declaration (see Appendix I), can only be seen as intended deliberately to blur the issue so that all parties could read into it what they wished. Soekarno must have known what the Tunku (and U Thant) had in mind when he agreed to that singularly unhappy piece of prose, after a lengthy process of hard bargaining.

The Tunku's negotiating position was an extremely difficult one. He had to be conciliatory enough to draw President Soekarno away from his initial unfriendly stand without giving in to any demands which might imperil Malaysia's formation. At the Wednesday session he made a considerable concession in agreeing to leave the detailed form of an ascertainment to U Thant to propose, without imposing specific conditions about what was acceptable to Malaysia. Implicitly this meant an abandonment of his insistence that Malaysia must be formed on 31 August. When questions were asked at a press conference later in the day about what would happen if U Thant decided there should be a referendum or that the formation of Malaysia should be postponed, the Tunku refused to say more than 'these questions are now in the hands of the Secretary General. We have now committed ourselves to this agreement and we cannot wriggle out of it.' It is hardly surprising that fears were aroused in British circles and in Singapore that the Tunku had been beguiled by the wily

Soekarno and was giving away too much for the sake of Pan-Malay brotherhood. But such a view did the Tunku scant justice. If he had merely dug his toes in from the outset, the conference would have broken down and he would have been cast in the role of villain. It later became obvious that he was not prepared to acquiesce in a lengthy ascertainment (in fact not even able to, since he could not commit the British — a consideration which must have been known to U Thant when he made his suggestions). A great deal was going to depend on the way in which U Thant replied to the request made to him. *The Times* reported that the Tunku believed (having in mind the earlier visits by Mr. Narasimhan to Borneo and Kuala Lumpur) that U Thant would not propose a referendum, but only a cursory assessment of political opinion in the Borneo territories. The Tunku was personally quite confident that any enquiry in Borneo would find in favour of Malaysia, more confident than the British authorities, according to some accounts. But a lengthy postponement of Malaysia Day would have involved too many incalculable risks for him to be able to contemplate. Moreover the British were showing great reluctance to accept any delay at all.[34]

U Thant's first cable in reply to the request from Manila to conduct an ascertainment did imply a very lengthy postponement. It was a full and rather literal reply to the question addressed to him as to the time he would need to conduct an assessment of opinion in Borneo 'in the spirit and letter' of Resolution 1541. He spelled out the implications of this request in detail — that some form of plebiscite was implied, that the General Assembly would have to be consulted, that action could be taken only on the request of the three governments concerned, that the administering authority (Britain) would have to approve, that the cost would have to be borne by the parties and that the problems of organizing such a mission, the size needed and the nature of the terrain meant that the result would probably not be known before December.[35] Obviously it was almost out of the question for the Tunku to accept such a long delay, pressed as he was by the promptings of Borneo politicians and the fact that the British still held authority there. He stated firmly on the Thursday (perhaps to refute earlier reports that he was wavering) that Malaysia must be established by 31 August and that a referendum was not acceptable; only within those limits was he prepared to allow some form of United Nations enquiry for the sake of amity with his neighbours.

A second cable from U Thant received on the following day was basically similar to the first in that it still implied a plebiscite, but it 'raised hopes by modifying the time required, since U Thant had decided that it would not be necessary to wait for authorization by the General Assembly before undertaking the enquiry and believed that six weeks might suffice to carry it out'.[36] This would have brought the delay down to about a fortnight, which the Tunku might have felt able to accept — and eventually did. But the form of the ascertainment was still unacceptable to him. The Malayan delegates were firmly resisting any commitment to a full-scale referendum. Nevertheless, Lopez again announced optimistically that progress towards a settlement was being made and the two extensions to the conference testify that neither party wanted to see the talks break down. Various forms of self-determination were being discussed, said Lopez after the Friday evening session. It was at this stage of the proceedings that Mackenzie reported to New York on the impossibility of reaching agreement on the basis of a referendum, as proposed in U Thant's first two cables. As a result, the third cable from U Thant, received on the Saturday, opened up new horizons by proposing a more limited form of enquiry along the line that was finally adopted.

U Thant's third cable did not immediately resolve the deadlock, but it seems to have significantly changed the strategy of the negotiations. Whereas the first two cables had proposed a procedure which put the Tunku in a defensive and embarrassing position, since he could hardly accept them, but would have incurred the blame for wrecking the conference if he had flatly refused to continue the negotiations, the boot was now on the other foot. He could agree to the new procedure in the confidence that it would entail very little risk of upsetting Malaysia. (Lopez is said to have been extremely angry at Mackenzie's action which brought forth the third cable.) On the Saturday night, Ghazali commented optimistically about the prospects of reaching an agreement, although further hard bargaining continued until Sunday night.[37] From the point of view of Soekarno and Macapagal, there was now little to be gained on the issue of self-determination except a procedure for saving face. It has been suggested that that was all they wanted from the start, but I do not think this hypothesis fits their behaviour in the earlier phase of the conference when they were angling for much bigger fish. It seems more likely that Soekarno's primary aim was to draw the Tunku into a commitment to some form of self-determination process which would at least delay Malaysia's formation and perhaps either drive a wedge between the Malayan and British governments or even frustrate the formation of Malaysia in some way. U Thant's first two cables, by presupposing conformity to General Assembly Resolution 1541, helped to serve Soekarno's purposes excellently. The third did not, and Soekarno was left with the choice of accepting a 'face-saving' form of enquiry or allowing the conference to collapse fruitlessly. But the latter alternative would have gained nothing and would have crushed the Maphilindo spirit at birth, whereas the former still held out some possibilities of being turned to Indonesia's advantage. Even if Malaysia could not be prevented, the Maphilindo connection could perhaps be utilized to draw the Malayans away from their dependence on the British.

Negotiations continued throughout the weekend before the last details of the Joint Statement were finally settled by the Heads of Governments at breakfast on Monday morning, only a few hours before the formal closing ceremony. Although on Saturday night only one clause of the Joint Statement remained to be settled (obviously paragraph 4, since the other contentious issue of the bases had been settled by this time), the *Manila Chronicle* reported that the meeting was still bogged down throughout the Sunday on the manner in which the ascertainment was to be conducted. Lopez favoured a 'cursory survey', but the composition of the survey teams remained a key problem, since Indonesia was now pressing for the inclusion of representatives of the three Maphilindo partners as full members.[38] Neither side appears to have given way completely on the crucial points of disagreement (the length and nature of the ascertainment) until the Tunku and Subandrio reached a compromise on Sunday evening. After the last Foreign Ministers' meeting that night to draft the request to U Thant to conduct the mission, Lopez characterized the ascertainment as 'neither a referendum nor an electoral commission, but something of both'. Next morning, after some minor last-minute adjustments, agreement was reached on paragraph 4 and the Joint Statement was signed.

The tortuous ambiguities of paragraph 4 of the Joint Statement show the influence of the hard-fought struggle to reach agreement in drafting it. For this reason we must be wary about the inferences that can be drawn from interpretations of the Manila Agreements as merely a formula for giving Soekarno and Macapagal a face-saving way out of their embarrassing political predicaments or as the 'true and genuine product of an Asian co-operative mind' embodying some deeper wisdom not perceived by outsiders. This part of their agreements was not easily reached and was not particularly desired by either party, except perhaps the Philippines. Its drafting was, in fact, a masterpiece of evasion and compromise. The Manila Agreements contained no specific assertion that the formation of Malaysia should be contingent upon a favourable verdict by the UN Mission, nor any specifically binding commitments upon Indonesia and the Philippines, except those entailed in the vague generalities of the Manila Accord that they would 'welcome' Malaysia if the UN Mission's report was favourable. From the fact that the task of the UN Mission was stated very vaguely in the introductory sentence ('... should ascertain ... the wishes of the people ... within the context of General Assembly resolution 1541 ... by a fresh approach ....') but was very specifically spelled out in the instructions about investigation of the Sabah and Sarawak elections, it can only be inferred that the latter was the agreed purpose of the Mission, even though its terms of reference were defined rather open-endedly so that the reference to the General Assembly Resolution could also be included. U Thant proceeded to interpret it this way in his instructions to the Mission and no protest was made at the time by Indonesia or the Philippines as to the adequacy of the terms of reference he gave it. Indonesians were later to argue, however, that a 'fresh approach was not apparent in the whole operation. This fresh approach should have ensured complete compliance with the principle of self-determination within the requirements embodied in principle IX of the General Assembly Resolution 1541 (XV).'[40] It is difficult to see how the words of paragraph 4 can be made to sustain this criticism in view of the circumstances that have been outlined. The reference to 'a fresh approach' was never spelled out — did it mean a different kind of approach to that of the Cobbold Commission, or that implied by the election results? — and in any case the words 'in the opinion of the Secretary General' clearly left its interpretation to U Thant, who was also to determine the criteria applicable to the issue of self-determination in Borneo. Since the words of this clause were unquestionably chosen with the greatest of care, it can hardly be claimed that the three signatories intended any other interpretation of those obscure phrases.

Filipinos and Indonesians later told me that certain provisions of the Manila Agreements were not carried out as had been agreed at the conference and, when pressed to specify, asserted that there were unstated understandings behind the ambiguous compromise committed to paper. I have been unable to obtain from them any satisfactory evidence for this assertion and it seems to me entirely incompatible with the course of the negotiations and the way the compromise was reached. The interpretation of the Joint Statement was left entirely to U Thant, who had been thoroughly informed about the course of the negotiations and the kind of ascertainment he was expected to carry out. Although the Indonesians and Filipinos had some valid grounds for complaint about the way the British and Malayan governments interpreted the Manila Agreement, they cannot justifiably argue that the UN survey was not carried out as agreed at the meeting. When they later cried: 'Let us go back to the Manila Agreements', what they meant was 'Let us return to our interpretation of what the Manila Agreements meant.'

One other aspect of the Manila Agreements which attracted great attention at the time, but which appears to have aroused far less argument at Manila, was the question of foreign bases and the security of the region. After agreeing that responsibility for the peace, security and independence of the area 'lies primarily in the hands of the Government and peoples of the countries concerned', the three Heads of Government went on in paragraph 11 of the Joint Statement to agree that

... foreign bases — temporary in nature — should not be allowed to be used directly or indirectly to subvert the national independence of any of the three countries. In accordance with the principle enunciated in the Bandung Declaration, the three countries will abstain from the use of arrangements of collective defence to serve the particular interests of any of the big powers.

The qualification 'temporary in nature' was a piece of transparent sophistry, for the Philippines-American bases agreement ran for 99 years from 1946 and did not at that time include any provision for prior revocability, as the Malayan-British defence agreement did, even though the latter specified no time limit. But on this issue the Philippines and Malaysia had similar interests in not being committed to any binding obligations on the length of their defence agreements, while Indonesia was apparently content with this vague commitment. The mutual assurances that foreign bases should not be used to subvert the independence of another Maphilindo partner were a more solid achievement; reassuring Indonesia on this point had been one of the original aims of the whole series of Manila talks, although by August it was rather overshadowed by the other issues in dispute.

At the closing session of the conference each of the three Heads spoke briefly in terms which illustrated their very divergent views on their region's place in the wider world. The Tunku uttered one of his customary denunciations of Communism ('a religion ... more destructive than Imperialism'), while Soekarno sat unsmiling and angry, visibly annoyed. Then he spoke briefly, without a prepared text: 'You cannot escape history now that Maphilindo has been formed ... now that Asia, Africa, Latin America and the Socialist nations will congregate together into a great force — the new emerging forces fighting against imperialism, colonialism, exploitation ....' Only Macapagal kept safely to the middle of the road with enthusiastic bromides about an Asian 'declaration of independence' from outside interests.

MAPHILINDO

The idea of Maphilindo blossomed suddenly and briefly in the weeks following the Manila Summit. Much talk was heard about 'the Manila spirit' and about *musjawarah Maphilindo* as the basis for a new, cordial relationship between the three nations of Malay origin. Even the war of words between Indonesia and Malaysia died down a little, at least at the higher levels (although border incursions continued), while the UN Mission set about its task of ascertaining the wishes of the people of Borneo. This interval of Indian summer was short-lived, however, for the resumption of confrontation with increased intensity after the creation of Malaysia on 16 September dissipated the basis of mutual trust on which the Maphilindo spirit depended. Yet even then Maphilindo was not entirely abandoned. Throughout the first half of 1964 the notion again came into vogue as the possible basis for a settlement of the conflict ('back to the Manila Agreements') and for future cooperation within the region. Until the Tokyo Summit meeting of June 1964 revealed the hopelessness of such a settlement, the Maphilindo idea exercised a beguiling influence on discussions of the region's future, not only in the countries concerned, but also in America, Australia and even Britain.

Like many of the more fruitful ideas that have swayed the course of human history, Maphilindo was important more for the significance that people read into it, both its supporters and its critics, than for what it explicitly proclaimed. Malay brotherhood, which was its core, is in itself no more reliable a basis for enduring political unity than Arab nationalism has proved to be, or the idea of European union. We can take with a fairly considerable grain of salt the enthusiastic platform oratory (most of it originating from the Filipinos, rather than from Indonesians or Malaysians) such as Macapagal's glowing vision that 'in Maphilindo and through Maphilindo, nourished constantly by their vision and enterprise, the Malay peoples shall be borne upon the true, the vast, the irresistible wave of the future'. Maphilindo could, potentially, be made to exercise a strong and wide appeal to people of Malay blood. But what brought the idea so suddenly into prominence was neither mass enthusiasm for it (which the

Malayan and the Indonesian governments barely endeavoured to foster) nor its credibility as an effective political association, so much as its momentary usefulness to the governments concerned in the political manoeuvring of 1963–4 as a visionary alternative to the existing political arrangements of the region. The facile generalizations with which it was embellished can easily give a misleading impression of what it entailed (for example, the description of it as a 'confederation') unless we notice just what use was and was not being made of it by the governments concerned.

In the Philippines, the Pan-Malay aspect of Maphilindo made a powerful appeal to politicians who wished to give a more 'Asian' cast to their foreign policy and develop closer ties with their neighbours. In Kuala Lumpur, it held a similar fascination (which lasted right through the period of confrontation and bitterness towards Indonesia) among Malay politicians who often looked upon Maphilindo as a means of counterbalancing the economic and political power of the local Chinese. Among the latter, however, the idea aroused either intense repugnance or, at the least, grave uneasiness — the latter even among undeniable anti-communists such as the leaders of the MCA in Malaya and Lee Kuan Yew in Singapore.[41] To the Peking government it was objectionable on various counts, as being both racially and politically anti-Chinese in character, as well as American-inspired. Both the Russian Communists and the PKI took the same view and opposed it equally. Paradoxically, the British too were by no means enthusiastic about Maphilindo at first, seeing it as a threat to the maintenance of their influence in their former colony. In Indonesian official circles, the anti-Chinese argument was muted somewhat, at least in public utterances, for Maphilindo was regarded primarily as a means of ensuring that responsibility for the defence and security of South-East Asia should be solely in the hands of the people of the area; in Djakarta, continued reliance on foreign troops was regarded as intolerable and no other basis for a regional security system had any chance of acceptance. In Washington, however, Maphilindo was welcomed for both these reasons, and more. Although it was not immediately clear just what Maphilindo was to mean in concrete terms of a political and functional association, it must sooner or later be made to mean something, many commentators argued, it must grow into an organic unity (an embryonic forerunner of the regional associations which were emerging in other parts of the world) if an orderly state system was to maintain itself in South-East Asia and ward off by its own efforts the threat of Chinese expansion.[42] Since the colonial period was at last ending and power in the region would henceforth depend on the efforts and strength of the people of the region, some such arrangement as Maphilindo seemed to offer the best hope of providing a framework within which the largest and most restless nation in South-East Asia could be encouraged to exercise a constructive and peaceful influence — preferably in an anti-Communist, anti-Chinese direction. Both historicist necessity and wishful thinking seemed to point toward something like Maphilindo as a solution.

Actually the men who negotiated the Manila Accord were under no illusions about the immediate scope of Maphilindo. No surrender of sovereignty or independence was involved (clauses 6 and 7): all that was envisaged was 'machinery for frequent and regular consultation' on matters of mutual concern. National secretariats were to be set up, co-operating and co-ordinating with each other until a central secretariat could be established. The Heads of Governments and Foreign Ministers were to meet at least once a year for consultations. That was all Maphilindo meant; much less than a confederation, hardly even an alliance. (The three nations all intended to maintain their strikingly divergent foreign policies.) Even the Association of South-East Asian States, ASA, had been a little more specific in designating particular fields of regional cooperation in the economic sphere. Razak himself looked upon Maphilindo as a mere first step in drawing Indonesia towards something of a more concrete and positive nature, like ASA; Pelaez also seems to have been more interested in ASA than Maphilindo, although neither his successor as Foreign Secretary, Lopez, nor President Macapagal was so inclined.[43] Soekarno, for his part, rarely mentioned it in his public statements and did not attempt to build up the idea of *musjawarah Maphilindo* into anything more than a mere consultative machinery. This is not to say that he disregarded it or saw no value in it. It is said that he briefly contemplated using the Maphilindo relationship as a means of drawing the Tunku away from the British connection and into a closer commitment to his own anti-colonialist principles. He even held out the prospect that a second Summit meeting might be held in Kuala Lumpur itself during October (which would have meant his first official visit to Malaya).[44] Maphilindo could serve him as an instrument of policy which might be useful, without in any way deflecting Indonesia from her own independent and active foreign policy. His partners in Maphilindo needed him more than he needed them!

The racial implications of Maphilindo have attracted much attention both from those who were alarmed by or critical of them, like Lee Kuan Yew, as well as by its advocates who regarded the ethnic and cultural affinities between the three nations as powerful bonds of association. The former group had understandable grounds for apprehension: no matter how limited and vague the actual terms of the Maphilindo relationship might be, its very *raison d'être* as an association of Malay peoples would have helped to strengthen the arguments of those who wished to uphold Malay supremacy and privileges, simply because it implied that the *bumiputra*, the 'sons of the soil', or the original inhabitants, were to be regarded as having prior title and rights within the three countries. Chinese in Singapore and Malaya who were hoping for a 'Malaysian Malaysia' in which the special rights of Malays would be kept to a minimum could hardly be expected to welcome a close association with the Philippines and Indonesia, which imposed severe discriminations against Chinese — especially at a time when the May riots in Java were fresh in their minds. Maphilindo was undoubtedly an essentially racial concept beneath its veneer of polite phrases: its appeal to Malays came, in fact, largely from its anti-Chinese overtones, among which there was no clear distinction between the threat posed by Communist China and that of the Overseas Chinese.[45] It would be wrong to overstress this aspect as if there were no more to it than that, but we should not underestimate it, either.

On the other hand, it is easy to attach too much importance to the platform oratory of enthusiasts for Maphilindo who spoke of it as 'the fruition of the dreams of generations of Filipino and Malay heroes' or 'the beginning of a new golden age for people of Malay stock'.[46] Pan-Malay sentiment certainly exists within each of the three countries and, like Pan-Slavism in eastern Europe in the late nineteenth century, could easily become too explosive a factor in the internal politics of each to be taken lightly. But it is a diffuse sentiment, a visionary ideal rather than a primary determinant of national policies. Significantly, the Pan-Malay aspects of Maphilindo attracted much more enthusiasm in the Philippines than in Indonesia. President Macapagal and Foreign Secretary Lopez put great stress on it in 1963-4 because it suited their foreign policy strategies to do so: Macapagal later dropped it almost as suddenly as he had taken it up, when the prospects of gaining substantial results began to fade and a presidential election drew uncomfortably near. His objective had been to create a more distinctively 'Asian' foreign policy which would reveal a greater degree of Philippines' independence of the USA by drawing into a closer relationship with Indonesia: he was also hoping to strengthen his hand in prosecuting the North Borneo claim against Malaysia.[47] These were his dominant political considerations, though the stated rationale of his policies was far more wide-ranging and idealistic — to promote regional cooperation, to open up a larger common market for Philippines' manufacturers, to exert joint pressures against the 'British colonialists', to exercise a moderating influence on Indonesia as a counter to pressures towards Communism there, to forestall any possibility of Indonesian disruptive activities in the southern Philippines. Neither Soekarno nor Subandrio stressed the Pan-Malay aspects of Maphilindo nearly as strongly, even during the brief period of euphoric enthusiasm for Maphilindo at the time of Macapagal's visit to Indonesia in early 1964. To them the anti-colonialist implications of *musjawarah Maphilindo* and the doctrine of 'Asian solutions to Asian problems' were the useful and appealing aspect. Maphilindo was described by a Foreign Ministry spokesman as 'a concept which in the long run could find a synthesis between the world as a product of colonialism with the world as aspired to by the new states of Southeast Asia.'[48] Malay unity was rather played down, for they were chary of showing too much enthusiasm for a doctrine which was intensely disliked in Peking. Even among the lower-ranking officials who were, no doubt, much more susceptible to Pan-Malay appeals, it would hardly have appeared necessary to invoke a closer association with despised little nations like Malaya and the Philippines simply to deal with the Chinese problem. The Malaysian leaders, for their part, skirted the racial aspect of the relationship in public statements for obvious reasons of domestic politics, regarding Maphilindo mainly as a framework within which friendlier consultative relations might be sought and an amicable resolution of the dispute with Indonesia obtained.

Actually, Malay solidarity and the 'Maphilindo spirit' were not very strikingly in evidence during the Manila conferences of mid-1963, in spite of all the high-flown oratory on this theme. Soekarno barely referred to Maphilindo in his speech at the Summit conference, or in his Independence Day address on 17 August, which was always an important key to his political thinking. The clouds of uncertainty about Malaysia's formation still hung heavily over Kuala Lumpur and Djakarta during this period, for Soekarno's outburst of anger during July had dissipated whatever mutual confidence was generated at the Foreign Ministers' meeting. During August there was a lull in verbal attacks at the official level (though the border incursions in Sarawak continued), but only lip-service to Maphilindo was being expressed by government leaders in Indonesia and Malaya — and positive apprehension in Singapore and North Borneo. The significance of this has been overlooked by those writers who have simply noticed the Pan-Indonesian aspect of Maphilindo and assumed that it made a strong appeal there because of 'long-standing expansionist sentiments' among the leaders and recollections of past empires like Majapahit.[49] Official Indonesian statements about Maphilindo were nearly all directed towards showing that it entailed no change of policies for her and would strengthen her influence in the region. For instance, General Yani envisaged that 'within the framework of Maphilindo' the primary responsibility for the security and stability of South-East Asia now rested with Indonesia.[50] For him and other Indonesian military leaders that was apparently its main attraction, although the Malaysian and Filipino governments would hardly have welcomed this interpretation.

The PKI continued to be very suspicious of Maphilindo, however, fearing that its anti-Chinese implications would outweigh its anti-colonialist aspects: American enthusiasm for the concept and the perils of closer association with two such committed Western-bloc nations as the Philippines and Malaysia were quite enough to make the Communists apprehensive of this Trojan horse in their midst. According to Arnold Brackman, the PKI later modified its opposition to Maphilindo and adopted a 'wait and see' attitude: Karel Supit commented in November that 'the first question is: "What kind of Maphilindo?" If it adheres to Manipol, we are all for it ....' That was after the break with Malaysia and the collapse of the stabilization programme, however. The drift to the right in Indonesian policy had been checked, the PKI had won a famous victory and Indonesia's main foreign policy objective now was to woo Macapagal by responding to his enthusiasm for Maphilindo. The PKI could afford to take a more acquiescent view during 1964 when 'the Maphilindo spirit' and 'a return to the Manila Agreements' became important planks in Subandrio's policy of 'confronting' Malaysia diplomatically at the Bangkok and Tokyo conferences.[51] The Indonesian government also showed more enthusiasm for Maphilindo during the first half of the year, as it tried to persuade the Malaysia leaders to compromise on a negotiated settlement of the dispute between them. But when the strategy of negotiation was abandoned, after the failure of the Tokyo conference in June and Indonesia switched to a more aggressive policy of direct physical pressure on Malaysia, Maphilindo was sharply down-graded in most Indonesian official statements. It also became the more necessary to deny the racial overtones of Maphilindo as the Djakarta-Peking *entente* developed. By the end of 1964, Ganis Harsono was speaking almost contemptuously of Maphilindo as merely a Filipino idea intended to embroil Indonesia with the *Nekolim*.[52]

THE UN ASCERTAINMENT MISSION

As a step towards a settlement of the Indonesia-Malaysia dispute, the Manila Agreement raised as many questions as it resolved. Would an ascertainment Mission entail a lengthy delay before Malaysia could be established? Would the British be willing to accept the risks it involved? Would U Thant be able to accept the request made to him — and how would he interpret it as to the scope of the Mission's operations? What would happen if the Mission found against Malaysia?

Even if it could be assumed that the object of the Agreements was simply to save Indonesian face by providing a rubber-stamp operation in Borneo, the Mission posed some delicate problems of political manipulation for Tunku Abdul Rahman, who had to convince the British and the other constituent states of Malaysia, as well as critics in his own party, that the concession he had made in the hope of winning Indonesia's goodwill towards the new Federation was a wise one. At a press conference on his return from Manila he had to admit that Soekarno had not called off confrontation. Moreover, border incidents in Sarawak and hostile comments from military leaders and politicians in Djakarta continued throughout August, although Soekarno and Subandrio themselves said nothing contrary to the Manila mood. The Tunku said publicly on his return from Manila that he was prepared to postpone the birth of Malaysia for a few days, if necessary — but he still had to persuade the British government to agree to this, and Whitehall preserved a stony silence until U Thant revealed his plans in detail.[53]

U Thant agreed on 8 August to carry out the task he was charged with, provided that his decision on the outcome be accepted as final and provided that Britain, as the administering power, were agreeable. 'It is my understanding that neither the report of my representative nor my conclusions would be subject in any way to ratification or confirmation by any of the governments concerned', he wrote. The time-table would have to be worked out by his representative on the spot. He 'noted' also that observers had been deemed desirable by the three Manila signatories, but went on to say that the working teams would be exclusively responsible to him. Britain expressed her approval for this procedure next day and on 12 August U Thant announced the membership of the nine-man Mission led by Laurence V. Michelmore, an American who was former director of personnel in the UN secretariat, with G. V. Janacek, a Czech official at the UN, as his deputy. U Thant said that the Mission had the task of deciding:

a. whether or not Malaysia was a major issue in the last election in the regions concerned;
b. whether the electoral registers were properly compiled;
c. whether the votes were polled and counted properly;
d. whether the elections were really free and without coercion.[54]

The time needed to perform this task was obviously a matter of crucial importance. U Thant said he expected it to take about four weeks, which would have meant delaying Malaysia Day until the middle of September. This meant a longer postponement than the 'few days' earlier mentioned by the Tunku, but it was much less than the two or three months which the Indonesians allegedly anticipated. However, Ganis Harsono expressed Indonesia's 'full agreement' with U Thant's proposals and with the persons selected for the Mission, so it began to seem that all might, at last, be well for the successful implementation of the Manila Agreements. The absence of harsh reference to Malaysia in President Soekarno's annual Independence Day speech on 17 August seemed to presage smoother waters ahead and he himself abstained from hostile comments on Malaysia during the rest of the month.[55]

Little time was wasted before the UN Mission reached Kuching on Friday 16th; preparations were made over the weekend for an early start to the investigation, part of the group proceeding thenceforth to Jesselton to begin the survey in North Borneo. Then followed an unexpected delay of over a week, while the Mission waited for the settlement of a dispute that blew up over the number and status of the Indonesian and Philippines observers who were to accompany the mission. Subandrio accused the British on 19 August of trying to sabotage the Manila Agreements by restricting the number of observers.[56] And in the days following, a deadlock developed which threatened to disrupt the tight time-schedule on which the success of the Mission depended.

The exact numbers of observers demanded by Indonesia and permitted by Britain in the early stages of the dispute is a matter on which various figures are cited. But the general point at issue is clear enough. Indonesia asked for a number which Britain considered suspiciously high. Britain offered a number which Indonesia considered so inadequate as to be downright provocative. Initially, too, a further point was involved — the status of the observers in the ascertainment process. When the dispute first arose, a Filipino official was quoted as saying that 'we are hoping that at some stage we will have consultations with the Secretary General before his findings are announced. This investigation is not a mere formality. The decision must be fully accepted by everybody.' (That view had been specifically rejected by U Thant at the outset.) Later the Indonesians were to argue that the function of the observers was to keep check on the actions of the colonial authorities, who had made the

Mission's arrangements, whereas the British asserted that the observers were intended to check the good faith of the UN team, not the British.

Yet the heart of the problem was neither the numbers nor the functions of the observers so much as the suspicions each side now began to develop regarding the other's intentions over the whole matter. The British were beginning to believe that 'Indonesia is bent upon postponing the Malaysia Federation as long as possible and disrupting it afterwards' — and because they felt Indonesia's demands were unreasonable, they became all the more suspicious of her aims and the less willing to 'appease' Soekarno with further concessions. However, they were also anxious not to embarrass U Thant, who would have to decide whether the Mission should go ahead without observers or not; U Thant was obviously reluctant to proceed with the investigation against Indonesian and Philippines objections — on 22 August he ordered the Mission to delay the start of its hearings until the issue was settled — and even for the British there were advantages in going on, now that the ascertainment scheme had already developed so far. But they were suspicious about how far Indonesia's appetite for concessions would extend, for 'it is clear that Indonesia is not to be appeased, and is as determined as ever to kill Malaysia at birth.'[57]

Was this fear valid, or the product of fevered British imaginations? It is difficult to believe that the dispute about the number of observers was crucially important in itself. Indonesia and the Philippines, after initially asking for thirty, reduced their request to nine and Britain finally accepted eight per country, after all, although half of these were only 'clerical assistants'.[58] What was more disturbing to the British, however, was the fact that both Indonesia and the Philippines nominated intelligence officers and suspiciously senior officials as members of their observer teams. The fear that these men might serve as contact agents to spark off another Brunei revolt by anti-Malaysia elements in Sarawak was a very real factor in the minds of British officials. Whether the Indonesians really had some such a scheme in hand, or were merely playing at psychological war with their adversaries, or simply could not resist a propensity to use cloak-and-dagger methods, remains obscure. For them, it was second nature to assume bad faith on the part of colonial rulers and to expect, from their experience of 1948–9, all manner of imperialist stratagems to pull the wool over their eyes and the UN Mission's. Hence their view that the observers were to keep an eye on what the colonial authorities were doing, not just on the Mission. We do not have to assume sinister intent as central to Indonesia's behaviour on the observer issue, but however charitably one looks at the matter, it is hard to reconcile some of her actions with the hypothesis that she was treating the UN ascertainment merely as a face-saving formality.

When on 23 August Britain accepted U Thant's compromise proposal that four 'clerical assistants' might accompany the four observers, the problem seemed to be solved: first the Philippines and then Indonesia agreed to the formula. The UN teams began their hearings on Monday 26 August, without waiting further for the observers to arrive.[59]

However, trouble persisted into the following week, because of a further dispute between the British and Indonesians over the granting of visas. It is not easy to discover just who was responsible for these further pinpricking delays or what the exact reasons for them were: the Indonesians alarmed the British by asking to use their own air force planes to transport their observers, while the British irritated the Indonesians by refusing to grant visas to certain members of the observer teams. The British Ambassador in Djakarta was not able to obtain access to Dr. Subandrio (having been subjected to the cold-shoulder treatment since his arrival several months earlier), so that top-level personal communications between the two countries had to be carried out through the Australian or American Ambassadors. By this time, both governments were almost unable to avoid attributing the worst of motives to everything the other did — and each was tending towards an intransigent rather than accommodating view of how their quarrel should be ended. Indonesians were becoming increasingly convinced that the British were attempting to sabotage the Manila Agreements and Maphilindo, while the British were less and less willing to believe that Indonesia was really prepared to accept Malaysia, some of them arguing that Indonesia wanted to wreck the UN Mission enquiry in order to avoid the humiliation of having to abide by a report favourable to Malaysia. The danger in this situation, which prompted the Tunku to attempt direct negotiations with Djakarta to resolve the dispute, was that both countries were coming perilously close to washing their hands of the enquiry regardless of the consequences this would entail for the UN Mission and the Manila Agreements.

At this point the Malayan government made one more effort to ensure Indonesian participation in the ascertainment. Tunku Abdul Rahman was in a difficult position as the end of August approached, for he had been under pressure since the Manila conference to commit himself to a definite date for Malaysia Day, but had avoided doing so as long as possible in order to avoid antagonizing the Indonesians. The uncertainties in Kuala Lumpur at this time were creating a good deal of uneasiness, partly about how far the Tunku was prepared to go just to humour Soekarno, partly about the possibility of an unexpected turn of events in domestic politics. The leaders of Singapore and Sabah had expressed strong misgivings about the Manila compromise, and Sarawak's were opposed to concessions to Djakarta over the observers. Even within his own party the Tunku had his critics, although he had no difficulty in passing the Malaysia bill through the Malayan Parliament on 20 August. The main danger lay in uncertainties about the political future of the new federation; some observers, and particularly the British authorities, were apprehensive that Lee Kuan Yew might make a bid for leadership of an opposition bloc by appealing to the Borneo politicians and other elements (like the Malayan Chinese) who were uneasy about the racial implications of Maphilindo and the consequences of being drawn into Indonesia's embrace. Whether or not it was for this reason that Duncan Sandys, the Minister for Commonwealth Relations, advanced the date of his departure for Kuala Lumpur by a week at the height of the observers crisis (he arrived in Kuala Lumpur on 23 August), the Indonesians have cast him for the role as villain of the piece, believing that it was he who now put pressure on the Tunku to 'sabotage' the Manila Agreements.[60] At any rate, the Malayan cabinet seems to have reached a firm decision over the promulgation of Malaysia Day a day or so later. It could hardly have been delayed much longer, indeed, with 31 August looming near and some amendment of the Malaysia agreement and the various legislative instruments which gave it legal force becoming urgently necessary.

After a cabinet meeting on Monday 26 August at which this decision must have been finally affirmed, the Tunku cabled an invitation to Dr. Subandrio to come to Kuala Lumpur — ostensibly to discuss the continuing dispute over the observers, but no doubt also to inform him of the necessity to promulgate a new Malaysia Day. Subandrio declined next day, on grounds of ill-health, but suggested that Tun Razak might come to Djakarta. That was said to be impracticable, but it was decided to send instead Inche (later Tan Sri) Ghazali bin Shafie, the tough, able permanent secretary of Malaya's Department of External Affairs.

Ghazali's visit to Djakarta on 29 August for talks on the two central issues of the moment, the deadlock over Indonesian observers and Malaya's intention to proclaim the date of Malaysia Day on that day, takes on, in retrospect, a significance which was barely apparent at the time. It did not attract particular attention from the press in either Indonesia or Malaya, nor did Dr. Subandrio react vehemently against the latter announcement then and there. Later, however, the Indonesians were to stress the 29 August announcement as their prime illustration of Malaya's ill-faith — but Subandrio raised no particular objection at that stage and the talks were mainly directed towards a solution of the observers issue, on which he directed his anger vehemently against the British. Thereupon Ghazali stepped in to play the part of mediator and embodiment of the Maphilindo spirit by prevailing upon the British to drop their objections then and there to the issue of visas to the Indonesian nominees, in return for Indonesian agreement to participate in the final stages of the ascertainment.[61] Presumably the full implications of the Malaysia Day announcement which was issued that day in Kuala Lumpur were overshadowed by the last-minute flurry of negotiations over the observers. At that stage, all seemed to be well again and the Manila spirit restored.

The official announcement that Malaysia would be formally proclaimed on 16 September was made in Kuala Lumpur several hours after Ghazali had informed Subandrio of it. Yet although it later drew forth a formal note of protest (and also a Filipino one), and was to become the most important of Indonesia's arguments against Malaysia, nothing that was said at the time of Ghazali's visit gave him any forewarning of the storm that was to arise three weeks later. On the contrary, Subandrio repeated to Ghazali a suggestion that had been made earlier that the first regular *musjawarah Maphilindo* might be held in Kuala Lumpur during October as a gesture of President Soekarno's friendship towards the Tunku. And over the following weekend, Indonesia despatched her observers to North Borneo, in spite of further last-minute irritations at British restrictions on them. The Indonesian government was apparently not, at that stage, looking for an excuse or opportunity to break with Malaysia and resume militant confrontation. Yet if that was really its purpose, it could have justified a break at the end of August more convincingly and achieved more effective political results than it was able to after the UN report was issued and Malaysia both established and widely recognized by other countries. Ghazali himself provided grounds for Indonesian complaint about the meaning Malaya attached to the Manila Agreements by his uncompromisingly rigid interpretation of them. To Subandrio he had stressed that the participation of the observers was not an integral part of the Agreements, but merely a *desideratum*. And in a statement as he left Djakarta he asserted that Malaysia was not conditional upon a favourable verdict by the UN Mission. Both propositions may have been legally valid, but they diverged far from the Indonesian view. Subandrio repudiated the second of these propositions next day in a press conference and asked: 'Why was the Manila meeting held and why has the UN team been sent, in that case?'[62] Even so, less outcry was raised than might have been expected if the Indonesian authorities were determined to be touchy or to exploit any good excuse to avoid having to recognize Malaysia.

Neither the official Djakarta reaction to the 29 August announcement nor Indonesian press comment was strikingly vehement. Dr. Subandrio commented on Monday 2 September that: 'We are watching for deviations from the Manila Agreements'. Next day a strong official protest was sent to Kuala Lumpur: it characterized the announcement as a 'unilateral action' which violated the spirit and the letter of the Agreements. (Malaysia rejected the protest two days later with the argument that the formation of Malaysia did not depend on the UN team's findings.)[63] But the Indonesian press was content at that stage merely to argue that the incident showed Indonesia's moral superiority over Malaya, rather than to urge that it should be used as a ground for abruptly breaking with her. Attention was by this time being focused more on the observers who were accompanying the UN teams on the last stages of their North Borneo investigations. Only after the leader of Indonesia's observer group, Otto Abdurrachmen, returned to Djakarta on 5 September did the statements of Indonesian leaders begin to harden on the question of its general acceptability, as if in anticipation of a report favourable to Malaysia.

When U Thant issued his findings on the report of the UN Mission on 14 September (along with the report and an *aide-memoire* from each of the observer teams), his verdict proved to be strongly favourable to Malaysia and a disappointment to the Indonesians, who had been hoping for a more critical or equivocal finding. U Thant's major conclusion was
... that the majority of the peoples of Sabah (North Borneo) and of Sarawak have given serious and thoughtful consideration to their future and to the implications

for them of participation in a Federation of Malaysia. I believe that the majority of them have concluded that they wish to bring their dependent status to an end and to realise their independence through freely chosen association with other peoples in their region with whom they feel ties of ethnic association, heritage, language, religion, culture, economic relationship, and ideals and objectives ... there is no doubt about the wishes of a sizeable majority of the peoples of these territories to join in the Federation of Malaysia.[64]

Dealing with the specific questions about the elections in Sabah and Sarawak on which he had been required to satisfy himself under Article 4 of the Manila Joint Statement, U Thant also gave categorical replies favourable to Malaysia. Less than 100 detainees had been deprived of votes in Sarawak through detention or imprisonment for political offences, he reported, and even fewer in Sabah; their votes would not have materially affected the result, nor was the campaigning potential of the groups opposed to Malaysia significantly reduced by the restriction of their activities or those of a further 164 persons who were not able to vote, or by the absence of a few hundred persons absent from the colony for political reasons. U Thant was indirectly and mildly critical towards the British and Malayan governments on several other matters — the necessity to squeeze the Mission's work within tight deadlines (although 'more time ... would not have affected the conclusions to any significant extent'), the hold-up over the matter of observers, which he regarded as 'a matter for regret' since a more congenial atmosphere might have been achieved for the enquiry, and the premature announcement of Malaysia Day.[65] But on the whole the report was much more favourable than the Malaysia side had expected and provided very little basis for further controversy on points of substance. Even the reservations expressed in the Indonesian observer team's *aide-memoire* — that there was 'no element of a fresh approach' and that the enquiry had been conducted in an atmosphere of colonial intimidation — were unlikely to carry much weight against the unanimous recommendations of the Mission.[66]

Soekarno is said to have been surprised and angered by U Thant's report, although he did not make any immediate comment or indicate what Indonesia's reaction would be until after a special KOTI meeting to consider it on 15 September. Probably even at that late stage he had simply not made up his mind what to do if the Mission's report favoured Malaysia. Throughout the year he had been keeping several options open — either to acquiesce in the formation of Malaysia and rely on the Maphilindo connection to draw the Tunku out of the British orbit into Indonesia's or, if opportunity arose, to frustrate the creation of Malaysia even at the cost of wrecking Maphilindo. There are reasons for believing that he did not make up his mind on the issue until it was made up for him by the course of events between 15 and 21 September. It was characteristic of his political tactics to wait for events to unfold before he revealed his intentions at all plainly. (It is also worth recalling that he was a sick man at the time, feeling his age — as he himself admitted — and beset with domestic problems which were not easily resolved.)[67] The two main clues to his thinking during August were his relatively mild references to Malaysia in his Independence Day speech and a phrase in his speech to a PNI conference at Purwokerto on 28 August (at a time when it looked almost certain that Indonesian observers would not be sent to the Borneo enquiry) in which he said that Indonesia would have no choice but to 'bow our heads and obey' if the people of North Borneo decided to join Malaysia: on the other hand, he went on to say that he was convinced they would reject Malaysia and he reiterated Indonesia's opposition to Malaysia.[68] The admission that Indonesia might have to acquiesce in Malaysia was stressed at the time by advocates of the theory that Soekarno was merely looking for a face-saving formula (with the further argument that the rest of the speech was ritualistic fulmination, for the people of Borneo had already made their choice, after all), whereas sceptics were inclined to interpret the speech as a Machiavellian hint to the Borneo dissidents that they should stage an uprising to demonstrate their opposition to Malaysia. Probably Soekarno was quite happy to let it be taken either way, for he was a master at exploiting the ambiguity and vagueness with which he enshrouded many of his utterances.

We may take it as axiomatic that Soekarno and his ministers did not abandon their long-term aim of trying to eliminate British influence from the region. Possibly they were still hoping until the eleventh hour to benefit by any opportunities the UN Mission might offer for delaying Malaysia or even sparking off some form of last minute revolt against it in Borneo. One could even explain their decision to send observers after Ghazali's visit and the surprisingly bland response to his message about Malaysia Day as merely tactical moves, not evidence of a real change of heart towards accepting Malaysia. Nevertheless, there remains the fact that the Malaysia Day announcement on 29 August was *not* made the occasion for a denunciation of Malaysia and the obligations incurred at Manila; on the contrary, observers *were* sent a few days later — a gesture which could only make it harder for Indonesia to justify any later repudiation of the UN Mission's report, not easier.

One consideration complicating any attempt to identify Soekarno's intentions towards Malaysia at this period is the fact that his government was equally preoccupied with domestic problems at the time, particularly the mounting pressures for some modification of the stabilization programme. The link between these two issues deserves some attention, for it has been suggested that the conflict with Malaysia was engineered deliberately by the government in order to provide an easy way out of a politically embarrassing commitment to budgetary stringency. It is certainly true that some groups in Indonesia (notably the PKI and its allies, but not only these) were urging a policy of militancy towards Malaysia because it would pull the country away from the Western bloc and help to undermine the stabilization programme. And that was, indeed, its effect in the second half of September. But to argue mechanistically from effect to cause would be a serious over-simplification. On the other hand, there are indications of divided counsels and conflicting interests among Soekarno's ministers on economic questions as well as on the Malaysia issue, and abundant evidence that the government was finding itself acutely embarrassed by the strains resulting from its sharply deflationary measures of 26 May. A liquidity crisis brought about by its tight money policy was causing an outcry amongst the 'national businessmen' and managers of State enterprises who should have been the government's strongest supporters in its efforts to curb inflation.[69] The pruning of government expenditures for the sake of a balanced budget was antagonizing politicians with vested interests in large government departments, particularly the leaders of the Armed Forces. The latter, in particular, had little reason to favour the stabilization scheme and stood to gain from an intensification of the conflict with Malaysia.[70] In addition to all this, rumours were prevalent in early September that the government was failing to keep its expenditures within the limits set down by the IMF as a condition for further financial assistance. The government reviewed the economic situation as it had developed during the three months since the May decrees at a KOTI meeting on 4 September (the first to be held since the Manila Summit), after which Djuanda said that the situation could be described as 'reasonable': the expenditure figures, he said, were still below the upper limits set out in the Budget that had recently been approved by the parliament. Djuanda admitted that the development projects were in difficulties and that there were severe strains on liquidity, but he anticipated some improvement in this regard. However, a day or so later the Central Executive of the National Front came out with a series of fiery resolutions attacking the stabilization scheme, one of which 'proposed to the President to immediately change the 26 May economic regulations'. The President himself made a statement to this body in which he expressed his agreement with the broad lines of its resolutions and urged it cryptically to go ahead and 'execute them'. Yet after a second KOTI meeting on 11 September Djuanda stated firmly that the government was not considering the withdrawal of the May regulations, but merely planning to supplement and amend them without any fundamental changes.[71]

Are we justified in concluding from this that Soekarno and his ministers were not at that stage anticipating abandonment of the stabilization scheme — or, at least, not to the extent of using the Malaysia issue as an opportunity to bring about a complete change of political course? It seems unlikely that they were thinking in terms of such clear-cut alternatives, although no categorical answer can be given on this matter. Some ministers, like Djuanda, were more strongly committed to the stabilization programme than others and the evidence suggests that their view was still prevailing down to mid-September, although they must have been in a weaker political position because of the unpopularity of the programme — and perhaps even shaken in their own confidence by the problems it was creating. A sharp rise in rice prices in the first fortnight of September added to their embarrassments, since it threatened to upset the hard-won price stabilization that had been achieved since May. It would be surprising, of course, if the other ministers who felt no strong identification with the stabilization scheme did not see the political implications for it of an intensified conflict with Malaysia — and temperamentally the latter course may have appealed more strongly to their revolutionary zeal. But there were other considerations, also, cutting across both these issues, which complicated the picture even more. Both Chairul Saleh and Subandrio were jockeying for the opportunity to step into Djuanda's position as First Minister and putative deputy and successor to Soekarno. (Djuanda had been in poor health for over a year and died two months later.) The prospect of a conflict could not be regarded lightly by Nasution and the Armed Services chiefs, either. Thus the political motivations of nearly all the major figures around Soekarno were tangled and ambivalent. In the circumstances, a firm line by the government on such contentious issues as Malaysia and the stabilization programme could hardly be expected. Hence the peculiar importance attaching to the extraordinary events of the week following the break between Indonesia and Malaysia.

THE BREAKING OF RELATIONS: SEPTEMBER 1963

The events of the week following the UN Mission's report and the formation of Malaysia were of decisive importance in the development of the conflict between Indonesia and Malaysia. A point of no return was passed, not only in relations between the two countries, but also in the domestic politics of Indonesia, where the Western-oriented course which had been followed earlier in the year now had to be reversed and a drift towards the left set in which continued throughout the next two years. Confrontation was intensified in the form of fierce verbal attacks based upon the slogan 'Crush (*ganjang*) Malaysia', as well as by open military and economic measures intended to force Malaysia to bid for a settlement on terms acceptable to Indonesia. Whereas confrontation had previously been an ambiguous and erratic policy which did not commit Soekarno unequivocally to a collision course with Malaysia, but left him the option of either stepping up clandestine border raids in Sarawak or wooing the Tunku away from the British with the honeyed phrases of the Maphilindo phase, the latter alternative was now virtually eliminated — at least until such time as a political settlement could be patched up. And that was to prove unattainable during the next two years, even though the three Maphilindo countries frequently expressed their desire to resolve their quarrel on the basis of a 'return to the Manila agreements'.

Because of the far-reaching consequences of that week's events it is a matter of some importance to determine how and why they developed in the way they did. To explain the whole affair just in terms of Soekarno's adventurousness and excitability, or of the PKI's machinations in bringing about a break with Malaysia in order to undermine the Indonesian government's policy of relying upon Western financial aid would be a gross over-simplification. Certainly the PKI was trying to pull Indonesia away from the West and had long been the foremost opponent of Malaysia: Communists played a prominent part in the events of that week which made the break with Malaysia irreparable and the PKI gained enormously from the wrecking of the stabilization programme, since Soekarno henceforth had little choice but to look increasingly to the left for political support. But the PKI was not solely responsible for what had happened and could not by itself have achieved all this if Soekarno and his ministers had been more determined to prevent it.[72] They were, in fact, resisting pressures from the PKI, as we shall see, but in doing so they allowed a situation to develop in which the affair got out of hand and they found themselves with no acceptable alternatives to intensification of the conflict.

Does this mean that there was some logical necessity or dramatic inevitability about the course of events in that turbulent week, or might they have turned out differently? In the account which follows, considerable emphasis will be put on the element of chance and the unforeseen twists of fate which contributed to the government's difficulties in keeping control of events at that time, for there are many indications that neither Soekarno, Djuanda nor Subandrio initially expected or intended that the affair would develop in the way it did. The course of events may have been not unwelcome to Soekarno, since he was temperamentally more inclined towards a 'revolutionary' struggle with an external enemy than to the prosaic domestic problems of managing a disinflation (although that was certainly not true of Djuanda, nor of Subandrio, at that stage), but it is clear from a close examination of the happenings of that week that Soekarno and his government were swept along by the tide of events to some extent. On the other hand, it might be argued that the damage was really done as soon as Soekarno decided not to accept the UN Mission's report and to withhold recognition from Malaysia. That was bound to precipitate the kind of deadlock that later developed in relations with Malaysia, it is said, since Indonesia had been so strongly predisposed towards conflict with Malaysia by the ideological indoctrination and sentiments of hostility generated in the previous months that Soekarno could not reverse his course even if he wanted to. The details of how the deadlock came about are regarded as of slight importance on this view. Others have even denied that September was a particularly significant turning-point at all: only the outer form and tactics of confrontation were changed, but the basic objective (to destroy Malaysia and root out British influence in the region) had been the same since soon after the Brunei revolt.[73]

A basic weakness of these interpretations is that they leave out of account the ambiguity of Soekarno's policies and the domestic pressures which largely determined the way in which he exploited that ambiguity. What distinguished his policy towards Malaysia before and after September 1963 was not so much the degree of intensity with which confrontation was pursued (for it remained an extraordinarily lackadaisical affair even after September) so much as the fact that it was no longer easy for him to 'get off the hook' if it suited him, as he had been able to do during the Maphilindo phase. Because he allowed the conflict to develop too far in September, he destroyed the possibility of obtaining large-scale Western aid and thus tilted the domestic political balance decisively against the anti-Communists within Indonesia. It is most unlikely that he meant to do this, or that he realized how far-reaching would be the international and domestic implications of September's events. The most plausible explanation is that he was not initially clear what response to make to the UN Mission report and the formation of Malaysia, that he intended some dramatic gesture of protest — not sufficiently serious, however, to jeopardize the foreign aid Indonesia needed — but that his hand was forced by the burning of the British embassy and the PKI-sponsored take-over of British firms. Thereafter, he set about making a virtue of necessity by attempting to force Malaysia to negotiate, justifying his efforts to do so by ever more militant assertions of the doctrine of the New Emerging Forces and ineluctable struggle with the *Nekolim*.

Before we look into the course and causes of these events in detail, it may be helpful to summarize them briefly in broad outline. On Sunday 15 September, Indonesia refused to accept the United Nations Mission report and decided to 'withhold recognition of Malaysia' when it was proclaimed next day. Diplomatic relations were formally severed by Kuala Lumpur on 17 September in reply. Two violent demonstrations were launched against the British embassy in Djakarta on the Monday and Wednesday (and against the Malayan on the first occasion), the second of these in response to a somewhat similar attack on Indonesia's embassy in Kuala Lumpur on the Tuesday. (Paradoxically, it was the British rather than the Malaysians who attracted the main thrust of Indonesian hostility during this period, since they were regarded as the real villains of the piece; yet diplomatic relations between Indonesia and Britain were not broken by either government, nor were British firms in Indonesia nationalized at that time, in spite of widespread popular demands for such action.) A series of unofficial 'take-overs' of the British firms by their workers began in the middle of the week, on the same pattern as the take-over of Dutch firms in December 1957, and obviously calculated to force the government's hand on an issue about which most ministers themselves had ambivalent feelings.[74] Yet the ministers concerned attempted to curb these 'revolutionary' actions or at least gain control of them, before they got out of hand; and they specifically denied that the British properties were nationalized. When KOTI and the Supreme Economic Command (KOTOE) met on Saturday, 21 September, to consider the report of a special committee appointed some days earlier to investigate the economic aspects of confrontation, it did not decide upon nationalization of the British properties, but upon the severance of all commercial and financial relations with Malaysia, including Singapore. By this time, the die was cast. Early in the following week both the IMF standby credits and further US aid were withheld and the DAC discussions on a loan for Indonesia abandoned. The stabilization policy was in ruins.

There are a number of mysteries about this swing from a relatively mild initial reaction to Malaysia's creation at the beginning of the week to the disastrous breach which had been achieved by the end. If Soekarno had intended such a break all along, why did he need two attacks on the British embassy to bring it about? (The excuse that the wrath of the multitude was 'provoked' by the other side can be applied more persuasively to the Monday's events than the Wednesday's.) If not, just what was the purpose of the second attack? Why did he resist the demands for nationalization of British firms instead of giving way to them? Are we to conclude that his mind was made up for him by the mobs who stormed the embassy and the unionists who took over the British companies? If so, why did the government not take firmer action to keep popular passions under restraint when matters of such delicate and far-reaching importance were at stake? It is at this point that the picture becomes indistinct. Certainly the highest authorities were well aware of the mass demonstrations against the British embassy that were to take place on the Monday and probably (some of them, at least, but perhaps not all) on the Wednesday. Such things do not happen without the approval of someone in authority under a Guided Democracy. The Monday affair was openly sponsored, publicized in advance and effectively controlled by the National Front, though Wednesday's was not. But it is questionable whether Soekarno or even the most fiery of his ministers expected that the demonstrations would go so far on either occasion or that they realized how seriously the snowballing effect of the week's happenings would jeopardize Indonesia's prospects of obtaining the international loans she sorely needed to make the stabilization policy succeed.

Even if any did foresee this (and some must have feared it), what were the immediate alternatives open to a man like Djuanda, who would have been dismayed to see the torpedoing of the development policies he had been waiting to put into effect for years? He could hardly resist demands for some gesture of protest against Malaysia; he could only hope to minimize the damage it might do to Indonesia's international credit rating. He may not even have greatly wished to resist. He was a patriot and a nationalist, not immune to the prevailing sentiments of bitterness against the British for what most Indonesians believed to be their part in pulling Tunku Abdul Rahman away from the Maphilindo connection.[75] There were certainly some among his colleagues who would not have been averse, either, to giving the British lion's tail a twist by having the embassy windows shattered and even the whole building consigned to flames. Many Indonesians seem to have been under the impression that the British needed only a small push to hustle them finally out of South-East Asia. The lion seemed to be getting old and losing its teeth: de Gaulle's rebuff to Britain's application to enter the Common Market and the Macmillan government's waning prestige at home — even the Profumo scandal — all these contributed to a belief that Britain was a declining force in the world, no longer capable of taking strong measures in defence of Malaysia. And if the head counselled caution, the heart was bound to be torn by the embarrassing predicament Indonesia's ministers found themselves in at that juncture. What reasons were there for believing that a policy of restraint, patience and grateful reliance on the still uncertain prospect of foreign aid would do the country more good in the long run than a bold and revolutionary girding up of the loins to confront the alien imperialists and capitalists of Singapore once and for all, who were not only sucking Indonesia's lifeblood, but also standing between her and her destiny in South-East Asia? Perhaps more to the point, would it do a minister's prospects of political survival any good to prefer the former to the latter?

It is hardly surprising that government policy (if it is meaningful to talk of such a thing) was far from clear. The issues themselves were blurred. The situation was too fluid for sharply defined policies, too rapidly changing, still contingent on too many uncertain factors — negotiations about the foreign credits, the state of the national budget, sharply rising rice prices and dissatisfaction with the stabilization programme, quite apart from the unpredictable Malaysian situation. Just how the 'decision-making process' worked in Djakarta at this vital stage is something that only a very well-informed and unprejudiced participant could really elucidate in full. Too little is known about the aims of the President himself, around whom all crucial decisions hinged. As usual, his public utterances on the subject were few and sphinx-like. There are signs that he was talking in different vein to different actors in the drama — telling his ministers to counsel restraint on the one hand, yet encouraging the National Front and youth leaders in their militant demonstrations on the other. He was presumably concerned as much with the problems of keeping control of the domestic political situation as with the way the Malaysia dispute developed, hence obliged to ensure that the hostility to Malaysia that had been aroused was not exploited against his government by the PKI or any other group. To resist the aroused national sentiment against Malaysia would have meant eating his own words, whereas to ride along with a 'revolutionary' upsurge and seek to steer it to his own advantage was characteristic of Soekarno's political strategy.

* * * *

Indonesia's reaction to the UN report was announced officially by Dr. Subandrio after a special KOTI meeting on Sunday 15 September. Indonesia could not endorse (*mengesjahkan*) the birth of Malaysia, he said and would withhold recognition of Malaysia 'as it was now', but this attitude could be changed if the UN made 'corrections' in the carrying out of the UN Mission's tasks; it would have to be carried out on the basis of the Manila Agreement, however, for even U Thant had referred to the survey's shortcomings and 'regretted' them. Subandrio's statement was on the whole milder than had been expected, commented the *Straits Times* next day; it did not seem to foreshadow more drastic measures and was so heavily qualified that Indonesia could easily change her stand if it suited her to accept Malaysia.[76] But other voices in Djakarta were much less restrained. Hardi, for the PNI, called for revolutionary action and urged President Soekarno to give the 'command' for action to oppose the formation of Malaysia. A mass meeting of youths and students on the Sunday under the Central Youth Front called for the breaking of relations with

Malaysia and Britain. Yet the Soekarno government did not accede to this demand; diplomatic relations with Britain were never entirely broken and even the formal break with Malaysia was proclaimed by Kuala Lumpur (not without provocation, one must admit, but there is reason to doubt that the provocation was deliberately intended to have that particular consequence). Mass meetings might influence government policy in Indonesia, but they did not determine it.[77]

'We do not anticipate trouble, but it could develop', said the Australian Ambassador in Djakarta, K.C.O. Shann, on the Sunday.[78] That was a reasonable assessment at the time, although troubles soon developed thick and fast. The Malayan and British embassies and the British consulates in Medan and Surabaja had already requested police protection on Malaysia-day, in anticipation of demonstrations which had been announced for the next day. A Malayan embassy reception to celebrate Malaysia's proclamation on the 16th was deprived of catering facilities because of a boycott by suppliers. But these could be regarded as mere ritual gestures, a letting off of steam, hardly a 'revolutionary' response to the new situation. So also could the first demonstration outside the British embassy on the Monday. There is no reason to believe that Soekarno had already decided to 'crush' Malaysia and carry confrontation to a point of open conflict. In the course of the week, however, the atmosphere in Djakarta became much more explosive and Soekarno found himself pushed on to a course from which it was difficult to retreat without humiliation and to which there were no advantageous alternatives for him. Although the two attacks on the British embassy were important steps down the slippery path, they do not appear to have been planned with the specific aim of precipitating the conflict which developed. Both appear to have got out of hand to some extent, even though the question of how far the authorities were willing to use force to maintain control and confine the demonstrations to a relatively limited protest remains an open and controversial one. What was apparently not foreseen was the intensity and consequences of these demonstrations at such a delicate stage in Indonesia's relations with Malaysia and her allies.

The circumstances of the two demonstrations on the Monday and the Wednesday were so different that one can hardly avoid the conclusion that on the former occasion, at least, nothing more than a breaking of windows was intended by the authorities. (This is almost becoming a standard form of diplomatic — or should one say undiplomatic — practice these days, worthy of inclusion in any revised edition of Satow.) Monday's demonstration had been widely publicized in advance, the police guard on the British embassy strengthened somewhat (although far from adequately, in the Ambassador's opinion) and the ostensible purpose of the demonstrators, organized by the Youth Front and the PPMI, was simply to convey the resolutions of the previous day's mass meetings to the Malayan and British Ambassadors.[79] The leaders of the Monday demonstration were prominent members of the organizations concerned (Anwar Nasution of *Pemuda Rakjat*, Mawardi and Ismail) and they were able to prevent the crowd getting out of hand, as it did on the Wednesday when there was no recognized leadership or organization. The police attempted to restrain the crowd for some time ('within the limits of their instructions the police behaved very well' commented the British Ambassador acidly) and even after the fence was broken down and the British embassy grounds were invaded, the building itself was not entered, although all the windows were broken. A meeting of KOTI was in progress in the President's palace at the same time as the stone-throwing against the Malayan and British embassies was taking place on Monday morning and the decisions reached at that meeting, whatever they were, did not seem to point towards an irrevocable breach with Malaysia or Britain then and there.[80]

Indonesians sometimes put the blame for much of what happened on 16 September and the days following on the 'provocative' behaviour of the British officials, which aggravated the seriousness of the Monday demonstration and, by making it harder for the 'moderates' to keep control of a difficult situation, played into the hands of the extremists who were trying to force a breach between Indonesia and the West. In support of this view they compare the different behaviour of the crowd at the Malayan and British embassies on the Monday. Some stone-throwing, window-breaking and defacing of embassy property occurred at the Malayan embassy also, which the demonstrators visited first, after meeting at the Youth Front Headquarters (*Gedung Pemuda*) early in the morning: but the leaders of the demonstration were received politely by the First Secretary (the Ambassador, Dato Kamarudin, having being summoned earlier by Dr. Subandrio to be told that Indonesia did not recognize a 'Malaysian' embassy in Djakarta) and their protest accepted for transmission to Kuala Lumpur. The Secretary co-operated with the leaders of the demonstration in addressing the crowd to explain the Ambassador's absence, with the result that it soon dispersed in the direction of the British embassy about a mile away down Djakarta's main highway.

In the middle of the morning about 10,000 demonstrators converged on the British embassy, a three-storey 'glass-house' opposite the Hotel Indonesia, at the end of Djakarta's most fashionable street. Barely a year old at the time, the building could hardly have been more unsuitably designed for such a volatile political climate. According to *Suluh Indonesia* what started the stone-throwing there was the 'provocative' bagpipe-playing of the assistant military attache, Major Rory Walker, who defiantly marched up and down the embassy grounds piping, in spite of appeals (or threats) to stop by the police chief and the leader of the demonstrators. A further cause of anger to the crowd was the lengthy argument and delay that ensued when the Military Attache, Colonel Beck, refused to admit more than six of the fifteen-man delegation to present their resolutions to the Ambassador. Then a demonstrator jumped the fence and tried to tear down the British flag, but was foiled by Colonel Beck and some of the guards. A second attempt on the flag succeeded, however, after the demonstrators pulled down part of the iron fence round the embassy compound and swarmed around the building, burning the Ambassador's car and the British flag. The security guards were by that time unable to restrain them, even though some tear-gas bombs were used. But the embassy building itself was not invaded on this occasion. Ambassador Gilchrist finally received the delegation coldly amidst the broken glass strewn across his office floor, cynically taunting them (as *Suluh Indonesia* reported it) with 'That's your mob' and, as they left, 'Long live U Thant'.

Would the story have been substantially different if the British officials had behaved differently on that day? Insofar as the events of that week developed in intensity snowball-fashion from then on towards a decisive break later in the week, one can only wish that the British embassy officials had shown more tact in the first place and less of the bulldog spirit, bowing a little before the storm and the indignities of the mob like their Malayan counterparts did, in order to keep the political temperature low. But that would have seemed demeaning in their eyes and temperamentally they were inclined more towards defiance in the maintenance of Britain's dignity — which the Indonesians regarded as 'provocation' and arrogance.

Major Walker was a dashing figure of obvious courage, who had once piped his troops into action at Dinan and had been the first man to break the hour for the scramble from Marble Arch to the Arc de Triomphe. The Ambassador, Sir Andrew Gilchrist, was a tough Scot whose previous diplomatic task had been to show the stiff upper lip in Iceland during a fisheries dispute involving fisticuffs and a war of nerves. His reaction to the various mob demonstrations was to stand stiffly and fearlessly on diplomatic protocol; he was not the sort of man who would invite the leaders in for coffee and try to play the game on their terms. Whether matters would have turned out very differently if he and his colleagues had been men of a different stamp is a contentious point. But by reacting defiantly as they did, they seem to have confirmed Indonesian suspicions that the British were implacably hostile to Indonesia and were trying to wreck the Manila Agreements and Maphilindo (since this would mark the end of British influence in the region) by affronting and humiliating Soekarno over the manner of Malaysia's formation. The suspicion was far-fetched, but it is hardly surprising that many Indonesians, including 'moderates' opposed to Soekarno, felt that it was borne out by British actions in the previous weeks.

On the other side of the picture, there is little doubt that, after eight months of confrontation and pinpricking, many British officials were in no mood to be accommodating to the Indonesians much longer. Few had much patience left for what was coming to be known as the 'Jones' line' of support for President Soekarno at almost any price. It was galling to be under pressure from the State Department to contribute to the DAC loan to Indonesia while she was behaving so provocatively. The feeling that 'someone must stand up to these people' was becoming widespread, and it tended to be compounded by the belief that Soekarno was over-reaching himself on the Malaysia question and might soon 'come a cropper' once and for all if he was firmly resisted. Indonesia's apparent dependence on foreign aid to sustain her stabilization programme reinforced the notion that the time had come for firmness towards her rather than acquiescence in Soekarno's whims and moods. Mixed up with these sentiments was also a strong dash of contempt for Indonesia's failure to deal with her economic mess, as well as moral indignation with her on many counts — at her bullying attitude towards little, defenceless Malaysia, at her twisting of the lion's tail throughout the previous months and at her pretensions to moral superiority over the old established forces, which often contrasted outrageously with some of the shoddy behaviour of her leaders. In British eyes, Soekarno was breaking the rules of proper international behaviour over and over, so he deserved to be punished, not humoured. One can hardly blame the British diplomats in Djakarta for feeling incensed and one cannot assert with complete confidence that events would have developed very differently if they had been less inflexible in their reactions, more patient and accommodating, in short, closer to Ambassador Jones' approach. But as it was, the chief beneficiaries from the day's business on 16 September were those Indonesians who wanted to force an irreparable break with Malaysia and pull Indonesia away from the orbit of the Western powers.

Despite the seriousness of Monday's demonstrations as a breach of diplomatic protocol, it did not immediately appear that Indonesian-Malaysia relations were irreparably broken. The atmosphere of Djakarta and the tone of the press on Tuesday and Wednesday mornings after the glass-breaking spree at the British embassy appear to have been relatively calm after the previous day's excitement. Matters were aggravated, however, by the second and far more serious attack on the British embassy on the Wednesday, which left the Indonesian government in a position from which retreat without humiliation would be far more difficult.

Several events on the Tuesday, although not in themselves decisive, were important links in the chain of developments. The first unofficial 'take-overs' of British firms began and British aircraft landing at Djakarta were boycotted by the trade unions concerned. A meeting of KOTOE was held 'in connection with confrontation', at which a special committee was set up to formulate proposals for a further meeting at Bogor on the Saturday. It was this committee which proposed the severance of all economic links with Malaysia. Curiously, neither Djuanda nor Soemarno, the two senior economists among Soekarno's Ministers, was on it: the ranking ministers were Leimena and Chairul Saleh. One can only assume that its recommendations were at that time not expected to be as fateful as the decision which finally emerged from the KOTOE deliberations on the Saturday.[81]

Also on Tuesday, 17 September, Malaysia formally broke off diplomatic relations with her two Maphilindo partners, in response to their refusal to grant immediate recognition, and a demonstration took place at the Indonesian embassy in Kuala Lumpur in which parts of the consulate building were burned and the Indonesian national emblem was torn down and desecrated. This was reported in Indonesia in a way that aroused great indignation there. It was made the pretext for the much more serious attacks on the British embassy in Djakarta next day.[82] *Suluh Indonesia* commented two days later, in accounting for the sacking of the British embassy, that the incident in Kuala Lumpur was 'uncivilised' and the Tunku's action in stamping on the Garuda 'insulting and difficult to excuse'. (The fact that the British and not the former Malayan embassy building were made the target of the rioters' wrath is merely another of the strange quirks of that week's events) although readily explicable in terms of neo-colonialism. Indonesians were particularly incensed by reports that the Tunku himself had trampled on the Indonesian national emblem, although according to Kuala Lumpur versions of the story he was bodily placed upon it much against his will by the youthful demonstrators who bore the emblem to the residency for his approval, after they had burned and stoned part of the consulate building. The Tunku chided them gently for their excess of enthusiasm, though he thanked them for their national spirit and, characteristically, treated them to soft drinks on the residency lawns before sending them home.[83] The whole episode seems so absurdly disproportionate to the two Djakarta demonstrations that it is hard to credit allegations that Soekarno's anger at the Kuala Lumpur episode was an important factor in what happened on the Wednesday. Yet it is not impossible.

The burning of the British embassy on 'Ash Wednesday', 18 September, was a much more serious and puzzling affair than the Monday demonstration. There was little indication beforehand that another major demonstration was to take place, as there had been on the first occasion, although a meeting at the Youth Front building had been called for Wednesday afternoon to protest against the Kuala Lumpur 'insult'. Signs of prior organization among the demonstrators (apparently through the National Front) were later discernible, but it seems undeniable that the affair blew up suddenly and then got out of hand in the course of the afternoon, that not all of what happened was intended to happen by whoever authorized the affair in the first place. The action was started by a few truckloads of unidentified *pemuda* ('youths'), who suddenly descended upon the now window-less embassy and immediately set it ablaze, without any prior warning, just as the great bulk of Djakarta's working population was streaming home along the adjoining highways at about 2.15 p.m. Very quickly a huge crowd gathered. Cars, furniture, papers and books were burned, people swarmed into the embassy through the broken windows, an attempt was made to seize incriminating documents, and for several hours neither the police nor fire brigade could control the situation. A group of 23 British personnel, including the Ambassador, spent several terrifying hours huddled against a wall outside the burning embassy, unable to move because of the encircling crowd which threw stones and bottles at them (Gilchrist himself being hit twice), while the police tried in vain to push the crowd back. Finally a police car forced its way in, with armed policemen manning its running-board, and began to evacuate the women. The crowd stoned it and tried to overturn it, but finally scattered when the car was driven straight through the throng of people. Thereafter the rescue proceeded without obstruction. Four Britons were reported hurt, but no serious bodily injury was done to anyone — a point which Indonesian spokesmen stressed time and again in the days following.[84]

The reactions of the authorities responsible for law and order are briefly summarized in the *Suluh Indonesia* account of the episode:

> Two fire engines which arrived at 4 p.m. were prevented from being put into operation by the crowd. All the fence around the embassy was torn down. With the aid of extension ladders from the fire engines, youths hoisted the Indonesian flag and the crowd sang the Indonesian national anthem. Only at 6 p.m. when the Mobile Brigade forces arrived, could the youths be kept out of the grounds and the fire engines start to extinguish the already dying fire .... [Later] youths emptied several English houses and burned the contents. They also located and overturned several English-owned cars and burned them in the streets. People who were discovered trying to steal any of the goods were handed over to the police. In the evening, youths stopped cars on the roads. When they came across British cars, they politely asked the passengers to get out, then turned the cars over, poured petrol over them and set them alight.

The extent of the rampage and destruction in nearly every British house in Djakarta is marvellously understated in this account. The leaders of the mob were equipped in advance with full and accurate lists of the British-owned houses (Australians and Americans in the same areas were not molested) and nearly all were systematically sacked during the afternoon. According to some reports, there was relatively little looting, but the testimony is conflicting on this point. Clearly, however, there was an element of prior organization and even discipline among the rioters involved, provided either by the National Front or its constituent organizations.

There are several curious features of the Wednesday affair which do not conform with clearcut theories that the attack was officially instigated or that it was provoked solely by the PKI with the aim of pushing the government further than it wished to go. It seems fairly certain that elements from both political wings were involved. The rioters were described by several observers as of a very different type from the youthful student demonstrators of the Monday, being generally older men from the working classes, which probably betokens Communists, but possibly their rivals also. Both Communists and anti-Communists later charged each other with the prime responsibility. The numerous allegations from PKI sources about 'provocation' and warnings about 'counter-revolutionary' elements seem to indicate that they were distinctly alarmed lest the confused situation might be exploited by others to their disadvantage. No-one was at all keen to take the credit for the action over the next few days, while both press and official comment conveyed a definite impression of alarm and even shock at this uncontrolled and destructive turn of events.[85] It is hardly surprising. The Djakarta 'new rich', living in the wealthy suburb adjoining the British embassy, must have had pause to think about the implications of 'revolutionary' mass actions as they watched the sacking of British houses in their midst, wondering whether their turn might come soon if things went on like this.

It is also noteworthy that the law-enforcing authorities, who had acted to keep the Monday demonstration within bounds, conspicuously failed to do so on the Wednesday until the damage was done. Why did the Army not appear on the scene until four hours after the fire started? What degree of collusion with the organizers are we to infer? It is difficult to piece together the various rumours which went around about their part of story. The Army leaders were not at all happy about mob actions which could be manipulated by the Communists to their own advantage and might easily bring the Army and police forces into conflict with the inflamed masses. In Medan, the Army refused to permit a second demonstration on the Wednesday. The Djakarta Military Commander, Brig.-Gen. Umar Wirahadikusumo, was aware that a meeting of eighteen different organizations in the Youth Front was to be held on the Wednesday afternoon, but he did not expect a situation where the Army would have to be called out to restore control. Even when the police called for military assistance, there was a lengthy delay because General Umar had to wait for a formal, written request before he was legally empowered to intervene.[86] Since the abolition of martial law several months earlier, delicate questions about the precise demarcation of authority as between the civil authorities, the police and military had arisen. The request for military assistance had to be channelled from the Police Chief to the Governor to the Military Commander — evidently no contingency preparations for rapid action on the Wednesday afternoon had been made. Just why this took four hours still remains a mystery. Muddle, accident and sheer misunderstanding could quite easily have been largely responsible. At any rate, by the time the Mobile Brigade began to move in the early evening, Djakarta was almost quiet again. It is significant, however, that Umar was immediately vested with powers tantamount to those he would exercise under martial law, which he retained until after the Games of the New Emerging Forces were held in November.

How much did the President or other senior members of the government know in advance about his attack on the British embassy? The fact that the National Front was involved suggest that some approval or hint must have been received from the very highest level. President Soekarno is said to have been angered by the Kuala Lumpur 'insults' to him and to Indonesia on the previous day and it is hard to believe that such an important step would have been taken without his knowledge. On the other hand, one story has it that the President was intensely angry with the ministers concerned (Sudibjo and Hanafi) for letting the affair develop too far. Sudibjo promptly made a broadcast condemning unauthorized and irresponsible actions beyond the limits of the National Front demonstration and ordering that all further mass actions to oppose Malaysia should be concentrated within the National Front framework.[87] It is quite possible that Soekarno's instructions to the National Front leaders were either ambiguous or misinterpreted (or both) and that during the demonstration they lost control over the various groups belonging to their loosely-structured organization. The fact that the rioters were supplied with accurate lists of British houses betokens some degree of prior liaison with someone in the Foreign Ministry or security organizations. But how much and with whom? The questions cannot yet be answered. At a later stage one might have suspected the sinister hand of Subandrio here, but he was out of the country on that day and seems to have been caught unawares by the new turn of events.

Next morning an official government statement was issued in the President's name expressing disapproval and regret for the previous day's events ('although the government understands the outpouring of popular anger') and again warning firmly against unauthorized actions. British firms were still being taken over and the atmosphere in Djakarta was tense and apprehensive, to judge from the jittery references in both the Communist and anti-Communist press to 'provocation' and 'counter-revolutionary saboteurs' as the instigators of the trouble. In several respects the confused situation was reminiscent of that which developed at the time of the take-over of Dutch enterprises in December 1957, after the unsuccessful attempt to assassinate Soekarno at Tjikini. Popular passions were inflamed on several counts. Startling and portentous events were occurring. Orders of the government were being disregarded with impunity in some matters and were ambiguous or obscure on others. The take-over of British firms by their workers and trade unions (mostly, but not solely, under PKI influence) had begun in a small way on the Tuesday. The Shell Oil Company offices in Palembang (but not the main office in Djakarta) were seized on Wednesday morning and later that day various British banks and trading companies in Djakarta also. An order was issued through Chairul Saleh that such actions must cease and the firms be returned to their owners, but the process continued throughout the Wednesday and Thursday.[89] Nationalization of the British firms had been the main demand of the PKI throughout the week, but Chairul Saleh, with the President's apparent support, was strongly resisting nationalization of the Shell Oil Company, since this would have created serious difficulties for the government with the other oil companies and the US government.

It was not going to be easy for the government to resist the demand for nationalization if the PKI chose to make a stand on the issue by refusing to surrender control over the firms which had been taken over although its authority was not as shaky as in 1957 and the PKI also had good reason to be apprehensive lest the military authorities should take advantage of the tense situation to re-impose martial law and suppress the PKI by force. Probably the decision to sever commercial ties with Singapore and Malaysia on 21 September was influenced to a great extent by the realization that unless some such action were taken, the PKI and the unions would be very difficult to handle. The thinking of Soekarno's ministers on this problem must have been very close to the sentiment expressed later by one of them about a similar situation; 'No Indonesian government can afford to bluntly resist popular movements of this kind: it must ride along with the tide and seek to regain control of it.' This seems to epitomize what the government tried to do on this occasion.

The government's reluctance to be forced into the nationalization of the British firms even after relations with Britain had deteriorated so far is noteworthy in the circumstances. Soekarno himself signed an order calling upon the workers to hand over the Shell installations in Palembang to the regional authorities for restoration to the management. Another instruction forbade further take-overs of oil installations. Finally, a decree of Friday 20 September brought all the taken-over firms under the 'protective custody' of the appropriate ministry 'for the sake of their own safety' and to ensure their continued operation.[90] It was stressed, however, that they were not being nationalized — although their precise status remained obscure and the British government sent an official Note seeking a definition of protective custody. The ambiguity of the order was characteristic: it enabled the Indonesian authorities to assume control of the seized enterprises from the workers while simultaneously being able to tell the British government and the British owners that only in this way could demands for their nationalization be fended off. In short, no irrevocable decision had to be made.

These measures served their purpose, for further take-overs ceased and the workers relinquished control in the following week, although some local difficulties persisted at the Shell Oil installations at Balikpapan.[91] (No doubt the unions were the more willing to acquiesce after the PKI had by then been assured of a major victory by the severing of Indonesia's links with the Western aid consortium.) Another round of take-overs was launched against the remaining British and part-British companies early in 1964 when the PKI again wanted to put pressure on the government on a foreign policy issue, but that is part of a different story.[92]

The decision to sever all trade links with Malaysia (about which there had been very little speculation earlier in the week), was taken at the end of the week after a six-hour joint session of KOTI and KOTOE; *inter alia*, the meeting was summoned to consider the report of the sub-committee set up on the Tuesday to consider the economic aspects of confrontation. Just why the decision went in favour of the trade break rather than nationalization is not entirely clear. But it is probably significant that Chairul Saleh and the newspaper most closely associated with him, *Berita Indonesia*, had been hinting at the former whereas the PKI had concentrated almost solely on the latter. Chairul Saleh also happened to be the man most likely to find a showdown with either the PKI or the foreign oil companies acutely discomforting. Probably it was also felt necessary for the government to take some dramatic action against the *Nekolim*, while avoiding the impression of giving in too blatantly to pressure from the PKI. In any case, the desire to end Singapore's grip on Indonesia's trade and, in particular, to break the ties between the Chinese merchants of Singapore and their confreres in Indonesia was of long standing and deeply felt in some circles. Only a few days earlier, Nasution had made a speech attacking foreign saboteurs of the economy who were responsible for the increase in prices and it was quite clear that he was referring to the Chinese.[93] The PKI would, of course, have avoided arguments and measures with anti-Chinese overtones; hence their preference for the direct nationalization of *British* firms — which may in itself have inclined the anti-Communists to the other side. Either course was likely to antagonize the Western aid consortium (but the trade break perhaps slightly less) and jeopardize the stabilization scheme, but to do nothing at all was practically unthinkable by that stage. Soekarno, with whom the decision ultimately rested, must have been inclined towards action both by his mercurial temperament and by his shrewd appreciation of the Indonesian political scene: either measure should mollify the PKI, but to do nothing would antagonize it seriously. Probably the decision against nationalization was also determined to some extent by a belief that the international repercussions of the trade break would not be so adverse, since no questions of compensation would arise. But if any single decision Soekarno took during that week spelled the end of the stabilization scheme, it was surely the trade break, for the attempt to divert nearly half of Indonesia's exports away from Singapore was bound to cause expense and disruption.

Just how serious the diplomatic effects of the week's events would prove to be was not immediately apparent. At first the Indonesian government seemed anxious to minimize the extent of the change that had been wrought. The British government hovered momentarily on the verge of breaking diplomatic relations with Indonesia on the day of the embassy-burning, but decided against it after receiving assurances from the Indonesian Ambassador in London that mob violence was deplored by the Indonesian government and that the safety of British lives and property in Indonesia would be guaranteed. The American government submitted oral complaints (but not formal protests) about the violation of diplomatic immunities, both through Dean Rusk to the Indonesian Ambassador in Washington and directly to President Soekarno through Ambassador Jones.[94] It did not, at that stage, immediately cut off foreign aid, however. That followed a week later, after the trade break and a further outrage when uniformed Indonesians were caught by the British trying to steal documents from the strongroom of the gutted and deserted embassy. On 24 September, the US government announced that it had come to the conclusion that the stabilization programme could not succeed, so it saw no further point in the DAC talks on credits. The IMF also suspended Indonesia's drawing rights on the unexpended portion of the $50 million stand-by credit granted several months earlier. Existing American aid programmes, running at a rate of about $70 million per annum were not cancelled, however, although it was later revealed that no new commitments were being authorized.[95]

Proposals for further talks between the leaders of the three Maphilindo nations to find a way out of the situation that had arisen began to be heard almost immediately, particularly from the Philippines, Japan and Thailand, who all had an interest in averting a serious conflict in the region.[96] Significantly, Indonesia seems to have shown rather more interest in these suggestions than Malaysia. Subandrio himself, who had left Djakarta early on 18 September for New York to put Indonesia's case to the UN General Assembly (and was therefore absent during the most critical phase), welcomed a suggestion for Japanese mediation and, after he saw Dean Rusk on 24 September, said that Indonesia wanted to find a peaceful solution. But the Tunku set stiff conditions for further talks and it was obvious that neither side was in a mood to back down publicly for the sake of a settlement, despite attempts by the Philippines to bring about another summit meeting on 25 September. Lopez commented that a cooling-off period was needed before there could be another Maphilindo conference.[96] About six weeks later, when the annual Colombo Plan Ministerial Conference was to be held in Bangkok, Subandrio made a point of attending, apparently in the hope of informal talks with Tun Razak, but the latter pointedly avoided meeting him. Negotiations for a settlement of the dispute did not begin, therefore, until the Bangkok conference of February 1964, after the intervention of Robert Kennedy. It is arguable that the delay merely increased Indonesia's intransigence, for as time passed she became more confident that she could weather the economic perils of the new course she was embarked on and the alternatives left open to the advocates of moderation became fewer and fewer. Negotiations in the last months of 1963 may have proved no more fruitful than they turned out to be in 1964, but it is a pity that they were not tried before the changes in the domestic political situation began to set firmly into a new mould after Djuanda's death and Subandrio's rapid rise to power.

[1]'British-Made Malaysia — Barrier to International Peace and Progress' in *New Forces Make a New World* (Djakarta, Department of Foreign Affairs, Indonesian Policy Series, 1964).

[2]This claim was made in Soekarno's speech of 10 July denouncing the London Agreement.

[3]Brief summaries of these speeches were published in *Harian Rakjat*, 8 June 1963.

[4]Narasimhan was one of U Thant's deputies who had visited South-East Asia in February and April, partly on West Irian business, partly to inform himself about the Malaysia dispute: he visited northern Borneo in April.

[5]This paragraph is based largely on discussions with various officials who attended the conferences. In the closed meetings Subandrio gave an impression of frankness and cordiality in order to win Razak's confidence. For instance, he explained Indonesia's attitude toward Malaysia largely in terms of her fear of the overriding threat from the Chinese, arguing that with the withdrawal of the Western powers from Asia only India, Indonesia and the Philippines had sufficient strength to stand in the way of China. Normally, Subandrio avoided the anti-Chinese argument in public. He also suggested at one point that Narasimhan might be called in to conduct the enquiry: 'after all, he is on your side'.

[6]See Appendix I, pp. 336-8.

[7]Quotations from the three major official or semi-official accounts of the Malaysia dispute published by the Indonesian Department of Foreign Affairs, *The Malaysia Issue; Background and Documents*, 1964; 'British-Made Malaysia — Barrier to Inter-

national Peace and Progress' in *New Forces Build a New World* (Indonesia Policy Series, 1965); and *The Problem of Malaysia* (The Indonesian Herald, 1963); see below, pp. 208–11 for a comment on the interpretations given in these accounts.

[8]*The Problem of Malaysia*, p. 9.

[9]The Malaysian view of the matter was forcefully put by Goh Keng Swee at the Bangkok Conference on 7 Feb. 1964: 'So the obligations of the Government of Malaya in regard to the Manila Agreement really boiled down to these. First, we would consult the three governments concerned, Britain, Sarawak and Sabah. Second, we would require them to cooperate in the ascertainment. Third, the Federation of Malaya would do its best to persuade Britain to extend its cooperation and facilities. Mr. Chairman, we have fulfilled our obligation in every detail, both in letter and in spirit.' Unofficial transcript of proceedings, in the possession of the author.

[10]Private information, but press reports corroborate the general impression.

[11]*Harian Rakjat*, 13 June 1963. Subandrio's enthusiasm for *musjawarah Maphilindo* was in striking contrast to the coolness of the PKI.

[12]*Harian Rakjat*, 15 June 1963. The conference communique was not identical with the Manila Accord and when Subandrio returned to Djakarta on 13 June, he said the contents of the agreement could not yet be published as they were only a recommendation to the Summit meeting to follow; but he stressed that there was no deviation from Indonesia's support for the struggle of the people of North Kalimantan. The Accord was published in Manila by Pelaez shortly afterwards.

[13]'U.S. imperialism' had just provided further proof of its villainy (see *Harian Rakjat*, 8 and 10 June) when Averell Harriman made a statement strengthening America's endorsement of Malaysia.

[14]The PKI's three conditions for an acceptable plebiscite in North Kalimantan were that British troops must be withdrawn; that political detainees must be released and Azahari be permitted to campaign; and that a similar referendum be held in Singapore and Malaysia because of opposition there. *Harian Rakjat*, 20 June 1963.

[15]Cf. the suspicious but mild comments on the 'confederation' idea in *Harian Rakjat* on 8, 11 and 12 June 1963 (when the stress was still on the difficulties of getting agreement on the idea) with the PKI's silence on the matter from mid-June until 11 July.

[16]See *Harian Rakjat*, 11 and 15 July 1963, for arguments that a Summit meeting was now unnecessary and even 'dangerous'. The slogan '*Ganjang Malaysia*' was used prominently on 11 July, but had presumably been coined before that.

[17]See *Harian Rakjat*, 16 July 1963.

[18]The Philippines government was reported as being reluctant to comment on Soekarno's speech, presumably to avoid offending him and further reducing the chances of holding the Summit meeting. (Macapagal would surely have spoken out in support of Soekarno if there had been any justification for his view in the Manila Accords.) See *Harian Rakjat*, 13 July 1963, which also reported (rather surprisingly) a Radio Malaya statement that the Philippines agreed that the decision to create Malaysia did *not* conflict with the Manila Accord.

[19]See pp. 70–1 above.

[20]For example, see *Indonesian Herald* (the semi-official mouthpiece of the Foreign Ministry), 27 May 1963, for a claim that the prospects of Malaysia's formation were not promising. Indonesian press comment on foreign news (and probably much official reporting too) frequently picked on the one aspect of an incident which seemed to conform with Indonesian hopes or expectations, without much appraisal of counterbalancing factors: e.g. the Sultan of Brunei was hailed momentarily in *Berita Indonesia*, 13 July 1963, for 'showing guts' when he refused to join Malaysia, but a few days later he was again written off as a British pawn.

[21]*Harian Rakjat*, 17 July; *Berita Indonesia*, 26 July; *The Age*, 17 July 1963.

[22]*Suluh Indonesia*, 31 July 1963.

[23]*Indonesian Involvement in Eastern Malaysia* (Kuala Lumpur, Department of Information, 1964), p.48. Compare the large raids on 4 and 6 July and 8 August 1963.

[24]Ibid. p. 9: Indonesians saw this as 'an insult to our dignity', according to *Berita Indonesia*, 27 and 29 July 1963.

[25]Soekarno's speech on 27 July developed the '*Ganjang Malaysia*' theme with a loving relish and ended with the statement that he was going to Manila 'to carry on our confrontation in opposing and nullifying the neo-colonialism of Malaysia': *Berita Indonesia*, 30 July 1963.

[26]Ganis Harsono, quoted in *Nation* (Rangoon, 1 Aug. 1963): *The Age* (Melbourne, 30 July 1963, 'took an optimistic view that if Soekarno was still intending to "confront" Malaysia, it was difficult to see why he came to Manila'.

[27]The *Straits Times*, 1 Aug. 1963, contrasted Soekarno's mood of Wednesday with that of the previous day when he 'seemed ready for a clash with the Tengku'.

[28]*Straits Times*, 1 Aug. 1963. Mackenzie's status at the conference was a matter of some uncertainty: his instructions from New York required him to act as the 'eyes and ears of U Thant', which implied a more active role than that of a mere purveyor of messages. Djakarta officials criticized him angrily for being more than that when recounting to me later that he consulted Inche Ghazali, the principal Malayan official, before he cabled New York. (See *Straits Times*, 1 August 1963, for corroboration that he did so.) It certainly appears that he later took some degree of initiative in his telephone report to New York on the deadlock that developed on 2 August, as a result of which U Thant sent his third cable next day proposing a limited form of ascertainment in Borneo, which was to break the deadlock and pave the way for a formula acceptable to Malaysia. This also angered the Philippines and Indonesian ministers.

[29]*The Times* (London), 1 Aug.; *Bangkok Post*, 2 Aug.: Principle 9 of the Annex to General Assembly Resolution 1541 (XV) of 15 December 1960 provides that where a territory is achieving self-government through integration with an independent state 'integration should have come about in the following circumstances:
   a. The integrating territory should have attained an advanced stage of self-government with free political institutions, so that its peoples would have the capacity to make a responsible choice through informed and democratic processes;
   b. The integration should be the result of the freely expressed wishes of the territory's peoples acting with full knowledge of the change in their status, their wishes having been expressed through informed and democratic processes, impartially conducted and based on universal adult suffrage. The United Nations could, when it deems it necessary, supervise these processes.'

[30]*New York Times*, 2 August 1963; *Sydney Morning Herald*, 2 August 1963. A statement by Duncan Sandys in the House of Commons on 2 August, in reply to a question about the postponement of Malaysia Day, confirmed the impression of British obtuseness about any suggestion of compromise.

[31]*Sydney Morning Herald*, 2 August: *Bangkok Post*, 1 August 1963. Salvador P. Lopez had replaced Vice-President Pelaez as Foreign Minister of the Philippines on the eve of the conference, after the latter had resigned in anger because Macapagal had implicated his name in the Stonehill scandal. Whereas Pelaez had played an influential part in the June meeting of Foreign Ministers, Lopez closely followed Macapagal's policy of siding with Indonesia rather than Malaysia from this time on.

[32]The information from which this account of the Manila conferences has been compiled is derived, unless otherwise specified, from press reports in *The Times*, *New York Times*, *Sydney Morning Herald* and the *Age* (Melbourne), corroborated by discussions with Mr. A. M. Mackenzie, whose help I acknowledge with gratitude. Former Vice-President Pelaez and Mr. Narcisco Reyes, Philippines Ambassador to Djakarta, Mr. Suwito, Deputy Foreign Minister of Indonesia, and Ganis Harsono all contributed towards my understanding of their countries' attitudes to the Manila Agreements, although my final interpretation of it has differed considerably from theirs.

[33]Kahin was present at the Manila conference with President Soekarno's delegation and his account in 'Malaysia and Indonesia', *Pacific Affairs*, Fall 1964, reflects the view generally offered by Indonesians at that time. The Manila Agreements provided 'what might have been a viable, mutually acceptable formula' for settling the Indonesia-Malaysia dispute: the resolutions could have enabled the Indonesian and Philippines governments to tell their peoples that Great Britain had had to consider their wishes and 'permitted Soekarno and Macapagal to climb down gracefully'. Both leaders had expected a verdict from the UN Mission favourable to Malaysia and 'had privately so advised U Thant', said Kahin (ibid. p. 269). Substantially the same view was commonly attributed to Ambassador Jones also; see *Indonesia: the Possible Dream*, pp. 281–4.

[34]*The Times*, 2 and 3 Aug. 1963.

[35]*The Times*, 3 Aug. 1963.

[36]*The Times*, 3 Aug. 1963.

[37]*Nation* (Rangoon), 4 Aug. 1963.

[38]*Straits Times*, 5 Aug.; *New York Times*, 4 Aug. 1963.

[39]*A Survey on the Controversial Problem of the Establishment of the Federation of Malaysia.* Memorandum released by the Permanent Mission of the Republic of Indonesia to the United Nations, 24 Sept. 1963.

[40]*Aide Memoire from the Observers of the Republic of Indonesia to the UN Malaysia Mission in Sarawak and Sabah*, para. 2.

[41]Since it was not politic for him to oppose Maphilindo openly, Lee Kuan Yew argued rather casuistically that he could approve the concept only as an instrument for economic and cultural cooperation, but that any political involvement would have to be ratified by the peoples concerned: see *Straits Times*, 10 August 1963. By mid-1964, when the Maphilindo spirit had almost completely disappeared, he was much more forthright in replying to an UMNO critic's challenge to say why the PAP was afraid of it: 'We are not afraid of Maphilindo. We will fight it because it is a racial concept. It will definitely break up Malaysia if the idea materializes.'

[42]For a characteristic formulation of the Washington view, see the editorial in *New York Times*, 6 August.

[43]Interview with Tun Razak, January 1965: Pelaez's attitude is discussed in Bernard K. Gordon, 'The Potential for Indonesian Expansionism', pp. 25–6.

[44]Interview with Ganis Harsono, December 1964.

[45]The point was bluntly made by Arifin Bey, editor of the *Indonesian Herald*, in a speech to the American Men's Association in Djakarta in August 1964 when he described Maphilindo as 'an attempt to domesticate the Overseas Chinese': typescript in possession of author.

[46]Gordon, op. cit. pp. 23–4.

[47]Ibid. pp. 19–34 for a brief survey of the various strands of Macapagal's new foreign policy ventures in 1962–3.

[48]Arifin Bey, loc. cit.

[49]'Indonesia is perhaps the only Southeast Asian state in which irredentism is openly cited by leading officials as a possible impetus for governmental actions.' Gordon, op. cit. pp. 80–7: see also Arnold Brackman, *Southeast Asia's Second Front*, pp. 122–5, 178–80.

[50]Brackman, op. cit. p. 187.

[51]Ibid. pp. 188–9.

[52]Interview with Ganis Harsono, December 1964.

[53]For the Tunku's press conference, see *Straits Times*, 7 August 1963. Nasution made statements denouncing the Sabah and Sarawak elections on 6 August and approving the continuation of guerrilla incursions into Sarawak on 31 August: *Straits Times*, 7 August, and *Far Eastern Economic Review*, 5 Sept. 1963.

[54]*New York Times*, 10 and 13 August 1963: U Thant's letter of 8 August is included in the *UN Malaysia Mission Report*, para. 2.

[55]*New York Times*, 14 and 18 August 1963. Soekarno's brief reference in his August 17 speech to the Manila Agreements was characteristic of his ability to give a misleading impression of the Agreements without too blatantly contradicting them: 'Malaysia is not to be established before the right of self-determination of the peoples of North Kalimantan has been exercised .... The UN will send working teams to arrange this self-determination ....' According to the *Far Eastern Economic Review*, 5 Sept, a meeting of parties and mass organizations was instructed on 11 August that Malaysia was not to be made the target for hostile comments.

[56]*Straits Times*, 20 August 1963.

[57]*The Times*, 21 and 22 August 1963: see also *New York Times*, 23, 24, 25 August for comment on the significance of the observers controversy and its resolution.

[58]An official British account of the dispute over observers was summarized in the *Philippines Free Press*, 19 Oct. 1963, p. 82. Britain initially agreed to permit the three Maphilindo countries each to send one observer to Sarawak and one to Sabah. Indonesia and the Philippines immediately demanded that 20 observers and 10 assistants be permitted. Britain then doubled the number from 2 to 4 for each country; Indonesia refused this but reduced her request to 9. Then U Thant proposed that 4 observers and 4 'clerical assistants' be permitted. Britain accepted this, subject to certain conditions regarding the assistants.

[59]The *UN Malaysia Mission Report* reveals (para. 5) that its hearings were originally scheduled for 22–31 August 1963, but because of the delay over the observers were rescheduled from 26 August to 2 September: additional hearings were held on 3 and 4 September also.

[60]See *The Problem of Malaysia* (Djakarta, the Indonesian Herald, 1963), pp. 15–16.

[61]Interview with Malaysian officials accompanying Ghazali.

[62]*Harian Rakjat*, 31 August.

[63]*Straits Times*, 6 September. Howard P. Jones also comments on the mildness of Subandrio's initial reaction to the August 29 announcement, but remarks that Soekarno was infuriated by it.

[64]For U Thant's statement of 14 September, issued simultaneously with the *UN Mission to Malaysia Report to the Secretary General* see *Malaysia, Select Documents*, pp. 200–1.

[65]Ibid. p. 199.

[66]The Aide-Memoires of the Indonesian and Philippines observer teams can be found in an appendix to *The Problem of Malaysia*.

[67]Soekarno's speech at Purwokerto on 28 August contained an unusually direct admission that he was feeling unwell and weary of the burdens of office: see *Suluh Indonesia*, 29 August.

[68]*New York Times*, 29 August.

[69]K. D. Thomas, 'Recent Developments in Indonesia', *Australia's Neighbours*, 4th series, no. 11–12, Jan.-Feb. 1964.

[70]This point is stressed by Donald Hindley in 'Indonesia's Confrontation with Malaysia; the Search for Motives'; but specific evidence that Army leaders were hostile to the stabilization scheme and therefore actively seeking to intensify confrontation at this time is not easy to find.

[71]*Suluh Indonesia*, 5, 7, 12 September.

[72]It would be wrong to suppose that the PKI was bending its efforts exclusively to the confrontation of Malaysia. Throughout mid-1963 it was more concerned with domestic goals and policies. Although the break with Malaysia was a major gain for the PKI, it did not come about in the way the PKI was urging and the events of September caused it a good deal of alarm as well as elation, for it was very apprehensive that the Army would seize the opportunity to re-impose martial law.

[73]This view was put to me very forcefully by a senior British diplomat in early 1965.

[74]The 'take-overs' of 1957 are described in K. D. Thomas and Bruce Glassburner, 'Abrogation, Take-Over and Nationalisation: The Elimination of Dutch Dominance from the Republic of Indonesia', *Australian Outlook*, vol. XIX, no. 2, August 1965, pp. 158–79. For a fuller account of the political background to the affair, see Herbert Feith, *The Decline of Constitutional Democracy*, pp. 578 ff.

[75]Djuanda was the minister most strongly committed to the stabilization programme; a sympathetic assessment of his role in Indonesian politics is given in Daniel S. Lev, *The Transition to Guided Democracy, Indonesian Politics, 1957–59* (Cornell Modern Indonesia Project, 1966) pp. 176–82. Even he spoke in favour of a radical transformation of Indonesia's economic relationship with Singapore, although the most vocal proponent of this seems to have been Chairul Saleh (with some encouragement from Nasution).

[76]Subandrio told the press after the KOTI meeting on 15 September that Indonesia could not endorse the birth of Malaysia, but that this attitude could be changed if the UN made 'corrections in the implementation' of the enquiry: the formation of Malaysia could be accepted if it were carried out on the basis of the Manila Agreement.

[77]Indonesian Foreign Ministry officials insisted that it was not Indonesia but Malaysia who formally broke off diplomatic relations, since their refusal to accept Malaysia did not amount to a severance of relations with Malaya. This subtle distinction was hardly acceptable in Kuala Lumpur, however.

[78]*The Sun* (Melbourne), 16 September 1963.

[79]*Bintang Timur*, 15 Sept: *Suluh Indonesia*, 16 Sept. 1963.

[80]The following account of the embassy attacks on the Monday is based largely on *Suluh Indonesia*, 17 Sept. and *The Times* (London), 18 Sept. 1963.

[81]The KOTOE committee consisted of Leimena, Chairul Saleh, Surachman, Munir, Jusuf Muda Dalam, Dr. Suharto, Ir. Abdulrahman, Mutalib, Dr. Surjadi, Achmadi, Sutikno Slamet and Dasaad.

[82]A headline in *Suluh Indonesia*, 18 Sept. 1963, proclaimed 'Tunku tramples on Indonesian national emblem'; cf. also *Harian Rakjat*, 18 Sept. (Curiously *Berita Indonesia* ignored the story until next day.) The *Suluh Indonesia* editorial two days later was a masterpiece of hyperbole, putting the blame for the Wednesday attack on the Tunku's 'incomparable insult.... The demonstration at the Malayan Embassy in Djakarta on the

16th was orderly. If there was one incident that was a very small matter. It cannot be compared with what happened to the Indonesian Embassy in Kuala Lumpur.'
[83]The Malaysian version of the episode can be found in *The Times*, 18 September.
[84]*Suluh Indonesia*, 19 September: *The Times*, 19 Sept. 1963.
[85]A headline in *Berita Indonesia* (20 Sept.) proclaimed: 'The counter-revolutionaries have mobilised ten thousand members'. On 18 Sept. (even before the burning of the British embassy) *Harian Rakjat* prominently displayed a Central Committee announcement calling for order and discipline, so that the British imperialists could not take advantage of the anger of the people (i.e. by provoking a military crackdown). A curious sidelight is that Wednesday's *Harian Rakjat* carried a violent attack on the newspaper *Pelopor*, the mouthpiece of its arch-enemy SOKSI (an anti-Communist union favoured by a number of Army-connected 'bureaucratic capitalists'), for not reporting the Monday demonstrations; SOKSI men and trucks were later alleged to have been involved in the embassy burning on Wednesday afternoon. It is quite conceivable that they took part, either to demonstrate their patriotic fervour or to provoke Army action against the PKI (or both!).
[86]Interview with Brigadier General Umar Wirahadikusuma, January 1965.
[87]*Berita Indonesia*, 20 September 1963: the term *tindakan liar* has beeen translated as 'unauthorized actions', although *liar* also connotes 'wild, untamed'.
[88]Subandrio had left Indonesia to lead the Indonesian delegation to the UN General Assembly, but he flew back to Djakarta within a few days of arriving in New York: on arriving in Tokyo on 19 Sept., he had welcomed a Japanese offer to cooperate in seeking a solution to the dispute and said that the road to a solution could be found in a week or two when the situation had calmed down: the Tunku had acted too impetuously, he said: *Suluh Indonesia*, 21 Sept. 1963.
[89]*Berita Indonesia*, 19 Sept. 1963: Chairul Saleh also quoted a statement by Subandrio that 'we've already got enough on our hands'.
[90]*Berita Indonesia*, 20 Sept. 1963: cf. *The Times*, 21 Sept. 1963.
[91]*The Times*, 23, 24 and 30 Sept. and 4 Oct. 1963. The attitude of the local commander seems to have been extremely important in all regions. In East Kalimantan, Lt. Col. Suharjo simply refused to obey the central government's orders. (He was removed some months later.)
[92]See below, pp. 225–6, 243.
[93]Nasution's speech at Lembang in which he stressed the need for economic confrontation of Malaysia in order to stop Singapore's 'subversion' of the Indonesian economy was given considerable prominence in *Berita Indonesia*, 19 and 20 Sept. 1963.
[94]*The Times*, 19 Sept.: *New York Times*, 20 Sept. 1963. See also Howard P. Jones, op. cit. pp. 262–3 — although his account gives a misleading impression that the Malaysians were the first to resort to embassy-stoning, not the Indonesians.
[95]See *New York Times*, 25 Sept., 8, 15 and 28 Nov. 1963 for details of American aid to Indonesia at that time.
[96]See *New York Times*, 20, 22, 26, 27 Sept. 1963; *The Times* (London) 21, 27, 30 Sept.; *Suluh Indonesia*, 27 Sept. The Japanese Prime Minister, Ikeda, who was just setting off on a goodwill visit to the Philippines and Indonesia, was reported at various times as having offered his services to bring about an amicable settlement of the dispute. Subandrio publicly welcomed his offer but it seems that Ikeda confined his efforts to informal discussions. The Thai Foreign Minister urged further talks, in a very general way, while in New York for the General Assembly session where moves were being made for another Summit. The Tunku insisted on three conditions for such a meeting — 'that whatever decision is reached every effort will be made to honour it: secondly, that they will normalise diplomatic relations with us, and the initiative must be taken by them, as they were the first to break off diplomatic relations with us; thirdly Indonesia must undertake to stop any aggressive actions direct or indirect, and all troops now concentrated on the border of Sarawak must be withdrawn.'

VIII

The Course of Confrontation 1963-1964

THE open breach between Indonesia and Malaysia in September 1963 constituted a major turning-point in the development of confrontation. Until then, Indonesia's efforts had amounted to little more than a strategy of exploiting any opportunities that might arise to frustrate the formation of Malaysia, without involving the two countries in open conflict. Soekarno was far from being wholeheartedly or irrevocably committed to confrontation. But the events of September pushed him into a commitment to 'crush Malaysia' ('*Ganjang Malaysia*', a phrase that was enthusiastically taken up in Indonesia at this time) from which it became increasingly difficult for him to draw back, mainly for reasons of domestic politics. Even in this new phase, however, the campaign against Malaysia was still pursued in a tentative and haphazard fashion, notable more for its high-flown rhetoric than for its effectiveness.

For several months, the political and military implications of the new course were not at all clear. Although border raids in Borneo were stepped up a little, the scale and intensity of Indonesia's military efforts there were not at all commensurate with her fierce threats to 'crush Malaysia'. Initially, the economic thrust of confrontation seemed more purposeful and specific — the diversion of Indonesia's export trade away from Singapore, with the aim of strengthening the Indonesian economy and weakening Malaysia's. During 1964, however, the emphasis changed. Confrontation became an intensely political affair, its purpose far more 'expressive' than 'instrumental' so far as Soekarno and his government were concerned. The emancipation of Indonesia's trade from Singapore domination was almost forgotten and smuggling to Malaysia was gradually resumed in 1964. Soon the economic consequences of the break began to prove more burdensome for Indonesia than for Malaysia, as many observers had expected from the outset, for the diversion of trade was bound to prove expensive and disruptive; yet dire predictions that Indonesian economy would 'collapse' in three or six months proved to be very wide off the mark.[1] Despite the resumption of serious inflation after the collapse of the stabilization programme in September 1963, economic dislocation did not greatly hamper the government in its campaign against Malaysia until late in 1964 (or even later), when the inflation began to accelerate and the shortage of foreign exchange became really acute. Even then, however, economic pressure did not force Soekarno back to the conference table in 1965. Domestic political forces proved to be far more important than sheer economic necessity in determining the course of confrontation.

Before we look further into these aspects of the campaign, however, some attention should be given to the way Indonesians formulated their case against Malaysia, the reasons why they felt so strongly that the conflict must be pursued to its end, despite its great costs, and the nature of the arguments they advanced. It is impossible to explain why the Indonesians followed the course they did unless one takes into account the way they saw the dispute, through the ideological lens of the doctrine of the New Emerging Forces.

INDONESIA'S PROPAGANDA OFFENSIVE

Indonesia's propaganda war against Malaysia revolved around four main categories of argument — the charge that Malaysia was a neo-colonialist puppet created by the British and imposed upon the people against their will; that it posed a threat to Indonesia's security and to the peace of the whole South-East Asia region; that the continuation of 'imperialist and neo-colonialist' influence in South-East Asia was doomed on historicist grounds ('the tide of history is against them'); that Indonesia was insultingly disregarded and humiliated by the manner of Malaysia's formation, particularly by the alleged breach of the Manila Agreements in September 1963, and by her later refusal, because of British pressure, to negotiate a compromise settlement in 'the Asian manner' of *musjawarah* (consultations).

In the Indonesian view, Malaysia's refusal to agree to the proposals for a compromise settlement of the dispute which Soekarno put forward during the 1964 negotiations could only be regarded as evidence that she was not really interested in a peaceful settlement. She was also regarded as seeking, with British support and encouragement, to overthrow the Indonesian government or, at the least, to 'divert the course of the Indonesian revolution'.

Unfortunately, while it is only fair to summarize these arguments as far as possible in the terms they were stated in at the time, some distortion and over-simplification is inevitable. It is not as easy to expound them persuasively to anyone who is disposed to rebut them as it was to Indonesians who were willing to accept the doctrine of the New Emerging Forces and its all-embracing *Weltanschauung*, which was ideologically congenial to them. Sometimes the official doctrines would evoke cynical or scathing comments in private from Indonesians who were critical of Soekarno, but such sentiments were rare and could not be uttered in public except at great personal risk. Most ordinary Indonesians who had few sources of information apart from the government-controlled media of press and radio accepted the broad outlines of these arguments. One often heard more plausible formulations of the case against Malaysia from unsophisticated Indonesians who had instinctive and honest attitudes to the whole affair, albeit muddled and inconsistent, than one found in the high-flown rhetoric of the Great Leader of the Revolution or the clever, quicksilver arguments of their diplomats.

First, because it was central to all Indonesian charges against Malaysia since the end of 1962, was the objection that Malaysia was merely a creation of the imperialists and neo-colonialists, a stratagem to maintain the reality of British power behind the facade of independence. It was engineered by the British to maintain their commercial and strategic interests in collaboration with Malaya's feudal rulers and the capitalist Chinese *towkays* who also have vested interests in the old established order created by the colonial rulers. 'Why is it that from the very beginning we said we did not agree with the formation of Malaysia?.... Because we are convinced that Malaysia is neo-colonialism....' Soekarno told a mass rally (overlooking the fact that he had not said so until long after the very beginning): 'The objectives of old-style colonialism or imperialism and of their new-style counterparts are the same. Firstly, their economic aims are the same. One nation can drain the economy of another country, control the economy of another nation by all kinds of methods.... Besides exploiting economic wealth, imperialism sometimes aims at military control... by means of new-style neo-colonialism.'[2]

Indonesian scepticism about the reality of Malaysia's independence was grounded in the bitter experiences of her own fight for independence through bloody struggle and revolution. Colonial rulers do not simply surrender their power for reasons of altruism or prudence: Indonesia's negotiations with the Dutch during her struggle for independence were remembered as a long series of frustrations and confidence tricks. Real independence can only be achieved if it is fought for and paid for with sacrifices, reiterated Soekarno. Even continued exposure to foreign economic and cultural influences was felt to be a detraction from true independence, so it was impossible for a country so lacking in 'individuality' (*kepribadian*) and a distinctive ideology as Malaysia to be considered free in the same sense as Indonesia. Its leaders were regarded as mere stooges of the British, just as Sultan Hamid of Pontianak, Dr. Mansur and other Federalist leaders of the United States of Indonesia were regarded as puppets of the Dutch.[3] Tunku Abdul Rahman had never had a good press in Indonesia. He differed entirely in temperament, political outlook and experience from Soekarno, while their two governments had both been mutually suspicious of the other's ultimate intentions towards each other since Malaya became independent in 1957. Relations were never cordial and often bad.

The following extract is characteristic of the way Indonesia's Foreign Ministry depicted the dispute with Malaysia:

'Malaysia' is an artificial federation of the British colonial possessions of Malaya, Singapore, Sarawak and Sabah (North Borneo). It did not arise out of a free association at the will of the people concerned, but was imposed by the British colonial authorities in connivance with the yes-men in the Kuala Lumpur regime whom the British had installed beforehand.

'Malaysia' is but British colonialism in new form, established in order to protect and to maintain British political, economic and military interests. In pursuance of this objective, not only does British-made 'Malaysia' neglect and suppress the interests of the people subjected to its rule; it also attempts to subvert, to deflect from its course and to contain the Indonesian Revolution, because that Revolution is pledged to the complete and final eradication of colonial and imperial domination.

These are the reasons why the people of North Kalimantan set up an independent state of their own. These are the reasons why various groups in Malaya and Singapore oppose the present Kuala Lumpur regime. These are the reasons why the Republic of Indonesia is conducting a policy of confrontation against the neo-colonialism of 'Malaysia'.

And this, in a nut-shell, is the 'Malaysia' problem.

It is not a dispute between the two sovereign and independent states. It is a struggle against the domination and exploitation which British neo-colonialism exercises against the peoples of Malaya, Singapore and North Kalimantan. It is a struggle against the interference, intervention, sabotage and subversion which British neo-colonialiam exerts against the Indonesian State and Revolution.

This problem of 'Malaysia' is disturbing the South-East Asia region, where colonialism and imperialism have been fighting to maintain their interests in country after country. 'Malaysia' is but the latest device of many, and it is directed against Indonesia.

The forces of colonialism, imperialism and neo-colonialism have been inflicting many sufferings upon the people of the whole region. And now the neo-colonialism of 'Malaysia' has brought a situation that threatens to erupt at any time into a conflict of much greater proportions, the fore-runner of a world conflagration.[4]

However distorted and inaccurate this view may seem to Westerners, there was enough *prima facie* resemblance to the truth in it to account for its widespread acceptance inside Indonesia. The contrary opinion, that Britain's reasons for establishing and defending Malaysia (and the Tunku's) were based on defensible and even worthy principles, would ring strangely hollow to anyone disposed to be suspicious of British intentions, especially after the Brunei revolt, the arrest of opponents of Malaysia in Singapore and Malaysia, the refusal to hold a referendum in Borneo about Malaysia, the continued reliance on Ghurka troops and British military might for the defence of Malaysia and the hostility in British circles to the idea of Maphilindo. Indonesians frequently heard statements by Azahari, Mangol, Ibrahim Yaakub and other anti-Malaysia leaders from Malaysia to the effect that resistance to British or Malaysian oppression was steadily rising there; every report of trouble in Sarawak or other parts of Malaysia was presented, often in lurid or distorted form, as yet another sign that the people of Malaysia were growing impatient with their feudal or neo-colonialist rulers, that Malaysia was splitting apart as Soekarno had always predicted it would. The race riots of 1964 and the separation of Singapore almost a year later were even more encouraging evidence to this effect, particularly as each came after long months of disappointingly little progress from the Indonesian point of view.

Whether or not Malaysia is viable in the long run is, of course, an arguable question to which no confident answer can be given even now. There is a sense in which it is an 'artificial' creation, although so are many other nations of the Third World and there is much to be said before it can be written off as a mere puppet of the British merely on that score. It is also, as the Indonesians reiterated, governed by the more conservative elements in Malay and Chinese society who have close ties with the British at many levels and little interest in the sort of radical changes that the brash young men who looked towards Djakarta or Peking for inspiration would like. In fact, their very moderation, pragmatism and restraint on some of the country's most explosive problems were not accounted as virtues in Indonesia, but as a lack of *semangat* (spirit, ardour) and revolutionary drive. How could such men stand up to their former colonial masters? How was it possible that their bland and unheroic approach to politics could produce better results than Indonesia's? It was better to suppress the question. Even 'moderate' Indonesians like Hatta expressed distaste for the sober, bourgeois character of the new Malaya as they saw it — presumably the towns mainly, more cosmopolitan or Chinese in character than Malay, and so much the less attractive for that.[5] No matter how much truth there may or may not have been in Indonesian characterizations of Malaysia as a British cats-paw, a house of cards lacking in identity and *raison d'être*, it is hardly surprising that they thought it. The contrast of political styles and ideologies reinforced the conflict of interests (in the short term at least), while the paucity of communication between and regarding the two countries helped to exaggerate the stereotypes the inhabitants of each country held about the other. Many Indonesians used to visit Singapore, but it was little more than a Chinese emporium to them. Many Sumatrans and Indonesian Chinese had relatives there and on the peninsula; some of them have lived there for considerable periods, usually amongst the ethnic community to which they belong. But those groups were generally uninfluential outsiders in Soekarno's Indonesia, in no position to spread opinions that might modify the stereotype, even if they wanted to do so.

The second broad category of arguments against Malaysia, based on the threat to Indonesia's security, were more varied and loosely connected. The belief that Singapore, as a huge British base and a haven for smugglers, was potentially a dagger posed at Indonesia's throat has been in general currency for many years. Memories of foreign intervention in Indonesia's internal conflicts in 1958–9 left a feeling of acute sensitivity to military threats from that quarter. Concern about the perpetuation of the British bases under the Anglo-Malaysian defence agreements has been one of the most plausible arguments given in explanation of confrontation since it was first launched in early 1963. Allegations of 'encirclement' by the imperialists (not only the British, but also the Americans with their bases in the Philippines and the Australians, who were allowing the British V-bombers to use Darwin) were a later elaboration of the same argument — a less valid one, perhaps, but none the less potent in the minds of people who had been conditioned by Soekarno's ideology to feel isolated, embattled and threatened by hostile forces pressing down upon them. By 1964–5, the feeling that 'If we don't get them, they'll get us' was very widespread, particularly after the scare in September 1964 when the possibility of a British air or naval attack on Indonesia's installations loomed ominously close for a brief moment. Yet the external threat was not usually visualized in narrowly military terms, except in the minds of the top military leaders like Nasution, who knew well enough the strategic vulnerability of Indonesia's armed forces vis-à-vis British or American military power. More commonly, the threat was stated in political and ideological terms, 'a struggle against the interference, intervention, sabotage, and subversion which British neo-colonialism exerts against the Indonesian State and Revolution'.[6] Not much effort was ever made by the Indonesian government to show concrete evidence of British sabotage or intervention in 1963–4, presumably because it was barely necessary for internal consumption — one naturally expected that sort of behaviour from the Nekolim. Instead, the Nekolim aim of containing or subverting the Indonesian revolution was stressed, for it was inherent in the dialectical nature of their conflict with the New Emerging Forces that they should seek to do so.

As it happened, the almost metaphysical, transcendental nature of this argument that the Nekolim must necessarily be in conflict with the New Emerging Forces came to be stressed step by step with the deterioration in their relations with both the British and the Americans after September 1963, and this only seemed to support the truth of the doctrine. It is interesting that the earliest Indonesian semi-official survey of the Malaysia dispute in September 1963 has almost nothing to say about any neo-colonialist threat to Indonesia (although this argument was being developed by early 1964), despite its fulminations against British neo-colonialist manipulation of the peoples of Malaysia.[7]

A third set of Indonesian arguments against Malaysia was based on the belief that Malaysia was a historical anachronism because of its continued dependence on Britain and close ties with her. The neo-colonialists were seen as attempting to 'stem the tide of history' by trying to prevent the peoples of South-East Asia working out their own destiny in their own way. This was not only unjustifiable in Indonesian eyes, it was also doomed to failure in this 'century of the revolutionary uprising of the people of Asia and Africa': in this universal conflict, it seemed obvious in 1963–4 that the imperialists and neo-colonialists were in retreat and disarray. America's embarrassing predicament in Viet-Nam could be cited as proof that the withdrawal of Western power which began when the former colonies proclaimed their independence in 1945 was now reaching its final phase.

This kind of view also came strongly to the fore in discussion of Maphilindo and the long-term problems of security in South-East Asia. It underlay the reasoning even of those Indonesians who spoke of China as the principal threat to the security of the region, which could not be admitted publicly by those who were strongly committed to the official ideology in which Indonesia and China were New Emerging Forces together. They would frequently demand of a questioner: 'How can you contain the threat from China with Western troops and arms? Does not the defence of the area have to depend in the last resort upon the people of the area? How much reliance could we place on the Western powers to defend Asia in 1941, when they still had huge vested interests here?' Most Indonesians were scornful of the argument that Malaysia had been created a bulwark against Communism or Chinese expansionism. If that were Britain's purpose, they would argue, why put more reliance on a fragile nation of 10 million (half of them Chinese) than on 100 million or more Indonesians? 'Is not a Maphilindo-type association of the three kindred nations of Malay race the best solution in the long run? Then why did the British try to sabotage Maphilindo? There must be a political solution to our disputes in the long run and all over the world there is a trend towards bigger regional units like the European Economic Community. Maphilindo is a natural development, for Malaya and the Philippines cannot rely on their defence treaties with the Western powers for ever.' This may have been a question-begging line or argument, but there was enough validity in it to cast doubts over alternative solutions to the long-term political and strategic problems of the area — except on the dubious assumption that American and British power would never be entirely withdrawn from the region. Perhaps that is conceivable, but an Indonesian would find it hard to believe and he would certainly not approve of it. 'Why is South-East Asia the concern of Britain? What right does the British government think it has to determine what constitutes peace or stability in this corner of the globe.' Outside interference has only bred wars and conflicts in Asia, he would argue, which would have been avoided if the peoples concerned could have sorted out the problems in their own way. Even the Filipinos were attracted towards this view as expressed in the Soekarno-Macapagal doctrine that 'Asian problems should be solved by Asians in the Asian way'.

All these arguments were based partly on what might be called a plain man's geopolitics, partly on the doctrine of struggle between the New Emerging Forces and the *Nekolim* in which the former were destined to triumph in the long run. They were essentially historicist arguments in their assumptions that the future course of South-East Asia's history will be simply an extrapolation of recent trends. Western-trained political scientists may easily question the basis of the analysis, yet it is not surprising that Indonesians did not. Soekarno himself was inclined to think in a Toynbee-esque, almost millenarian vein. And his successes on the international stage over recent years were due in large part to his perceptive assessment of the changing balance of power in Asia, in the Communist bloc and in the non-aligned world. He suffered set-backs too, of course, notably at the Cairo Conference of Non-aligned Nations in October 1964: but it must be conceded that he generally succeeded to a degree in maximizing Indonesia's bargaining power beyond what her economic and military resources might seem to warrant. So long as he was able to keep on claiming successes, few Indonesians could easily oppose him on this matter. His intense diplomatic activity among the Afro-Asians in 1964–5 was largely intended just to maintain the outward impression that successes were still being achieved, although the pretence was becoming rather threadbare by then.

The fourth class of arguments against Malaysia, those based on the assertion that the manner of its formation violated the Manila Agreements, had a rather different character from the others. They did not have the same broad metaphysical or ideological sweep, but were more specific and legalistic in nature. This made them more suitable for persuading foreigners who had not been indoctrinated with the ideology of the New Emerging Forces, whereas the latter carried more weight at home, where it was less necessary to prove that the *Nekolim* were at fault, for that was only to be expected. The charge that the Manila Agreements had been violated was used by the Indonesian government as the basis for its refusal to accept the UN Mission's report and to grant immediate recognition to Malaysia on September 16.[8] It was also the main issue in the negotiations subsequently in Bangkok and Tokyo. Because the argument hinged on the interpretation of texts, it was susceptible to debate on the basis of specific documents and evidence, to an extent that the other arguments were not. But it was not so important to the Indonesian case that these charges should stand up in a court of law, as that they should have a superficial plausibility. For the issue was essentially a political one, not legal. What was required, from Indonesia's point of view, was simply a *prima facie* case that there was at least a matter for discussion here, whether by negotiation, conciliation or adjudication. These arguments served that purpose well, for the Malaysians' counter-arguments were seriously weakened by their tactical error of August 29 in announcing Malaysia Day in the terms they did.

It would be wrong to suggest, however, that Indonesia's charge that Malaysia violated the Manila Agreements was solely a piece of sophistry, as if we could distinguish sharply between some 'real' reason for her hostility and the stated reasons. Many Indonesians felt very strongly that it *was* Malaysia who had cast the first stone and that she grievously humiliated Indonesia in doing so, in order to wreck the Manila Agreements and Maphilindo. Instead of giving Soekarno a face-saving and honourable opportunity to scale down confrontation and accept Malaysia within the Maphilindo framework, the Malayan and British governments repeatedly went out of their way to make it impossible for him to do so, according to some Indonesians. The announcement on 29 August, long before the UN Mission had completed its enquiry, that Malaysia would come into being on 16 September was seen as a gratuitous provocation — not merely a blatant violation of the Manila Agreements, but a mockery of the negotiations in which Soekarno had magnanimously (but with grave misgivings) agreed to participate.[9] We have already noticed that the matter was not, in fact, as clear-cut as most Indonesians assumed, that Indonesian interpretations of the Manila Agreements were strained and tendentious. But it is not surprising that most Indonesians, who had no opportunity to assess the matter fully or impartially, believed that the whole incident was a deliberate insult which must have had a sinister purpose — and that the purpose must have been to wreck Maphilindo, because it would have meant an ending of British influence over Malaysia.

Another interpretation put upon the same episode was that it revealed how strong British influence over the Malayan government still was. Duncan Sandys allegedly induced Tunku Abdul Rahman to violate the Manila Agreements, thereby confirming Indonesia's worst fears that the Tunku was a mere puppet and that Maphilindo could not succeed until British control had been eliminated.[10] This view did not depend so much on the legal niceties of the matter as on the general plausibility of the interpretation in Indonesian eyes, an interpretation which would also be relatively easy to put across in other countries disposed to be suspicious of neo-colonialism.

The Indonesians also asserted that the Manila Agreements were breached in the manner of the ascertainment process in Borneo, in the inadequate time allowed for it, which they attributed to British obstruction, and in the oppressively close 'colonial' supervision maintained by the British throughout. 'The element of a "fresh approach" as mentioned in article 4 of the Manila Joint Statement ... was not apparent in the whole operation', according to the *Aide-Memoire* of the Indonesian Observers accompanying the Mission. These charges are spelled out more fully in that document and in the speeches of the Indonesian Representative to the UN General Assembly on 27 and 30 September and 8 October. They served Indonesia's purpose of underlining to Afro-Asian delegations the fact that the UN Mission had to be carried out under the eyes of the colonial authorities, although they do not stand up to close examination in the light of what was originally intended at Manila.

The various elements that were interwoven into Indonesian formulations of their case against Malaysia may best be seen in a Foreign Ministry pamphlet on Malaysia, published early in 1965.[11] This reveals a hardening of opposition against both the Malaysians and the British, if compared with earlier accounts, and is interesting because it represents a rewriting of the events of 1963 to conform better with the requirements of the prevailing political myth about the origins of confrontation. Little stress was now put on Maphilindo, but far more on the machinations of the British neo-colonialists.

Decolonization, according to this account, was merely a new tactic on the part of the British imperialists, behind which they devised their neo-colonialist strategies in order to maintain their grip on their old imperial life-line. But when the Brunei revolt revealed that 'there were now at work two processes of decolonization in the British colonial territories

bordering Indonesia', one of them an artificial creation of the old established forces, the other a 'genuine nationalist movement of the entire people
of North Kalimantan', Indonesia had to make a choice and unequivocally
sided with the latter. Harsh suppressive measures by the British authorities failed to eliminate the hard core of resistance by freedom fighters of
North Kalimantan to whose requests for help Indonesian now responded.
Hostile statements from Kuala Lumpur and provocative British military
activities along Indonesia's borders followed, yet talks between the Indonesian and Malayan leaders were still possible and revealed that they could
still 'find common ground' in dealing with problems of the security and
stability of the region: the Manila Foreign Ministers' talks raised hopes
that 'before the British-made Malaysia project could be instituted, some
arrangements could be made between the three countries to secure their
peoples against neo-colonialist designs, and that the Philippines' suggestion
for a Musjawarah Maphilindo might become a useful channel for this and
other common endeavours'. But then came 'the first of a series of proofs
as to how un-free an agent Tunku Abdul Rahman really is'. First, the
London Agreement establishing Malaysia, which contained no alterations
to the earlier scheme, 'notwithstanding Tunku Abdul Rahman's promise
to President Soekarno in Tokyo and the arrangements so recently entered
into' at the Manila Foreign Ministers' conference, which 'made nonsense
out of earlier hopes for what Summit might accomplish'. Then, when
another effort was made to reach an acceptable solution at the Manila
Summit conference, the British interfered in the negotiations and in the
implementation of the Manila Agreements to sabotage them. Finally,
the announcement of August 29 from Kuala Lumpur, that 'Malaysia
would be established on September 16 no matter what the results produced
by the UN,' revealed that 'vis-à-vis the British, Tunku Abdul Rahman was
not a free agent .... It was Britain's will, and no one else's, which counted
in this matter' — and by acquiescing in it, the Tunku had flagrantly
violated the Manila Agreements. It was precisely this British dominance
and the imposition of the idea by a colonial power which Indonesia had
opposed as neo-colonialism from the start.
   It was in these circumstances that open conflict developed, the pamphlet
goes on to explain.

   Protest demonstrations took place on a wide scale on 16th September. On
17th September the Kuala Lumpur regime severed diplomatic relations with
both Indonesia and the Philippines, and stirred up especially anti-Indonesian
feeling; that day the Indonesian Embassy in Kuala Lumpur was set on fire and
ransacked. The British Embassy in Djakarta was burnt out on 18th September,
and in it documented evidence was found that the 'Malaysia' project was indeed
aimed at 'containing' the Indonesian Revolution.
   Convinced that, at least for the time being, co-operation with Malaya would
not be possible, Indonesia now severed the economic relations with Malaya
and Singapore which had been a source of difficulties for some time past.

   The British now began to tighten their military and economic grip in
Malaysia through further repressive measures against opposition there and

the extension of the Anglo-Malayan defence treaty to cover the whole of Malaysia. 'But if the old established forces had strengthened their position, the New Emerging Forces which repelled their domination were to show that they were far from weak.' And the struggle to unify the latter through the various diplomatic manoeuvres of 1964 was seen as evidence of their increasing solidarity in the face of the *Nekolim*.

Misleading though it was in many particulars, this kind of account had enough plausibility to find general acceptance within Indonesia in 1964-5 and a good deal in the world outside also. The various techniques of propaganda utilized by the Indonesian government during those years, sometimes with considerable skill (among uncommitted countries), sometimes very crudely, make an intriguing study in themselves. The diverse uses that were made of this strange war of words and symbols, both on the domestic political scene and the international, deserve closer attention than we can give it here — to mobilize national unity within Indonesia, to foment opposition to the government in Malaysia and to colour the opinions of the diplomats and governments of other countries which might exert some influence on the course of negotiations. Soekarno and his lieutenants were highly talented and experienced operators in this field, but it can hardly be said that their efforts were very successful on this occasion. Indonesian radio broadcasts to northern Borneo and Malaya failed to stir up opposition or disaffection there, despite their blatant exploitation of racial issues. Likewise, on the international stage, their case did not win them the kind of support that they had obtained in their earlier struggles for West Irian or for independence. Yet within Indonesia itself, the sheer weight of government propaganda ensured that there was little overt dissent from the policy of confrontation until 1966, when the reaction against Soekarno's policies revealed that the effects of indoctrination were little more than skin-deep after all.

MILITARY ASPECTS

In the two weeks immediately following the formation of Malaysia, six separate incursions were made into Sarawak from Indonesian Borneo by forces numbering between 60 and 90 men, followed by many smaller raids in the last quarter of 1963. But the scale of military activity was not stepped up significantly beyond the earlier level of reconnaissance and probing raids, despite the strident threats to 'intensify confrontation'.[12] Few of these earlier incidents involved more than half a dozen men. Their objectives appear to have been primarily to gain information and make contacts in Sarawak. Only one substantial attack was launched against Sabah, against the Malay Regiment at Kalabakan, near Tawau, in December. This angered the Malaysians as an outrageous mockery of Indonesian protestations about Maphilindo brotherhood; it was also a serious blow to the morale of the Malay troops, who suffered quite heavy casualties. But on the east coast of Borneo the Indonesians subsequently attempted only a few pin-pricking border incidents around Sebatik Island

and some half-hearted attempts to subvert the substantial colony of Indonesian estate labourers and timber workers near Tawau.

A logical pattern can be discerned in the military tactics followed by Indonesian forces in their attempts to encourage and assist the 'freedom fighters' of Sarawak and other parts of Malaysia.[13] As seen by the British security forces, the military operations fell into five main phases. The first was the Brunei revolt and its aftermath of mopping-up operations in the early months of 1963, in which there was little direct Indonesian involvement. The second phase began with the Tebedu raid on 12 April, which was followed by a series of incursions from the Indonesian side, many of them penetrating quite deeply into Sarawak. These raids seem to have had a three-fold purpose of setting up semi-permanent camps, mainly in the remote jungle areas of the 3rd and 4th Divisions, of recruiting or stirring up disaffected groups in the population to oppose Malaysia and of intimidating others in order to emphasize their vulnerability — all intended, apparently, to precipitate another Brunei-type revolt before Malaysia Day. British forces were initially insufficient to prevent these incursions, but gradually their strength was built up to seven battalions in Sarawak by September 1963.[14] Up to this stage, the insurgents were apparently TNKU irregulars for the most part. The Indonesian Army made no attempt to deny that it was training them (Nasution visited a TNKU training camp in West Kalimantan during July and made sure the fact was well publicized), but it still maintained the outward pretence that regulars were not involved.

In the third period of military operations, between September 1963 to about April 1964, regular Indonesian troops were used more and more openly, although still ostensibly as 'volunteers' who had been released from their Army units to join the 'Pramuka' irregular units along the border. More than 20 incursions by groups of 25 or more men were reported during the 9 months between Malaysia Day and the Tokyo Summit conference in June 1964, despite the official 'cease-fire' agreement in January: seven of these groups contained more than sixty men. By far the greatest number of clashes occurred in the 1st and 2nd Divisions of Sarawak, close to the Indonesian bases around Pontianak. The purpose of these raids seems to have changed, however; it was now mainly to create disturbances and discontent among the inhabitants of the exposed border areas, rather than to establish permanent camps, which were now proving impracticable because of the build-up of forces on the Malaysian side. (At least one attempt was made to build up such a camp, however, near the border behind Lundu, on the extreme western tip of Sarawak.)[15] The British and Ghurka troops put great stress on mobility, constantly patrolling the remote jungle paths and harrying the intruders whenever they found them, so that it would be impossible for them to establish themselves strongly. They were fast learning the value of helicopters in this type of jungle war, for they were now able to drop troops behind the insurgents and cut off their retreat to the border. British officers later attributed their success in containing the Indonesian challenge primarily to the improvement in their tactical use of the helicopter, rather than to any great increase in their forces. The increased availability of helicopters for support services was also a crucial factor in enabling the security forces to do more in their 'hearts and minds' operations among the Dayak longhouse dwellers near the frontier, by air-lifting the wounded and sick to Kuching for hospital treatment.

A fourth phase in the Borneo operations, which can be dated from about April 1964, was marked by the establishment of clear military superiority by the defending forces and a change in the tactics of the Indonesians. Deep penetration was now abandoned and incursions were practically confined to brief night raids on longhouses or ambushes close to the border, so that retreat was relatively easy. The British, however, could never afford to forget that Kuching was dangerously vulnerable to substantial military assault if the Indonesians ever chose to launch it. No such attempt was ever made, although there was a minor flurry of alarm at the end of 1964 resulting from reports of a substantial Indonesian build up of forces in the border areas (not unconnected, one suspects, with the need to give some semblance of credibility to Soekarno's oft-repeated threats that 'before the cock crows' in the following year, the enemy would be crushed). In general, the main thrust of Indonesia's military probes was shifted away from Sarawak in mid-1964 towards the mainland of Malaya, beginning with the attempted landings at Pontian and Labis (described below) and continuing with a number of smaller raids. Something like a military stalemate ensued along the Borneo border from that time on, although there was some intensification of Indonesian activity there during 1965.[16]

Tactically the Indonesians had one great advantage in Borneo — their own territory was inviolate, so that they could mount their operations with impunity anywhere along the 970 mile border in Borneo and withdraw to safety whenever they were being hard pressed by British or Malaysian forces. To this must be added the latent advantage that the frontier represented a political division across which the Chinese, Ibans, Land Dayaks, Kayans and Kenyah all had ancient family and tribal connections. The Indonesians occasionally accused the British of violating the frontier, but without much air of conviction or corroborating evidence; British field commanders were under strict orders to obey Marquis of Queensberry rules in this regard so that there would be no excuse for the Indonesians to demonstrate blatant aggression against their territory. (Occasional minor breaches may well have occurred in such terrain, however.) But one great disappointment to the Indonesians was the almost complete lack of support for the insurgents among the local population: according to the Malaysians, 'far from circulating among the people like fish swimming in water, they are almost completely isolated from them'.[17] The guerrillas captured in early 1964 had been led to expect that they would get food, shelter and assistance from the opponents of Malaysia in Sarawak and Sabah: they were completely unprepared for the actual situation confronting them. But it would be wrong to give the impression that there were no elements at all on the Malaysian side which cooperated with them.

In the early stages some raiding parties did get through to areas where dissident groups were prepared to hide and protect them, while fear of reprisals sometimes drove the luckless Dayaks of the border regions to hedge their bets by giving information about troop movements to both sides indiscriminately. Nevertheless, it is obvious that there was by no means enough support from the Sarawak population to create the classic conditions for a guerrilla war, and even less in Sabah. The purpose of the raids soon came to be limited to terrorizing the Dayak communities of the interior in the hope of making the British position untenable, an essentially negative aim. Another purpose was to provide appropriate background noises to the government's diplomatic manoeuvres in Manila or Bangkok. The Indonesians' problem was that they wished to provoke a native rebellion in Sarawak, not a Chinese one, but the only well-organized rebel groups consisted of Chinese who were uneasy about the Indonesian government's treatment of its own Chinese.

The little information that is available about Indonesia's military dispositions in this period gives the impression that her armed forces were not initially geared to anything much more than guerrilla operations and that their leaders were probably caught by surprise when the breach with Malaysia occurred in September 1963. Not until May 1964, following Soekarno's nationwide call for 'volunteers' and his proclamation of the *Dwikora* (The 'People's Twofold Command', to be described below), was a special command, called *Komando Siaga* (KOGA), created for operations against Malaysia and this seems to have been plagued by organizational problems and shortage of suitable troops throughout the following year. KOGA was to include elements of all four armed services (Army, Navy, Air Force and Police) and was under the command of Air Vice Marshal Omar Dhani, the Air Force commander, assisted by Deputy Commanders from the other services. Soekarno's selection of Dhani for this purpose aggravated the antipathy that the Army and Air Force leaders had long felt towards each other, largely because of the latters' political inclinations towards Soekarno and the PKI. Friction soon arose between Dhani and the Army leadership over the scope of KOGA's jurisdiction, about which Soekarno had given ambiguous instructions.[18] This problem was partly resolved after the failure of the Malayan landings of August-September (responsibility for which is attributed by Army informants to Subandrio and KOTI Section V, not to the Army), when KOGA was reorganized as an area command, now called KOLAGA (*Komando Mandala Siaga*), from which Java was excluded and within which the Army officers were to have a greater influence, especially after Major General Suharto, the former commander of the West Irian operation and commander of the Strategic Reserve (KOSTRAD) in 1962, became First Deputy Commander under Dhani. But even then there were difficulties and delay in obtaining Army battalions for the Borneo front — ostensibly because of inadequate equipment and transport, but possibly also because of deliberate obstruction to their despatch for essentially political reasons. Certainly, Army officers were later to claim that they had played a restraining role in the later stages of the conflict to prevent its escalation beyond a level that Indonesia could handle without undue risk. Their political opponents took a less charitable view, of course, accusing them of 'dragging their feet' for political purposes, either because they were afraid of the dangers involved or because they were too concerned with domestic political problems. For instance, at his later trial for complicity in the October 1965 coup attempt, Brigadier-General Supardjo, commander of one of the operational units in West Kalimantan, said that while he could not say there was actual opposition to confrontation from the Army higher command, 'we felt that things were not being done wholeheartedly and were even being sabotaged'.[19] He cited as an example his experience with three brigades which he took to Kalimantan, only to find them transferred by the General Staff from his command to that of the local divisional commander, on whose loyalty Yani could rely.

It is hardly surprising that charges such as these were heard in the later stages of confrontation, when the Army leaders must have been very conscious of the danger that any substantial escalation of the conflict would precipitate a British counterblow against Indonesia's home bases. They should be balanced against several other considerations, however. Both the prior experience and the military doctrines of the Indonesian Army leaders, as well as the general political background of confrontation, would have inclined them towards low-posture quasi-guerrilla operations, rather than a textbook assault with regular forces, which would have involved a conflict on terms most favourable to the British in terms of their superiority in resources and organization. Moreover, the government's broad political strategy until June 1964 was based on the fiction that the conflict in Borneo was a 'people's struggle' backed only by 'volunteers' from Indonesia: to have mounted a large-scale offensive by regular forces at that stage would have undermined such a claim. And it was only after that time that serious attention seems to have been given at a national level to the organizational and logistical problems involved in a major military operation. (Neither Nasution nor Yani seem to have been particularly reluctant to give encouragement and training to the guerrillas from North Borneo in the earlier stages.)[20] Thus, while it could be argued that a more vigorous military effort in the months immediately after Malaysia-day might conceivably have caused enough disruption and hardship among the Dayaks of the 1st and 2nd Divisions of Sarawak to undermine their loyalty to the new federation, there were good reasons why this was not attempted. And after the military crisis of September 1964, the risks of an intensified war were just too great.

Sheer lack of battle-ready troops was apparently also one of the main factors inhibiting the Army leaders. There is probably some truth in the quip that in mid-1964 the Army was deploying more troops to crush Andi Selle's revolt in South Sulawesi than it had launched against Malaysia. The Army had about 100 battalions in mid-1964, but most were under strength and only 25 were assessed as being really good, according to a

KOSTRAD survey.[21] Plans were drawn up in October 1964 to have 7 brigades in the border areas, 4 in Kalimantan and 3 in Sumatra, most of them being Army units under KOSTRAD command, but also some units from the Navy and Police. As a result, the number of Indonesian troops on the border in Kalimantan increased considerably at the end of 1964, with estimates ranging from 15–20,000 up to 30,000 men, in contrast to estimates of about 2,500, about one-third irregulars, in mid–1964.[22] On the basis of these figures, it seems clear that the Indonesians were simply not capable of launching more vigorous operations in Sarawak before the end of 1964, but they would have been in a position to operate in much greater strength there by 1965. There are some indications that their attacks were being stepped up towards the middle of that year, although still without much success. But Britain had 10,000 troops (excluding Australian and New Zealand troops) in Borneo in January 1965, and 50,000 in the whole of South-East Asia, so the risks involved in a major assault would have been considerable.

The use of refugee 'freedom fighters' from Sarawak and Sabah in the border operations seems not to have been very fruitful, although they apparently played the most important role up till the middle of 1964. It may well be that the increased use of Indonesian regulars and the nation-wide campaign for 'volunteers' in President Soekarno's *Dwikora* speech was related to the realization that the people of Northern Borneo were not going to rise up against the *Nekolim*. Little was ever heard about the military role of the TNKU remnants who fled to Indonesia after the Brunei revolt. According to a Malaysian account, most of the so-called TNKU units were made up of Indonesian citizens who were either 'volunteers' recruited in West Kalimantan or regulars — the former often being 'press-ganged' or joining 'to escape unemployment, starvation, reprisals against their families or imprisonment', while others were promised land or jobs.[23] Some of the insurgents on the eastern coast of Borneo had previously been barter traders shipping into Tawau, who had been captured and offered the choice of imprisonment or service as 'volunteers'. In West Kalimantan unemployed young men from Sambas and Singkawang were said to have been rounded up *en bloc* by their village heads and recruited into the TNKU by a mixture of inducements and pressures; some were recruited through Partindo. Although allowances must be made for the element of hyperbole in these frankly propagandist allegations — for the Malaysians delighted in stressing the unemployment and hunger in Indonesia, which they often exaggerated grossly — they sound fairly plausible. Not much was revealed, however, about the role of Chinese SCO insurgents who crossed the border for military training. The number of these was generally estimated as between 1000 and 2000, though not all were trained and armed. They probably outnumbered the Malays and other non-Chinese who went over, who were said to be 'less than 50 of Azahari's followers who were trained in Indonesia before the revolt'.[24] Some of the Chinese were apparently incorporated into TNKU raiding parties, but never more than a mere handful in each unit. Not all the SCOs who defected were used in them. No exclusively Chinese units were ever mentioned publicly, though the SCO themselves had some in the border areas. The Malaysians circulated stories to the effect that the Chinese were neglected or ill-treated by the Indonesians, or that those who came back with raiding units lacked shoes and equipment, or were merely used by the Indonesians as guides or bearers: these should be taken with a grain of salt since they were probably intended mainly to deter other SCOs from defecting. Such stories were not corroborated by British military officers early in 1965, though there was said to be some friction on racial grounds. It appears that the Indonesians made no substantial attempt to send arms to Sarawak to the SCO cadres hiding in the jungles, although one might have expected that this would have been a most effective way to foster an insurrection there. On the other hand this may have been because proper 'hides' for their reception had not been prepared by the SCO.

Certainly it was a very minor war if measured in terms of the casualties involved. In contrast with the West Irian campaign of 1962, the Indonesian authorities never put much stress on the Army's role in the Borneo confrontation, although they gradually abandoned the fiction that the clashes in Sarawak were simply the work of freedom fighters or irregular 'volunteers'.[25] But the Malaysians and the British had too much at stake to take the conflict lightly, for the very future of Malaysia and the continuance of British influence in the area were indeed in the balance. Moreover, the war was expensive and frustrating to them, for there was no easy or quick way of bringing it to an end, except by a politically self-defeating strike against Indonesian base areas. Indonesian military pressure had to be contained, they felt, since even a compromise settlement would just breed increase of appetite in Djakarta. Moreover, Indonesia's attitude towards tiny Malaysia smacked too much of sheer bullying for the liking of many British officers, who frequently averred that Soekarno had to be given 'a bloody nose' before British troops could be safely withdrawn from the area. The moral sentiments inspiring latter-day 'imperialism and neo-colonialism' were more prosaic than those of Kipling's hey-day, but they were still influential.

The cost of defending Malaysia became very onerous for the British during 1964, particularly at the end of the year, when a substantial military build-up had to be undertaken shortly after the new Labour government's first sterling crisis.[26] The Indonesians had good reasons for hoping that sooner or later the British would cut their losses and give up the attempt to maintain a military presence in South-East Asia. It is quite possible that this consideration had some influence on the scale of their military operations in Borneo. Confrontation did not directly create an intolerable financial burden for Indonesia, so long as the war was confined to small-scale raids, but it could be made increasingly heavy for the British. The crudely Leninist conception of imperialism prevalent among Indonesians may well have coloured their assessments of the British reaction — if the war could be made expensive enough to the British it would outweigh the profits derived from their investments there, and compel them to negotiate a settlement, just as their struggle against the Dutch had done in 1945–9. That was the way they expected imperialists and neo-colonialists to behave.

ECONOMIC ASPECTS

Indonesia's severance of her commercial ties with Malaysia had an immediate impact on both countries. In Singapore, it brought a perceptible loss of trade and, with it, some unemployment, although less than might have been feared. If the trade ban had been effective, it would have been a major landmark in the history of Indonesian-Malayan economic relations, bringing to an end the long era of Singapore's dominance. But in the short run Indonesia had to pay a high price to achieve this long-desired goal, not only a severe disruption of her exports, but also the loss of large-scale Western aid, both of which intensified the inflation which had been curbed briefly by the stabilization scheme. Prices rose sharply in September, continuing to do so until early 1964, aggravated by a bad harvest which brought about a doubling of rice prices in a matter of weeks.

Since the achievement of political independence, many Indonesians had been impatiently awaiting the golden dawn of 'economic independence' as well — the final elimination of foreign capital and a reorientation of the nation's trade channels so as to break the grip of the 'parasitic' Chinese traders of Singapore and to ensure that Indonsian commodities were sold direct to the final consumers without any extraction of 'middleman's profits' by foreigners. It was all very well for Western economists to point out that Singapore provided essential commercial services more efficiently than Indonesia could provide them herself, but many Indonesians saw the matter in a quite different light. To them the essential problem was to liberate Indonesia's trade from the grip of the capitalist Singapore merchants who were hand in glove with the *Nekolim*. This was primarily a political act, demanding will-power, sacrifices and reorganization within Indonesia. (Confrontation, and the whole 'course of the Indonesian Revolution' was very largely a matter of will, self-confidence and related moral qualities.) It also offered a prospect of forcing Malaysia to her knees by disrupting Singapore's economy, a subject on which Indonesia's 'guided press' gave grotesquely misleading reports in the latter part of 1963. In any case, whatever the outcome of the struggle against Malaysia, Indonesia would increase in stature and self-confidence as a result of the trade break. The humiliating subordination of a proud people to a mere bunch of foreign merchants (mostly Chinese) would be ended. 'The sweat of one hundred million Indonesians is being sucked by two million Malayans. Such things cannot go on. One hundred million people are no longer willing to be made coolies by two million people', said Chairul Saleh, one of the foremost advocates of the break.[27] Since the revolutionary spirit of the people had to be sustained at a high pitch for domestic political reasons, the trade break suited most of Indonesia's leaders well, for it required immediate action and determination in a clearly understandable cause rather than the compromises and delicate phraseology of diplomacy. The trade break did not necessarily preclude a political settlement, if a favourable opportunity arose, nor did it amount to open hostilities. The only people in Indonesia who were likely to regard the move with disapproval were the Chinese traders in league with the Singapore bloodsuckers. No Indonesian could object to the stated objectives of economic independence and greater self-reliance, and the trade break was widely welcomed by the politically articulate, in spite of the disruptions and hardships involved. Many argued that 'in the long run we shall emerge stronger from it', or that Indonesians needed to be jolted out of their acquiescence in the former state of affairs by some drastic, irreversible action of this kind, analogous to the long-desired expropriation of the Dutch in 1957–8. In some respects, the summons to show determination, resourcefulness and sacrifice was not unwelcome to people who had lost their bearings and goals of purposeful action in the turmoil and disappointments of the previous decade.

A spate of new regulations and plans had to be devised in the weeks after 21 September in order to ensure that the trade ban was carried into effect. Its adverse consequences in particular parts of the economy also had to be remedied by emergency arrangements. New organisations had to be set up to arrange for the channelling of trade direct to overseas customers. Smuggling had to be stopped, in the name of patriotic duty. Draconian punishments, including death, imprisonment for up to 20 years and fines of up to Rp.30 million for 'subversion', were announced in a new Presidential decree, which gave an all-embracing definition of the term to include profiteering and (putatively) smuggling, as well as ideological deviations and expressions of sympathy for unfriendly countries. Listening to Radio Malaysia became a punishable offence — although this did not prevent a good deal of clandestine listening. Malaysian-owned rubber remilling plants and other properties (mostly owned by Singapore Chinese) were nationalized and efforts made to export the remilled rubber direct from Sumatra, not altogether successfully, it would seem. The 'de-dollarization' of Riau archipelago had to be carried out and its close ties with Singapore broken, even though this required that water as well as foodstuffs should be shipped in from Djakarta in badly-needed boats. Altogether there suddenly seemed to be a great flurry of activity again in high government circles, all directed towards the execution of this revolutionary new trade policy. And Indonesia's revolution was recharged by new activity, new goals to strive for, new positions of power to be achieved, regardless of the odds against success which the average Indonesian was in no position to calculate realistically, and his leaders in no mood to.

A great deal of prominence was given to the creation of a free port at Sabang (off the northern tip of Sumatra) as a rival to Singapore, as if this could be done easily by mere administrative *fiat*. It was little more than a symbolic gesture, needless to say, a castle in the air, of a kind which became more and more frequent and fantastic in the months that followed.

So also was a KOTI order for the establishment of 'free trade areas' in Tandjung Priok, Makassar and Belawan, a quite meaningless arrangement in a country so shackled by trade and currency controls. More realistic was the designation of nine 'ocean ports' which were to handle the commodities formerly flowing to the Singapore entrepot, channelling them directly to the 'final consumer' (the magic phrase of that time) without benefit to foreign middlemen. This was a logical way to simplify the control of trade, by concentrating in a few large ports the harbour facilities and customs inspection services needed for ocean-going ships, leaving the smaller ports to the domestic shipping services. But many of the latter had been heavily dependent on the small boats of the Singapore Chinese; these could not immediately be replaced by Indonesian shipping companies, whose services were already in serious disarray. Overseas shipping lines could not immediately be rescheduled to serve the ocean ports, either, and it took many months before the new system was operating at all satisfactorily. How effectively it was working by 1964-5 cannot be ascertained, for reports varied greatly; surprisingly, the recorded value of exports was slightly higher in 1964 than in 1963, if that is a significant clue.[28]

Smuggling in small boats to Singapore and Malayan ports practically ceased for a few months, but then it resumed gradually until August 1964, when the traffic in small boats was banned by Malaysia. But Indonesia was also suffering a serious loss of foreign exchange through underdeclaration and wrongful documentation of cargoes exported in ocean-going vessels from the main ports, which became a major scandal during the following years. The new trade system did not bring any improvement in foreign exchange control, despite the more potent sanctions the government was now able to brandish. Instead, the system came to embody the worst excesses of mercantilism, in which corruption and extortion flourished more than ever. At least one 'palace millionaire' made a fortune at the expense of the poor rubber farmers of Djambi whose produce had piled up after the cessation of small-boat traffic across the Straits: he obtained virtual monopoly rights to buy it up at a low fixed price and ship it overseas, paying someone in Djakarta a handsome percentage, presumably. This kind of arrangement seems to have become much more prevalent in the more restricted trading conditions of 1964-5.[29]

From the statements of Indonesian ministers in the weeks following the trade break, it seems clear that they did not anticipate that the conflict with Malaysia would last so long or have such adverse effects for Indonesia. Subandrio commented after a visit to Sumatra in October that within six months the disruptions produced by the trade break would be overcome. His oft-quoted remark at the end of 1964 that 'Indonesia had decided to put politics before economics' probably reflected the government's view of the situation fairly accurately. There was little it could do to stop the inflation while confrontation lasted, except try to remedy the dislocation of trade by stop-gap measures. The government formally repudiated the unpopular 26 May regulations in response to demands from the political parties, but the gesture meant little, since the government had no clearly defined policy to keep the inflation under control.[30] Yet there are indications that by about April 1964 Subandrio was becoming more confident that Indonesia was over the worst of the economic disruption resulting from the trade break and that she could weather the rising seas of inflation. ('Indonesians have learned how to live with inflation', it was often said in reply to foreign critics who were eternally predicting imminent economic collapse.) The increases of prices and the money supply during the middle of the year were of manageable proportions, until about October. This probably had a bearing on Indonesia's hard line towards Malaysia during that period, at the Tokyo talks and the Security Council debates, for the government had earlier been anxious to reach a settlement if possible, at the time of the Bangkok conference when rice prices were rising alarmingly.

It turned out, of course, that confrontation eventually had disastrous effects on the Indonesian economy, although it proved far more resilient than most of the experts anticipated.[31] Inflation was intensified, but for about twelve months it seemed to be controllable. A brief survey of the major factors involved will help to put the matter in perspective.

First, deprivation of over $250 million of expected aid from the West removed the main prop of the earlier stabilization scheme. Balanced budgets and stable prices could not now possibly be maintained, especially as government expenditure was bound to be increased by confrontation, instead of being reduced. For some years Indonesia had been spending roughly $200 million *per annum* more foreign exchange than she had been earning; now her sources of foreign credit were drying up and her foreign exchange reserves were almost exhausted, while her repayment obligations were mounting steeply. This meant less foreign exchange was available for imports. Moreover the cessation or diminution in 1964 of American rice shipments under the Surplus Agricultural Commodities Act was likely to have a serious effect on food prices, for the Indonesian government had become heavily dependent on substantial rice imports. Since a high level of imports was Indonesia's most powerful anti-inflationary weapon, this loss was of critical importance.

Secondly, exports were disrupted by the deflection of trade away from Singapore and Malaysia. Just how much of her export trade had been flowing abroad through Malaysian ports is a matter of some disagreement, but the estimates range between about 25 and 45 per cent, excluding oil which was in a special category as it poses peculiar problems in the Indonesian trade and payments statistics. Some of her products could be diverted to other markets (at some cost and only after a major reorganization of the trade channels), but for a few commodities the Singapore outlet was irreplaceable.[32] Recorded exports, other than oil, showed a very distinct fall in the first six months after September 1963 ($200 million, compared with about $240 million in the same period of the two previous years), but the decline was not as disastrous as many commentators had anticipated. It was certainly not enough to force the government to call off confrontation out of sheer economic necessity, as many had predicted during the rice shortage and rising prices of early 1964. In fact, exports appear to have improved later in the year. (The fact that smuggling was also curbed by the ban on trade with Malaysia may have diverted some illegal trade into legal channels, at least until early 1964, when smuggling was reported to be on the increase again.)[33] But although the immediate situation was not desperate, the disruption of old trade channels and the long-established credit links between the Indonesian exporters, mostly Chinese, and their agents in Singapore had many adverse effects on efficiency. As foreign exchange became scarce and the discrepancy between the black market and official rate of exchange widened, the machinery of export trade tended to break down and by 1965, the foreign trade situation was becoming very serious indeed.

Thirdly, declining exports meant reduced imports, for the government held virtually no foreign exchange reserves. This had a two-fold inflationary effect: the prices of goods rose, while budget deficits increased because relatively less revenue was being received from import taxes, which had previously been the government's most lucrative source of revenues. Since debt repayment obligations were also increasing, the squeeze upon Indonesia's capacity to import was becoming acute, but throughout 1964 the government managed, in various ways, to tap bigger reserves of (illegally held) foreign exchange and foreign credit than had been expected.

Fourthly, the budget deficit mounted steadily, with proportionate effects on the volume of money and prices, as revenues shrank while expenditures rose inexorably. The deficit approximately equalled government revenue in both 1963 and 1964, years in which the volume of money rose by 97 per cent and 156 per cent respectively: then, in the first nine months of 1965, it jumped to 240 per cent.[34] By that time, however, a whole series of processes were interacting to generate an accelerating rate of inflation within Indonesia. Prices were increasing at roughly the same rate, while the government was rapidly losing its capacity to control the economy effectively in any way. But it was not until late 1965 that the inflationary spiral spun out of control. Throughout the first twelve months of confrontation, the mystery was rather that it had not done so and that the economy seemed to have been damaged so little by what seemed the disastrous measures of September 1963.

DIPLOMATIC CONFRONTATION

Soekarno's strategy in the confrontation of Malaysia resembled that which he had successfully applied against the Dutch in the West Irian campaign in its combination of direct (but very limited) military pressure and a strident propaganda offensive with tortuous diplomacy which served to veil his immediate intentions and to bring international pressures to bear upon his adversaries to negotiate on his terms. But whereas on the former occasion his objective had been obvious, to force the Dutch to negotiate a transfer of sovereignty, in the latter case it was far from clear just what Indonesia's goals really were, or on what terms a compromise settlement might have been reached. In fact Soekarno sems to have deliberately fostered the uncertainty that prevailed as to his intentions, perhaps because of the diverse domestic pressures which he had to consider, but perhaps also because his goals were not at all clearly spelled out in his own mind except in the vaguest terms. He seems to have been constantly 'playing it by ear', adjusting to changing circumstances as they developed.

It is not surprising, therefore, that interpretations of his motives and diplomatic tactics varied greatly at the time. According to one theory, Soekarno was genuinely seeking a political settlement of the dispute in early 1964 in order to get 'off the hook' on which he had been caught by the events of September 1963, provided he could do so under a face-saving formula which would enable him to silence domestic critics. Opponents of this theory argued that he was simply trying to 'crush Malaysia' at the conference table by outwitting the Tunku, since he had failed to do so by subversion or armed invasion.[35] Neither of these interpretations can be entirely accepted or rejected *in toto*, nor are they entirely incompatible with each other; from time to time Soekarno's diplomacy was directed towards quite divergent purposes. It is fruitless to debate whether or not he 'genuinely' wanted a settlement of the conflict. No doubt he did — provided that it was on his terms, which would probably have amounted, in effect, to Malaysia's admission that she was at fault in the affair. But what were the terms on which Soekarno might have been willing to accept a compromise? That was the key question throughout the negotiations of 1964–65, but at no stage did the Indonesians give any clear indication or hint of what the answer would be, except in terms of the question-begging phrase; 'Let us return to the Manila Agreements'. Both sides meant different things by those words, however. And the very vagueness of Indonesia's demands during the course of the Bangkok and Tokyo talks of 1964 proved to be a major obstacle to any settlement of the dispute by a horse-trading process of mutual concessions.

In the weeks immediately after the breaking of relations, Indonesia had shown rather more interest than Malaysia in mediation proposals put forward by the Japanese and others who wanted to reconcile the Maphilindo partners and restore peace in the region. Indonesia's leaders appeared anxious to avoid further deterioration in their relations with the USA, so the prospects of a peaceful settlement of the Malaysia dispute seemed reasonably good at the beginning of 1964, when Robert Kennedy was sent to the region by President Johnson with the aim of 'getting the war out of the jungle and back to the conference table', before it escalated out of control. Throughout the next few months of intense diplomatic activity, there was a degree of plausibility in the argument that Soekarno was anxious to achieve a settlement if only Malaysia would make some face-saving concession of a symbolic nature. As the year drew on, however, this theory became less persuasive, for many Indonesian actions were not easy to reconcile with the hypothesis that Soekarno was really seeking a solution of the conflict in good faith. After the failure of the Tokyo Summit Conference in June, the chances of achieving a peaceful settlement faded rapidly and the several spasmodic efforts that were made to resume formal talks later in 1964 and again in 1965 had little chance of success.

Before we plunge into the details of these negotiations, some attention should be given briefly to the attitudes of the major powers to the dispute, particularly as they affected Indonesia.

America's responses to Indonesia's actions were again a matter of considerable but indirect importance to Soekarno, as in the West Irian campaign and the events of 1963. The Kennedy and Johnson administrations both wanted to see the dispute settled peacefully so as to prevent the growth of Communist influence in the region at a time when they were increasingly preoccupied with Viet-Nam. Soekarno was able to exploit their anxieties on this score by directing American pressure against Malaysia and Britain to make them more amenable to negotiations. The State Department, for its part, endeavoured to keep a 'foot inside the door' in Djakarta, despite Congressional limitations on further foreign aid to Indonesia, by continuing its existing programmes as long as possible into 1964.[36] But after the failure of the negotiations arising out of the 'Kennedy cease-fire' and Soekarno's realisation that he could not hope for much more economic or diplomatic help from the United States — his vehement 'To Hell with your aid' in March 1964 marking the moment of truth in this respect — there was a steady hardening of attitudes on both sides and a deterioration of relations between the two countries. In July the meeting between President Johnson and Tunku Abdul Rahman marked a distinct shift in America's relatively non-commital policy on the dispute towards sympathy for Malaysia. So did Adlai Stevenson's strongly critical speech in the Security Council debates in September. Moreover, America's increasing involvement in the Viet-Nam war after the Gulf of Tonkin incident in August also contributed to the deterioration, since it was seen by the Indonesians as a further sign that the *Nekolim* powers were becoming locked in a global struggle with the New Emerging Forces. Soon afterwards as Soekarno's new policy of alignment with China began to unfold, Indonesia's relations with the USA began to deteriorate seriously, almost to the point of an open breach in early 1965, when pressure from the PKI and the general thrust of Soekarno's policy of 'Living Dangerously' were pushing him steadily towards the left. Both governments seemed anxious to avoid taking the extreme step, but there was now little reason for either to be particularly accommodating to the other.

British policies and interests in the dispute diverged significantly from the American in early 1964, since the British were far less anxious for a negotiated settlement until Soekarno had been given a sharp rebuff to show that he could not get away with his blustering tactics against them as he had against the Dutch. Negotiations were tantamount to putting pressure on Malaysia to make concessions, in their eyes, whereas the British saw the blame as being essentially on Indonesia's side.[37] In any case, they were finding the military aspects of confrontation manageable and were still in no mood to urge compromise. They were also more sceptical, in general, of Ambassador Jones' view that Soekarno really wanted a settlement of the dispute. In May 1964, however, the British Foreign Secretary began to speak with a belated enthusiasm for Maphilindo as the basis for a political settlement. But the Tokyo Conference soon dashed any hopes in this direction. British policy remained much the same thereafter until the coup, even after the Labour government came into power, despite the burdensome costs of their increased military commitment in Malaysia made necessary by confrontation. Australia and New Zealand, who were also committed to support for Malaysia, took broadly the same approach as the British, although with rather different nuances reflecting their more sensitive relationships with Indonesia. Russia showed less interest in fishing in troubled waters during this dispute than she had during the West Irian affair, for her relations with Indonesia were soured by that country's unsatisfactory repayment of the instalments falling due on its enormous loans from Russia and by Soekarno's closer association with China. She made no significant move to exploit the embarrassments of America and Britain to her advantage. She cast her vote in favour of Indonesia in the Security Council debate of September 1964, ensuring that Malaysia's complaint was vetoed, but gave her little diplomatic or verbal support beyond that. The reason for her coolness must, of course, be sought in the Sino-Soviet rift and her strained relations with the PKI. It is salutory to reflect that for all the influence Russia had earlier been said to be establishing in Indonesia through her vast military and economic aid programs, she was able to exert very little leverage over Soekarno in either direction at the most critical time. China, on the other hand, was able to play an important part in the affair in 1965, as we shall see in due course (though her influence was not very significant before then), despite the fact that she could provide Indonesia with relatively little help in concrete terms.[38]

Of the Afro-Asian states, only the Philippines and Thailand played a role of any significance in the dispute, the latter simply in an intermediary capacity when requested to provide her services. As we will see later, Indonesia's absorption with Afro-Asian diplomacy in 1965 showed that she considered moral support to be nearly as valuable as material, for her aim was to isolate Malaysia among the nations whose sympathy and respect she sought in order to deny the charge of neo-colonialism. President Macapagal of the Philippines found himself in a difficult position after September 1963, for the breach with Malaysia and his flirtation with Soekarno could be used as electoral ammunition against him by his opponents if the drift to the left in Indonesia continued. Hence, after his brief attempt to commit Soekarno to a solution by *musjawarah* — 'an Asian solution to Asian problems' — at the beginning of 1964, he endeavoured to withdraw from too close an embrace with such an unlikely soul-mate. On the other hand, it suited him to be pursuing an actively 'Asian' and anti-colonialist foreign policy and he could claim that by attempting to mediate in the dispute between the other two Maphilindo partners, the Philippines was exerting a measure of restraint upon Indonesia, since Soekarno could not afford to alienate her and wreck the Maphilindo relationship altogether. Consequently, despite an agreement to restore diplomatic relations at the consular level with Malaysia in early 1964, Macapagal made only the most minimal moves in this direction, so as to avoid antagonizing Soekarno and incurring his wrath for appearing to have changed sides. Much later in the year, he uttered a mild and qualified criticism of Indonesia's assaults on mainland Malaysia (not of those in Borneo, however), but by this time he had little hope of exercising any leverage to bring Soekarno back to the conference table in any case. Nevertheless, his dissociation from Indonesia did not entail a dramatic *rapprochement* with Malaysia, for hard bargaining continued in respect of the Sabah claim, on which no progress was made in 1964–5, so that relations between the two were virtually in cold storage during the last year of Macapagal's presidency and only began to thaw again in 1966, after the coup in Indonesia and the election of Marcos to the Malacanang.

The negotiations involving the two Bangkok conferences and the Tokyo Summit talks followed directly from Robert Kennedy's intervention in January-February 1964. Kennedy's aim was simply to induce the two antagonists to agree to an immediate cease-fire and so establish a more cordial atmosphere in which talks between them could proceed towards a political settlement of their dispute. He was concerned primarily with getting the negotiations started, not with their ultimate outcome, but both sides seemed to agree in principle with what he was proposing, although each had reservations on matters of detail which gave rise to some stubborn arguments.

Malaysia was initially lukewarm about the value of holding talks unless Soekarno was willing to call off confrontation and recognize her. The Tunku queried Soekarno's sincerity, since he was still saying publicly in Indonesia that negotiations were simply another means of attaining the objectives towards which confrontation was directed, i.e. the repudiation of 'British Malaysia' and the establishment of an 'Asian Malaysia'. (Indonesian countered the Tunku's conditions for talks with the assertion that she too had a pre-condition, the withdrawal of British troops from Borneo.) But despite its misgivings, the Malaysian government was anxious to reach a peaceful settlement of the dispute if there was a chance of obtaining it on reasonable terms.

Kennedy seems to have had little difficulty in persuading both governments to abandon those preconditions for talks which were obviously unacceptable to the other side. And he succeeded in obtaining their agreement to a cease-fire (announced on January 23, just after he left Djakarta) as a preliminary to ministerial-level negotiations. Soekarno's real intentions remained obscure, however. On the very evening the cease-fire order was issued, he declared that confrontation would go on, that tactics might change, but not the principle of support for freedom struggles. He was under heavy pressure from the PKI at that time to avoid an accommodation with Malaysia and the *Nekolim:* a further wave of 'take-overs' of British firms just before Kennedy arrived in Djakarta could be interpreted as a PKI warning to the government against weakening its opposition to Malaysia. And although the government made some attempt to resist this pressure from the left, the episode raised serious doubts about Soekarno's capacity to override the PKI on the confrontation issue.[39]

Another reason for doubting Soekarno's ultimate intentions arose over the nature of the cease-fire order. It soon became clear that whereas the Malaysians regarded the order as implying a withdrawal of all Indonesian troops from Malaysian Borneo, Soekarno looked upon it as no more than an end to the shooting, a stand-fast order. (He later claimed that his interpretation had been put to Kennedy and specifically accepted by him and the Tunku.)[40] An angry exchange of recriminations occurred over this issue almost immediately, after the Malaysians had air-dropped leaflets issued by the British commander of the Borneo operations, giving instructions to insurgents on how to surrender. This greatly annoyed the Indonesian authorities, who countered with a radio order to their guerillas on 30 January urging them to secure their positions and retaliate against any violations of the cease-fire. Next day, Indonesian aircraft intruded into Malaysian airspace as far as 30 miles inside Sabah in order to drop 'stand-fast' leaflets.[41] Thus, even before the Ministers met in Bangkok, the political atmosphere was clouded by suspicions on both sides.

The first of the two Bangkok conferences of Foreign Ministers of the three Maphilindo nations (Razak again deputizing for the Tunku in this role) lasted from 5 to 10 February and was mainly devoted to the details of the cease-fire agreement, with the aim of creating a better atmosphere for talks between the Heads of Government on the broader political issues in dispute. Some discussion of these political issues also occurred at Bangkok and provided a revealing insight into the strategies and ideas of the two governments. But the immediate stumbling block was the question of how the cease-fire was to be implemented. While some agreement was reached on certain general principles to be followed and the supervisory measures to be undertaken by the Thai government as a neutral arbiter, a deadlock occurred on the issue of whether the cease-fire implied a withdrawal of Indonesian forces, either regulars or irregulars, from Malaysian territory. The Malaysians insisted on this as a necessary condition for an effective cease-fire and further talks on the political issues, but Subandrio would not commit himself to it; he was not authorized to agree to anything more than a cease-fire, he said, and would have to refer the question to Soekarno. (He himself seemed to regard it as a relatively minor issue. The forces involved were very small.) The conference ended on a strangely indeterminate note. The communique issued made no reference whatsoever to the withdrawal of troops, but included a statement by Razak reserving his government's position on the matter (in peculiarly convoluted terms), presumably to put on record that the point was not conceded by default.[42] In addition, Subandrio agreed verbally that he would try to obtain Soekarno's approval for a withdrawal of the volunteers when he returned to Djakarta and would then cable the other Foreign Ministers within 48 hours so that arrangements could be made for another meeting between them before the end of the month in order to pave the way for a Summit meeting. As it turned out, he did not get Soekarno's approval for a withdrawal and did not sent any word on the matter until much later in the month, after other issues had arisen.

Enough information has become available about the Bangkok negotiations to give us some insight into the diplomatic tactics involved.[43] The Malaysians felt strongly that it was up to the Indonesians and Filipinos to make concessions; they regarded themselves as the aggrieved party who was being attacked after having carried out their obligations under the Manila Agreement. They should not now be expected to offer concessions in the face of armed aggression. The Indonesians, on the other hand, felt that they had already made a concession in agreeing to accept a cease-fire and come to the conference table. Negotiations involve give-and-take, argued Subandrio: we cannot be expected just to give and give. What the Indonesians wanted was a 'return to the Manila Agreements' as they understood them. Neither they nor the Filipinos were very specific about what this phrase meant, except insofar as it entailed a tacit admission that there had been a deviation from them, an inadequate implementation of them for which Malaysia was at fault. This issue was debated at some length during the Bangkok conference and the wide gulf between the two standpoints became all too clear. The Malaysians asserted that they had faithfully carried out the three obligations laid upon them in the Manila Agreements in both letter and spirit. They challenged the other delegates to specify in exactly what respect the Agreements had been improperly implemented. Suwito and Sudjarwo, the Indonesian delegates, tried to steer the discussion away from arguments of this kind, which they considered merely legalistic, and, in order to avoid disturbing the atmosphere of cordiality in which the conference began, they proposed that the delegations should merely 'exchange points of view' rather than dwell on disagreements. They put the blame for the disruption of the Manila spirit on 'outside forces' (i.e. the British): 'We are not here to sit in judgment on each other, but only to find ways and means to solve our present difficulties', they stressed, over and over again. They were anxious to discuss *why* there had been defects of procedure, not *what* those defects consisted in. Then, when a stalemate was reached on the question of the Manila Agreements, the Indonesian delegates shifted their ground and invoked the spirit of *musjawarah* to urge mutual concessions for the sake of each agreement, instead of harping on contentious issues. They called on the Malaysians to help Soekarno to reach a compromise by offering concessions to match those he had made in even coming to the conference table against the wishes of domestic critics. But Suwito would not indicate just what particular concessions the Indonesians wanted, although he had hinted that the presence of British troops and bases was the main source of offence to them. Evidently what he wanted was simply Malaysia's admission of the central principle that she had been in error in implementing the Manila Agreements. This was just what the Malaysians would not concede in any way, and probably could not without fundamentally undermining their entire position. So appeals to their generosity failed to move them.

Quite apart from the rights and wrongs of the matter, the bargaining tactics of the Indonesians made it difficult for the Malaysians to compromise. 'What do you want us to do about the British?' asked one of their delegates. 'Please be more precise.' This Indonesian reluctance to come down to brass tacks was a crucial aspect of the problem. Another was put with characteristic bluntness by Ghazali.

Whatever Malaysia does, it has never been satisfactory to Indonesia. You ask us to do something today and we accommodate you. Tomorrow you will create a new difficulty, a new problem. We have done nothing which is acceptable to you. Now what do you really want? Let's get to the crux of the matter. You don't accept U Thant's report. Therefore, you say you don't like the British bases and British troops in Malaysia. So, will you accept Malaysia if we get rid of the British bases and British troops from Malaysia?

Sudjarwo's reply was also characteristic.

I did not put it quite like that. What we mean is this. The present situation ... should be studied in the projection of the Manila Agreement.

In other words, what mattered to him was not a particular aspect of the problem, but the essential principles involved in it, the *rangka*, or frame of reference within which it acquired significance.

Conversely, the Malaysian intransigence in negotiating was felt by the Indonesians (and to some extent the Filipinos) to be a fundamental obstacle to agreement on the basis of *musjawarah*. Far from showing any willingness to adopt a spirit of 'give-and-take', they seemed to be behaving in a 'take-it-or-leave-it' manner, as if they were bargaining from strength and had no need to reach a settlement. This intransigence was even more marked at the second Bangkok conference in March, when both sides were beginning to take up much more rigid positions.

On 18 February, Indonesia notified the Thai government, as the cease-fire supervisory authority, that she wished to airdrop supplies to her 'volunteers' in North Kalimantan. This outraged the Malaysians, for it implied that the Indonesians had some right to be there. It was also regarded as a sign of Soekarno's obduracy on the issue of withdrawal. The Tunku immediately announced that he would not attend any conference with Soekarno until the guerrillas were withdrawn from Malaysian soil: he also threatened that any who were captured would be dealt with under Malaysian law, not treated as prisoners of war. Next day, Subandrio proposed to Lopez that the second ministerial meeting due on 25 February should be postponed. He also accused the Malaysians of a breach of confidence in revealing the verbal agreement about his consultations with Soekarno, implying that they had thereby spoiled the opportunity for a quiet withdrawal without loss of face, since the disclosure that withdrawal was a pre-condition of further talks left the Indonesian government no choice but to keep the guerrillas there and try to supply them. He also threatened on 22 February that if the Malaysians conducted mopping-up operations in spite of the cease-fire,

Indonesia would 'respond accordingly', announcing that she intended to airdrop supplies to the guerrillas without waiting for permission. Malaysia promptly closed her airspace over Borneo and warned her not to attempt any such action. Evidently she did not, since nothing further was heard about the matter. But the mood on both sides was now too uncompromising to offer much hope of further talks proving fruitful.

It seems clear that even if Soekarno entered into the Kennedy cease-fire and the Bangkok negotiations with a genuine desire for a peaceful settlement, his attitude hardened considerably during or soon after the first Bangkok conference. This can probably be attributed to two factors. One was the PKI pressures mentioned above, which were maintained for several weeks against officials who appeared reluctant to take strong action against the British firms taken over in January; although the government stopped short of nationalizing them, it avoided an open collision with the left-wing unions and trimmed its sails to the wind as far as possible. The other factor in Soekarno's hardening attitude was the realization that there was little hope of inducing Malaysia to make any substantial concessions for the sake of a political settlement.

At the second Bangkok conference on 4 March, Razak immediately and uncompromisingly insisted on withdrawal of all Indonesian forces as an essential condition for any political talks. He recalled that Subandrio had promised at the previous meeting to take back to Djakarta a compromise proposal on this matter, but had failed to gain his government's assent to it. Subandrio denied that he had given any assurances that he could obtain Soekarno's assent for withdrawal: the proposal had been found unacceptable by the Indonesian government which now wanted to 'sweeten the pill' by linking a step-by-step withdrawal to the progress of political talks. Razak refused to budge on this point, despite attempts by Lopez and Thanat Khoman to break the deadlock by compromise proposals.[44]

Despite the collapse of the Bangkok talks, hopes of further negotiations did not entirely vanish. The cease-fire agreement had practically lost any meaning it ever had, but the fiction was not entirely abandoned: Indonesia did not dramatically step up her military pressure in Borneo, as the Malaysians feared she might. Lopez kept up his mediation efforts and both sides avoided slamming doors on an alternative proposal he was reported to have submitted to them. But with elections pending in Malaya, nothing much could be done for several months.

The interval between the Bangkok and Tokyo talks was marked by more than usual uncertainty, for neither side was willing to make any substantial concessions, yet neither wanted to be put in the position of appearing responsible for a breakdown in negotiations. The domestic aspects of confrontation became more interesting than the diplomatic. Both countries began to adjust themselves to the probability that a long drawn-out battle of wits and wills lay ahead. The Alliance government lost no popularity when, in the aftermath of the Bangkok fiasco but before the election, it announced the imminent call-up of 100,000 national servicemen (conscripts) from amongst men registered in the 21–29 year age-group. The move was of symbolic rather than military importance, for only a few thousand could quickly be absorbed into Malaysia's tiny army and the main burden of resisting Indonesian attacks still had to be borne by British and Ghurkha troops. But it was an earnest of Malaysia's determination to continue the struggle and all the main parties in the Malaysian Parliament found it expedient to support the measure. The Tunku's resounding victory in the Malayan elections at the end of April demolished any hopes the Indonesians may have entertained that domestic opposition to Malaysia would drive him to seek an accommodation with Indonesia at any price. Soekarno's response to the Malaysian call-up was to proclaim the creation of his Volunteers' Command (*Komando Gerakan Sukarelawan*) a few days later, which claimed a membership of 21 million 'volunteers' pledged to crush Malaysia. It certainly made Malaysia's few thousand reservists appear trivial by comparison, thus highlighting the point that without British support Malaysia would be virtually defenceless against Indonesia's supposedly revolutionary masses.[45]

Soon after the Malayan elections, the Philippines resumed its mediation efforts in one last attempt to bring about the Summit conference which had not transpired earlier in the year. Lopez, who had just been replaced as Philippines Foreign Minister, shuttled back and forth between Kuala Lumpur and Djakarta on a special mission to bring the two sides close enough together to warrant a meeting of the Heads of Governments. The drawn-out preliminary haggling that then preceded the Tokyo Summit Conference in June reveals as much about the aims of the three countries as the Summit meeting itself, which deadlocked hopelessly almost as soon as it started. To judge from what was said on both sides during the preceding weeks, little more was ever seriously expected of it by any of the three governments.

As in February, it was proposed that the Foreign Ministers should meet first to create a favourable mood for conciliatory Summit-level talks on the central political problems. Each side would demonstrate its sincerity and willingness to establish more cordial relations by modifying its previous demands on the implementation of the cease-fire. Subsequently both Indonesia and Malaysia have claimed that they made great concessions for the sake of peace, but that the other showed itself to be utterly unreasonable and unwilling to compromise. As it was, hard bargaining took place even before Lopez could induce the two sides to make sufficient concessions to warrant formal talks, for neither showed much sign of the give-and-take spirit needed if a *musjawarah*-type settlement on the basis of mutual compromise was to be at all feasible. On the contrary, each was careful not to concede any points which might be of tactical value in the negotiations.

The obstacles Lopez had to overcome in the course of his efforts to bring Soekarno and the Tunku to the conference table turned out to be far more formidable than he initially expected. On 13 May he said he was hoping for a Summit meeting in Tokyo within ten days or so, the Heads of Governments meeting to take place after two days of preliminary talks at the Ministerial level, during which the withdrawal of Indonesian forces would be verified. But it was not until 18 June that the conference began, roughly along the lines initially suggested, after lengthy and bitter arguments about the prior withdrawal of troops.

Initially Subandrio offered only a token withdrawal as Indonesia's gesture of conciliation. Malaysia promptly rejected this as insufficient, the Tunku objecting that he could not be expected to enter into negotiations until the invading forces had fully withdrawn from Malaysian soil, since this would leave him in an inferior position at the conference table. (He ultimately did so, however.) The Indonesians then proposed that they 'accept withdrawal in principle', the withdrawal to commence simultaneously with the Ministerial conference — although they still refused Malayan demands for a complete withdrawal. Then the Malaysian government dropped its insistence on this condition and on 25 May a Philippines spokesman announced that Indonesia would begin the withdrawal of troops simultaneously with the commencement of talks between the three Foreign Ministers to pave the way for a Summit meeting on 5 June. The Thai government agreed to supervise and verify the 'withdrawal'.

Then began a curious new series of pin-pricking delays and arguments. Soekarno had cabled a message to Lopez in Kuala Lumpur on 25 May qualifying what was to be meant by the word 'withdrawal': plans for the Foreign Ministers' meeting therefore had to be delayed while Lopez again visited Djakarta to resolve the disagreement. From the terms for a Summit meeting on which agreement was announced by Lopez on 29 May, it was clear that Indonesia was offering little more than a token withdrawal and acceptance of the principle that she should withdraw her troops.[46] More disturbing still, from the Malaysian point of view, the official Indonesian announcement of this agreement in Djakarta included an additional clause to the effect that further withdrawal of troops would only take place in conformity with the progress made in the political negotiations. When asked by the Malaysian government to obtain an explanation of this unexpected new development, Lopez replied blandly that it was intended merely for domestic consumption with Indonesia and was not considered to be part of the text of the agreement. This answer was far from satisfactory to the Malaysians, of course, but Lopez was not able to obtain assurances that the Indonesian government would abide by the text until a week later, the day before Soekarno left for Tokyo.[47] The episode further increased the suspicions in Kuala Lumpur about Indonesian slipperiness in negotiation and it set the Malaysians more than ever on guard against loopholes in any agreement made with Subandrio and Soekarno.

Two further points of dispute arose before the Tokyo talks finally began, while a series of pin-pricks and new border incursions eroded away any hopes that an atmosphere of trust and cordiality might be created. The Malaysians wanted Soekarno to issue a public order that all Indonesian guerrillas were to withdraw, claiming that Lopez and the Tunku had agreed upon this; but the Indonesians refused to comply, alleging that a secret order had already been issued. Malaysia finally gave way on this point, which was only of symbolic importance since there were so few guerrillas in Sarawak. More controversial was the question of how many checkpoints were needed along the border to verify the withdrawal, on which the Malaysians wanted firm agreement before finally committing themselves to attend the conference. The Malaysians wanted 'a substantial number' of check-points in both Sabah and Sarawak, but the Indonesians claimed that only one pair had been provided for in the earlier agreement with Lopez. In the end, Malaysia gave way on this matter also in order to allow the conference to proceed.

All these disputes caused considerable delay, suspicion and a hardening of attitudes on both sides. Although Soekarno was waiting in Tokyo from 8 June, it was not even certain that the Tunku would attend the conference until several days later; in response to domestic criticisms that he should not go until Indonesia had demonstrated her good faith more convincingly, he commented that 'it would be undignified to keep President Soekarno waiting', but he did not finally reach Tokyo himself until 14 June. Next day, agreement was finally announced on the question of the check-point (to be situated at Tebedu) and the procedure for withdrawal. Then another flurry of charges and counter-charges of military clashes in the border area ensued before all was finally ready for the Foreign Ministers' meeting on 18 June. That night thirty-two Indonesian guerrillas duly withdrew through the Tebedu check-point. (The Malaysians claimed that they had been sent into Sarawak only a short time before in order to carry out this charade, for they did not bear the signs of prolonged jungle-bashing.) Next day the Thai verification report was solemnly transmitted to the Foreign Ministers, so that they could recommend to the Heads of Government that the withdrawal had begun and they could now meet at the Summit.

It was hardly surprising, in such inauspicious circumstances, that the Summit meeting turned out to be an uncompromising confrontation rather than an occasion for negotiations. Soekarno began bluntly by proclaiming: 'I cannot accept this Malaysia'. It was not formed in accordance with the Manila Agreements, he asserted, because the British had wrecked them. 'If I had known at Manila that you were going to change the date, I would not have signed the Manila Agreement.' The session quickly became bogged down in arguments about Ghazali's visit to Djakarta in August 1963 and the meaning of the Manila Agreements. There was no hint of a conciliatory approach. Seeing that nothing fruitful could be expected of the conference, Macapagal then put forward his proposal that a settlement of the dispute should be sought by *musjawarah* within the framework of a four-nation Afro-Asian Conciliation Commission.[48]

The discussion of this proposal quickly revealed how little hope there was for compromise on the basic issues in dispute. Razak called for immediate cessation of all forms of confrontation, withdrawal of all Indonesian forces within four weeks, then a meeting of the Foreign Ministers to establish the Afro-Asian Conciliation Commission. Subandrio refused to accept these terms, arguing that they implied that the existence of Malaysia was a *fait accompli* and that the guerrillas had no right to be there: to the Indonesians, he said, this was a conflict about the formation of Malaysia, a political problem, not just a military one. Indonesian volunteers were fighting for a principle, against colonialism. Later he carried his argument a stage further: 'We are not aggressors, since Malaysia is not in existence.' Razak replied that if there was to be conciliation, the fighting must first stop: what was the use of the agreement on a cease-fire and check-points for the withdrawal otherwise?

The abrupt, angry final session of the Heads of Governments brought matters no closer to a solution. Soekarno stood firm in his insistence that withdrawal of the guerrillas could only be considered step by step with the progress of political talks, in effect calling upon the Afro-Asian Conciliation Commission to adjudicate during the process. The Tunku rejected this as unacceptable, since it involved a diminution of Malaysia's sovereignty. The final communique simply recorded their divergent views. Soekarno proclaimed his full agreement with Macapagal's proposal for an Afro-Asian Conciliation Commission and even went further in giving an assurance that he would abide by any recommendations it made. The Tunku agreed in principle, but with the proviso that all acts of hostility against Malaysia must cease forthwith.

What were Soekarno's purposes in agreeing to the Tokyo Conference, if he was so unconciliatory in his behavior at it? Or the Tunku's for that matter? There is no clear answer on either side, beyond the general observation that both the Indonesian and Malaysian governments felt it necessary to respond positively to the Filipino mediation attempt and to test the other's good faith. If they were initially hoping for any real progress towards a settlement, their hopes must have dwindled before the conference began. By the time the Heads of Government actually met, each seems to have been manoeuvring primarily with the aim of showing that the other was not prepared to compromise in good faith. This is implicit in two semi-official accounts of the conference.[49] According to the Indonesians:

> The 'Malaysian' side has arrogantly insisted on dictating its terms with regard to check-points etc .... The arrogant and stubborn pose taken by 'Malaysia' thus far throws a serious doubt as to the sincerity of their intentions. While pouring out a constant barrage of accusations and contradictory statements invariably picturing Indonesia as the villain, it is they who are dragging their feet and bickering endlessly over insignificant details. Their delaying tactics and transparent manoeuverings give the impression of trying to score a 'victory' even before the talks have begun .... The facts are that it is Indonesia, which, having committed itself to the principle of withdrawal, has shown all possible restraint and goodwill ....

A Malaysian spokesman gave precisely the opposite interpretation:

Malaysia's desire for a peaceful settlement was clearly established in Toyko by the numerous concessions that were made for the sake of the Summit conference. Before the Malaysian delegation left Kuala Lumpur it said it would stand firm on a number of principles before the talks could begin .... We gave in on all these requirements. We finally accepted only one pair of check-points on either side of the border in Sarawak and agreed that the withdrawal should begin in Sarawak alone. There was no public order from Sukarno for the withdrawal of his men. The Foreign Ministers' meeting began without a verification report from Thailand.

Both Soekarno and the Tunku later pointed to the Tokyo Conference as evidence that it was impossible to negotiate with the other, the Tunku in his appeal to the Commonwealth Prime Ministers' Conference and to President Johnson, Soekarno in his bid to have Malaysia isolated in the Afro-Asian community for stubbornly refusing to *musjawarah* in the Asian manner.

Nothing ever came of the Macapagal proposal for an Afro-Asian Conciliation Commission, but it served as a basis for some desultory diplomatic football over the next year whenever a renewal of talks came under discussion. Outwardly it seemed a perfectly feasible alternative to the three-nation 'Maphilindo' framework within which the negotiations had been conducted up till this time. (Macapagal was anxious to disengage from the increasingly difficult position he was finding himself in before the 1965 elections loomed too close — hence the proposal to set the issue in a wider context, but still one in which the principle of 'Asian Solutions to Asian Problems' could find expression.) Macapagal's plan was simple: 'Each of us will select an Asian or African nation. Then these will unanimously elect one more.' The four-man commission would recommend measures to reconcile the three countries within a specified time limit. Pending this Commission's report, the three governments should refrain from any actions likely to aggravate the situation. Soekarno immediately and unconditionally agreed to this, but the Tunku would only agree subject to a number of conditions about withdrawal of troops and the cessation of confrontation and all hostile acts, which Soekarno refused to accept. The Indonesians later made great play of their willingness to accept in advance whatever recommendations the Commission might make, chiding their adversaries for being so unwilling to match their generous concession. And, superficially, the scheme looked very reasonable; the Security Council later commended it as a means of reaching a solution after the Malaysian complaint against Indonesian aggression. But there can be little doubt that Malaysia would have found herself under heavy pressure to make concessions in such a body, for the sake of consensus and 'the Asian approach'. Even if three of the four nations were definitely sympathetic to her, it was only necessary for Indonesia to nominate one member who would press her case strongly in order to make consensus impossible, or possible only on terms agreeable to her.

Such are the politics of consensus, *musjawarah* — and the Malaysians were probably right in suspecting that unless they could ensure in advance that Indonesia had called off confrontation, they would be asked to make greater concessions for the sake of peace than they were prepared to. But neither country was eager to plunge into a new set of negotiations immediately after Tokyo, in any case, and by the time the question arose again, towards the end of the year, other developments had intervened which made the prospects of agreement even more remote.

[1] See *The Bulletin* (Sydney), 14 December 1963, pp. 54–5 for a discussion of the likely costs of Indonesia's attempt to divert her trade away from Singapore. For a discussion of why the economy did not 'collapse', see J. A. C. Mackie, 'Inflation and Confrontation in Indonesia', *Australian Outlook*, vol. XXVIII, no. 3, December 1964, pp. 278–98.

[2] Soekarno's speech at anti-Malaysia rally in Jogjakarta, 25 September 1963, cited in Modelski, *The New Emerging Forces* (Canberra, 1963), p. 80.

[3] See Kahin, *Nationalism and Revolution in Indonesia*, ch. 12–13, for an account of the Federalist policy pursued by the Dutch in 1948–9 and the Indonesian nationalists' view of the Federalist leaders as 'puppets'.

[4] 'British-Made 'Malaysia' — Barrier to International Peace and Progress' in *New Forces Build a New World* (Djakarta, Department of Foreign Affairs, Indonesia Policy Series, 1964), pp. 43–4.

[5] See Mohammad Hatta, 'One Indonesian's View of the Malaysia Issue', *Asian Survey*, vol. V, no. 3, pp. 139–43.

[6] 'British-Made 'Malaysia' — Barrier to International Peace and Progress', p. 46.

[7] See *A Survey on the Controversial Problem of the Establishment of the Federation of Malaysia*, circulated in roneo form by the Permanent Mission of the Republic of Indonesia to the United Nations, 24 September 1963. Compare the later publications of the Indonesian Herald, *The Problem of 'Malaysia'* (n.d. — published about November 1963) and of the Department of Foreign Affairs, *The 'Malaysia' Issue, Background and Documents* (n.d. — 1964?).

[8] See the speech by L. N. Palar, Indonesian Delegate to the UN before the General Assembly on 27 September 1963: also Indonesian Herald, *The Problem of Malaysia* (Djakarta, 1963).

[9] Ibid.

[10] Ibid.; also 'British-Made 'Malaysia' — Barrier to International Peace and Progress', pp. 55–6.

[11] Ibid.

[12] Details of the various border incursions are given in *Indonesian Involvement in Eastern Malaysia*, pp. 24, 45–6, 67–74. For a brief account of the Long Jawi raid in late September by a force said to number 100, see 'The Azahari Myth', *Nation* (Sydney), 14 December 1963, p. 7. Long Jawi is situated well inside the Sarawak border on the route used by Indonesian migratory workers coming down the Batang Balui to the sawmills of the 4th Division of Sarawak.

[13] Much of the information in this paragraph and elsewhere in this section is based upon briefings by the public relations officers of the British military forces in Singapore and Kuching in early 1965. A brief account has been published by the Commander British Forces, Borneo, General Sir Walter Walker, 'How Borneo was Won', *Round Table*, Jan. 1969, LXIX, i, no. 233. Some informative articles on the Borneo war were written by Dennis Bloodworth of *The Observer* (London): in particular, see 'Borneo War' and 'Borneo Today; Under the Shadow of Terrorists', *The Age* (Melbourne), 16 June 1964 and 4 July 1964. Three articles in *The Times*, 12–14 August 1964, entitled 'The Malaysia Campaign' are useful.

[14] There were 5 British battalions in Borneo just after the Brunei revolt (2 infantry, 1 Gurkha and 1 commando battalion): the number was increased to 7 in September 1963, 10 by mid-1964 (including 3 Malaysian and 6 Gurkha battalions) and 13 by March 1965; for further details, see Walker, op. cit. Indonesia had 7 battalions and a para-commando regiment, plus 13 irregular units, in Kalimantan in mid-1964; *Indonesian Involvement*

in Eastern Malaysia, p. 45. *The Times*, 12 August 1964, published an estimate of 11,000 Indonesian troops and 2,000 'volunteers' there, of which only 3,000 were disposed in small units close to the border. The Secretary of State for Commonwealth Relations told Parliament on 9 February 1965, after the build-up at end of 1964, that there were 10–12,000 Indonesian troops in the border area and 15–20,000 in the whole of Kalimantan: *Hansard*, vol. 706, p. 191. According to Gen. Walker, the Indonesian forces were tripled in strength to 'two or three times' the British forces.

[15]An attempt was made by two platoons of irregulars to establish a liberated area near Gunong Gading, west of Lundu, in the first quarter of 1964. They were aided by local peasants who were members of SUPP. On 9 May, the Lundu branch of SUPP was proscribed: *Sarawak Tribune*, 11 May 1964.

[16]For a list of alleged British border violations see the speech of the Indonesian delegate Sudjarwo Tjondronegoro, at the Security Council debate on 9 September 1964; they were relatively minor episodes.

[17]*Indonesian Involvement in Eastern Malaysia*, p. 3. Both Malays and Chinese around Paloh and Binatang, near the mouth of the Rejang, sheltered a sea-borne band of armed Indonesian insurgents in September 1963: *Sarawak Bulletin*, 16 December 1963. As late as July 1965 it was necessary for the Sarawak government to move 1,000 Chinese families from the Serian road area into 're-settlement camps' after they had been implicated in harbouring Indonesian insurgents during attacks; *The Age*, 7 July 1965.

[18]According to Peter Polomka, whose MA thesis on 'The Indonesian Army and Confrontation: an enquiry into the functions of foreign policy under Guided Democracy' (University of Melbourne, 1970) is the source for most of the material in this paragraph, Dhani regarded his jurisdiction as extending over all of Kalimantan, Sumatra and Java and as entailing the authority to create an offensive striking force; Yani saw it only in terms of command over a retaliatory force in the event of a British attack. Soekarno, when consulted on the matter, merely said that he had had in mind 'something like the Mandala command' (i.e. Major-General Suharto's command in East Indonesia during the West Irian campaign) and left it to Subandrio to sort out the details.

[19]Ibid. p. 175. Polomka also mentions that Brig.-General Rukman was transferred from command of Kostrad to a less crucial command in Makassar because Yani had doubts about his political reliability; in North Sumatra, the battle units from Kostrad under Brig.-General Kemal Idris included Siliwangi division units which 'could be relied on not to act indiscreetly'.

[20]There are some indications that Nasution was distinctly more 'hawkish' than Yani in the early months of confrontation (perhaps because he had suffered a set-back during the West Irian campaign, perhaps to regain the initiative on a military matter): Yani is said to have reacted strongly against a movement of troops to West Kalimantan by Hasan Basri, the All-Kalimantan Commander, and an officer close to Soekarno, early in 1963.

[21]Polomka, op. cit. p. 172–3. The revolt by Ande Selle in South Sulawesi in April 1964 seems to have caused a good deal of alarm in Indonesia, as the old Darul Islam leader, Kahar Muzzakkar, was also still at large there and his revolt created dangerous opportunities for arms smuggling and foreign intervention: see *Suluh Indonesia*, 5 May, and *Sketsmasa*, no. 15, May 1964.

[22]See *Indonesian Involvement in Eastern Malaysia*, p. 33, and statement by Tun Razak on 27 Jan. in *Malaysia News* (Canberra), 3/65. Radio Pontianak announced a build-up to 30,000 men in West Kalimantan in late December and British military authorities said they believed this was the level to which the Indonesians planned to bring their forces: it represented a three-fold increase of the force in Kalimantan a few months earlier. According to General Walker, the pattern of Indonesian incursions began to change soon after, with larger and better trained (regular) troops for long-range patrolling in company strength: op. cit. p. 17. The Indonesian forces were stiffened by regulars during 1964 and began to provide much more professional opposition. The campaign now involved 'long range patrolling, often in company strength, ambushing and attacking large bodies of the enemy, often dug in. It had become a company commander's war. The enemy fought with tenacity and skill. He had mortars and guns and used them efficiently. Gone were the days when the immediate reaction to a contact was to charge the enemy.'

[23]*Indonesian Involvement in Eastern Malaysia*, pp. 15–35.

[24]Ibid. p. 81: cf. Bunnell, 'Guided Democracy Foreign Policy: 1960–5', pp. 517–18, and Brackman, *Southeast Asia's Second Front*, p. 207, who reports that the first phase of

the Borneo campaign was directed by Zaidi, the former *Barisan Pemuda Sarawak* school teacher from the Rejang, who had been in Indonesia during the Revolution.

[25]Lt.-General Yani asserted in July 1965 that only Indonesian 'volunteers', not 'regulars' had been used against Malaysia; *The Age*, 16 July 1965. But General Nasution had frankly admitted their use in September 1964 and Sudjarwo made no attempt to deny the charge in the Security Council debate later that month.

[26]The cost of the war to Britain was estimated at $1.25 million per week in early 1964: *The Times*, 13 April 1964. The casualties on the British-Malaysian side were stated roundly at 125 men killed and 200 wounded in June 1966, on the Indonesian side at 500 dead and 735 prisoners: see Neville Brown, 'The First Steps Towards Disengagement', *New Statesman*, 3 June 1966, p. 801.

[27]*Berita Indonesia*, 21 September 1963.

[28]The value of exports, excluding oil, was $457 million in 1964 compared with $428 million in 1963, according to *Bulletin of Indonesian Economic Studies*, no. 5, October 1966, p. 77. Some of the formerly smuggled goods (barter trade) probably had to be shipped through official channels.

[29]See the rubber-exporting arrangements of PT Karkam, described in Lance Castles, 'Socialism and Private Business: the Latest Phase', *Bulletin of Indonesian Economic Studies*, no. 1, June 1965, pp. 37–8.

[30]Parliament was invited to make proposals for new measures to replace the May decrees, but the political parties had conflicting ideas on how to tackle the inflation and there was virtually no scope for any substantial alternative to the government's essentially hand-to-mouth economic policy: see *Suluh Indonesia*, 4, 5 and 6 April for the ambiguous and contradictory ideas of the Parliamentary committee. The 17 April regulations used the language of 'social control' but represented, in effect, an admission that inflation could not be checked by any act of government policy.

[31]The paradox is discussed in Mackie, 'The Resilience of the Economy' in *Problems of the Indonesian Economy*, ch. 4.

[32]Indonesian export statistics are quite misleading on the matter of destination of exports. Some notion of the export to Singapore was available in the Malaysian trade statistics; these were conveniently summarized in the Economist Intelligence Unit, *Three Monthly Economic Review*, from which the estimates given here have been calculated.

[33]Tables of quarterly exports and imports in the 1961–4 period are given in Mackie, 'Inflation and Confrontation in Indonesia', p. 288.

[34]See Mackie, *Problems of Inflation*, pp. 98–101 for statistics of the increase in prices and money in the period 1963–5.

[35]According to Bernard K. Gordon, *The Dimensions of Conflict in Southeast Asia*, p. 108, there was much evidence that Soekarno wanted a settlement: 'he decided to end the confrontation soon after it began, but found that he would not be able to do so until he could convince the more rabid opponents of Malaysia that he had extracted every concession....' This theory reflected a view frequently attributed to Ambassador Howard P. Jones: a more sophisticated formulation may be found in Kahin, 'Malaysia and Indonesia', *Pacific Affairs*, Fall 1964. For a more critical but superficial interpretation of Soekarno's motives, see Arnold Brackman's account in *Southeast Asia's Second Front*, ch. 17–21.

[36]See above p. 193 on the gradual reduction of American foreign aid programmes after September 1963. U.S. policy towards Indonesia at this time is briefly summarized in Bunnell, op. cit. pp. 667–80.

[37]See Michael Leifer, 'Anglo-American Differences over Malaysia', *The World Today*, vol. XX, no. 4, April 1964, pp. 566–71.

[38]Nadia Derkach, 'The Soviet Policy towards Indonesia in the West Irian and Malaysia Disputes', *Asian Survey*, vol. V, no. 11, November 1965, pp. 566–71; see also Uri Ra'anan, 'The Coup that Failed: a Background Analysis', *Problems of Communism*, vol. XV, no. 2, March-April 1951, for a useful summary of Russian and Chinese policies towards Indonesia in 1964–5.

[39]See below p. 243.

[40]Soekarno's version of his agreement with Kennedy was given in his 'Dwikora' speech of 3 May: see *Gelora Konfrontasi Mengganjang Malaysia* (Djakarta, Department of Information, 1964), pp. 377–8.

[41]*The Age*, January. The cease-fire came into effect on 25 January, but Subandrio later charged that mopping up operations were still continuing: *Suluh Indonesia*, 29

January. The cease-fire was never formally abrogated, despite allegations of breaches by both sides: but it was merely a threadbare fiction after the second Bangkok conference in March and was discarded entirely in July.

[42]Razak's reservation of his Government's position on the Bangkok cease-fire terms reads as follows:

'It is the sincere desire of the Malaysian Government to adhere to the cease-fire arrangements. However, as there are members of Indonesian Armed Forces, Regulars as well as Irregulars, on the Malaysian side of the border, their presence will provoke incidents. The Malaysian Government therefore considers that the cease-fire would not be fully effective unless the Governments concerned agree to limit the activities and movements of their Armed Forces, Regulars as well as Irregulars, within their respective territories.'

In all other respects, the Joint Press Communique of the Bangkok Conference was a singularly vague and general document.

[43]A good deal of information on the Bangkok conference, slanted somewhat against Malaysia, was published in the *Philippines Free Press*, in articles by Napoleon Rama on 22 February and 21 March. The account given here is based partly on these and partly on an unofficial transcript of proceedings of the Bangkok and Toyko conferences, some extracts of which have been published in Gordon, op. cit. pp. 106–15.

[44]See *Philippines Free Press*, 21 March 1964.

[45]See chapter 9 below for further details of domestic developments in Malaysia and Indonesia at this time.

[46]For the terms of the agreement, see *Straits Times*, 29 May, 1 June 1964.

[47]*Straits Times*, 2, 6, 9 June 1964: for the additional paragraph of the Indonesian communique, see *Suluh Indonesia*, 1 June 1964.

[48]Some excerpts from a Malaysian official transcript of the Tokyo Summit proceedings have been published by Peter Boyce in *Malaysia and Singapore in International Diplomacy—Documents and Commentaries*, Sydney University Press, 1968, pp. 92–6.

[49]For the Tunku's version of what happened, see the talk over Radio Malaysia by Patrick Keith on 23 June (published by the Office for the High Commissioner for Australia and New Zealand, Canberra, in 'Malaysian News', no 29/64): for the official Indonesian version, see the 'Position Paper' of 13 June in *Dokumentasi Konperensi Tingkat Tinggi* and *New Forces Build a New World* (Department of Foreign Affairs, Indonesian Policy Series, 1965), pp. 60–3: a Philippines account is given by Napoleon Rama in the *Philippines Free Press*, 27 June 1964.

IX
'Vivere Pericoloso'

WHILE there may have been some possibility in early 1964 that the dispute between Indonesia and Malaysia could be settled by negotiations and mutual concessions, a number of developments in the middle of that year brought about a hardening of attitudes on both sides. Race riots broke out in Singapore in July; shortly afterwards Indonesian forces were twice landed on the west coast of Malaya in what appeared to be attempts to stir up communal strife there. These events precipitated a sharp crisis in September, when Malaysia complained to the Security Council about Indonesia's aggression and the British seemed at one point to be contemplating a major naval and air strike against Indonesian bases. Malaysia's internal strains seem to have inclined Indonesia's leaders to believe that the new federation would collapse from within if they maintained their pressure on it. Meanwhile, political developments within Indonesia — and on the broader international scene — were strengthening the hands of those who wanted to continue confrontation at the expense of those who might have favoured bringing it to an end. These latter factors came to exercise an increasing influence on the course of confrontation by the end of 1964.

THE INDONESIAN POLITICAL BACKGROUND, 1963–1964

Some time after the open breach between Indonesia and Malaysia, Herbert Feith commented that the events of September 1963 constituted a distinctive landmark in Indonesia's domestic politics since it ended a period of right-wing predominance and introduced a distinct new swing towards the left.[1] There was not a dramatic and major shift in the balance of power, nor any clearcut victory for the left, but the trend was soon discernible in a number of 'retoolings' of local government officials such as governors and regency heads, frequently after vigorous campaigns against them by the PKI and related organizations, and their replacement of men with less strongly anti-Communist inclinations. Cabinet reshuffles occurred in November 1963 and August 1964, but the changes on both occasions were relatively minor, despite persistent PKI demands for a *Nasakom* cabinet. The first of these became necessary after the death of First Minister Djuanda and another minister, but it brought no increase in overt PKI representation: if anything, the rival Murba faction was strengthened.[2] However, Nasution's position was weakened, as he was not included in the new inner Presidium of a cabinet which was now too large to function effectively. More significantly, Dr. Subandrio now began to emerge as a major contender in the struggle for power around the President, defeating Chairul Saleh and Dr. Leimena (the other members of the Presidium) in the tussle for Djuanda's mantle, under the new title of First Deputy Prime Minister.

Subandrio's role in the Indonesian political drama became much more important about this time, as he gathered more and more strings of power into his hands, to the discomfiture of other contenders.[3] Previously he had been regarded as a politically colourless technician, but he was soon being mentioned as a probable successor to the President in the event of the latter's death, for he now showed himself to be both ambitious and unscrupulous as he became the most prominent and powerful of Soekarno's ministers. He did not stand as close to the Army leaders as Djuanda had done: in fact, by 1965 he was obviously aligned against them. The PKI had earlier distrusted him for his foreign policies, particularly his support for the American-oriented course of mid-1963, but in 1964 it found his handling of the Malaysia policy far more suitable to its purposes. Although some of its personal distrust for him remained, the PKI increasingly regarded him as its most favoured candidate for the succession, since he was not overtly anti-Communist and had no other source of political support, as his rivals had, so that in a post-Soekarno struggle for power he would have been heavily dependent on PKI backing. By 1965 Subandrio was generally regarded as having thrown in his lot with the PKI in support of Soekarno's policy of a close alignment with China and a more militantly anti-American policy, but it is an over-simplification to regard him as simply a Communist or crypto-Communist.[4] He does not seem to have had any very settled political convictions, being essentially a political technician and manipulator. He clashed sharply with Aidit on several issues late in 1964 and it seems that he threw himself eagerly on to the left-wing band-wagon only after Soekarno had foreclosed all other avenues by his decision to leave the UN in January 1965. Subandrio's uneasy balance between the Army leaders and the PKI throughout 1964 reflected not only the delicate internal balance of forces, but also the ambiguities of Indonesia's relations with the major foreign powers; he was apparently reluctant to break openly with the Americans or the Russians, yet the logic of events was pushing steadily in that direction. The Army leaders' suspicions of him increased accordingly, of course, although not until early in 1965 did Subandrio identify himself unequivocally with the 'progressive' forces and lash out at 'reactionaries' who were obstructing the leftward course of the revolution.

The declining influence of Nasution and other Army leaders who shared his strongly anti-Communist inclinations, coinciding, apparently, with a loss of immediate political purpose in 1964 (at least in contrast with their actively political role in 1960–2), roughly corresponded with the growth of a new vigour among the political parties, both Murba and PNI as well as PKI. The suspension of martial law during 1963–4 may have contributed something to this, for banned PKI publications were permitted to reappear and restrictions on PKI activities in the provinces were lifted. But there was also a new assertiveness and militancy among other parties too, on both left and right, in their claims to be 'instruments of the Revolution' in mobilizing the people to accomplish its tasks — of which 'crushing Malaysia' was the most obvious and concrete. The PKI threw itself fairly eagerly into this cause, which it found a very convenient stick for beating the heads of conservative or cautious officials who did not sufficiently trust the people in advancing the cause of the revolution. All sorts of activities could be shown to have relevance to this patriotic aim and to the struggle against the *Nekolim* and their agents at home and abroad. The other parties tried to counter the PKI in various ways — without great success, it must be said, although the Communists were not in a strong enough position during 1964 to launch the kind of vehement campaign to cut down their enemies that developed in the following year, after Soekarno had led Indonesia out of the UN and into a closer alignment with China. But the PKI was able to prevent any attempt at a *rapprochement* with Malaysia or reversion to the policies of mid-1963. And as time drew on, with the economic situation steadily deteriorating and the chances of achieving a compromise settlement with Malaysia gradually fading into the distance, it became increasingly hard for anti-Communists to find any basis on which they could make a firm stand to reverse the drift to the left.

One of the most striking features of the Djakarta political scene during 1964 was the gradual demoralization and decline of the anti-Communists. They seem to have been unable to regain the political initiative from the Communists as the latter went from strength to strength, except during two periods of intense 'polemic' between the anti-Communists and the PKI, in June–July and December–January, in each of which the former suffered setbacks. The apparent impotence of the Army leaders to check the growth of Communist strength was sometimes puzzling. The estrangement of Nasution and Yani was one factor behind their unwillingness to take action.[5] Another was its reluctance to allow itself to be outflanked by the PKI on the Malaysia issue as the proponent of patriotism and militancy, as it had been during the West Irian campaign. Thus it came to be competing with the PKI on ground advantageous to the latter and it ultimately found itself caught in a situation from which it could go neither backwards nor forwards without taking grave political risks. It could not repudiate confrontation, yet the political benefits of confrontation were being reaped by its rivals, Subandrio and the PKI, who took more and more advantage of the Army's discomfiture as they pushed Indonesia's revolution further towards the left.

Although the Malaysia issue suited the PKI very well by weakening Indonesia's links with the West, the party was also apprehensive about the risks it involved and apparently opposed to any escalation of military activities, lest the Army leaders be provided with the opportunity to reimpose martial law and again restrict the PKI's activities, as in 1960–2.[6] In its New Year message for 1964, the PKI stressed that the main problems to be solved that year were the *sandang-pangan* (food and clothing for the people) and land reform problems. Malaysia was mentioned only in third place. The official PKI view of the Malaysia campaign in the latter part of 1964 was that three distinct approaches could be discerned among the nation's leaders. The 'reformist' approach looked towards negotiations and a compromise with imperialism. The 'adventurist' approach, favoured by the 'Bonapartists' who had set in motion the adventurist landings in Malaya, was directed towards an increase of military activity in the hope of provoking a British attack so as to justify the re-imposition of martial law and an Army seizure of power. The 'revolutionary' approach involved total confrontation in all fields — economic, political (through the mobilization of the Indonesian people against the *Nekolim* and their domestic lackeys and other 'diehards'), diplomatic (through recognition of North Kalimantan and the severence of diplomatic relations with Britain), cultural and military. But military confrontation should be confined to sending volunteers to North Kalimantan to assist the guerillas there. The imperialists would seek to encourage the reformist and adventurist trends, so the revolutionary approach had to be strengthened by the PKI through active support for the *Dwikora* volunteers campaign, preventing secret sabotage of the struggle by rightists and increasing the revolutionary consciousness of the people. In short, the PKI was broadly content to defend what it had achieved on the Malaysia issue — i.e. to prevent a compromise settlement and any *rapprochement* with the West (its role in precipitating the union actions against British companies at the time of Robert Kennedy's visit was an example of that) and to exploit the issue for its own domestic purposes. The Malaysia campaign also suited the PKI in its long-range campaign to focus attention on the USA as the leader of the imperialist world and the most dangerous enemy to be resisted. Some 'progressives' (i.e. Soekarno) still harboured illusions about this, according to PKI leaders, for they wished to confine the struggle to British imperialism, but the reactionary role of US imperialism could be demonstrated by reference to Michelmore's role in the UN Mission of Enquiry to Borneo, by Robert Kennedy's attempt to reach a 'reformist' solution (abetted by Howard P. Jones, against whom a savage verbal attack was launched in April), by the provocative movements of the Seventh Fleet in Indonesian waters, by the Johnson-Abdul Rahman joint statement of July 1964 and, of course, by American increasing involvement in Vietnam after the Gulf of Tonkin incident. Towards the end of 1964, the PKI was able to spearhead a campaign to exclude American films from Indonesia, to force the closing of USIS libraries in several cities and, early in 1965, to bring Indonesian-American relations very close to breaking-point.[7] This was not the only benefit it derived from the Malaysia campaign, but it was probably the most far-reaching, since the anti-Communists could not afford to take the risk of appearing pro-American at such a time.

On the surface, Indonesian politics became more than usually amorphous and circumlocutory during 1964. The tug-of-war between left and right became increasingly intense over a series of issues, some of which aroused far more concern than the conflict with Malaysia. But Soekarno still controlled the situation through his power to determine how far he would let either side pull the other on any particular issue before he called a halt in the name of national unity. The aim of nearly all contestants in the struggle for power became concentrated on manoeuvring Soekarno into policies which would foreclose the opportunities for their rivals to achieve their objectives. Neither the Army leadership nor the PKI was prepared to risk disassociating itself openly from the President's policies or to make any premature bid for greater power so long as the President was alive and able to maintain the *Nasakom* formula for national unity, although it was generally expected that a struggle for power would develop as soon as he was gone, in which the Army would have many advantages in its favour. The PKI leaders still believed that the party would not be ready for many years to take over power in Indonesia, so their strategy was to rely on the President's protection, to identify with him while pushing him towards policies they favoured and, so far as possible, to make themselves indispensable to him.

President Soekarno's attitude to the PKI and its opponents during 1964 was even more cryptic than usual. He made gestures in both directions. No one could ever be sure which way he was going to turn next — which made it dangerous to do anything except follow him. At the time of Robert Kennedy's visit in January, Soekarno approved measures to thwart the PKI's attempt to have all British properties nationalized, but soon afterwards he stiffened in his attitude towards a negotiated settlement with Malaysia.[8] Several times during the year he gave countenance to attempts by non-Communist radical nationalists to clip the wings of the PKI in various ways, but later decided against them when he saw which way the wind was blowing. Some observers were convinced that he was trying to resist the PKI but could not afford to abandon the confrontation of Malaysia unless he was given a face-saving compromise. An equally plausible case could be made to the contrary, however — that he could no longer disregard the PKI and may not have wanted to. If there were any dominant strands in his thinking during the first 12 months after the break with Malaysia, they were his heightened emphasis upon the importance of inculcating a revolutionary spirit and ideology, upon national unity and upon ensuring the mobilization and participation of the people for the tasks of carrying Indonesia's revolution to its goals.[9] The maintenance of confrontation enabled him to stress these themes, whereas domestic issues would have called for different approaches.

The struggle with Malaysia also enabled him to divert attention away from domestic dissensions by calling for demonstrations of national unity and solidarity. The most obvious example of this was the great stress put on the Volunteers' Command in March, a response to Malaysia's call-up of national servicemen, and the 'Peoples' Twofold Command' (*Dwikora*) a few weeks later. Few episodes in the whole history of confrontation illustrate so well the essentially expressive, symbolic character of much Indonesian political activity in those years as the Volunteers' Command. For weeks it provided a theme for public oratory, press exhortation and resounding personal declamations of patriotism and self-sacrifice. Soekarno's daughter Megawati was one of the first to enrol — and her inspiring lead was promptly hailed and emulated by student groups. Partindo promptly declared all 250,000 of its members to be volunteers, without any further ado. Within a week eighteen million volunteers had come forward, according to the Minister in charge of the National Front; soon afterwards the conventionally accepted figure was twenty-one million.[10] Such numbers really meant very little, for they were mere aggregates of the membership claimed by the various mass organizations and parties which enrolled *en masse* (frequently bodies with overlapping memberships at that), as Partindo did. Yet large numbers of people undoubtedly did volunteer personally, many out of ardent patriotism, of course, and many out of opportunism, for it would have been impolitic or even perilous to be branded as reluctant to answer the call. How much all this sound and fury amounted to is quite another matter. Very few of the volunteers were ever sent to the battle zones, though a small number were used in the raiding parties sent across the Malacca Straits later in the year and some were reportedly sent to West Kalimantan to render support services to the Army there, growing vegetables and generally acting as a reserve labour corps. In Djakarta and many other towns, volunteers were formed into detachments under the local military commanders and given drill, physical training and, in some instances, distinctive uniforms. All in all, the Volunteers Command was used for a variety of purposes, many of them only remotely connected with the crushing of Malaysia. In 1965, the training of Communist Youth (*Pemuda Rakjat*) volunteers at Halim air base in the weeks before the 1 October coup was one of the factors that particularly disturbed the Army leaders.

The climax to the Volunteers' movement came on 3 May when President Soekarno announced his *Dwikora* to a mass rally of (allegedly) one million volunteers outside the Merdeka Palace. Following the pattern of the *Trikora* which had preceded the infiltration attacks in West Irian in late 1961, this speech was less significant for the commands themselves — 'Assist the Struggle of the People of Malaya, Singapore, Sarawak, Brunei and Sabah to dissolve Malaysia' and 'Intensify the Defence of the Indonesian Revolution' — than for the status which it subsequently acquired as the hallowed source of moral authority for the struggle against Malaysia.

When something like Martial Law had to be re-imposed later in 1964, a new office of Regional Executors of the *Dwikora (Pepelrada — Penguasa Pelaksanaan Dwikora Daerah)* was created, analogous to the former Regional Martial Law Administrators.[11] Obeisance to *Dwikora* came to be required in almost every public utterance about confrontation. The myth that the commands were issued 'at the urging of the Indonesian people', not at the whim of Soekarno himself, had to be established by sheer reiteration, for there was no basis in fact for it, except the flood of 'volunteers'. Neither Parliament nor the Consultative Assembly (MPRS) had been consulted about it. Rather, the whole episode has the appearance of being an elaborate exercise in drumming up national unity in the face of an external enemy at a time when rifts in the facade of domestic unity were causing serious anxiety. Hints that the imperialists might be about to assault Indonesia and 'set back the course of Indonesia's revolution' were also prominent in Soekarno's *Dwikora* speech, although at just that time the British imperialists were belatedly bringing themselves to see some good in Maphilindo, in hopes if negotiating a settlement of the conflict. Another element in this curious piece of shadow-play was an eagerness to create the impression abroad that the campaign against Malaysia was a genuinely popular campaign in which people and leaders were strongly united, for on other matters they were far from united at that time.

A series of vehement controversies broke out in May-June 1964, which revealed the state of acute tension that was building up behind the facade of national unity. The main storm-centre was a 'polemic' stirred up in the press and political parties during June and early July over a kite-flying proposal by anti-PKI elements for the abolition of political parties, or, alternatively, for the creation of a single 'Vanguard Party' *(Partai Pelopor)* or the 'simplification of parties' through the reduction of approved parties from 10 to 3, each representing one of the main *Nasakom* streams. The vehement but strangely convoluted debate on political principles which raged over this question revealed a state of acute political tension over other issues also, quite out of keeping with the outer facade of national unity. The most interesting feature of the episode was the emergence of the Murba Party leaders (notably Adam Malik and Chairul Saleh) as the most active opponents of the PKI and the leaders of a rather heterogeneous band of anti-Communists seeking a new battleground on which the PKI could be fought.[12] Their strategy in the matter was to associate themselves as closely as possible with President Soekarno, his ideas and his language of revolution, even hinting that their ideas were Soekarno's own and that his doctrine of the Indonesian revolution was in principle incompatible with Communism. The idea of a Vanguard Party had been in Soekarno's mind ever since August 1945, claimed Chairul Saleh's mouthpiece, *Berita Indonesia*, asserting that as an 'instrument of the Revolution' it must naturally expound the President's ideas.[13] The establishment of a single party system would mean the submergence of the PKI as such. Even if it tried to take over the new party surreptitiously and impose its doctrines from within, they would be seriously watered down in the process:

advocates of the new system hoped, in any case, to exercise a dominant influence in it. Even the less extreme idea of party simplification could be turned to the disadvantage of the PKI, since the latter could be required to share its place in the Communist or Marxist stream with Murba and could be weakened in that way.

The newspaper polemic on this issue developed into a most unusual storm for Indonesia's 'guided press'. The major parties (PKI, PNI and NU) attacked the single party proposal as undemocratic and unconstitutional, arguing that parties were an essential instrument of the Indonesian revolution. They were not so wholeheartedly opposed to the idea of party simplification, however, for there were elements in the PNI and NU which were far from averse to a measure which might help to clip the wings of the PKI. The alignment of forces was blurred, however, for on other issues the PNI was ranged against Murba elements, over the policies of Education Minister Prijono, and against the NU over demands by the PKI for the banning of the Muslim student organization, HMI.

A much more explosive cause of social and political tension which began to develop at this time was a series of 'unilateral actions' (aksi sepihak) over land reform issues, arising out of measures taken by the PKI and its affiliated peasant organization to hasten the implementation of reforms incorporated in the 1960 Agrarian Law.[14] These had involved regulations intended to guarantee a large proportion of the harvest to share-farmers under crop-sharing agreements and a limit on individual landholdings, coupled with a distribution of surplus land to landless peasants. The economic rationale behind this legislation was highly dubious, but need not be analysed here. More importantly, it was bound to sharpen antagonisms between rich and poor peasants and between different aliran at the village level, since it raised expectations which could not be met and it disrupted existing relationships between landowners and share-croppers with disadvantageous consequences for both sides. The richer peasants and many of the local officials who were connected with them had been doing their best since 1960 to evade or frustrate the implementation of the land reform programme, while the Communists and their allies were becoming increasingly impatient and militant in their insistence on carrying through the crop-sharing laws in particular. In this, Soekarno seemed to have given them his support. Energetic and consistent implementation of the land reform programme suited the PKI's political strategy well if it meant the isolation and weakening of their opponents, but admonitions to resolve local disputes by musjawarah on a Nasakom basis in organizations which were dominated by rich land owners and their friends made little appeal to the PKI and its peasant organization, the BTI (Barisan Tani Indonesia). Hence the resort to 'unilateral actions' against the 'reactionary' elements. The first of these to be widely publicized occured in Klaten in May 1964, one of the most densely populated regions of Java, in the notorious 'Red Triangle' just west of Surakarta. Many other incidents occured in the latter part of 1964 and 1965, often spilling over into fights and bloodshed on both sides. The bitterness engendered by these episodes not only aggravated the struggle for power in Djakarta (for it made nonsense to talk about *Nasakom* and *musjawarah* as a basis for unity in the capital if *musjawarah* was giving way to open violence or frustration of the law in the rural areas) but also sharpened the antagonisms within the villages. This was later to result in the bloody massacres that followed the coup of October 1965, when the anti-Communists turned upon their opponents to destroy them as soon as the opportunity presented itself.

Soekarno was in Tokyo when the storm in Djakarta blew up, but even when he returned he did not immediately make any comment on the issues in dispute. His silence on the single party notion was interpreted by some to mean that he was not averse to it, for some of his closest political cronies were actively supporting it.[15] Probably, however, he was waiting to gauge the strength of the two sides before committing himself. His benediction or ban was sure to be the decisive factor in the tug-of-war going on, for no-one could afford to espouse doctrines known to be in conflict with his; so each side sought to manoeuvre the other into a position which could be condemned as opposed to the views of the President and national unity. However, Soekarno finally ordered a ban on all further 'polemics', declaring at the same time that political parties were a necessary instrument of the Indonesian revolution and would not be 'simplified' or merged.[16] It was a set-back for the anti-Communists although it was not followed by any further political changes. A minor cabinet reorganization was announced in August, marked by the elevation of Njoto of the PKI to the Presidium, but this was counter-balanced by the appointment of several anti-Communists to important positions. There was no other significant change in the power balance (apart from the creation of quasi-Martial Law in September, which only slightly strengthened the Army's powers and confidence) until the end of the year, when a dramatic swing to the left occurred involving a severe set-back for the Murba group.

It is understandable, therefore, that in such circumstances, the determination of policy towards Malaysia was essentially left to Soekarno. No other party or group dared to risk the opprobrium of openly opposing the continuation of the conflict, despite the diminishing prospects of victory and the burdensome consequences it entailed. The PKI, on the other hand, fully supported the President's policy of maintaining the conflict at an ambiguous, low-keyed level. Consequently, the course of the confrontation throughout 1964 was very much a matter of Soekarno's immediate response to particular developments at any moment, domestic as much as external, rather than of clearly planned policy.

MALAYSIAN POLITICAL DEVELOPMENTS, 1964

It was generally assumed in Indonesian comment on Malaysia during 1963–4 that Malaysia would be forced to come to terms with Indonesia or else crack under the strain of confrontation, either because of a popular reaction against the Tunku's government or from the inherent tensions and contradictions of its neo-colonialist character. Domestic developments within Malaysia were eagerly scanned for signs of the expected disintegration. The Indonesian government's strategy in 'crushing Malaysia' seems to have been influenced at certain points by the course of events there — for example, the lull in diplomatic activity just before the April elections and the resumption immediately after, or the attempt to exploit racial conflict after the Singapore riots of July 1964. But if one can judge by the frequent Indonesian news reports of opposition to the Tunku and his government or of incipient fissures in the ranks of the 'puppets' who had supported Malaysia, the significance attached to events within Malaysia was fantastically distorted in Djakarta. No Indonesian journalist or public speaker could have brought himself to state openly the awkward truth of the Malaysian situation, which was that both the Tunku and Lee Kuan Yew found their domestic political position much strengthened by the creation of Malaysia and by the threats from Indonesia, that their domestic critics and opponents were not the confident vanguard of a swelling band of revolutionary fighters inspired by the doctrine of the New Emerging Forces, but a set of politically impotent and demoralized parties which had little hope of upsetting any government in Malaysia either by lawful means or unlawful.

It would be intriguing to reconstruct a composite picture of Malaysia's political life in this period as revealed in the Indonesian press and indoctrination media in order to discover how the basic political mechanics of Malaysia were understood there: one was often left with the impression that few Indonesians had access to any sources of reasonably objective information on the matter (although many listened to Radio Malaysia in the quiet of their homes — not that it could be called objective). But the picture obtained by a simple Djakarta newspaper-reader would not have been the same as the picture in the minds of Soekarno or Subandrio who had much wider and better sources of information. So it would not be very fruitful to depict the Malaysia scene as seen through Indonesian eyes, except if this were our sole purpose in telling the story. The story needs to be filled in, however, for the tensions which began to build up in Malaysia in the latter half of 1964, after the Singapore race riots, must be set in perspective. It came to be widely believed in Djakarta — and elsewhere — that Malaysia might collapse from its own political strains long before Indonesia was forced by economic necessity to bid for a settlement.

Far from cracking up under the pressure of confrontation, however, Malaysia was in some respects welded together more strongly because of the external threat than might have been the case in happier circumstances. The contentious problems which could easily have arisen in the difficult early stages of adjustment to a new set of political and economic arrangements were made less troublesome because the ranks had to be closed in the face of the enemy. The parties opposing Malaysia were left in a position of acute political difficulty because they could not escape the stigma of being characterized as pro-Indonesian. The disastrous defeat suffered by the *Barisan Sosialis* in the election suddenly sprung by Lee Kuan Yew on 21 September, just after Malaysia Day, was perhaps not solely due to this factor, but it must have contributed, as it certainly did in the defeat of the Socialist Front in the Malayan elections six months later. In Sarawak, SUPP was set back disastrously because of the security situation.[17]

Singapore felt the immediate economic effects of confrontation more severely than any other part of Malaysia after Indonesia's severance of commercial relations, but the prospect of wider economic opportunities in Malaysia offered her some compensation. (Penang also suffered some loss, without any compensating advantages: Indonesian tin ore was diverted away from the big smelter there and the small but lucrative 'barter trade' with Atjeh was stopped — or driven into more dangerous and expensive smuggling channels.) A good deal of unemployment in Singapore resulted from the cessation of rubber and copra imports, which had been processed there for re-export, and from the general loss of entrepot trade. Lee Kuan Yew estimated that alternative employment might have to be found for 15,000 persons, while Goh Keng Swee assessed the possible decline in the national income at 8.2 per cent, a figure which was considered rather too high by some economists, since the government was able to mop up some of the unemployment by other means. During 1964, Indonesian low-grade rubber began to flow back to Singapore in defiance of the trade ban, although not in sufficient quantities to offset the earlier loss.[18]

The *Barisan Sosialis* was unable to make political capital out of the unemployment situation, however, for it was now so weakened in the Legislative Assembly and shaken by its various setbacks of the previous year that it was no longer in any position to challenge the PAP. Its one serious attempt at industrial action through SATU, the Singapore Association of Trade Unions, a strike at the naval dockyard and a general strike on 7–8 October, merely resulted in the arrest of more *Barisan* leaders under the Internal Security Regulations, which both the Federal authorities and Lee Kuan Yew were now able to invoke with more justification than before. The *Barisan* was torn by disagreements over its strategy and leadership during this period, so that Lee Kuan Yew had virtually no serious parliamentary opposition to contend with in his own state. Some of the former leaders who had been detained were released at the end of 1963 (including Woodhull, and the Puthucheary brothers) but they did not go back into political life and dissociated themselves from the *Barisan*, as also did Lim Chin Siong himself at the end of 1965.[19]

The greatest danger to Malaysia in 1964 arose from the risk of internal racial strife, which flared up briefly in July and September. This, in turn, can be related directly to the political consequences of the PAP government's decision to campaign in the elections on the Malayan peninsula in April 1964, a decision from which followed many of Malaysia's troubles of the next 18 months, culminating in the expulsion of Singapore from the Federation in August 1965.

Instead of using the threat from Indonesia as an excuse to postpone the elections due to be held in 1964, the Tunku decided just after the failure of the first Bangkok conference to hold them forthwith. His aim was partly, no doubt to exploit the atmosphere of national emergency in which he could utilize the appeal to patriotism, national unity and the need to defend the country's territorial integrity as a central election issue, and partly to demonstrate to Soekarno that the government had the solid support of the Malayan people on the question of Malaysia. His confidence was amply justified, for in the elections on 25 April the Alliance had a landslide win over the parties which had opposed Malaysia, winning 59 per cent of the vote and 74 out of 102 seats, after an election campaign fought mainly over the issue of Malaysia and confrontation. But the main political interest of the election was focused on the entry of the PAP on to the mainland political scene.

The opportunity to stress the issues of the national emergency and the external threat was very convenient to the Alliance, since it made it easier to relegate to the background more basic questions of economic and social policy. The Alliance had proved vulnerable in the 1959 election on contentious and difficult issues such as language policy, Chinese education and equality of civil rights. In 1964, the Alliance campaigned on its record as the party which had achieved independence for Malaya in 1957 and Malaysia in 1963, the only party which could be relied upon to safeguard the peoples' happiness and security. It castigated the two major opposition parties, the Pan-Malayan Islamic Party and Socialist Front, for taking the same side as Soekarno: '... the declared policy of Soekarno and his government is to 'crush Malaysia' and overrun our sacred country .... Among the parties which are seeking your sacred vote are the PMIP and the Socialist Front who openly support Soekarno and want us to be part of Indonesia'. The effectiveness of the Alliance appeal to fears of Indonesia's intentions was later acknowledged by a Socialist Front leader in a postmortem on the party's failure in its former stronghold of Penang.

... Although we kept on refuting the allegation of being pro-Soekarno ... we could not convince quite a good section of the electorate. The consensus of opinion is that while we appeared to be strong critics of whatever wrongs the Alliance did, we refrained from criticizing whatever wrongs the Indonesian Government has done. This gave the impression that, notwithstanding our utterances of not being pro-Soekarno, such lack of criticism of what appeared to be wrong in the minds of the people, indicated a pro-Soekarno tendency.[21]

As the Penang electorate was predominantly Chinese, it could be argued that fears of Indonesia were more easily exploited there than in Malay electorates, but it is noteworthy that the PMIP vote was also much lower than in 1959. The opposition simply failed to attract votes with its charge that the Alliance had dragged Malaysia into a war with Indonesia because of its subservience to the British ('if you want war, vote for the Alliance: if you want peace, vote for the Socialist Front'); in challenging the government on its own ground, the Socialist Front neglected to stress its economic and social platform on which it might have made a more effective case, as in 1959.

When the PAP's Deputy Prime Minister announced the decision to contest the elections at the beginning of March, he said that only a token number of seats would be contested, the purpose being simply to establish the principle that the PAP was a national party with a right to organize outside Singapore.[22] After the first hostile reaction from the Alliance, the PAP withdrew its candidates from seats where they would have been opposing UMNO representatives, announcing that the party did not intend to fight UMNO, but to co-operate with it. However, no bones were made about its intention to fight the MCA. Lee Kuan Yew displayed open contempt for the MCA leaders and had earlier expressed doubt whether the MCA would succeed in delivering to the Alliance the votes of the 'urban masses', who were mostly Chinese, of course. (In the 1959 elections, the MCA had done so badly that its future as UMNO's partner in the Alliance did seem to be in jeopardy for some time.) Lee stated his position as follows: 'Our enlightened self-interest demands that we should do nothing to hinder or embarrass the present Malay leadership .... But while the present Malay leadership of Tunku and Tun Razak is vital to the survival and success of Malaysia, the Chinese leadership in the Alliance as represented by the MCA is not irreplaceable.'[23] However, the UMNO leaders were not as grateful for Lee's solicitousness as perhaps they should have been, for they regarded the PAP intrusion as a threat to the Alliance as a whole. 'The PAP move in calling on the urban voters — who are mostly Chinese — was a clear indication that its participation in the election was to kill the MCA and later force UMNO to accept the PAP as a partner or compel UMNO to work with it. If the PAP succeeds in destroying the MCA it will no doubt later turn on UMNO itself.'[24] A more extreme version of the UMNO distrust of Lee was: 'Mr. Lee is just like a hungry dog. You feed him out of pity when you see his pathetic look. But when he is well he turns around and bites you!' The Tunku reacted to Lee's attempt to drive a wedge between the two Alliance partners by stating firmly that he would have nothing to do with the PAP and would retain the MCA in the Alliance regardless of its result.

As it turned out, the PAP polled surprisingly badly in all nine seats it contested except one, which it managed to win.[25] Thus it achieved very little for its pains except the hostility of Kuala Lumpur politicians and a considerable deflation of the PAP's reputation for vote-winning. (The fact that it had attracted the biggest crowds during the campaign was little consolation.) The MCA, on the other hand, managed to poll much better than in 1959 and thus re-established its position in the Alliance on a firmer basis than in the uncertain years between.

The intensity of Kuala Lumpur distrust and dislike for Lee Kuan Yew throughout the following months was extraordinary. It had many causes, one of which was the widely spread belief among Malays that in contesting the election Lee had broken an agreement not to bring the PAP directly into mainland politics.[26] (When questioned on this point later, Lee denied that any such agreement had been made, but conceded in rather vague terms that the Malayan leaders may have been under the impression that the PAP would not contest the *first* post-Malaysia election.) But even if there was no specific agreement or understanding on this, it seems clear that Malay politicians were strongly inclined to believe that the PAP was committed to keep out of the Federation, for the very essence of the political agreement underlying the creation of Malaysia, as they saw it, was that UMNO dominance (hence the Alliance pattern) should not be shaken by the increase in Chinese voting power. And they looked upon the PAP as simply another Chinese party, based beyond their reach in Singapore, and threatening the delicate political balance upon which the Alliance had been maintained on the mainland. Singapore had been granted a specially favourable degree of autonomy when she entered Malaysia, they believed, in return for the provision that Singapore's solid

TABLE 5

PARTY STRENGTHS IN MALAYA:
MALAYAN ELECTIONS FOR FEDERAL PARLIAMENT 1959 AND 1964
SEATS WON BY EACH PARTY AND PERCENTAGE OF TOTAL VOTE POLLED
(in brackets)

	1959		1964	
Alliance	74	(51.1)	89	(58.7)
UMNO	52	(36.0)	59	(38.6)
MCA	19	(15.1)	27	(18.6)
MIC	3	(1.0)	3	(1.5)
Socialist Front	8	(12.8)	2	(16.0)
Malay candidates	1	(2.9)	—	(5.9)
Non-Malay candidates	7	(9.9)	2	(10.1)
PMIP	13	(21.7)	9	(14.3)
PPP	4	(6.3)	2	(3.6)
UDP	—	(—)	1	(4.2)
PAP	—	(—)	1	(2.0)
Party Negara	1	(2.1)	—	(0.3)
Independents	4	(5.7)	—	(0.6)
Total	104	(100.0)	104	(100.0)

Source: Figures in this table extracted from Table 9 of R. K. Vasil, 'The 1964 General Elections in Malaya, International Studies, vol. VII, no. 1, July 1965.

Note: In 1964, the Federal Parliament also contained 16 Sabah members (all Alliance), 24 Sarawak members (20 Alliance, 3 SUPP and 1 Independent) and 15 Singapore members (12 PAP and 3 Barisan Sosialis).

block of Chinese voters would not tilt the balance of voting power in the Federation against the Malays. The Singapore government had agreed to accept only 15 seats in the Federal Parliament, so the Malays had believed themselves politically secure, but here was Lee posing a new kind of threat, challenging the essential compromise of the Malaysia Agreement not in the letter, perhaps, but in the spirit. UMNO leaders later charged the PAP with upsetting the racial harmony which had been achieved in the Federation under the Alliance system of government; paradoxical though it may seem to those who take the more familiar PAP view of Malayan politics, they regarded Lee Kuan Yew as the one who had raised the communal threat, since the PAP was primarily bidding for Chinese votes, even though it spoke in terms of multi-racialism. In effect, the PAP was setting out to create a Chinese party which would not be content to act merely as a junior partner in the Alliance, but would constitute a vigorous rival to UMNO, seeking the support of all non-Malay communities in Malaysia. (One PAP slogan in the election had been: 'You will vote PAP eventually — why not right from the start?') This was not what the Malays had expected Malaysia to mean. But in the year following the election Lee's concept of a 'Malaysian rather than a Malay Malaysia' was elaborated with such clarity and force that their worst suspicions were confirmed.

The PAP had persuasive answers to these arguments, of course — that there could be no such obligation on any party to keep out of Malayan politics indefinitely; that Singapore had paid the price for her wider domestic autonomy in the labour and education fields with her smaller representation in the Federal parliament; that the recognition of Malay rights and a special position for the Malays must not be extended to the point of implying a 'Malay Malaysia'. But the very persuasiveness of the PAP case tended to be regarded by Malays as merely another manifestation of Lee Kuan Yew's excessive cleverness, which aggravated his devastating flair for making enemies. Much of the rancour against him seemed to have had personal origins as much as political. No doubt PAP entry into Malayan politics would have had to be accepted sooner or later. But Lee was regarded by Malays as in too much of a hurry in 1964, too ambitious for a more important role or a larger political stage, as if the Prime Ministership of Singapore was not enough for him ('Why should he be a Prime Minister, when other states have only a Chief Minister or *Mentri Besar*? He is no more important than they are, but foreigners think he ranks with the Tunku.') and as if he were aspiring to dominate Federal politics as he had long dominated Singapore's. Later in the year, when Singapore ministers were feeling rather chastened by the race riots, some of them were prepared to admit that it had been a mistake to contest the election since it frightened the UMNO leaders.[27] (The very word betrays their implied superiority which so irritated the Malays. 'Why should we be frightened of the PAP when it can only win one seat?' they replied.) One can only speculate whether the outcome would have been very different if the PAP had not made its move until later; after the 1964 election it might have been less contemptuous of the MCA's vote-winning power, less brash in its claim to be the natural leader of Malaya's urban masses and less abrasive of Malay susceptibilities. The racial strife of mid-1964 might have been avoided and the political battle between the UMNO 'ultras' and the PAP, which led up to the separation of Singapore in 1965 never have occurred. The 'might-have-beens' can be pursued *ad infinitum*.

The political differences between the Alliance and the PAP were steadily widened in the months after the election, although they were masked to some extent by the intensification of the Indonesian threat after the failure of the Tokyo Summit meeting in June and the atmosphere of emergency created by the race riots in July and September. But as the smoke cleared later in the year, the PAP leaders found that they could no longer count on the Tunku's avuncular sympathy for them as they had been able to, for he had his own problems to worry about in controlling the so-called 'extremists' in UMNO.[28] Any hopes they had ever harboured that the PAP would be taken into some sort of partnership by the Tunku and perhaps even given cabinet representation were dashed soon after the election by a statement of the Tunku's that it would not be appropriate to include the PAP in the cabinet. Increasingly the PAP found itself in a position of opposition to the government in the Federal parliament in late 1964 and early 1965, not on the issue of confrontation (on which it had nothing in common with the main opposition parties), but in its advocacy of the ideal of a 'Malaysian Malaysia' as an alternative to a 'Malay Malaysia'.

Soekarno is said to have commented after the Malayan elections that as the Tunku now had secure parliamentary backing Malaysia could afford to resume negotiations in a more accommodating frame of mind than she had shown at Bangkok. The *pourparlers* that ultimately led to the Tokyo Summit meeting were begun shortly after the election, but it soon became apparent that neither side was prepared to make concessions on what it considered the essential matters in dispute. Although the Indonesians attributed the blame for the failure of those negotiations to the Tunku's stiffnecked refusal to compromise on the Manila Agreements, it is hard to resist the conclusion that it was Soekarno's attitude to the conference which ensured its failure and that in doing so he threw away a golden opportunity. If he had chosen instead to exploit the domestic tensions in Malaysia at that time by talking softly and reviving the idea of Maphilindo, he might have been able to embarrass the Tunku acutely. Even the British had come around to seeing some good in Maphilindo by this time and among Malay politicians it was still regarded as something of a lifeline. The vehemence with which Syed Ja'afar Albar denounced Lee Kuan Yew[29] shortly afterwards for attacking Maphilindo as a communal concept was merely one among many indications that UMNO politicians would have welcomed its resuscitation at that time. Unfortunately for them, the 'spirit of Maphilindo' was even weaker in mid-1964 than it had been a year earlier. Soekarno showed no enthusiasm for it, presumably because it would have involved him in difficulties with the PKI, or because he needed a militant display of confrontation at that stage, rather than a more equivocal and restrained policy. Yet it seems probable that if he had followed a hot-and-cold policy, as in 1963, with the aim of widening the rift between UMNO and the PAP over the Maphilindo concept, the Tunku would have found the task of maintaining Malaysian unity even harder.

Instead, the intensification of confrontation in mid-1964 helped to paper over this rift and postponed the development of PAP opposition to the government. (For example, an amendment of the National Security Act in July requiring university students to obtain a security clearance would probably have been bitterly resisted by the PAP in more normal times.) But a Malay counter-attack on the PAP had begun as early as March, in a series of articles in *Utusan Melayu*, the UMNO Malay-language newspaper, directing personal abuse at Lee and aiming to discredit the PAP government. They did this by focusing attention on the depressed condition of the 240,000 Malays of Singapore and the PAP's refusal to extend to them the 'special position' enjoyed by Malays and natives everywhere else in Malaysia. The articles even charged that the government was discriminating against Malays and in July the attacks came to a head over a government decision to evict and rehouse Malays in one area in order to make room for one of its vast new housing projects (which were the pride of the PAP, but disliked by Malays, who preferred their old *kampong*-style habitations to living in the huge, anonymous new concrete skyscrapers). Lee Kuan Yew summoned a group of Malay non-political organizations to meet him on 19 July to discuss their grievances, but by excluding UMNO from the meeting he provoked a vehement Malay response in Singapore which culminated in the riots of late July.

Different accounts have been given by the Federal and Singapore governments of the origin of the racial riots which broke out on 21 July.[30] The trouble began during a Muslim procession to celebrate *Maulud*, the Prophet's Birthday, but the precise question of who cast the first stone has never been settled, for the Commission of Enquiry set up after the riots never met. According to the police report cited by Tun Razak, someone threw a bottle into the middle of the procession: the fighting which broke out between Muslims and non-believers, Malays and Chinese, continued intermittently, despite the curfew proclaimed, for several days. Chinese secret society gangs then joined vigorously in the affray. The PAP version of what happened is that the Malay community of Singapore had been incited to a high pitch of excitement by a meeting 10 days previously at which the UMNO Secretary-General, Syed Ja'afar Albar, made a highly inflammatory speech and a Malay National Action Committee was set up to press for special privileges for the Malays of Singapore. This committee was responsible for a leaflet which was circulated among the Malay community during the following week urging Malays who had supported the PAP to 'come back to their own people and fight shoulder to shoulder with them .... If the Malays do not resist now, there will be no Malays left after 20 years ... let us fight the PAP government before it is too late.' It also claimed that the Chinese were planning to kill the Malays of Singapore and concluded: 'Before Malay blood flows in Singapore, it is best to flood the state with Chinese blood'. (There had been a serious communal clash at Bukit Mertajam in Province Wellesley on 12 July, causing two deaths, so racial tension was already very acute.) In the explosive situation of that time, the out-break of the *Maulud* riot was merely the final spark. The Malay National Action Committee contained adherents of several groups noted for their 'bigotry, racialism and Indonesian sympathies'. One member was Isa Zain, a man who had been named in the Malaysian government's White Paper earlier in the year as an Indonesian agent. Inevitably, allegations of Indonesian provocation of the riots were put forward,[31] but according to senior officials in Singapore there was no Indonesian involvement in the July troubles, although there was in the September riots.

The riots were the most serious racial disturbances in Singapore's postwar history. The fighting and killings continued for several days, mainly on the fringes of the relatively few Malay areas, but it was nearly a week before Singapore was calm and the curfew could be relaxed. Altogether 22 people were killed and nearly 500 injured. But the most serious aspect of all was the sudden revelation of how easily Malaysia's fragile unity could be shattered. If racial conflict recurred and spread, it could easily achieve the destruction of Malaysia which had proved beyond the powers of Indonesia's military forces. 'The fate of Malaysia is in the balance at its fulcrum, Singapore', wrote one commentator. But the danger was not solely in Singapore, for there have been racial clashes in other parts of the Federation in recent years and it was reported that during the Singapore riots a substantial band of Johore Malays set out with knives and *parangs* to do battle alongside their Singapore brothers, but were turned back at the causeway. Communal feelings, like communal politics reached throughout the entire nation.

The Tunku was still in the USA when the riots occurred, but he visited Singapore for talks with the PAP leaders soon after his return and relations between the two governments seemed to be much improved. (There had been a distinct coolness between the PAP and Tun Razak.) Lee spoke warmly of his trust in the Tunku: 'If we rely on constitutional and legal rights and obligations, then I say there is very little hope for the actual success of Malaysia. It has got to rest on more than that ... on faith and trust. Therefore we accepted the Tunku's leadership. Not just as leader of the Malays, but also leader of all the other races in Malaysia. Otherwise, we should not have embarked on Malaysia.'[32] He may well have believed this — for the Tunku evoked much warmer feelings than Razak — but Lee also needed the Tunku's help to keep Syed Ja'afar and the UMNO 'ultras' in check and to calm down the Singapore Malays. The Tunku was apparently prepared at this stage to give his help, if only for the sake of national unity. By the following month he was less obliging, however, and relations between the two governments began to deteriorate.

The Indonesians did not overlook the potentialities opened up for them by racial conflict in Singapore. Their attempt to land troops at Labis on 2 September was not only intended to re-ignite the embers of the (largely communal) Emergency, but also coincided with a renewal of racial clashes in Singapore. There was no immediate political explanation for the various incidents between 2 and 7 September, which were largely instigated by gangs of both Malay and Chinese strong-arm men, presumably hired, who perpetrated cold-blooded and brutal murders in public with the sole aim, apparently, of precipitating communal conflict.[33] They were unsuccessful, on the whole, and racial harmony was not seriously threatened this time. The people of Singapore seemed to realize that the aim of the killings was simply to provoke them and, in any case, the military threat from Indonesia was then more imminent than it had ever been.[34] It is extremely significant, in fact, that obviously provoked racial incidents such as these proved to be less dangerous in the last resort than the earlier riots, which arose out of political and communal tensions. Perhaps Malaysia was not quite as vulnerable to Indonesian subversion and instigation to communal conflict as she seemed, although she could easily have destroyed herself by her own follies.

The Tunku and other federal ministers again visited Singapore after the second riots to look into measures to improve the conditions of the Malays in Singapore, shortly after an UMNO annual conference where there had been much criticism of the PAP. This time the Tunku was sharply critical of the Singapore government for using the 'goodwill committees' set up after the July riots as virtual instruments of the PAP: they were disbanded soon after and replaced with 'peace committees' which acted in close cooperation with the police (an agency of the central government, not of the state). In an important speech on 20 September he also charged that 'some politicians in Singapore have not been free from blame' for the riots, criticizing the PAP for the unsatisfactory conditions of the Malays in Singapore. He went on to attack the PAP for intruding in Malayan affairs and accused them of trying covertly to undermine his leadership by depicting him as the leader of the Malays only.[35] The very serious political implications of this speech, which conformed more closely to the UMNO view of the PAP than any of the Tunku's earlier statements, were recognized by the PAP, which avoided any immediate public response. Lee and his senior colleagues flew to Kuala Lumpur on 24 September for talks at which a 'truce' was arranged — an agreement by the two sides to avoid raising contentious communal and party issues for the next two years.

Shortly after this, preparations began for the establishment of National Solidarity Committees throughout Malaysia in anticipation of National Solidarity Week, 16–22 November, which was intended to foster intercommunal solidarity and harmony and 'provide opportunities and media for people to express their loyalty in concrete forms'. Three opposition parties declined to participate in these worthy proceedings, however. In the prevailing atmosphere of high emergency caused by the Indonesian landings, a great deal of publicity was given to the various 'nation-building' activities of the moment — civil defence, local vigilante corps, the call-up of National Servicemen and so on. The Trade Unions and Malayan Employers' Association agreed on a no-strike arrangement during the Emergency. The Tunku spent part of National Solidarity Week in Sabah in the hope of patching up a simmering quarrel in the Alliance there (and to make amends for its earlier neglect by federal ministers) — although the Sabah quarrel erupted even more bitterly as soon as he had gone, as also did the Kuala Lumpur-Singapore dispute.

The truce of 24 September was soon forgotten. In fact doubts about its terms and even its very existence were being expressed in Kuala Lumpur a little later, after PAP spokesmen charged Khir Johari with a breach of the truce in October. When the federal Parliament met for the budget session in the last weeks of 1964, the PAP's vigorous criticisms of some rather inept tax measures aroused a quite disproportionate response from the Alliance parties. In the following months, a new and even more bitter phase of the Alliance-PAP controversy began, which led step by step to the separation of Singapore in August 1965.

MILITARY FLASHPOINT

After the collapse of the Tokyo conference, an intensification of Indonesian pressure on Malaysia was generally expected. Next day, in a sharp, fierce clash at Rasau, over 100 insurgents attacked a Gurkha force for six hours in one of the biggest engagements of the Borneo campaign. In Djakarta, Brigadier-General Achmadi ordered the Volunteers to prepare for a 'long-term guerrilla war'. On the Sarawak border, however, military activities tended to dwindle over the next few months. There was little activity except scattered attacks on border villages with no other apparent purpose than to terrorize them by random shelling. Another substantial engagement occurred in October, but the general aim of Indonesian patrols there in the later part of the year was apparently little more than reconnaissance, to make the security forces reveal their positions.[36]

The focus of Indonesian attention now seemed to shift to Singapore and the peninsula, where various cases of sabotage occurred in late June and July — an attempt to blow up the Merdeka bridge in Singapore, to cut the Singapore water supply line in Johore and to derail the Singapore-Kuala Lumpur express. These were disturbing incidents, but not in themselves especially dangerous. Moreover, Indonesia seemed to be interested in resuming negotiations again within the framework of the Afro-Asian Conciliation Commission suggested by Macapagal, although not under the conditions on which Malaysia was insisting. Soekarno and Subandrio had worries enough at home at that time, as Subandrio admitted with unaccustomed frankness after the first post-Tokyo meeting of KOTI, when asked about Indonesia's response to Macapagal's latest call to return to the conference table. 'All the matters we have previously been putting aside have to be taken up for the sake of consolidation within the country. We must intensify confrontation in the spheres of development and economic affairs and subsequently in the diplomatic sphere.'[37] Earlier, too, he had spoken of 'heightening confrontation in the fields of information and education' — in both of which fierce domestic 'polemics' were raging. But soon afterwards came another major step in the 'heightening' of confrontation.

The Singapore race riots at the end of July revealed opportunities for trouble-making in Malaysia which were too tempting to be overlooked. Indonesia had had nothing (or very little) to do with the July riots, but her two landings in the peninsula in August and September seem to have been hastily-contrived attempts to stimulate communal uprisings there, first among the Malays and then among the Chinese. The second wave of Singapore race riots on 2 September were deliberately instigated by *agents provocateurs* who were probably acting in connivance with Indonesian agents. They coincided exactly with the Indonesian paratroop landings at Labis, in Johore, which were intended to kindle again the flames of Communist insurrection among certain Chinese communities in Malaya. If the two operations had succeeded both Singapore and the peninsula might have burst aflame with communal conflict. Malaysia promptly reported the Labis landings to the UN Security Council, while British naval and air forces were alerted to strike at Indonesian bases if any further major attacks were launched. All this made September 1964 the period of most dangerous tension during the entire period of confrontation. 'Vivere pericoloso', the President had told his people on 17 August — and the following month he was certainly putting that advice into effect.

A fortnight previously, on Indonesia's Independence Day, a substantial force of Indonesians had landed near Pontian, at several points along a stretch of swampy coast little more than 30 miles north of the Straits of Johore. About 40 well-armed guerrillas were estimated to have landed, about half of them regulars from the Indonesian Army ('sergeant-major's volunteers', according to a British officer), the rest dissident Malays or Chinese. In that part of Johore there is quite a heavy population of Javanese immigrants and it seems likely that the object of this first substantial incursion into the Malay peninsula so soon after the first Singapore riots was either to arouse pro-Indonesian elements among the Malay communities there or to provoke further communal conflict in an area where serious anti-Chinese riots had broken out in 1946.[38] The argument that their Malay brothers in Singapore were being oppressed as well as outnumbered by the Chinese there might have been expected to arouse their sympathy. If the raiders had received any significant degree of local support, they would have imposed a serious strain on the British and Malaysian forces, who would have had to deploy a substantial number of men in a new theatre of operations, and perhaps even reduce their Borneo force. But things turned out very differently.

The immediate threat posed by the Pontian landings was so quickly dealt with that the Malaysian government did not even bother to proclaim a state of emergency or seriously consider an appeal to the Security Council, though it reported the landing to the Security Council for information. Indonesia completely denied the incident. About half the infiltrators were captured soon after they landed and the rest had no success in arousing the local population. The area was promptly organized under a series of security guards and armed vigilante forces: a curfew was imposed and mopping-up operations carried out by regular forces in the swampy coastal region for several weeks. A few of the insurgents apparently remained at large until late October, but they found little or no support among the local population. Militarily, the landing was no more significant than the border incursions that had been taking place in Borneo throughout the previous 18 months, although its political significance was far greater, as it was 'the first invasion-like landing in strength in the peninsula'.[39]

The Labis air-drop on the night of 1–2 September was a much more substantial operation, with roughly 100 troops involved (mostly para-commandos of the Indonesian Air Force with about 10 Malaysian Chinese defectors, including 2 girls) using 3 Hercules C-130 aircraft of the Indo-nesian Air Force, one of which crashed in the Malacca Straits before dropping its paratroops, according to the Malaysian account.[40] Labis had been a Communist stronghold during the Malayan emergency and 'a very tough nut to crack.' It is situated close to the central mountain spine of the southern peninsula and has a large Chinese population in the vicinity, many of them working on nearby plantations. Apparently, the Indonesian aim was to set up a jungle camp deep in the forest reserve near the mountains and to use local Chinese defectors to recruit other dissidents who would help to stir up the embers of the earlier Communist insurrection. But the operation was very badly executed, for the 2 plane loads of paratroops were dropped some miles apart and they were dispersed erratically over such a wide area that they were unable to regroup during the night. The commander of one of the two forces, Lt. Sutikno, later recounted that he spent 20 days wandering around with only one of his followers trying to locate the others, but was finally driven by hunger to take the risk of disclosing himself. Mopping up of the scattered guerrillas was still continuing well into October. They posed no serious military danger by then, but this was not initially apparent, nor was it certain that Indonesia did not intend to escalate her attacks against the mainland further, which would have created a serious strain on the available military forces there. The outbreak of race riots in Singapore, obviously provoked, on the same day aggravated the threat. The Malaysian government immediately decided to refer the landing to the UN Security Council and proclaimed a State of Emergency. The Security Council debate, to which we shall return shortly, took place against a background of high tension arising from the possibility that the conflict might still escalate into full-scale war.

Indonesian press reports of that week make very strange reading after the event. Nothing was said about the Labis landing or Malaysia's complaint to the Security Council until the day before it met, after the departure of the Indonesian delegation — described as an 'active-offensive fighting-unit' (*satuan tempur*) which had gone to the UN to disclose the truth about imperialist subversion in Indonesia; only a careful reader of several papers would have been able to infer that it was Malaysia who had laid the charges and not Indonesia. Surprisingly little significance was attached even to the Singapore riots (this was particularly striking in the left-wing press), hardly enough to reveal how serious a situation they had created. But an atmosphere of emergency was built up by an order from KOTI on 2 September cancelling all leave for military personnel and civil servants, followed by orders to the Armed Services to 'sharpen their preparedness' (*pertadjam kesiap-siagaan*) and to the entire population to stand by for a 'command' from the President.[41] On the 4th Soekarno conferred with Subandrio and the Armed Service chiefs, ostensibly about the presence of foreign warships cruising in Indonesian waters: Subandrio described the situation as 'very tense' and the threat of 'British provocation' was strongly headlined, along with suggestions that the British were trying to create an opportunity for a 'second Tonkin' by their naval and air manoeuvres. But the much-heralded announcement by the President never came. (A speech widely advertised for 7 September turned out to be all about land reform!) Had he been expecting that a 'liberated zone' in Malaysia could be proclaimed as a result of the Labis landings? For whatever reason, there seemed to be a change of emphasis at the end of the week, after an emergency KOTI meeting on Sunday 6 September, towards a quite new line of argument which veiled a more defensive tactical course behind a more forthright and challenging new formulation of the Indonesian case. Incursions into Malaya and Borneo by Indonesian 'volunteers', as well as Kalimantan 'freedom fighters' were now admitted — by Nasution and others in Djakarta and by Sudjarwo in the Security Council.[42] But the British had been committing aggression too, it was insisted, infiltrating agents and weapons into Sumatra, Kalimantan and Sulawesi. Air space had also been violated by both sides on various occasions. The Malaysian charges were a case of the pot calling the kettle black.

The crisis created by the Labis landing (from the Malaysian-British point of view) and the movement of British warships in Indonesian waters (from Indonesia's) brought the British air and naval forces in Singapore to the brink of a retaliatory attack on Indonesia. It is not easy to sort out the truth about the entire episode from its embellishments. Air raid precautions were instituted in Djakarta and an atmosphere of crisis persisted until the middle of September. At the height of the crisis the government announced a new form of virtual martial law, vesting emergency powers in the President as Executive Authority of the *Dwikora* — although three days later Soekarno flew off on a world trip *en route* to the Cairo Conference, due to be held early in October![43] The main concern of the British, for their part, was to deter the Indonesians from any repetition of the Pontian-Labis incursions. Neither the Foreign Office nor the Tory government, which had to face an election only six weeks later, wanted to see the war escalate, although it is reported that the Ministry of Defence and some senior officers in the Far East were anxious to take advantage of the provocation offered and to cripple the Indonesian air force and navy.[44] Lee Kuan Yew, then in London, also spoke in a very hawk-like vein. It is said that the Indonesian Air Force (or, more precisely, that part of it which was not grounded by mechanical troubles) was promptly shifted far to the east to be out of harm's way — a tactic which, if this report is true, can hardly have endeared it to the unprotected military and naval forces. A British naval force consisting of an aircraft carrier and two destroyers which was then in the Indian Ocean *en route* from Singapore to Australia was ordered to return. There was much press speculation in Britain about the possibility that it would insist on passing through the Sunda Strait, which Indonesia claimed as territorial water, with the aim of defying her to close it. However, the ships were diverted to the Lombok Strait after the Indonesians announced that naval manoeuvres in the area would make passage through the Sunda Strait dangerous, a face-saving compromise which revealed that neither side really wanted to risk a showdown there and then.[45]

Just how close the British came to an air strike on Indonesian bases during that tense week before the diversion of the ships was announced is a matter on which reports differ. Stories that they came within an ace of launching a massive air attack against Indonesian naval and air forces during the second week of September were in widespread circulation at the time, but they seem to have been exaggerated on all sides. No doubt contingency plans for such a strike had been drawn up, in order to retaliate promptly and heavily if Indonesia again attacked Malaysia in strength. And it suited the British that the Indonesians should believe in the possibility and be deterred by it. A Foreign Office spokesman dropped a hint that Britain might be going to follow the precedent set by President Johnson in the Gulf of Tonkin several weeks before, but this can hardly have been more than a bluff.[46] A deterrent strike would have completely undermined Malaysia's political strategy in appealing to the Security Council. Moreover, it would have had far-reaching and unpredictable consequences for Indonesian domestic politics, weakening the advocates of moderation and, if successful, creating havoc among the Armed Forces leadership, to the great benefit of the PKI and other advocates of a militant 'peoples' war' against Malaysia. The very fact that British ships were diverted at the height of the Sunda Straits crisis reveals that the British government was not anxious to provoke a showdown. But it seems that the episode did have the effect of discouraging the Indonesian military leaders from taking any further risks of provoking a deterrent strike by the British, for their military effort from then onwards was distinctly lukewarm.

The Indonesians launched no further attacks of any size against Malaysia until late in October, when a rather amateurish landing by 52 saboteurs was attempted at Kesang, near the Muar estuary. Thereafter, the small raiding parties which continued to be sent across the Malacca Straits throughout the next few weeks were merely of nuisance value to the defenders and were never of sufficient size to trigger a violent British response. Most of these seem to have been launched from the Riau

Islands, which were not under direct Army control: apart from a handful of NCO's and regular soldiers, they were mainly composed of irregulars — volunteers and pressed men — trained merely for sabotage and trouble-making rather than for purposive military operations. A change in the character of the operations in December was discerned by the military authorities in Malaysia: the raiding parties became larger and contained more regulars, but the objectives were still essentially to sabotage and stir up trouble rather than to establish 'liberated zones'. It was believed in Malaysia that they were under the control of Subandrio's Border Area Command, rather than the Army leaders themselves, and that the latter became increasingly angry at the pointless and hopeless nature of missions their men were being sent on, because of the demoralizing effect it was having on others. (Malaysia was rubbing in the point here by threatening not to treat the men they captured as prisoners of war, but to try them and execute them under domestic law.)[47] Accusations that the Army leaders were lacking in enthusiasm for the Malaysia campaign became increasingly common towards the end of 1964. But the blunt fact was that little more could be done except at very great risk, after the two probing raids at Pontian and Labis had failed and the British had been provoked almost to the point of a counter-strike.

A build-up of forces on both sides at the very end of 1964 attracted a great deal of publicity and contributed to an atmosphere of emergency in both Indonesia and Malaysia, but it proved to be rather an anti-climax. Soekarno had so often threatened that Malaysia would be crushed 'before the cock crows in 1965' that there was a good deal of apprehension among the British and Malaysians that a major assault might be launched just before the old year ended as an earnest of Indonesia's determination. Indonesia's forces on the Sarawak border and in the Riau islands were considerably increased (to 15–20,000) during December, accentuating fears of an intensified military effort.[48] The New York Times reported that Chen Yi had urged a change of strategy from guerrilla raids to a massing of conventional forces on the borders so as to overstrain the defenders and encourage insurrection within Malaysia, but there is little corroborating evidence that such a strategy was later followed.[49] The British countered with an ostentatious increase of their own Far Eastern forces, dramatized by the arrival in Singapore of HMS Eagle, Britain's newest and largest aircraft-carrier, two battalions of troops and some ancillary units, including paratroopers, and a simultaneous visit to Malaysia by her Minister of War. (Actually, the number of British troops in the area was not increased very significantly, although the additional ships and equipment were important. One suspects that the British were trying to maximize the psychological impact of the increase, not merely to give the Indonesians pause, but also to dramatize the 'East of Suez' policy being followed by the new Labour government.) The Indonesian press attacked the British build-up as 'provocative' and throughout early January harped on the theme of British 'aggression' against Indonesia, but whether out of real fear that the British were preparing to strike at

Indonesian bases or simply to heighten the atmosphere of crisis at the moment after Soekarno had withdrawn his country from the United Nations one cannot tell.

At any rate, the pattern of military activities in early 1965 did not radically change. Scattered and ineffectual raiding parties landed in Johore during January. Then there was a brief lull while peace feelers were being put out in February. On 9 March, a force of 80 Indonesian regulars landed in swampy land at Kota Tinggi, about 23 miles north-east of Singapore, the largest and most professional force since the Labis landing: it had an initial success in an engagement with units of the Singapore regiment, then headed inland for a remote rubber plantation. But ultimately lack of food and maps proved to be the downfall of this force like its predecessors. On 27 April, a substantial incursion occurred in Sarawak (the biggest since July 1964) when a force of 100 men attacked near Balai Ringin, near Bau. Indonesian forces on that part of the frontier were said to have been considerably strengthened and a month later there were reports of more determined pressure in that area, involving a change of tactics from the former hit-and-run raids close to the border.[50] Patrols were being carried out more frequently and persistently than before, although there is no indication that any serious military threat to Kuching was developing at that time. A more alarming prospect for the Malaysians was conjured up by reports that Indonesia was trying to contact Chin Peng's remnants of the Malayan Communist Party on the Thai-Malaya border in the hope of inciting them into a renewal of the Emergency; it is surprising indeed, that no effective use was made of the MCP's potential for stirring up trouble among the backward Malays of the northern border regions (on both sides of the frontier), as also that more attention was not directed to the east coast of Malaya. But there was no significant development in either quarter during 1965 before confrontation was quietly scaled down after the October coup.

THE SECURITY COUNCIL DEBATE

The Malaysian government reacted to the Labis landing by immediately calling for a meeting of the UN Security Council under Article 39 of the UN Charter, charging that Indonesia's action constituted a 'blatant and inexcusable aggression against a peaceful neighbour, an act which is in itself a breach of the peace and involves a threat to international peace and security in the area'. Even though there was little likelihood that the Security Council would take positive action to intervene in the dispute, or even condemn Indonesia bluntly as an aggressor (for Russia's veto was almost certain to be used in her defence, despite the growing chilliness of relations between Russia and Indonesia), the evidence of Indonesian aggression would be published before the world — and, at the very least, Indonesia might be temporarily restrained from further aggressive actions while the UN was discussing the matter.

The Security Council debate opened with touches of drama on both sides. The Malaysian delegate, Dato' Dr. Ismail, displayed on the table of the Security Council itself a mortar, rifles and other paratroop equipment with Indonesian markings captured after the Labis landing. In reply, Dr. Sudjarwo, the Indonesian representative startled the Council by making no attempt to deny the Labis landing and completely ignoring his government's earlier refutations of it. Never before had a nation charged with aggression in the Security Council so bluntly conceded the immediate charge against her and set out to argue the case on the basis of such an unconventional and 'revolutionary' logic. Sudjarwo's reply was simply that Malaysia's accusations were made 'out of context and without reference to the deeper and broader conflict which regrettably exists between our two Governments'.[51] Indonesia had suffered aggression and confrontation from imperialism and colonialism since the outbreak of her revolution, he said; she had been subjected to foreign intervention and bombing and violations of her territory in 1958–9, to economic subversion and manipulation from Singapore, as well as a long series of British incursions in Kalimantan, Sumatra and Sulawesi in 1963–4. Sudjarwo itemized these in detail, mentioning one raid on the Riau islands by a group as large as the one Malaysia accused her of dropping at Labis. Earlier Indonesia was too weak to respond to this confrontation, he went on, but to-day we are strong enough to react:

I would not deny that our volunteers, our guerrillas, together with the militant youth of Sarawak and Sabah, some of whom have been trained in our territory, have entered so-called 'Malaysian' territory in Sarawak and Sabah. They have been fighting there for some time. This is no secret. And in the absence of a peaceful solution to the problem of 'Malaysia' ... the fighting on both sides could only become aggravated or even escalate. And now this fighting has spread to other areas in 'Malaysia' such as Malaya. Why is 'Malaysia' so greatly concerned now that it requests a meeting of the the Security Council? Why was it not equally concerned much earlier when the fighting broke out in Sarawak and Sabah, which is also a part of this 'Malaysia'? As a matter of fact, the fighting in Malaya is only on a very small scale compared to the magnitude of the fighting in Sarawak and Sabah .... Why then all the fuss? Is it because very serious riots recently broke out in Singapore? .... Is it because the present 'Malaysian' Government feels unable to overcome its own internal troubles, the weakness left to it by the British colonial policy of divide and rule?[52]

Confrontation and the guerrilla activity were not the cause of the Malaysia dispute, argued Sudjarwo. Its cause was the existing political dispute. But Malaysia had been less willing to seek a solution than Indonesia. The Security Council should reflect before making any decision that it was not a mere resolution that was called for in the situation, but a solution, a peaceful settlement.

Except in Dato' Ismail's opening speech, the Labis landings were barely discussed again in the six sessions of the Security Council which were spread over the following week. The debate was essentially a rehearsal of the familiar arguments about the neo-colonialist nature of Malaysia.

the Manila Agreements and the responsibility for the failure of the Bangkok and Tokyo talks. There is no better elaboration of the arguments of the two sides than this debate, punctuated with the supplementary observations of the other Council members. Within the terms of its own logic, Indonesia's argument was ingeniously and persuasively presented — sufficiently persuasive to make a condemnation for 'aggression' most improbable — but on the bald facts of the matter the Malaysian delegate had a more impressive body of evidence on his side and succeeded in meeting Sudjarwo's case at point after point.

Malaysia had asked that the Security Council judge Indonesia guilty of aggression and condemn her for it. Even if the Security Council could not take any action, Malaysia hoped that she would be able to obtain a resolution expressing support for her territorial integrity which could provide a basis for a future appeal to the UN if Indonesian attacks continued.[53] She soon had to abandon any hope of obtaining a 'strong' resolution condemning Indonesia's attacks, however, since the Moroccan and Ivory Coast delegations, which were taking the initiative in trying to formulate a draft resolution which would be acceptable to all parties, were unable to gain Indonesia's agreement to any suggestions on that basis. When the Ivory Coast delegate first spoke, he said that his country would support a resolution 'deploring' Indonesia's attacks, but would avoid the word 'condemnation' which would only create further difficulties. Morocco was even more equivocal in its attitude. For Malaysia the choice lay between trying to obtain an agreed resolution which Indonesia would accept and the Council would pass unanimously (otherwise Russia would impose her veto on Indonesia's behalf) or else seeking a 'strong' resolution condemning Indonesia and thus forcing the Russian veto, so as to show that Indonesia could count only on Communist support. But if the latter became necessary it was desirable for Malaysia to have the support of as many Council members as possible, including the Afro-Asian and Latin-American members. Morocco and the Ivory Coast were reluctant to be put in a position where they would have to vote against Indonesia and they were being lobbied intensively by her, but they were unable to find a form of resolution acceptable to both Malaysia and Indonesia during the meetings on 14 and 15 September. Consequently, the Norwegian delegation stepped in and proposed a similar but slightly stronger resolution which was intended to be moderate enough to win the support of the Ivory Coast and Moroccan delegates — the word 'aggression' was still avoided — although it was known to be unacceptable to Indonesia.[54] According to the resolution, the Security Council

1. Regrets all the incidents which have occurred in the whole region;
2. Deplores the incident of 2 September 1964 which forms the basis of the complaint ...;
3. Requests the parties concerned to make every effort to avoid the recurrence of such incidents;
4. Calls upon the parties to refrain from all threat or use of force and to respect the territorial integrity of each other, and thus to create a conducive

atmosphere for the continuation of their talks;

5. Recommends to the Governments concerned (to resume their talks on the basis of the Macapagal proposal).

When this resolution was put to the vote on 17 September, after being criticized and pronounced unacceptable by Indonesia (mainly on the score of clauses 2 and 4), it was passed by 9 votes to 2, but was vetoed by Russia in order to rescue Indonesia from further embarrassment.[55]

The result was better than Malaysia had expected and a disappointment for the Indonesian delegation, for it had not won the support of the Afro-Asian members as it had hoped; Indonesia's uncompromisingly ideological arguments did not overcome their reluctance to condone her blatant and admitted attacks on Malaysia. (Since the vote was technically defeated, however, because of the Soviet veto, the Indonesian press presented it at home as a defeat for Malaysia, since she could not get even such a mild resolution through the Security Council.) But the episode helped to underline Soekarno's dissatisfaction with the UN as a creation of the Old Established Forces. Thereafter demands for its 'retooling' or reorganization became more frequent. The fact that Malaysia was scheduled to become a member of the Security Council in 1965 added to Indonesia's irritation with the UN. She now began to address her diplomatic efforts almost obsessively to the task of convincing the Afro-Asian world that it must unite against the old order to break its domination and transform its institutions.

The Second Conference of Non-Aligned Countries which was held in Cairo early in October was not as suitable an arena for Soekarno to advance his new doctrines in as an Afro-Asian conference, since the former tended to be dominated by countries advocating peaceful co-existence and a restrained approach to major world problems — Yugoslavia, UAR and India — whereas Soekarno was now urging that there could be no co-existence or non-alignment in his crusade against the Old Established Forces. However, he had no choice but to attend the Cairo conference and try to achieve whatever he could by way of committing the members to more militant doctrines, despite the risk of diplomatic setbacks. In his opening speech, Soekarno put heavy emphasis on the need for unity in the struggle against imperialist domination and endeavoured to modify the doctrine of peaceful co-existence which had been a major theme of the 1961 Belgrade Conference. There was no longer any need for the non-aligned to press for co-existence between the two world blocs in order to prevent a world conflagration: Washington and Moscow could work out their own *rapprochement*. 'Ideologies will not create a big power conflict .... What endangers world peace is the conflict of national interests in the international field .... The ideological conflict is merely a disguise to involve the innocent on one side or the other.' Referring to troubles in Vietnam, Yemen, Cyprus, Cambodia and Malaysia, he asked: 'How can peaceful co-existence be applied in cases such as these? .... Peaceful co-existence needs a balance, an equilibrium of forces.' Solidarity between the developing countries was essential if the imperialists were to be confronted with equal strength.[56]

This view did not appeal to the Yugoslavs or Indians, naturally enough, the original advocates of the Belgrade conference of the non-aligned. Tito's displeasure was manifest, while in the political sub-committee set up to draft the joint declaration, a distinct cleavage developed between the radical group led by Indonesia and the 'moderate' group led by Yugoslavia and India.[57] On the whole, Indonesia was supported only by the smaller African nations — Guinea, Ghana, Mali, Tanzania and Burundi — and was not able to exercise much influence in imposing her radical stamp on the final conference declaration. She tried unsuccessfully to amend resolutions urging respect for established frontiers (Article V, clause 2) and abstention from all use or threat of force against the integrity of other states (Article IV, clause 5), which could be regarded as criticisms of her attitude towards Malaysia. Since Malaysia was not a non-aligned country within the terms of the conference, no question of her exclusion was involved (she had two diplomatic representatives in Cairo lobbying against Indonesian propaganda, but had not attempted to obtain an invitation) and there was no specific mention of Malaysia in the declaration. Some attempts were made in the Indonesian press to interpret this as a sign of Malaysia's isolation in the Afro-Asian world and, conversely, to play up those items on which Indonesia had been able to influence the conference resolutions, but on the whole the results of the conference were not very satisfactory to Indonesia. Soekarno's hopes of winning the endorsement of the Afro-Asian world for his ever more uncompromising doctrines at the forthcoming Afro-Asian conference must have been somewhat chastened and, as we shall see, in 1965 he devoted a remarkable amount of time, energy and political capital towards the building up of a militant bloc of supporters for his increasingly radical views in order to ensure that next time it would be India and the 'moderates' who would find themselves isolated and embarrassed.[58]

Although there was continued talk in the chancelleries of South-East Asia during the last months of 1964 about the possibility of reaching a settlement of the Indonesia-Malaysia conflict within the framework of an Afro-Asian Conciliation Commission, the chances of success in such a venture were becoming increasingly remote. Flurries of hope that Soekarno might be anxious to get back to the conference table arose on at least three occasions in early 1965, but nothing came of them, for there was only a slim possibility that talks would succeed in resolving the dispute on a basis acceptable to both sides. Three distinct but intertwined questions were involved. How seriously was either side really seeking to achieve a settlement from such talks, as distinct from some immediate tactical advantage? What price was each willing to pay, in terms of concessions to the other's point of view? And, assuming that some prospect of ultimate agreement might be discernible, on what basis could negotiations be started? The general division of opinion on the answers to these questions is of some interest for the light it throws on the diplomatic aspects of confrontation during its final stages.

Advocates of negotiation generally argued from the proposition that Soekarno was sincerely anxious to end the conflict, that he wanted to 'get himself off the hook' of confrontation, but that he had been forced by the Tunku's intransigence and by the pressures of domestic politics into a situation from which it would be very difficult for him to retreat without considerable loss of face. Therefore, it was argued, Malaysia should be urged by her allies to offer some concession that would enable negotiations to be resumed and a mutually acceptable compromise to be worked out. Macapagal's proposed Afro-Asian commission was suggested as a favorable venue for such negotiations, since it would be regarded as an entirely new framework, quite distinct from that of the tripartite Manila conferences which had come to grief so dismally. It would provide for the 'Asian solution to Asian problems' that Soekarno desired (without the suspicions of a 'Made-in-Washington' label that Maphilindo had evoked), yet it would also serve to reassure Malaysia that the dispute would be resolved in accordance with commonly accepted Afro-Asian principles of consultation and in front of neutral participants.

Even if a settlement could not be immediately achieved, some people argued, confrontation must be scaled down from the level of military conflict to a mere 'political confrontation', lest some incident suddenly blow up uncontrollably and cause serious escalation of the war. The September crisis weighed heavily on the minds of many people in Djakarta in the months that followed, for any intensification of the conflict would almost certainly benefit the PKI, especially if the Armed Forces suffered a major defeat, and increase the risks of foreign intervention. Many of the anti-Communists in Indonesia, including most of the Army leaders (and Soekarno himself, in the opinion of Ambassador Howard P. Jones), were therefore genuinely anxious to end or reduce the level of the conflict, for they recognized the political dangers of maintaining it or allowing it to escalate; even a stalemate would leave them vulnerable to PKI accusations. But if the abandonment of confrontation was not to look like a defeat for Soekarno (since he had invested so much political capital and indoctrination in the campaign to crush Malaysia) it was necessary that Malaysia should offer some gesture for the sake of peace that would help Soekarno to head off the PKI; either she should agree to 'return to the Manila Agreements' or at least accept the Macapagal proposal to resolve the dispute without British or American interference in an Afro-Asian context, as suggested by Macapagal. For had not Soekarno already given an earnest of his sincerity when he agreed publically in advance to abide by whatever decision was reached there? The Tunku's insistence that Soekarno must first demonstrate his good intentions by abandoning hostile actions against Malaysia was unrealistic, his critics argued, because domestic political pressures made it too difficult for Soekarno to enter into negotiations requiring several stages, as envisaged at Bangkok and Tokyo earlier; the only hope was to bridge the gap between the two governments before formal talks started and achieve a sufficient degree of mutual trust to make it possible for them to proceed directly to a political settlement in one step. Then Soekarno could 'make it stick' against PKI opposition.

Among the opponents of this view, however, such trust was entirely lacking. Two forceful objections were raised against the arguments in favour of compromise and a resumption of negotiations. Such a step implied that Malaysia should make concessions even though it was she who had been attacked and who, in her view, at least, was the wronged party in the dispute. Since the Afro-Asian method of resolving disputes was likely to be based on the principle of *musjawarah* (deliberations leading towards a mutually acceptable consensus) it was inevitable that Malaysia would be under pressure to compromise further in the course of negotiations; yet there was no guarantee that Indonesia wanted such talks for the sake of reaching a settlement in good faith, rather than for her own tactical purposes in manoeuvring the Malaysians into an awkward bargaining position. They would be negotiating under duress, in any case. They could no longer be expected to trust too much to Soekarno's good intentions just because he was said to be faced with domestic difficulties in dealing with PKI opposition to abandonment of confrontation. Secondly, and perhaps more to the point, how convincing was the argument that Soekarno really did want to reach a peaceful settlement — or that he could make the PKI accept it if he did?

British, Malaysian and Australian diplomats were much more sceptical than some of their American and Filipino colleagues on the answers to these questions. They were not so trustful of Soekarno's intentions or inclined to put much confidence in his ability to override PKI opposition. Until he showed clear proof that he could and would do this, the Malaysian government would be very reluctant to take the risks entailed in entering into negotiations again. They were more inclined to look upon Soekarno as by now the prisoner of the PKI, willing or unwilling, and they disputed Ambassador Jones' contention that Soekarno exercised such a decisive and independent influence in the political scene that he alone could determine the course of Indonesian policy in a matter like this. In any case, Jones' view became less and less plausible by the end of 1964 as Soekarno swung sharply towards the left and tied his political fortunes far more closely to the PKI and the new association with China, while Indonesian relations with the USA deteriorated rapidly. Perhaps this might not have happened if he had been able to present the country with a settlement of the Malaysia conflict that symbolically vindicated the policies of the previous two years, but this argument is not at all convincing. The tide of events was running too strongly to the left by this time; it could be reversed only by a major shift in the domestic political balance, such as occurred after the coup of October 1965. But the changes which were occurring at the end of 1964 and early 1965 were all pointing in quite the opposite direction.

There was also another obstacle in the way of a resumption of negotiations on the basis of a single-stage conference leading to a compromise settlement. Such a move presupposed that both sides would have a fairly clear notion in advance of the likely outcome, that the terms on which the other would probably settle and the concessions each would be required to make should at least be foreseeable. But it was impossible to get any specific indication from Indonesian officials of the kinds of concession they might require Malaysia to make at the bargaining table, of their maximum or minimum requirements in the matter, except insofar as they kept coming back to the vague and question-begging demand for a 'return to the Manila Agreements'. When pressed to elaborate what that would mean in concrete terms — the unscrambling of the Malaysian federation as it stood? a referendum in the Borneo states? the immediate withdrawal of British troops and their bases? — they always avoided discussing the matter in such terms, suggesting that this was not the way to approach it. 'No, we do not expect that the Tunku can agree to such demands immediately' replied one group of officials.

We are realistic about his problems and we want him to appreciate ours. It is the spirit of the agreement that matters, not just the letter. We must resolve these questions by consultations in the right atmosphere, within the appropriate framework. Let us first get back to the Manila Agreements and the spirit of Maphilindo, so that we can approach the problem in the Asian way without outside interference. What we object to is the continuation of British neo-colonialist influence. Why can't the Tunku show more independence of Britain and co-operate with us in a Maphilindo solution to regional problems?

(One official went further along this line of reasoning; 'If the Tunku was pushed aside we could work with Razak. He's got some spice of nationalism in him.') This concern with the general framework and spirit of an agreement rather than its details, which had been observable in the exchanges at Bangkok earlier in the year — and which was a characteristically Javanese way of approaching a problem — made it almost impossible to enter into negotiations on a basis of down-to-earth horse-trading of concessions, quite apart from the the willingness and confidence of both sides to take the plunge.

[1]Herbert Feith, 'President Soekarno, the Army and the Communists: the Triangle Changes Shape', *Asian Survey*, vol. IV, no. 8, August 1964, pp. 969–80.

[2]Adam Malik's inclusion in the cabinet strengthened the Murba faction around Chairul Saleh, although the latter was defeated by Subandrio for the post of First Deputy Prime Minister. The left was strengthened shortly afterwards by the addition of Astrawinata as Minister for Justice and Oei Tjoe Tat as Minister attached to the Presidium.

[3]In October, Subandrio was appointed head of the new Crush Malaysia Border Area Command (KOPEDASAN): he also controlled Section V of KOTI, the so-called BPI or Central Intelligence Bureau, which was built into a powerful rival to the Army's intelligence section. In May 1964 he became Vice-Chairman, under Soekarno, of KOTRAR, the new authority for 'retooling', purging and anti-corruption drives, which replaced a former body headed by Nasution. He also gained considerable influence over news media through his position as chairman of the Supervisory Board of the *Antara* news agency.

[4]See below, p. 280.

[5]The rift between Nasution and Yani became so serious that in January 1965 a special commission of three high-ranking Javanese generals was deputed to try to restore unity between them. Their efforts were not immediately successful, however, and throughout 1965 the Army leaders were under heavy pressure from Soekarno and the PKI to agree to the arming of the peasants as a 'Fifth Force'.

[6]Ruth McVey, 'Indonesia', *Survey*, no. 54, Jan. 1965, p. 121. The rest of this paragraph is based on information kindly supplied by Dr. Rex Mortimer, who discussed the political situation with PKI officials in September 1964.

[7]McVey, op. cit. pp. 116–18.

[8]The wave of PKI-sponsored take-overs of 18–21 January occurred during the President's absence and just after his first meeting with Robert Kennedy in Tokyo — ostensibly in protest against the British seizure of two Indonesian ships in Hong Kong. The government resisted the process, although left-wing pressure to have the firms nationalized was maintained for several weeks. (Like those seized in September 1963, these firms were merely put under the supervision and custody of the local authorities.) Soekarno maintained a firm line against the take-overs, but he began to speak in more uncompromising tones about continuing confrontation, immediately after agreeing to the cease-fire sought by Kennedy: *Suluh Indonesia*, 24, 25 January 1964.

[9]These themes were most in evidence in his 17 August speech later that year, entitled '*Tahun Vivere Pericoloso*' (The Year of Living Dangerously): see also his Dwikora speech of May 6 in *Gelora Konfrontasi* (Department of Information, 1964).

[10]*Suluh Indonesia*, 1 April 1964.

[11]See p. 261 below.

[12]Chairul Saleh later denied that he was a member of Murba (in January 1965,when Murba was proscribed), but he had always been closely associated with the group of '1945 Generation' politicians who were its leaders, Malik, Sukarni and others.

[13]*Berita Indonesia*, 5 June 1964, *Suluh Indonesia*, 13 June 1964: the idea of party simplification or elimination was first raised in *Sketsmasa* (Surabaya), a weekly which generally reflected the strong anti-Communist views of the East Java Army leadership: see also Frank Palmos, 'Indonesia and the One-Party State', *The Bulletin* (Sydney), 18 July 1964.

[14]The Land Reform and Crop Sharing legislation of 1960 is briefly summarized in Selosoemardjan, 'Land Reform in Indonesia', *Asian Survey*, vol. I, no. 12, February 1962, pp. 23–30. On the tension that had built up about it at the end of 1964, see Daniel S. Lev, 'Indonesia: the Year of the Coup', *Asian Survey*, vol. VI, no. 2, February 1966, pp. 103–10. Lev had been in Central and East Java when the controversy over the 'unilateral actions' by the BTI (Communist-led peasant organizations) was at its height. Soekarno had required in 1961 that land reform be 'implemented within three years' in Java, so in 1964 the BTI took 'unilateral action' to do so in regions where the local officials and richer peasants were resisting the application of the laws. An excellent study of the subject is Rex Mortimer, *The Indonesian Communist Party and Land Reform 1959–1965* (Monash Papers on Southeast Asia, 1972).

[15]For example, B. M. Diah, former editor of 'Merdeka'.

[16]*Berita Indonesia*, 13 July 1964.

[17]For a detailed study of the Singapore election, see Osborne, op. cit. pp. 29–39 and 95–112. On Sarawak, see below pp. 301-2.

[18]See Osborne, op. cit. pp. 74–5 for an assessment of the immediate economic consequences of confrontation. Singapore's rubber imports in 1963 (not solely from Indonesia, of course) declined in value from a 1961–2 level of $960–970 million to $814 million in 1963 and $501 million (as recorded) in 1964. The effect on Singapore's total trade may be seen from the following figures:

	Imports	Exports
	Imports	*Exports*
1962	$3308 mill.	$2475 mill.
1963	3522 "	2463 "
1964	2686 "	1846 "

A careful statistical analysis of the impact of confrontation is given in H. V. Richter, 'Indonesia's Share in the Entrepot Trade of Malaya and Singapore prior to Confrontation', *Malayan Economic Review*, vol. XI, no. 2, Oct. 1966, pp. 28–45. The conclusion reached is that the smuggling and diversion of Indonesian commodities to Singapore during 1964 could hardly have reached 25 per cent of the previous levels. According to the *Straits Times*, 12 July 1964, however, *Antara* reported that 20–25,000 tons of rubber per month were being smuggled into Singapore and Malaysia, compared with

35,000 tons previously. (This figure was probably far too high, but it has been quoted extensively.) Singapore's registered unemployment figures, which hovered around the 45,000 mark in 1961–2, rose to 48,649 in June 1964 and 55,386 in 1965.

[19]The Barisan Sosialis chairman, Dr. Lee Siew Choh, resigned in May 1964 over the party's reaction to mobilization. The party boycotted the Singapore Legislative Assembly in 1966.

[20]For a penetrating analysis, see R. K. Vasil, 'The 1964 General Elections in Malaya', *International Studies* (New Delhi), vol. VII, no. 1, July 1965, pp. 20–65 to which I am much indebted throughout this section. The Malayan constitution provides for elections at least once every five years.

[21]Ibid. p. 52.

[22]Quoted from *Straits Times*, 2 March, 1964, in R. K. Vasil, 'Why Malaysia Failed?', *Quest* (Calcutta), no. 49, April–June 1966, p. 56.

[23]'It is fairly obvious that if it were possible for the MCA to hold the towns in Malaya then the present structure of the Central government and the policies it pursues can be unchanged. But if the towns decisively reject all MCA candidates, then there must be a reappraisal by UMNO. They will have to decide whether they can come to terms with a leadership that can command the loyalty of the sophisticated urban populations, Chinese, Indians, Eurasians and others, or govern without the support of the leadership of the towns.' Cited in Michael Leifer, 'Singapore in Malaysia: the Politics of Federation', *Journal of Southeast Asian History*, vol. VI, no. 2, Sept. 1965, p. 60.

[24]Ibid. pp. 60–1.

[25]See ibid. p. 62 for the voting figures in electorates contested by PAP. The MCA's poor showing in the 1959 elections and its internal troubles in 1959–62 must have caused the Tunku some apprehensions in those years as to the Alliance's chances in the next election of winning the urban, Chinese-dominated seats from the Socialist Front. Ironically, the PAP intervention deprived the Socialist Front of probable victory in 5 seats and thus helped the MCA to rehabilitate itself — although MCA candidates could still only win under the Alliance banner in seats where there was a solid base of Malay voters who could be relied upon to vote for them as Alliance candidates! Vasil, 'The 1964 General Elections', p.62.

[26]Ibid. p. 67 for the Tunku's statement to this effect on 21 Sept. 1964. In 1963, Lee had reacted vehemently against an attempt by the MCA to organize in Singapore ('merchant adventurers' out to loot the spoils of Singapore).

[27]Ibid. p. 63.

[28]PAP leaders frequently pointed out that Singapore was not represented in the Federal cabinet — although after the election they said it was preferable not to be!

[29]Speech by Dato Syed Ja'afar Albar at Pasir Panjang UMNO meeting, 12 July 1964. 'Why on earth should he [Lee Kuan Yew] denounce Maphilindo at this moment? .... No reason at all. It is not his business to poke his nose on [sic] Maphilindo. He wants Mao Tse-Tung to know that the whole Malay nation in this part of the world is uniting, and he therefore wants the Chinese too to unite and be up and awake.' (From English language transcript provided to the author by courtesy of Dato Albar.)

[30]See Michael Leifer, 'Communal Violence in Singapore', *Asian Survey*, vol. IV, no. 10, October 1964, pp. 1,115–21, for a brief background to the July riots: cf. Dennis Bloodworth, 'Crush Malaysia — From Within?', *The Bulletin* (Sydney), 1 Aug. 1964, for the PAP version, putting the blame squarely on Albar, who duly issued a rebuttal implying that the whole affair was provoked by Lee Kuan Yew.

[31]See statements by Khir Johari, 29 July, and Tunku Abdul Rahman, 11 Aug. 1964.

[32]*Straits Times*, 19 Aug. 1964.

[33]Based on information from officials of Singapore government and security forces in Singapore, January 1965.

[34]Speaking at the UMNO General Assembly just after the riots, the Tunku spoke of 'Indonesian agents going round the kampungs telling Malays to side with Indonesians rather than let the country fall into the hands of other races.' He did not put the blame on the Chinese as such, though he implied that the PAP's failure to improve the lot of the Malays in Singapore was at the root of the troubles.

[35]*Straits Times*, 21 Sept. 1964.

[36]On the Rasau clash see *The Age*, 23 June 1964. The October engagement at Terbat Besar involved the largest single party since the beginning of hostilities, approximately 120 men.

[37]*Suluh Indonesia*, 27 June 1964.

[38]The 1946 race riots are described by K. O. L. Burridge, 'Racial Relations in Johore', *Australian Journal of Politics and History*, vol. II, no. 2, May 1957.

[39]The quotation is from the speech by Dr. Ismail before the Security Council on 9 Sept., published as *Malaysia's Case In the UN Security Council* (Kuala Lumpur, Ministry of External Affairs, 1964), p. 4.

[40]Ibid. p. 5–6 for brief details of the Labis landing as revealed in Dr. Ismail's statement to the Security Council; this account referred to only one plane load of paratroops, however. A fuller account by Second Lieutenant Sutikno, who commanded one group of the paratroops, was published shortly after his capture in the *Straits Times*, 1 October 1964. The final stages of mopping-up were described in *Straits Times*, 28 Oct. 1964. Sutikno was later induced to issue a message instructing his men to surrender. On 2 Nov., leaflets written by Sutikno were air-dropped over Riau and Sumatra by Malaysian planes, urging Indonesians not to be misled about the attitude of the people of Malaysia. The reaction of the Indonesian authorities to this incident was curious: far from reviling Sutikno, they presented him as something of a hero. The Indonesian people should be proud that it had taken 5,000 Gurkha, British, Australian and New Zealand troops to capture Lt. Sutikno, commented Ganis Harsono, portraying him as an example of courage and revolutionary spirit: see *Suluh Indonesia*, 4 November 1964.

[41]*Suluh Indonesia*, 3 and 4 September 1964.

[42]Nasution's admission to Melbourne correspondent, Creighton Burns, that Indonesian 'volunteers' had been entering Borneo and Malaya for some time was reported in *The Age*, 8 Sept. 1964. Indonesia continued to draw a distinction between 'volunteers' and 'regulars', however; e.g. Sudjarwo on 'our guerrillas, our volunteers' in the Security Council on 10 Sept.: 'Volunteers in Indonesia come from all quarters of the population and not only from Indonesia but also from the territory now called Malaysia. It is a peoples' fight for freedom against colonialism and neo-colonialism, against Malaysia as a political notion. For the volunteers, national boundaries do not exist. Their boundaries are political ones.'

[43]For the text of the new quasi-martial law regulations, see *Harian Rakjat*, 17 Sept. 1964. Regional military commanders were designated as *Penguasa Pelaksanaan Dwikora Daerah* in every military command area except Bali, Riau and Nusa Tenggara and West Irian, with powers similar to their former powers under the State of Emergency. They were required to consult with the local *Pantja Tunggal* and were responsible directly to the President for the use of their powers.

[44]See the report from London by Herbert Mishael in *The Age*, 16 Sept. 1964.

[45]For a rather sensational account of the naval crisis see *The Australian*, 12 and 14 September 1964, which also carried a more balanced assessment of British policy towards Indonesia at that time from the *Washington Post* service.

[46]*The Australian*, 18 Sept. 1964.

[47]An Indonesian Air Force corporal who had taken part in the Pontian landing was sentenced to death in a Johore court on 17 October after the judge had ruled that he could not be regarded as a prisoner of war and was subject to the mandatory death sentence under civil law: *Straits Times*, 22 Oct. 1964. The sentence was not carried out, but the status of Indonesian prisoners was left obscure until 24 April 1965 when the Malaysian Attorney General withdrew the charges (at a stage when peace talks were under discussion) and announced that members of the Indonesian Armed Forces would not be prosecuted, but would be treated as prisoners of war. The repatriation of 478 such P.O.W.s was announced in *Suara Malaysia*, 13 October 1966.

[48]See statement by the Secretary of State for Commonwealth Relations in the House of Commons, 9 Feb. 1965: *Hansard*, vol. 706, p. 191. These estimates seem to have been inflated for political effect, however.

[49]*New York Times*, 8 Jan. 1965.

[50]The major military engagements of early 1965 were described in *The Herald* (Melbourne), 14 April 1965; *The Sun* (Melbourne) 28 April; *The Age*, 25 May, 2 July 1965.

[51]The proceedings relating to Malaysia at the Security Council meetings of 9–17 Sept. 1964 are published in full in *Malaysia's Case in the United Nations Security Council* (Kuala Lumpur, Ministry of Exernal Affairs, 1964), from which all quotations below are taken.

[52]Ibid. p. 15.

[53]Good appraisals of the Malaysian and Indonesian strategies in the debate are given in Bruce Grant's reports from New York in *The Age*, 10, 11, 12, 15 Sept. 1964.

[54]*Malaysia's Case in the Security Council*, p. 71: for the crucial statements by the Morocco and Ivory Coast delegates, see ibid., pp. 54–8 and 76–8. The Indonesian Department of Foreign Affairs maintained in its pamphlet on the debate (*The 'Malaysia' Issue Before The UN Security Council* — which contained only the Indonesian delegate's speeches and the draft resolution) that Malaya did not succeed in obtaining any significant decision at all, since even the Norwegian resolution avoided use of the term 'aggression'.

[55]Bolivia, Brazil, China, France, Ivory Coast, Morocco, Norway, USA and United Kingdom supported the draft resolution: Czechoslovakia and USSR opposed it.

[56]Soekarno's speech at the Cairo Conference and the Conference Declaration are printed in *The Era of Confrontation* (Djakarta, Department of Information, 1964).

[57]*Suluh Indonesia*, 9 Oct. 1965.

[58]Bunnell, op. cit. pp. 68–70.

X
'Storming the Last Ramparts of Imperialism'

AFTER her diplomatic setbacks in the Security Council and the Cairo Conference, Indonesia's efforts to 'crush' Malaysia during the next few months amounted to little more than a series of nuisance raids across the Straits of Malacca which, as we have already noticed, were singularly ineffectual. The Malaysia conflict did not exactly slip into the background in the year that followed, but no significant new developments occurred to 'heighten confrontation' apart from a much-publicized build-up of troops in the border areas at the end of 1964 and the somewhat metaphysical transformation of the campaign into a grander confrontation of the entire imperialist world in 1965.

Domestic political tensions and the related question of Indonesia's new international alignment with China became the dominant concerns of Djakarta politicians during the twelve turbulent months that preceded the attempted coup of October 1965. A few half-hearted attempts to negotiate a settlement with Malaysia were made, but they were of relatively little importance in the overall scene. Within Indonesia, this was an extraordinary period of turbulent political conflict and rapidly rising prices, of demoralizing uncertainty and apprehensiveness about the future, compounded by an alarming increase in day to day lawlessness. Indonesia's revolution seemed to be spinning out of control, or out of the normal world of political realism into a fantasy realm in which only ideology mattered. Soekarno's obsession with the *romantik, dialektik* and *dynamisme* of the Revolution became more visionary than ever — at least in his public statements, and apparently in his political calculations also — while the scope of his ambitions seemed to grow even as the means of achieving them atrophied. His abrupt New Year decision to withdraw Indonesia from the United Nations was the most dramatic expression of the new spirit. Its logical corollary was the rapid growth of the 'Djakarta-Peking axis' in 1965, paralleled by a sharp deterioration in relations with the USA, almost to breaking-point. Within Indonesia the PKI seemed to be carrying all before it as one after another of its opponents was politically defeated or isolated. The party was making dramatic gains as

Soekarno inclined his weight to its side on one issue after another in the months before the abortive coup of October, which suddenly transformed the political situation by bringing about the virtual destruction of the PKI.

In the face of Indonesia's spiralling inflation at this time, her political disunity and her patent failure to crush Malaysia, Soekarno's flights of ideological fantasy soared off to ever greater heights. Two themes were stressed to an almost hypnotic degree, as if the magic of words could conjure up reality. One was the invocation of ever more revolutionary spirit in confronting difficulties, opposition and struggle, the spirit of self-reliance, of daring to live dangerously and of fidelity to the revolutionary course regardless of its consequences. The other, which was presented as proof of the rightness of this course, was the assertion that the revolutionary assault by the New Emerging Forces on the citadels of imperialism had already entered its last victorious phase.

A mighty storm against imperialism is now raging in Asia, Africa, Latin America. These continents of ours, so long subjected to humiliation, enslavement, plunder, are no longer prepared to bear the crazy burden of imperialism upon their shoulders. We have cast this burden aside! We today stand firmly upright in the mighty ranks of the new emerging forces, and we are now storming the last bulwarks of imperialism! There is no power in the world that can prevent the peoples of Asia, Africa, Latin America from emancipating themselves! It is no longer possible for the imperialists, colonialists and neo-colonialists to rule over us, as they did in days of yore, and we are no longer prepared to be ruled over as we were in days of yore. This means that a revolutionary crisis on a world scale has occurred. We must grasp, grasp this opportunity, for if not, if we lose this opportunity, we will never get it back again![1]

There was an element of whistling in the dark, of course, in these brave words, yet behind them was also a shrewd assessment that by espousing an ever more militant role as leader of the have-not nations and threatening to kick over yet more international applecarts Indonesia was as likely to be able to exercise some political leverage in world politics (and certainly to attract world attention) in her straitened condition as she could hope to by withdrawing passively into a penitent silence. One wonders whether Soekarno really did believe that the troubles of the *Nekolim* in Vietnam or Malaysia or the United Nations might presage an imminent collapse of their world power, or how far he was simply clutching at any straws which would seem to support the validity of his own doctrines. His flight from reality into a magical world of words and symbols reached dizzier heights than ever, ending up with the incorporation of mystic talismans (*djimat*) in his arsenal of political concepts in June 1965.

Of course we have to make all kinds of sacrifices, face various difficulties in our day-to-day life, but heed this well — we do not collapse, we do not starve, we have not been ruined! .... For us the fight against 'Necolim' is nothing but beneficial to the Indonesian Revolution, beneficial to the Indonesian Soul, beneficial to Indonesia's development, beneficial to Indonesia's independence. The anti-Necolim struggle has given Indonesia a new spirit, has brought powerful unity, has given a resolve of steel, has given the freedom to organise its own national affairs, 'the freedom to be free'. We are prepared to pay for all this, to pay a fee for growth, to pay with sacrifice and with dedication. We have now come to the stage of the spirit of self-reliance, thanks to the fighting method of putting first things first, of 'Ambeg Parama Arta'. Once our Revolution has reached this stage of the Spirit of Self-reliance, further development is but a question of implementation .... You who fought for those foundations, making all kinds of sacrifices, now make the Spirit of Self-reliance and the Five Talismans your weapons, make them your heirlooms with which to serve the Revolution. Remember you have given the Revolution its Spirit, so you have to remain loyal to the Spirit of the Revolution, to keep on maintaining and developing the Spirit of the Revolution. The Spirit of the Revolution has come of age, and will develop in 'self-propelling growth'.[2]

The movement towards much closer association with China in international politics during 1964–5 was paralleled by a steady drift to the left in domestic politics. The two trends were sometimes attributed to the explosion of the first Chinese atomic bomb in October 1964, or to the growth of PKI influence, or to Soekarno's awareness of his own mortality after a sudden deterioration of his health in September 1964, and his desire to strengthen the domestic position of the Communists before he died, so as to forestall a right-wing reaction against the PKI after he was gone. A struggle for succession seemed to be developing, in which Subandrio came to be supported by the PKI during 1965 in his bid to establish himself as indisputably the strongest candidate.[3] All these factors contributed to tensions that arose at that time, but there is no simple explanation for the interplay of domestic and external developments. One thing led to another with bewildering speed — Soekarno's flirtation with Peking, the intensification of domestic political conflict, the departure from the United Nations, pressure from the PKI for a break with the USA, increasingly desperate stop-gap measures in 1964–5 to preserve national unity as the political temperature rose and inflationary pressures mounted inexorably.

Most of Indonesia's prominent anti-Communists, the men most likely to urge a settlement with Malaysia and a scaling down of confrontation, had been politically isolated or reduced to silence by the middle of 1965; every attempt to create an anti-Communist political bloc had been defeated and many people were beginning to take a fatalistic view about the PKI's seemingly invincible surge towards power, even to the point of becoming reconciled to the possibility of a PKI take-over. The Army itself, the ultimate bastion of anti-Communist power, came to be threatened by the PKI's demand for the creation of a 'Fifth Force' in the Armed Services, the arming of peasants and workers, which Soekarno endorsed in spite of Army resistance.[4] It is questionable, however, whether the tide of events really was running as strongly towards the left in the months before the coup as many people believed at the time — for the impression created by Djakarta political ferment was by no means reflected in the provinces, where anti-Communist elements were becoming increasingly militant also — and there are some grounds for believing that Soekarno was still trying to restrain the PKI and play his old balancing role in order to preserve national unity against the looming threat of social conflict. If this was his aim, however, he was being carried to the left in the process and his arguments generally left the initiative to the Communists rather than their opponents. But his objectives, as always, were diverse and, instead of lowering the political temperature, his temperamental addiction to the 'thrill of a political surf-tide' seems to have urged him on towards a glorification of the revolutionary aspects of Indonesia's situation in 1965 rather than towards the dampening down of controversial issues for the sake of economic stabilization. In any case, he had gone too far along the revolutionary road to turn back now to a political strategy which repudiated the radicalism and ferment he was advocating. There was little more he could hope to do than to maintain some degree of control in order to consolidate national unity before his health gave out or the inflation began to spiral uncontrollably.

WITHDRAWAL FROM THE UN

Soekarno's sudden decision on New Year's Eve of 1965 that Indonesia should withdraw from the United Nations because Malaysia was about to take a seat on the Security Council was the most striking sign of the change taking place in Indonesia's foreign policy and in the nature of confrontation. Whether it should be regarded as an effect or a contributing cause of that change is a matter for debate — the latter insofar as it left Indonesia little alternative but to look towards China for diplomatic support; the former insofar as Chinese blandishments or pressure had already inclined Soekarno in that direction. But its immediate cause must be sought in the circumstances of an acute domestic crisis then raging within Indonesia.

This crisis, which came to a head over a controversy between the PKI and the Murba Party leaders, Chairul Saleh, Adam Malik and Sukarni, concerning the attempt by the latter to build up an overtly anti-Communist organization known as the Body for the Promotion of Soekarnoism (BPS — *Badan Pendukung Soekarnoisme*), was another classic example of the way domestic political forces could influence Indonesian foreign policy, and vice-versa, at a critical moment. While it has only an indirect bearing on the Malaysian conflict (despite a simultaneous flurry of threats and alarms over the build-up of military and naval forces on both sides of the Indonesian-Malaysian border), the crisis is relevant to our story for several reasons: foreign policy considerations resulting from the Malaysia conflict played an important part in the drama. Moreover, the increase of domestic political tensions resulting from it largely accounts for the dwindling of Indonesia's military threat to Malaysia during 1965 and for the virulent outburst of violence after the '*Gestapu*' coup attempt which heralded the ending of confrontation.

The strains and rivalries of Djakarta politics which had threatened to imperil national unity earlier in 1964 again came to the surface in the last quarter of the year, partly as the result of a sudden deterioration in Soekarno's health during a lengthy overseas tour and partly because of the intensification of political party conflicts over the land reform issue in Central and East Java. The question of who would succeed Soekarno in the event of his death now gave rise to a great deal of speculation, with Subandrio emerging as an increasingly strong contender.[5] There was no one else of comparable political influence within the government who commanded sufficient backing or who would prove sufficiently acceptable to all the groups represented within the *Nasakom* framework. Chairul Saleh was too close to Murba for the liking of the PKI. An overt seizure of power by the Armed Forces seemed unlikely because of the personal estrangement of Nasution and Yani, which was aggravated by significant differences of opinion on political issues between and within the several services. It was widely believed that, if Soekarno died, the Army leaders would have agreed to some form of triumvirate or presidium composed of Subandrio and several other national leaders, maintaining the old Soekarno formula of a loose *Nasakom* government and ideology at least for an interim period. Subandrio had drawn many strings of power into his hands over the previous year, largely at Nasution's expense, and he was more likely to have PKI support in the event of a struggle for power in the post-Soekarno era than either Chairul Saleh or anyone identified with the Army, if only because his policy towards Malaysia suited the PKI so well. But he was not strongly beholden to the PKI at first: in fact, his foreign policy had been attacked by the PKI during 1963 and even as late as October 1964, when he clashed openly with Aidit after he condemned the Chinese nuclear explosion. Because of Subandrio's later association with the PKI in 1965, when he seems to have staked his political future on the success of Soekarno's Peking-aligned foreign policy and to have accepted the possibility of an ultimate PKI victory in Indonesia as historically inevitable, there has been some tendency to misinterpret his earlier political position. Certainly he began to espouse Soekarno's doctrine of 'living dangerously' with great enthusiasm in early 1965, just after Indonesia left the UN, for he must by then have recognized that the point of no return had been passed in Indonesia's relations with the West. But until a few weeks earlier his political position vis-à-vis the anti-Communist leaders in the Armed Services or even the Murba politicians, Chairul Saleh and Adam Malik, was far from clear-cut.[6] While he would hardly have wished to see any of them gain appreciably in political prestige, he was not bent upon their destruction, as he seemed to be after the BPS affair.

The Body for the Promotion of Soekarnoism was a rather amorphous movement which mushroomed in the major towns of Indonesia, mainly among the newspapermen and anti-communist politicians, after the publication of a series of articles on 'Soekarnoism' in *Berita Indonesia*, the paper most closely associated with Chairul Saleh and the Murba Party and the most unspokenly anti-Communist.[7] The articles were written by an old PNI stalwart, Sajuti Melik, with the aim of showing that Soekarnoism was an ideology quite distinct from Communism and that it was being misinterpreted by the Communists as a cloak for their own very different purposes. Opponents of the PKI eagerly seized upon this line of argument, since 'Soekarnoism' seemed to be a splendid ideological rallying-point from which they could attack the PKI without being accused of being reactionary or anti-revolutionary. The Murba leaders came to be most prominently identified with the new movement, notably Adam Malik, Sukarni and, to a lesser extent, Chairul Saleh, along with the Navy chief and various other strongly anti-Communist officers in the armed services; but support for the BPS came from many other sources to the right of the PKI and left wing of the PNI. Essentially, this was much the same political alignment as during the Single Party controversy six months earlier, but in a new guise. Once again, Soekarno remained cryptically silent about his views of the BPS for some time while he gauged its strength — which was interpreted variously as a sign of approval in some quarters and disavowal in others.

By early December, a vehement polemic was raging over the rapid spread of BPS chapters, with the PKI and Ali Sastroamidjojo's supporters in the PNI attacking it bitterly as an attempt to split the nation and under-mine *Nasakom* unity. Ideology, far from uniting the country, was now becoming a cause of dissension; Subandrio felt constrained to issue an appeal for the avoidance of 'ideological confrontation' in an attempt to calm the storm. 'Do not let -isms be used as an instrument for splitting us.... Soekarnoism, Pantja-Sila-ism, Nasakom-ism' he pleaded.[8] But more than mere exhortation was now needed to restore national unity, for tension between the Communists and their opponents was breaking out in many parts of Java over the issue of land reform. The 'unilateral actions' which the Communists had instigated earlier in the year, mainly in Central and East Java, multiplied towards the end of the year, thus intensifying the antagonism between the PKI and local PNI and NU branches, which were backed by the richer peasants. This tension was transmitted to Djakarta, where the central organizations of these parties were under orders from the President to maintain *Nasakom* unity even while their own supporters were complaining of violations of the *Nasakom* spirit by their rivals. The struggle for power which arose over the BPS issue was to some degree a projection of this deeper antagonism.

Soekarno could do little to reconcile these tensions. To have called off the land reform programme would merely have antagonized the PKI and been tantamount to an admission that the programme was wrong, which would have run counter to his whole political philosophy of spurring on revolutionary and radical elements, not restraining them. So he simply resorted to his customary strategy of urging the two sides to resolve their differences by *musjawarah* and emphasizing the need for national unity against the common enemies, Malaysia and the *Nekolim*. A lengthy con-ference with representatives of the government and all political parties met at Bogor on 12 December to discuss, *inter alia*, the questions of land reform and the BPS; only with considerable difficulty could a threadbare compromise be patched up, committing the parties to a series of pious generalities for the sake of national unity. Neither side had yet gained the ascendancy in the contest for his support. Yet, a few days later, quite out of the blue, Soekarno announced that the BPS was to be banned and must dissolve itself forthwith.[9]

This decision was the first of several which transformed the political scene in Djakarta over the next few weeks. The PKI had been very much on the defensive just beforehand, while Chairul Saleh and Adam Malik seemed to be the rising stars in the political firmament, but henceforth the trend of events in Djakarta was strongly in its favour, while any of its opponents who had been associated with the BPS came under heavy attack. The decision to withdraw from the UN, announced equally suddenly and unexpectedly, confirmed the impression that Soekarno was now leaning towards the side of the PKI in the political struggle, causing consternation and dismay among its opponents, who realized that it would isolate Indonesia still further from any possibility of restoring her links with the West and leave her no choice but to align more closely with China. The Communists and their allies were already mounting violent demonstrations against the American embassy, consulates and USIS reading rooms with the aim of forcing a breach of diplomatic relations with the USA and were able to exploit the prevailing climate of hostility to the *Nekolim* which had been generated by the Malaysia issue.

Soekarno's motives in all this were a puzzle at the time, for it was not clear why he had suddenly decided to abjure the BPS and its leaders after earlier seeming sympathetic towards them. Nor was it known whether he had decided to leave the UN in a fit of pique when faced with the unpalatable fact that Malaysia was about to take a seat on the Security Council, or because of pressure from Communist China. With the advantage of hindsight, we can see that Chen Yi's visit to Djakarta at the end of November presaged the development of the 'Djakarta-Peking axis' early in 1965, but there was little outward sign that Soekarno was preparing to move so far and fast in that direction before the New Year.[10] And while his actions at this time conform to a general strategy of 'turning the wheel of the Revolution' still harder towards the left, it is debatable whether he deliberately decided to embark upon a course involving closer relations with China and a further severing of ties with the West, with all its implications in both domestic and foreign policy, or whether he simply found himself swept along by the momentum of events which he could only control intermittently.

There seems to be little doubt that Soekarno made the decision to withdraw from the UN at very short notice, with little or no prior discussion of its implications with his ministers.[11] Although it had long been known that Malaysia was to take a seat on the Security Council in 1965 under an earlier gentlemen's agreement with Czechoslovakia for a split-term sharing of an available seat, no plans appear to have been made for an Indonesian riposte, certainly not for anything as dramatic as this, and the Foreign Ministry was thrown into consternation by it. Soekarno is said to have made the decision abruptly at a Presidium meeting shortly before the speech in which he announced it (ironically, at a rally to celebrate the eradication of illiteracy, an occasion on which his luckless Education Minister chose to express his thanks to UNESCO for the help it had given in this worthy cause!), though he did not make it clear for over a week whether the withdrawal would be complete and absolute or limited and symbolic — for instance, from the General Assembly only — but not from the UN as a whole or its specialized agencies, which were giving Indonesia badly needed technical assistance. The whole affair was characteristic of his political style — to act on impulse in accordance with his general political inclinations and then adjust his further actions to the requirements of the situation. By taking Indonesia out of the UN, he was merely applying the doctrine of 'living dangerously' and 'standing on our own feet' a little more uncompromisingly. The decision also had the advantage for Soekarno of being a sharp, almost irreversible change of course, something that the gradually evolving relationship with China would not be otherwise, which his anti-Communist ministers could not easily resist. The latter were thrown into a state of dismay and confusion by the manoeuvre, as he doubtless intended. There was some muttering in private that 'This time he has gone too far', but no effective action to stop him, since the President exploited the uncertainties and ambiguities of the situation too skilfully for his adversaries to mobilize effective opposition to the new course that was emerging.

An atmosphere of acute crisis persisted in Djakarta for several weeks until the implications of the President's decision became clear. It was skilfully exploited to the disadvantage of the anti-Communists by Subandrio, who now began to identify himself much more openly with the swing to the left. In a speech on 4 January, he predicted that

1965 will be a year of crystallisation of the forces of the Indonesian Revolution ... and possibly there will be some of our comrades in the struggle whom we will have to leave behind because they can no longer follow the course of revolution and have even become counter-revolutionary.[12]

The reference here to the former BPS leaders was obvious and the hint was taken up by the PKI and its allies as a signal for a vehement campaign against counter-revolutionaries of all kinds, both at home and abroad. Subandrio had also spoken of the need to 'tidy up' the press to remove anarchistic elements, an indirect pointer at newspapers which had been supporting the BPS against the Communists, of which the most prominent was Chairul Saleh's mouthpiece, Berita Indonesia. (A bitter struggle was still continuing in the press and the Indonesian Journalists' Association.) The left wing now began to press vigorously for the 'retooling' of the cabinet with the aim of eliminating Adam Malik and Chairul Saleh. At this point, the President issued an order banning the Murba Party (strictly speaking, ordering it to 'temporarily cease its activities') which was taken to signify that he was no longer giving any protection to the former BPS group at all. Adam Malik was now left in a dangerously exposed position, while Chairul Saleh scurried for cover with a statement repudiating his associations with Murba and the BPS. In such a manner did Soekarno and Subandrio contrive to emasculate the opposition to the PKI and to the President's new course of foreign policy. Because of the prevailing atmosphere of emergency and crisis created by the military build-up in Borneo, the insistent ideological indoctrination on the theme of confronting Malaysia and the *Nekolim* and the political risks of appearing at all lacking in revolutionary zeal, there was little the anti-Communists could do to regain the initiative.

As it happened, Soekarno soon damped down the pressures for a cabinet reshuffle and set out to calm the storm of political strife, characteristically contriving to avoid leaning too far towards one side or the other in the struggle for power which went on being fought over a whole series of other issues, each relatively minor in itself, throughout the first three quarters of 1965.[13] It would lead us too far away from the Malaysia story to try and trace all the convolutions of Indonesian domestic politics during this period but several aspects must be mentioned briefly.

First, it would be difficult to distinguish whether Soekarno was consciously trying to bring the PKI closer to power during 1965, but moderating the steps he took to avoid provoking the Army to resistance, or whether he was simply concerned to preserve national unity on the old *Nasakom* basis and compelled to make constant concessions to the PKI as its price for maintaining the facade of unity. From the way he flirted with the idea of the 'Fifth Force' (arming the peasants and workers) which Aidit and the Chinese were urging upon him in 1965 one might assume the former, but from other evidence one could argue the latter. Probably he was not entirely sure of himself. So the combination of revolutionary slogans and indeterminate actions allowed him to have the best of both worlds.

Second, it was largely on foreign policy issues that the 'revolutionary' thrust of Soekarno's ideology was now expressed, not domestic ones. By stressing the threats from the *Nekolim* and urging the doctrines of 'living dangerously' and 'standing on our own feet' in international affairs, Soekarno was able to make it impossible for his right-wing critics to develop any alternative doctrine to oppose him. Thus, although some of them wanted a settlement with Malaysia in order to check the drift towards China, they could never seize the initiative to achieve this, for it remained always in Soekarno's hands.

Third, the tension between Communists and anti-Communists continued to increase in the provinces, where the former were still by no means as powerful as they were becoming in Djakarta. In East and Central Java, resistance to the PKI and its affiliates over the land reform issue aroused certain fundamentalist Muslim groups to a pitch of militancy which even the PKI recognized as dangerous: a clash in Malang in March demonstrated their power briefly, while attacks on Communist officials and organizations by Muslim flying squads in East Java showed how explosive the tension there had become. Communist organizations were demanding that the Muslim student organization HMI should be banned, but this was too dangerous even for Soekarno to consider and he refused to do so right down to the end of September. His heavy emphasis on the Afro-Asian conference celebrations in April, which was directed largely towards the goal of ensuring Malaysia's exclusion and isolation from the Afro-Asian family, seems to have been intended also to help restore national unity by enabling him to silence statements critical of the government and of other groups until after the conference celebrations.

THE SINO-INDONESIAN ENTENTE

The *rapprochement* between Indonesia and China developed so dramatically at the end of 1964 that it is important to recall that it was not a sudden new trend (except negatively, insofar as it entailed the weakening of ties with Russia and the West). As David Mozingo put it at the time:

Rather, it was the culmination of a gradually evolving sense of the harmony between certain aims of Indonesian nationalism and Peking's drive to create a China-centred political order in the Far East that would exclude the presence of major Western powers, particularly the United States. Chinese policies in relation to Indonesia have been linked to a broader Asian strategy that emerged a decade ago at the Bandung Conference. This strategy was predicated on the assumption that the aims of Asian nationalism would result in a long period of conflict with the Western powers and that Peking could exploit this conflict to restore the Middle Kingdom's pre-eminence in the Far East by promoting wherever possible a convergence between 'anti-imperialist' nationalism and Chinese Communism.[14]

By 1964, this convergence of China's and Indonesia's aims in the matter of eliminating American and British power from Vietnam and Malaysia respectively was giving the two countries similar interests in their relations with the great powers, both Russia and the USA, and with the Third World, which they also hoped to embroil in their anti-imperialist campaign. The process of *rapprochement* was furthered by the perceptible cooling of Indonesian-Russian relations during 1963–4 and the fact that Indonesia's chances of obtaining substantial political or economic help from the USA faded steadily in the twelve months after September 1963.

But the *rapprochement* was not just an accident of history, as was often assumed by people who believed that there was some basic conflict of national interests between the two nations because of the widespread antipathy between Malays and Chinese in South-East Asia and the geo-political notion of Indonesia as a 'counter-balance' to China in the area. Peking's leaders had 'consistently striven to shape their policies towards Indonesia so as to maximize the area of common agreement between the two countries', observed Mozingo. He regarded their handling of the problem of overseas Chinese nationals in Indonesia as restrained and tactful, with the one exception of the dispute in 1959 over exclusion of Chinese rural store-keepers from Indonesia's villages, when Peking briefly tried to bluster and bully Subandrio into withdrawal of the measure. Even on this issue she finally backed down in order to mend her fences with Indonesia in 1960–1, when Russian influence in Djakarta began to increase. On the other hand, it suited Soekarno's political temperament and his tactical purposes to maintain good relations with Peking, as well as Moscow and Washington, while the Chinese leaders were prepared to applaud both his anti-imperialist stand in foreign policy and his restraints on anti-Communist and anti-Chinese sentiments at home.

Although the Chinese leaders must have welcomed the increasingly militant tone of Soekarno's foreign policy in 1963 and gave open support for Indonesia's confrontation of Malaysia on several occasions, they initially did so in rather guarded and qualified terms. The two nations did not see entirely eye-to-eye on the Malaysia issue.[15] China appears to have been trying to push Indonesia into more militant support for the North Kalimantan rebels in 1963 than Subandrio wanted to undertake, while Peking was far from happy about Indonesia's handling of the Malaysia issue at the Manila conferences. The Soekarno-Liu Shao-chi communique of April 1963, in which support was expressed for the North Kalimantan freedom fighters could hardly have said less than it did on the subject and seems to indicate that there was at that time no close identity of views on the Malaysia question. If the Peking government had been entertaining hopes of ultimately gaining greater leverage within the Malaysian region through the overseas Chinese there (a possibility that may have occurred to them during the previous years of political crisis in Singapore), they may have been uneasy about Indonesia's bid for hegemony over the region, especially during the Maphilindo phase. But they seem to have been more concerned to commit Indonesia to a strongly anti-imperialist line over Malaysia than to extend their own influence there, for a friendly (and dependent) Indonesia in close alliance with them against the Western powers was a more realistic objective to work for than Chinese dominance of Malaysia.[16]

During 1964 the Sino-Indonesian relationship developed from a rather tentative similarity of interests in the common anti-imperialist struggle early in the year to the remarkable cordiality between the two governments which grew up in 1965. Developments affecting the wider international balance of power in South-East Asia were obviously of primary importance in this. Both countries became more inclined towards a militantly anti-imperialist course by the changing fortunes of war in Vietnam and Borneo, partly because of the prospect of a Communist victory in Vietnam which was seen in Indonesia and China as evidence that the strength of the imperialistic Americans and British was beginning to crumble, partly for the converse reason that Britain's reinforcement of her military forces in Malaysia required that Indonesia's struggle to expel them be waged within a broader context. Three other factors also contributed to the new alignment — Indonesia's loss of her previous sources of economic aid and political support during 1964 and her need for any crumbs of help she could find elsewhere; the sharp deterioration of her relations with Russia, largely over Russia's right to attend the Second Afro-Asian Conference, which China was contesting; and the explosion of China's first nuclear bomb in October 1964.

China's nuclear bomb seems to have had an indirect influence upon Indonesian politics, but in a quite unexpected way.[17] It was not that it frightened or impressed the Indonesians into an acknowledgement of China's new military might, but rather that Soekarno seems to have set out to gain some benefit from China's nuclear prowess. The rapid change in Soekarno's politics towards China in the period immediately after the October explosion is noteworthy. Soekarno was still abroad at the time and the first Indonesian comment came from Subandrio, who condemned the Chinese explosion as contrary to the 1963 Test Ban Treaty, to which Indonesia was a signatory. Shortly afterwards, Soekarno called unexpectedly at Shanghai for talks with Chou En-lai and Chen Yi on his way home and soon after his return Indonesia's policy towards the Chinese tests was significantly modified. Chen Yi visited Djakarta at the end of November, also unexpectedly, and apparently at China's initiative, for a week of talks during which the basis was apparently laid for the new 'Djakarta-Peking axis', whose detailed implications were later worked out by Subandrio's visit to Peking in January 1965.

Chen Yi presumably came to Djakarta in order to dangle some substantial bait in front of Soekarno to keep him on a leftward course both domestically and internationally, perhaps also to induce him to curb the efforts of the anti-Communists in Djakarta who were seeking to restore Indonesia's ties with the West. But the nature of the bait was not immediately clear. China's offer of a $50 million line of credit to Indonesia ($10 million of it in desperately needed cash) was hardly sufficient to buy Indonesia into her camp. The joint communique issued after their talks contained little to indicate any major changes in policy on either side, though the harmony of interests in the struggle against imperialism was acknowledged more clearly than ever before. After Subandrio's mission to Peking in January, however, the implications of the new relationship were spelled out much more specifically.[18] Indonesia went further than ever before in attacking the USA as the leader of imperialism and colonialism, while China promised that if the British or American imperialists dared to impose a war on the Indonesian people 'the Chinese people will not stand idly by'. Military and 'technical' (i.e. nuclear?) cooperation were to be undertaken for the first time, with exchanges of delegations in these and other fields — though Subandrio denied that these engagements amounted to a military alliance or that Indonesia had departed from her traditional policy of non-alignment. Uri Ra'anan attaches great significance to the fact that the police chiefs of the two countries played a prominent part in these talks, but that none of the top Army leaders were included in the Indonesian mission, despite the heavy emphasis on military matters. Significant evidence for his hypothesis that cooperation on nuclear research was one of the major subjects of discussion at both sets of talks was the prominent part played by Wu Heng, who was believed to head the section of China's Scientific and Technological Commission concerned with nuclear affairs.

Whether the Chinese ever went so far as to offer, or hint at, the prospect of a joint Sino-Indonesian nuclear test, possibly in Indonesian waters, with some token participation by Indonesian technicians, we can only speculate. Soekarno threw out hints of this kind in the middle of 1965 and there was a remarkable flurry of talk about the need to develop nuclear weapons and nuclear technology, although the earliest Indonesian statement about her plans to produce a bomb (which was something between a jest and a misunderstanding) dated back to a period even before the Chen Yi visit and could not conceivably have had any solid foundation.[19] All this stress on nuclear weapons had a quality of desperate over-compensation about it at a time when Indonesia could barely afford to import the simplest of spare parts for her industries or generate enough electric power to supply Djakarta with adequate lighting continuously. It seemed the propensity to fantasy encouraged by Soekarno's grandiloquent speeches was running to extremes when he spoke about Indonesia's plans to produce a bomb. Yet it is conceivable that Soekarno was hoping he could thereby create the impression of a Chinese commitment to share nuclear secrets (and perhaps even a test in Indonesian waters) and that they were at least humouring him, rather than flatly refusing. China has generally been extremely cautious in the uses she has made of her nuclear capacity.

What did the Sino-Indonesian *rapprochement* amount to in practical terms during 1965? Did it significantly influence the course of Indonesian politics or her relations with other nations? It did not quite bring her to a breach of diplomatic relations with the USA, although she came perilously close to the brink. Her relations with Russia deteriorated too, but not quite so seriously. It did not prevent her from negotiating with Malaysia on two occasions for a resumption of peace talks, although it is doubtful if there was much likelihood that these would have succeeded. It was mainly in her Afro-Asian diplomacy and plans for CONEFO (Conference of the New Emerging Forces) that the Chinese association had most impact, for China supplied the money to begin the construction of the lavish conference centre which Soekarno now ordered, while the support of China and her client states, North Korea, North Vietnam and Cambodia, helped Soekarno considerably in giving credibility to his plans to hold such a Conference in 1966. The new axis (Soekarno always referred to it as the Djakarta-Phnom Penh-Hanoi-Peking-Pyongyang axis, no doubt in order to give it a CONEFO flavour and avoid the charge of having become harnessed solely to Peking's chariot) was useful to him in the context of the Afro-Asian politics looming up before the Algiers conference — although there was a significant divergence of interests between Indonesia and China even there. But beyond these essentially 'symbolic' fringes, it made little difference to the hard realities of Indonesia's situation in 1965. The Chinese leaders gave Indonesia advice on how to crush Malaysia, but no practical help. The credit of $50 million they gave was no doubt welcome, but it was a mere drop in the bucket for a country which desperately needed to find well over $200 million a year more than she was earning from exports — a sum which China could not possibly contribute. Moreover, Soekarno himself was still trying to avoid becoming entirely beholden to China alone (hence his desire to incorporate the new relationship within a broader CONEFO framework) or to the PKI. But in the circuitous domestic politics of early 1965, the steady drift towards the left in Indonesia seemed almost irresistible and it was perhaps here that the impact of the new relationship was most strongly felt, for the militantly revolutionary spirit epitomized by the CONEFO concept became part of the new legitimacy. How far the Sino-Indonesian partnership would have led if the coup of 1 October had not intervened one can only guess, for it could not offer any resolution of Indonesia's fundamental problems of political instability (except in the unlikely event of producing a Communist regime capable of achieving stability on the basis of economic self-sufficiency almost overnight) and it could only continue so long as the now shaky Indonesian economy could be kept under control. It provided Soekarno with an opportunity to provide yet newer and better political circuses, but not bread.

AFRO-ASIAN DIPLOMACY, 1965

Preparations for the Second Afro-Asian Conference at Algiers absorbed an extraordinary amount of Indonesian diplomatic energy and attention in the first half of 1965. The reasons for Soekarno's almost obsessive concern that the conference be held were complex, however, and as the conference approached it seemed more likely to prove embarrassing for him than fruitful on the Malaysia issue.

One of his principal aims was to ensure that Malaysia would be excluded from the Afro-Asian family of nations so as to leave no doubt about her diplomatic isolation and inferior status as a British client state. If she had been excluded it would have been a further endorsement of Soekarno's charges that she was not truly Asian, and a severe blow to Malaysia's self-esteem, although it would hardly have had a decisive effect on her ability to resist Indonesian confrontation. Conversely, it would have been a severe set-back for Soekarno if she had been admitted. There were several indications that the Indonesians were hoping that Malaysia might be sufficiently alarmed by the possibility of exclusion to make the concessions Soekarno was demanding for the sake of a negotiated settlement of the Malaysia dispute.[20] If this was the case, they had misjudged the Malaysian leaders badly, but one wonders how realistic their political assessments on these issues were by this stage and how coloured by their own preconceptions and wishful thinking. Indonesian diplomats were extremely confident early in the year that Malaysia would be excluded, but as the conference approached in June many foreign observers believed it was more likely that she would be admitted.[21]

The question became entangled also with that of Russia's inclusion in the conference, which cut both ways. Russia wanted Indonesia's support vis-à-vis China who was opposing her application, so the issue gave Indonesia some political leverage over her in this regard. On the other hand, the necessity for Indonesia to choose between Russia and China was bound to be an embarrassment. At an earlier preparatory meeting on the Conference, no agreement could be reached about the eligibility of Malaysia and Russia, whom India had supported but Indonesia and China had opposed. Regarding Malaysia, who was obviously entitled to attend in the eyes of some delegations, the hope was expressed that 'obstacles which prevented reaching a consensus on the invitation would be eliminated' (i.e. confrontation be brought to an end). But no agreement was reached even on the question of how or by whom the issue of invitations should be settled, although it was later accepted that the preliminary meeting of Afro-Asian Foreign Ministers in Algiers immediately preceding the Conference would make the final decisions.[22] Russia therefore put pressure on Indonesia to support or cease opposing her claim for membership, but there was a curious connection between the Russian and Malaysian case which made the political tactics involved quite unpredictable. Indonesia had no particular interest in excluding Russia (except insofar as she needed to side with China on this matter), but she did want to exclude Malaysia and was presumably hoping to take advantage of the former issue to strengthen her stand on the latter. India, for instance, had a stronger interest in achieving Russia's inclusion (as a counter-weight to China) than Malaysia's, however strongly she believed in Malaysia's right to be there: some Indonesians were hoping that she could be pressed to drop her support for Malaysia in order to ensure Russia's inclusion. Even China and Indonesia had divergent aims on the membership question, although they were in broad agreement about the radical ideological themes they wanted the Conference to adopt. It was reported that Chou En-lai informed Dr. Subandrio at the end of May that China might have to drop her opposition to Malaysia in order to win other Afro-Asian votes against Russia.[23] Indonesia was in precisely the reverse predicament. But in spite of increasing uncertainty that she could keep Malaysia out, she remained the most enthusiastic advocate of holding the Algiers meeting, even when it became clear that not all Afro-Asian states were willing to attend.

Three different Afro-Asian meetings were held in Indonesia during March and April to focus attention on the forthcoming conference and to celebrate the original Bandung meeting ten years earlier. It is difficult to account for all this expensive and time-consuming activity just in terms of the concrete benefits to be expected from the Algiers conference in the struggle against Malaysia. Equally significant was the fact that all this diplomacy served domestic purposes also, by providing Soekarno with an international stage and an opportunity to demonstrate his stature as a world leader, by providing immediate objectives and tasks for the politicians around him and key dates in the political calendar upon which other political decisions had to wait. The abrupt timing of the tenth anniversary of the original Bandung Conference in April seems to indicate that it was conceived at least partly in order to provide a display of national solidarity at a time of acute political tension.[24] Domestic attention was also focused on the broader confrontation taking place upon the Afro-Asian stage and away from the less tractable Malaysia problem. But even the extravagant tinsel and glitter of the occasion was barely sufficient to disguise the lack of political substance in the whole affair. Coming as it did at a time of severe economic difficulties, just after Soekarno had proclaimed to his people the need for a new economic policy of self-sufficiency and austerity ('Standing on Our Own Feet'), the anniversary celebration represented the apotheosis of Soekarno's forays into political showmanship pure and simple.[25]

The overthrow of President Ben Bella by the Algerian Revolutionary Council under Col. Boumedienne on 19 June, only a few days before the Afro-Asian delegates were due to assemble for the forthcoming Algiers Conference, gave a dramatic twist to the whole episode and was eagerly seized upon by some governments as a reason for postponement. But it has been aptly observed that 'Ben Bella's fall provided the occasion but not the explanation for the postponement'.[26] It was not so much uncertainties about the new regime's policies or apprehensions about the security situation in Algiers which weighed upon most of the participants so much as the fact that many were glad to seize any credible excuse to avoid holding the conference at all by this time. Both China and Indonesia announced recognition for the new Boumedienne regime with almost indecent speed on 20 June, although Indonesia did not subsequently go quite so far out on a limb as China in her efforts to bulldoze waverers into holding the conference during the following week. However, a bomb explosion in the conference hall just before the proceedings were due to begin provided a decisive reason for postponing the meeting until November. Soekarno's hopes of Afro-Asian solidarity in the struggle against the *Nekolim* and Malaysia fell to the ground.

The Algiers conference had a paradoxical epilogue, for by November it was China and Indonesia who wanted a further postponement. The entire situation had changed fundamentally by then because of the coup in Indonesia and the consequent Sino-Indonesian rift and, to a lesser extent, the complications introduced by the India-Pakistan war and the intensification of the Sino-Soviet split. When the Standing Committee met late in October, China submitted several preconditions for the holding of the conference which she must have known would be unacceptable to some members. When they were not accepted, she announced that she would not attend. Indonesia made no protest this time, for Soekarno's power had already been greatly reduced in fact, although not yet in form, as a result of the coup. She no longer wanted the conference either. Subandrio was not even allowed to attend the Standing Committee meeting. India administered the ultimate indignity with a motion proposing the inclusion, *inter alia*, of Malaysia and the Soviet Union! The meeting then adjourned *sine die*. The myth of Afro-Asian solidarity was dead.[27]

SINGAPORE'S SEPARATION FROM MALAYSIA

For nearly a year, Indonesia had made little concrete progress towards her goal of 'crushing' Malaysia when suddenly the summary ejection of Singapore from the Federation, which owed nothing whatever to Indonesia's efforts, brought new life to her flagging hopes. It was promptly seized upon as proof that Soekarno had been right all along in regarding Malaysia as a ramshackle and unnatural creation of the *Nekolim*. Did it not presage the further disintegration of Malaysia? As matters turned out, it did not, but perhaps there was some ground for expecting so, in view of the fierce controversy that had preceded Singapore's separation throughout the early part of 1965, to which we must briefly turn.

Reconsidering their political strategy towards the end of 1964 in the light of their set-back in the Malayan election and the race riots, the PAP leadership decided to launch an ideological offensive, in the hope of attracting Malays to the PAP through ideology, 'not by the present PAP leaders taking an aggressive lead and setting the pace of politics, but more by helping to quicken the emergence of like-minded leaders domiciled in the Peninsula'.[28] This new policy was expressed in the formation of the Malaysian Solidarity Convention under PAP leadership in April 1965, and in the emergence of the doctrine of 'Malaysian Malaysia'. This vaguely tendentious, but terribly effective slogan, with its implication (frequently made explicit) that opponents of the PAP stood for something less than this, for a 'Malay Malaysia' or Malay dominance, served Lee Kuan Yew's purposes brilliantly — far too brilliantly, as it turned out — by serving as a rallying point for all who were dissatisfied with the existing arrangements, by presenting a persuasive image to the outside world and by putting UMNO critics of the PAP into a defensive and disadvantageous position. The essentials of the new doctrine are summarized in the following statement of 'fundamental principles' on which Malaysia had been founded.

(a) Malaysia should be a democratic society where legitimate differences of views provided they accept undivided loyalty to the Malaysian nation should be permitted and where individuals and political parties should have full freedom to persuade its citizens, by constitutional means, to their particular point of view.

(b) Malaysia being a multi-racial and multi-cultural society must show respect and tolerance for legitimate diversity provided these do not weaken Malaysian unity or hamper loyalty to Malaysia.

(c) Malaysia was conceived as belonging to Malaysians as a whole and not any particular community or race.

But in the PAP view, Malaysia had degenerated into a non-Malaysian Malaysia where there were people who identified 'the spirit and essence of Malaysia with the interests and norms of one particular community or with the authority of one particular political party. For them, being a Malaysian means all other communities and groups adjusting themselves to the views and specific aspirations of a particular community'.[29] The PAP leaders did not directly oppose the Malay and native rights and privileges embodied in the constitution of Malaysia, but they did indirectly threaten them by arguing that special privileges alone would not advance the economic and social condition of the Malays. What was needed they suggested, was a 'rational economic method of abolishing rural poverty', which the PAP knew how to produce, since it had already begun to abolish urban poverty by realistic planning and efficient administration in Singapore. They attacked the 'feudal' nature of the old Malay society which the defenders of Malay rights and advocates of Malay as the sole national language wanted to preserve, pointing the way instead to the Malaysia of the future, a new multi-racial society based on democratic socialism, instead of 'Alliancism, i.e. the policies of conservative Malay traditionalist leaders collaborating with Chinese compradores and capitalists for mutual benefit'. Like the Socialist Front five years earlier, the PAP wanted to see parties appealing across the racial barriers on the basis of policies, doctrines and rational argument, embracing the poor Chinese and Indians as well as poor Malays, against the existing parties dominated by the upper classes.[30] Unfortunately, however, this beautiful dream has never exerted an effective political appeal in Malaya.

The PAP arguments were spelled out with a beguiling persuasiveness (to all except Malays, it sometimes seemed) at nearly every point. The 'moderate' Malay leaders such as the Tunku were never attacked, but were regarded as sharing an identity of purpose with the PAP. In fact they had to be helped in dealing with the 'ultras' who were forcing them to take up untenable positions in defence of the special rights of Malays and the old conservative social order in Malaysia. If necessary, they had to be compelled to dissociate from the latter by being made aware of the risk of communal conflict towards which the country was being pushed by advocates of Malay dominance within the Alliance. If such conflict was going to come, argued PAP spokesmen (in private quite frankly, but more discreetly in public), it would come at a time and place of our choosing next time: 'we are not afraid to show the mailed fist'. There was a fiercely Puritan sense of moral fervour in the PAP advocacy of 'Malaysian Malaysia', a belief that passivity and lack of specific loyalty to this goal had left opportunities open to their more assertive and bigoted opponents, the 'ultras' or 'five mad Mullahs' as Lee was later to call them, to stir up racial strife. There must be no more compromise now that the lines of battle were drawn. The moderates in Malaya had to be forced, if necessary, to take a stand against the UMNO extremists, who were now constantly attacking the PAP through their mouthpiece *Utusan Melayu* in a bitter polemic which persisted through 1965. Unless they did so, there was a danger of Malaysia breaking up through internal conflict.[31] Although there were no further outbreaks of racial violence after September 1964, the fear that it might recur at any moment (especially when the Muslim and Chinese New Year holidays coincided at the end of January 1965) remained acute until the following August.

However, the Tunku's reaction to Lee's 'foolish and harmful and dangerous' argument was quite the opposite to that which Lee was urging. Instead of repudiating the 'ultras', he set out to strengthen the Alliance by making more explicit its basic philosophy of coexistence between communally based parties on a basis of mutual accommodation (a safe and traditional doctrine reminiscent of earlier Malay and Chinese modes of adjustment to multi-racial situations in the region) and by formally establishing a 'Malaysian Alliance Party' as a merger of the Alliance parties of all four states in April.[32] He urged the Singapore leaders to concentrate their thought and efforts on making Singapore into the foremost city and biggest port in Asia, instead of bidding for political power in Kuala Lumpur on the basis of an appeal to non-Malay voters. The Chinese should concentrate on economic power and leave political power to the Malays, he was virtually arguing. He had one undeniably valid point in his favour: no matter how much the PAP talked about multi-racialism and offering a new leadership to the rural Malay voters, its basic political support was bound to come from the urban Chinese — and this was precisely the threat it offered if it entered the peninsula as a vigorous political force. (The very fact that it had only contested urban seats with mainly Chinese voters in the April elections in order to avoid a conflict with UMNO could be thrown back in its teeth here.) The PAP simply could not escape its Chinese-ness — with all the disadvantages and advantages vis-à-vis Malays that this entailed. In the Borneo states, the notion of 'Malaysian Malaysia' appealed mainly to the non-Malays who were uneasy about an UMNO-dominated Alliance. It is hardly surprising that Malay moderates, as well as the 'ultras', found the implications of the 'Malaysian Malaysia' doctrine too much to swallow. One of the former, Musa bin Hitam, argued that PAP talk about multi-racialism was itself evidence of the party's communal base.

The very subtle insinuations of the PAP leaders by propagation of non-communalism and equality of status in Malaysia at the moment naturally provoke communal sentiments. And as long as the PAP leaders imply in their speeches that no race should enjoy privileges and protection from the other so long will there be a hardening of attitudes in the different communities in Malaysia.[33]

Putting essentially the same point rather differently, it could be said that equality of political rights was almost certain to prove disadvantageous to the Malays even if they were numerically equal to the non-Malays (which they no longer were) so long as they were inferior in economic and educational status in an individualistic and competitive society. 'All the business, the wealth, and the trade in this country are in the hands of non-Malays. Hardly 1 per cent of the Malays are in business and hardly 15 per cent of those in Universities abroad or at home are Malays. If these rights are taken away what hope is there for the Malay to survive in his own country.'[34] Hence the Malay stress on maintaining their unity to meet the challenge of other races and their savage attacks on 'traitors to their race' in Singapore who went so far as to join the PAP. (The bitterness of these attacks on Malays in the PAP far exceeded that directed against *Party Ra'ayat* left-wingers or collaborators with Indonesia; the attacks contributed greatly to the anger within the PAP against the 'ultras', since it was desperately anxious to win Malay members so as to appear genuinely multi-racial.) One of Lee Kuan Yew's intellectual blind spots was an inability to appreciate the peculiar importance of loyalty to the Malay *ra'ayat* — loyalty to their race, their leaders and their religion — and the concomitant stress on unity. To him, the Cambridge-educated cosmopolitan brought up in the thrusting and individualistic Chinese society of Singapore, these were merely attributes of a 'feudal' society which had to be transformed. His multi-racial political parties based on ideology would recruit members on an individual basis, regardless of community. (But if the Malays would not join him and parties remained essentially communal, he could probably expect to attract Chinese support in the long run, so it was a 'Heads I win; tails you lose' strategy in a sense.) The Tunku saw the dangers of Lee's challenge as clearly as Syed Ja'afar Albar, though his response was milder. Lee's strategy was forcing him to a choice between the devil and the deep sea, for the UMNO extremists might easily gain control of the party if the Tunku could not contain the threat from the PAP. To side with the latter, metaphorically, by acquiescing in the PAP doctrines and letting their challenge succeed by default, would merely have provoked the UMNO extremists and split both UMNO and the Alliance. The Tunku was well aware of the dangers of communal extremism, but he was hard put to formulate an alternative doctrine that could be held up as a counter to 'Malaysian Malaysia' and unite both moderate Malays and the 'ultras'. The Alliance philosophy of accommodation and gradual change was not a very exciting or attractive alternative, but in the circumstances it was probably the best available — as even Donald Stephens' highly critical *Sabah Times* was to acknowledge later, after a flirtation with 'Malaysian Malaysia' which proved disastrous to Stephens' political fortunes.[35] Unfortunately, it made less appeal to transient foreigners who were delighted by the sophistication of Lee Kuan Yew's arguments and horrified by the intolerance of *Utusan Melayu*, which the Tunku seemed powerless to control — with the result that the Kuala Lumpur authorities became excessively sensitive to outside criticisms. Lee's trip to Australia in early 1965, which was a *tour de force* in public relations, alarmed the UMNO leaders greatly and contributed further to the tensions that the Tunku was finding ever harder to resolve.

The creation of the Malaysian Solidarity Convention was a concrete manifestation of the 'Malaysian Malaysia' sentiment, but it is questionable whether it was in itself an immediate threat to the Alliance, for its long list of member parties accounted for only four seats in the federal parliament.[36] Potentially, however, it might have constituted a future focus of much broader electoral opposition to the Alliance which could prove far more cohesive and determined than the flaccid opposition of PMIP and Socialist Front in the past. Donald Stephens' UPKO was restless within the Sarawak Alliance and openly sympathetic to the 'Malaysian Malaysia' doctrine: if the MSC succeeded in undermining the Alliance in Sabah, it might succeed in doing likewise in Sarawak, where the SUPP leaders were definitely sympathetic to it and even some of the Alliance parties inclined towards its point of view.

From May onwards, the political tensions built up rapidly. At an UMNO Assembly in the middle of the month, the Tunku and Dr. Ismail had difficulty in persuading the delegates to keep calm and ignore Lee's 'childish statements' against the Malays. A resolution calling on the government to detain Lee could only be watered down to a demand for 'strong action' against him. Lee added fuel to the flames by a speech in which he said: 'If we must have trouble, let us have it now instead of waiting for another five or ten years. If we find Malaysia cannot work now then we can make other arrangements.[37] This was interpreted by many Malays as a threat to secede, although Lee denied any such intention strenuously (and sincerely, it seems, for his commitment to the Malaysia concept was still beyond question, however dissatisfied he was with the terms of the association): in the vicious dialectics of his quarrel with *Utusan Melayu*, his pugnacious manner of challenging his opponents to follow out the implications of their own utterances could be too easily twisted into a misinterpretation of his own views. The May-June session of Parliament was stormy and when the Tunku flew off to London in June, he must have been full of foreboding about the future. He later said that he took the decision to separate Singapore from Malaysia while he was lying in hospital in London.

In his absence, the situation deteriorated further. Another attempt by Tun Razak to reach agreement with Lee (strongly opposed by the UMNO Youth Organization) was a failure. And, ironically, one of the last scenes in the drama was another by-election in the Singapore constituency of Hong Lim, in which Lee's campaign speeches were directed as much against the Alliance and the UMNO 'ultras' as against the now debilitated *Barisan Sosialis;* he even charged the Singapore branch of the Alliance with supporting the pro-Communist, anti-Malaysian *Barisan* in the election.[38] The PAP, he said, was the only alternative to Communism and a Malaysian Malaysia was the only alternative to Malay domination which would drive the Chinese into opposition. There is a tragically appropriate symbolism in the contrast between the second Hong Lim by-election and the first.

The separation of Singapore was announced by the Tunku on 9 August, just after he returned from overseas and three days after he first raised the issue with Lee and the federal cabinet.[39] The broad outlines of the story are now too well-known to need repeating — how the federal government kept the decision a closely-wrapped secret until it was ready to confront the world (and particularly Malaysia's beholden defenders, Britain and Australia, who were almost sure to oppose the decision) with a *fait accompli;* how three Singapore ministers refused to sign the separation agreement until the Tunku himself sent a letter stating that ' ... if I were strong enough and able to exercise complete control of the situation I might perhaps have delayed action, but I am not' (a letter which Toh Chin Chye promptly published, to the annoyance and embarrassment of the Tunku) and how Lee Kuan Yew, in his press conference explaining why Singapore was no longer a part of Malaysia, broke down briefly in anguish before the television cameras when he came to the words: '... all my life ... You see ... the whole of my adult life I had believed in merger and the unity of these two territories ... as a people connected by geography, economics and ties of kinship ....' Lee said he had tried to persuade the Tunku to maintain some formal constitutional link between the two states, but the Tunku insisted that their disagreements had reached a stage where Singapore must leave the federation if further racial conflict was to be avoided and 'I finally became convinced that the Tunku was right on this'.

Singapore's expulsion was, of course, a great boost to Indonesian hopes, since it opened up new possibilities of exploiting rifts between Kuala Lumpur, Singapore and London. A speech by Lee Kuan Yew expressing a desire to resume trade and friendlier relations with Indonesia struck a different note from the Tunku's speeches — and was angrily rebuked by the latter. Subandrio immediately offered to recognize Singapore and establish diplomatic relations with her if she 'declared her independence', but statements by Soekarno and other Indonesian leaders were too uncompromising to encourage any feelers in this matter.

SABAH AND SARAWAK IN MALAYSIA

The incorporation of the Borneo territories in Malaysia, which had originally seemed the most questionable part of the Malaysia experiment, was achieved, paradoxically, with far less initial strain than the incorporation of Singapore. During the first two years the strains and difficulties of readjustment were relatively minor ones, not sufficient to disrupt the Alliance pattern in either state or to cause serious dissension between those two wings of the Alliance and the central government in Kuala Lumpur. Serious strains became manifest only in 1965–6. No doubt confrontation helped to mask or delay the development of the fissiparous tendencies which became manifest soon after the expulsion of Singapore and the effective ending of confrontation, but it was to the former rather than the latter that we can mainly attribute the political conflicts which developed in both Sabah and Sarawak in 1965–6, to the aftermath of the debate over 'Malaysian Malaysia' and to the fears of federal domination which were aroused by Singapore's separation. It was inevitable, of course, that strains would develop within the two state Alliances sooner or later. They were, after all, hastily contrived coalitions whose main unifying bond had simply been their common support of the Malaysia idea in 1962, but they included groups with significantly different views about the nature of the Alliance pattern and the kind of relationship they wanted to have with Kuala Lumpur.[40] Perhaps the most surprising feature of the first two years was that these differences first began to create difficulties in Sabah which had earlier seemed so tranquil, rather than uneasy Sarawak, where the opportunities for Indonesian subversion were greatest because of the SCO threat which loomed constantly in the background of the political picture.

The Sabah Alliance, which assumed the reins of government in September 1963, held all 18 seats in the Legislative Council, which meant that the politics of Sabah were essentially thrashed out within the Alliance and the Cabinet, rather than the Legislative Council itself. The Alliance was a three-legged affair, for the Chinese party SANAP (Sabah National Party) with 4 seats held a balance of power between the Malay-Muslim party, USNO (United Sabah National Organization), led by Datu Mustapha, with 8 seats, and Donald Stephens' essentially Kadazan party, UNKO (United National Kadazan Organization), with 5. The *Pasok Momogon* also had 1 seat, but it was soon drawn into a merger with UNKO to create UPKO (United Pasok Kadazan Organization) in early 1964. It was agreed at the outset that Stephens would be Chief Minister and Datu Mustapha the first Head of State (*Yang di-Pertua Negara*) — a position which he is said to have chosen in preference to Chief Minister because of a misapprehension that it would be of similar importance to that of the colonial Governor, which of course it was not. Unfortunately, frictions soon developed between the two men on both personal and political grounds, with the result that twice in 1964 the Tunku had to be invoked as mediator to sort out crises in the Alliance. The first of these, in June, arose from various causes, partly USNO criticisms of Stephens' leadership (he appears to have antagonized many people at this time by his high-handedness) but also from fears in the other parties that Stephens was aiming to build UPKO into a position of predominance in the Alliance by presenting it as a multi-racial party and an example of 'the way people should get together'. There was a direct threat to SANAP here, if UPKO should succeed in recruiting large numbers of Chinese away from it, and an indirect one to USNO, which based its support almost entirely on the Malay-Muslim communities (though it claimed to be multi-racial also) and leaned towards the UMNO concept of communal parties. Among the nine conditions on which the June 1964 crisis was resolved was a stipulation that only 'natives' should be admitted to 'native' parties, while Chinese should only join SANAP.[41] The cabinet was reconstituted with 3 UPKO, 3 USNO and 2 SANAP ministers (with one nominated assemblyman, Thomas Jayasuriya, to keep the highly desirable portfolio of Natural Resources — i.e. timber concessions — in neutral hands) and an USNO man became Deputy Chief Minister.

Friction continued, however, as both USNO and UPKO ministers continued to score points off each other over various issues for the rest of 1964. There were difficulties between the government and the Deputy Federal Secretary, whom UPKO leaders accused of trying to establish Kuala

Lumpur domination over Sabah, and a growing cleavage between the 'states rights' attitude of the UPKO leaders and the 'federalist' views of USNO, which was suspected by its enemies of negotiating to establish a close relationship with UMNO as its Sabah wing. Although there was a slight lull in the running battle between the two parties during September and again when the Tunku visited Sabah for 'National Solidarity Week' in November, another crisis arose in the following month over a controversial appointment by Stephens to the politically sensitive position of State Secretary.[42] USNO threatened to move a vote of no-confidence against Stephens and UPKO countered with a similar threat against Datu Mustapha! Again the Tunku's mediation was sought, but this time he could not resolve the impasse and it was intervention by the Chief Minister of Sarawak which finally brought a solution. The party representation in the cabinet remained the same, but Stephens had to step down as Chief Minister and join the federal cabinet as Minister for Sabah Affairs (an honorific post which carried little power and required him to be exiled from his home base) while Peter Lo of SANAP, the former federal Minister, assumed the Chief Ministership and the USNO Deputy Chief Minister gave way to an UPKO man. The change represented a significant shift in the balance of power in Sabah, for SANAP had, in effect, thrown its weight on to the USNO side; thus UPKO had lost its advantageous position in the Alliance, which it did not regain. Although Peter Lo had earlier been appointed to the federal cabinet by Stephens, he was said to have acquired a 'federal' point of view while in Kuala Lumpur, and there was less friction between the Jesselton and federal governments in the following year, despite the explosive potentialities of the 'Malaysian Malaysia' issue in 1965.

Donald Stephens and his fiery young lieutenants in UPKO continued to talk about the need for a multi-racial party in terms startlingly like Lee Kuan Yew's, with whose views they were beginning to discover a closer affinity than they had felt for the UMNO view of political parties and the nature of the Malaysia relationship. UPKO would doubtless have thrown in its lot with Lee Kuan Yew's Malaysia Solidarity Convention in 1965 had it not been bound to the Alliance, with which Stephens was finding himself increasingly out of sympathy. The UPKO leaders maintained in early 1965 that they would return to power in the next elections (for which preparations were already being made, although it was to take two more years before they were held) by making a broader appeal as a multi-racial party than USNO, which they characterized as narrowly communal and subservient to Kuala Lumpur, or SANAP, which they despised in much the same way as Lee Kuan Yew despised the MCA.[43] This philosophy was bound to alienate SANAP and drive it closer to USNO, in the hope of preserving its position as the party representing the Chinese in a classical Alliance system, even though a Chinese-Muslim affiliation may seem a more unnatural arrangement than a Chinese-Kadazan one. UPKO's principles may have been admirable, but the harsh realities of power worked against them, just as they had worked against Lee Kuan Yew.

Months before the exclusion of Singapore brought the problem to a head for them, UPKO politicians were having second thoughts about Sabah's entry into Malaysia and dreaming wistfully about a looser relationship with the federal government, though not of leaving the federation. Their apprehensions about Kuala Lumpur's high-handedness were increased by the way Singapore was summarily ejected from the Federation, without any consultation with the other constituent states. A statement was issued by UPKO on 16 August calling for a reconsideration of Sabah's terms of participation in Malaysia. The Sabah Alliance set up a committee to look into the matter. Then the Tunku flew to Jesselton and Stephens was required either to dissociate himself from UPKO or resign from the federal cabinet: he chose the latter and withdrew from the UPKO leadership soon after.[44] But UPKO's call evoked no response amongst its Sabah Alliance partners and it was in no position to do much about it while it remained in the minority there. Its disillusionment with Malaysia was no doubt a sad commentary on the high hopes of the 1961 Malaysian Solidarity Consultative Committees, but it was not by any means enough to bring about Sabah's withdrawal.

As matters turned out, UPKO did not even withdraw from the Alliance after Singapore's separation, although there was a good deal of discussion about doing so, about fighting the forthcoming elections alone and even adopting a secessionist policy. The latter would probably have meant courting dissolution under the Internal Security Regulations, while the former would certainly have meant exile to the political wilderness, at the very least. So the party decided, instead, to live and fight again.[45] Even during the 1966 Sarawak crisis, which again brought up the question of how far the federal government should be able to interfere in state politics, UPKO avoided any clash with its partners in the Sabah Alliance. And at the end of that year, not long before the 1967 election which it contested in harness with (but also against) its Alliance partners, UPKO formally abandoned its earlier claim to be a non-communal party by limiting its membership to 'natives' (*bumiputera*). It explained this change in terms which showed that it had learned the lesson of Lee Kuan Yew's sad fate (or Donald Stephens', though he was to attempt a come-back shortly after, in a more chastened frame of mind): 'UPKO desires a better understanding with other parties ... and realises the need to comply with the Alliance pattern of having racial parties working within a multi-racial framework .... The best system is that which has worked successfully in Malaya'.[46]

The Sarawak Alliance, in contrast with its Sabah counterpart, enjoyed nearly three years of outward tranquility before it cracked under the strain of communal tensions and personal rivalries among its member parties, although the latter were at least as acute as Sabah's. But the sheer arithmetic of party representation in the Council Negri contributed a degree of stability there, in contrast to the rather precarious balance in Sabah, for no one party, or even two, could hope to win a majority immediately. In fact, the Chief Minister, Stephen Kalong Ningkan, became an avowed advocate of the need for communal cooperation within a multi-racial Alliance in which the experienced and wealthy Chinese of the SCA (Sarawak Chinese Association) would play a prominent part.[47] The main cleavage that began to develop — and finally undermined the unity of the Sarawak Alliance in 1966 — stemmed largely from differences of opinion between supporters of Ningkan's view and those who wanted the Alliance to give preponderant influence to 'native' parties, a cleavage with many similarities to that which existed in Sabah between the UPKO and USNO views on the nature of the Alliance system and the relationship between the State governments and the Federal government or Alliance in Kuala Lumpur.

It may be remembered that the Sarawak Alliance had emerged from the 1963 indirect elections with an overwhelming majority in the Council Negri, 27 out of the 36 elected seats there, while the two parties outside the Alliance, PANAS and SUPP, had only 8 seats between them. Within the Alliance 11 seats were held by Temenggong (later Tan Sri) Jugah's PESAKA party, based essentially on the Iban of the 3rd Division, while SNAP, the 2nd Division Iban party led by the Chief Minister, Stephen Ningkan, had only 7, BARJASA (the Malay-Melanau party) had 6 and SCA 3.[48] The latter two had fared very badly at the polls and had to be given nominated seats in the Council Negri, as even their leaders had been defeated; but they were both represented strongly in the Cabinet and proceeded to play a very active part in Alliance politics there.[49] Personal antagonisms seriously exacerbated party rivalries within the Alliance, although its stability was assured so long as Ningkan had the backing of Tan Sri Jugah and PESAKA, as he did until June 1966. He was able to survive an abortive bid in May 1965 by the BARJASA leaders to create a frankly anti-Chinese 'Native Alliance Party' and overthrow Ningkan's government. While confrontation posed an immediate threat to Sarawak, the tensions within the Alliance were muted, of course, whereas a considerable political ferment seems to have developed in early 1966 as the threat began to recede and politicians became more concerned with the problem of how to widen their party's basis of popular support in anticipation of the next general election in 1968 or 1969.

Confrontation helped the government indirectly by creating serious difficulties for SUPP, the only party opposed to the Malaysia experiment and without doubt the best organized and largest in Sarawak. Many of its members were either involved or suspected of involvement in SCO activities; others actually crossed the border to join the Indonesians, creating a serious embarrassment for the party leaders, who were hesitant to condemn or disavow them but who could be taunted with the charge of disloyalty if they did not. Many of the government's measures against the SCO affected SUPP disadvantageously (although they cut two ways, insofar as the arrest of the militants helped the moderates like Ong Kee Hui and Stephen Yong to maintain their positions) and at one stage during 1964 there was a possibility that SUPP might be banned altogether.[50] But although SUPP was probably still supported by a considerable majority of the Chinese in Sarawak, who had some reason to feel aggrieved by the disadvantages to which their party was being exposed, the Chinese were not as severely victimized under the new political dispensation as some of the SCO's earlier prophecies might have led them to fear. (In fact, it was they who reaped the most immediate benefits, on the whole, from the economic boost Sarawak enjoyed after its entry to Malaysia from increased Federal expenditure and the bonanza of defence forces' spending.) Ningkan's government, moreover, showed that it was willing to alleviate some of the hardships confronting the Chinese, notably their shortage of land, and he was more inclined towards a moderate concept of a multi-racial Alliance system than some of his colleagues.

On several contentious issues such as language and education policy, 'Borneanization' of the civil service and Federal interference in Sarawak affairs, Ningkan found himself at odds with the federal government and the Sarawak advocates of an essentially 'Malay Malaysia'. He resisted pressures to hasten the replacement of British expatriates by Malaysians (which was likely to mean Malays rather than Ibans or other natives) or to substitute Malay for English as the medium for school instruction and official business. Although some tensions arose between Kuching and Kuala Lumpur during 1964–5, they did not create such serious threats to Malaysia's political stability as those of Sabah and Singapore. It is significant that Lee Kuan Yew's campaign for a 'Malaysian Malaysia' evoked less response within the Sarawak Alliance than in its Sabah counterpart: the only Sarawak representatives at the Malaysia Solidarity Convention in 1965 were Ong Kee Hui, Stephen Yong and other non-Alliance politicians.[51] But it was essentially on the same questions of the special political position of 'native' parties with the Alliance system that Ningkan's rivals, particularly the BARJASA leaders and some PESAKA politicians, manoeuvred to build up opposition to him.

The first rift in the Sarawak Alliance occurred in May 1965 when the BARJASA leaders withdrew with the aim of establishing a 'Native Alliance Party' with PESAKA. The immediate cause of this rift was a set of land bills introduced by Ningkan into the Council Negri which would have made it easier for Chinese to obtain land. The opposition from the 'native' parties was so strong that Ningkan had to back down, but by ensuring the continued support of PESAKA and threatening to bring the other Malay party, PANAS, into the government in place of BARJASA, he succeeded in isolating the latter and preventing the overthrow of the government. The crisis soon blew over, with BARJASA returning to the fold, and the Cabinet was enlarged with two PESAKA ministers and one from PANAS (now received back into the Alliance after two years in opposition), but the tensions it revealed persisted into the following year when a more formidable challenge to Ningkan finally brought about his overthrow.[52]

The separation of Singapore from Malaysia caused few ripples on the surface of Sarawak politics. Confrontation was still causing serious concern there and Ningkan's speech immediately after the separation crisis was simply a homily on the need for unity and avoidance of subversive sentiments. Even the coup in Indonesia soon afterwards, which was to mark the beginning of the end of confrontation, was not hailed as enthusiastically in Kuching as in Kuala Lumpur, for border raids into Sarawak continued until well into 1966, although on a reduced scale. Ironically, just as Indonesia and Malaysia were finally patching up a settlement of their quarrel in 1966, a major crisis exploded in the Sarawak Alliance which two years earlier would have ideally served the purposes of Indonesian propaganda about Kuala Lumpur's high-handed treatment of the Borneo states.

Gradual shifts in party affiliations and alignments were only to be expected, of course, in view of the rather hasty formation of parties and the Sarawak Alliance four years earlier. PESAKA was beginning to make inroads into SNAP's political base among the 2nd Division Iban, aided by the fact that Ningkan's personal influence there was crumbling. He was losing popularity for various reasons (and he had never been a strikingly charismatic leader) — partly his alleged neglect of native interests and close association with James Wong, the wealthy Chinese Deputy Chief Minister, partly that his behaviour offended both the sophisticates who deplored some of his longhouse mannerisms and Iban traditionalists who felt he had become too aloof and westernized. Several prominent SNAP politicians, including Penghulu Tawi Sli, who was later to supplant him, switched over to PESAKA, which was relatively under-represented in the Cabinet in proportion to its strength as the major Iban party. Ningkan was converting SNAP into a more multi-racial party, with Chinese members and a branch in the 1st Division, and he was in much closer sympathy with the PANAS leaders, who also espoused a doctrine of multi-racialism, despite their essentially Malay following, than with PESAKA and BARJASA which were quite frankly communal and anti-Chinese in their political doctrines.[53] The latter were also more inclined to look to Kuala Lumpur for help in attaining power, like their Sabah counterpart, USNO. Attempts were made by the Tunku and other UMNO leaders to create a united Malay party through the merger of PANAS and BARJASA, but without success.[54] While personal antagonisms dating back to the Cession controversy evidently had a lot to do with this, so also did the basic difference of opinion between those who wanted a Malay communal party affiliated with UMNO (the BARJASA view) and those who favoured a single multi-racial Alliance.

The crisis which led to Ningkan's dismissal in June 1966 is of interest to this story mainly because it epitomizes essentially the same conflict between two conceptions of Malaysia as the earlier troubles in Singapore and Sabah did. It started on 12 June when Ningkan dismissed Abdul Taib, the BARJASA Minister of Works and Communications (who had been the storm centre the previous year also), charging him with instigating plots against the government. But BARJASA had the support of Temenggong Jugah and PESAKA this time: their ministers resigned and a delegation from these parties flew to Kuala Lumpur for talks with the Tunku. The Tunku then announced that he had a letter from a majority of the Council Negri calling for Ningkan's resignation and, in his capacity as Federal Head of the Alliance, called upon the Governor of Sarawak to demand Ningkan's resignation.[55] Constitutionally, the Tunku's action was an extraordinary incursion into state politics, though he asserted that it was normal practice for Chief Ministers or *Mentri Besar* of Alliance-governed states to be chosen by the Head of the Alliance Party. Moreover, the constitutional situation was complicated by the fact that Ningkan avoided a showdown with his opponents in the Council Negri, where he no longer commanded a majority, by suspending it in their absence and refusing to summon it.[56] On 15 June the Alliance National Council in Kuala Lumpur chose Penghulu Tawi Sli to succeed Ningkan as Chief Minister and he was duly installed. But the Sarawak Alliance was deeply split by the affair and when Ningkan withdrew SNAP from the Alliance early in July, he was supported by PANAS: moreover, it was only after some heart-searching that the SCA decided to remain in Tawi Sli's government. Ningkan then contested the legality of his dismissal in court and in September the verdict was given in his favour. But the federal government again intervened to prevent his return to office by declaring a State of Emergency in Sarawak.[56] While there may have been more justification for its action than met the eye, its intervention in Sarawak politics was so heavy-handed that it bore out many of the worst fears aroused earlier about Kuala Lumpur's disregard for state rights within the Malaysia framework. Ningkan and his allies were able to gain a good deal of popular sympathy as a result of his apparent victimization, but as an election was not due until 1968 or 1969, he could not do much to shake the new government's majority in the Council Negri.

One consequence of the affair was that SNAP and PANAS began to draw closer to SUPP in opposition to Tawi Sli's government. Here again, the opposition parties were more inclined to stress the need for multi-racial parties and an approach to major political issues that was closer to the 'Malaysian Malaysia' ideal, whereas their opponents were more concerned with a special relationship with the Kuala Lumpur government and a frankly communal party system in which 'natives' (as variously defined) would enjoy a privileged position. Somewhat fortuitously, it had come about that each of the three main communities of Sarawak was strongly represented in one of the parties on either side of the political spectrum — a situation which is certainly preferable to a straight-out cleavage on communal lines. The pattern might very well change after the second election, of course, and the party system in Sarawak has not yet stabilized by any means. Compromises and accommodation between the parties, within them and between the governments in Kuching and Kuala Lumpur will continue to be necessary. The degree of tact and wisdom shown by the federal government in its dealings with Sarawak will be a vital factor determining the viability of the political system there. From the experience of the first three years of Malaysia, it could not be argued conclusively that Sarawak's incorporation either had or had not demonstrated that the Malaysia experiment had succeeded.

[1]Extract from Soekarno's speech at the opening of the Tenth Anniversary Celebrations of the Bandung Conference: see *Ten Years After Bandung* (Djakarta, Department of Information, 1965), pp. 37–8.

[2]Extract from Soekarno's Independence Day Address, 17 August 1965, *Reach to the Stars! A Year of Self Reliance* (Djakarta, Department of Information, 1965), pp. 47–8.

[3]Uri Ra'anan, 'The Coup that Failed', *Problems of Communism*, vol. XV, no. 2, March-April 1966, pp. 37–9; H. Feith, 'President Soekarno, the Army and the Communists: the Triangle Changes Shape', *Asian Survey*, vol. IV, no. 8, August 1964, p. 978.

[4]See above, pp. 82–4, for contradictory estimates of the Army as an anti-Communist force; also Daniel S. Lev, 'Indonesia in 1965: The Year of the Coup', *Asian Survey*, vol. VI, no. 2, February 1966, pp. 103–10.

[5]On Subandrio's position vis-à-vis the PKI, the Army and Murba Party leaders in 1964, see Uri Ra'anan, op.cit. pp. 40–2 and Guy J. Pauker, 'Indonesia in 1964: Toward a 'People's Democracy'?' *Asian Survey*, vol. V. no. 2, February 1965, pp. 90 ff.

[6]See above p. 240.

[7]See Pauker, op. cit. pp. 92–5 for a fuller account of the BPS movement and its significance in the domestic power struggle; also Howard P. Jones, *Indonesia, the Possible Dream*, pp. 352–8.

[8]*Suluh Indonesia*, 4 December 1964.

[9]For the text of the Bogor Declaration, see ibid. 14 December 1964; compare the interpretations given in *Harian Rakjat* and *Berita Indonesia*, 14 and 15 December 1964. There was no reason to infer from these that Soekarno was at that stage preparing to side with the PKI against the BPS.

[10]On the Chen Yi visit, see above p. 287.

[11]The information on which this paragraph is based was obtained in discussions with Foreign Ministry officials and others in Djakarta in January 1965: Soekarno's speech on 7 January announcing his decision to break with the UN completely was published as *Mahkota Kemerdekaan Bukan Keanggautaan PBB, tetapi Berdiri diatas Kaki Sendiri.* ('The Crown of Independence is not Membership of the UN but standing on One's Own Feet'), (Djakarta, Department Penerangan RI, Penerbitan Chusus 355, 1965).

[12]*Suluh Indonesia*, 5 January 1964.

[13]For further details, see Lev, op. cit.

[14]D. P. Mozingo, *Sino-Indonesian Relations: an Overview, 1955–1965* (Memorandum RM-4641-PR, The Rand Corporation, California, 1965), p.v.

[15]Mary F. Somers Heidhues, 'Peking and the Overseas Chinese: the Malaysian Dispute', *Asian Survey*, vol. VI, no. 5, May 1966, pp. 280–2, discusses the various reasons for Peking's reticence in commenting upon the Malaysia issue — her hopes of gaining influence in the area through the Chinese of Malaysia and wariness about being identified with Chinese communal opposition to it. Cf. Mozingo, op. cit. p. 60.

[16]Mozingo, op. cit. p. 62, suggests that around September 1963 the Peking leaders decided to accept Indonesian domination of the southern extremity of South-East Asia as 'an acceptable price for a long-term alignment with that country on the basis of a common interest in excluding Western imperialism'.

[17]Uri Ra'anan, op. cit. p. 41.

[18]The joint statement is analysed in Mozingo, pp. 71–2. For the full text see *Suluh Indonesia*, 29 January 1963.

[19]Uri Ra'anan suggests that the Chinese 'intended merely to "train" a few Indonesian scientists and then stage what would have been billed as a "joint" Sino-Indonesian nuclear test. In fact this would still have been a purely Chinese bomb, while giving Soekarno the prestige he thirsted for'. Most of the references to an Indonesian bomb occurred in late July 1945 when an Indonesian delegate, Mrs. Utami Suryadarma, was attending the World Congress against Atomic and Hydrogen Bombs in Tokyo; Indonesia here defended the right to produce atomic weapons to resist imperialist aggression, so long as imperialism continued to threaten national independence and world peace. She may have felt constrained to do so on behalf of China rather than herself, but in a written message to the Congress, Soekarno claimed that Indonesia was *considering* the production of a bomb herself. See also his speech to the Muhammadiyah in Bandung on 24 July in which he was reported to have said 'God willing, Indonesia would soon produce its own atomic bomb'. Brig.-Gen. Hartono, Director of the Army Logistics Command (who was responsible for the original facetious reference to an Indonesian bomb in November 1964) said on 28 July in an interview with *Angkatan Bersendjata* that Indonesia would test its first atomic bomb after the Afro-Asian Conference.

Indonesia at that time had one small American reactor, quite insufficient to produce the fissionable material needed, but a much more powerful Russian reactor was under construction. It was barely conceivable that she had the facilities to produce a bomb on her own, but she was giving a good deal of publicity to every development in the nuclear field. The Chinese, by contrast, were being very reticent about their cooperation with the Indonesians.

[20]Indonesian officials endeavoured to convince me in January 1965 that the Malaysian government would be eager for a negotiated settlement before the Algiers conference because exclusion would be such a blow to them. The feelers put out through the Japanese envoy, Kawashima, at the end of April, just after the Bandung Conference 10th Anniversary, may have been intended to catch the Malaysians in a mood of diminished confidence; evidently Tunku Abdul Rahman was not prepared to make the concessions Soekarno wanted, however, for it was the latter who torpedoed the Kawashima mediation bid.

[21]For the view that 'the large majority of members would support Malaysia', see T. B. Millar and J. D. B. Miller, 'Afro-Asian Disunity: Algiers, 1965', *Australian Outlook*, vol. XIX, no. 3, December 1965, p. 315. But the decision on membership would not necessarily be a matter of majority vote: it was more likely to be a package deal. A more cautious view was expressed by Creighton Burns, South-East Asian correspondent of *The Age*, 28 May.

[22]The preparatory meeting of Afro-Asian Foreign Ministers held in Djakarta in April 1964 has been dealt with fully in Franklin B. Weinstein, 'The 2nd Afro-Asian Conference: Preliminary Bouts', *Asian Survey*, vol. V, no. 7, July 1965, pp. 359–73.

[23]Guy J. Pauker, 'The Rise and Fall of Asian Solidarity', *Asian Survey*, vol. V, no. 9, September 1965, p. 428. See also Uri Ra'anan, op. cit. for details of Russian attempts to induce Indonesia to support, or at least not oppose Russian membership.

[24]The *Dasawarsa* celebrations were only announced in late March, so late that it was not easy to obtain a reasonable number of Heads of State or senior dignitaries. A poorly-attended Afro-Asian Islamic Conference had been held in Bandung a short while before. The announcement came not long after the 'Malang incident', at a time of acute tensions between left and right wings in both Djakarta and the provinces. On 29 March a ban on all 'controversial statements and actions' was ordered, until the *Dasawarsa* celebrations were over.

[25]An entertaining but informative account of the *Dasawarsa* celebrations was given by Creighton Burns in *The Age*, 27 April 1965, p. 2 ('Djakarta Runs a Party'). For Soekarno's speeches at the *Dasawarsa* Conference (and some others) see *Ten Years After Bandung*. Creighton Burns drew attention to the almost complete neglect of the original Ten Principles of Bandung in the militant rhetoric encouraged by the Indonesian hosts.

[26]Millar and Miller, op. cit. p. 306.

[27]The November denouement is outlined briefly in Millar and Miller, op. cit. pp. 318–19.

[28]*Our First Ten Years*, PAP Tenth Anniversary Souvenir, 21 Nov., 1964, pp. 111–12, cited in R. K. Vasil, 'Why Malaysia Failed?', *Quest* (Calcutta), no. 49, April-June 1966, p. 58.

[29]Vasil, op. cit. p. 59, quoting mimeographed paper circulated by Convenors of the Malaysia Solidarity National Conference.

[30]The Socialist Front argument for organizing political parties on ideological grounds, cutting across communal divisions, was summarized in Charles Gamba, 'Labour and Labour Parties in Malaya', *Pacific Affairs*, vol. XXXI, no. 2, pp. 117–30; cf. K. J. Ratnam, op. cit. pp. 171–4.

[31]This paragraph is based largely on discussions with three PAP ministers in January and March 1965; not all the points quoted here were (or could be) mentioned publicly, but most can be found in the various publications of the Singapore Ministry of Culture, particularly *Towards a Malaysian Malaysia* (Ministry of Culture, 1965).

[32]*Straits Times*, 18 April 1965. The new Alliance National Council had 40 members, allocated as follows: Malaya 27, Singapore 4, Sarawak 5, Sabah 4.

[33]*Straits Times*, 9 Feb. 1965, cited in Michael Leifer, 'Singapore in Malaysia: the Politics of Federation', *Journal of Southeast Asian History*, vol. VI, no. 2, Sept. 1965, p. 69. Musa bin Hitam later replaced Syed Ja'afar Albar as Executive Secretary of UMNO.

[34]*Straits Times*, 25 April 1965.

[35]See above, pp. 297–300.

[36]See Jean Grossholtz, 'An Exploration of Malaysian Meanings', *Asian Survey*, vol. VI, no. 4, April 1966, p. 230–1, and R. S. Milne, 'Singapore's Exit From Malaysia: the Consequences of Ambiguity', *Asian Survey*, vol. VI, no. 3, March 1966, p. 181. The Chairman of the Malaysian Solidarity Convention was Dr. Toh Chin Chye, Singapore's Deputy Prime Minister. Only parties which accepted Malaysia were invited to the inaugural meeting, not the Socialist Front or *Barisan Sosialis*. The SUPP leaders, Ong Kee Hui and Stephen Yong, attended and supported the new movement, but were repudiated by their party for doing so, although they later regained control.

[37]Grossholtz, op. cit. p. 232. For Lee Kuan Yew's denial that he had in mind any intention to secede, see his speech to the Federal Parliament on 27 May and his press conference on 3 June, published as *The Battle for a Malaysian Malaysia*, 1 & 2 (Singapore Ministry of Culture Publication, 1965).

[38]An account of the Hong Lim by-election of 1965, in which the Alliance openly supported the anti-Malaysia candidate of the *Barisan Sosialis* is given in Grossholtz, op. cit. pp. 233–5.

[39]The events immediately preceding the separation of Singapore are usefully summarized by Peter Boyce in 'Singapore as a Sovereign State', *Australian Outlook*, vol. XIX, no. 3, Dec. 1965, pp. 259–63. See also Milne, op. cit.

[40]Robert O. Tilman, 'The Alliance Pattern in Malaysian Politics: Bornean Variations on a Theme', *South Atlantic Quarterly*, vol. LXIII, no. 1, Winter, 1964.

[41]SANAP refused to take sides in the June crisis: *Straits Times*, 5, 9 June 1964.

[42]The December crisis developed out of a speech by Stephens at Benoni on 22 November in which he accused the Malayan Alliance leaders of putting UPKO in a difficult position in relation to USNO and threatened to reconsider UPKO's position in the Alliance. (There had been some suggestions of an UMNO-USNO merger in previous weeks, although nothing came of them.) The crisis came to a head over Stephens' controversial appointment of a Sabah man as State Secretary.

[43]Interview with various UPKO leaders in Jesselton, February 1965.

[44]*Straits Times*, 17, 19, 23 August 1965.

[45]Margaret Roff, 'Pre-election Politics in Sabah', *Australia's Neighbours*, series IV, no. 41, January-February 1967.

[46]*Sabah Times*, 29 December 1966, cited in Roff, op. cit. For a later and fuller account of the 1967 election in Sabah see Margaret Roff, 'Sabah's Political Parties and the 1967 State Election', *International Studies*, vol. IX, April 1968, pp. 431–56.

[47]Michael Leigh, 'The Development of Political Organization and Leadership in Sarawak, East Malaysia' (Cornell University, Ph.D. thesis, 1971), pp. 143–6, 167–71.

[48]Craig Lockhard, 'Parties, personalities and crisis politics in Sarawak', *Journal of Southeast Asian History*, vol. VIII, March 1967, p. 116.

[49]Leigh, op. cit. pp. 36–9, 53–7, 144, 173–5.

[50]Michael Leigh, *Sarawak in Malaysia*, pp. 3 and 7; SUPP members near Lundu, mostly scattered Chinese smallholders on the outskirts of the jungle, had assisted Indonesian attempts to set up a 'liberated zone' in that area between Jan.-March 1964 and the Lundu branch of SUPP was proscribed on 9 May; *Sarawak Tribune* 11 May.

[51]*Towards a Malaysian Malaysia* (Singapore, Ministry of Information, 1965), no. 2.

[52]*Sarawak by the Week*, nos. 20–3 of 1965; *Straits Times*, May, 15 June 1965.

[53]Lockhard, op. cit. p. 118.

[54]The *Straits Times*, 13 April 1966, reported that despite the urgings of the Tunku and UMNO leaders, PANAS had decided against merger with BARJASA in a single Malay party to be affiliated with UMNO. The leader of PANAS, Datu Abang Othman (brother of the Datu Bandar) had been working closely with Ningkan towards a single multi-racial Alliance party.

[55]*Straits Times*, 15 June 1966. If the Tunku were able to take action in his capacity as Head of the Alliance Party of a kind that would be considered a blatant invasion of States rights if taken in his capacity as Prime Minister, the federal structure of government (and the Alliance system) would come under very heavy strain.

[56]Ningkan had refused to summon the Council Negri where he was sure to be voted out of office by his opponents in the Alliance: under the constitution the Governor had no power to summon the Council Negri independently of him, so there was some danger of a serious constitutional crisis which might conceivably have been exploited by SCO elements.

XI

The Final Phase:
October 1965 - August 1966

THE abortive coup of 1 October and its bloody aftermath marked the beginning of the end of confrontation, for it led to the destruction of the PKI and a radical shift in the balance of power in Indonesia. Although it was to be nearly a year before a new group of Indonesian leaders were prepared to sign an agreement with Malaysia bringing the dispute to an end, confrontation quickly receded into the background. A few incidents continued to occur on the Sarawak border and several half-hearted attempts were made to exploit the rift between Kuala Lumpur and Singapore, but these did not amount to much. Soekarno indulged in one final flurry of sabre-rattling of a more alarming nature in February 1966, when he briefly seized the political initiative in Djakarta and tried to reactivate confrontation and the Chinese alliance; but this was a last desperate bid which soon failed. After Lt.-General Suharto took over the reins of government in March, he and Adam Malik moved as swiftly as they could to bring the fruitless conflict with Malaysia to an end.

Within a few days of the coup the Tunku and other Malaysian ministers began to express hopes that the new supremacy of the Army in Indonesia would soon bring an end to confrontation. This interpretation of events was promptly denied in Indonesia by Subandrio's spokesman at the Foreign Ministry, Ganis Harsono, who announced that there would be no change in Indonesia's foreign policy. Army spokesmen also retorted that Indonesians would now be stronger than ever and more united in their struggle to resist the *Nekolim*, since the 'traitors to the Revolution' had been cast out.[1] These pious sentiments were little more than whistling in the dark, of course, for Soekarno's 'Old Order', as it soon came to be called, quickly began to crumble under the anti-Communist onslaught. Moreover, the Army leaders had more urgent tasks for their loyal troops than the fruitless war in Sarawak. The rapid deterioration of Indonesia's relations with Communist China undermined the major pillar of the old foreign policy, while the notion of *Nasakom* unity became a mockery over the next six months. (The term '*Nasakom*' quickly lost its former respectability, while Radio Indonesia, closely following the winds of change, immediately suppressed the official *Nasakom* song and various other propagandist jingles it had been broadcasting endlessly under the Old Order.) Nevertheless, the possibility that confrontation might again be intensified could not be ruled out entirely so long as Soekarno and Suban-drio retained formal control of the government and its foreign policy, for it represented their last remaining hope of tilting the political balance back in their favour by drumming up national unity against an external enemy.

From the point of view of the Malaysia story, therefore, the most important feature of this period was the strangely tentative process by which Soekarno was finally stripped of effective authority and gradually reduced to impotence. The coup attempt itself was a small-scale and make-shift affair which was put down with ease in little more than twenty-four hours by troops of the Strategic Reserve (KOSTRAD) under Major-General Suharto. From that day onwards, Suharto had effective military control of the capital and the Army soon established itself as the dominant political force throughout the whole of Indonesia. Yet Soekarno remained Presi-dent, not merely in name, but to an important degree in fact also, for both Suharto and Nasution, his titular superior, were reluctant to defy him openly while he was still the symbol of legitimacy. Although they soon found themselves in open opposition to him on fundamental political issues arising out of the coup attempt and quite blatantly resisted or dis-regarded his instructions on many matters, they avoided a showdown for nearly six months, until Soekarno's attempt to get rid of General Nasution brought to a head the conflict between the Old Order and the New. In the meantime occurred the terrible explosion of communal conflict throughout the whole of Indonesia in which hundreds of thousands of PKI supporters (and some of their opponents too) were slaughtered or gaoled in one of the most extraordinary bloodbaths in modern times. This horrifying out-burst of violence was both a cause and a consequence of the piecemeal destruction of the PKI, coinciding with the emergence of the Army as the controlling force in Indonesian politics, that brought about the end of the Soekarno era.

THE COUP AND ITS AFTERMATH

The attempted *coup d'état* by Lieutenant-Colonel Untung and his associates on 1 October occurred at a time when the political atmosphere was so tense that only a spark was needed to cause an explosion. Political tensions had been building up alarmingly during the previous year because of the spectacular increase of Communist influence in Djakarta and the accelerating economic and administrative decline brought about by the now uncontrollable inflation.[2] In the circumstances, the brittle facade of *Nasakom* unity could hardly withstand the shock effects of a major act of violence directed towards a change of regime.

Throughout the middle of 1965, the PKI had seemed to be succeeding more dramatically than ever before in pushing the 'course of the Indonesian revolution' towards the left, with the evident approval of President Soekarno. The manifestations of this trend were various — the steady isolation and silencing of anti-Communists; intensified Communist control over the press and propaganda media; Soekarno's increasing use of Communist concepts and slogans, as well as his attacks on 'counter-revolutionaries' guilty of 'Nasakom-phobia' or hypocritical lip-service to the revolution. Most important of all was the controversy over the PKI's demands for a 'Fifth Force' in the struggle against Malaysia and the Nekolim, to be created by arming the peasants and workers. The Army leaders (but not the Air Force and Navy) were strongly averse to any such scheme, for it threatened, once started, to erode away the Army's vitally important quasi-monopoly of armed force. (The Chinese provenance of the idea also aroused their worst suspicions.) But they had to be very careful how they resisted it, lest they expose themselves to attack as reactionaries and Nasakom-phobes; Soekarno's open support for the proposal put them in a particularly difficult position, since it left them tactically on the defensive, while the President and the PKI enjoyed the political initiative. For that very reason, the training and arming of anti-Malaysia 'volunteers' (including some Communist Youth Corps members) at Halim Air Force base near Djakarta in July aroused considerable alarm among the generals, since it posed a danger that this precedent would be used as the thin edge of the wedge.

Another major set-back for the anti-Communist forces was the purging of the right wing of the PNI in August, on Soekarno's orders. This had little immediate effect on the overall balance of power (though it was a serious set-back for the anti-Communist leadership of the PNI in Central Java, where the PNI and PKI were bitterly at odds over the land reform issue), but it was an alarming indication of the way the wind was blowing, for there were few remaining political organizations which now dared to stand up to the PKI openly. The only prominent one was the Muslim Student Association, HMI, whose dissolution the PKI was demanding clamorously, but without success. During August and September, the PKI's vehement denunciation of its remaining enemies reached an unprecedented pitch, not only the HMI, but also 'bureaucratic capitalists' (PKI jargon for the Army-connected heads of State business enterprises) and corrupters being attacked in a more daring and defiant way than ever before. Rice prices had again begun to spiral uncontrollably in September, several outbursts of violence between Armed Forces units in Djakarta seemed to signify a serious breakdown of law and order, while an atmosphere of apprehension and expectancy contributed to a fin de siècle sense of impending catastrophe, a modern counterpart to the dreaded kali-yuga of Hindu mythology. There were various signs that by September the PKI was striving to increase its power base in the Soekarno regime with a sense of sudden urgency, as if its leaders realized that time might now be desperately short for it.

According to official accounts of the coup, which emphasize the role of the Communists as the master-minds behind the attempt, Soekarno had suffered a severe illness in early August and Chinese doctors attending him had tipped off the PKI leaders that his death was imminent. The PKI therefore stepped up its preparations for a seizure of power, using Untung and his associates with whom the PKI had been in contact for some time, in order to forestall any similar move by the Army leaders: and on 1 October, shortly after a second brief collapse by Soekarno, Untung took action with just this purpose. Other accounts treat Untung as an almost independent agent and the PKI as an almost unwitting accomplice in the affair.[3] Just what his relations with the PKI were in the matter of responsibility for the coup, whether Aidit and his colleagues were its masterminds or mere dupes who let themselves become involved in it, and whether the Central Committee was seriously divided on the strategy to be followed (Aidit perhaps favouring a seizure of power and Njoto supporting continued reliance on the association with Soekarno) are questions on which the evidence is still not clear. In any case, the question of how far the PKI was involved in the planning of the coup attempt is of limited relevance to our story here. For in the circumstances of September 1965, the mere fact that the PKI came to be associated with an attempted left-wing coup was bound to give rise to the suspicion that the PKI was behind it. If the coup had succeeded, the elimination of the most anti-Communist generals would have enormously strengthened the PKI's position — and the Indonesian revolution would have spun almost irresistibly towards the left, whether the PKI gained power immediately or not. There are many puzzles about the tactics of Untung and the PKI leaders on 1 October, particularly the failure to use the party's mass following to any substantial extent in support of the coup, even though it was implicated to a disastrously incriminating extent. But there is nothing puzzling about the consequences of its failure.

Untung undertook the coup with a mere handful of troops in Djakarta, about six battalions, and the support of some units in Central Java. Elsewhere there was no overt support for his bid. In such conditions, the key to his success lay in his ability to confront the President and the rest of the Armed Forces with a *fait accompli*, the elimination of the senior generals and the seizure of the capital, and to obtain the President's public endorsement of his 'Revolutionary Council'. Why he did not attempt to do away with the two generals in Djakarta who had troops at their direct command, Suharto and Major-General Umar Wirahadikusuma, the Djakarta garrison commander, is one of the great mysteries of the affair. For Suharto's action in moving promptly to assume command of the Army, neutralize Untung's forces and thus compel the President to dissociate himself from Untung seems to have been the crucial factor leading to the failure of the coup.[4] (Nasution's narrow escape from death may also have had some effect on the President's calculations, but he played almost no part in the day's events.) By the morning of 2 October, Suharto had effective military control of the capital and President Soekarno was virtually within his power. Untung, Aidit and the other leading figures in the coup had fled from Halim to Central Java where they could hope for a greater degree of safety and popular support while they decided what to do next. If they intended to fight on in the hope of ultimately gaining power through armed struggle, Central or East Java was the logical base. And for several months the danger that they might still be able to plunge Java into civil war inclined the Army leaders towards caution in their dealings with President Soekarno, since they were reluctant to precipitate any further breakdown of national unity.

After the failure of Untung's coup in Djakarta, the PKI leaders had to decide whether to try and fight on from a 'Yenan' in Central Java or to lie quiet and rely on President Soekarno to protect them from Army reprisals with the argument that the coup was solely an affair within the Armed Services in which the PKI was not involved. They chose, at least initially, to rely on Soekarno. Apparently they miscalculated the damaging effect of the episode on Soekarno's political position, for it soon became apparent that Soekarno was quite unable to save the PKI from the whiplash of anger and emotional reaction against it. By the time the PKI (or some elements of it) began to organize resistance in Central Java late in October, it was too late.[5]

Despite their suspicions of Soekarno's role in the coup attempt (later intensified by his attempts to shield the Air Force and the PKI from Army recriminations) neither Nasution nor Suharto made any move to usurp his authority. In fact, in the days immediately following the coup, they showed a surprising willingness to entrust to him the responsibility for working out 'a political solution' to the nation's problems. At the first cabinet meeting after the coup on 6 October (attended by Njoto and Lukman of the PKI), Soekarno set out to regain the initiative and restore the political *status quo ante* with an amazing degree of blandness and nerve, as if nothing irreparable had happened. Calling for a restoration of national unity, he urged that demands for revenge should be avoided lest it 'provoke the *Nekolim* to launch an attack against Indonesia.' The events of 1 October were merely the kind of upheaval one must expect during a revolution, he said: while he did not condone the murder of the generals, he refused to ban the PKI or condemn any participants in the coup until the full facts were known. Meanwhile he accepted a PKI statement that the affair had been purely an internal problem of the Army. But already Soekarno's old magic was waning. Suharto had quickly established himself as the key figure in the situation. After the bodies of the murdered generals were found in a well at Lubang Buaja on the outskirts of Halim air base, they were exhumed in Suharto's presence and he grimly challenged the President's earlier assertion that the Air Force had not been involved in the affair. Next day the generals were solemnly buried amidst scenes of high emotion. Rallies condemning the PKI and demanding its dissolution began to snowball in intensity throughout the following week. The PKI headquarters in Djakarta was burnt by an invading mob several days later and the Army authorities took no action to prevent it. Similar attacks on other institutions with PKI affiliations or sympathies quickly followed as the hostility towards the PKI which had been pent up during the previous three years or more suddenly burst out. Not long afterwards, one after another of the

Army's regional commanders took action to 'suspend' the PKI. The President disapproved of their actions and steadily resisted Army pressures to ban the PKI, but he was now powerless to reverse the tide or prevent the piecemeal destruction of that party.[6]

Because neither Nasution nor Suharto was willing to defy the President openly or risk plunging the country into civil war until they were confident of their own authority over the Army, the grim struggle for power in the capital was fought out on a host of minor issues during the next five months, with few spectacular or decisive gains by either side. Soekarno still had two enormous assets on his side, legality and his charismatic appeal. These were sufficient to sustain his position for some time, despite the groundswell of anti-Communist support for the Army leaders in their efforts to change the character of the government.

Outwardly, the only major changes of key personnel were Suharto's elevation to command of the Army (and hence Ministerial status), the replacement of Omar Dhani as Air Force commander, reconstitution of the crucially important Army General Staff and two minor reshuffles of KOTI. But behind the facade of continuity, a substantial shift in the balance of power was occurring. Subandrio's influence was quickly circumscribed — he was deprived of control over the notorious Central Intelligence Bureau and was not even permitted to attend the Preparatory Committee meeting for the postponed Algiers Conference at the end of October. Government departments and the Armed Forces were purged of persons suspected of involvement in the coup (which in effect meant suspected Communists) and PKI trade unions and mass organizations were banned. Nevertheless, Soekarno hung on tenaciously in refusing to yield any ground to his opponents if he could avoid it, either in the matter of reconstituting government bodies like KOTI or in his basic approach to a political solution of the nation's troubles. He still insisted that the course of the Indonesian revolution must be maintained: it must not be 'diverted' towards the right because of the coup, which he tried to characterize as merely an inevitable ripple in the turbulent stream of revolution, 'a minor thing' when measured alongside the supreme requirement of national unity in the face of enemies of the revolution.[7] The political and ideological foundations of that unity had to be maintained at all costs, he argued — and that meant preserving *Nasakom* and the PKI.

By the middle of November, Soekarno still had not revealed what his long-awaited 'political solution' to the coup and its consequences would be; the Army leaders and their bandwagon of supporters were strongly demanding that he ban the PKI, while in province after province action had already been taken to suspend it despite the President's orders. The rift between the Army and Soekarno was so blatant that Nasution called upon him to ban the PKI 'in order to clear up the question of unanimity between the President and the Armed Forces'.[8] Soekarno still refused, but his inability to assert much effective authority at all was now becoming increasingly obvious as the power of the Army leaders in the regions was consolidated. Yet despite the widening rift between the President and the

Army leaders, the latter seemed less and less likely, as time passed, to attempt an overt move to displace him or radically circumscribe his power, partly because of tactical dangers involved in any such bid for supremacy, partly because they had to secure their own power base within the Armed Forces first and reestablish control over Java and Bali. While this was being done and the deadlock continued in Djakarta, the widespread slaughter and gaoling of Communists throughout the country destroyed not only the PKI but also the very basis of the political system Soekarno was trying to restore.

The horrifying bloodbath of 1965–6 cannot yet be fully explained until a great deal more information becomes available about the numbers killed and the circumstances of the slaughter in different regions.[9] Some of the killings in the early weeks seem to have been a consequence of sporadic fighting and raiding that occurred because of the paralysis of authority and governmental power during the period of uncertainty following the coup. Much of it, however, was a consequence of the methods used by regional Army commanders and the RPKAD, the para-commando brigade, particularly in Central and East Java and Bali, in re-establishing control there. Apart from the numerous arrests (and frequently the summary executions) of local PKI leaders by Army teams, there seem to have been many cases where local anti-Communists were permitted or encouraged to 'clean out' the Communists, while the local Army officers turned a blind eye. All kinds of old scores were settled in the dark of the night with few questions asked afterwards. In some areas, the Army authorities were too precariously in control of the situation to be able to curb the killings, or else reluctant to antagonize the anti-Communists, such as the militant Muslim flying squads in East Java, by trying to restrain them. It could be argued that many of the prisoners who were herded into makeshift detention centres for screening, imprisonment and, in the case of hard core Communists, summary execution, were safer there than they might have been if exposed to the wrath of their enemies outside, although the death-roll from disease and under-nourishment in the camps was appallingly high. Significantly, the killings seem to have been less indiscriminate in West Java, where the Siliwangi division moved promptly in early October to arrest the PKI leaders and destroy their organization, so that there was not the same power vacuum as in eastern Java during the weeks before the arrival of the RPKAD.

The whole affair must also be seen, however, as a bursting forth of the tensions that had been building up behind the facade of *Nasakom* unity during the previous years. W. F. Wertheim has commented that: 'The extreme cruelty and the mass scale of the murdering as well as its regional distribution and the accompanying impact on the implementation of the land reforms, could not be explained without taking account of the basic class-struggle character of what happened.'[10] While the term 'class-struggle' has connotations that are not entirely appropriate to the more complex *aliran* conflict that underlay the killings in Central and East Java, it is certainly true that they were worst in areas where the PKI had been strongest and where social tensions had been building up over the land reform issue during the preceding years — and these were generally areas where, with some exceptions, the pressure of population and incidence of landlessness was most acute. The wealthier farmers who stood to lose land or income if the land reform laws were thoroughly implemented or who had been threatened by the PKI during 1964–5 (generally associated with the Nahdatul Ulama in East Java and the PNI in Central Java) now seized the opportunity to turn upon the Communists who had been harassing them while they were at a disadvantage. Violent clashes occurred between *Ansor* (the NU youth organization) flying squads and PKI gangs in East Java, which was one of the few regions where the Communists attempted resistance briefly. Estimates of the numbers killed have ranged widely from several hundred thousand to over a million. And from official figures it appears that at least a quarter of a million people were gaoled.[11] Central and East Java and Bali accounted for by far the largest numbers.

Only after the struggle for power in Djakarta was resolved and the supremacy of the Army leaders had been firmly established throughout the country in 1966 was control gradually re-established. But although the destruction of the PKI further weakened Soekarno's chances of effectively restoring his former authority, it did not directly lead to his overthrow. Its main significance in the central power struggle was to embolden his opponents to take action against him at long last, although even then Nasution and Suharto seemed strangely reluctant to do so until compelled to by the course of events in Djakarta.

Three developments between mid-December and early March finally brought about a crystallization of opposition to the Soekarno regime and forced the Army leaders to brace themselves for the long-predicted show-down with him. These were the spiralling inflation, the street demon-strations by the student action fronts, and Soekarno's last desperate attempt to tilt the balance back to the left by a cabinet reshuffle in which Nasution was dismissed. Together they served to reveal the impotence of Soekarno's government if it lacked Army support, for it was no longer able to take any action to arrest the economic decline or to curb the growing anarchy in Djakarta. Even so, his opponents remained extra-ordinarily hesitant to move openly against him and finally did so in a very roundabout manner so that they did not formally violate the legitimacy which he alone could bestow. Ironically, it was the schoolchildren and students of Indonesia, the very people whom one might have expected to be most thoroughly indoctrinated by the years of propaganda, whose actions finally led to the collapse of Soekarno's regime by forcing the Army leaders to act against him.

The economic background to this last phase of the drama was one of runaway inflation, unprecedented even in Indonesia's rich experience of the malady. In mid-December, the government issued a series of regula-tions (including a money-cutting measure which incorporated a 10 per cent tax on cash assets) in the hope of curbing the rise in prices, which had doubled in the two months since the coup. It had earlier raised the price of petrol from the absurdly low figure of Rp. 4 per litre to 250 and then 1,000 in order to eliminate a costly built-in subsidy which was contributing to the budget deficit, a step in the right direction, but in the circumstances rather quixotic. In fact, the entire problem was handled so ineptly that panic buying and economic disruption were simply intensified, without achieving any check on the rising prices, which again doubled in the first two months of 1966.[12] By this time the government no longer had any weapons in reserve to use against the inflation. Exports had declined seriously in 1965 and the foreign debt repayment problem was becoming acute. Soekarno and his ministers continued to utter platitudes about 'standing on our own feet' (or, as the cynics of Djakarta put it, 'standing on our own foot') but nothing they could do offered any real hope of checking the inflation, unless the government could miraculously discover new sources of overseas aid or of political strength to tackle the basic problem of bringing budget expenditures and into line with revenues. This now seemed to be out of the question. In fact, when the students took direct action to prevent any increase in petrol prices by the retailers, Soekarno simply gave in and directed his ministers to lower them again. The Army leaders ostentatiously disassociated themselves from the economic policies of the government, leaving the burden of unpopularity to be borne by the President and Chairul Saleh. Early in January, Suharto and Nasution participated in a seminar at the Economics Faculty of the University of Indonesia at which the government's economic policies were attacked by professors and students alike, in a way that had been unknown under Guided Democracy. It was from this period that the students began to emerge as the catalysts of political change in Djakarta.

The student demonstrations occurred in two waves, being directed initially against rising prices and then continuing as a series of protests against the remnants of Communist or 'Old Order' influence in the government.[13] From 10 to 17 January, during the Economics Faculty seminar, university students demonstrated daily against the government on the streets of Djakarta, obviously with the Army's approval. In fact they were openly encouraged by some of the strongly anti-Communist officers such as Sarwo Edhie, the commander of the paratroop brigade that had just swept through Java and Bali. The students went so far as to invade the grounds of the Presidential palace at Bogor on 17 January during a cabinet meeting there and would only disperse after Lt.-Gen. Suharto himself came out to address them. Next day the government banned further street demonstrations. The students flouted the ban on the following day, but after that there were no further demonstrations for nearly a month. Soekarno attempted to regain the initiative in the struggle for power by organizing a counter-force within a National Union of Students and simultaneously mobilizing popular support within a 'Soekarno Front', through which all mass actions were to be channelled. Regional Army leaders paid lip-service to the President's instruction on this matter, but made little attempt to hide their hostility to it and did what they could to frustrate his intentions, although still without openly disobeying him.

For several weeks a tortuous tactical battle was waged over the establishment of the Soekarno Fronts in various regions, with the Army leaders taking over control of them where they could not prevent their establishment; but by the middle of February there were signs that the pro-Soekarno forces were beginning to win the tug-of-war. Then, on 21 February, Soekarno made his last major bid to reassert his authority. A cabinet reshuffle was announced, in which Nasution was deprived of office and various minor changes were made with the aim of weakening the position of the anti-Communists in the government. At the same time, Soekarno and Subandrio made statements indicating that the confrontation of Malaysia would be intensified and that relations with China must be repaired. Also KOTI was renamed KOGAM, the 'Crush Malaysia Command'.

Next day the students of Djakarta again took to the streets. Several days later an official ban on KAMI was ordered, but street demonstrations continued, now under the banner of KAPPI (the high-school students action front): Soekarno's complaints that the ban on KAMI was not being carried out give some indication of the extent to which the Djakarta military authorities were supporting the action fronts.[14] Clashes occurred between pro- and anti-Soekarno student organizations, but the latter were clearly far stronger. In the second week of March the anti-government students were repeatedly bringing all traffic in central Djakarta to a standstill. And since only a few military units (notably the palace guard) were willing to take a stand against the students, there was nothing Soekarno could now do about it.

Finally, on 11 March Suharto decided to take action. (Nasution's failure to give any lead to the anti-Soekarno forces after his dismissal a fortnight earlier cost him the opportunity to step into Soekarno's shoes which Suharto was now to take.) Soekarno's palace was surrounded and he was virtually compelled to agree to transfer executive power to Suharto. He signed a document giving Suharto power to 'take any steps necessary to ensure security, calm, the stability of government and the progress of the Revolution, and to guarantee the personal safety and authority of the President'.[15] It was on the authority of this 'Letter of March 11' that Suharto now proceeded to take over the reins of government in Indonesia. Next day he banned the PKI throughout the country.

Suharto still had to move very cautiously vis-à-vis the President during the next few months, until his authority as the effective bearer of executive power was endorsed by the Peoples' Consultative Congress in July. (It was extended at two further sessions in early 1967 and 1968.) Although fifteen Ministers from the previous cabinet were arrested in the middle of March and the cabinet was reshuffled shortly after, many of Soekarno's former ministers were still retained. Outwardly, continuity was preserved as far as possible, so as to minimize resistance to the abrupt change that had occurred; but power was now effectively concentrated in the hands of a 'triumvirate' consisting of Suharto, Adam Malik, the new Foreign Minister, and the Sultan of Jogjakarta. It was these three who now presided over the dramatic reversal of Soekarno's economic and foreign policies, through a threefold drive to curb inflation, end the confrontation of Malaysia and restore Indonesia's relations with the West in the hope of obtaining desperately needed foreign aid. The Sultan revealed on 12 April that Indonesia's foreign debts amounted to $2400 million and that there was virtually no possibility of meeting her repayment obligations for 1966. There was simply no alternative but to change course in foreign policy as quickly as possible. Yet this was no light matter, for the Indonesian people had been intensively indoctrinated to believe that their campaign against Malaysia was just and necessary; the President himself was actively opposed to the abandonment of confrontation and even the chief figures of the New Order had been too closely associated with the campaign to be able to repudiate it lightly. Until they were more confident that the new regime was securely based, a *rapprochement* with Malaysia had to be handled very delicately, so that it did not look as if Indonesia was simply abandoning the case for which she had been fighting and for which men had been giving their lives as recently as a few weeks earlier.

THE END OF CONFRONTATION

The new Suharto regime did not waste much time before giving indications that it was keen to scale down confrontation or even end it entirely. On the other hand, the triumvirate of Suharto, Malik and the Sultan was not sufficiently sure of its power at first to run the risk of suddenly flouting all the beliefs and slogans on which confrontation had been based, or to make concessions to Malaysia which implied that Indonesia had been in the wrong on the matter of the Manila Agreements. In fact Radio Indonesia still insisted for several weeks after Subandrio's downfall that it was not true that confrontation was just a PKI-Subandrio policy: official statements by the new leaders that confrontation would continue were proof of that. Malik himself denied a statement by the Tunku that confrontation would end automatically now that the PKI had been banned and an anti-Communist regime established.[16]

This line was soon modified, however, to assertions that confrontation would continue until a peaceful settlement was reached. Other indications were soon given that the triumvirate was definitely anxious for a settlement, although it continued to play diplomatic poker for a few weeks in the hope of extracting some concessions from Kuala Lumpur.[17] For their part, the Malaysian leaders were not willing to give much away until they were sure of the new regime's sincerity and durability: but even when they became convinced on these counts after negotiations in April and May, it was still not easy to reconcile the two countries' conflicting arguments about the implications of the events of 1963.

Malik quickly made a bid to recognize Singapore and establish diplomatic relations with her, but as he said he was doing this on Soekarno's instructions as part of a policy of intensifying confrontation (i.e. of diplomatic rather than military confrontation), hackles were naturally aroused in Kuala Lumpur. The *Indonesian Herald* made matters worse by describing it as part of a plan to isolate Malaysia internationally.[18] The Tunku treated it as such when he once again reacted very heavy-handedly in publicly warning Lee Kuan Yew not to swallow this bait. Yet within three weeks Malik was saying openly that recognition of Singapore was now only a matter of time (as it indeed turned out to be: it followed immediately after the Bangkok talks between Malik and Razak), so it seems far more likely that Malik's reference to intensifying confrontation was merely a device to avoid an open clash with Soekarno as he took the first steps towards a resumption of friendlier relations. In a relatively conciliatory statement at about the same time (12 April) Suharto said that Indonesia would accept Malaysia provided that the people of North Borneo really wanted it. Secret contacts between the Indonesian and Malaysian governments must by this time have been leading towards the *rapprochement* that was to follow, for by the end of the month both Malik and Suharto were talking in a very conciliatory vein. Malik held brief talks in Bangkok with the Philippines Foreign Minister, Ramos, who was anxious to extricate his government from the embarrassing predicament it had stumbled into earlier and to restore diplomatic ties with Malaysia.[91] Malik suggested that mediation might help to bring the two adversaries together again, but this idea was dropped a fortnight later in favour of direct ministerial talks between Malik and Tun Razak, also in Bangkok.

The thaw in Indonesian-Malaysian relations developed quickly in May, after both Malik and Suharto had indicated that they did not regard the withdrawal of British troops from Singapore as a necessary pre-condition for a peaceful settlement, nor were they insisting on a referendum in Sabah and Sarawak. Little was said publicly about a return to the Manila Agreements, either. Apparently the only point at issue was the diplomatic mechanics of how to reach an agreement to end confrontation.

Soekarno was still opposed to the new policy, however, and was still in a position of formal authority, although no longer of effective power. 'I am keeping silent in one thousand tongues', he cryptically told a gathering of military officers on one occasion, alluding to his disagreements with Indonesia's new masters.[20] Apparently the triumvirate was still endeavouring to avoid any open conflict with him over Malaysia, hence the Janus-quality of statements from KOGAM, even in May, about 'confrontation continuing' and volunteers still being sent to the border.[21] Malik told student demonstrators that Soekarno had been 'furious with him' over the peace talks — which was probably a better way to win their support for his policies than explaining them would have been — but Soekarno was always associated with KOGAM decisions and Malik did not attempt to by-pass him altogether. (A suggestion by one correspondent that Malik's very rapid reversal of confrontation in May was intended to force a showdown with the President is rather fanciful: there were far more complex economic motives for his policy than that.) No secret was made about Malik's plans to meet Tun Razak at the end of May with the aim of negotiating an end to confrontation. The only surprise was the sudden visit to Malaysia of an Indonesian mission of high-ranking KOGAM officers just before the Bangkok talks opened, to be feted and publicized as a symbol of the end of confrontation and the restoration of Indonesian-Malaysian friendship.[22]

The Bangkok talks did not bring complete agreement, however. Although both sides were keen to end confrontation, neither could bring itself to make the concessions the other required if the agreement was to be formalized in a written treaty. Consequently, after nearly three days of tough bargaining, the two delegations merely exchanged sealed packages containing proposals about the method of moving towards normal relations between their two countries. The meeting ended amidst enthusiastic speeches, popping flashlights, bubbling champagne and Muslim prayers, but neither in the brief communiqué issued nor in any of Malik's press statements was it said in so many words that confrontation had ended. Even Tun Razak merely spoke of 'laying the foundations of peace'. Some pessimistic commentators were still inclined to doubt whether the Indonesians could yet be trusted not to resume military confrontation again if it suited them, whether it might not again be a diplomatic trick on their part. Nothing specific was said about when Indonesia would recognize Malaysia, nor about the contentious question of whether a referendum should be held in Sarawak and Sabah. These continued to be matters of dispute in Indonesia for some weeks. It was later alleged that these matters were spelled out in a secret Bangkok Accord, of which an unauthorized version was soon circulating in the rumour markets.[23] This is quite plausible, since they constituted the key clauses of the final Djakarta Agreement of 11 August, but the question of real interest is the terms in which they were set out, for Soekarno later alleged that the Djakarta Agreement was different from the Bangkok Accord, while Malik denied this. Until the Accord is published it will be impossible to tell who was right.

The failure to reach an open and specific agreement at Bangkok has been attributed to Malik's inability to carry his 'prestige conscious' military colleagues in the delegation along with him in his haste to reach a settlement: they were determined not to humiliate President Soekarno unduly, it was said, and insisted on gaining some satisfaction on the matter of Sarawak and Sabah. Another explanation was that Malik hesitated about committing himself openly to a definite agreement until he was sure he could get it ratified by the President or some other appropriate authority. He would have been left in a dangerously exposed political position at home if he had openly committed himself to recognizing Malaysia before obtaining any satisfaction about the return to the Manila Agreements, for even many supporters of the new regime would have found this hard to swallow. It probably suited Malik quite well to be able to leave the awkward questions open and to imply that they were still under negotiation.

The Malaysians were said to have been disappointed that the Bangkok talks did not result in a more positive agreement, although they seem to have been satisfied that the Indonesians were genuinely anxious to end confrontation, which was their primary concern. They apparently did not expect formal recognition immediately, in any case.

The problem of obtaining ratification of the Bangkok Accord in Djakarta remained the chief obstacle to further progress during the two months which followed, for the power balance in Indonesia was still unsteady. Parliament ducked the responsibility for ratifying it (though the constitution empowered it to do so), the Speaker expressing general but rather qualified approval of Malik's report on the conference, then passing the buck by saying that 'Indonesia is still waiting for President Soekarno to approve or reject the proposals'. At one point Malik even suggested that ratification by the President might not be necessary, that the signature of the Foreign Minister would suffice.[24] (The 1945 constitution was not being closely followed on this matter. The supreme representative body, the People's Consultative Congress, might have been the most convenient body to approach for ratification, as it was due to meet late in June and was now vehemently opposed to Soekarno; but no attempt was made to invoke its authority on the matter — perhaps because there was little constitutional basis for doing so, but also because popular opinion could not yet be relied on to accept Malik's concessions on a matter of such firmly established belief.) A KOGAM meeting on 10 June, at which Soekarno was present, endorsed the Bangkok Accord as having 'established mutual trust and goodwill between the two countries', but it then went on to authorize General Suharto, not Malik, to promote further contacts with Kuala Lumpur and 'seek clarification of certain matters'.[25]

Several days later, Ghazali bin Shafie visited Djakarta for secret talks with Suharto and shortly afterwards an Indonesian mission under Lt.-Col. Moerdani (who had been Suharto's representative in the secret negotiations earlier in the year) was established in Kuala Lumpur to constitute the *de facto* Indonesian representation there, even though recognition and mutual exchange of formal diplomatic relations still had not been agreed upon. By this time both nations were apparently willing to shelve their arguments about the diplomatic issues, while they brought confrontation to an end in substance if not in word. On the Malaysian side, preparations for the withdrawal of British troops both from Borneo and the South-East Asia area now began to proceed quite rapidly. A blind eye was turned to continued clashes on the Borneo frontier. Indonesia began to withdraw units from the Borneo frontier and the Riau islands. No objection was raised in Kuala Lumpur when Singapore and Indonesia formally recognized each other in June and prepared to resume barter trade. Indonesia's relations with Britain began to improve after her Foreign Minister visited Djakarta to talk about the reduction of British forces in Malaysia and the possibility of rescheduling Indonesia's £10 million debts to her.

Yet although the substantive issues were being settled, the old symbols could still not be disregarded. Even Nasution seemed to be differing from Malik (perhaps deliberately, for he was no longer as influential as he had been and may have found an issue of this kind a useful lever) when he said on 17 June that although the battle with Malaysia may be over, the struggle against imperialism still went on and 'the Manila Agreements, using Asian means to settle Asian matters, must be utilised in bringing about a peaceful settlement'. Soekarno was also insisting that confrontation would continue until Malaysia 'adhered to the Manila Agreements', the only change being that it would now be carried out peacefully, instead of militarily. The NU was taking the same line quite assertively. Hence the government simply could not afford to flout Indonesian interpretations of the Manila Agreements openly, at least until it had strengthened its domestic authority. Added point was given to Indonesian arguments for making an issue of the right of the Borneo territories to decide their own destiny after the Sarawak crisis blew up in June over the Tunku's ham-fisted sacking of the Chief Minister, Stephen Kalong Ningkan.

General Suharto's position vis-à-vis President Soekarno was considerably strengthened in July after the People's Consultative Congress (duly shorn of its Communist-sympathizing elements who were replaced by more reliable members) rebuffed the President bluntly and called for a cabinet under Suharto's leadership. On 28 July, Suharto completed the formation of a new cabinet which bore the stamp of the new regime a good deal more strongly than its predecessor. After the first cabinet meeting on 4 August, it was announced that confrontation would end before Independence Day, 17 August. After further exchanges with the Malaysian government Tun Razak visited Djakarta to sign the agreement on 16 August ending hostilities and normalizing relations between the two countries.

The final agreement was brief and vague, providing merely for cessation of hostile acts (the word 'confrontation' was again not used), for immediate establishment of diplomatic relations — but not yet diplomatic representation — and, 'in order to resolve the problems between the two countries arising out of the formation of Malaysia', for the Malaysian government to afford an opportunity to the people of Sabah and Sarawak 'to reaffirm in a free and democratic manner through general elections, their previous decision about their status in Malaysia'.[26] The last sentence was a masterpiece of compromise in reconciling the conflicting views about the earlier choice by the Borneo states. Indonesians could interpret it as a triumphant vindication of their argument that the 1963 act of self-determination was unsatisfactory and should be repeated. Malaysians could feel that their interpretation of the 1963 decision had been upheld, but that they were now making a generous concession to Indonesian objections, without being committed specifically to anything more than the elections in those states which were due, in any case, within a year or so. (A legalist might even point out that Malaysia was committed only to 'reaffirming the previous decision'; it gave no hint of the possibility that the people of Sabah and Sarawak might vote in a way which could be interpreted otherwise — which was by no means improbable.) Meanwhile recognition and full diplomatic representation would be withheld until honour was satisfied on this point.

[1]See statement by Brigadier General Sugandhi, spokesman for the Armed Forces, on 9 October in reply to statements by Inche Senu several days earlier; compare also the statement by the Tunku on 12 October. For a fuller account of the ending of confrontation which differs in some respects from the interpretation given here, see Franklin B. Weinstein, *Indonesia Abandons Confrontation. An Enquiry into the Functions of Indonesian Foreign Policy* (Cornell Modern Indonesia Project. Interim Reports Series, 1969).

[2]Figures indicating the seriousness of the inflation in 1965 may be found in the *Bulletin of Indonesian Economic Studies*, no. 2, September 1965, pp. 10–11 and no. 4, June 1966, p. 21; and Mackie, *Problems of the Indonesian Inflation*, pp. 42 and 100.

[3]Out of the numerous accounts of the coup and its aftermath, I will here merely list a group of English-language articles (of varying degrees of reliability) presupposing a high degree of PKI responsibility for what happened, against which must be set those which assume a low degree. In the former category, see Nugroho Notosusanto and Ismail Saleh, *The Coup Attempt of the 'September 30 Movement' in Indonesia* (Djakarta, 1968), the most plausible statement of the 'official' version; Arthur J. Dommen, 'The Attempted Coup in Indonesia', *China Quarterly*, vol. X, no. 2, Summer 1966; and John Hughes, *The Indonesian Upheaval* (New York, 1967). In the latter category, see D. Lev, 'Indonesia: The Year of the Coup', *Asian Survey*, vol. VI, no. 2, February 1966; Lucien Rey, 'Dossier of the Indonesian Drama', *New Left Review*, no. 36, March-April, 1966; W. F. Wertheim, 'Indonesia Before and After the Untung Coup', *Pacific Affairs*, vol. XXIX, no. 1–2, Spring-Summer, 1967; and Ruth McVey, 'Indonesian Communism and China' in Tang Tsou (ed.) *China's Policies in Asia and America's Alternatives*, vol. 2 (University of Chicago Press, 1968), ch. 13: and the so-called 'Cornell paper', first circulated unofficially in 1966 and published in an identical version in 1971, in which the argument that the PKI was not wittingly involved in the Untung coup was most strongly stated — *A Preliminary Analysis of the October 1, 1965 Coup in Indonesia* (Cornell University Modern Indonesia Project, 1971). For a judicious analysis of the issues and the current state of the controversy, see Rex Mortimer, 'Unresolved Problems of the Indonesian Coup', *Australian Outlook*, vol. XXV, no. 1, April 1971.

[4]Suharto's account of his actions on 1 October, as related to a meeting of the National Front two weeks later, is published in *Indonesia* (Cornell University, Modern Indonesian Project), no I, pp. 160–78.

[5]According to Australian journalist Frank Palmos who was in Central Java soon after the coup attempt, PKI branches had received instructions after the coup to take no action and to lie low in the hope that the storm would pass. If Aidit's alleged confession, as published in *Asahi Shimbun* and in Dommen, op. cit. pp. 168-70 can be believed, however, Aidit was making preparations for a PKI uprising in Solo (Surakarta) on 23 October, but was foiled by the arrival of the RPKAD on the previous day. The confession has been challenged (by W. F. Wertheim) as a 'crude fake', but there seems to be some evidence that the PKI made a last-minute attempt to prevent the RPKAD reaching Solo.

[6]The PKI headquarters was burned on 8 October: attacks on the Youth Front building and Respublica University (both regarded as hot-beds of PKI influence) occurred in the following week. On 17 October, KOTI ordered a ban on all groups involved in the coup, but Soekarno was still refusing to charge the PKI with complicity and strongly condemned the uncontrolled attacks on Communists. Next day, Suharto instructed regional military commanders to 'temporarily ban mass organizations of political parties where there are clear indications of their involvement in the coup', and the Djakarta military commander banned the PKI in Djakarta. On 21 October, all government departments were ordered to be purged of persons involved in the coup. PKI deputies in Parliament were suspended on 23 October; SOBSI was also banned and all members of the PKI were ordered to report regularly to the military authorities. By the end of October, the PKI was reported to have been banned or 'suspended' in East Java, South Sulawesi and South Kalimantan: the ban was ordered in North Sumatra and West Kalimantan on 9 November, in West Java on 19 November. Early in November, the press reported that the President was under heavy pressure to order the PKI dissolved and that he was 'considering' it; but despite a resolution to this effect by Parliament and a mass rally in Djakarta on 17 November, he refused to give in on the issue and it faded into the background soon after. But by that stage, 10,000 people were reportedly under arrest as a result of the coup and the PKI was almost past saving. Aidit was captured and shot on or about 23 November 1965.

[7]*The Age*, 25 October 1965.

[8]*The Age*, 10 November 1965.

[9]Seymour Topping quote estimates from 150,000 to 'far more than half a million' in *New York Times*, 24 August 1966. Frank Palmos indicated a substantially higher number in *The Sun* (Melbourne), 5 August 1966: compare also *The Economist*, 20 August 1966 and *New Statesman*, 5 August 1966.

[10]Wertheim, op. cit. p. 125.

[11]Herbert Feith, 'Indonesia — Blot on the New Order', *The New Republic*, 13 April 1967.

[12]For fuller details, see 'Survey of Recent Developments', *Bulletin of Indonesian Economic Studies*, no. 3, February 1966, pp. 1–26.

[13]This paragraph is based on material supplied by Mr. Stuart Graham from a dissertation on student politics in Indonesia.

[14]*Angkatan Bersendjata*, 3, 5, 9, 11 March 1966.

[15]Ibid. 12 March.

[16]See statements by Malik, 22 March, and Ali Sadikin, 23 March; also Weinstein, op. cit. pp. 32–3. Radio Indonesia was still saying as late as 11 May that confrontation would continue and troops were reported as still being sent to the Borneo front on 22 March and 16 May.

[17]Suharto commented on 31 March that 'the door is open to peace'; Malik repeated this after a KOGAM meeting on 4 April, although Soekarno urged on the same occasion that confrontation must be intensified. *The Australian*, 5 April 1966.

[18]*The Age*, 11 April 1966; *Indonesian Herald*, 11 April 1966.

[19]*Straits Times*, 14, 30 April 1966. Ferdinand Marcos, the new President of the Philippines, had made clear his intentions to recognize Malaysia and restore normal relations with her. A move in this direction in February provoked a hostile reaction from Soekarno which caused Marcos to modify his plans, to the displeasure of Malaysia.

[20]*The Age*, 30 May 1966. The formal relationship between Soekarno and Suharto at this stage was utterly obscure, as the executive authority being exercised by the latter was based on Soekarno's letter of 11 March. After the 4th MPRS session in June, Suharto could claim its authority as MPRS 'mandatory'; at a special session in February 1967, he became Acting President and at the 5th session a year later full President.

[21]*The Age*, 16 May 1966. Part of the official communiqué of the KOGAM meeting of 15 May reads: 'confrontation will continue, but the door for peaceful negotiations on the basis of the Manila Agreements is still open. This can be implemented directly without mediation and can be on a Foreign Ministerial level.'

[22]*Straits Times*, 28 May 1966.

[23]*Straits Times*, 2 and 11 June 1966; some further details were given by Creighton Burns in *The Age*, 15 June 1966.

[24]*The Age*, 10 June 1966.

[25]The domestic politics of ratification are related more fully in Weinstein, op. cit. pp. 57–69.

[26]For the text of the Agreement to Normalise Relations, see Weinstein, op. cit. pp. 93–4.

XII
Conclusion

WHEN confrontation ended in 1966, it was not easy to believe at first that a post-Soekarno regime would be able to change the direction and character of Indonesia's foreign policy as radically as President Suharto and his Foreign Minister, Adam Malik, soon managed to do. Because confrontation had seemed to be a manifestation of Indonesia's deep-seated political instability, the causes of which could obviously not be eliminated by a mere change of government, it was widely believed that Indonesia would remain a restless and potentially disturbing element in the South-East Asian international system long after Soekarno's disappearance from the scene. The question 'Will confrontation recur?' still seemed a valid one. One could answer it by giving a number of particular reasons why a recurrence seemed unlikely (see p. 333 below), but even then a general question remained about the significance to be attached to confrontation itself. Was it simply an aberration from Indonesia's traditional foreign policies, for which Soekarno can be held to blame? Or should its causes be seen as more deeply rooted in the Indonesian political system, either in popular attitudes towards 'Greater Indonesia' or in the inherent tendency of a nation suffering from such serious political and socio-economic problems to project its aggressive tendencies against either domestic scapegoats or external enemies?

To regard Soekarno as wholly or primarily responsible for confrontation, without noticing how far he himself was a prisoner within Indonesia's tangled web of political forces in 1963–5, would, of course, be a considerable oversimplification. The causes of confrontation were obviously far more complex and deep-seated than that. But they were neither as ineluctable nor as mechanistic as some of the theories advanced to explain the conflict implied. Soekarno almost certainly could have extricated himself from it in the early stages, at least if he had been willing to contemplate the implications of such a move, a distinct shift to the right in domestic politics and greater dependence on foreign aid. General Suharto found no great difficulty in bringing about such a reversal of policy in

1966-7, but the whole political environment had been radically changed by then through the destruction of the PKI. Soekarno had a far more difficult team of horses to drive and he was committed by the doctrine of *Nasakom* unity to the belief that they must be kept harnessed together, not separated. And for that purpose, an issue like confrontation suited him well by helping to preserve national unity. Only if he had been a very different kind of man could one have expected him to repudiate the opportunities it offered him.

THE SEARCH FOR EXPLANATIONS

Amongst the various interpretations of confrontation that have been advanced, three main classes of explanation can be discerned, which may be designated as expansionist, diversionist and ideological theories. None is entirely satisfactory by itself, though they all have a grain of truth in them and elements of all three must be invoked to account for particular parts of the story.

The hypothesis that confrontation resulted from an expansionist drive or irredentist sentiment directed towards the re-establishment of *Indonesia Raja* is not at all convincing in its cruder forms and deserves only passing attention. Several writers have given undue prominence to a Malaysian government propaganda paper based on Mohammed Yamin's yearnings for *Indonesia Raja* and his contributions to the 1945 debates about the extent of Indonesia's national territory, but, as we have seen above, this can hardly be taken as satisfactory evidence of attitudes held in 1965 without further corroboration.[1] And the almost complete absence of any appeal by Soekarno or his ministers in the years 1963–5 to the historic glories of Majapahit and Srivijaya is most striking. Enthusiasm for confrontation was generated on quite different grounds, anti-colonialism and ideological fervour. (There may have been more invocation of past glories and historic destiny at lower levels of propaganda activity than appeared on the surface — for instance, in schools and indoctrination courses — but little evidence is available about the extent of this.)[2] There is a more tenable form in which the expansionist theory could be stated, however. If Indonesia had succeeded in driving the *Nekolim* from South-East Asia by her assertive tactics in 1963–4, she would in effect have established a moral hegemony over the region which her neighbours would have found difficult to resist. But the explanation of this is best summarized in Kahin's account of the 'powerful, self-righteous thrust of Indonesian nationalism' and the widespread belief that 'because of their country's size and armed power, and because it won its independence through revolution, it has a moral right to leadership in Asia ...'.[3] Indonesians gave little thought to the concrete ways in which their dominance would have been manifest and there is no need to disbelieve their denials of any attempt to incorporate the Borneo territories or Malaya; they saw the matter only in vague terms of 'liberation from imperialist domination' or a solution 'based on the will of the people', phrases which were not just cynical double-think but the product of their blurred, millenarian notions of the future.

It is in this respect that the interpretation put forward by the foremost advocate of the expansionist theory, Bernard Gordon, is seriously misleading:

...at least let it [confrontation] be understood for what it is: not the unfortunate by-product of Indonesia's internal circumstances, but the actions of a state the leaders of which appear to have a set of external goals. No doubt Indonesia's deep internal divisions have contributed to Soekarno's decision to 'crush' Malaysia. But the argument that confrontation is the result of Indonesia's need for crisis — to keep together 'the various balanced pieces of the governing coalition' — over-emphasizes domestic politics to a point where it ignores a fundamental hypothesis: that important internal groups may nevertheless have common external goals .... Indonesia's foreign policy is not merely the functional product of internal troubles. If that were so, Soekarno could have embarked on almost any new campaign to weld together the dissident elements; according to this view he settled on the confrontation with Malaysia largely because it best satisfied internal requirements. But the facts seem to indicate otherwise; the decision to oppose Malaysia was made in an environment already conditioned for that goal.'[4]

Because of the great stress he puts on the argument that Indonesia's leaders 'have a set of external goals', Gordon's explanation of their strategy and tactics fails to take account of the tentative, erratic development of confrontation in 1963–4. In fact, there was no single 'decision to crush Malaysia' as he implies, for the most striking feature of Soekarno's policy up till September 1963 was its ambivalence, characterized by the pursuit of a diplomatic strategy at the Manila talks simultaneously with guerrilla raids into Sarawak and verbal bombast. But the latter was largely a smoke-screen and should be recognized as such.

It cannot be denied that there was an aggressive, disruptive element in Indonesia's foreign policies in 1963–5, but this was a matter of the threats and illegal methods she resorted to rather than the dimly-specified objectives she was pursuing. The dynamic was not crude 'expansionism' but the 'revolutionary' nature of her ideology; and it is to the latter that we should look for an explanation of the driving forces, not the peripheral fantasies of men like Yamin.

There is a great deal more to be said for diversionist or scapegoat theories of confrontation which interpret it as essentially a projection into foreign policy of the nation's domestic instability. They receive *prima facie* support from the fact that confrontation developed so soon after the ending of the West Irian campaign, at a time of domestic economic difficulties, and had the effect of enabling Soekarno to turn attention away from the task of economic rehabilitation. The crudest versions of this theory — that external adventures served as a means of distracting attention from internal problems or that a foreign crisis helped to maintain national unity and the authority of the government — have only a small element of validity in this case, although they may have been relevant to several key turning points of the West Irian campaign. One cannot adequately explain the development of confrontation at its most decisive points by reference to this hypothesis, even though one must admit that domestic problems were frequently swept aside by the clamour of Soekarno's foreign policies. But confrontation certainly served a variety of purposes for various actors in the Indonesian political drama which enabled them to avoid alternative policies that would have been less advantageous to them.

A persuasive statement of this kind of argument was given by Hindley in his interpretation of confrontation in terms of President Soekarno's twin objectives of welding a nation out of 'the heterogeneity that is Indonesia' and of maintaining his central position in the struggle for power there.[5]

Both these objectives are furthered by a situation of crisis involving real or supposed threats from foreign powers. With foreign enemies and subversives threatening Indonesia, its many peoples move closer together and feel as one people within the protective walls of strident nationalism. With a foreign crisis, the various balanced pieces of the governing can stay together with a common goal; while if domestic problems, such as economic deterioration, were tackled there would be strong clashes of interest within the coalition. Soekarno might then have to choose between the PKI and the Army.

Confrontation certainly enabled the government to focus attention on the struggle against the *Nekolim* and to insist that national unity on this issue must be maintained at all costs: differences of opinion on economic and political issues could be subordinated to this primary goal. But was that an intentional or secondary effect? Did the government deliberately step up the level of confrontation in September 1963, for instance, in order to distract attention from the embarrassing political and economic problems arising from the May stabilization policy? The effect was certainly to undermine that policy; and some groups seem to have intended that this should happen, but their primary purposes were too complex to be explained away as merely 'diversionary'.

A related and more sophisticated aspect of this hypothesis has been emphasized by Herbert Feith in his discussion of the Soekarno regime's addiction to symbol-wielding and 'expressive' rather than instrumental policies.[6] At a moment of national emergency, real or imagined, policies and leaders of one type are required whereas in a period of economic reform quite other priorities and skills will be called for. 'If the government were to speak less and less of the need to complete the revolution and instead to declare economic development as the principal challenge of the present period, describing this as a slow and difficult task, then men in (positions of authority)... would soon have their positions contested in the name of the government's ideology by others who could claim greater technical competence.' 'Revolutionary diplomacy' and assertive foreign policies served to divert energies from more mundane tasks, but they were not just diversionary in the anthropomorphic sense of distracting attention from hungry bellies. The people whose bellies were empty were not likely to forget the fact just because they had been thrilled momentarily by cheering patriotic speeches at a stirring mass-rally. The reaction in 1966 revealed that many were cynically aware of the ironic contrast.

As an explanation of how and why confrontation developed in 1963, the diversion theory implies both too much and too little. Too much insofar as it is wrong to imply that Soekarno was driven to seek an external issue just to distract attention from insoluble problems at home. On several occasions he had to make difficult political decisions on domestic issues (early 1963, for example), but when it came to the point he did make the decisions, not evade them; confrontation helped him to get them accepted, indeed, but it was not just a way of escaping from his difficulties. Rather, it became an intrinsic part of his grand political and ideological strategy. On the other hand, the diversion theory implies too little if interpreted strictly. Soekarno certainly found the issue a useful manipulative instrument throughout 1963, particularly for keeping the PKI in line while he was pursuing policies they detested. In this respect confrontation was not so much a diversion as a bribe, or a bait. Similarly, the Army leaders found confrontation a useful means of preserving their power and privileges at a time when alternative policies would have threatened them. So, too, did the political parties: as Hindley has shown, even the PKI leaders found it useful as a means of justifying their policy of cooperation with the 'bourgeois' nationalists to their restless followers.[7] By 1965 confrontation was serving Soekarno in a variety of ways to maintain national unity, this time mainly to keep the anti-Communists in line.

Perhaps the clearest case of Soekarno's foreign policy having a diversionary effect at a time of acute domestic tension, serving to create an atmosphere of emergency and apprehensiveness, so that opponents could easily be caught on the wrong foot, was Soekarno's abrupt decision to leave the United Nations on 31 December 1964. The threat of national disunity was acute at the time. His plunge towards an extension of confrontation to embrace the United Nations and almost half the world is impossible to explain except in terms of the President's psychology. When under pressure, he seized the initiative, no matter how extreme the consequences. Certainly the tactic worked momentarily at that time. The political crisis passed, national unity was patched up for a few months, at least on the surface, and all major supporters of the regime were induced to express support for the new and higher goals of confrontation.

Going beyond these types of hypothesis, we find that the explanation of confrontation as an expression of the ideology President Soekarno was expounding to his people in the years 1963–6 brings us much closer to the heart of the matter. The doctrine of the New Emerging Forces not only served to justify the dispute with Malaysia in Indonesian eyes, it also made it politically necessary, and thus acceptable to the newspaper-reading public there. Two questions must be asked about this explanation, however. How far do these doctrines provide the key to Soekarno's foreign policies in 1962–5? And why was ideology so extraordinarily influential and all-pervasive in Indonesia at that time, when its effects on the economy and administrative structure of the country were patently disastrous?

In 1963, at a time when many people were trying to divine Soekarno's intentions towards Malaysia by looking for a pattern in what he was doing rather than what he was saying on the ground that his speeches were generally intended primarily for domestic consumption and should be regarded as largely of 'symbolic' importance rather than as statements of what he was actually going to do, the former Secretary of Australia's Department of External Affairs, Sir Alan Watt, urged that Soekarno's utterances should be taken very seriously as meaning just what he said.

President Soekarno is not a weak politician struggling precariously to maintain power by diverting his people from domestic economic difficulties by seeking foreign adventures. He is the clear leader of his people, a self-styled 'revolutionary' pressing with skill and pertinacity to expand the bounds of Indonesian influence and power and to steel his people to the necessary sacrifices. His ideology should be studied, understood and believed.[8]

The observation was an apt one so far as it went. Soekarno's ideology was undeniably revolutionary in its implications, while one of the major purposes behind it was to 'steel the people to sacrifices' as well as to unite them in a struggle against common enemies. Indonesia's foreign policy since 1960 cannot be explained without reference to the ideological indoctrination which was being systematically inculcated in almost every sphere of public life.

The roots of that ideology must be sought partly in the nation's need for cultural and moral orientation at a time of confusing political conflict, partly in what Frederick Bunnell has called, inelegantly but appropriately, the deep-seated 'psychological-ideological impulses of a fervent nationalist'.[9] The confrontation of Malaysia suited the moral and political requirements of that ideology almost perfectly. But we must still consider whether the meaning that Soekarno and other Indonesians read into defiant phrases about the struggle to overthrow imperialism and to 'crush Malaysia' was the same as was read into them by foreigners. The meanings attached to words and concepts depend in large part on the cultural frame of reference within which they are used. Because of the vagueness and ambiguity of Soekarno's doctrines, a search for their 'literal meaning' is less likely to be fruitful than an examination of the ways they were utilized.

Another student of international relations, George Modelski, has also stressed the importance of Indonesia's ideology as 'the basis of its foreign policy ... a carefully thought out body of ideas that serves as the guide, inspiration and also rationalization of its international position'.[10] He commented that Soekarno had attempted to base Indonesia's foreign policies on a set of principles, the doctrine of New Emerging Forces, 'the doctrine guiding the country's international behaviour'. Modelski also observed, however, that ideological preoccupations provided 'no more than a partial guide to Indonesian international behaviour', but he merely noted the divergence between words and actions without analysing it in any detail. That is what we have to do, however, for there was certainly a great deal of hyperbole about Soekarno's utterances, many of which were intended to veil his deeper thoughts as well as to reveal them. To regard him as literally a 'revolutionary' or a Socialist without noticing how little he had in common with many of the revolutionaries and Socialists whose terminology he borrowed would be very misleading. Soekarno's ideology may have influenced most aspects of Indonesian politics, but it was by no means the sole determinant of them and its meaning was not always clear-cut by any means.

There is no question, however, that the ideology of the time, particularly the doctrine of the New Emerging Forces, contributed to the development of confrontation in various ways. In the first place, it coloured Indonesian perceptions of the world in such a way that Indonesians could hardly have been expected to see the British and their Malaysian 'lackeys' as anything but agents of sinister *Nekolim* forces antagonistic to the Indonesian revolution. On the basis of Indonesia's experience with Dutch 'puppet' governments in 1946–9, Malay Sultans and Dayak chiefs who were prepared to collaborate with the colonial power were irredeemably 'feudal' and reactionary: so too were wealthy Chinese *towkays* of the same ilk. We all perceive the world through an ideologically tinted lens, but some lenses are more strongly tinted than others, while some people have more opportunities than others to try alternative lenses and become aware of the distortions. That was almost impossible for ordinary Indonesians by 1963, unless they listened to foreign radio broadcasts — and even these came under an increasingly damaging stigma of being propagandist in purpose and irredeemably *Nekolim* in sympathy, so that they were not really an acceptable alternative except for a tiny minority of Indonesians. The press dared not stray beyond prescribed doctrinal limits and anyone relying solely on one or two Indonesian newspapers for his information about Malaysia in 1963–4 would have found it almost impossible to interpret what was happening there except in terms of the government's version of a *Nekolim* plot against Indonesia.

Second, confrontation was ideologically necessary for Indonesia in the sense that a government proclaiming the doctrine of the New Emerging Forces could not afford to ignore the Brunei revolt and subsequent developments in Malaysia without being accused of denying or abandoning its own principles. Whenever Soekarno or his ministers too flagrantly diverged from their oft-stated doctrines, the PKI and other critics were always eager to seize upon the issue. Because the national ideology had been elevated to such extraordinary status as the touchstone of all political activity, it would have been almost out of the question to ignore it, or to justify more cautious policies on colourless pragmatic grounds of expense or prosaic considerations of national interest. In any case, few of Soekarno's ministers would have greatly wanted to do so. Most would have seen the conflict with Malaysia through much the same ideological filter as the President and would have shared his sentiments about it.

Third, confrontation itself served to reinforce the doctrine of the New Emerging Forces by adding proof of its validity in the eyes of most Indonesians. As the conflict with Malaysia developed, both the British and their lackeys in Kuala Lumpur behaved in precisely the ways that the

Nekolim might be expected to behave. Nothing they could have done would effectively have expunged the taint upon them. Hence it was almost impossible to settle the Malaysia-Indonesia conflict on the basis of a compromise political settlement during 1963–4, for the Indonesians could not be convinced that the Malaysians had changed their spots. The converse was also true, of course. Neither was prepared to trust the other.

Finally, Soekarno's revolutionary, quasi-scientific and strongly millenarian doctrines made a strong appeal not only with Indonesia but even beyond borders — and this, too, was not unwelcome, for it helped to confirm their universal validity and to forward Indonesia's political aims, particularly when these were broadened to embrace 'Building the World Anew'. That was why the intensely ideological character of Indonesian foreign policy made her a 'high pressure area' and source of alarm to her neighbours. They all had discontented minorities or groups of frustrated individuals who had been uprooted by technological and cultural change, and who were dangerously susceptible to millenarian appeals, whether in the crude form of cargo cults or in more sophisticated ideological guises.[11] Soekarno's picture of the world as divided into *Nekolim* and New Emerging Forces conformed at many points to their own experience of the foreigners and their culture. His doctrines offered also a doctrine of struggle (part of a world-wide struggle in which the New Emerging Forces must ultimately win) and thereby a sense of purpose and national dignity. Transparent though much of this ideology proved to be on closer examination, many groups in South-East Asia were hungering for just such spiritual fare. Upon the doctrines of permanent revolution, solidarity with the New Emerging Forces and continuous confrontation ('confrontation with all the obstacles obstructing the course of the revolution...with the counter-revolution...with subversion...with vested interests'). Soekarno based his call for moral regeneration and personal dedication to the nation's struggle against the numerous enemies of Indonesia's revolution. He gave his people an inspiring cause and purpose to devote themselves to, definite goals (the destruction of the *Nekolim* and their accomplices) and a set of political doctrines which provided identifiable points of reference for Indonesians in the confused and rapidly changing world they found themselves in. It is true that there was much in his ideology that was vague and ambiguous — as a political theorist, Soekarno was not a Lenin or a Trotsky — but Indonesians pride themselves on their eclecticism and would not worry greatly about the finer points. The general thrust of Soekarno's teachings was clear enough — radical, anti-capitalist, intensely nationalist, obsessed with the 'romanticism and dialectic of revolution', with *Umwertung aller Werte*.

The new stress on a dynamic, ideologically-inspired foreign policy came after a period of intense domestic indoctrination and ideological exhortation in the years 1960–2, directed towards the welding of national unity on the basis of the President's Political Manifesto and the *Nasakom* principle. This had succeeded to such an extent that these were never publicly questioned by 1962, although they were interpreted in radically different ways. The reasons for this shift from an internal to an external stress in slogans and ideological concerns have been dealt with in chapter V. No doubt the West Irian campaign had a lot to do with it, coinciding as it did with economic and administrative failures at home and an overall change in the world situation which opened up new opportunities for an assertive foreign policy. But the main point to be emphasized is simply that by 1962 Indonesians were accustomed to intense indoctrination and prepared to acquiesce in it, at the same time often manipulating official slogans to serve their own political purposes. Ideology was an accepted element in the political system. Few would ever have challenged the proposition that Indonesia needed an ideological *grundlage*, though there was deep disagreement about the acceptability of different ideological principles, Islamic or Marxist, traditionalist or modern.

WILL CONFRONTATION RECUR?

The singular importance of Soekarno's ideology in creating the predisposition towards a militantly anti-imperialist foreign policy in the mid-sixties is one of the factors that attracts our attention when we are faced with the question: 'Is a confrontation-type foreign policy likely to recur?'. There have been various reasons for giving a confident 'No' to that question in the years immediately after Soekarno's downfall — the sheer economic pressures upon the Suharto regime and need to avoid antagonizing potential aid donors, the strongly anti-Communist orientation of the new regime and its preoccupation with domestic issues. In addition, one could point to the very different ideological environment in which Soekarno's grandiloquent doctrines developed and that in which any latter-day emulator would have to operate. If Suharto or his successor or any challenger for power from within the Army were to make a bid for widespread popular support by advocating a more 'Soekarnoist' foreign policy or a resumption of Indonesia's crusade against imperialism and neo-colonialism, he would find himself obliged to formulate such a policy under far less favourable circumstances than those in which Soekarno was able to commit Indonesia to militant confrontation of Malaysia and the *Nekolim*. It is worth noting some of the factors which assisted him to do this. Moreover, it should be noticed that several important elements in the rather singular constellation of circumstances in which confrontation developed (and which happened to make it unusually easy for Soekarno to develop the sort of foreign policy he did in 1963–5) are most unlikely to recur.[12]

In the first place, Soekarno and his ministers were able to involve Indonesia in the confrontation of Malaysia in 1963–4 without much domestic resistance because it seemed likely that the campaign would succeed, and at not too great a cost, that Malaysia would be forced to bid for terms and the British to withdraw from South-East Asia. The stakes were attractive and the chances of success would have appeared to many Indonesians reasonably high. Soekarno seemed to be riding a wave of success after the acquisition of West Irian and the vindication of his political doctrines. The *Nekolim* could be depicted in a state of disarray elsewhere in the world at that time, so it was easy for Indonesians to accept his assertions that the tide of history was running strongly in favour of the New Emerging Forces. By applying a modicum of pressure against Malaysia, that jerry-built edifice (as they saw it) could be pushed over, Britain's position in the Far East made quite untenable and Indonesia's power demonstrated as a major force in the region.

Secondly, it happened that the strategic moment for Indonesia to apply her pressure against Malaysia and Britain came just at the time when Soekarno was developing the kind of foreign policy which inclined him strongly towards confrontation and when, moreover, the international situation was peculiarly favourable to the attempt from Indonesia's point of view. She was no longer inhibited by the need for support in her claim to West Irian. Britain and Malaysia were not likely to be strongly supported by any other power, except Australia, who clearly wanted to avoid a war with Indonesia. Neither America nor Russia had much effective leverage over Indonesia to dissuade her from a foreign policy based on 'Vivere Pericoloso' if she chose to apply it. On the contrary, just because the entire international system was beginning to thaw out of the rigidities of the Cold War era in 1962–3, mavericks like de Gaulle and Soekarno were discovering that they could thumb their noses at the super-powers to a quite unprecedented degree. They had to pay a price for it, but the price was not as crippling as before, for there were new possibilities of playing off one country against another. We have seen that Soekarno began to formulate the doctrine of New Emerging Forces in 1961–2 deliberately as an alternative foreign policy doctrine for an era when the old division of the world into the two contending blocs and the non-aligned Third World was no longer relevant. By 1964, he was trying to minimize Indonesia's dependence on both USA and USSR — in part by moving into closer partnership with China, whose star was then at its brightest.

Thirdly, it should be remembered that Soekarno was able to get away with the extravagant policies he was pursuing in 1962–5 only so long as he had access to external sources of finance, so that he could run Indonesia into debt without reaching the point where the brakes of economic necessity or social discontent began to check his course. Indonesia was able to live beyond her means because she was able to draw on a considerable sum of foreign credits and loans in the years 1961–4. The importance of those credits should not be under-rated, for Indonesia was still drawing on them (to a rapidly diminishing extent, it is true) until 1965, well after the cessation of US aid.[13] Thus Soekarno was able to disregard warnings of impending economic disaster, despite the ruinous economic disruption which proved to be tolerable for much longer than most people initially expected. Those credits were something of a windfall, however, having mostly been negotiated in the unusually favourable economic and political atmosphere of 1960–1. It is doubtful that such a favourable situation will repeat itself in a similar way.

Finally, we come back also to Soekarno himself. He exercised an enormous influence in the years 1960–5, largely because he provided Indonesia with an ideology of struggle and continuing revolution which evoked a response from his people and conformed to their view of the world around them. The ideology developed and changed step by step with his advance to semi-dictatorial power within a gradually changing political system. The Soekarno of 1959 could not have carried the country into a campaign like confrontation even with the PKI's support. In 1961, he had difficulty in carrying it into a militant confrontation of the Dutch in West Irian. By 1963, however, his authority was vastly greater and the validity of his ideas was widely accepted. But success was essential to the credibility of the doctrines on which his regime depended — and as successes on substantial matters eluded him, the ideology became more fantastic and unreal, sustained only by symbolic victories and the constant anticipation of some miraculous transformation. Confrontation, therefore, suited Soekarno's personality and political requirements almost perfectly in the last flamboyant stage of 'living dangerously'. Once the ideological facade was shattered, however, the bankruptcy of his policies could no longer be hidden.

[1]See above, pp. 21-3. Such interpretations were offered in Gordon, *The Dimensions of Conflict in Southeast Asia*, and in his 'The Potential for Indonesian Expansionism', *Pacific Affairs*, vol. LXXXVI, no. 4, Winter 1963–4, pp. 378–93: Garth N. Jones, 'Soekarno's Early Views upon the Territorial Boundaries of Indonesia', *Australian Outlook*, vol. XVIII, no. 1, April 1964, pp. 30–9. Compare also Tregonning, *North Borneo*, p. 121: 'in Indonesia ..., the claim for all Borneo is made only less frequently than that for New Guinea'.

[2]See Robert Curtis, 'Malaysia and Indonesia', p. 23: 'It is common talk in Indonesia that the real aim is for Djakarta not Kuala Lumpur to control North Borneo.' An Australian military officer who attended the Indonesian Staff and Command School in Bandung (SESKOAD) informed me that a great deal of Yamin-type history was included in Army training courses (as in the armed services of most nations, of course).

[3]Kahin, 'Malaysia and Indonesia', pp. 260–1.

[4]Gordon, op. cit. pp. 95–6.

[5]Donald Hindley, 'Indonesia's Confrontation with Malaysia: a Search for Motives' *Asian Survey*, vol. IV, no. 6. June 1964, pp. 904–13.

[6]Herbert Feith, 'The Dynamics of Guided Democracy', p. 387.

[7]Hindley, op. cit. pp. 910–11.

[8]'Soekarno's Ideas and Ambitions', *Sydney Morning Herald*, 28 November 1963. Modelski, *The New Emerging Forces,* pp. ii-viii.

[9]Frederick Bunnell, 'Guided Democracy Foreign Policy: 1960–65', *Indonesia*, II, October 1966, p. 38.

[10]Modelski, *The New Emerging Forces*, p. iv.

[11]In the Philippines, the left-wing group of radical students and intellectuals associated with the *Progressive Review* took over some of Soekarno's phrases and concepts in 1963–4, although using them in rather different ways.

[12]For a fuller treatment of these arguments see J. A. C. Mackie, 'Indonesia's New Look: An End to Confrontation?', *New Guinea* (Sydney) no. 7, October 1966, pp. 55–8.

[13]Details of $295 million of foreign credits provisionally negotiated between January and September 1965 are set out in *Bulletin of Indonesian Economic Studies*, no. 2. September 1965, p. 6.

Appendix I
The Manila Agreements

(A) THE MANILA ACCORD

REPORTS and recommendations of the Conference of the Foreign Ministers of the Federation of Malaya, the Republic of Indonesia and the Republic of the Philippines, to their respective Heads of Government.

1. The Governments of the Federation of Malaya, the Republic of Indonesia and the Republic of the Philippines, prompted by their keen and common desire to have a general exchange of views on current problems concerning stability, security, economic development and social progress of the three countries and of the region and upon the initiative of President Diosdado Macapagal, agreed that a Conference of Ministers of the three countries be held in Manila on 7th June, 1963, for the purpose of achieving common understanding and the close fraternal cooperation among themselves. Accordingly, Tun Abdul Razak, Deputy Prime Minister of the Federation of Malaya, Dr. Subandrio, Deputy First Minister/Minister for Foreign Affairs of the Republic of Indonesia, and Hon. Emmanuel Pelaez, Vice-President of the Philippines and concurrently Secretary of Foreign Affairs, met in Manila from 7th to 11th June, 1963.

2. The deliberations were held in a frank manner and in a most cordial atmosphere in keeping with the spirit of friendship prevailing in the various meetings held between President Soekarno of the Republic of Indonesia, and Prime Minister Tunku Abdul Rahman Putra of the Federation of Malaya, and President Diosdado Macapagal. This Ministerial Conference was a manifestation of the determination of the nations in this region to achieve closer cooperation in their endeavour to chart their common future.

3. The Ministers were of one mind that the three countries share a primary responsibility for the maintenance of the stability and security of the area from subversion in any form of manifestation in order to preserve their respective national identities, and to ensure the peaceful development of their respective countries and of their region, in accordance with the ideals and aspirations of their peoples.

4. In the same spirit of common and constructive endeavour, they exchanged views on the proposed Confederation of Nations of Malay origin, the proposed Federation of Malaysia, the Philippine claim to North Borneo and related problems.

The Macapagal Plan

5. Recognising that it is in the common interest of their countries to maintain fraternal relations and to strengthen cooperations among their peoples who are bound together by ties of race and culture, the three Ministers agreed to intensify the joint and individual efforts of their countries to secure lasting peace, progress and prosperity for themselves and for their neighbours.

6. In this context, the three Ministers supported President Macapagal's plan envisaging the grouping of the three nations of Malay origin working together in closest harmony but without surrendering any portion of their sovereignty. This calls for the establishment of the necessary common organs.

7. The three Ministers agreed to take the initial steps towards this ultimate aim by establishing machinery for frequent and regular consultations. The details of such machinery will be further defined. This machinery will enable the three Governments to hold regular consultations at all levels to deal with matters of mutual interest and concern consistent with the national, regional and international responsibilities or obligations of each country without prejudice to its sovereignty and independence. The Ministers agreed that their countries will endeavour to achieve close understanding and cooperation in dealing with common problems relating to security, stability, economic, social and cultural development.

8. In order to accelerate the process of growth towards the ultimate establishment of President Macapagal's plan, the Ministers agreed that each country shall set up its own national secretariat. Pending the establishment of a central secretariat for the consultative machinery, the national secretaries should co-ordinate and co-operate with each other in the fulfilment of their tasks.

9. The Ministers further agreed to recommend that Heads of Government and Foreign Ministers meet at least once a year for the purpose of consultations on matters of importance and common concern.

Malaysia and North Borneo

10. The Ministers reaffirmed their countries adherence to principle of self-determination for the peoples of non-self-governing territories. In this context, Indonesia and the Philippines stated that they would welcome the formation of Malaysia provided the support of the people of the Borneo Territories is ascertained by an independent and impartial authority, the Secretary-General of the United Nations or his representative.

11. The Federation of Malaya expressed appreciation for this attitude of Indonesia and the Philippines and undertook to consult the British Government and the Governments of the Borneo Territories with a view to inviting the Secretary-General of the United Nations or his representative to take the necessary steps in order to ascertain the wishes of the people of those Territories.

12. The Philippines made it clear that its position on the inclusion of North Borneo in the Federation of Malaysia is subject to the final outcome of the Philippines claim to North Borneo. The Ministers took note of the Philippine claim and the right of the Philippines to continue to pursue it in accordance with international law and the principle of the pacific settlement of disputes. They agreed that the inclusion of North Borneo in the Federation of Malaysia would not prejudice either the claim or any right thereunder. Moreover, in the context of their close association, the three countries agreed to exert their best endeavours to bring the claim to a just and expeditious solution by peaceful

means of the Parties' own choice, in conformity with the charter of the United Nations and the Bandung Declaration.

13. In particular, considering the close historical ties between the peoples of the Philippines and North Borneo as well as their geographical propinquity, the Ministers agreed that in the event of North Borneo joining the proposed Federation of Malaysia the Government of the latter and the Government of the Philippines should maintain and promote the harmony and the friendly relations subsisting in their region to ensure the security and stability of the area.

14. The Ministers agreed to recommend that a meeting of their respective Heads of Government be held in Manila not later than the end of July 1963.

15. The Ministers expressed satisfaction over the atmosphere of brotherliness and cordiality which pervaded their meeting and considered it as a confirmation of their close fraternal ties and as a happy augury for the success of future consultations among their leaders.

16. The Ministers agreed to place on record their profound appreciation of and gratitude for the statesman-like efforts of President Macapagal whose courage, vision and inspiration not only facilitated the holding of this historic meeting but also contributed towards the achievement for the first time of a unity of purpose and a sense of common dedication among the peoples of Malaya, Indonesia and the Philippines.

(B) THE MANILA DECLARATION

The President of the Republic of Indonesia, the President of the Philippines and the Prime Minister of the Federation of Malaya, assembled in a Summit Conference in Manila from July 30th to August 4th 1963, following the meeting of their Foreign Ministers held in Manila from June 7th to 11th, 1963:

Conscious — of the historic significance of their coming together for the first time as leaders of sovereign states that have emerged after long struggles from colonial status to independence,

Desiring — to achieve better understanding and closer cooperation in their endeavour to chart their common future,

Inspired — also by the spirit of Asian-African solidarity forged in the Bandung Conference of 1955,

Convinced — that their countries, which are bound together by close historical ties of race and culture, share a primary responsibility for the maintenance of the stability and security of the area from subversion in any form or manifestation in order to preserve their respective national identities and to ensure the peaceful development of their respective countries and their region in accordance with the ideals and aspirations of their peoples, and

Determined — to intensify the joint and individual efforts to their countries to secure lasting peace, progress and prosperity for themselves and their neighbours in a world dedicated to freedom and justice,

Do hereby declare —

First — that they reaffirm their adherence to the principle of equal rights and self-determination of people as enunciated in the United Nations Charter and the Bandung Declaration,

Second — that they are determined, in the common interest of their countries, to maintain fraternal relations, to strengthen cooperation among their peoples in the economic, social and cultural fields in order to promote economic progress and social well-being in the region, and to put an end to the exploitation of man by man and of one nation by another,

Third — that the three nations shall combine their efforts in the common struggle against colonialism and imperialism in all their forms and manifestations and for the eradication of the vestiges thereof in the region in particular and the world in general.

Fourth — that the three nations, as new emerging forces in the region, shall cooperate in building a new and better world based on national freedom, social justice and lasting peace, and

Fifth — that in the context of the joint endeavours of the three nations to achieve the foregoing objectives, they have agreed to take initial steps towards the establishment of Maphilindo by holding frequent and regular consultations at all levels to be known as Mushawarah Maphilindo.

(C) THE MANILA JOINT STATEMENT

The President of the Republic of Indonesia, the President of the Philippines, and the Prime Minister of the Federation of Malaya met at a Summit Conference in Manila from July 30th to August 5th, 1963.

1. Moved by a sincere desire to solve their common problems in an atmosphere of fraternal understanding, they considered, approved and accepted the report and recommendations of the Foreign Ministers of the three countries adopted in Manila on June 11th, 1963 (hereafter to be known as the Manila Accord).

2. In order to provide guiding principles for the implementation of the Manila Accord the Heads of Government have issued a Declaration known as the Manila Declaration, embodying the common aspirations and objectives of the peoples and Governments of the three countries.

3. As a result of the consultations amongst the three Heads of Government, in accordance with the principles enunciated in the Manila Declaration, they have resolved various current problems of common concern.

4. Pursuant to paragraph 10 and 11 of the Manila Accord, the United Nations Secretary-General or his representative, should ascertain prior to the establishment of the Federation of Malaysia the wishes of the people of Sabah (North Borneo) and Sarawak within the context of General Assembly resolution 1541 (XV), Principle 9 of the Annex, by a fresh approach, which in the opinion of the Secretary-General is necessary to ensure complete compliance with the principle of self-determination within the requirements embodied in Principle 9, taking into consideration:

(I) The recent elections in Sabah (North Borneo) and Sarawak, but nevertheless, further examining, verifying and satisfying himself as to whether —
    (a) Malaysia was a major issue, if not the main issue,
    (b) Electoral registers were properly compiled,
    (c) Elections were free and there was no coercion, and
    (d) Votes were properly polled and properly counted, and

(II) The wishes of those who, being qualified to vote would have exercised their right of self-determination in the recent elections had it not been for their detention for political activities, imprisonment for their political offences or absence from Sabah (North Borneo) or Sarawak.

5. The Secretary-General will be requested to send working teams to carry out the task set out in paragraph 4.

6. The Federation of Malaya, having undertaken to consult the British Government and the Governments of Sabah (North Borneo) and Sarawak

under Paragraph 11 of the Manila Accord on behalf of the three Heads of Government, further undertake to request them to cooperate with the Secretary-General and to extend to him the necessary facilities so as to enable him to carry out his task as set out in paragraph 4.

7. In the interests of the countries concerned, the three Heads of Government deem it desirable to send observers to witness the carrying out of the task to be undertaken by the working teams, and the Federation of Malaya will use its best endeavours to obtain the cooperation of the British Government and the Governments of Sabah (North Borneo) and Sarawak in furtherance of this purpose.

8. In accordance with paragraph 12 of the Manila Accord, the three Heads of Government decided to request the British Government to agree to seek a just and expeditious solution to the dispute between the British Government and the Philippine Government concerning Sabah (North Borneo) by means of negotiations, conciliation and arbitration, judicial settlement, or other peaceful means of the Parties' own choice in conformity with the Charter of the United Nations. The three Heads of Government take cognizance of the position regarding the Philippine claim to Sabah (North Borneo), after the establishment of the Federation of Malaysia as provided under paragraph 12 of the Manila Accord that is, that the inclusion of Sabah (North Borneo) in the Federation of Malaysia, does not prejudice either the claim or any right thereunder.

9. Pursuant to paragraph 6, 7, 8 and 9 of the Manila Accord and the fifth principle of the Manila Declaration, that is, that initial steps should be taken towards the establishment of Maphilindo by holding frequent and regular consultations at all levels, to be known as Mushawarah Maphilindo, it is agreed that each country shall set up a National Secretariat for Maphilindo affairs and as a first step the respective national secretaries will consult together with a view to coordinating and cooperating with each other in the study on the setting up of the necessary machinery for Maphilindo.

10. The three Heads of Government emphasised that the responsibility for the preservation of the national independence of the three countries and of the peace and security in their region lies primarily in the hands of the Government and the peoples of the countries concerned, and that the three Governments undertake to have close consultations (Mushawarah) among themselves on these matters.

11. The three Heads of Government further agreed that foreign bases — temporary in nature — should not be allowed to be used directly or indirectly to subvert the national independence of any of the three countries. In accordance with the principle enunciated in the Bandung Declaration, the three countries will abstain from the use of arrangements of collective defence to serve the particular interests of any of the big powers.

12. President Soekarno and Prime Minister Abdul Rahman express their deep appreciation for the initiative taken by President Macapagal in calling the Summit Conference which, in addition to resolving their differences concerning the proposed Federation of Malaysia, resulted in paving the way for the establishment of Maphilindo. The three Heads of Government conclude this Conference, which has greatly strengthened the fraternal ties which bind their three countries and extended the scope of their cooperation and understanding, with renewed confidence that their Governments and peoples will together make a significant contribution to the attainment of just and enduring peace, stability and prosperity in the region.

Appendix II
Joint Communique of the Malaysian Socialist Conference on Malaysia, January 1962

AN APPROACH TO MALAYSIA

THE Conference welcomes the closer cooperation in all spheres of life of the peoples of the Federation of Malaya, Singapore, Sarawak, Brunei and Sabah and expresses the hope that in the years to come this cooperation will bring about peace and stability in the region.

The Conference has deliberated on the submissions of the delegates present and is of the view that any form of constitutional change for the peoples of the territories mentioned must only be brought about with their express consent.

The Conference has noted with some concern the attempts in some quarters to foist upon the peoples of the territories a constitutional arrangement inimical to their interests and regardless of their feelings.

The Conference also notes with regret that little opportunity is being afforded to the people for a genuine expression of their views. Instead there appears to be a deliberate effort to by-pass the people and, under cover of an intense propaganda campaign, to rush through a constitutional arrangement for Malaysia that is not in harmony with the sentiments and aspirations of the people.

For this reason the Conference feels morally bound to deplore the conduct of the Malaysia Solidarity Consultative Committee for attempting to speak for the peoples of the territories when it has not the mandate or the competence to do so, and calls upon the Consultative Committee to desist from such outrageous behaviour.

The concept of Malaysia was considered and the Conference is in support of the views expressed in the most definite terms by the delegates from Brunei and Sarawak, that the three Bornean territories should exercise the right of self-determination before the concept of Malaysia is to be further examined.

The Conference has also noted the opposition of the socialist parties in Singapore to the constitutional proposals for bringing Singapore under the jurisdiction of the Federation Government. The Conference supports the stand taken by these parties in opposition to the White Paper proposals on 'merger' and wishes to express its conviction that these proposals would only lead to racial disharmony and greater divisions among the peoples.

Merger between Singapore and the Federation should only take place on a basis of equality, that is all Singapore citizens should become national citizens and should send representatives to Parliament on a proportional basis. This the Conference declares should be an essential precondition to the acceptance of any merger proposals.

Considering the present state of political growth in the Federation, the Conference realizes that the conditions are not favourable for a full and complete merger and therefore supports the desire of the people of Singapore for full self-determination.

The Conference wishes to make it clear that whatever happens it is the people of the territories who must decide their future, and that any attempt to ignore the people must be resolutely resisted. The people can only decide if representative forms of government are fully established in all the territories.

In the field of Foreign Affairs, the Conference supports the policy of non-alignment with the power blocs as enunciated by the Asian African Conferences in Bandung in 1955. The Conference supports the struggle of the Indonesian people for the recovery of the territory of West Irian from the Dutch.

It is also recognised that the main danger to peace in South-East Asia comes from such aggressive organisations as the South-East Asia Treaty Organisation. The Conference resolved that on no account must the people allow their territories to be used in the service of SEATO.

Signed by the Leader Delegates to the Conference of the following parties:

1. The Sarawak United Peoples Party.
2. The Workers Party, Singapore.
3. The Barisan Sosialis Singapore.
4. The Partai Rakyat Singapore.
5. The Partai Rakyat Malaya.
6. The Partai Rakyat Brunei.
7. The Labour Party Malaya.

This communique was issued at Kuala Lumpur on 28 January 1962.

Appendix III
Indonesian Borneo
(Kalimantan): a Footnote

Political developments in British North Borneo had no observable impact on the Indonesian segment of the island until confrontation was intensified in the latter part of 1963. Historically, relations between the two parts have never been very close and in recent years they have only been of peripheral importance. Smugglers from Indonesia used to flock into Tawau, but more from north Sulawesi than the unproductive and thinly populated east coast of Kalimantan. Some pepper and rubber was smuggled across the border from the region around Pontianak on the shoulders of Dayak bearers, a trade which was quite lucrative for some people on both sides, but of slight economic importance for the rubber growers and Chinese *towkays* of West Kalimantan in comparison with their trade to Singapore, with which the latter have traditionally had much closer links. Many of the Chinese farmers on both sides of the border are descendants of the original Hakka goldminers who came to the region nearly two hundred years ago. To them, as to the Dayaks of the remote interior, the frontier has probably not been much more than a geographical feature obstructing movement; only on a few occasions in colonial times has it been a matter of political concern to the two governments. Tiny groups of Indonesians were to be found in Kuching, Jesselton and Sandakan and one larger community of over 12,000 Indonesian migrant labourers on rubber plantations and in timber camps near Tawau, but most of these came from Timor, Sulawesi and more distant islands rather than East Kalimantan.[1]

Yet there were other reasons why the Indonesian government had an interest in what was happening on the northern side of the frontier. Since independence, the Indonesian government has administered Kalimantan with a fairly loose rein. Communications are rudimentary and the major centres of populations scattered and small. Government officials from Java have often been unpopular and have generally disliked being sent there. In any case, it was usually politic to appoint prominent local men to key positions in order to gain their co-operation and political support, for the central government agencies could not operate effectively without the assistance of the regional leaders, even though their interests and outlook have frequently diverged from those of the Djakarta authorities. (Sometimes it has been necessary to appoint more reliable outsiders, but that is rarely a popular move.) Little money has been made available by the central government for development projects there, nor has very much been done to bridge the gap between the primitive and isolated tribes of the interior and the more sophisticated urban communities of the coast, except insofar as the former have been attracted down to the river towns by the prospect of health services, education or trading opportunities there. The extent to which the central government has simply made use of traditional authorities in the various communities of Kalimantan as its agents of government, as it seems to have done to a considerable extent in Sulawesi, is hard to assess; some of the former Sultans were seriously discredited in nationalist eyes by their support for the Dutch during the revolution and were unable to retain their political influence in this way. But there are indications that the Djakarta government has played off one community against another from time to time in order to control the balance of power in particular areas. It is probably true to say that the central government has wielded less effective control in Kalimantan than in either Sumatra or Sulawesi — and some of its concern with what was happening on the British side of the border may well have been due to apprehensions on this score.

A brief glance at the ethnic and political situation in the four provinces of Kalimantan will help to fill in some of the gaps in our understanding of this huge but little-known island. Most of their four million inhabitants are clustered in two areas around Bandjarmasin, capital of South Kalimantan, and Pontianak, capital of West Kalimantan.[2] Elsewhere, except around the oil town of Balikpapan, the population is widely scattered throughout many small coastal and riverine settlements. In general, the Dayaks are mostly dispersed throughout the interior, Bandjarese and other 'Malay' (i.e. Muslim) groups around the coast and the 370,000 Chinese mostly in the Pontianak-Sambas area or the main towns.[3] The two provinces of Central and East Kalimantan have very small populations (about half-a-million each) which are predominantly Dayak; consequently they have had very little political influence at the national level — in fact, in the 1955 parliamentary elections, no party in East Kalimantan even reached the electoral quotient necessary to gain a seat. Locally, the Dayaks have had a good deal of political influence in South and West Kalimantan. In South Kalimantan, on the other hand, the Muslim parties have had overwhelming strength, as table 13 shows.

Bandjarmasin is the largest town and was the administrative centre until 1956, before Kalimantan was divided into four provinces. The region surrounding it is also important for political reasons, since it is the homeland of the Bandjarese, the largest single ethnic group in Kalimantan, numbering between $1\frac{1}{2}$ and 2 million, a Muslim trading people who can be found scattered throughout many coastal regions of Borneo and the other islands of the archipelago (like the Buginese), far more advanced economically than the Dayaks and politically more closely-knit and influential. They have generally been at odds with both the former colonial government in Batavia and the Djakarta authorities since 1950, sympathetic to the Muslim parties, Masjumi and NU, and generally anti-Communist. During the struggle for independence, the Bandjarese of south-east Kalimantan actively opposed the Dutch, in contrast to the Dayak leaders, most of whom backed the Dutch-sponsored *Dewan Dayak Besar* (Greater Dayak Council) within the Dutch federal framework because they feared that they would be dominated politically and economically by the more numerous Bandjarese if the latter gained control. The Dayak communities were small and scattered widely through the interior where the only means of communication was by river; few of them had achieved much education or wealth, or even come in contact with the down-river manifestations of twentieth-century civilization. They had very little hope of attaining positions of influence in the early years of the Republic and their political power was nugatory. But the situation began to change around the time of the regional rebellions of 1957–8, when the Bandjarese were inclined to sympathize with the anti-Djakarta forces (although they sat rather uneasily on the fence until they saw who was going to win), with the result that the Dayaks came to be favoured by the central government as a more compliant and reliable set of allies. The latter had succeeded shortly beforehand in inducing Djakarta to create a separate province of Central Kalimantan, no longer subordinate to Bandjarmasin; although it contained a substantial Bandjarese population along the coast, the predominance of the Dayaks within the new provincial assembly was ensured by a little political juggling. The better-educated of the Christian Dayaks in the new province got most of the key posts there, which they could barely have hoped for under the old dispensation. Consequently, the central government found them generally amenable to its policies, in contrast to the Bandjarese of South Kalimantan (for example, over contentious questions about the PKI and the establishment of the National Front in 1961). A major road construction was undertaken, with Russian aid and technicians, from the new capital of Central Kalimantan at Palangka Raja, 60 miles up the Kahajan River in virgin jungle, to the coastal port of Sampit, which is an important timber-producing centre with a substantial population of Javanese labourers.

In South Kalimantan, the central government employed a different strategy to establish its control. The power of the foremost Bandjarese leader, Hasan Basry, the military commander who had been regarded as the local champion since the revolution when he led a guerrilla movement against the Dutch, was being gradually whittled away by the Djakarta authorities. He was virtually kicked upstairs in 1960 to a more prestigious but less powerful military position and replaced by another Bandjarese officer, Col. Jusi, who was considered more amenable to Djakarta control. Jusi was also strongly anti-Communist and resisted the establishment of the National Front in the area under his command; he supported Nasution in his attempts to put pressure on the PKI in 1960–1 by banning the party in South Kalimantan, but he was soon transferred after Nasution's replacement by Yani in 1962, as also was the strongly anti-Communist Bandjarese governor of the province, Hadji Maksid. The National Front was then established and the Communists regained freedom of action there. In effect, the strongly anti-Communist and potentially anti-Soekarno elements among the Bandjarese population had been politically neutralized in South Kalimantan by mid-1963, although the new political balance was precariously maintained, since regional sentiment and discontent with economic conditions still constituted a potential danger to Djakarta's authority there.[4]

In the province of West Kalimantan, there is no dominant group comparable with the Bandjarese, but the most striking feature of the region is its very large proportion of Chinese, 20% of the population of the province, which is the highest percentage of Chinese to be found anywhere in Indonesia. Dayaks and 'coastal Malays' are the two major ethnic categories, the former predominantly found up the main rivers and the latter (descendants of Buginese, Javanese and others, for a large part) closer to the coast.[5] The Chinese and a few Arabs are also concentrated in the coastal regions, apart from a few in the trading centres of the interior. Most of the population is clustered in the north-west corner, between Pontianak and Sambas, or up the great Kapuas river, which runs almost parallel with the Sarawak border towards the homeland of the Sea Dayaks in the deep interior of the island. The pattern of settlement and the ethnic politics of West Borneo strongly reveal the legacy of the region's turbulent history over the last 200 years, to which some attention must briefly be given.

Three Malay sultanates have played an important part in the history of West Kalimantan — Sukadana, Sambas and Pontianak. The oldest was Sukadana, a famous trading port on the south-western corner of Borneo from the 16th to the 19th century, that can trace its origins back to the days of Majapahit. But it has been superseded in importance over the last two centuries by Sambas and Pontianak, the former established as far back as the early 17th century, but more renowned for its piratical proclivities than honest trade, whereas the latter has flourished as the preferred resort of traders in the area since it was established towards the end of the 18th century, enjoying the support of the British and the Dutch against its rivals for this reason. The Sultanate of Pontianak remained one of the most loyal props to Dutch power in the island right up to 1949, when Sultan Hamid II took a leading part in the Dutch Federalist movement during the Revolution. (His political influence collapsed entirely in 1950, when he was gaoled for his association with a coup attempt by 'Turk' Westerling.) How far the social and political influence of the old aristocracies buttressing these Sultanates still survives in regional affairs it is difficult to discover, for singularly little is known outside about West Kalimantan politics. In Dutch times, West Borneo was a classic example of 'indirect rule'; the so-called 'self-governing' native states had only loose contractual relationships with their overlords, who had little reason for trying to interfere or establish intensive control there, provided the peace was kept — except in the heavily Chinese sub-district of Mempawah-Mandor, which was under direct Dutch administration because of the special problems it posed. The Dayaks were generally under the rule of Malays, at least in the coastal regions, so the Dutch were able to maintain control with fairly light reins, once the unruly Chinese *kongsis* of West Borneo had been subdued in 1855.[6]

The origins and growth of the Chinese communities of West Borneo constitute a remarkable chapter in the story of the Chinese in the Nan Yang, for here they created for some time an almost independent Chinese republic. A few Chinese miners were brought in by a vassal of the Sultan of Sambas around 1740 to dig for gold there, under the control of Dayak headmen. Soon a number of settlements were established, organized in self-governing *kongsis* which soon made themselves practically independent of the Sultan and his servants. The Dutch East India Company endeavoured to discourage this Chinese intrusion, although its effective power in Borneo was slight in the 18th century and in 1791 it had to withdraw its forces altogether. A big Chinese influx followed and some 30,000 were estimated to be mining there in 1812. The *kongsis* were virtually independent of both the Sultan of Sambas and the Dutch during the first half of the 19th century. There was a good deal of rivalry and conflict between them, particularly as the gold became worked out in the later decades, but three became dominant in the main mining areas around Montrado, Mandor and Pemangkat. In 1850, the Dutch decided to enforce stricter control over 'smuggling' by the Chinese and became embroiled in a major campaign to reduce the Montrado *kongsi* to subjection: this was finally achieved in 1855 with the occupation and complete dissolution of the *kongsi*, so that a system of direct rule over the region was necessary.[7] The mines were becoming exhausted by this time, but many of the

Chinese stayed and turned to farming or trading instead. Pontianak (which they had long preferred to Sambas as a trading centre) flourished as a consequence of their enterprise, particularly after the introduction of rubber cultivation early in the twentieth century. The rubber production of West Kalimantan today is almost entirely in their hands.

The Chinese population of West Kalimantan has increased nearly six-fold since 1912 and is estimated to have reached about 315,000 by 1961.[8] In the town of Pontianak itself the Chinese make up roughly 60 per cent of the population. Many are rubber-growers and farmers, unlike the Chinese in nearly all other parts of Indonesia, to whom land ownership is barred by law. Most belong to the Hakka speech-group, the descendants of the miners and farmers of inland Kwangtung province who opened up this part of Borneo over the last two centuries, but the great increase of population since the 1930 census (which recorded 108,000 Chinese) indicates that a substantial immigration of Chinese into the area has occurred since then too. As elsewhere in the Nanyang, the Chinese of West Kalimantan should really be considered as several distinct communities with significant differences of language and political outlook. Rivalry between pro-Communist and Kuo Min-tang elements has been intense in West Borneo and in 1957–8 the Indonesian authorities were capitalizing on it by playing off one group against another. It is not surprising that they were apprehensive about such a large, wealthy and culturally distinct Chinese minority in West Kalimantan, and this may well have seemed to them the safest way to handle it.

The threat to Indonesian Kalimantan if Sarawak fell under the control of its Chinese population (with or without Sabah and Brunei) was often mentioned as one of the reasons for Indonesia's opposition to the Malaysia scheme. However improbable such an eventuality may have been, it is obvious that a very awkward situation would have arisen for the Indonesian authorities in West Kalimantan if it had come about. There are more than half a million Chinese in that corner of Borneo, on the two sides of the border, many of them militant, chauvinistic and politically sympathetic to Communist China. The Indonesian government's authority in the province has not been very firmly grounded there and, essentially it has rested on the civil service and the Army rather than the backing or dominance of a particular ethnic group. The 'Malays' of the coastal regions are politically suspect for various reasons, but the Dayaks are not yet advanced enough economically or educationally to be relied upon alone. The government has always had difficulty enough merely to curb the Chinese smuggling trade between Pontianak and Singapore.

The Djakarta government has, therefore had ample grounds for concern about the difficulties of maintaining control in West Kalimantan. It would be interesting to discover how far military leaders like Nasution were influenced in their assessment of the Malaysia problem by concern with the strategic difficulties of holding Pontianak if it became necessary. They seem to have been far more concerned with West Kalimantan than with the sparsely populated and relatively stable north-east. Military confrontation on the Sarawak border served some useful defensive purposes for them. It justified the build-up of military forces in an area where the Army has probably been one of the strongest instruments consolidating the Indonesian government's rule. It also enabled the government to bring in 'volunteers' from Java as support units for the Army, then turned them to food production and development tasks in this still-backward province. (Over a long period, this might have had the same effects in tilting the ethnic balance in the region to Djakarta's advantage as transmigration has had over several decades in South Sumatra.) It must have strengthened the authority of the military commanders in Kalimantan greatly in the face of awkward demands from civilian politicians. It provided an opportunity to suppress the Chinese smuggling trade to Singapore and Sarawak. It even served as a means of facilitating the removal of politically unreliable battalions out of Java to be deployed on the frontier. In these respects, confrontation may have made some contribution towards the process of 'nation-building' or national integration in Indonesia, despite its great cost in other respects.

TABLE A. POPULATION OF KALIMANTAN

	1930	1961
West Kalimantan	802,000	1,581,000
South Kalimantan	835,000	1,473,000
East Kalimantan	329,000	551,000
Central Kalimantan	203,000	497,000
	2,169,000	4,102,000

Source: McVey, Indonesia, pp. 14–15, compiled from 1930 and 1961 census figures: these can be regarded as approximately accurate, but not entirely so.

TABLE B

VOTING PATTERNS IN KALIMANTAN, 1955 PARLIAMENTARY ELECTIONS

	West Kalimantan	South Kalimantan*	East Kalimantan
Masjumi	155,000	252,000	44,000
Nahdatul Ulama	37,000	381,000	20,000
PSII	3,000	7,000	7,000
PNI	64,000	46,000	43,000
PSI	16,000	5,000	13,000
PKI	8,000	17,000	8,000
IPKI	7,000	19,000	—
Party Daya	146,000	12,000	—
Parkindo	11,000	11,000	3,000
Katolik	3,000	—	4,000
Baperki	—	2,000	—

*South Kalimantan includes present-day Central Kalimantan.

Source: H. Feith: The Indonesian Elections of 1955 (Cornell Modern Indonesia Project), pp.69-70. (Figures rounded.)

TABLE C

POPULATION OF WEST KALIMANTAN, 1920–1961

Afdeling (kabupaten)	1920	1930	1961
Singkawang (Sambas)	179,000 (44,000)	251,000 (67,000)	413,000
Pontianak*	228,000 (20,000)	309,000 (34,000)	379,000
(Pontianak municipality)			150,000
(Sanggau)			220,000
Sintang*	160,000 (3,000)	134,000 (4,000)	176,000
(Kapuas Hulu)			87,000
Ketapang	65,000 (1,000)	82,000 (2,000)	157,000
TOTAL:	605,000 (68,000)	802,000 (108,000)	1,581,000 (315,000)

Source: Volkstelling, 1930; Sensus Penduduk, 1961.
Note: Figures in brackets indicate Chinese population of districts concerned (not available for 1961, except estimated provincial aggregate). The very great increase of population in the area of Pontianak and Sanggau (81,000 in 1930) is most striking, as also of Sambas to a lesser extent.

In the 1920–30 census returns, Pontianak afdeling included Pontianak municipality and Sanggau onderafdeling, which have since become separate second-level autonomous units (kabupaten or kotapradja). Likewise, Sintang afdeling included Kapuas Hulu which has since become a separate kabupaten. The boundaries of the present-day kabupaten appear to follow the old afdeling and onderafdeling boundaries, so far as one can judge from available maps.

TABLE D

ETHNIC CHARACTER OF THE POPULATION OF WEST KALIMANTAN, 1930

	Dayaks	Malays	Chinese	Others or Unknown
Singkawang	55,000	61,000	67,000	66,000
Pontianak	141,000	74,000	34,000	57,000
Ketapang	36,000	42,000	2,000	—
Sintang	103,000	52,000	4,000	—
TOTAL:	335,000	229,000	107,000	124,000

Source: Volkstelling, 1930.
Note: Slight discrepancies between Tables C and D are due to rounding of figures.

[1]'The Indonesian community consisted of about 20,000 members over the age of 12, largely made up of immigrant workers on plantations and timber camps. Some 13,400 were concentrated in the Tawao Residency and about 2,800 in the Sandakan Residency', *Indonesian Involvement in Eastern Malaysia*, Department of Information, Kuala Lumpur, 1964, p. 5. According to the *Sabah Annual Report 1963*, pp. 8 and 231, the proportion of Indonesians employed on the estates and timber camps has increased sharply since 1956. An Indonesian consulate was established in Jesselton in January 1962; in July 1963 two officials of the consulate were accused of fostering subversion among the Indonesians and declared *persona non grata*.

[2]See Table A for population of Kalimantan by provinces in 1930 and 1961. The present-day province of West Kalimantan is the former Dutch residency *Westerafdeling van Borneo*, while the old *Zuider- en Oosterafdeling van Borneo* has been divided into the three provinces of Central, South and East Kalimantan since 1956. (For some years the Indonesian part of the island was a single province, administered from Bandjarmasin.) The political complexion of these provinces, as revealed in the 1955 parliamentary elections is shown in table B. It may be assumed, on a very crude basis of assessment, that relatively few of the non-Muslim Dayaks would have voted for the Muslim parties, but would have preferred *Party Daya* or one of the secular or Christian parties. Probably the proportion of Chinese eligible to vote was very small — but the absence of *Baperki* candidates in West Kalimantan is puzzling.

[3]The estimate of Chinese population (in 1961) is by G. W. Skinner in McVey, *Indonesia*, p. 99.

[4]For much of the information in this paragraph I am indebted to Mr. Douglas Miles of Sydney University. A vivid picture of life in Central Kalimantan in 1963 is given by Judith M. Hudson in 'Letters from Kalimantan', *Indonesia*, nos. I and II, April and October 1966.

[5]See Tables C and D, the latter providing the only available data on ethnic origins of the population in different areas.

[6]Except in the case of Pontianak, which retained a 'long contract' with the Dutch government, most of the districts or sub-districts of West Borneo were categorized as '*zelfbesturenden landschappen*' (self-governing lands) under the uniform 'short contracts' which replaced the former long contracts in the early decades of this century. Details of these relationships are given in the *Encyclopaedie van Nederlandsch Indie*.

[7]For a good short account of the Chinese mining *kongsis* of West Borneo, see Graham Irwin, 'Nineteenth Century Borneo — A Study in Diplomatic Rivalry', *Verhandelingen van het Koninklijk Instituut voor Taal-, Land- en Volkankunde*, 1955, XV. The most useful Dutch sources are P. M. van Meeteren Brouwer, 'De Geschiedenis der Chineesche Districten', *De Indische Gids*, 1927, ii, pp. 1057–1100; J.J. M. de Groot, *Het Kongsiwezen van Borneo*, 1885; S. H. Schank, 'De Kongsis van Montrado', *Tijdschrift voor Indische Taal-, Land- en Volkenkunde*, 1893, pp. 498–612; P. J. Veth, *Borneo's Westerafdeling*, 2 volumes.

[8]An estimate of 53,000 in the Westerafdeling van Borneo is given in T. J. Bezemer, *Beknopte Encyclopaedie van Nederlandsch Indie* (Martinus Nijhoff, 1921), p. 83. G. W. Skinner has calculated the 1961 figure as a projection from earlier estimates, as the census of that year did not record the ethnic composition of the population: see his discussion of 'The Chinese Minority' in McVey, *Indonesia*, pp. 100 et seq.

Glossary

abangan: The syncretist, nominally Muslim *aliran* (QV) amongst the Javanese adhering to practices and beliefs stemming from the pre-Islamic era (Hindu, Buddhist and animist).

aksi sepihak: Unilateral action. Actions taken by pro-Communist peasant organizations in 1964-5 outside the consultative framework of the *Nasakom*-based land reform committees.

aliran: 'Stream' (lit.). The term applied to the main ideological or socio-cultural groupings such as *santri*, *abangan* and *prijaji* (QV).

Ansor: A Muslim youth movement affiliated with NU.

Barisan Sosialis: Socialist Front. The Singapore party formed by the left-wing breakaway group which left the PAP in July 1961 and became the major opposition party, opposed to merger with Malaysia.

Barisan Pemuda Sarawak: Sarawak Youth Front. A strongly anti-British organization expressing Malay cultural nationalism and anti-colonialism, mainly among anti-cessionist Malays, in the 1950s.

Barjasa: *Barisan Ra'ayat Jati Sarawak*—Sarawak Native Peoples' Front. A Sarawak Malay-Muslim party represented in the Sarawak Alliance.

BPS: *Badan Pendukung/Penjebar Soekarnoisme* — Body for the Promotion of Soekarnoism. An anti-Communist organization established in late 1964 aiming to attack the ideology of the PKI in the name of the doctrines of President Soekarno.

BTI: *Barisan Tani Indonesia* — Indonesian Peasants' Front. The PKI-affiliated peasant organization.

CCO: Clandestine Communist Organization. The term initially applied by the British to the underground Communist movement in Sarawak, later designated officially as the SCO (Sarawak Communist Organization).

DAC: Development Assistance Committee. The aid-coordinating arm of the Organization for Economic Cooperation and Development (OECD).

Darul Islam: 'The Abode of Islam' (lit.). The Muslim rebel movement in West Java between 1948–62, supported by similar groups in Atjeh and South Sulawesi, which advocated the establishment of an Islamic theocratic state.

Dwikora: *Dwikomando Rakjat* — The People's Twofold Command. President Soekarno's speech of 3 May 1964 calling upon Indonesians to assist the struggle of the people of Malaya, Singapore, Sarawak etc. against Malaysia and to intensify the defence of the Indonesian Revolution.

HMI: *Himpunan Mahasiswa Islam* — Islamic Students' Association. The leading Muslim students' organization; strongly anti-Communist in the late Guided Democracy period.

Harian Rakjat: People's Daily. The PKI daily newspaper.

KAMI: *Kesatuan Aksi Mahasiswa Indonesia* — Indonesian Students' Action Front. A federation of anti-Communist university student organizations.

KAPPI: *Kesatuan Aksi Pemuda dan Peladjar Indonesia* — Indonesian Youth and Students' Action Front. Similar to KAMI, but drawn from the secondary school level.

KOGA: *Komando Siaga* — Alertness Command. Established May 1964 after Soekarno's *Dwikora* speech to take responsibility for the military campaign against Malaysia; headed by Omar Dhani.

KOGAM: *Komando Ganjang Malaysia* — Crush Malaysia Command. The name applied to the former KOTI (QV) following Soekarno's attempted reshuffle of his cabinet and government in February 1966.

KOLAGA: *Komando Mandala Siaga* — Alert Theatre Command. Established late in 1964 to replace KOGA; headed by Omar Dhani, with Suharto as Deputy.

KOSTRAD: *Komando Strategis Angkatan Darat* — Army Strategic Reserve Command. The strategic reserve corps, formed in 1964 under the command of Major General Suharto.

KOTI: *Komando Tertinggi* — Supreme Operations Command (originally 'for the liberation of West Irian'). Established April 1962 as a small inner group of senior ministers, headed by Soekarno as Commander in Chief. Reconstituted July 1963 without Nasution.

KOTOE: *Komando Tertinggi Ekonomi* — Supreme Economic Command. One of the several functional committees of KOTI.

kongsi: A trading company or firm (Chinese).

Majapahit: East Javanese kingdom of 14–15th century, the last and greatest of the Hinduized states prior to the spread of Islam.

Manipol-Usdek: The Political Manifesto of President Soekarno, enunciated on 17 August 1959 as the programme and philosophy of Guided Democracy, of which USDEK was an acronym referring to its five main features.

Masjumi: *Madjelis Sjuro Muslimin Indonesia* — Council of Indonesian Muslim Associations; an Islamic party founded in 1943 under the Japanese, re-established as a federation of Muslim associations in November 1945; banned in August 1960 for supporting PRRI rebellion.

MCA: Malayan Chinese Association. The Chinese component of the Alliance: established 1948, formed Alliance with UMNO in 1952.

MCP: Malayan Communist Party. Established 1930, banned 1948, but remained active as an underground organization with bases on the Malaysia-Thailand border.

MIC: Malayan Indian Congress. The Indian component of the Alliance.

MPRS: *Madjelis Permusjawaratan Rakjat Sementara* — Provisional People's Consultative Congress. Designated in the Constitution as the 'supreme embodiment of the people's sovereignty', an (interim) Assembly was appointed in 1960 by Soekarno as the highest organ of the state.

Murba Party: A small national-communist or Marxist party stemming from the radical-nationalist group around the old 'Trotskyist' leader, Tan Malaka, in 1945–48; its leaders in the 1960s were Adam Malik and Sukarni.

musjawarah: A meeting, discussion or deliberation directed towards achievement of a consensus (*mufakat*).

Nasakom: *Nasionalisme-Agama* (religion)-*Komunisme:* an acronym referring to the principle of cooperation between nationalist, religious and Communist streams, advocated by Soekarno as the basis of national unity, especially after 1960.

National Front: A nationwide coordinating body of mass organizations. It was established at Soekarno's behest in 1960 to mobilize popular energies to national causes like the West Irian issue. In many areas it was dominated by local military authorities, but in some others was under strong PKI influence.

Nekolim: An acronym referring to 'neo-colonialism, colonialism, and imperialism'.

NKKU: *Negara Kesatuan Kalimantan Utara* — Unitary State of North Kalimantan. The state proclaimed by Azahari following the Brunei revolt.

NU: *Nahdatul Ulama*. Established in 1926 as a conservative Muslim counter to the reformist Muhammadiyah; later one of the constituent organizations within Masjumi, from which it seceded in 1952; after the banning of Masjumi it was the largest Muslim party.

PANAS: *Party Negara Sarawak*. The second oldest political party in Sarawak, founded April 1960 as a multi-racial party, but with a strongly-pro-indigenous slant: led and supported mainly by Malays.

Pantja Tunggal: Five in One. An enlarged form of the *Tjatur Tunggal* (QV) to which a representative of the regional National Front was added.

Partai Pelopor: Pioneer Party. One of the proposed forms of a 'single party' concept advanced in 1964.

Party Rakyat (also Ra'ayat): Peoples' Party. The small Malay component of the opposition Socialist Front in Malaysia; led by Boestamam.

Pasok Momogon: The name of a short-lived political party, initially opposed to the Malaysia concept in 1962, backed by the non-Muslim (mainly Murut) people in the interior of Sabah. Later merged with UNKO into the United Pasok Kadazan Organization (UPKO).

PEPELRADA: *Penguasa Pelaksanaan Dwikora Daerah* — Regional Executive Authorities of the *Dwikora*. Authorities vested with virtual martial law powers (usually local military commanders) after the September 1964 military crisis.

PESAKA: *Party Pesaka Anak Sarawak*. An Iban political party drawing support mainly from the 3rd Division.

PKI: *Partai Komunis Indonesia* — Indonesian Communist Party. Established May 1920, suppressed after 1926–7 revolts, re-established late 1945 and the fourth largest political party in the 1955 elections.

PMIP: *Pan-Malayan Islamic Party*. Founded 1955; supported mainly by east coast Malays opposed to the more 'establishment' orientation of UMNO.

PNI: *Partai Nasional Indonesia* — Indonesian Nationalist Party. Originally founded by Soekarno in 1927, then banned in 1930: a successor party, to which Soekarno was close but not formally a member, was formed in 1945 and emerged as the largest political party in the 1955 elections.

prijaji: The term embracing the upper class of government officials in Java: more generally, the upper strata of the non-*santri* stream (*aliran*) among the Javanese.

PRRI: *Permesta: Pemerintah Revolusioner Republik Indonesia* — *Perdjuangan Semesta* — Revolutionary Government of the Republic of Indonesia — Universal Struggle Charter. The 1957-8 regional dissident movements based on West Sumatra and North Sulawesi.

PSI: *Partai Sosialis Indonesia* — Indonesian Socialist Party. Established February 1948 and led by Sutan Sjahrir until 1960; a small party with influential following among intellectuals but little mass support. Banned by Soekarno in August 1960.

Pemuda Rakjat: Peoples' Youth. The PKI-affiliated youth front.

RPKAD: *Resimen Pasukan Komando Angkatan Darat*. The Army commando (paratroop) regiment, under the command of KOSTRAD, which played a major part in the destruction of the PKI in 1965–6.

santri: 'A pupil' (lit.). A devout Muslim: in general the more self-consciously Muslim stream (*aliran*) among the Javanese.

SCA: Sarawak Chinese Association. A small Chinese party based on the MCA model, but far less influential.

SCO: Sarawak Communist Organization. The latter-day name for the CCO.

SNAP: Sarawak National Party. Supported mainly by Second Division Iban, led by Stephen Kalong Ningkan.

SUPP: Sarawak United Peoples' Party. The oldest Sarawak political party, established 1959; officially multi-racial, but mainly backed by Chinese. The foremost opponent of the Malaysia concept in Sarawak. Leaders were Ong Kee Hui and Stephen Yong.

Tjatur Tunggal: Four in One. The body which in 1963 replaced the former Regional War Administrators' committee operating under martial law regulations between 1957–62, consisting of the regional military commander, local governor or *bupati*, chief of police and chief prosecutor.

TNKU: *Tentara Nasional Kalimantan Utara* — North Borneo National Army. The Brunei-based guerrilla organization opposing the Malaysia concept; launched Brunei revolt, December 1962, later continued struggle mainly from Indonesian Borneo.

Trikora: *Trikomando Rakjat* — The People's Threefold Command. Issued by Soekarno on 19 December 1962 as a signal for intensification of the struggle for West Irian.

UDP: United Democratic Party. A Penang-based party, officially multi-racial, but supported mainly by Chinese and Indians.

UMNO: United Malays National Organization. The senior party of the Malayan Alliance, established in 1946 by Dato Onn bin Ja'afar.

UNKO: United National Kadazan Organization. Established by Donald Stephens among the Kadazan people of Sabah.

UNTEA: United Nations Temporary Executive Authority. Established to administer West Irian under UN auspices during the period of transfer from Dutch to Indonesian control, August 1962 – May 1963.

UPKO: United Pasok Kadazan Organization. The main non-Muslim party in Sabah, formed early 1964 by fusion of the *Pasok Momogon* (QV) and the *Kadazan* party UNKO.

UPP: United People's Party (Singapore). The party led by Ong Eng Guan between 1961 and 1963.

USNO: United Sabah National Organization. The Malay-Muslim party led by Datu Mustapha.

Utusan Melayu: The leading Malay (Jawi script) newspaper.

Select Bibliography

Since a comprehensive bibliography would be unwieldy (and almost inevitably incomplete), the list of books, pamphlets and articles set out below includes only those works (other than newspapers) most commonly referred to in this study and the most significant contributions in English on the topics with which they deal, for the sake of readers seeking to pursue the subject further.

A. GENERAL

AUSTRALIA: Department of External Affairs, *Select Documents on International Affairs*, no.I. of 1963, *Malaysia.*

BOYCE, PETER, *Malaysia and Singapore in International Diplomacy, Documents and Commentaries* (Sydney University Press, Sydney, 1968).

BRACKMAN, ARNOLD C., *Southeast Asia's Second Front. The Power Struggle in the Malay Archipelago* (Frederick A. Praeger, New York, 1966).

CURTIS, ROBERT, 'Malaysia and Indonesia', *The New Left Review*, no. 28, November-December 1964, pp. 5–32.

GORDON, BERNARD K., *The Dimensions of Conflict in Southeast Asia* (Prentice Hall, New Jersey, 1966).

—— 'The Potential for Indonesian Expansionism', *Pacific Affairs*, vol. XXXVI, no. 4, Winter 1963-4, pp. 378–93.

HATTA, MOHAMMAD, 'One Indonesian View of the Malaysian Issue', *Asian Survey*, vol. V, no.3, March 1965, pp. 139–44.

HEIDHUES, MARY F. SOMERS, 'Peking and the Overseas Chinese: the Malaysian Dispute', *Asian Survey*, vol. VI, no.5, May 1966, pp. 276–87.

HILSMAN, ROGER, *To Move a Nation. The Politics of Foreign Policy in the Administration of John F. Kennedy* (Doubleday, New York, 1967).

HINDLEY, DONALD, 'Indonesia's Confrontation of Malaysia: a Search for Motives' *Asian Survey*, vol. IV, no.61, June 1964, pp. 904–13.

HYDE, DOUGLAS, *Confrontation in the East* (Bodley Head, London, 1965).

INDONESIA, DEPARTMENT OF FOREIGN AFFAIRS, *Aide Memoire from the Observers of the Republic of Indonesia to the United Nations Mission in Sarawak and Sabah* (1963).

—— *The Era of Confrontation* (1965).

—— *Gelora Konfrontasi Mengganjang Malaysia* (1964).

–––––– The 'Malaysian' Issue: Background and Documents (Djakarta, n.d (1964?)).

–––––– The 'Malaysia' Issue Before the UN Security Council (Djakarta, 1964).

–––––– New Forces Build a New World (Indonesia Policy Series, 1965).

–––––– A Survey on the Controversial Problem of the Establishment of Malaysia (Memorandum released by the Permanent Mission of the Republic of Indonesia to the United Nations, 24 September 1963).

INDONESIAN HERALD, The Problem of 'Malaysia' (Djakarta, 1963).

JAMES, HAROLD and SHEIL-SMALL, DENIS, The Undeclared War (Asia Pacific Press, Singapore, 1971).

KAHIN, GEORGE McT., 'Malaysia and Indonesia', Pacific Affairs, vol. XXXVII, no.3, Fall 1964, pp. 253–70.

LYON, PETER, War & Peace in Southeast Asia (London, 1969).

MALAYSIA, Background to Indonesia's Policy Towards Malaysia (Government Printer, Kuala Lumpur, 1964).

–––––– Indonesian Aggression against Malaysia (Ministry of External Affairs, Government Printer, Kuala Lumpur, 1964).

–––––– Indonesian Intentions Towards Malaysia (Ministry of Internal Security, Government Printer, Kuala Lumpur, 1964).

–––––– Malaya-Indonesia Relations, 31 August 1957 to 15 September 1963 (Department of Information, Government Printer, Kuala Lumpur, 1963).

–––––– Malaya-Philippines Relations, 31 August 1957 to 15 September 1963 (Department of Information, Government Printer, Kuala Lumpur, 1963).

–––––– Malaysia in the United Nations Security Council (Ministry of External Affairs, Kuala Lumpur, 1964).

–––––– A Plot Exposed. (Government Printer, Kuala Lumpur, 1965).

MILLAR, T. B. AND MILLER, J. D. B., 'Afro-Asian Disunity: Algiers 1965' Australian Outlook, vol. XIX, no.3, December 1965, pp. 306–21.

MODELSKI, GEORGE, 'Indonesia and the Malaysia Issue', The Yearbook of World Affairs, 1964 (Stevens, London, 1964), pp. 128–49.

–––––– The New Emerging Forces (Department of International Relations, Australian National University, Canberra, Documents and Data Papers no.2, 1963).

PAUKER, GUY J., 'The Rise and Fall of Afro-Asian Solidarity', Asian Survey, vol. 5, no.9, September 1965, pp. 425–32.

UNITED NATIONS, Final Conclusions of the Secretary General regarding Malaysia (Document SG/1583/13 September 1963).

B. INDONESIA

ADAMS, CINDY, Soekarno: an Autobiography as told to Cindy Adams (Bobbs Merrill Inc., New York, 1965).

ANDERSON, BENEDICT, 'The Languages of Indonesian Politics', Indonesia, no.1, April 1966, pp. 89-116.

BONE, ROBERT, The Dynamics of the West New Guinea (Irian Barat) Problem (Cornell Modern Indonesia Project, Monograph Series, 1958).

BUNNELL, FREDERICK P., 'Guided Democracy Foreign Policy: 1960–65', Indonesia (Cornell Modern Indonesia Project), no.2, October, 1966, pp. 37–76.

DERKACH, NADIA, 'The Soviet Policy towards Indonesia in the West Irian and Malaysia Disputes', Asian Survey, vol. V, no.11, November 1965, pp. 566–71.

FEITH, HERBERT, *The Decline of Constitutional Democracy in Indonesia* (Cornell University Press, Ithaca, N.Y., 1963).

—— 'The Dynamics of Guided Democracy', in Ruth McVey (ed.), *Indonesia* (Human Relations Area File Press, New Haven, 1963), ch.8.

—— 'President Soekarno, the Army and the Communists: The Triangle Changes Shape', *Asian Survey*, vol. IV, no.8, August, 1964, pp. 969–80.

—— 'Indonesia's Political Symbols and the Wielders', *World Politics*, vol. XVI, no.1, October, 1963, pp. 79–97.

HINDLEY, DONALD, *The Communist Party of Indonesia* (University of California Press, 1964).

—— 'President Soekarno and the Communists: the Politics of Domestication', *American Political Science Review*, December 1962, pp. 915-26.

HUGHES, JOHN, *Indonesian Upheaval* (Mackay, New York, 1967).

JONES, HOWARD P., *Indonesia: The Possible Dream* (Harcourt Brace Jovanovich, New York, 1971).

KAHIN, GEORGE MCT., *Nationalism and Revolution in Indonesia* (Cornell University Press, 1952).

KROEF, J. M. VAN DER, *The Communist Party of Indonesia* (Vancouver, University of British Columbia, 1965).

LEGGE, J. D., 'Indonesia after West Irian', *Australian Outlook*, vol. XVII, no.1, April 1963, pp. 5-20.

—— *Soekarno* (Penguin Books, 1972).

LEV, DANIEL S., 'Indonesia: the Year of the Coup', *Asian Survey*, vol. VI, no.2, February 1966, pp. 103–10.

—— 'The Political Role of the Army in Indonesia', *Pacific Affairs*, vol. XXXVI, no.4, Winter 1963–64, pp. 349-64.

—— *The Transition to Guided Democracy: Indonesian Politics, 1957–59* (Cornell Modern Indonesia Project, Monograph Series, 1966).

MACKIE, J. A. C., 'Inflation and Confrontation in Indonesia', *Australian Outlook*, vol. XVIII, no.3, December 1964, pp. 278–98.

—— *Problems of Inflation in Indonesia* (Cornell Modern Indonesia Project, Monograph Series, 1967).

MCVEY, RUTH (ed.), *Indonesia* (Human Relations Area File Press, New Haven, Conn., 1963).

—— 'Indonesian Communism and China', in Tang Tsou (ed.) *China's Policies in Asia and America's Alternatives*, II (University of Chicago Press, 1968), ch.13.

—— 'The State of the Parties, Indonesia', *Survey*, no.54, January 1965, pp. 113–22.

MORTIMER, REX A., 'The Ideology of the Communist Party of Indonesia under Guided Democracy 1959–65' (Monash University, Ph. D. Thesis, 1971).

MOZINGO, DAVID P., *Sino-Indonesian Relations: an Overview, 1955–1965* (Rand Corporation Memorandum, RM-4641-PR, California, 1965).

—— 'China's Policy towards Indonesia' in Tang Tsou (ed.) *China's Policies in Asia* (Chicago, 1968), ch. 12.

POLOMKA, S. PETER, 'The Indonesian Army and Confrontation. An Enquiry into the functions of Foreign Policy under Guided Democracy' (University of Melbourne, M.A. Thesis, 1970).

PAUKER, GUY J., *Communist Prospects in Indonesia* (Rand Corporation Memorandum, RM-4135-PR, November 1964).

——— 'The Role of the Military in Indonesia', in J. J. Johnston (ed.), *The Role of the Military in Under-developed Countries* (Princeton University Press, 1962).

REY, LUCIEN, 'Dossier of the Indonesian Drama', *New Left Review*, no.36, March-April 1966, pp. 26–40.

RA'ANAN, URI, 'The Coup that Failed', *Problems of Communism*, vol. XV, no.2, March-April 1966, pp. 37-43.

RICHTER, H. V., 'Indonesia's Share in the Entrepot Trade of Malaya and Singapore Prior to Confrontation', *Malayan Economic Review*, vol. XI, no.2, October 1966, pp. 28–45.

SUBANDRIO, *Indonesia on the March* (Department of Foreign Affairs, Djakarta, 1963).

SUKARNO, Independence Day Addresses (Department of Information, Djakarta).

——— 1965. *Reach to the Stars. A Year of Self Reliance.*

——— 1964. *A Year of Living Dangerously.*

WEATHERBEE, D. E., *Ideology in Indonesia: Soekarno's Indonesian Revolution* (Yale S.E. Asia Studies, New Haven, 1966).

WERTHEIM, W. F., 'Indonesia Before and After the Untung Coup', *Pacific Affairs*, vol. XXXIX, nos.1-2, Spring-Summer 1967, pp. 115-27.

WEINSTEIN, FRANKLIN B., *Indonesia Abandons Confrontation. An Inquiry into the Functions of Indonesian Foreign Policy* (Cornell Modern Indonesia Project, Interim Reports Series, 1969).

C. MALAYSIA

ANGEL, J. R., 'The Proposed Federation of North Borneo, Brunei and Sarawak' (Sydney University, M.A. thesis, 1965).

ARMSTRONG, HAMILTON FISH, 'The Troubled Birth of Malaysia', *Foreign Affairs*, vol. XLI, no.4, July 1963, pp. 67–93.

CLARK, MARGARET. 'The Malayan Alliance and its Accomodation of Communal Pressures' (University of Malaya, M.A. thesis, 1964).

COBBOLD REPORT, See under 'Great Britain'.

GEDDES, W. R., *Nine Dayak Nights* (Oxford University Press, Oxford Paperbacks no.35, 1961).

GREAT BRITAIN, COLONIAL OFFICE, *Report of the Commission of Enquiry, North Borneo and Sarawak, 1962.* (The Cobbold Report.) London, HMSO, 1962. Cmnd. 1794.

——— Colonial Office and Commonwealth Relations Ministry, *Malaysia. Agreement concluded between the United Kingdom of Great Britain and Northern Ireland, the Federation of Malaya, North Borneo, Sarawak and Singapore* (The Lansdowne Commission Report), London, HMSO, 1963. Cmnd. 2094.

GROSSHOLTZ, JEAN, 'An Exploration of Malaysian Meanings', *Asian Survey*, vol. VI, no.4, April 1966, pp. 227–40.

GULLICK. J. M., *Malaya* (London, Ernest Benn, 2nd. ed., 1964).

HANNA, WILLIARD A., *The Formation of Malaysia* (American Universities Field Staff, 1964)·

FLETCHER, NANCY McH., *The Separation of Singapore from Malaysia* (Cornell University, S.E. Asian Studies, Data Paper, no. 75, 1969).

HARRISON, TOM, *Background to a Revolt* (Light Press, Brunei, 1963).

—— *The Malays of South-West Sarawak before Malaysia: a Socio-ecological study* (London, 1970).

—— *The Peoples of Sarawak* (Government Printer, Kuching, 1959).

INTERNATIONAL BANK FOR RECONSTRUCTION AND DEVELOPMENT, *Report on the Economic Aspects of Malaysia* (The Rueff Report), (Government Printer, Kuala Lumpur, 1963).

KRAUSE, D., *Die Panindonesische Idee. Entstehung und Entwicklung in Malaya and Singapur bis 1963* (Freiburg in Breisgau, 1967).

KROEF, J. M. VAN DER, *Communism in Malaysia and Singapore: a Contemporary Study* (The Hague, Martinus Nijhoff, 1967).

LANSDOWNE REPORT, See under 'Great Britain'.

LEE KUAN YEW, *The Battle for Merger* (Government Printing Office, Singapore, 1962).

LEIFER, MICHAEL, 'Anglo-American Differences over Malaysia', *The World Today*, vol. 20, no.4, April 1964, pp. 156–67.

—— 'Politics in Singapore: the First Term of the Peoples' Action Party, 1959–63', *Journal of Commonwealth Studies*, vol. XX, May 1964, pp. 107–19.

—— 'Communal Violence in Singapore', *Asian Survey*, vol. IV. no.10, October 1964, pp. 115–21.

—— 'Singapore in Malaysia: the Politics of Federation', *Journal of Southeast Asian History*, vol. VI, no.1. September 1965, pp. 54–70.

LEIGH, MICHAEL B., *The Chinese Community of Sarawak: a Study of Communal Relations* (Malaysia Publishing House Ltd., Singapore Studies in History, no.6, 1964).

—— *The Development of Political Organization in Sarawak and Eastern Malaysia* (Cornell University. Ph.D. thesis. 1971).

MILNE, R. S., *Government and Politics in Malaysia* (Houghton Mifflin, Boston, 1967).

—— 'Singapore's Exit from Malaysia: the Consequences of Ambiguity', *Asian Survey*, vol. VI, no.3, March 1966.

NORTH BORNEO, COLONY OF, *Annual Report*, London, HMSO, 1947 to 1962. (See also Sabah Annual Report).

ORTIZ, P. A., 'Legal Aspects of the North Borneo Question', *Philippines Studies*, vol. XX, January 1963, pp. 18-64.

OSBORNE, MILTON E., *Singapore and Malaysia* (Southeast Asia Program, Data Paper no.53, Cornell University, Ithaca, 1964).

PRINGLE, R., *Rajahs and Rebels. The Ibans of Sarawak under Brooke Rule, 1841–1941* (London, Macmillan, 1970).

RATNAM, K. J., *Communalism and the Political Process in Malaya* (University of Malaya Press, Kuala Lumpur, 1965).

RATNAM, K. J. AND MILNE, R. S., *The Malayan Parliamentary Election of 1964* (University of Malaya Press, Singapore, 1967).

ROFF, MARGARET, 'Sabah's Political Parties and the 1967 State Election', *International Studies*, vol. IX, April 1968, pp. 431–56.

—— 'The Rise and Demise of Kadazan Nationalism', *Journal of Southeast Asian History*, vol. X, 1969.

ROFF, W. R., *The Origins of Malay Nationalism* (Yale University Press, New Haven, and University of Malaya Press, Kuala Lumpur, 1967).

RUNCIMAN, STEVEN, *The White Rajahs. A History of Sarawak from 1841 to 1946* (Cambridge University Press, 1960).

Sabah Annual Report, 1963 (Government Printing Department, Jesselton, 1963).

SARAWAK, COLONY OF, *Annual Report* (London, HMSO, 1947 to 1962).

SILCOCK, T. H. AND FISK, E. K. (eds.), *The Political Economy of Independent Malaya* (A.N.U. Press, Canberra, 1963).

SILCOCK, T. H. AND UNGKU ABDUL AZIZ, 'Malayan Nationalism' in W. L. Holland (ed.), *Asian Nationalism and the West* (Institute of Pacific Relations, New York, 1953), pp. 269–346.

SINGAPORE. GOVERNMENT PRINTING OFFICE, *Singapore Annual Yearbook* (*1962*).

―――― *The Battle for a Malaysian Malaysia* (1965).

―――― *Malaysia Comes of Age* (1964).

―――― *Towards a Malaysian Malaysia* (1965).

―――― *Separation* (1965).

―――― *Some Problems of Malaysia.*

SMITH, T. E., *The Background to Malaysia* (RIIA, London, 1963).

―――― 'The Brunei Revolt: Background and Consequences', *The World Today*, vol. XIX, no.4, April 1963, pp. 135–8.

SOENARNO, RADIN, 'Malay Nationalism, 1900–1945', *Journal of Southeast Asian History*, vol. 1, no.1, March 1960, pp. 1–28.

TILMAN, ROBERT O., 'The Alliance Pattern in Malaysian Politics: Bornean Variations on a Theme', *South Atlantic Quarterly*, vol. LXIII, no.1, Winter 1964, pp. 60–74.

―――― 'Elections in Sarawak', *Asian Survey*, vol. III, no.10, October 1963, pp. 507–18.

―――― 'The Sarawak Political Scene', *Pacific Affairs*, vol. XXXVII, no.4, Winter 1964–5, pp. 412–25.

TREGONNING, K. G., *North Borneo* (Corona Library Series, HMSO, London, 1960).

―――― *Under Chartered Company Rule* (*North Borneo 1881–1946*) (University of Malaya Press, Singapore, 1958). (Republished as *A History of Sabah*, 1964.)

VASIL, R. K., 'The 1964 General Election in Malaya', *International Studies* (New Delhi), vol. VII, no.1, July 1965, pp. 20–65.

―――― 'Why Malaysia Failed?', *Quest* (Calcutta), no.49, April-June 1966, pp. 51-9.

―――― *Politics in a Plural Society. A Study of Non-communal Political Parties in West Malaysia* (Kuala Lumpur, 1971).

WANG GUNGWU (ed.), *Malaysia. A Survey* (F. W. Cheshire, Melbourne, and Donald Moore, Singapore, 1964).

WRIGHT, LEIGH R., 'Historical Notes on the North Borneo Dispute', *Journal of Asian Studies*, vol. XXV, no.3, May 1966, pp. 471–84.

Index

ABDUL RAHMAN (*see* Tunku Abdul Rahman)

Achmadi, Brig.-Gen., 258

Afro-Asian Conciliation Commission, 232–4, 268–9

Afro-Asian Conference: Bandung (1955), 27; Algiers (1965), 4, 97ff, 288

Afro-Asian Journalists' Conference, Djakarta (1963), 127

Afro-Asian People's Solidarity Conference, Moshi (1963), 127

Aidit, D. N., 83, 134, 280, 311

Alisjahbana, S.T. (cited), 91

Angkatan Pemuda Revolusioner Melayu (Malayan Revolutionary Youth Force), 106

Anglo-Malayan Defence Agreement (1957), 32, 43, 104, 130, 151

Asian Games, 103

Association of South-East Asian States, 33, 129, 131, 167

Aziz Ishak, 52

Azahari, A. M., 42, 48, 61, 73, 104–18

BALAI RINGIN, attacked, 264

Bangkok Accord (1966), 320

Barisan Pemuda Sarawak (Sarawak Youth Front), 63–4

Barisan Ra'ayat Jati Sarawak (*see* BARJASA)

Barisan Sosialis, 8, 40, 45–51, 128, 143, 248–9; arrest of leaders, 48, 128; Malay Socialist Conference, 50; party strength, 41 (table)

BARJASA (Barisan Ra'ayat Jati Sarawak), 63, 68, 301–2

Belgrade Conference of Non-aligned Nations, 96

Ben Bella, overthrow, 291

Benda, Harry J., cited, 2

Bloomfield amendment, 136

Body for Promotion of Soekarnoism (*Badan Pendukung Soekarnoisme*), 279–81

Boestaman, Ahmad, 19, 26, 49, 51, 104, 128, 139; arrest, 27, 52, 128, 139; policy on Malaysia, 51

Borneo: British North Borneo, 36–7, 41–2, 56–78; closer association proposed (1958), 8, 59, 65–6, 72, 114; UN Ascertainment Mission 150, 170–6 (*see also* Brunei; Sabah; Sarawak; Kalimantan)

Brooke, Rajah Charles, 62

Burhanuddin al'Helmy, Dr., 27–8, 49, 51

Britain: Anglo-Malayan Defence Agreement, 32, 43, 104, 130, 151; British Embassy burnt, 3, 181–93; British firms taken over, 181, 225–6, 243

Brunei: attitude to 1958 Borneo closer association call, 114; to Malaysia proposal, 115–17; decision not to join Malaysia, 141–2; population, 61, 113; revolt (Dec. 1962), 6, 69, 74, 111–43 (*see also* Azahari, A. M.; Party Ra'ayat)

Bunker, Ellsworth, 100

Bunnell, F. (cited), 330

CAIRO CONFERENCE OF NON-ALIGNED NATIONS, 207

Chairul Saleh, 93, 124, 179, 191–2, 240, 245, 279–80, 282

Chen Yi (Foreign Minister of China), 263, 282, 287

Clandestine Communist Organization (CCO), (*see* Sarawak Communist Organization)